Rabbi Berman
from
J. S. Lewis

THE

Abraham and Hannah Oppenheim

MEMORIAL PUBLICATIONS

VOLUME I

PUBLISHED BY

THE HEBREW UNION COLLEGE PRESS

CINCINNATI, OHIO, U.S.A.

TEXTS AND STUDIES

IN JEWISH HISTORY AND LITERATURE

BY

JACOB MANN, M.A., Litt.D. (London)

Professor of Jewish History and Literature,
Hebrew Union College

VOLUME I

WITH 27 FACSIMILES

HEBREW UNION COLLEGE PRESS
CINCINNATI, OHIO, U.S.A.
1931

PRINTED AT
THE HEBREW PRESS OF THE
JEWISH PUBLICATION SOCIETY OF AMERICA
PHILADELPHIA, PA.

לזכר נשמת אבי,
מורי ורבי,
אשר חנכני על פי דרכי התורה והיהדות,
ר׳ ניסן מאנן,
שו״ב בקהלת פרעמיסלא,
נפטר ביום כ׳ שבט התרפ״ט לפ״ג.
ולזכר נשמת אמי היקרה,
מרת מינדיל מאנן,
נפטרה ביום ט׳ טבת התרפ״ח לפ״ג.
תנצב״ה.

CORRIGENDA

Page XV, l. 10. *For* 41 *read* 40.
,, 17, l. 23. *For* 11–12 *read* 15.
,, 187, l. 4 from bottom. After "what" insert "was."
,, 292, l. 4. *For* שיר אחיו no doubt *read* נְזִיר אחיו (cp. Deut. 33.16). Hence delete note 88.
,, 534, l. 13. *For* בית הלוי *read* לבית הלוי.

PREFACE

THE studies presented in this volume were determined by the manuscript material that formed their starting points. This material, culled from diverse sources scattered in several libraries, is but a kaleidoscopic reflex of Jewish life in the Middle Ages as it found expression chiefly in the countries under the sway of Islām. The nature and variety of the material precluded a unified presentation construed on the framework of a central theme. The studies with their accompanying texts are primarily designed as contributions to a more comprehensive and intimate understanding of Jewish affairs in the past in its various manifestations, institutions and interests.

Apart from the political and economic conditions that were on the whole controlled by his Gentile masters, with now and then a high Jewish official, like Ḥisdai ibn Shaprūṭ in Spain, protecting actively Jewish interests, the Jew lived his own communal life in devotion to his traditional ideals and practices. The focus of the internal Jewish life lay in the study and the cultivation of Judaism in its various aspects and disciplines. Hence the affairs of the seats of learning and of their representatives figure so much in the sources at our disposal. The Gaonates of Babylon, Palestine, Egypt and Syria are discussed through the letters of the presidents of the academies. The economic difficulties of the schools, the rivalry between the Geonim, the contacts with numerous communities of several countries, the inner organization of the Yeshibot, the conflict between the Gaonate and the Exilarchate in their final stages and other topics are passed under review in the course of the investigation of the new material.

Other data throw new light on events in the life of European Jewry, notably among them are the diplomatic endeavors of Ḥisdai ibn Shaprūṭ on behalf of Jewry in Christian Europe. Conditions in Palestine and in Egypt under Muhammedan rule are further illustrated by new material forming a supplement to what has been incorporated in my work on the Jews in Egypt and in Palestine under the Fāṭimid Caliphs and elsewhere. One section deals with the Jews in Mosul and in Ḳurdistān, a district hitherto very scantily represented in the annals of Jewish History. The purely literary side of the present volume is composed of fragments of Halakhic writings of the Gaonic period and also of Genizah booklists that testify to the Jewish cultural interests of the bygone ages.

An important factor in Mediæval Jewry under Islām was Ḳaraism which extended also to Christian countries. New material on the external history of this sect and its spread to various countries right down to modern times will form the basis of volume II of the present Texts and Studies accompanied by a detailed index covering both volumes.

All these studies, based as they are on new material, which supplements and illumines the already known, will, it is to be hoped, be appreciated by scholars and students who, like the writer, are averse to fanciful theories spun out as a rule from a minimum of available data—a new type of "making bricks without straw," or of rearing castles in the air. Only by a cautious and laborious inductive method and by adding constantly to our knowledge of the actual realities of the Jewish past (as against the speculative imaginings of which we have enough and to spare) can we understand this past fully and truly and ultimately hope to obtain the synthesis that every research worker sets before himself as his ultimate goal. The more the material stored up in manuscripts is made accessible in a scientific manner, the better will the history of Jewish life and activities in the course of the past ages be reconstructed anew. With the widening of the horizon new perspectives are revealed and events, movements and personalities, are placed in a different setting and proportion.

As for those, who in their vaunted superiority condescend to look down pityingly on studies of this kind as consisting of dry minutiæ culled from dusty and worn out writings and who either cannot or will not accompany in spirit the seeker for truth in his quest for the evidence of the realities of the past wherever it can be discovered—for such persons research studies of this nature are frankly never intended and their inherent lack of appeal is a foregone conclusion. In the true process of research experience has, however, shown over and over again how seemingly small data become missing links in whole chains of evidence which thereby obtain a significance never realised before.*

* * *

There remains now to express my thanks to the staffs of the libraries for courtesies extended to me in the course of gathering the new material whether while copying it on the spot or when obtaining photostats of required items. These libraries include the three great depositaries of Jewish manuscripts in England, the Bodleian at Oxford, the British Museum at London and the Cambridge University Library. Another great depositary is the Government Public Library at Leningrad. During my visit to Leningrad I was assisted by Prof. David Maggid in locating manuscripts, a task rendered difficult by the brief handlists available mostly in the Russian language. Mr. Jack Mosseri of Cairo kindly made possible for me to go through his Genizah collection and has also supplied me with a number of facsimiles. Mr. A. S. Oko has placed at my disposal a number of manuscripts of the Hebrew Union College Library. To all and sundry my sincere gratitude is herewith rendered.

Finally special thanks are due to the Board of Governors of the Hebrew Union College for defraying the expenses of many photostats needed in preparation of the present work. This my particular request was kindly sponsored by the President of the College, Dr. Julian Morgenstern. The Board of Governors have also made possible the publication of this work issued by the Hebrew Union College Press.

J. M.

Cincinnati, Ohio, October 12, 1930.

* Attention should be drawn to the following procedure in transliterating Hebrew words. a=א, ʻa=ע; h=ה, ḥ=ח; k=כ, ḳ=ק; s=ס, ṣ=צ; t=ת, ṭ=ט.

In the Judaeo-Arabic texts the diacritical points are given as follows. ג̇=ج, ג̇=غ, כ̇=خ, ת̇=ث.

The frequent references to Mann I or Mann II are to Mann, *The Jews in Egypt and in Palestine under the Fāṭimid Caliphs*, vol. I, 1920; vol. II, 1922.

CONTENTS

Section III

PALESTINIAN AFFAIRS IN THE 11th CENTURY

Section IV

EGYPTIAN AFFAIRS AND PERSONALITIES (10th–15th CENTURIES)

Section V

DOCUMENTS CONCERNING THE JEWS IN MOSUL AND ḲURDISTĀN

Section VI

FRAGMENTS OF LEGALISTIC WRITINGS OF THE GAONIC PERIOD

Section VII

GENIZAH INVENTORIES OF BOOKS

LIST OF FACSIMILES

SECTION I

DOCUMENTS CONCERNING EUROPEAN JEWRY

1.

ḤISDAI IBN SHAPRŪṬ AND HIS DIPLOMATIC INTERVENTION ON BEHALF OF THE JEWS IN CHRISTIAN EUROPE

Introduction

THIS prominent Jewish statesman of Cordova has established for himself an everlasting memorial in the annals of Jewish history by his endeavors on behalf of his brethren within the borders of the Spanish Caliphate and without. It was no vain boasting when in his famous letter to Joseph, the king of the Khazārs, he stated that his exalted position in the court of 'Abd ar-Raḥmān III had brought about an improvement in the status of the Jews in Andalusia. "And although we are children of the diaspora"—he writes—, "the remnant of Israel, (yet) the servants of my lord, the king, are dwelling in peace in our country, for our God has not forsaken us nor has He removed His protection from us. And it came to pass that when we disobeyed our God, He brought us to judgment and placed distress on our loins; He aroused the spirit of the officials that were over Israel so that they appointed tax gatherers over them, who made heavy their yoke and oppressed them with fierce anger, so that they (the Jews) were humiliated under them and many evil troubles befell them. But when our God beheld their poverty and trouble, He caused that I be presented before the Caliph and extended kindness to me turning the Caliph's heart towards me, not on account of my own righteousness but through His kindness and because of His covenant (with Israel). Thereby the downcast Jews were exalted with salvation and the hands of their oppressors slackened and shrank from further imposition, and their yoke was lightened through the mercy of our God."[1]

[1] Letter to king Joseph, beginning: ולפי (=ואף על פי) שבני הגולה אנו, פליטת ישראל, עבדי אדוני המלך (היינו: הכליף) שרוים בשלוה בארץ מגורינו, כי אלהינו לא עזבנו ולא

Evidently by Ḥisdai's influence as treasurer of the Caliph the previous method of arbitrary exactions from the Jews was considerably modified. The contemporary Hebrew poets in Spain, like Menaḥem b. Sarūḳ, Dunāsh b. Labrāṭ and the former's disciples, greatly eulogise Ḥisdai for his being a tower of strength to his coreligionists.[2] Menaḥem's disciples describe how the statesman's absence from Cordova afforded the enemies of the Jews an opportunity for intrigues and how his return to the capital meant the frustration of all their evil designs.[3]

Again in his letter to King Joseph, Ḥisdai alludes to his diplomatic endeavors on behalf of the Jews outside the Spanish Caliphate when interviewing the foreign ambassadors that would visit Cordova in order to negotiate certain state agreements. He made it his practice to inquire of these envoys about the Jewish position in their respective countries hoping in addition to hear ultimately of an independent Jewish dominion in some distant

סר צלו מעלינו. ויהי כאשר מעלנו באלהינו הביאנו במשפט וישת מועקה במתנינו, ויער את רוח הפקידים אשר היו על ישראל וישימו עליו שרי מסים ויכבדו עולם וילחצום בחמה עזה, ויכנעו תחתיהם ותמצאן אותם צרות רבות ורעות. וכראות אלהינו את ענים ועמלם ואפס עצור ועזוב, היתה סבה מאתו ויציבני לפני המלך ועלי הטה חסד ויסב את לבבו (היינו: לב הכליף) אלי, לא בצדקתי כי אם בחסדו ולמען בריתו, ובזאת עניי הצאן קודרים שנבו ישע ותרפינה ידי לוחציהם ותקפץ ידם מעונש ויקל עולם ברחמי אלהינו.

The expression עונש is used here, as in the Gaonic responsa and elsewhere, in the meaning of arbitrary impost and heavy taxation (see Mann, *JQR.*, *N. S.*, X, 126, note 187 and *Jews in Egypt*, II, Hebrew Glossary s. v.).

[2] Thus Menaḥem in the introductory poem to his well-known letter of complaint to Ḥisdai for the treatment meted out to him (in Brody-Albrecht, *Sha'ar Hashshir*, 1906, p. 1, l. 9): גם היה היה. לכל שארית השביה. חומה ובצרון. Likewise Dunāsh in the poem wherewith he dedicated his refutation of Menaḥem's Dictionary to Ḥisdai (ibid., p. 4, l. 31): לעמו טוב דרש. וקמיהם גרש. ושבר רע חורש. ונזר מתגרים.

[3] In the dedicatory poem to Ḥisdai accompanying the defence of their master's Dictionary against the strictures of Dunāsh (ibid., pp. 5–6, ll. 5ff.): ותגל הערבה. ותפרח בתנובה. לראש כלה כי בא. בשמחה ובשירים: אשר מדי הלכים. פעמיו בדרכים. מאורות נחשכים. והיו נקדרים: ועיר ההללה (היינו: קרטובה). ביופי נגבלה. לאחריו משפלה. וישביה עכורים: ושממו אביוניו. בהעלימו עיניו. ולא ראו פניו. מאירות כמאורים: ומשלו הזדים. בלכתו—בשרידים (היינו: היהודים). והיו כעבדים. קנוים ומכורים: והשתוממו כלם. למען סר צלם. ומקל את עלם. גדולים וצעירים: אשר נפשם חיה. וגם היה היה. כפלג בציה. וגם מים קרים: והסיר את סבלו. לעמו גם חבלו. ונפשו עגמה לו. ורחמיו נכמרים: ושבט נגש בו. שברו מקרבו. וגם מנע מבוא. עליהם אכזרים: אשר אין בלעדיו (היינו: השם). ברחמיו וחסדיו. שלחו לשרידיו. למחיה ומזרים:

region.[4] This allusion testifies to his great concern for the Jews in other countries, and the inference is justified that he pleaded with the ambassadors to make their influence felt at their respective courts on behalf of the Jews. Positive proof of his diplomatic intervention on behalf of Byzantine Jewry we have now in the Genizah leaf given below (sub No. I), unfortunately very damaged, which is evidently a copy of the original diplomatic missive of Ḥisdai to the court of Byzantium. In pleading for a better treatment of the Jews in Christian Byzantium he could proudly refer to his own record in showing a benevolent attitude towards the Christians in Andalusia (recto, l. 19).

It is interesting to note that his correspondence was in *Hebrew*, in the same Paiṭanic style as the letter to king Joseph of Khazaria which reminds one immediately of its author, the fine stylist Menaḥem b. Sarūḳ, Ḥisdai's Hebrew secretary. Evidently some Jews accompanied the Byzantine envoys to Cordova in the role of interpreters, especially as their coreligionist Ḥisdai was the person delegated by the Caliph to receive all the embassies and to introduce them in due course to him.[5] These Jewish interpreters would upon their return to Constantinople translate Ḥisdai's Hebrew letters to the persons addressed. It is from these Jewish interpreters that Ḥisdai probably obtained the real information about the actual Jewish position in the various countries and also ascertained to whom to appeal in order to obtain effective intervention. Ḥisdai was experienced enough to realize that from the official envoys, skilled in diplomatic discretion, the whole truth could not be secured. It is also probable that these Jewish interpreters, accompanying the

[4] ואת כל השלוחים האלה, מביאי המנחות, אני שואל אותם תמיד בעד אחינו ישראל, פליטת הגולה, אם (probably read ואם) שמעו שמע לדבר הדרור לשרידים אשר כלו בעבודה ולא מצאו מנוח. Thus Ḥisdai would as a rule inquire about the Jewish position and also about "the report concerning the freedom for the remnants" (viz. about an independent Jewish dominion).

[5] Thus Ḥisdai reports in his letter to king Joseph: ומלכי הארץ כשמעם את גדולתו ואת תקפו (היינו: של הכליף) יובילו לו שי ויחלו פניו במנחות ובחמודות, ומהם מלך אשכנז, ומלך הגבלים שהם אלצקלאב, ומלך קשטנטיניה ומלכים אחרים, ועל ידי תבאנה מנחתם ועל ידי תצאנה גמולתם. תבענה שפתי תהלה לאלהי השמים אשר הטה עלי חסדו לא בצדקתי כי אם ברוב רחמיו.

envoys, transmitted to Ḥisdai letters from the Jewish communities appealing for the use of his influence on their behalf.[6]

Ḥisdai's fame spread all over the Diaspora and the letters sent to him by whole communities and by individuals must have been numerous. Whether these epistles together with copies of his replies have been systematically preserved during his lifetime is impossible to ascertain owing to lack of evidence. Whatever may have been the case, they are hardly likely to turn up again in Spain. But the few Genizah fragments available show that there was in Egypt a desire to procure copies of the correspondence of this Jewish statesman, both his own epistles as well as those sent to him; at least the correspondence that concerned the larger Jewish issues in the various countries of the Diaspora. Ultimately fragments of these copies found their way into the lumber room of the Palestinian synagogue at Fusṭāṭ and from there in recent years to various libraries as Genizah manuscripts. So far we have an incomplete fragment of two letters from Ḥisdai to the Empress and the Emperor of Byzantium respectively, to be discussed here under I, and a fragment of 2 incomplete letters to Ḥisdai from Italy, to be discussed subsequently under II. A copy of a letter from French Jewry to him is given under III.

There is further an epistle from the Babylonian schools (or school), soon after the honorary title of Rosh Kallah had been bestowed upon him, appealing for his sustained interest in the welfare of scholarship at the ancient seats of learning in Baby-

[6] Of such Jewish interpreters special mention is made in the letter to king Joseph as having come in the company of the envoys from the king of the Slavs (והנה שלוחי מלך הגבלים באים ועמהם ב' אנשים מישראל, שם האחד מר שאול ושם הב' מר יוסף). For further information about these interpreters see infra sub No. III.

Reference should also be made to the Jew Isaac who accompanied Charlemagne's embassy to Harūn ar-Rashīd and who was its sole survivor on the return journey to the Emperor's residence at Aix-la-Chapelle bringing with him the Caliph's reply and gifts in 802 (see Aronius, *Regesten zur Geschichte der Juden im Fränkischen u. Deutschen Reiche*, 1902, p. 26, No. 71).

About the Jew Ibrāhīm ibn Ya'ḳūb, who is supposed to have been in the company of the envoys of the Caliph of Cordova to Germany (cp. Aronius, ibid., p. 56, No. 130), see now Georg Jacob (*Arabische Berichte von Gesandten an germanische Fürstenhöfe*, 1. Heft, 1927, p. 6) who denies his official connection with this embassy.

lon.[7] This epistle was probably copied in Fusṭāṭ during its transmission from Bagdād to Cordova via the capital of Egypt.[8] The biography of Sa‘adyah Gaon, sent to Ḥisdai by the late Gaon's son, Dosa,[9] has unfortunately not turned up in the Genizah, though it may be surmised that it too had been copied in Fusṭāṭ during its transit to Cordova. Also Dunāsh b. Tamīm of Ḳairwān corresponded with Ḥisdai ibn Shaprūṭ on matters of astronomy.[9a] Who knows whether Jewish communal affairs did not also form the subject of their correspondence?

The most famous correspondence of Ḥisdai's was, of course, the letter to king Joseph of Khazaria and the latter's reply. Of this copies were available in Spain in the 12th century. Abraham ibn Daud of Toledo refers to it[10] and also Judah b.

[7] See the fragment published by Mann, *Hebrew Union College Jubilee Volume*, 1925, pp. 252–57, where the probability of its having been addressed to Ḥisdai has been demonstrated.

[8] About this procedure at Fustāt of copying Gaonic responsa and other writings destined to communities beyond Egypt, see Mann, *JQR.*, *N. S.*, VIII, pp. 355–8.

[9] This biography is cited by Abraham ibn Daud (ספר סדר הקבלה, in Neubauer, *Med. Jew. Chron.*, I, p. 66, top): ויתר דברי רב סעדיה והטובות אשר עשה לישראל הנם כתובים על ספר הגלוי ועל אגרת ר' דוסא בנו שכתב לר' חסדאי הנשיא בר רב יצחק מנוחתו בכבוד. It is doubtful whether Abraham ibn Daud ever used Dosa's letter when writing his chronicle, else his account of Sa‘adyah would have been more satisfactory than it is.

[9a] See the passage from Dunāsh's commentary on Sepher Yeṣirah (cited by Munk, *Notice sur Abou'l Walid Merwan ibn-Djana'h*, p. 52, note 1): וכבר בארנו זה ושמנו לו תבניות בספרנו אשר חברנוהו ושגרנוהו אל אבי יוסף חסדאי בן יצחק בתשובות שאלות שהגיעו אלינו ממדינת קסטנטינה והוא שלשה חלקים. החלק הראשון בידיעת תכונת הגלגלים, והחלק השני ההכרח בחכמת הגלגל מצרך חשבון. והשלישי בדרך הכוכבים. Munk suggests that this work probably related to the Jewish calendar and further surmises that Ḥisdai sent the question to Dunāsh of Ḳairwān via Constantinople because direct communications between Cordova and Ḳairwān were very difficult owing to hostilities between ‘Abd-ar-Raḥmān and the Fāṭimid Caliph of North-Africa. The very corrupt version of Dunāsh's commentary from MS. Bodl. 2250 (published by M. Grossberg, ס' יצירה המיוחס לאברהם אבינו ע"ה עם פרוש הרב הקדמון אבוסהל דונש בן תמים, London 1902, p. 31, bottom) has this passage in a defective manner: וכבר בארנו זה ושמנו לו תמונה בספרנו אשר חברנו בתכונה ובספרנו אשר עשינו אותו שליחות אל אא (אבו) יוסף בנו חסדאי (sic !) והוא ג' חלקים וכו'.

[10] Ibid., p. 78, bottom: ויוסף מלכם שלח ספר לר' חסדאי הנשיא בר' יצחק בן שפרוט והודיעו שהוא על דעת הרבנות וכל עמו.

Barzillai of Barcelona,[11] in addition to Judah Hallevi who, in his Kuzari, evidently drew from the reply of King Joseph to Ḥisdai. It is of interest, however, that Isaac ʻAḳrīsh, who first edited this correspondence in Constantinople (about 1577), evidently obtained his copy in Cairo. He describes his journey from Constantinople to Egypt in 1562 and the stories he heard on board ship of the whereabouts of an independent Jewish kingdom. Aroused by this tittle-tattle he made further inquiries at Alexandria and then in Cairo where it seems he also came upon a copy of the Khazār correspondence and was induced by this excitement concerning the "ten lost tribes" to edit the correspondence as further evidence of the existence of an independent Jewish dominion.[12] In his naiveness Isaac

[11] The interesting remarks of Judah al-Barceloni have been published by S. Assaf (*Jeschurun*, ed. Wohlgemuth, XI (1924), Hebrew part, pp. 113–117). See also Dubnow (*Livre d'Hommage . . . Poznański*, 1927, Hebrew part, pp. 2–3 = Anhang 3 in his *Weltgeschichte des jüd. Volkes*, IV, pp. 479–83). R. Judah mentions another epistle from a Constantinople Jew about the wars between Byzantium and the Khazārs: וזה שהוצרכנו לכתוב על (r. כל) זה מפני שמצאתי נוסח כתב אחר שכתב יהודי בלשונו בקונסטנטינופולי ממלכי קונסטנטינופולי (viz. concerning the Byzantine emperors) והזכיר מלחמות שאירעו בין מלכי קונסטנטינופולי ובין אהרן, וכן נמי מלחמות בין בני אותם המלכים של גוים ובין יוסף המלך בן אהרן. Assaf (ibid. p. 115) rightly remarks that this letter is unfortunately lost. But Dubnow (ibid. p. 3, note 1) is ready to identify it with the fragment published by Schechter (*JQR.*, *N.S.*, III, 181ff.) which is hardly likely. This letter from Constantinople, of which R. Judah had a Hebrew copy, seems to have been written *originally in Greek* and hence he was careful in stating שכתב יהודי ב ל ש ו נ ו בקונסטנטינופולי after mentioning the reply of king Joseph to Ḥisdai which was in *Hebrew*: וראיתי במקצת נוסחאות (i. e. in some MS. texts) נוסח כתב שכתב יוסף המלך בן אהרן הכהן כוזרי (evidently a corruption of הכנן, Khagan!) לר' חסדאי בר יצחק. Moreover the Schechter fragment was clearly sent by a Jew living in Khazaria and not in the Byzantine capital. This identification therefore should be dropped. When this Constantinople epistle was written, whether to Ḥisdai, as seems likely, and whether before the disastrous onslaughts of the Russians on Khazaria (966–69) or afterwards, remains still problematic as long as a copy of it is not forthcoming.

[12] Isaac ʻAḳrish's publication, which is very rare, contains first the Bustanai story (מעשה בית דוד בימי מלכות פרס, fols. 1a–5a) and then קול מבשר (fol. 5b ff.) dealing with reports about the whereabouts of the "ten lost tribes." (fol. 6b) יודע לפני כל יודעי דת המקוים ומחכים לישועת ה' כי בשנת השכ"ב ליצירה (=1562) נסעתי מקושטנדינא לארץ מצרים דרך ים, ובספינה לא היה שם (r. שום) יהודי זולתי, והיו בספינה ישמעאלי' ותוגרמים וערביים והיו באים אצלי להתוכח עמי כי אני בעונותי נכה רגלים

'Aḳrīsh did not realise that several centuries had already passed since the Khazār kingdom had ceased to exist. He also seems to have had no idea as to who Ḥisdai b. Isaac, the king's correspondent, really was.

Of course it is possible that a copy of this correspondence was brought to Egypt by the Spanish exiles after 1492 and onwards, but as there was an interest in Egypt in Ḥisdai's activities on behalf of Jewry several centuries before, as evidenced by the Genizah fragments that date certainly of the 11th century, if not earlier, it is only natural that a copy of this famous Khazār correspondence was in vogue in Fusṭāṭ still in the lifetime of Ḥisdai. This is further established by the fact that the Genizah has preserved a fragment of a letter sent by a Jew of Khazaria to Ḥisdai (published by Schechter, *JQR*, *N.S.*, *III*, 189–219). The original has evidently been transmitted via Constantinople to Cordova and indeed the author alludes to Ḥisdai's messengers who travelled to Constantinople.[13] Subsequently a copy of this epistle found its way to Fusṭāṭ.

All these data testify to the strong interest the Egyptian Jews took in the activities of their famous coreligionist of Cordova, activities that concerned the welfare of כלל ישראל and hence deserved to be known all over the Diaspora. It is only by new finds in Egypt that more of these noble activities of Ḥisdai will be made manifest in the annals of Jewish history.

נגוע הטיול מוכה הבטלה, והיו מלעיגים עלי ואני הייתי גם כן מלעיג עליהם כן משפטנו כל היום וכו'; (fol. 7b) ואני יצחק כשמעי את הדברי' האלה מפי הזקן מסיח לפי תומו שמחתי ונתתי שבח והודאה לש"י שזכני לשמוע אלו הדברים וכיוצא בהם. וכשהגעתי לאלכסנדריא של מצרים שמעתי רמז מה בין היהודים ובלבול על אודות השבטים . . . וכשהלכתי מאלסכנדריא למצרים (i. e. Cairo) מיד בעת ההיא הלכתי אצל החכם הנזכר (היינו: הרופא שמואל שולם) . . . (8b); וכששמעתי אלו הדברים ו ר א י ת י אגרת ששלח (i. e. Ḥisdai) למלך הכוזר ותשובתו (he evidently saw the copy in Cairo) אמרתי להדפיסם בעט ברזל ועופרת לחזק ולהאמין אמונה אומן שיש ליהודים מלכות וממשלה וכו'.

The other version of king Joseph's reply (printed from a MS. Firkowicz by Harkawy, מאסף נדחים No. 8, reprinted at the end of Kuzari, ed. Zifrinowitz) probably also emanates from Egypt (cp. also Schechter, *JQR.*, *N. S.*, III, p. 183).

[13] Ibid. p. 210, ll. 86–7: והו (=והוא) מימין לים הבא מארצכ[ם] אשר עברו בו שלוחיך לקוסטנטינא. The reading מארצכם is visible from the facsimile on p. 211. Schechter's suggested reading (note 47) מהמלכות is certainly unlikely

I.

Ḥisdai's Intervention on Behalf of the Jews in Byzantium

The two incomplete letters, given under No. I, forming the starting point for our discussion of Ḥisdai's correspondence, are evidently both written to Byzantium. The first, the beginning of which is missing, is addressed to a lady of great power and influence. Ḥisdai appeals to her by stating that "I know that you can achieve everything and that nothing is impossible for you by your intelligent plan when you will it wholeheartedly" (recto, ll. 15–16). He alludes to two requests made in his letter (l. 2) the nature of which was no doubt described in the missing part of the epistle. He continues further to plead for religious liberty to be granted to the Jews that they be not compelled to forsake their faith (ll. 4ff.) and suggests that the lady addressed should appoint one of her subordinates to take special care of the Jewish affairs so that the Jews would be placed under her direct protection (ll. 11ff.). He points to his own benevolent attitude towards the Christians in Cordova and in the whole of Spain (ll. 18–9) and evidently to his close relations with the Caliph (l. 20). In conclusion he elegantly draws her attention to the fact that all persons of intellect and knowledge desire that their deeds be remembered by posterity and thus by her kindness to the Jews, the exalted lady will leave a lasting memorial of her deeds (verso, ll. 3ff.).

The remainder of verso (ll. 9ff.) contains the beginning of an epistle addressed to a "great ruler" who is much eulogised. The writer informs him that his letter has reached 'Abd ar-Raḥmān, the Spanish Caliph (ll. 17–18).

It is very much to be regretted that the bottom of the leaf is so damaged that the reference to the "land of the Khazārs," contained at the end of recto, is altogether obscure. But it is evident that the persons addressed are the Empress Helena and her royal husband Constantine Porphyrogennetos (912–959). The latter was a scholar and for a long time allowed his father-in-law Romanos Lekapenos (919–44) to be the actual ruler of Byzantium. Romanos started a plot in 944 against his son-in-law in order to put his own sons in the saddle, but the latter turned on their own father and had him imprisoned. Shortly afterwards, in January 945, Constantine got rid of Romanos' sons making them join their father in the same prison monastery and became again supreme ruler while in reality the government was conducted by his wife Helena.[14] Romanos towards the end of his regime (viz. in 943) had instituted a religious persecution against the Jews of which mention is made in the letter of the Jew from Khazaria to Ḥisdai published by Schechter.[15] The Khazār king Joseph in retaliation persecuted the Christians in his own dominion.

It seems that after the overthrow of Romanos Ḥisdai found the opportune occasion for appealing to the royal couple for religious tolerance towards the Jews, especially to the all powerful Helena. Ḥisdai was thus accurately informed when he alluded

[14] See Gibbon, *History of the Decline and Fall of the Roman Empire*, ch. 48; Hertzberg, *Geschichte der Byzantiner u. des osman. Reiches*, 1883, pp. 156–7.

[15] *JQR.*, *N. S.*, III, 208, ll. 61ff: וגם בימי יוסף המלך אדני... ב ה י ו ת ה ש מ ד ה ב י מ י ר ו מ נ ו ס ה ר ש ע [כשנודע] הדב[ר] לאדוני סילה רבים ערלים. Cp. also Krauss, *Studien zur byz.-jüd. Geschichte*, 1914, p. 45. About Romanos' persecution see now the Hebrew apocalypse (printed by Ginzberg, גנזי שעכטער I, 1928, p. 320, top): ואחר כך יקום מלך ויצערם בהגרשה ולא בהשחתה אבל ברחמנות, ויתן פניו באלים (r. באלים=באלהים) ולא יצליח, במהרה ישנה (r. תשנה) מלכותו. Dr. Ginzberg (p. 316) rightly interprets this passage as referring to Romanos and his persecution, which was not as serious as the previous ones in Byzantium. It chiefly involved the exile of a number of Jews who fled to Khazaria as Mas'udi reports (Murūj adh-dhahb; the edition of this work being unavailable to me, the extract in Hebrew translation (given in Kahana, ספרות ההסטוריא הישראלית, I, 53) is appended here: ורבים מהיהודים מן שאר ארצות הישמעאלים ומן רום (Byzantium) נלוו לו (היינו: למלך הכוזרים), כי בשנת של"ב (943 C. E.=H.) ארמנוס (Romanos) המלך אנס את היהודים בארצו להכניסם אל הדת הנוצרית).

On the other hand a rather legendary account of a letter from Petrus, Doge of Venice, to Henry I of Germany would indicate that the religious persecution of Romanus, forcing the Jews of his Empire to embrace Christianity, took place between 932–36 (see Aronius, *Regesten*, pp. 53–4). But the expression "ad Romanum imperatorem" is rather vague and the whole account belongs rather to the realm of legend. Further data are needed to clarify the whole question of the cause and the date of Romanos' religious persecution of the Byzantine Jews. Cp. however Franz Dölger, *Regesten der Kaiserurkunden des oström. Reiches*, I (1924), No. 624, where there is cited an order (jussit) by Romanos I, at the suggestion of the Patriarch of Jerusalem, that all Jews in Byzantium should be baptised (about 932–6 C. E.).

to her being able to achieve all she undertook (above, p. 10). The royal husband, known for his scholarship, Ḥisdai could well compliment on his intellectual abilities (verso, ll. 9–12).

Ḥisdai probably became acquainted with conditions in Byzantium in general, and with the Jewish position in particular, through his close contact with the embassy sent by Constantine (in about 944–49) to 'Abd ar-Raḥmān. The envoys brought as a gift a copy of the famous medical work of Dioskorides and as no person in Cordova could translate it from the Greek, word was sent to Constantine, who despatched the monk Nicolas to help translate it into Latin, whereas Ḥisdai by his knowledge of medicine and of Latin, assisted in the final rendering of the work into Arabic.[16] The Byzantine envoys could clearly realize the exalted position held by the Jewish statesman in Cordova and report their findings to the court at Constantinople. How far Ḥisdai was successful in his pleadings on behalf of Byzantine Jewry is at present unknown and only new finds of source material will illumine the obscurities that surround his endeavors on behalf of his coreligionists.

II.

Ḥisdai's Relations with the Jews of Southern Italy

The fragment, given under No. II, has been published and commented upon in a rather haphazard manner by Mr. E. N. Adler (*REJ*, LXVII (1914), 40–3).[17] However he rightly identi-

[16] About the translation into Arabic of the medical work of Dioscorides see Graetz, *Geschichte der Juden*, V, 4th edition, p. 536, and Steinschneider, *JQR.*, XIII, 98. On the basis of Ibn Joljol, who relates that the monk Nicolas was sent by Romanos in 948–9, Steinschneider (see also his *Arab. Liter. der Juden*, p. 115) declares the Byzantine embassy to 'Abd ar-Raḥmān to have been despatched by the Emperor Romanos II and not by Constantine and therein he is followed by Eppenstein who corrects Graetz accordingly (ibid. p. 342, note 1). But this is chronologically impossible. Romanos I Lakapenos was thrown into prison in December 944 whereas Romanos II, Constantine's son, only came to the throne in 959. Ibn Joljol no doubt confused Constantine with Romanos I. Indeed Ibn Adhari (cited by Graetz, ibid. p. 537) states: ופיהא (פי סנה̈ 334) וצל אלי קרטבה̈ רסל מלך אלרום אלאכבר ק ס ט נ ט י ן—צאחב אלקסטנטינה̈—בכתאב מן מלכהם אלי אלנאצר. 334 H. corresponds to 945 C. E.

[17] Cp. also Poznański, ibid. 288ff. Cassuto wrote a special article on the fragment (Una lettera ebraica de secolo X, in *Giornale della Societa Asiatica*

fied the person addressed with Ḥisdai ibn Shaprūṭ. The second epistle, of which only a few introductory lines in heavy Paiṭanic style are preserved (verso, ll. 19–26), has the superscription: כתב ר' יהודה בן יעקב מרומה ז"ל למרב חסדאי נ"ע. Both are mentioned as departed, a fact which clearly shows that we have a later copy of the original sent to Cordova. But the first letter, the beginning of which is missing, has also been addressed to the same dignitary as the phraseology indicates. He is addressed as "the holy one of God honored in splendor" (r., l. 2), "our nobleman" (l. 3); allusion is made to his "greatness and authority" (l. 22), combining "wisdom, humility and power" such as unheard of since the Biblical kings of Israel (ll. 24–5). He is further called "the pride of the scattered sheep" (viz. Israel, v., l. 1)[18] and "our leader and guide" (v., l. 14)—all these attributes apply fittingly to our Ḥisdai in his exalted position at Cordova which he utilized on behalf of Jewry all over the Diaspora.

This letter, probably emanating from the important Jewish community of Bari,[19] is evidently in answer to a previous communication from Ḥisdai which, owing to the troublesome times, could not be replied to immediately (r., l. 2f.). The communities in Southern Italy experienced a brief persecution lasting 2 days, and when this letter was written already 9 months seem to have passed since that event (see verso, l. 3). The nature of the persecution is rather obscure but it seems to have involved the burning of Jewish writings (in recto, l. 11, Torah is evidently a general term for the Jewish religious literature having its basis in the Bible). The destruction by fire started in Bari whence the Jews of Otranto were secretly warned to be on their guard and hide their books (r., l. 12). Probably there was a general prohibition involving the study of Judaism and those caught were tortured unless they accepted Christianity. In Otranto 2 scholars, R. Isaiah and R. Menaḥem, and their disciple R. Elijah died as martyrs

Italiana, vol. 29, pp. 97–110). The corrected version given here removes several difficulties raised by these scholars.

[18] In this phrase גאון שה פזורה no official title Gaon should be sought as Adler (ibid., p. 40) does.

[19] As Cassuto (ibid., pp. 104–5) has rightly suggested.

(r., ll. 4ff.). The raid on Jewish literature and its students lasted for 2 days and was soon stopped (r., ll. 12ff.).

In the epistle there are enumerated the scholars that escaped the persecution, among them R. Abraham b. Yehoshaphaṭ, formerly Rabbi of Oria (r., l. 16–17), a community so well known from the Aḥima'aṣ Chronicle. The Oria community is referred to as "scattered" (המפוזרה) which shows that the local Jews were in dispersion on account of exile. Perhaps we obtain here a clue for the date of our epistle. The Saracen raid on Oria in 925 during which Sabbatai Donnolo was captured is too early to be considered in this connection.[20] But Oria was overwhelmed again in 952 when Paltiel, of Aḥima'aṣ Chronicle fame, was among the prisoners soon to become the favorite of al-Mu'izz, Crown Prince and subsequently Fāṭimid Caliph of North Africa (and of Egypt after 969). Hence our letter dates after 952. But if the persecution, evidently engineered by the Byzantine authorities of Southern Italy, was one phase of the general religious persecution in Byzantium under Romanos,[21] then the phrase "scattered" for the Oria community would apply to the state of affairs after the raid of 925 which resulted in many previous members abiding in those places where they happened to be ransomed and did not subsequently return to their former habitations.[22]

Our epistle further enumerates the names of the scholars

[20] Cassuto, ibid., p. 103–4, maintains that the condition of the Oria community after 925 is meant here. However his argument about the account of the raid on Oria (given in the Aḥima'aṣ Chronicle, ed. Neubauer, *Med. Jew. Chronicles*, II, p. 125) to refer also to that of 925 cannot be accepted. There al-Mu'izz, the Fāṭimid Crown Prince, is clearly mentioned. To say with Cassuto (p. 103, note 1) that the mention of al-Mu'izz is a scribal error, is impossible as the whole subsequent account concerning Palṭiel, one of the captives from Oria, and his close connection with the Crown Prince, and subsequently with him when already Caliph till the conquest of Egypt in 969 and beyond, hinges on this prince. We have to take this account to refer to the raid of 952 (see also Kaufmann, *Ges. Schriften*, III, 29, where 962 and also 852 (p. 28, n. 3) have to be corrected to 952) shortly before al-Mu'izz ascended the throne.

[21] Cp. also Cassuto, ibid., pp. 108–9.

[22] Sabbatai Donnolo was ransomed in Tarento while his parents and relatives were brought as captives to Palermo and North-Africa (see the introduction to his commentary on Sepher Yeṣirah, חכמוני, ed. Castelli).

that escaped from the persecution in Otranto (r., l. 19ff.). Finally an excuse is sent on behalf of a certain Samuel, called "trustworthy" (evidently he was the bearer of the epistle to our Ḥisdai; about his official connection with Ḥisdai, see infra sub No. III), who after the persecution undertook to copy the famous Yosippon for Ḥisdai, but was robbed by brigands on his way to Bari, near נפיאה,[23] losing the copy together with all the epistles he was bearing. An attempt has been made by Abraham, the son of Sason the physician and president of the Bari community, together with other companions to overtake on horseback the brigands but it evidently was not successful (verso, ll. 1–9). This copyist Samuel underwent terrible tortures (evidently during the persecution), but he remained steadfast in his faith (v., ll. 11–13).

What the aim was of the correspondence from Bari to Ḥisdai, which Samuel was to bring (he had also other letters with him when the brigands fell upon him), and what the occasion was for Ḥisdai's previous communication to this community, still remains obscure. But it may be taken for granted that the Jewry of that part of Southern Italy which was subject to Byzantium, appealed to him to use his influence in pleading with the court at Constantinople for a larger measure of religious tolerance towards the Jews within the Empire.

If the identification with Ḥisdai as the recipient of the letter and its dating in connection with the persecution of Romanos be correct, we have here the earliest reference to the book Yosippon so popular in the Jewish circles of the Middle Ages. It also disposes of the dating of the book after the crowning of Otto I in Rome as Emperor (962), as accepted by modern scholars (see e. g. Vogelstein-Rieger, *Geschichte der Juden in Rom*, I, 193–4, 196ff.). The description of the crowning of an Emperor in Rome can just as well refer to Charlemagne (Christmas, 800). But it seems that through Ḥisdai's interest the book was for the first time introduced among the Jews of Spain, as it is to be assumed that our Samuel ultimately finished a new copy for

[23] This place is certainly not identical with Naples (Napoli) as Adler thinks (cp. also Cassuto, p. 101, note 1).

Ḥisdai. That the first copy took him 9 months to complete would indicate that it was the more extensive version, of which Judah Mosconi speaks (אוצר טוב, 017ff., in *Magazin*, III), and from which our existent texts are but abbreviations.

III.

A Letter from French Jewry to Ḥisdai Bearing on the Community of Toulouse in the Provence

The epistle given under No. III, the beginning of which is evidently missing, emanates from "the congregations of France" (קהלות פרנצא, r., l. 6). No indication is given as to which communities were represented in the drawing up of this letter and where the communal leaders met in order to address the prominent Jewish dignitary eulogised therein by many flattering terms. The spokesmen of these communities report of the arrival of 3 persons, Saul, Joseph and Judah, who had visited this dignitary and related of his great position (r., ll. 11 ff.). There has further arrived an agent of this dignitary, Samuel by name, with instructions to ascertain from the communities as to what services his master might render to them in using his influence on their behalf. The communities decided to ask him to seek to abolish the disgraceful practice at Toulouse where the Jews were compelled to supply annually at Easter 30 pounds of wax for the Church (לעבודה זרה, r., l. 21) and the bearer of which tax in kind was given a wound on his neck. When Samuel the agent had heard of this request, he assured the communities that the task would be easy for his master to accomplish (r., l. 17—v., l. 2). The letter concludes with expressions of thanks to Divine Providence for raising up such a worthy leader in Israel and of good wishes for the continued greatness of this person styled נשיא ישראל (v., l. 19).

This barbaric practice of Toulouse is known from other sources.[24] Only at the beginning of the 12th century was the practice changed into a tax to the Church. A specious reason for the practice was given that the Jews had once betrayed the

[24] See Israel Lévi, *REJ*, LII, 162–3, and cp. Saige, *Les Juifs du Languedoc*, 1881, p. 11; Dubnow, *Weltgesch. d. jüd. Volkes*, IV, 128.

city to the Saracens and as a punishment a representative of the Jewish community was boxed in the ear once a year (or three times according to one story). But Israel Lévi is probably right in tracing the insult as a revenge for the maltreatment of Jesus (Matthew 26.67, John 18.22). This is corroborated by the detail in our text of the 30 pounds of wax (for candles) which the Jews had to supply on that occasion, the number 30 evidently corresponding to the 30 pieces of silver Judas Iscariot had received for his betrayal of Jesus (Matthew 26.15).

The identity of the dignitary asked to abolish this practice is nowhere indicated in our text. The nearest thought would be to assume that he was the Nasi of Narbonne of the family of R. Makhir, the so-called "Roi Juif." If we further assume that our letter dates from the beginning of the 12th century when, as a result of the intervention of this Nasi, the practice was modified into a monetary exaction, then we would have here an epistle to R. Ḳalonymos b. Ṭodros who reached a great age of 90 that extended from the second half of the 11th century to the first half of the 12th century.[25]

Yet this obvious identification is to be rejected for the more likely alternative that our epistle really dates from the 10th century and has been addressed to no less a person than Ḥisdai ibn Shaprūṭ. We have seen above (p. 11–12) that a certain Samuel was Ḥisdai's representative (נאמן) in Southern Italy and here too the dignitary's agent is thus styled. Moreover, there are mentioned Saul, Joseph and Judah who had arrived after paying a visit to this dignitary. Curiously enough in the company of the embassy from the king of Slavonia to 'Abd ar-Raḥmān there were 2 Jews, called *Saul* and *Joseph*, who volunteered to forward Ḥisdai's letter to the king of the Khazārs.[26] The

[25] Abraham ibn Daud (ס' סדר הקבלה, in one MS. version given by Neub., *Med. Jew. Chron.*, I, 82–3) reports: והיה שם (בנרבונה) לגאון רב טודרוס הידוע הנשיא ובניו מזרע זה ר' מכיר הנשיא ולא פסקה מהם גדולה וממשלה ותורה כמו הנשיא הגדול והידוע מרנא ורבנא קלונימוס הגדול. הוא התנהג השררא הגדולה (read בשררה גדולה) והיטיב לישראל בימיו והאריך ימים בגדולה והיו ימיו תשעים שנה ומת. About the date of this Ḳalonymos see Régné, *REJ*, LXII, p. 9.

[26] Letter to the Khazār ruler: אני טרם אכלה לדבר אל לבי, והנה שלוחי מלך הגבלים באים ועמהם שני אנשים מישראל, שם האחד מר שאול ושם השני מר יוסף, וכשמעם את מהומתי נחמו אותי, ואמרו לי: „תנה לנו אגרותיך ואנחנו נגיען אל מלך הגבלים, ובשביל כבודך

order of the names, first Saul and then Joseph, is the same, only in our text a third person is mentioned, Judah. They are styled 'our great ones' (גדולנו, r., l. 13) which shows that they were men of standing as befitting persons travelling in the company of an embassy. The envoys of king Hunu of Slavonia visited Cordova in 952–3[27] and it would have to be assumed that for some unknown reason instead of travelling by sea from a part in the Adriatic to Spain, they preferred a land route over northern Italy to southern France and from there to Cordova; or perhaps the embassy first visited Germany, then France and finally Spain for diplomatic negotiations in each country. At least this route in the reverse order would have to be assumed so that these Jewish companions met in France on their home journey the leaders of the 'French communities' (קהלות פרנצא) and acquainted them of what they beheld in Cordova of the exalted position of Ḥisdai.[28]

If this reasoning be correct, then we have to think of Samuel as a regular representative of Ḥisdai visiting several Jewries on a mission from his master. We find him in Southern Italy, where he underwent hardships during a religious persecution. There he busied himself also with copying the Yosippon for his

ישנר כתבך אל בני ישראל היושבים בארץ הנגרין (Hungary), וגם כן (הם read) ישלחוה אל רוס (Russia), ומשם אל בלגאר (Bulgaria), עד שיגיע כתבך כרצונך אל המקום אשר אתה רוצה״.

[27] Cp. Ibn Adhari (cited by Graetz, 5^{4}, p. 537): פי סנה (H.) 342 קדמת רסל חוניא מלך אלצקאלבה אלי אלנאצר.

[28] Some corroboration of the assumption that the Jewish companions of the embassy came to Cordova via a land route appears from another passage in Ḥisdai's letter to the Khazār ruler: ואותם שני אנשים אשר מארץ הגבלים מר שאול ומר יוסף, אשר ערבו לי להוביל אגרתי אל אדוני המלך, אמרו לי כי .היום כמו שש שנים בא אלינו איש ישראלי סגיא נהור, איש חכם ונבון, ושמו מר עמרם, ואמר כי הוא מארץ אלכזר והיה בבית אדוני המלך ובאוכלי שלחנו ונכבד אצלו״. וכשמעי שלחתי אחריו מלאכים להשיבו אלי ולא השיגוהו. It seems that these Jews came across again or heard of the further wanderings of this blind Jew from Khazaria somewhere in France or Northern Spain and hence Ḥisdai dispatched messengers to recall him. Had they come by boat from Slavonia to Spain, there would have been no purpose in sending messengers for him, nor is it indicated that these messengers of Ḥisdai took a sea journey to search for him. The whereabouts of 'Amram must have been somewhere in Southern France or Northern Spain and Saul and Joseph met him or heard of him again just on their journey to Cordova in the company of the embassy.

master but met with ill fortune by being robbed near Bari and losing the copy together with other documents. To justify him in the eyes of his master, the community of Bari, at his request no doubt, set forth what befell him. He must have come back to Spain and sometime after 952–3 he was in France on a new mission when it was suggested to him to request Ḥisdai to intervene so that the barbaric Toulouse practice be abolished. Samuel, thinking Ḥisdai's influence to be universal, regarded this intervention as quite easy to accomplish successfully. How Ḥisdai was to achieve it, is not clear, but he could request high clergymen in the Christian kingdoms of Northern Spain to induce their colleagues in Toulouse to abate their revengeful zeal for their Savior.[29] But how far Ḥisdai succeeded is also not clear, but a complete success it certainly was not. Our text speaks of a wound inflicted on the neck of the bearer of the 30 pounds of wax. It may be that it was modified into a box in the ear only to be entirely abolished at the beginning of the 12th century. The impost that was given then instead was not so much for the abolishment of the slap on the face as for the 30 pounds of wax which the Jews naturally regarded as a violation of their religious conscience as the wax was to burn in the form of candles in the church.

This whole argument may be regarded as a hypothesis based on the coincidence of the similarity of names which may be merely accidental. However the style of our letter is rather archaic and fits in better in the 10th century than in the 12th. Moreover the designation פרנצא or צרפת in the 12th century usually denoted northern and central France (and originally the so-called Île-de-France), over which the Capet dynasty ruled, as against the Provence (פרובינצא)[30]. The latter district ruled

[29] About Ḥisdai's diplomatic successes in his negotiations with Tota, queen of Navarre, and her son Sancho, king of Leon, see especially Dozy, *Geschichte der Mauren in Spanien*, 1874, II, 52ff. Ḥisdai's triumph in inducing them to come in person to Cordova with a large retinue of noblemen and churchmen and seek an alliance with 'Abd ar-Raḥmān is eulogised in the poem of Dunāsh b. Labrāṭ (see Brody-Albrecht שער השיר, p. 4, ll. 20ff.).

[30] Thus Abraham b. Nathan of Lunel in his Manhig (ספר המנהיג, Berlin 1855) distinguishes with regard to liturgical customs between צרפת and פרובנצא (10a bottom, 17a top, 18a top, 19a top, 24a, § 4, etc.)

by various Dukes and Barons was politically independent of the French kingdom and one would rather expect that in writing to the Nasi of Narbonne the Provence communities (קהלות פרובינצא) would interest themselves in the bad plight of the Toulouse Jewry and not the קהלות פרנצא. Moreover Narbonne too was a part of Aquitania bordering on the Provence (both forming Southern France) and the Nasi Ḳalonymos would not thus receive a letter from the Provencal communities as if these were abroad. The impression is rather that the dignitary addressed was living outside France and hence the writers introduced themselves as representing קהלות פרנצא. Only if the letter dates from the tenth century can we understand the general expression קהלות פרנצא as a common term for the French communities including the Provence because since the times of Charlemagne and his son Louis the Pious, when the country was united,[31] the Jews of France must have had a combined communal organisation and the lot of the Toulouse Jewry concerned all the Jews of France. This must have continued till Hugo Capet became king of the Île-de-France (987) when the Provence formed a different political entity and צרפת or פרנצא became designated as the former's territory and in general for northern and central France as against פרובינצא for the south. Thus we find that at the Jewish communal assemblies in the time of Rashi and of his grandsons, R. Tam and R. Samuel, the Jewish communities of the Provence are not represented.[32] All this militates against the assumption of the

About פרנצא, פראנציאה, Île-de-France, see Gross, *Gallia Judaica*, 485ff., and about פרובינצא, Provence, p. 489ff. Cp. also Güdemann, *Gesch. d. Erziehungswesens u. d. Cultur d. abendl. Juden*, I, 13, n. 1.

[31] After the death of Louis (840) there takes place in course of time a division between the Western and the Eastern Frankish empires (later to be designated as France and Germany). The former is broken up and with Hugo Capet becoming king of Francia (Île-de-France) in 987, the South becomes independent of the North. Yet the Jewish communal organization must have still retained for a considerable time its former united character till in the time of Rashi and the Tosafists the Jews of פרנצא and of פרובנצא act separately in communal affairs.

[32] Cp. the Taḳḳanot of R. Tam and his brother Samuel and other leaders of several communities including those of the districts of Troyes, Auxerre, Sens, Orleans, Chalon-sur-Saône, the Rhine boundary, Paris, Melun, Etampes

letter dating at the beginning of the 12th century and strengthens the earlier date of the 10th century with Ḥisdai as the dignitary addressed. In the case of our letter, evidently a copy of the original one, we would have another fragment of Ḥisdai's correspondence with the Jewries of the Diaspora that found its way in copies to Egypt and ultimately a resting place in the Genizah. This document thus adds to the comprehensiveness of Ḥisdai's interest in the welfare of Jewry and is moreover the oldest Hebrew document we possess of French Jewry more than a century before Rashi started to become prominent in its spiritual life.

Texts

I.

[A wrapper in T.–S. Box J2, marked No. 71, contains 3 pieces of paper leaves, very damaged and faint, 2 of which have no connection with the one given below.]

(Recto)

ולעצור כוח להתאמץ בכל . . . . [ל]שאול . . . .
בעד שני הדברים האלה החקוקים באגרת [הז]את [ומבקש אני]
ממך ומפיל תחנתי ל[פני הדרת] יקרך . . . . לביב . . . .
כבודו וגם . . . . לשאול באשר בש . . . .
ממנו על [יתר] הפליטה הנותרת אצלכם מקה[ל ישראל]
הכמֵיהִ[ים] . . . . . אשר נשארו מן השבי ומן המצ[ר] . . .
ביד מו . . . . דתות אלהינו אשר למולו עובדים והאל [ית׳ש׳][1]
צום לבלתי הרחיקם מעל גבול חוקיהם ולבלתי [הדיחם]
ממסלול משפטיהם אשר הם אוחזים בו יען כי לא . . . . .

Normandy and the maritime district, Anjou, Poitiers, and Lorraine (see the text in Finkelstein, *Jewish Self-Government in the Middle Ages*, 1924, 152ff.). The Provence is entirely unrepresented. One text incorporates a decision arrived at independently by the leaders of Narbonne and its district which subsequently the leaders of Île-de-France (צרפת), Anjou, Poitiers and Normandy adopted (ibid., p. 163, and cp. p. 164).

[1] =יתברך שמו.

. . . . בחוקי כל איי הגוים וגם לא בדת ודין . . . .
. . . . כם ואם תמלאי משאל [ה]קשט[2] בפרשך כנפיך עלימו או
. . . . .בהסתוככם במחסה צילך [אז תמני] את אחד מעבדיך. . .
. . [ת]מיד עליהם ואל תשליטי אחר זולתו לנגע במו ויהיה [שמך
הנכבד] נקרא עליהם למען יתמנעו קמימו להציר להם . . . .
. . . . לחו[יות] נפשם בגלילך וידעתי כי כל תוכלי ולא יבצר
[ממך מאומה ב]מזמת תבונה ברצונך עו[ל]יהו בלב חפץ. ובזאת . .
. . . . . תיך ושמועות המלך אדוני ותגענה אל קצוי ארץ וג . . .
. . . . יד הטובה עלי ואל[הי ישר] יודיע תעלומי ונקיון סעיפי
. . . [קה]לת הנוצרים הגרים . . . במדינת קרטבה ובכל
[ארץ ספרד] כי אחותי קשורה בלבתו[3] ואהבתו לא תמוט . . .
. . . . .בכל אשר יחפצון בו. וכי גם המה[4] מעידים
. . . . ים בטוב ידי וחוסן פעלי. וגם שלוחי דברתי[5]

[There are traces of 4 more lines of which very little is legible. In the last line but one from the bottom there are discernible the words [ארץ הכזר[יים!]

(Verso)

. . . . . אנייה מאניות המלך ה . . . .
. . . ה הוא ואנשיו הבאים עמו. וגם בזאת . . . .
. . . [תשובחנה פ]עולותיך ותאושרנה טובותיך ובל ת . . .
. . . . כי לא בקשו אנשי התבונה והמדע זולתי
. . . . זוכרים ולהעצים יתור מִפְּעולתם [לדור] אחרון
. . . . . ואחרימו למען יבואון ויספרון ויגידון את
מ . . . . . ם וטעם מעבדיהם ואני בטוח כי כן יותרין

[2] This phrase recalls the one in the letter to king Joseph, beginning: אבל נשענתי בקשט נתיבה ומעגלי מישרים.

[3] Evidently the Caliph, but perhaps the chief bishop of the Christian population of Cordova and Andalusia is meant with whom Ḥisdai maintained friendly relations.

[4] Viz. the Christians in Spain.

[5] The messengers of 'my word' (my letter) will testify to my good treatment of the Christians.

[מפעל]י [הג]ברת ואומץ חסדיה סלה.
. . . מאמרי במרחבי גיליון. לאפודת[6] מלך הגדול ההו[שם]
עליון. אשר אין ערוך אליהו בדמיון. מכל יצורי תבל . . . . .
הגיון. המבין חידות במערכי הרעיון. ולא עממוהו . . . .
[ח]נוכי החביון. הנאצר[7] בצאתו בבגדי תופש[8] ותלבוש[ו] . .
שריון. לדרוך פורה בהמון קמיו לשכלם בכיליון. יהי [רצון לפני]
צורו הנותן אפיק בציון[9]. להטות עליו חנו וחסדו ב . . . .
ולבלתי תת לפעל כפיו רפיון. כי אם לעודדו . . . .
לחזקו בכל אשר ישאלהו בהגיון. כן יעש וכן . . . .
בטובו אל עליון. אודיע את יקר אדוני המלוך כי הגיעה]
אגרתו היקרה אצל עבד אלרחמן מלך ספ[רד] . . . . . .
יועצם . . . [וי]שמח לבו ויגל כבודו במע . . . .
ש . . . . . במחמדי הא . . . . ם החקוקים ב . . . .
אגרתי יתבונן אדני המלך [א]ותי ובאה . . . .

[There are traces of 4 more lines of which very little is legible.]

II.

[MS. Adler 2156, published in *REJ*, LXVII (1914), pp. 42–3; re-examined by me. A facsimile of recto is found in *Catalogue of Hebrew Manuscripts belonging to Elkan Nathan Adler*, Cambridge 1921, plate 4.]

(Recto)

קדש[10] עליו שורה. וששתי אני להקביל פניו בציווי ואזהרה. והשגתיו
. . . לפי . . . . ראווית מכתב לקדוש ייי מכובד בתפארה. ולא

[6] Cp. also the commencement of the letter to Joseph: אפודת נזר לשבט מושלים.

[7] Probably read הנהדר. Cp. the old phrase recurring in several versions of the Yom Kippur 'Abodah: 'אמת מה נהדר היה כהן גדול בצאתו מבית קדשי הקדשים וכו probably going back to the Hebrew Ben Sira (50.5) מה נהדר בהשגיחו מאהל בצאתו 'מבית הפרכת (6) ככוכב אור וכו.

[8] The meaning of בגדי תופש is not clear to me.

[9] 'In the wilderness' (צִיּוֹן).

[10] The preceding word probably was רוח, viz. the holy spirit is resting upon him.

הספקנו לכתוב לפי כבוד אצילינו לפי שהיתה השעה ממוהרה. ולי מה
יקרו ריעיך אל ישי[11] עצמו ראשיהם להדרה. ואף עדת אודרנטו
הקדושה שלשה רעים חסרה. כשנאנסו אותה גזירה הארורה.
ושמותם רב ישעיה גברא רבא צנא מלא ספרא. חסיד וצדיק ועניו אשר
עיננו כמותו לא סקרה. ור׳ מנחם חכם וירא שמ׳[12] וטורח בכל מצות הזהרה.[13]
ומר אליה תלמידם תם וישר ובעל סחורה. ר׳ ישעיה בידיו נעץ סכין
בגרונו ונשחט כשה הנזבח בעזרה. ור׳ מנחם נשמט וינער בתוך
הבורה[14]. ומ׳ אליה נחנק בראותו כי שמשו קדרה. והודיה לאל אפילו
אות אחת מן תורה. שם[15] לא הובערה. לפי שהאש מעירינו הוסקה
ובערה. ושיגרנו בסתר והודענו הדבר להם מהרה. ובין בארצינו בין[16]
בארצם הצרה עד שני ימ׳[17] גברה. ביום הג׳ יצאנו מאפילה לאורה.
כי נרצה לפניו קרבן חסידיו כעלתא תדירא[18]. וישב ייי מחרון אפו ומחמתו
ההוצתה להבעירה. וכמעט רגע היתה תחנה מאת ייי אלהינו פליטה
לנו להשאירה. ובקהלינו נשאר ר׳ אברהם בן יהושפט ההיה רב לעדת

[11] Read מה, cp. Ps. 139.17.

[12] =שמים.

[13] Probably read בכל מצוה ואזהרה, i. e. all עשין ולאוין of Judaism.

[14] For הבור to suit he rhyme.

[15] i. e. in Otranto.

[16] Read ובין.

[17] =ימים.

[18] =כעולת תמיד, cp. Onkelos to Num. 28.6.

אורס המפוזרה. ר̇ שמואל[19] בן יהודה אשר בעירינו רבה ופרה. ור̇ אברהם בן[20] ור̇ אליה בן אברהם ור̇ משה הכהן בר אפרים ור̇ אביתר

[בר] יחזקאל ושאר תלמידי חבורה[21]. ובאודרנטו נשאר ר̇ הודיה ור̇

[א]מתי בנו רבי התורה. ור̇ חייא הכהן חתנו ור̇ מרדכי ור̇ ליאון ור̇ שבתי

[ור̇ א]ברהם בר עזרא. וכולם מבקשים כבוד מר ושמחים שלומו[22]

[שתגדל ג]דולתו ותכון ממשלתו מחננים לאל נורא. תחלה . . . . . לשני[23]

[אשר] אהבתו בלבם נקשרה. ואחר כן למר שכתב לנו . . . . .

[מכתב מלא חכמ]ה וענוה וגבורה. מה שלא שמענו מימי המלכים במקרא.

(Verso)

ועוד נודיע לגאון שה פזורה. אודות זה מר שמואל נאמן כעבד לרבו וכשפחה לגבירתה. הטורח ומתעסק . . . מפני רצינו[24]

גומרה. ואחרי המלטו מטומאת אותה המאירה. [קי]בל ובי[25] ט̇ חד[שים]

[19] Read 'ור. As against R. Abraham b. Yehoshafaṭ, who came from Oria, Samuel was raised in 'our city', i. e. Bari.

[20] The dots above and inside the Bet indicate that the whole word should be omitted. Hence Abraham is a separate person whose father is not mentioned. Elijah b. Abraham is not his son, else the wording would have been ור' אליה בנו.

[21] i. e. school, just as the Palestinian school was styled (see Mann, *Jews in Egypt*, I, 54, note 2).

[22] Read בשלומו.

[23] Greetings are sent to 2 persons with whom Ḥisdai was on affectionate terms.

[24] Read שרצינו, we wanted to finish it (viz. the task stated in the lacuna).

[25] Probably to be read זה, 9 months ago.

לכתוב ספר יוסף בן גור̇[26] במהרה. ובבואו הנה הנה קרוב לנפיאה יב̇ מיל
בספירה[27]. פגעו בו ליסטין ונטלו ממנו הספר וכל האגרות ומה שמצאו בידו
ועלו ההרה. ויבא הנה סר ונזעף ורוחו סרה. בוכה ואומר איך אשא פני אל
אדוני ובמה אמצא כפרה. והיה . . . . לחזרה.
ומאהבת מר רוח מר אברהם . . . [בר] ששון הרופא ראש הקהלה נעור[28]
וירכב על סוסו הוא ואנשיו והוא . . . מינים בגבורה[29] ∴ ועתה
בבקשה מן מר לפי [צדקת]ו השפורה. בחכמתו ובתבונתו[30] יושא נא פשעו וחטאתו
העבירה. כי סופו מוכיח כי שגה בבלי דעת כשוגה בשכירה. וביסורים
הרבה ככידודי אש ושוטים [ו]כבלי ברזל נפשו יוסרה. ומאהבת [יוצר] השמ̇[31]
סבל הכל וחייתו לא קצרה. ימצוא[32] מחילה וסליחה ובצרור החיים יחידתו
היות צרורה ∴ ומי שעולמו בחסד ברא. יאמר גדולת מנהיגנו ומורנו

[26] =נוריון.

[27] Instead of the more usual במספר for the sake of the rhyme.

[28] i. e. on account of his love towards you, the spirit of Abraham b. Sason was aroused to ride in pursuit of the brigands in order to recover the booty. Hence there is no such person Revaḥ mentioned here as Poznański (*l. c.*, p. 289) thought (cp. also Cassuto, *l. c.*, p. 101, note 3). The name ששון (and not ששנא as Adler has it) is also found among the Egyptian Jews (see Mann, *l. c.*, II, Index).

[29] It is not stated what success Abraham's endeavors had, but from the following lines it is evident that he did not recover the copy of Yosippon.

[30] These 2 words are on the righthand margin; for יושא read שא.

[31] =השמים.

[32] Read ימצא.

להגבירה. לבלות ימיו בטוב ושנותיו בנועם להכבירה. להנגידו ולהצליעו[33]
בנאה וחסודה והגונה לו לעזרה. וליתן לו בנים ובני בנים עושקים[34]
במפנינים יקרה. מנהיגי דור ומתעסקים בכל צרכי ציבורה[35]. וכל
משאלותיו ימלא בטוב סברה[36]. אמן א׳[37] כן יהי רצון מפני הגבורה ∴
כתב ר׳ יהודה בן יעקב מרומה ז״ל למרב חסדאי נ״ע

[Follow seven lines in heavy Paiṭanic style forming the beginning of Judah's epistle to Ḥisdai.]

III.

[T.-S. Loan 45, paper.]

(Recto)

סהר אשר גיהץ[38] צור בעדינו. עומד בפרץ לחזק ולתקן
ולגדור פרצותינו. פותח יד לכל צד לפרוק ניר[39] צוארינו.
צופה בעלבון חלכאים ועשירי דורינו[40]. קשוט וענוד
וחמוש בכל מצות תורתינו. רביד מופלא וענק לצוארנו.
שוען ומשעינה[41] לחזקנו ולעזרנו. תומכנו ושלט וצינה
ורותק פרודינו[42]. ממנו קהלות פרנצא עבדיך. אבק

[33] From צלע, Adam's rib from which the first woman was formed. Here in the meaning of having (or continuing to live with) a worthy wife.

[34] =עוסקים, who busy themselves in the Torah (cp. Prov. 3.15).

[35] For צבור to suit the rhyme.

[36] For סבר, hope, for the sake of the rhyme.

[37] =אמן.

[38] To polish, to make bright (cp. Ben-Jehuda, *Thesaurus Totius Hebraitatis*, II, 712, col. 2, and 713, col. 1, where he quotes from a Piyyuṭ: ניהץ שני פנסים להבהיק ביהולם, referring to the creation of the sun and the moon).

[39] In the meaning of heavy yoke of the gentile rule (cp. Ben-Jehuda, VII, 3652).

[40] Viz. interesting himself in the indignities perpetrated both on poor and rich coreligionists.

[41] Cp. Is. 3.1, hence read here משען for שוען.

[42] 'Joining together our separated ones' (i. e. Diasporas); פרודינו=פזורינו.

הדום רגליך. קנייך ופרחיך[43]. נזמיך ואפעיך[44]. החוסים בצילך ומתחופפים תחת כנפיך. מתחננים אנחנו לפני בוראנו על שלות גושיך[45]. ובריות גופיך. ועל זקיפת קרנך שייגבר למעלה כתועפות ראם[46] עלוי כבודך ויקר הדרך. ידע כבוד אדוננו שאנו שרויים לשלום שבח והודיה לפני מי שאמר והיה העולם בגוף ובלב מבשורות טובות שבישרו לנו גדולנו. מ̇[47] שאול ורב יוסף ומ̇ יהודה כשבאו מאצל אדוננו. וגם נגלה לכל כי הסתופפו בנוה נשיאנו. בכן בירורו חכמים בעוז בינה. ניאום[48] צרופה וסנונה[49]. ידהן מן דקרב לגבי דוהנא[50]. ניכר דבר זה לפרנסנו ב[ס]בלונות וביזבינה[51]. בלב[52] מבשורות שבישרנו מ̇ שמואל שליח אדוננו ונאמנו. ופייס ממנו למצוא מצוה נאה לבחיר אלהינו. ובילשנו[53] ומצאנו מקום לאדוננו. בטולושא[54] המדינה שנותנין היהודים משם מס לעבודה זרה ל̇ ליטרי קירה[55] בפרשת

[43] Cp. Exod. 25.31ff. with regard to the branches and flowers of the Menorah.

[44] What נזם, nose-ring, has to do with אפעה, viper, is not clear. For אפעיך read perhaps עכסיך (cp. Is. 3.18) or more likely טבעותיך (cp. Is. 3.21: הטבעות ונזמי האף).

[45] Literally 'clod of earth', here as a metaphor for the human body created from earth.

[46] Cp. Num. 23.22; 24.8.

[47] =מר.

[48] Read נאום.

[49] For סנן, filtered, purified, thus סנונה is a synonym of צרופה.

[50] Cp. Sheb. 47b: קרב לגבי דהינא ואידהן.

[51] זבינה=זבינא, merchandise. The meaning is here that "our Parnās" knows the truth of this Rabbinic statement by the gifts and presents he has to give to the officials and courtiers.

[52] Here some words are missing, like ושמחנו שמחה גדולה בגוף ובלב (cp. above, l. 12, where too the words ושמחנו שמחה גדולה should be inserted). See verso, l. 3.

[53] From בָּלַשׁ, to search.

[54] Toulouse in the Provence.

[55] 'Wax'.

אור[56] שלהם בכל שנה ושנה ובשעת נתינת הקירה נותנין פצע אחת על צוארו לאותו שיוליך אותה וכששמע

(Verso)

מר שמואל [נאמ]ן אדוננו כך אמר דבר זה קליש[57] [ב]עיני אדוננו לבטל ואמרנו אולי יש בלאטיי[58] [אדו]ננו לעבור גזירה זו ושמחנו שמחה גדולה בלב ובנפש ונתננו שבח לצור מעוזנו וברכנו את שמו הקדוש אשר לא עזב חסדו ואמתו מעמו ישראל והקים לנו רועה נאמן וקדוש וחסיד וישר כזה ובחסידותו ובצדקתו ובעינוותו נחיה בגוים וברוך המקום שהקים את דבר נואמו[59] כי לא אלמן ישראל ויהודה [בימיו ת]צמיח ישועה[60] על יד נטע מובחר ומעולה כמוהו בכרמו הכורם זכיות וצדקות כבני אדם המקניפים[61] תבואתם שיהי ר[צ]ון מלכנו מקים רועים וממליך מלכים ומעמיד רוזנים שיקיים הודו וגאונו וממשלתו ותפארתו לא[ו]רך ימים] ושנים ותאיר[62] עינינו בעצתו המפוארה ותתנהו[63] לחן ולחסד ולרחמים בעיניו ובעיני כל רואיו ולפני מלכי ארץ ולכל שומעים להרבות חיל ורחב[64] וישועה ועושר וכבוד וירים קרנו לעד מתחננים אלו שלא יושט[65] בעיניו כתב

[56] At the season of light of the Christians, i. e. Easter.

[57] Light, easy.

[58] From לאט, to speak gently (Job 15. 11), the noun לָאָט being used Paiṭanically in the meaning of prayer (see Ben-Jehuda, V, 2584), here: perhaps it will be possible by the pleadings of our lord to abolish this shameful practice. For לעבור read להעביר.

[59] Jer. 51.5.

[60] Viz. the Messiah should come in the person of a member of the Davidic family as worthy as the leader to whom the letter is addressed.

[61] Read המנקיפים, from נקף, beating down the produce of the trees (cp. כנקף זית, Is. 17.6; 24.13), here in the general meaning of gathering in the harvest.

[62] Read ויאיר.

[63] Read ויתנהו. [64] Read ורכב.

[65] From שוט, to despise.

עבדיו כי אין אנו ראויים לכן אלא מרוב אהבת אדוננו וב[טחוננו] בעוונותו[66] הגדולה וברוב חסידותו לכן כתבנו רמז מקצת דרכי רבנא ומרנא נשיא ישראל נמשלה דבר זה למלך שיש לו אלף אלפים קנטרי זהב ומקלסין אותו בשני קנטרי כסף והופחדנו להרבות דברים פני יקור[67] מחמדנו. יופי כלילת[נו]. משוש [לבנו]. ורוח אפנו. גדולתו ותפארתו יפה[68] וירבה וישגה גזר וייצמר[69] ויִתְּצֹר לעדי עד . . . .

[66] Read בעינוותו as above l. 7, but בענותו would in both cases be more correct.

[67] Read יקר.

[68] Read יפרה.

[69] Probably read וישמר. The next word is to be deleted as indicated by the dots above.

2.

A DOCUMENT CONCERNING A MEMBER OF THE FAMILY OF R. ṬODROS, NASI OF NARBONNE

The fragment given here consists of a circular letter of appeal on behalf of a widowed proselyte hard hit by fate. This lady, of a wealthy and prominent Christian family, forsook her home and her faith and arrived at Narbonne where she accepted Judaism. Subsequently R. David, of the family of R. Ṭodros of Narbonne, married her. After six months, on hearing that his wife was being sought by her relatives, he escaped with her to the place whence our fragment was written. How long they lived there is not stated, but several years must have passed since the marriage which was blessed by 3 children, the second of which, a girl by the name of Justa, is stated to have been 3 years old. Then an attack on the Jewish community took place during which R. David was killed in the synagogue, 2 of his children were taken captive and all his possessions despoiled. There only remained the unfortunate widow with a child a few months old and in abject poverty. The fragment is an appeal on her behalf to help her in her endeavors to obtain the ransom money for her captured children.

The letter seems to originate from the congregation of Anjou in France though the reading אניו is doubtful.[1] The MS. seems to be of the 11th century. R. Ṭodros, mentioned as departed, of whose family the martyred R. David was a member, is thus identical with the celebrated R. Ṭodros I, Nasi of Narbonne, who is mentioned in a legal document of the year 1064.[2] Should we therefore say that this attack in Anjou took place during

[1] For the spelling אניו among others, see Gross, *Gallia Judaica*, 64ff.; Salfeld, *Das Martyrologium des Nürnberger Memorbuches*, p. 163.

[2] See Neub., *Med. Jew. Chron.* I, 82, bottom: והיה שם (היינו בנרבונה) לגאון רב טודרוס הידוע הנשיא ובניו מזרע זה ר' מכיר הנשיא ולא פסקה מהם גדולה וממשלה ותורה וכו' *Régné*, *REJ*, LXII, p. 9, cites a document of 1064 wherein the estates of Tauros, the Hebrew, are mentioned, probably identical with our Ṭodros.

the first Crusade? But so far we have no data as to how the local Jews fared on that occasion. The earliest mention of troubles in Anjou during the preaching of a new Crusade refers to 1236 when about 3000 Jews were killed in Bretagne, Anjou and Poitou.[3] We have to await further material in order to ascertain the nature of the persecution alluded to in our epistle. Maimonides mentions a great slaughter of Jews in Lyons (about 1060–70) as a result of a Messianic movement (cp. Mann, *Hattekufah*, XXIV, 356–58, and infra, p. 664, top) but Anjou is too far removed from Lyons to connect the above persecution with this event.

[T.–S. 16.100, vellum.]

(Recto)

ממנו קהל אניו*[3] צעירי הצאן הלחוצים והרצוצים השוכבים בתוך
[אריות וזאבי ערבות אשר אכלונו בכל פה][4]
עד שנשארנו מעט מהרבה כתורן אשר על] ההר וכנס על הגבעה
לחורב ביום ולקרח בלילה[5] [יהי שם י"י
מבורך לעולם ולנצח נצחים ועם [תוקף דו]חקינו. ואומץ מצוקינו.
מעריכין אנו חין[6] ושוע פני מושגבנו. להחיש הבשורה]
הטובה ולהחביר גליותינו. ולקבץ נפוצותינו. יחד בכסא כבוד
מרום מראשון ככ׳[7] ונשא נס לגוים ואסף נדחי יש׳ וגו׳[8] ואנו]
מודיעים כבודכם רבותינו עסק אלמנה זו הגיורת שהיה בעלה
ר׳ דוד נ׳נ׳[9] מבני קהל נרבונה [מבני משפחתו]

[3] See Lewin, *M. G. W. J.*, XVIII (1869), 101 ff. The apostate Nicolas Donin, who later on became notorious by his disputation about the Talmud with R. Yeḥiel of Paris in 1240, seems to have had a hand in this massacre (cp. ויכוח רבינו יחיאל, Thorn 1873, p. 10, bottom: הלא כמה (i. e. Donin) ויען הנבל רבבות נפלו מכם בחרב ברייטנא ואניוב ופוייטוב, ואיה הם הנפלאות והאותות אשר עשה לכם אלהיכם אם אתם עם סגולה כאשר אמרתם?). These martyrs of Bretagne, Anjou and Poitou are evidently listed in the prayerbook of the 14th century (Salfeld, *l. c.*, p. 80, bottom): איינגו ופייטוא ובירטיינא.

*[3] The reading is doubtful. [4] Cp. Jer. 5.6, Is. 9.11.

[5] Cp. Is. 30.17, Gen. 31.40.

[6] A Paiṭanic form instead of תחנה.

[7] =ככתוב, Is. 11.12. For the previous phrase cp. Jer. 17.12.

[8] =ונומר. [9] =נוחו נפש.

של ר̇ טודרוס זצ̇ לב̇[10] שבנרבונה ויצא לכאן היום שש שנים על עסק זו אשתו הגיורת שהיתה . . . .

הק̇ ויצאתה מבית אביה מעושר הרבה ומארץ רחוקה ובאתה לשם אלהינו ולחסות תחת כנפי [השכינה ועזבה את]

אחיה וגדולי משפחתה והיא יושבת בנרבונה ונשא אותה ר̇ דוד זה הנפטר והיה עמה יותר משנ[ש]ה [חדשים ושמע]

שהיו מבקשים אותה ברח עמה אל מקומינו עד שגזר הקב̇ה גזירה זו עלינו צדיק הוא וצדיק ה[בא עלינו[11] ונהרג בעלה]

בבית הכנסת ונשבו שני בניו נער אחד ששמו יעקב ושם הנערה יושתא[11a] והיא מן שלשה שנים [ונשלל כל מה שהיה לו]

ונשתיירה האלמנה בוכה וצועקת על רוב דלדולה וענ[ל] עניותה ואין מישגיח[12] עליה ונשתייר [לה ילד מן] . . .

חדשים ונשתיירה בצמא ובעירום ובחוסר כל ולא יש לה מה שתוציא על עצמה ועל יתומה . . . .

רבותינו ולהודיעם דחקה וצערה ועכשיו רבותינו שאו לשמים עיניכם וחוסו על עני[ותה] ועל הו[12]* . . . . . . [ועל]

בניה שהלכו בשבי ועל עסק בעלה שנהרג אולי יחנן י״י צבאות ונפדה אותם ותקבלו[ה] בסבר [פנים יפות ותעשו]

עמה כמידתכם הטובה כמו שאתם עושים על[13] כל עובר ושב וכו׳

[Follow 4 more lines of appeal on her behalf.]

Signatories:

יהושע בר עובדיה נ̇ע̇

. . . . . [בר] יצחק נ̇ע̇ יצחק בר . . . . .

[Follow 5 more lines of which only a few letters are preserved.]

[10] זכרו לברכה=.

[11] Cp. Neh. 9.33.

[11a] Justa.

[12] Read מי שישגיח or משגיח.

*[12] The reading is doubtful.

[13] Read עם.

3.

A MESSIANIC EXCITEMENT IN SICILY AND OTHER PARTS OF SOUTHERN EUROPE

The fragment given here is of a puzzling nature affording hardly any clue of the time of the extraordinary excitement described therein. The style is far from elegant betraying hasty composition by the writer who evidently sent an account to some correspondent of what he saw and heard in the Sicilian port of Catania after his arrival there together with a fellow-traveller.[1] The former is evidently Mikhael b. Samuel who tells our story jointly in his own name and in that of his companion Samuel b. X. Upon their arrival at Catania, where the writer had a son-in-law R. Sabbatai (fol. 2, verso, l. 24), they heard of a prophesying Jewess in San Torbo (either a suburb of or a locality near Catania) who, though pregnant for nine months, gave no birth to a child. She would stand outside the synagogue during the prayers and her presence would be noticed by a pleasant scent. Then she would return home in a feverish state and summon people to behold the miraculous things about to take place. Such a scene is described in our fragment how this woman after one service summoned the whole congregation to witness the manifestations of the coming of the Messiah. She claimed to do this at the behest of "the holy one" (fol. 1, r., l. 9; v., ll. 8 and 19). This "holy one" can of course merely mean God (הקב"ה=הקדוש). However it may also refer to some martyr or saint famous in Catania in those days.

In her feverish state the lady demanded several covers and on these there would appear certain letters in saffron color, thus on one אני יי'י אחד, on another אֹס אֹו סֹו (probably=אמן סלה אמן ואמן סלה ועד) and on a third הֹזֹחֹד (perhaps=ה' זכר חסדי דוד). There were other miraculous signs such as blood appearing on

[1] As this account was found in the Genizah, the recipient of the letter apparently lived in Cairo-Fusṭāṭ.

the shawls and letters forming themselves thereon with certain magic lines surrounding a circle. The hysterical lady asked that these covers be exhibited among other congregations in order that they do proper repentance. The "holy one" gave assurance by oath in the presence of the angels and of Moses that the "End" was near at hand and that unless the evildoers repent, they will all perish by sword, famine or religious persecution. The lady's hysterics also affected other Jews. A scene is described how on a Saturday during the afternoon service a fire entered the synagogue and two worshippers, who had collapsed, related after their recovery their vision of an angel ready to strike them, apparently for not mending their ways.

Thus the whole atmosphere in Catania was charged with Messianic expectations and while the writer was recording "these prophecies" (fol. 2, r., l. 8) on the Sunday after this Sabbath, the date being Tishri 28, the excitement increased still more with the arrival of a non-Jew from Morea (Southern Greece) who was surprised to find the Jews of Sicily still tarrying. The tale of this non-Jew was still more phantastic than the miracles of the hysterical lady. He hailed in the streets a local Jew, Leon, and told him of the arrival of the ambassadors of "the hidden king" (i.e. the Messiah).[2] Leon summoned other Jews and the interview of the newcomer in the presence of the writer, Elijah the Parnās of the Catania community, Leon and David the teacher, was "the sensation" of the day. The "hidden king," the non-Jew related, had sent letters to the rulers of Spain and Germany with the peremptory command to aid his ambassadors on their mission to gather all the Jews of the Diaspora and lead them back to Jerusalem without any obstacle. The credentials of these ambassadors also contained instructions for the Jews to aid each other, the rich enabling the poor to start on their return

[2] There were several ideas about the whereabouts of the Messiah. According to the so-called Apocalypse of Zerobabel (ed. Lévi, *REJ*, LXVIII, p. 132) he was kept in prison in Rome till the 'End' would come (זו היא רומא רבתי שאני אסור בה . . . ויאמר אלי אני משיח יי' [בן חזקיה] שאני אסור בכלא עד עת קץ). Cp. 134, top: ויאמר לי זה משיח יי' צ פ ו ן בזה המקום עד קץ . . . וזה נולד בימי דוד מלך ישראל וישאהו רוח ו י צ פ נ ה ו בזה המקום עד עת קץ (see variants, notes 4–6, and p. 146, notes 3, 5).

from Exile.[3] The non-Jew took an oath that these ambassadors would soon reach the island of Sicily and that the authorities would receive them with the respect due to them.

This interesting reporter also related the engaging story of the upheaval he himself beheld in Spain where in a certain locality the bishop (or governor, הגמון) did not agree to let the Jews leave their homes for Jerusalem unless they had parted first with their money to which proposition they actually agreed. Then there follows a description of the ambassadors originating from among "the hidden ones" (fol. 2, v., ll. 8 and 13)[4] and being 12 in number (evidently corresponding to the 12 Tribes). They are accompanied by a bodyguard of 200 horsemen. Their credentials were in Hebrew signed by 12 gold seals. These 12 ambassadors claimed to represent an army of 12,000,[5] a ridiculously low number to impress the European rulers, and yet, our reporter went on to say, the kings of Spain, Germany, Hungary and France were mobilizing the wealth and the troops of their respective dominions to buy off "the hidden ones" or else fight them.

Continuing his story of what happened in Spain he depicted the reception of these ambassadors by the Spanish monarch, how he went out to meet them with great pomp in the company of the local Jews all riding on horseback. The ambassadors with their bodyguard refused the monarch's invitation to visit "the city" (his capital) but encamped along the river outside fraternising with the local Jews, the entertainment being at the expense of the king. All this the non-Jew declared to have witnessed himself and he added that the Marchese (המרקשי, fol. 2, v., l. 19), evidently a high government official, would bring instructions to the officials (in Sicily) as to how they should act in this emergency.

[3] Similar advice to the rich to spend all their money on the poor was given by the Pseudo-Messiah of Yemen and Maimonides in his Iggeret Temān (ed. Holub, p. 46) is very sarcastic about it (cp. also Mann, *Hatteḳufah*, XXIV, 350).

[4] Here "the hidden ones" are evidently members of the descendants of Moses (בני משה) and of other Lost Tribes who are closed up in their territories only to appear with the coming of the Messiah (see Mann, *Hatteḳufah*, XXIII, 255, notes 3, 5).

[5] After the model of the Israelitish army that was sent to fight the Midianites (Num. 31.4–5).

A further item of news was that in Germany a massacre of the Jews was impending but it was averted by the priests who restrained the mob from violence by making clear to them that if the local Jews were attacked, "the hidden ones" would avenge their blood.

All this interview, given out on that memorable Sunday, Tishri 28, was indeed sensational enough to have created a stir in the bazaars of Catania. On Monday the above mentioned Jews together with the writer's son-in-law R. Sabbatai (from the title רבנא it would appear that he was the Rabbi of the community) interviewed this non-Jew again. He repeated the whole story adding 2 more items to it and again took an oath that the ambassadors would arrive in Sicily together with the Marchese (Marquis). Here our MS. breaks off.

It is difficult to account for this phantastic report and to ascertain the underlying connection of this excitement in Catania with one of the hitherto known Messianic movements of the Middle Ages. Although the form מַרְקְשִׁי suggests more the Italian spelling Marchese than the Spanish one Marqués, yet it would seem as if this Marquis was to come from Spain to Sicily with documents to the local authorities containing instructions about the ambassadors who were accompanying him. Hence this account would reflect the time when Sicily was a dependancy of a Spanish ruler. This could apply either to the Aragonian period (beginning with Peter of Aragon, 1282, and ending with Ferdinand the Catholic, 1516) or to the Habsburg-Spanish period (1516–1700). The latter one is out of question, because of the expulsion of the Jews from Spain and also because of Hungary being mentioned as a separate kingdom. If we consider the early Aragonian period, a possible connection could be sought with the Messianic movement of Abraham Abulafia who stayed for a time in Sicily where he came out (in 1289) with his theory of the approaching End (קץ) in 1290.[6] Should we say then that he is meant by "the holy one" in our fragment? However Abraham's calculation of the Ḳeṣ does not seem to have led to an extended Messianic movement such as is described here.[7] Moreover our MS. rather appears

[6] See Graetz, *Gesch. d. Juden*, VII, 4th ed., p. 195.

[7] Solomon ibn Adret (Responsa I, No. 548) indicates that Abraham's movement was stopped quite at the beginning (ואחד מהם היה אותו הנבל שם רשעים

to be one of the 12th century and although our present knowledge of Hebrew paleography does not yet afford a definite criterion for fixing the dates of MSS. on the basis of their outward appearance, I hardly think that our fragment belongs to the end of the 13th century. We must therefore await further data to throw light on this amazing Pseudo-Messianic movement that agitated the Jews of Catania and probably of the rest of Sicily and of other countries in Southern Europe. There remains only to refer to a Genizah fragment (published by Mann, *REJ*, LXXIV, 150–52) which speaks of the reappearance of the Bnē Mosheh from behind the Sambaṭyon river and of the grouping of enormous armies to fight all enemies of Israel with one corps already 4 days' distance from Rome. But this MS. is of much more recent date and probably belongs to the time of David Reubeni (cp. my remarks, ibid. 148–49). There is no ground for connecting the two fragments as belonging to the same entourage of David Reubeni that fished in the troubled waters of European politics on the one hand and held out a phantastic mirage of Messianic hopes to the Jews on the other.

[T.–S. Loan 26, 2 paper leaves, damaged and torn.]

(Fol. 1, recto)

מים קׄר[נים עׄל] נפש עי[פׄה][1]

כאשר באנו אנחנו מיכל ברׄ שמואל וצׄי[2] ושמו[אל ברׄ] . . . [אל]

ירקב אותו אברהם ששם שמו נביא ומשיח בשסיליאה ופתה בכזביו כמה מבני ישראל ולולי שסגרתי הפתח בפניו בחמלת השם עם רב כתבי וכתבי קהלות הקדש כמעט שהתחיל והיה מכלה וכו'). Unfortunately Ibn Adret's letters to the Rabbi of Palermo, Aḥiṭub, on this affair have not been preserved. And indeed Abraham Abulafia denied that he had any intentions to act as a Messiah. Cp. his letter to Judah Salmon of Barcelona (in Jellinek, נגזי חכמת הקבלה, 18): ואמנם כתבתי ג"כ זאת האגרת השנית להודיע לכם אחי כי מה שחשב הרב ר' שלמה ב"ר אברהם ז"ל בן אדרת על עניני או מה ששמע היה הכל הבל ורעות רוח. See also p. 19: ועתה הכריחני לדבר עמך בזה המעט, הכתב ששלח הרב לבני פלירמו לר' אחיטוב שהיה מלא נאצות ולא היה שום דבר חכמה כי אם חרופים וגדופים כמנהג הנערים הקטנים שאינם בעלי דעת עד שרבים מרואיו הכחישו חתימות ידו וקראוה מזוייף ואמנם אני שהכרתי מדבריו ענינים ידועים (supply באתי) לענות לו על דבריו להודיע לך והדומים לך שהדברים שחשב או ששמע היו להפך.

[1] Prov. 25.25. This forms evidently the end of the exordium of the letter which began on the previous page (or pages) now missing. There is space after this line to indicate that this exordium is ended.

[2] Read צׄי = יצׄ ישמרו צורו.

שיקיליאה באנו בקהל אחד ושם המקום קטניא[ה][3] ושמענו [שיש
אשה אחת שנתנבאת בְּשֶׁיְנְטוֹרְבוֹ[4] והל[כנו לשם לראות]
אותה והיתה מעוברת ועבר לה זמן של ט̇ חדש[ים ולא ילדה]
ושם בעלה ר̇ חיים והלכנו בבית הכנסת ושמענו[5] ריח טוב [שהיא]
עומדת בחוץ ואחר התפילה אחזתה רעדה והלכה בביתה ונפלה
על פניה ושיגרה אחרינו בבית הכנסת והלכנו עם בעלה ואמרה
לבעלה כך נגזרתי מפי הקדוש שיבואו ויראו כל הקהל וראינו
אותה נופלת על פניה ומתחננת ובוכה ואמרא[6] לבעלה הביאו
טלית והשליכו עלי והביאו טלית ועד ש[ה]ביאו הטלית מן הבית
עלו על הטלית שהיתה עליה מקודם לכן אותיות והם אנ̇י̇ [ו]אחרי
כן
עלו ג̇ יודין כך ייי ועוד אחר[7] על קצה אחרת של טלית עלה
אחד[8]
והכתיבה היתה בזעפרן[9] והיו האותיות לחין והיו משימן[10] כל
אח[ד]
ואחד מן העומדים לשם אצבעו ולא היה נדבק בידינו [מן]
הלחלוחית כלום והייתה[11] צועקת כסו אותי טלית[12] [והביאו
הטלית]
וראינו אותו הטלית ולא היה בו שום דבר אבל ה[שימוהו עליה
ועלו עליו א̇ס̇ ועוד א̇ו̇ ועוד ס̇ו̇[13] ואמרו [13a] תקחו גם אח[ר]

[3] Catania, a part on the eastern side of Sicily. About the Jewish community of Catania, see Zunz, *Zur Gesch. u. Liter.*, 506.

[4] San Torbo was evidently a locality near Catania, or a district of the city of Catania, named after the church of San Torbo that was situated there.

[5] A peculiar expression. Better והרגשנו.

[6] Read ואמרה. [7] =אחרי כן.

[8] Three words of 3 letters each comprising אני יי'י אחד.

[9] Arabic Za'frān=Saffron.

[10] Read משימין. [11] =והיתה.

[12] Read בטלית.

[13] Three marks of 2 letters each standing perhaps for: אמן סלה, אמן ואמן, סלה ועד.

[13a] Read ואמרה.

ולקחו אותו והביאו אחר ועלו גם עליו הזחד[14] והיא [שוכבת]
באימה וברעדה והוציאה את ידה השמאל[ית] . . . . .
ומלטה[15] באותו היד נראה דמות אדם והיה יורד[15*] [ממנה כעין]
זעפרן ולקחנו וטעמנו כולנו שהיינו עומדים לש[ם והיה טעמו]
כטעם לשד השמן וריחו נאה כמר דרור[16] ושמענו ב[תפלתה]
שמע ישראל אי'י[17] אלהינו י'י אחד אל ארך אפים ורב חסד [ואמת]

(verso)

. . . . .נו כולנו גם [אנחנו ה]יינו מתחננים
[עמה ואחר] כך[17*] נשאה את ידיה [כמו שנוש]אים הכהנים
[בעלותם לדוכן ו]עלה דם על הטלית ואחרי כן עלו אותיות
. . . . . לה דם שירטוט אחד ובתוך השרטוט עגול
. . . . . [ו]ראינו בעינינו אילו א'[18] האותות והאותיות
[אשר על הטל]יתות ואמרה לנו תנו שבח והודאה ליי' ותחזרו בתשובה
[שלימה ג]ם אתם גם כל המקומות אשר תעברו תראו את הכתבים
[ו]את הטליתות ויחזרו בתשובה כי כך צוותי מפי הקדוש וביום השבת
לאחר התפילה הלכנו עם בעלה בביתה שנאכל ביחד ועד שלא
ברכנו ברכת המזון ראינו אותה כי עלתה בעלייתה ונפלה על
פניה והיתה מצטערת ועלינו עם בעלה לראותה ברצונו[19] וראינו
אותה כאילו אוכלת וידי[ניה] היו בחיקה ואחר כך ראינו אצבעותיה

[14] The meaning of this abbreviation is not clear to me. Perhaps=ה' זכר חסדי דוד (cp. Is. 55.3, 2 Chron. 6.42).

[15] More correct המליטה (cp. Is. 66.7), evidently the woman brought forth something from her body with her left hand on which there appeared a human figure.

[15*] The 'ד is uncertain.

[16] Cp. Numb. 11.8 and Exod. 30.23.

[17] Read י'י.

[17*] The reading is uncertain.

[18] The mark on top indicates that this letter should be deleted.

[19] =ברשותו, by his permission.

השלשה והיו נובעות כמו שמן ולקח בעלה ונתן לכל אחד ואחד ואכלנו והיה בו טעם כדבש וריחו כמר דרור ואחר כך קינחה [אצבע]ותיה בְּמַנְדְּלִין[20] שלה והיה כל המנדיל לח כמו שישרוהו [במים] והיה בו טעם כדבש וריחו טוב מאד מה שאין ריח [בעולם דומה לו] ואחֹ[21] כך ישבה והתחילה להתפלל י'י שמע י'י אלהיֹ[22]

[חוס ורחם ו]נאנחה ואומרת אוי לרשעים ואוי להם שאינם [עושים תשובה] כי כך נשבע לי הקדוש לפני המלאכים ולפני משה [רבינו] כי קרוב הוא הקץ ואם לא ישובו הרשעים הנה [יגועו רב]ים [בח]רב וברעב ובשמד ואם יחזרו בתשובה [ימלטו] כי קרובה ישועתי לבוא[23] ואותו שהיתי[24] אוכלת . . . עתיד הקבֹה ליתן לישרֹ[25] ואמרה לנו לכו בכנסת [והתפללו ה]תפילה והלכנו והתפללנו וראינו את הפרוכת כעומז . . . .א טוב וחזק וראינו גם אש שנכנס בבית הכנסת

(fol. 2, recto)

והלך בקרן האחרת ונפלו שני אנשים מ[ה]מתפללים על האר[ץ והיו מכים את עצמם בארץ ואחר כך כ[שעמדו מן הארץ] שאלנו להם מה ראיתם זה שלא בפני זה ואו[מֹ[26] האחד וחבירו] לא היה שומע אמֹ לנו ראינו את המלאך ו[חרב בידו ובידו] האחרת אש גדול ובא להכות אותי כמו כן [היה מספר השני] ואומֹ גם הוא כחבירו. שישו ושמחו ועשו תשובה [שלמה] ותענית ותחנונים על השמועה אשר באה אלינו בעשרים ושמונה לירח תשרי ביום אֹ כי בעודי כותב אילו הנבואות לא הוספקתי להשלימלם[27] והנה בא לועז אחד מן מוריאה[28]

[20] Arabic denoting a veil, head-band.

[21] =ואחר. [22] =אלהינו or אלהים. [23] Cp. Is. 56.1.

[24] =שהייתי. [25] =לישראל. [26] =ואמר.

[27] The ל' with dot is to be deleted.

[28] Morea (Southern Greece).

ובא עם דוגים[29] באנדרבידה[30] ובא והיה רואה את היהודים והיה תמיה קרא לר׳[31] למ׳ ליאון ואמ׳ לו יהודי אתה אמ׳ לו הין אמ׳ לו הגיעו הנה השלוחים אשר שיגר המלך שהיה גנוז כאשר שמע הדברים נתזעזע[32] ורץ אילנו[33] וסיפר לנו האמת והלכתי עם ר׳ אליה הפרנס ועם מר לאון ועם ר׳ דוד המלמד והלכנו במקום אחד וכך סיפר לנו כי שיגר המלך הגנוז שלכם כתבים למלך שְׁפַנְיאַה ולמלך אַלַמָנו[34] ולכל אותם המלכיות והם כתובים כך בגזירה אני כותב לכם שתשגרו כתבי ממקום למקום וממלך למלך ולתת סיוע לשלוחיי ללכת ל[כ]ל קהילו׳[35] ישראל שיתקבצו כולם ללכת בירושל׳[36] ולא יוכלו המל[כים] למונעם ולא ירעו להם ולא יאמרו להם מטוב ועד רע והכתבים [האלה כך] כתובים כי העשירים יתנו לעניים ימכרו[37] כל אש[ר להם וכשאתם] בירושלים ולא אמצא אתכם מסחרים[38] והיה [הלועז הזה] משביע לנו על אותם השלוחים אם באו ואם [לא] . . . כי עדין לא שמענו כזה הענין וכך נשבע [כי בעוד איזה] ימים ויגיעו הנה השלוחים אל ה[מושל ואל כל שריו והמושל]

[29] Fishermen (more correct דַיָּגִים).

[30] This locality in Sicily is unknown to me.

[31] To be deleted for the next word למ׳=למרנא.

[32] More correct נזדעזע.

[33] Read אלינו.

[34] Germany.

[35] =קהילות.

[36] =בירושלים.

[37] Read וימכרו.

[38] The meaning of the sentence seems to be that 'the hidden king' wrote in his letter to the Jewish communities that "if you come to Jerusalem, shall I not find for you opportunities of business?" Hence they should not be concerned about their possessions in their former places of residence.

(verso)

[וכל שרי המו]של יקומו להשתחוות וכאשר ראה[39] הבלבול [אשר היה באש]פניא אשר אין מספר לאלפים והם עברו [י]רושל בראש חודש תשרי ונתקבצו כל בני . . . . [המקום של] ההגמון כֹאשר[40] היו תחתיו ולא היו מניחים [אותם ואמֹ לו ב]על הכתבים[41] דע לך מה אתה עושה [ויען] אין אני מונע אתכם אבל תתנו לי הממון שלכם ואתם לכו לשלום אמרו לו ברצון נתנו הממון והלכו לכם ואתם תעמדו כמכם[42] שהיה ביחד והשלוחים הן מן הגנוזים והם מאתיים . . . רוכבים והיֹבֹ הם החשובים שבהם והכתב אשר הביאו כתב יהודית והוא חתום מלמעלה ומלמטה משניהם[43] עשר חותמות של זהב והיֹבֹ אמֹ למלך כי אני יֹבֹ אלפים ומלך שפניא ומלך אלמנו ומלך אונגריא ומלך צרפת הם באימה וברעדה ומקבצים ממון רב וחייל כבד אם יתרצו הגנוזים בממון ואם לא יעמדו כנגדם וכאשר באו השלוחים באשפניא עשה להם המלך כבוד גדול ויצא לקראתם עם כל חילו ועם היהודים אשר היו תחת ידו כל היהודים רוכבי סוסים אמֹ להן המלך הכנסו בעיר אמֹ לו אין אנו רוצים שנכנס אבל היה מחוץ לעיר נהר וישבו לשם באוהלים מיד הוציאו ל[ח]ם ויין ובשר ואכלו ושתו ביחד והמלך היה משגר להם די מחסור[ם כל] אלו היו בפני הלועז וגם המַרְקְשִׁי[44] הוא עתיד להביא

[39] This non-Jew (לועז) also related of the upheaval he saw in Spain where many Jews left their homes to proceed to Jerusalem. About this informant's supposed stay in Spain cp. also v., l. 19.

[40] The 'כ is to be deleted.

[41] Viz. the leader of the Jews, who had recieved the dispatches from the 'hidden king,' spoke to the bishop or governor (הגמון).

[42] =כמוכם.

[43] Read משנים.

[44] Marchese = Marquis. In l. 26 spelt מרקשין, perhaps plural.

הכתבים [א]ל הראשים מה יעשו וגם בני אלמן[45] עמדו להרוג את כל [היהודים עמד]ו הגלחים ואמרו להם הזהרו בכם שלא תרעו אותם [כי המרע אותם] וכל הנוגע בהם נוגע בבת עינו[46] ולא לעצמו לבד [גורם רעה אלא] לכל העולם כי אם יבואו וישמע[47] כי הרגו יהודים [יהרגו אתכם] תחתם וגם ביום שני הלכנו עם חתני רבנא שבתי [אל הלועז הזה ושמע]נו כאלו הדברים ועוד ב̇ דברים אחרים אשר [לא הזכיר ל]הם וכך נשבע [לנו] כי השלוחים יבואו עם מרקשין

(Here the MS. breaks off.)

[45] Germany.

[46] Cp. Zech. 2. 12.

[47] Passive.

4.

DOCUMENTS BEARING ON BYZANTINE JEWRY

The Genizah has yielded a number of valuable documents which add to our knowledge of the altogether obscure history of Byzantine Jewry. This information is the outcome of the commercial and communal relations which the Jews of Egypt had with their brethren in Byzantium. In the 11th century a number of Byzantine Jews were forcibly brought to Egypt as captives of Saracen pirates who raided Byzantine merchant ships. They were not allowed to remain in servitude in a strange land but rather were ransomed by their Egyptian coreligionists who cared for them and enabled them to return to their homes (see Mann I, 87–94; II, 87–96, 363–5; infra, p. 366ff.). The Messianic excitement in Byzantium during the first Crusade was duly reported to Fusṭāṭ (see the latest discussion by Mann, *Hatteḳufah*, XXIII, 251–261) whereas on the other hand the troubles of Fusṭāṭ Jewry through a high Christian official were the cause of correspondence with the congregation of Constantinople (see Mann, I, 210–212). Further data on the relations between the Jews of these two countries are to be gathered from the fragments given by Mann (II, 248, 306–7).

The letter given under I adds several points of interest. The handwriting is clearly of the 11th century. The writer, Elijah, living probably in Salonica,[1] kept up his correspondence with his brother (evidently in Fusṭāṭ) who seems to have been a prominent scholar. When a certain Abū ʻAlī, a resident of Elijah's city, visited Fusṭāṭ he was given by Elijah's brother letters for him and also for the Rabbi of the city, Elijah b. Sabbatai, dealing with the case of an imprisoned Jew.[2] In return for a present of the

[1] Salonica community figures in the Messianic movement during the First Crusade and also in the letter of introduction for a Russian Jew about to visit Palestine (Mann, II, 192).

[2] Whether in Fusṭāṭ or in Byzantium is not clear. About a Jew imprisoned in Constantinople, cp. Mann II, 248.

Scroll of Esther on parchment, Elijah sent his brother Piyyuṭim about the safe arrival of which he is very anxious to hear.

Of special interest is the mention of the Ḳaraites in Elijah's place of residence. Since when these sectaries spread to Byzantine is unknown. They are found early in the 11th century in Anṭalia as the letter of 1028 concerning the Byzantine captives testifies (*JQR*, XIX, 252, l. 35, cp. Mann, I, 89). Also Tobias b. Eli'ezer, the author of Leḳah Ṭob, who lived in Castoria during the First Crusade, had frequent occasions in his work on the Pentateuch to combat the views of the Ḳaraites, evidently because of his contact with them in Byzantium.[3] The celebration of the Festivals by the Ḳaraites on different dates from the Rabbanites was the occasion for friction between the two sections leading to denunciation to the authorities by the former and to the subsequent imposition of fines on the latter. Our fragment shows that in the 11th century the Ḳaraites of Byzantium followed the fixing of the calendar according to the ruling of their coreligionists in Palestine who went by the condition of the crops (אביב) in establishing the dates of the Festivals. It thus turned out that owing to the lateness of the crops the Ḳaraites in Palestine and in Byzantium had their Tishri a month after the Rabbanites. However the Ḳaraites in Babylon gave up the Abīb feature of calendation already at the beginning of the 11th century and the Byzantine sectaries followed suit later on.[3a] Elijah's brother in Fusṭāṭ was asked to take a hand in combating the views of the Ḳaraites, and in letters

[3] Cp. Buber's edition, Wilna 1884, Introduction, pp. 34–5. About Tobias' probable stay in Salonica during the Messianic excitement cp. Mann, *Hatteḳufah*, XXIII, 256, note 6.

More about the Ḳaraites in Byzantium will be found in vol. II of our *Texts and Studies*. Cp. also infra, p. 372.

[3a] Thus Levi b. Yefet b. 'Alī reports in his ספר המצות (composed in about 1007 C. E.): והקראין אשר בארץ שנער ובשאר המקומות הרחוקות מא"י רדפו אחרי הרבנין בעבור שמצאו המעוברות שלהם תמימות במרבית העתים (cp. Mann, *JQR*, *N. S.*, XII, 270, note 140). About the later Ḳaraites in Byzantium cp. Aaron b. Elijah who reports in his גן עדן, composed in Constantinople in 1354 (fol. 58a), about a difference of one month in the fixing of Tishri 5096 A. M. between the Byzantine Ḳaraites and their fellow-sectaries in Palestine who went by the Abib (מבקשי האביב, fol. 22b). Another such occurrence is reported by Elijah Bashiatsi for the year 1479–80 (אדרת אליהו, הר"ם, fol. 22d).

to his nephew, 'Obadyah b. Elijah, he undertook the championship of the Rabbinic cause. These epistles were read at a meeting of the community on Ḥol-ha-Moed of Tabernacles and met with full approval. There were present also Jewish merchants from Russia, where they had their own friction with the Ḳaraites, who too bestowed their eulogy on the author of these polemical writings.

There are mentioned several other people including the writer's father-in-law Samuel. The writer was living in poverty. He seems to have been occupied on a certain mission about which he reported to the Nagid of Egypt. He was evidently a native of Egypt but for some reasons he took up his residence in Byzantium (Salonica according to our suggestion) where also his wife's father lived.

Whether הרב הגדול (l. 8) refers to Elijah or to his father Sabbatai cannot be ascertained. In this connection attention should be drawn to Bodl. 2615[14] containing the end of a vellum codex of the Pentateuch with the five Scrolls evidently emanating from Byzantium. The colophon reads:

אני שבתי בריבי אליא מכרתי החומש עם חמש מגלותיו לר מיכ[אל] שטפילש[4]
שהוא מקום אטליא מ . . . בשלשה דינרים כירטא[5] שיולינ[ן] אותו לבן אחיו מׄ
יהודה בן מׄ שבתי המקום יזכהו ללמוד א . . .

MS. Adler 4009 (see Facsimile 5 in *Catalogue Adler*) contains a letter of introduction from the Nagid and the congregation of Ḳairwān[6] on behalf of a R. Sabbatai b. Yehudah b. Amittai.[7] Whether there is any relationship at all between these Sabbatai namesakes is at present impossible to say.

The colophons given under II clearly refer to Jews in Byzantium as evident from such names as Evdokia, Magdiel and Mebin. Colophons 1 and 2 are certainly genuine and refer to

[4] The meaning of this Greek word in not known to me.

[5] The nature of these coins is obscure to me.

[6] L. 13: מנו אנו נגיד הגולה נר ישראל . . . והזקנים ושאר קהלינו אנשי קהל קירואן. In Wertheimer's גנזי ירושלם, II, 18a, מנו has been wrongly read as מה and also the whole purport of the letter has been misunderstood (see Introd. pp. 8–9).

[7] Last line. נצר גדולים שרש חסידים אלופים בתורה ומסובלים במצות ר' שבתי ב"ר יהודה ב"ר אמתי והוא ר' שבתי זה קרובו של מרנו ור[בנו] . . .

transactions of 1252 and 1265 C. E. respectively. A codex of the whole Bible fetched the price of 250 silver-pieces called עֲזִרִינָא. The city קלעאשת or קלעאשר is unknown to me. Item 3 can also be genuine, viz. that later owners of half the codex, Jacob and Isaac, donated it to the synagogue in the name of their mother. But the remaining items are evidently spurious and contain Ḳaraite forgeries, especially item 7. Of the Crimean cities mentioned, Ṭaman, Kaffa and Sulkhat are known.[8] But there are also quoted in these spurious colophons the places of פשורי, כפר טרכיאש, קלבנה and אמניאקו which I am unable to identify at all.

I.

[T.-S. 20.45, vellum, top torn; verso blank.]

(Recto)

. . . .

ת אצל כבודך . . . .

לכבודך . . . .

נטרפה . . . .

מן התחלואים . . . .

אל[1] תאשימוני כי אתה חכם . . . .

גם בעת שבא לשם אבו עלי[1a] . . . .

נתת לו האגרות אחת לשלומנו ואגרת . . . .

[ואחרת לר' א]ליה בר שבתי הרב הגדול והיה כתוב בה על עסק

[ה]נאסר בבית האסורים וגם שיגרת לי ולאחינו . . . .

[ומגל]ת אסתר גויל והם עמנו לזכרון וכתבתי אני . . . .

[דברים][1b] על אותם האיגרות ששיגרת לי . . . .

[8] Cp. Deinard, משא קרים, pp. 109, 195, 196. More about these places in vol. II of our *Texts and Studies*.

[1] The reading is doubtful.

[1a] This Abū 'Alī was evidently a resident of the place where the writer of our letter lived. Abū 'Alī visited the place of the correspondent and on this occasion the latter sent with him the epistles referred to here.

[1b] The reading is doubtful.

[ביד אבו עלי] . . . . אותם התשובות שכתבתי אליך כל . . [כי לא כתבתי אותם] באגרת פשוטה אלא היו לי ג קונטרסים [של] [סליחות שחנן] האל ופייטתי אותם ושגרתים אליך תחת [מגלת] [אסתר גויל] ששגרת זכרון להיות בינינו וביניכם ועל חצ[י] [הקונטרס כת]בתי כל תשובות הדברים תחת אגרת . . . . אדו . . . . תק[2] החשובה בעד התשובות . . . . [או]תם האיגרות ששיגרת לי ביד אבו עלי כי לא כתבתי אותם באגרת פשוטה אלא היו לי ג קונטרסים כתובים בם סליחות שחנן האל ופייטתי אותם ושיגרתים אליך תחת מגלת אסתר ששיגרת להיות זכרון בינינו וביניכם ועלי חצי הקונטרס כתבתי כל תשובות הדברים תחת אגרת[3] ואמר לי אבו עלי תן לי תשובות הדברים שכתבת אל אחיך ואשגרם אני עם ערל מולפיטיאנין[4] עם אגרות שלי ונתתים לו לשגרם אליך ובאמונת שמים טרחתי ונתעסקתי מאד על אותם התשובות ואמרתי אכתוב אותם בביאור להודיעו כל דבר וכששיגרת עוד הכתבים אל בני ר׳ עובדיה ה . . . המפורשים על עסק הקראים המחליפים ארורים הם ולא שמעתי תשובת דבר בשביל אותם הסליחות והתשובות אם באו לידך ואם לאו נתעצבתי מאד. אבל זה ידוע לך אחי חביבי כי עוד נתגרו עלינו הקרעים[5] בשנה שעברה וחיללו את מועד[י] י״י המקודשים ועשו ראש השנה בחד[ש] השמיני כי קבלו מכתבים מארץ יש כי לא נראה אביב בניסן

[2] Here begins the continuation of the letter on another piece of vellum. The first 2 lines (lines 17–18) are overlaid by the bottom of the first piece of vellum and hence they can only be partially read. As the fragment is encased between glass, it was impossible for me to straighten up the pieces.

[3] Lines 19–23 seem to be a repetition of lines 11–16.

[4] Either the proper name of this non-Jew or "from ולפיטיאנין."

[5] Read הקראים or it may be a pun on הקראים.

ונעשה הפסח באייר ולפי הזמן נתקלקלו והממם האל ונפלה שנאה ואיבה גדולה בינינו ונהיו מחלקות גדולות והלשי[נו] את הרבנים ונהיה עונש בקהל קרוב אלף דינר׳[6] איפרנייר ובתוך אותם המחלקות והשנאה כי רבה הגיעו איגרותיך ששיגרת לבני ר׳ עובדיה ובחלו׳[7] שלמועד של[סוכו]ת עשו קיבוץ ונתוועד כל הקהל כאיש אחד בכנסת הגדלה[8] וקראו האיגרות וכשמוע העם את דברי האיגרות ואיך החליפו כל המצוות המו כל העם וברכו אות[ך] בשם ויענו כל העם אמן ויצא שמך הטוב . . . . . על כל העולם וגם ממקום ר ו ס י א ה[8a] מזקני [הקהל באו] הנה סוחרים ושמעו דברי האיגרת ומ . . . . . . נמצאו הנה ונשאו אותך על כל שבח וב[רכו אותך] גם אותי רואים ואומרים אחיו של ר׳ אליה זה כתב כל הסיפור הזה והכל אומרים א[שרי] יולדיו ואשרי רבותיו שלמדוהו תורה. ועתה אחי אם ייטיבך האל תכתוב לי אגרת ותשגר לי בעד בריאותכם ושלומכם וזיכר׳[9] הסליחות ששיגרתיך ובם מפורשים כל תשובות הדברים ואל תאשימני שלא הרבתי[10] שבחך כי שבחך ותפארתך מודעת בכל הארץ אלהי יש׳[11] יאריך ימיך ושנותיך בטוב ויזכך

[6] =דינרים. The meaning of איפרנייר is not clear to me. Probably read: איפרפרי, Hyperperi, Byzantine gold coins.

[7] Read ובחולו.

[8] Read הגדולה.

[8a] About a Jew of Russia who visited Salonica in the 11th century and obtained a letter of introduction to help him on his visit to Palestine as he knew neither Greek, Hebrew nor Arabic but only his native tongue, see Mann, I, 165–6; II, 192.

[9] =וזכר.

[10] Read הרביתי.

[11] =ישראל.

לשמוח עם חמודך בן בנים ובן בנות[12] ונשמע ונשמח על שמך הטוב ועם כל המקדים נקבלת התשובה ומי שהדיחנו בארבע קצות הארץ הוא יקבצנו ויבואו[13] גואל בימינו לקיים הנחמות והבשורות שהבטיחנו ביד עבדיו הנביאים ושלומכם ירבה

(Postscript in smaller hand).

וידוע לך אחי חמודי חביבי חשק נפשי מאור עיניי כי זה האיש מ׳ יצחק דודנו[14] שטרח והביא האיגרות ששיגרת בידיו והובילם לר׳ יוסף׳ ומ׳[15] דויד בני ר׳ עובדיה הצורף לא נתנו לו פרוטה אחת ולא השגיחו עליו אפילו לזמנו במאכל או לשגרו מנחה שוה פרוטה ואפילו לשאול לשלום לו לא הם ולא אדם אחר מבני קהלנו אלא על כי הוא קרוב אל חמי מ׳ שמואל הזקן כי קרובים הם ועל ביתו היה דר והודיע לנו את סודו והיה מתעצב אלינו והשביעני שאודיע לך האמת וגם אני אחי בכל יום הייתי רואה אותו ומתבייש ממנו ולא זכיתי לעשות עמו טובה מקוצר יד שהוכבד עלי והעניות וברוך הגוזר צדיק הוא יי׳ כי פיהו מריתי[16]. ועוד אני מזכיר אותך אם נא מצאתי חן בעיניך תודיעני בכתבך המיוקרה[17] על אותם הקונטרסים ששיגרתיך הסליחות ובתוכם סיפור שליחתי מבואר כל דבר גם בשביל הנגיד[18] הזכרתי בסיפור כתיבתי ועל זה כתבתי זו האיגרת מקוצרת ונזכה לשמוע בריאותכם ושמחתכם.

[12] Read בני בנים ובני בנות.

[13] Read ויביא.

[14] Here in the meaning of friend and not uncle.

[15] =ומרנא.

[16] Cp. Lam. 1.18.

[17] Better המיוקר.

[18] Evidently the Egyptian Nagid is meant here.

II.

[MS. Harkavy, B., Nos. 24–5, 2 leaves of vellum. Fol. 1, recto contains the end of Deuteronomy in 3 columns and fol. 2, verso, the beginning of Joshua. The colophons given here are to be found on fols. 1, verso, and 2, recto; they are very faded.]

1.

(Fol. 1, verso, right-hand column.)

[זכרון] עדות שהיתה בפנינו אנו החתומים מטה ביום . . . . . [לשבוע בחדש] אדר בארבעה עשר לחדש לשנת חמשת אלפים ושנים עשרה שנים לבריאת עולם[1] בעצם היום הזה קרב כלב בן שבתי לפני בית דין עם אחי אמו אברהם בן ר׳ שבתי אודות כי היתה להם [קרייה[2] שנפלה בירושה] לאם זה כלב ולאברהם בן ר׳ שבתי ושמה אבדוקייא[3] והיו לה שתי[4] בנים כלב ושבתי[5] וכשנפטרה היא לבית עולמה ובנה שבתי לא נמצא כאן והיה לזה כלב בן שבתי חוב וקרב לפני בית דין ואמר רבותי אני נפל לי חוב והנושים מגישים[6] לי מאד ואין לי מכל מקום לפרוע רק הקרייה שיש לי ולאחי אצל אברהם אחי אמי קראוהו כאן וחלקוהו כי אני רוצה למכור חלקי לפרוע חובי קראוהו בית דין ונתנו ולקחו במשא ובמתן

[1] =1252 C. E. [2] Bible.

[3] Kaleb's mother was called Evdokia (Εὐδοκία). Cp. the same name in the Ketubah of 1022 C. E. drawn up at Mastaura by the river Meandros (in Mann, II, 94, l. 4).

[4] Read שני.

[5] Since her husband was also called Sabbatai, this second son was either posthumous or from another husband.

[6] From נגש.

בדברי דין ובסוף הדין גזרו שיחלקוהו וחלקוהו לפני בית דין תשעה הספרים חלק אחד מן בראשית עד [ימי חייו][7] ומן ישעיה עד לטובה[8] חלק אחר והשליכו גורלות ונפל גורל התורה[9] לאברהם והכתובים והנביאים לכלב אמרו בית דין לכלב שמא תמכרנו ויבא אחיך ויערער עליך דברים אמר להם אני שו[מע] שהוא נפטר ומי יתן ויבא חי ואני ארצהו בכל דבר הכריזו לפני בית דין להמכר ענה שלמה בן יוסף ואמר אני אקנה אבל לא אוכל לקנות חלקך שנפל בגורלך אם יתן בחלקך שמא לא יהיו לי דברים .... אחכ׳[10] עם אחיך ענה אברהם ואמר יקח שני [החלקים] ונתפשרו שניהם והביאו חלקו של אברהם בג .... ונמכרו לזה שלמה במאתים וחמשים כספים עֲזְדִינָא[11] וקבל אברהם הדמים מיד שלמה ולא נשאר אצלו פרוטה ומסרו לו מכירה שלמה חלוטה ופסוקא[12] ברצון לבב בלי אונס וטעות ושגגה והחרימו לפני בית דין למערער [שיבוא ויערער] למחר מחרתים [על מכיר]ה זו מכירת התורה והנביאים וכתובים [לשלמה בן] יוסף לו ולזרעו אחריו ....

[7] Viz. end of 2 Kings, thus this part contained the Pentateuch, Joshua, Judges, Samuel (1 and 2) and Kings (1 and 2); in all 9 books.

[8] End of Nehemiah. Chronicles was probably placed in this codex before Psalms (see Mann, *REJ*, LXXII, p. 163).

[9] Together with the נביאים ראשונים.

[10] =אחרי כן.

[11] The identity of these coins is obscure to me. They seem to have been named after a certain ruler, 'Izz ad-Dīn.

[12] Read ופסוקה.

. . . . בית דין זה . . . .

. . . .

. . . . . בן שבתי[13] . . . .

. . . . בן אברהם . . . .

. . . . אברהם בן . . . .

2.

(Left hand column.)

עדות ההויה בפנינו אנו חתומי מטה
ביום דׄ לשבוע בחדש מרחשון ביבׄ[14]
יום בו שהיא שנת חמשת אלפים
וכׄהׄ שנים לבריאת עולם[15] בעצם
היום הזה בא לפנינו משה בן מׄ שלמה[16]
ממדינת קַלְעַאַשְׂת[17] ואמר היו עלי
עדים נאמנים כי אני מכרתי לזה
נתנאל בן ניסי זה חצי המקרא שלי
שהישיג[18] לי נחלה מאבי תורה וחצי
נביאים טׄ ספרים דמי נייר ודיו כפי
השעה במאתים וחמשים לבנים וחמ[שים][19]
בוקורדוביא עובר לסוחר חצים קכׄהׄ

[13] Here are evidently the names of the witnesses.

[14] This reading is doubtful.

[15] =1265 C. E.

[16] Evidently the son of Solomon b. Joseph who bought the codex in 1252 C. E.

[17] The reading קַלְעַאַשְׁר is also possible. I could not identify this place.

[18] Read שהשיג, in the meaning of שהגיע, cp. also l. 13. Evidently another child of Solomon b. Joseph received the second part as an inheritance.

[19] The letters חמ are doubtful. Perhaps read [חצ]ים, viz. half of the sum was given in coins called בוקורדוביא and the other half in 125 לבנים (in l. 12 for חצים read וחצים). Perhaps read also בקורדוביא, viz. in coins of Cordova, but the usual spelling of Cordova is קרטובא as in Arabic.

לבנים והישיגו[20] הלבנים לידי זה משה
בן מֹ שלמה לא נשאר אפילו פרוטה
אחת וכל מי שיערער דברים
יהיו דבריו כחרס הנשבר ואני
משה לא אנוש[21] ולא תועה ולא
מוכרח כי אם בשלום דעתי מכרתיו
מכירה צמיתות שיהיה לזה נתנאל
שריר וקיים.

[There follow the signatures of the witnesses.]

בנימין בן שלמה נֿנֿ[22] שבתי בן רֿ יהו[דה]
מגדיאל בר מבין רֿיֿתֿ[23]
הרופא זֿצֿל יצחק בן משה
שלמה בן חנניה פד[24] עד

3.

(Bottom of left hand column after No. 2 in large letters.)

זאת חצי המקרא
הקדישה יעקב
ואחיו רֿ יצחק
על שם אמם
חנה בת אברהם
ויזכו לקרוא בה בחייהם
ובניהם ובני בניהם לעלם[25]
ועד אחריהם אמן נצח
סלה הללויה

[20] Read והשינו=והגיעו, cp. note 18.
[21] =אנוס.
[22] =נוחו נפש. [23] =רוח י'י תניחנו.
[24] Read עד.
[25] =לעולם.

[The following colophons are spurious and some seem to be later forgeries which antedate the above transactions.]

4.

(Middle column.)

זיכרון עדות שהיה בפנינו
בחמישי בשבת בירח שבט
בשישה עשר בו בשנת
ארבעת אלפים ושמונה
מאות וז[26] לברית עולם[27] תחילת[27a]
למחזור רנ֗ד

[The rest is illegible; mentioned are שבתי, אברהם ביר֗ אלנתן and other people.]

5.

(Fol. 2, recto, right hand column.)

בשם אלהי ישראל.
סימן טוב לכל ישראל.
בבוא לציון גואל.
ובניין אריאל אריאל.
אנה חוה[28] בת אברהם בעת שכיב מרע
הנחתי לבני צואה יעקב ויצחק
לפני אביהם אהרן כדי שיקנו בעבורי
ספר ויהיה קדש בקהל טמן והנה הקימו
בניה דבריה וצואה שלה והאל יברך
אותם ויזכם שיקראו הם ובניהם ובני

[26] Can also be ה׳. But since Cycle 254 began in 4808 A. M., read וח׳.

[27] =1048 C. E; לברית=לבריאת.

[27a] Read תחלה.

[28] But in No. 3, l. 5, her name is given as חנה; for אנה read אני.

[בני]הם ויכתבו בספר חיים:
וזה החמש עם ספר יהושע ומלכים
יהיה קדש לאלהי יש׳ בקהל טמן לא
ימכר ולא יגאל עוד לעולם. וכן הקדישה
. . . . התורה הזאת שיהיה בכניסת[29] אלא
עזבתי אותו[30] ביד בני אחרי שילמדו
ממנו ויקראו עליו במושב ובבית אבל
וברוך שומרו וברוך מצניעו. והלומד
ממנו והקורא בו. וארור מוכרו וארור
קונהו. וארור מי ישימהו משכון לו.
וארור גונבו ומוציאו מקדושתו.
אלהי יש׳ ירחם את מ׳ חוה[28] בת אברהם
ואת בניה יעקב ויצחק והאל יזכם
ברצון עמו ויפקדם בישועתו. ככת׳[31] זכרני
י׳ ברצון עמך פקדני בישועתך.
ואותה יתן חלקה עם שרה ורחל ולאה
וכל יש׳ ברוכים. מפי מלך המלכים.

6.

(Lower down in different handwriting.)

אלה מספר ומנין ספרי תורות
והם סב׳ ול׳ חומשים וראשונים
ואחרונים וכתובים וג׳ קראיות
את אלה הוליכו הקהל לכפא
מעיר סולכטי קירים

[29] =בבית הכנסת. The form כניסת is after the Arabic كنيسة. The sense requires the insertion of לא after שיהיה.

[30] If the reference is to התורה, then better אותה, and so with the other genders.

[31] =ככתוב, Ps. 106.4.

7.

(Left hand column.)

זיכרון עדות שהיתה בפנינו
ברביעי בשבת בירח שבט באחד עשרה
בו שנת שית למחזור רנ̇ב[32] . . . .
פסיקת המקרא הקדיש . . . . . [לקהל]
פשורי בפני עדים נאמנים בפני
ר̇ משה ור̇ אליה ור̇ אלישע ור̇ אלנתן
ור̇ שבתי ור̇ יהודה השונה[33] ומ̇ר
יוסף̇ ומ̇ר שבתי ושאר כל קהל

(In different handwriting.)

פשורי מקטון ועד גדול איך כי
אמרו לנו שבתי ויהודה
הוו עלינו עדים וקנו מנו
בכל לשון של זכות
וכתבו וחכ̇[34] וחתמו ותנו
לר̇ מאיר ולמ̇ר אליקים
בני ר̇ שמריה בקינין גמור
ובכל תקנות שתיקנו רבנן
מכירה שרירה חלוטה
די לא להשניה וירש[35] ויש להם
רשות להחליף̇ וליתן במתנה
וכל אנש דאתי מארבע
רוחי עלמא בר ובת אח ואחות
קרוב ורחוק ויקונן ויהגה

[32] The reading is doubtful.
[33] The student (=התלמיד?) or the teacher (=המלמד?).
[34] To be deleted as scribal error.
[35] Lapsus calami of the following ויש.

וישתעה[36] דינא עם ר׳ מאיר דנן יהיו דבריו בטלים כחספא וגבירא[37] וכל מי שיערער או מהם או ממשפחתם יהי מוחרם ובשמתא דתקינו רבנן ובשמתא דיהושוע בן נון ואין לו חלק בעולם הבא וישבר כשבר נבל[38]. ונחתמו עדים נאמנים מר אברהם השונה מן כפר טרכיאש ר׳ כלב מקהל מְנַלִיאַ ר׳ מאיר מקלבנה[39] ושאר כל קהלות אמניאקו עדים שריר וקים וכל קהל פשורי החתומים למעלה עדים נאמנים בעדות ברורה.

[36] Read וישתעי.

[37] Probably read וטינא, clay.

[38] Cp. Is. 30.14.

[39] This reading is doubtful.

SECTION II

GEONICA

1.

THE LETTERS OF THE BABYLONIAN GEONIM

A detailed analysis of all the epistles hitherto published including several that are here edited for the first time.

Introduction

THE Gaonic letters, whether addressed to whole congregations or to individual scholars or patrons of the schools, enable us more and more, as they are brought to light from among the Genizah finds, to understand the internal conditions prevailing in the academies, the mutual relations of the Geonim and their contacts with the various communities and their prominent leaders. In this correspondence there is reflected the specific personality of each Gaon; the mental picture, which one carries away from the persual, is at any rate vivid, if not always pleasant, as the writers stand revealed in their thoughts, impulses and actions and not merely as names of persons going about by the time-honored title of Gaon. Unlike the responsa, the subject matter of which demanded on the whole an obliteration of the ego on the part of their authors—though much can indeed be gleaned from them too about the intellectual stature of the various Geonim—, the Gaonic letters reveal the human side of the heads of the schools more fully and their importance in helping to fill up many gaps in our knowledge of the events of their times is obvious.

And yet these epistles were committed to oblivion and only thanks to the Genizah a number of them have been brought to light. Elsewhere[1] I have already suggested the desirability of a scientific edition of all these Genizah letters in a collected form to serve as a sort of an historical text-source illustrating the Gaonic period. But the time of 'ingathering' will have arrived only after all the Genizah material has been made accessible. Herewith several new letters of the Babylonian Geonim are given

[1] *Hebrew Union College Jubilee Volume*, 1925, p. 249.

accompanied by a detailed analysis of all those already published. Through a close observation of their style and manner in addition to their contents other fragments, though incomplete, will be more readily identified.

All the epistles discussed belong to the tenth and the eleventh centuries. The earlier Geonim no doubt had many occasions for such correspondence in connection with their responsa and otherwise, but these letters have been entirely lost, a fate which fortunately did not befall all their responsa. How valuable for historical purposes would, for instance, be the correspondence of R. Yehudai Gaon (2nd half of 8th century) with the scholars of Palestine concerning several Palestinian customs which he unsuccessfully endeavored to abolish.[2] Only rarely are here and there to be found in the responsa of the 9th century items which usually were dealt with in the other Gaonic epistles. Thus R. 'Amram, at the beginning of the responsum which incorporated his famous Siddur to Spain, mentions a detail pertaining to the donations for the school.[3] Similarly R. Naṭronai, seemingly in a responsum to R. Natan b. Ḥananyah of Ḳairwān, alludes to the sum of money brought to the academy by R. El'azar Alluf of Lucena.[4] But perhaps this

[2] See פירקוי בן באבוי (ed. Mann, *REJ*, LXX, p. 136, l. 6ff.): ואף הוא כתב לארץ ישר׳ בשביל סירכא ובשביל כל המצות שנוהגין בהן שלא כהלכה אלא כמנהג שמד ולא קבלו ממנו ו ש ל ח ו לו מנהג מבטל להלכה וביקש להתחזק עליהם והתחזק שלא יהיו אפיקרסין והניח אותן. Here allusion is made to R. Yehudai's letter to the scholars of Palestine, the latter's reply to him and the final rejoinder of the former warning them not to oppose the Rabbinic authorities of Babylon, as the "heretics" (viz. those that were led by 'Anan, a contemporary of Yehudai Gaon) did. With this rejoinder Yehudai Gaon let the matter rest. Ginzberg's interpretation (גנזי שעכטער, II, 560, note to l. 8) is forced and unacceptable.

[3] See סר״ע, ed. Warsaw, I, 1a = ed. Frumkin, I, 24b–25a (and cp. Marx, *Untersuchungen zum Siddur des R. Amram*, 1908, Hebrew part, p. 1): עמרם בר ששנא ריש מתיבתא דמתא מחסיא לרבנא יצחק בריה דרבנא שמעון חביב ויקיר ונכבד עלינו ועל ישיבה כלה (=כולה) . . . שאו שלום ממנו ומן רב צמח אב בית דין ומן אלופים וחכמי ישיבה ובני ישיבה של עיר מחסיא . . . שגר לפנינו רבנא יעקב בן רבנא יצחק עשרים זהובים ששגרת לישיבה ה׳ שלנו וחמשה עשר לקופה של ישיבה וצוינו וברכנו אותך וכו׳. Cp. also the headings in תה״ג, ed. Lyck, No. 56, and *Geonica*, II, 326.

[4] See Samuel b. Jacob's (ibn Jama') additions to the 'Arukh (ed. Buber, *Graetz-Jubelschrift*, Hebrew part, p. 17; cp. Mann, *JQR*, *N. S.*, XI, 448): (אבאס .s. v) הדא מלתא ב כ ת ב י ר ש ו א ת א מרב (r. דמרב) נטרונאי כתב (r. כתוב) בשדר (r. דשדר) ליה למר נתן בר מר חנינא (r. חנניה) לקירואן ולשאר אתרואתא דיש (=דישראל) כי אתא מר אלעזר ריש כלא להא (=להכא) ואייתי מה דאייתי פרענא מקצת אבאס (debts).

was really contained in one of R. Naṭronai's epistles which are thus indicated as כתבי רשואתא as against the usual designation of תשובות שאילות for responsa.[5] Evidently R. El'azar on his journey from Lucena to Babylon visited Ḳairwān and other communities and was entrusted with forwarding the donations for the schools. R. Naṭronai subsequently acknowledged the amount received by the Sura academy to Ḳairwān and to other places (ולשאר אתרואתא דישראל). Another responsum with a beginning that deals with matters pertaining to the school we have in ed. Assaf, pp. 76–7, wherein the correspondent is urged to appeal on behalf of the academy and to forward the yield of the appeal to R. David and R. Mebasser in Damascus, the local representatives of the seat of learning.[6] It is interesting to note the manner in which the Sura Geonim in the 9th century express their regret in their responsa that their correspondents are not present at the school where the instruction received would be more complete and comprehensive. Thus R. Sar Shalom complains that the intricacies of the laws of יין נסך could be solved much better by oral discussion than in writing.[7] Especially R. 'Amram would air such sentiments as is evident from the interesting ending of a pamphlet of responsa in ed. Assaf, p. 46.[8] The editor assigns it to either Sar Shalom or R.

מתיבתא' (was pleased, r. ונייחא) דילנא וריחא. About Natan b. Ḥananyah see Poznański, אנשי קירואן, p. 44, and infra, p. 564.

[5] Cp., e. g., the book-list published by Mann, *REJ*, LXXII, p. 170, top, l. 10.

[6] See תשובות הגאונים מתוך ה„גניזה', 1928, p. 76f., ll. 4–8: וכל נדבה דאית תמן שדר אלתר (=לאלתר) לקדמנא על יד ר׳ דויד ור׳ מבשר מן דמשק שהם עומדין בעסק ישיבתנו ודעתינו נוחה מהם. Evidently the person addressed lived in Egypt and hence the donations would be sent to Damascus to be forwarded from there to Babylon. That this person stayed before in Babylon, as Assaf states, is not evident.

[7] See תשובות גאונים קדמונים, ed. Cassel, No. 46, beginning: כולן מסובכות זו בזו ומאפילות ביותר, ואם היה רצון (היינו: לפני השם) והייתם לפנינו היה אפשר לפרשן יפה יפה ולבררן יפה יפה זו מזו כמות דבר דבור על אפניו, מפני שכשתלמיד יושב בפני רבו וישא ויתן בדבר הלכה יודע רבו לאיזה צד לבו נוטה ומה מתעלם ממנו ומה מתברר לו ומה מתעקש עליו ופושט לו עד שמאיר עיניו ומראה לו פנים בהלכה, אבל בכתב כמה אפשר לו (היינו: לרב) אלא מקצת צוינו וכתבו לכם כללות של יין נסך.

[8] Line 20ff.: והוו יודעין שהרבה חשובים ויקרים [ונ]כבדים אתם לפנינו ושמחים אנו בשאילותיכם וכל זמן שאנו רואין חכמתכם ובינתכם ודקדוק שאתם מדקדקים בשמעתא ובסבארא ובפלפולא נותנין הודאה ושבח לפני הקב"ה שנתן בכם חכמה [ותב]ונה ודעה והשכל ויזכה

Naṭronai (p. 40), but a comparison with a similar passage in *Geonica*, II, 326, shortened forsooth by the copyist, makes it probable that the former emanates also from R. ʻAmram.[9] There are a number of other personal touches interspersed here and there in the responsa,[10] but the personal element is fully in evidence only in the Gaonic letters.

I. The Letters of Saʻadyah Gaon

Only a few letters have been preserved dating from the period of his Gaonate. His disturbed career as Gaon of Sura no doubt gave him plenty of opportunity to inform the outside communities of his doings, especially during the years of his conflict with the Exilarch David b. Zakkai. A circular letter of Saʻadyah to several communities in Spain, cited by Abraham ibn Daud, may

(r. וזיכה) אתכם לישא וליתן במלחמתה שלתורה ומיתקומטין (כלומר: ומצטערין) אנו הרבה [וחלישא] דעתין טובא ש ג ר ם ע ו ן ומרוחקים אתם מן הישיבה שאלו הייתם בישיבה היינו [אנחנו ו]אתם מוספים חיכמה (r. מוסיפים חכמה) והשכל ובינה הרבה (supply).

9 Line 11ff., in the heading of the responsa to questions, that arrived in Adar (1)169 Sel. (=858 C. E.), R. ʻAmram, in addressing his correspondent Meir b. Joseph, remarks: וכשהגיעו לפנינו שאלות ששאלת ממנו ששנו ושמחנו בהם הרבה ונתננו הודאה ושבח לפני המקום שאף על פי ש ג ר מ ו ע ו נ ו ת וכו'. Dr. Ginzberg (p. 302) regards it as possible "that our Responsum contained an allusion to the recent death of the Gaon's predecessor (viz. R. Naṭronai), running somewhat like this: שאף על פי שגרמו עונות ונסתלק מר רב נטרונאי גאון זכרו לברכה בכל זאת לא פסקה תורה מישיבתנו." But this is hardly likely in view of the fact that R. ʻAmram was in opposition to R. Naṭronai as rival Gaon for some time prior to the latter's death (see Sherira's Letter, ed. Lewin, p. 115). The passage cited above (note 8) clearly suggests that the continuation here was: שאף על פי שגרמו עונות [ומרוחק אתה מן הישיבה שאילו היית בישיבה היית מוסיף חכמה והשכל ובינה הרבה]. Cp. also J. N. Epstein (ציונים in memory of Simḥoni, 137, note 3), who rightly rejects Ginzberg's filling in of the lacuna without however offering an alternative, and Aptowitzer (תרביץ I, No. 4, p. 99, note 16) whose remarks are now untenable.

10 Thus R. Matityah of Pumbedita (Mann, *JQR*, *N. S.*, XI, 447, note 9; *Gaonic Responsa*, ed. Assaf, 144): סימן יפה לכל ישראל. שאילות אלו יצאו לפנינו לשער הישיבה שלאדונינו מתתיה ראש ישיבת גאון יעקב חמוד אדונינו רבי והגיע לפניו בחודש ניסן בערב הפסח של שנת אלף ומאה ושבעים וארבע שנים (=863) לאחר שנפטרו אלופים וחכמים מלפנינו בשלום איש לביתו ולאחר שיצאו ימי הפסח צוינו ושגרנו על החכמים ובאו לפנינו וצוינו אותם והתבוננו בהם ולפי מה שכתוב בהן ניראה לנו. Cp. further the ending of the responsum in *Geonica*, II, p. 158, and especially the endings of the responsa

belong to this time, but this chronicler has unfortunately failed to mention its contents, not to speak of reproducing it.[11]

1. The beginning of an epistle to Egypt at the time when he assumed the office of Gaon of Sura (928)[12] has been published by Lewin (גנזי קדם, II, 34, from a Genizah fragment belonging to Grand Rabbin Israel Lévi of Paris), bearing the heading:

כנתא]ב ראס אלמתיבה אלפיומי ז"ל [כ]תבה בבגדאד
פי וקת אן ולי אלראסה (r. אלריאסה) [ר]סלה אלי אהל מצר.

The fragment is clearly a copy of the original the superscription emanating from the copyist when Sa'adyah was no longer alive (after 942). By the "people of Miṣr" obviously the Fusṭāṭ community is meant which is expressly mentioned in l. 5. The fragment in *Geonica*, II, pp. 87–8, is no doubt the conclusion of this letter,[13] but between the 2 fragments there is an obvious lacuna which has not yet turned up in the Genizah fragments available.

In this epistle Sa'adyah mentions explicitly his residence in Bagdād, but the question cannot as yet be decided whether the Sura academy was actually transferred to the capital, or whether

of Sherira and Hai (ג"ה, pp. 31–2, 97, 104, 156, 172, 185, 234–35); Lewin, גנזי קדם, II, 21 (similar to ג"ה, p. 172); *Gaonic Responsa* (ed. Marmorstein, in אוצר החיים, IV (1928), pp. 37–8; his version is very corrupt). See further the beginnings of the responsa in ג"ה, p. 270 (which however is really part of a letter, see infra, p. 94), and תה"ג, ed. Assaf (1927), 33 (on the latter passage cp. Mann, *JQR., N. S.*, XI, p. 438). Cp. further Sherira's remarks to Jacob b. Nissim (ג"ה, No 257, end): ומתוך שאתה תלמיד חבר לנו והר גבוה בתורה גלינו לך את רחישות לבבנו.

For further characteristic statements in the responsa of Sherira and Hai, see Mann, *l. c.*, p. 458–9 (=Lewin, גנזי קדם, I, 69ff.), pp. 462–3.

[11] ספר סדר הקבלה (in Neub., *Med. Jew. Chr.*, I, 74): ושח לי ר' מאיר בן ביבש שראה גליון של רב סעדיה ז"ל וכתוב עליו לקהל קורטובא ואלבירה ואליסאנה ובגאנה וקלסאנה ואשביליא ומרידה העיר הגדולה וכל ערי ישראל אשר סביבותיה, viz. to the congregations of Cordova, Elvira, Lucena, Bajjana (near Almeria, now in ruins), Kalsana, Seville and Merida.

[12] The exact date, viz. Rosh Ḥodesh Sivan (or Iyyar 29th) = May 23rd (or 22nd) 928, is now established from a fragment of a list of his works drawn up by his sons (published by Mann, *JQR, N. S.*, XI, 424–5). The date calculated there (p. 423) should be corrected as above (cp. Simḥoni, התקופה, XXII, p. 500).

[13] As rightly recognised by Lewin (*l. c.*, p. 33) and by Epstein (דביר, II, 325–6).

Sa'adyah subsequently proceeded to Sura to supervise there the affairs of the school.[14]

Sherira and Ḥai in a responsum (נ"ה, p. 133, No. 259) state: ובני ישיבת מחסיה בזמן שהיה (r. שהיתה) בסורא היו מקילין הרבה בדבר זה. It could be inferred from this that at the time this responsum was written the Sura school was no longer in Sura but in Bagdād (just as the Pumbedita school was transferred thither already in 890, see Mann, *JQR, N. S.*, VII, 467ff., VIII, 348ff., XI, 434ff.). But such a conclusion would be fallacious as the passage means "when the school *existed* in Sura" because on the date of the responsum the school did not function at all having been closed some time after Sa'adyah's death. The date of this responsum can be approximately fixed because it is a part of the collection of responsa (Nos. 230–64) sent to Jacob b. Nissim of Ḳairwān (see p. 108 and cp. p. 132, No. 257 end, cited above, note 10). Now one responsum of this collection, No. 244, is referred to in another collection of responsa sent to Ḳabes (Nos. 351–69), viz. in No. 364: ושמועה זו כבר נשאלנו עליה בשנה הזאת מן קירואן וכן צוינו וכתבו את התשובה אל מר רב יעקב בן מר רב נסים. This collection to Ḳabes is expressly stated as emanating from Sherira and Hai Ab (p. 179 top: שאלות בני קאבס לפני גאון מר רב שרירא והאיי אב בנו), hence between 985–1004 (when Hai became Gaon). From the above consideration it appears that both collections of responsa, the one to Jacob b. Nissim and the other to Ḳabes, written in the same year, were completed before the Sura school was reopened under the Gaon Isaac Ṣemaḥ b. Palṭoi. The passage in *Geon.*, II, 206, l. 7ff. (in a responsum of Sherira, cf. *JQR, N. S.*, VII, 467, bottom): וכל הדברים הלילו היו נוהגין בהם החכמים בזמן שהיו בנהרדעא גם סב... (probably r. בסורא) ובפומבדיתא אבל עכשיו שנין בענו (read שנקבענו) בבגדאד המדינה הגדולה ראו החכמים וכו' probably also refers to the time when the Sura school was closed and hence all the scholars were congregated in Bagdād around the Pumbedita school that flourished in the capital.

But as regards the time of Sa'adyah's Gaonate he calls himself in the letter under discussion ראש ישיבה של עיר מחסיה and likewise Sherira in his Iggeret, in speaking of the closed Sura school,

[14] See Mann, *H. U. C. Jubilee Volume*, 225, note 7. Herewith the matter is given the required additional consideration.

refers to it as being במתא מחסיא, במחסיא (ed. Lewin, p. 118). Moreover Sa'adyah in this letter sends greetings on his own behalf as well as on behalf of the scholars, who are established 'in the house of our master' and the prominent coreligionists of Bagdād (l. 15ff.: שאו שלום ממנו ומן האלופים ומן שארית בחור שלנו ומן חכמי ישיבה כולם ומן המשנים הקבועים בבית רבינו ומבעלי בתים חשובים ונכבדים אשר בבגדד). Does this italicized phrase refer only to the משנים or also to the Allufim and the other members of the school? And where and what was this בית רבינו?

The משנים were probably identical with the תנאים who taught the Tannaitic statements (Mishnah and Baraitot) to the younger students while there were other teachers who taught the Amoraic comments and accordingly were called אמוראים or אמורי התלמוד.[15] In Sura it seems that these teachers preparing the young generations of students were established in the old synagogue of Rab known as בית רבינו, whereas the members of the school proper occupied another building.[16] But at any rate it would appear that Sa'adyah's

[15] See the Gaonic letter, probably by Sherira, published by Mann (*JQR*, *N. S.*, IX, 147, l. 21ff.): ומדרש (=בית המדרש) התנאים כמו שומם כי כל נער מאור עינים היה מובל למדרש המשנה ועתה אין איש מביא בנו. ותחבולות נעשה להביא אחד אחר אחד כדי שלא תשתכח (supply למוד) המשנה. וגם אמורי התלמוד רבים בבניהם יוצאים למלאכות אחרות וכו'. These so-called Tannaim and Amoraim are mentioned several times in the Gaonic letters (cp. ibid. XI, 450). See further Natan Habbabli's account (in the Arabic original, *JQR*, XVII, 755): פנזלו בני בירב ואלתנאין מע גמיע אלתלמידים. In the Aḥima'aṣ Chronicle (in Neub., *Med. Jew. Chron.*, II, 130, ll. 13–14) we have the expression Tannaim mentioned also in connection with the Palestinian school (ואל הישיבה לתלמידים ולתנאים).

[16] The identity of בית רבינו (cited in Meg. 29a: בית רבינו שבבבל) has given rise to numerous theories (see their enumeration by Marx, *Unters. z. Siddur Amram*, 9–10, and the long note of Ginzberg, *Geon.*, I, 41–3). Halevy (דוה"ר, III, 53a, note 15) doubts the identity of the Talmudic בית רבינו with the one mentioned by the Geonim, the latter being according to him the synagogue of the Exilarch. But this theory is not acceptable because the Geonim always referred to the Exilarch by his title ראש גלותא and not by the vague term רבינו, especially in our case where there would have been a confusion with the Talmudic designation referring to no less a person than Rab. The Geonim certainly had no such exalted opinion of the Exilarchate as to designate the holder of this office by the title רבינו.

S. Albeck (in his edition of ס' האשכול, p. 73, note 4) has the fanciful idea of a Bagdād school (ישיבת בגדאד) called by the Geonim בית רבינו שבבבל, but

school was in Sura, only at the beginning of his Gaonate he remained for a time in Bagdād till all the necessary arrangements were made and hence he alludes to his stay there (*Geon.*, II, 87, l. 2: כי אז נצוה את בעלי בתים חשובים אשר בבגדד אשר א נ ח נ ו י ו ש ב י ם ב י נ י ה ם).[17]

Interesting is his promise to his correspondents in Egypt that their political requests would be taken care of in Bagdād by the influential sons of Neṭira and of Aaron who would intervene on their behalf at the seat of the government. He does not include the Exilarch, David b. Zakkai, which shows that his political influence was then inferior to that of the above prominent Jews. The power of the ʻAbbāsid Caliphate was more strongly in evidence in Egypt since 905 when the Ṭūlūnid dynasty in the country of the Nile had been overthrown and the rule passed into the hands of governors appointed by the court of Bagdād. Thus Ben-Meir before 921 went in person to the capital to strengthen the cause of Rabbinism in Palestine against the encroachments of the Ḳaraites.[18] Likewise in 928 Saʻadyah could hold forth to

all his remarks are beyond the point. Meborakh b. David, who asked a legal question of R. Nissim בבית המדרש בשבתא דריגלא, a place Albeck thinks to have been our בית רבינו with R. Nissim being really the blind Nissi al-Nahrwāni, *actually visited Ḳairwān in the first half of the 11th century* (see infra, p. 329). Hence, of course, Meborakh b. David could not have been Nissi's contemporary of the first half of the 10th century, and neither the son of David al-Muḳammaṣ (sic!) nor the brother of the Gaon Hai b. David (sic!). True there was a Bagdād academy but this was the Pumbedita school transferred there in 890.

The view of Rappoport (ערך מלין, ed. Warsaw, I, 251) that the Geonim referred to the old synagogue in Sura, known as Rab's synagogue (Meg. 29a), is justified by the evidence now available (so also Marx, Ginzberg and now Aptowitzer, תרביץ I, No. 4, p. 94). Attached to this synagogue was a house of study where the so-called Tannaim and Amoraim of the Sura academy taught the younger students preparing them to join later on the Yeshibah proper which was housed in another building. The בית רבינו was evidently in Sura proper whereas the academy was in a suburb called מתא מחסיא.

[17] One could argue from Natan Habbabli's report of the conflict between Saʻadyah and David b. Zakkai that the former lived then in Bagdād since Judah, David's son, went hither and thither from his father to Saʻadyah and vice versa as if all this were taking place in the capital of the Caliphate. But the vague phraseology does not warrant any conclusion.

[18] See Mann, I, 62–4.

the Fusṭāṭ Jews the promise that he would induce their influential coreligionists in Bagdād to intervene at the court on their behalf.

2. In this epistle Sa'adyah indicates that another letter of general import, containing admonitions, would follow. This second one has been published by Revel (דביר, I, 183ff.) from a MS. dated 1438.[19] The text is very corrupt.[20] Noteworthy is Sa'adyah's reference to his inaugural speech when he was installed as Gaon.[21] It is to be regretted that this sermon has not been preserved. Very likely it was delivered in Arabic, the language current among the Bagdād Jews. Sa'adyah gives 30 admonitions to his Egyptian brethren, all commencing with the appellation בני ישראל, urging them to accept "Musar," to be aware of sins committed, to reflect before being carried away by passion, not to think that an additional fast or prayer is effective side by side with sinning but rather to abandon transgression, to fear God even in time of affluence and not only in adversity, to do a Miṣvāh with cheerfulness, not to scoff at the approaching Ḳeṣ and day of judgment, not to regard the Oral Law as having been changed (here there is a polemical thrust at the Ḳaraites), not to separate oneself from the congregational activities and duties, to rely on the Torah and finally to support the students of the Torah. At the end he urges them to send their legal difficulties to him and his school.

Of special interest are his remarks about too much fasting

[19] As has rightly been pointed out by Epstein, ibid. 189ff., cp. II, 325. Revel's remarks about the purpose and destination of this letter (pp. 180–83) are irrelevant and need no longer be discussed as it has no doubt been sent to Egypt.

There is an allusion in the first letter to the second one (l. 8ff.): ואחרי זה אנו מצוים עוד וכתבים (=וכותבים) אליכם כתבי הזהרות ותוכחות לעורר את לבותיכם ולהקיץ את שרעפיכם על מצות יי׳ אדונינו, and in the second to the first (fol. 1b, ll. 11–12): ו ב א ג ר ת ה ר א ש ו נ ה הודענו אתכם כי אחריה נצוה לכתוב אליכם אזהרות ותוכחות אשר תתעוררו בהם לשמוע כאשר תלמדו. The conclusion of both epistles is the same: ושלומכם וברכותיכם וטובותיכם וכל הצלחותיכם ירבו (ויעצמו) לעד.

[20] Fol. 1a, ll. 5–6, r. ומן האלופים והתלמידים כולם; fol. 1b, l. 2, read אגרת ב ש ו ר ה, viz. the good news of his appointment described in the missing part of the first letter; l. 19 is unintelligible; p. 188, l. 5, r. החסידים.

[21] Fol. 1b, l. 4ff.: ודקדקנו במסכיות (היינו: בסודות התורה) וביארנו טעמיהם והבינום הכל (היינו: כל הקהל הנאסף) והוסיפו שמחה כי רצה י׳׳י אדנינו להשכיל תורתו לעמו ולגלות להם כל סתום ועמום אשר בה והבינו מה שיש במשנה ובתלמוד להבין.

and praying (fol. 1b, l. 25ff.: בני ישראל אם יבקש לבבכם לצום תענית נדבה או להתפלל אל י״י תפלה תוספת הניחו עבירה אחת והיא גדולה מכולם כי העושים כן (היינו: שצמים או מתפללים ועושים עונות בבת אחת) נאמר בהם כי יצמו אינני שומע אל רנתם וכי יעלו עלה ומנחה אינני רוצה כי בחרב וברעב אני מכלה אותם ואמרו חכמים מצוה הבאה בעבירה הקב״ה שונאה). Yet later on, during his conflict with David b. Zakkai, his enemies attacked him for his too many public fasts especially during a plague.[22] But, as Harkavy rightly pointed out (ibid., p. 224), he followed then the general tendency prevalent in the Sura school where, for example, one public fast every year was a regular custom whereas in the Pumbedita school such a fast was declared only during a great emergency. Sherira must have experienced several such emergencies as he had to proclaim such public fasts several times.[23]

3. The beginning of a letter by the Gaon to a certain Ephraim b. Judah (?) is found in Schechter's *Saadyana* (p. 58). It is evidently in reply to a communication from Ephraim concluded by a poem (cp. p. 57, l. 9: אדני סעדיה בן יוסף; l. 10 read אוגר for (?)אמר, l. 11 אשר for אש). The text has not been properly edited. Herewith the fragment is given (p. 58, ll. 13–21) in the hope that the continuation may yet turn up among the Genizah fragments. The heading of the letter is indicated by the copyist in ll. 13–4.

. . . כאב (read כתאב) מראגׄעהׄ ראס

[א]ל[מתׄי]בהׄ רחמה אללה

סעדיה בן יוסף ראש ישיבה [ש]ל[נימי]ן[24] שלעיר

[22] Cp. Harkavy, *Studien u. Mitteil.*, V, p. 229, and 232; especially p. 233, bottom (if the completion of the lacuna be correct): ולא כזה (היינו: סעדיה) שגוזר תענית צבור ששה פעמים בשנה.

[23] See the interesting responsum (ג״ה, No. 259, discussed above, p. 68): ובני ישיבת מחסיה בזמן שהיה (r. שהיתה) בסורא היו מקילין הרבה בדבר זה ותמיד בכל שנה היו קובעין תענית כזאת בבי רב. אבל בני ישיבתנו (היינו: פומבדיתא–בגדאד) היו מחמירין ולא היו עושין כך אלא בצרה גדולה ובמקום שיש חכמים הרבה או חכם גדול מובהק ובאילו הורידו עצמן לסכנה וברחמי שמים הנהיגום שאין חוזרין ריקם. ואנו כבר קבענו כמה פעמים תעניות כאלה.

[24] This designation of Sura is mentioned several times. Cp. ג״ה, No. 551, and *Saadyana*, p. 66, l. 10: המשפט כחקו בימין להיזכר where בימין stands for בישיבה שלימין, viz. Sura (mentioned in l. 8: לתת נדר למחסיה הפרוצה). Sa'adyah himself in his Sepher Haggalui (see the fragment edited by Chapira,

מחסייה. לר[בנא] אפ[רים ב]ן רבנא [יהוד]ה*[24]
המבין בדברי חכמה. ודורש כי (r. כל) קנצי דעת
ומזמה. ושת את [לבו] לקחת מוסר השכל
וחשוב לפנינו ויקר יעזרך צורנו ויצליח לך.
אפני שלום וצפו[ני ב]רכות וספני תבונות
ותס פת (r. ותוספת) חיים ורצון וכבוד ואורה ושמחה

These are all the letters known from the period of his Gaonate. The interesting fragment (published by Mann, *JQR*, *N. S.*, IX, 148–50, cp. *H. U. C. Jubilee Volume*, 260) may have emanated from him because allusion is made therein to his stay in Bagdād (p. 150, top: הלא ידעת אם לא שמעת כי אנחנו יושבים בבגדאד מלמדים את העם וכו'). The whole tenor of the fragment in defending the Rabbinic tradition against Ḳaraism is in accordance with his well-known rôle as a champion of Rabbinism.

4. For the sake of completeness Sa'adyah's letters prior to his becoming Gaon should be mentioned. He had special occasion for many epistles during the Ben-Meir dispute about the calendar in 921, and also subsequently as Alluf of the academy (of Pumbedita-Bagdād) till 928. While still in Egypt he corresponded with

REJ, LXVIII, 11, ll. 1ff.) writes: (i. e. David b. Zakkai, ויהי [כאשר ראה] ידוד (i. e. והזבובים אשר על ה ש מ א ל י ת nickname for דוד, cp. Harkavy, רס"ג, p. 166) the members of Pumbedita school under Kohen Sedeḳ who sided with the Exilarch) וכל מתי סודם [את אש]ר הצליח ייי לעמו ישראל [ביד ס]עדיה ראש ה י מ נ י ת (i. e. head of Sura called ישיבה שלימין). See the other passages cited by Lewin, רב שרירא גאון, p. 2, note 2.

The whole designation of "right" for the Sura school and "left" for the Pumbedita is taken from the ceremony of installation of the Exilarch when the Sura Gaon sat at the right hand of the Exilarch and the Pumbedita Gaon at the left hand (see Natan Habbabli's report in Neub., *Med. Jew. Chron.*, II, 84, top: וראש ישיבת סורא יושב לימינו וראש ישיבת פומבדיתא יושב לשמאלו). Misunderstanding the whole thing, Malter (*Saadia Gaon*, p. 394), following Chapira, explains in the above passage in Sepher Haggalui the "right" to refer to Sa'adyah's party and the "left" to the Exilarch and Sarjadah (sic!). (The correct explanation is found already in Harkavy, רב שמואל בן חפני, p. 29, note 73). Also Obermeyer (*Die Landschaft Babylonien*, 252) has a fanciful theory that the Pumbedita school was called 'the left one,' because the city of Pumbedita was in the north (=left) whereas Sura was in the south (=right).

*[24] The lacuna could also be filled in as [שלמ]ה.

his prominent countryman, Isaac Israeli, court physician in Ḳairwān, on many occasions about scientific matters.[25] He also corresponded with R. Judah, Gaon of Pumbedita-Bagdād, while still staying in Palestine prior to his proceeding to Babylon.[26] Of all this correspondence prior to 928 only a few fragments have been preserved. There are 2 Hebrew letters written from Bagdād in 922 to his disciples in Fusṭāṭ (published by Neubauer, *JQR*, IX, 37–8 and Schechter, *Saadyana*, 24–26, reprinted by Bornstein, ס' היובל לסאקאלאוו, 81–85). The fragment in *Saadyana* has an Arabic address in which the words מן סעיד בן יוסף ראס אלכאל, i.e. from Sa'adyah Rosh Kallah (=Alluf), can still be deciphered.[27] The end of another letter, dated 17th Tammuz, 922, and signed by Sa'adyah Alluf, is given in *Saadyana*, p. 15.[28] There is finally

[25] Cp. the introduction to the commentary of Dunāsh b. Tamim on Sepher Yeṣirah (MS. Parma 3818, where it is attributed to Jacob b. Nissim, fol. 88a, col. 2): עד שהגיע אלינו (היינו: לקירואן) מארץ ישראל אַבוּדַּאני ודוד הֶחָרָשׁ שהיו ממדינת פאס ויביאו בידם (88b, col. 1) ספר זה (היינו: ס' יצירה) פתור ומפורש מפי רב סעדיה הפיתומי זצ"ל ואעיין בפירושו ואבונן בדבריו בו למען דעת והבין מעלתו בחכמה החיצונית שהיא חכמת פילוסופיאה ולאי זו מדרגה הגיע בה לפי שכתביו פעמים רבות באו למדינתנו הידועה קירואן לזקננו רבינו יצחק בן שלמה ז"ל בשאילות מחכמות החיצוניות והוא עדיין בפיתום טרם לכתו לבבל והיה רבינו יצחק מראה אותם לי ואנכי אז בן עשרים שנה והייתי מעמידו על מקומות טעותו והיה שמח לכך מפני מיעוט שני וכבוא אלינו פירושו לספר זה ועמדתי על המקומות שהצליח בפירושם ושטעה במו וסר מדרך הישר ולא הבין מאומה מרזי סודותם ויסבור כי הבין וידע. ודברים רבים הרגיש בנפשו כי לא הבינם ויט מעליהם ויחדל מלפרשם והרבה ליכנס (להכניס .r) דברים אחרים אינם מענייני סברת קובץ עיקר הספר ומייסדו לכך ראיתי לעזוב מה שבידי מזולת זה הספר ולהתעסק בפירושו ולגלות מה שצפן בו קובצו ואוספו הראשון [ואשר supply] שגה רב סעדיה בענייניהם והמקומות אשר טעה בו למען השאיר זכרינו אצל בני עמינו וכדי היות לנו שום שכר לפני בוראינו וכו'. In the very defective edition of this commentaty by M. Grossberg from MS. Oxford 2250 (London 1902, p. 17) the text is corrupt.

Sa'adyah left Egypt in 915. Prior to this date he corresponded with Isaac Israeli when Dunāsh was already 20 years old, hence he was born before 895. This makes it almost impossible that this commentary emanates from Jacob b. Nissim (as it is attributed to him in MS. Parma) because he died in 1006.

[26] See the responsum of Sherira (printed by Mann, *H. U. C. Jubilee Vol.*, p. 248): . . . אחת השאלות אשר שאל מר רב סעדיה גאון עודנו בארץ ישראל טרם [בא] בבל[ה] את אדונינו מר רב יהודה [ג]און זקינינו זכרם שניהם לברכה.

[27] See Halper, *Descriptive Catalogue of Genizah Fragments in Philadelphia*, 1924, pp. 175–6.

[28] כבודך ירב ירום וינושא ויתמך לעדי עד נצח. ונכתב ביום חמישי בשבת ב"ט יום לחדש תמוז שנת אלף ר"לג לממשלת חכמים סעדיה בן יוסף אלוף ישועה. The ending ישועה, salva-

an Arabic letter to persons in Egypt (published by Hirschfeld, *JQR*, XVI, 295–97)[29] which, although it has the heading: כֹּט גאון פיומי זֹכ לבֹ, was evidently written before he assumed the Gaonate. It belongs to the time when the conflict with Ben Meir was still an issue. He explicitly mentions that a letter of his correspondents had reached the then Gaon (of Pumbedita-Bagdād, viz. R. Mebasser, fol. 1, r., l.11: אֹד וצל כתאבכם אלי ראס אלמתיבהֿ אעזה אללה) and therefore Sa'adyah was then still Alluf.

II. The Letters of Nehemiah, Gaon of Pumbedita–Bagdād

Five epistles of his are now available, all couched in that unpleasant, abusive style peculiar to him.

1. The first chronologically is the one published by Lewin (אגרת רש"ג, 133–34), dating soon after the time when Nehemiah declared himself rival Gaon to Aaron b. Sarjādo who succeeded R. Ḥananyah, Sherira's father, in 942–3. Several years had already passed since Aaron assumed the Gaonate when Nehemiah broke with him, but only a minority of the scholars followed into his camp.[30] Nehemiah writes as head of a properly organized school having his brother Ḥofni with him as Ab and the latter's 3 sons, Samuel (the later prominent Gaon of Sura), Isaac and Ḥayyim as promising students, in addition to Allufim, Sopherim, Tannaim and disciples.[31] The epistle was evidently sent to Fusṭāṭ

tion, is a usual conclusion of letters expressing the Messianic hope similar to the endings ישע יקרב, ישע רב. Misunderstanding this, some writers explained that Sa'adyah was given the title "Alluf of salvation" (sic!) for his activities in opposing Ḳaraism (cp. Bornstein, *l. c.*, 86, note 2; Malter, *Saadia Gaon*, 64, for his activities in the Ben-Meir dispute about the calendar). For the right explanation cp. Mann, *REJ*, LXXIII, 107–8, and *Jews in Egypt*, II, 378.

[29] Cp. Hirschfeld's translation ibid., 291–3, and Yellin's corrections, 772ff. A new edition with a Hebrew translation is given by Bornstein, *Hatteḳufah*, vol. 16, p. 246ff.

[30] As Sherira reports (ibid., 121): ובתר כמה (supply שנין) פליג עליה מר רב נחמיה בר מר רב כהן צדק בתר דיתיב קמיה ומר אהרן הוה עדיף מיניה ולא פרשו רבנן מניה.

[31] By comparison with the letter given below (p. 79) lines 8–10 in ed. Lewin should read thus: ממנו ומן אב בית דין אחינו בן גאון אבינו ומן טובי בחור[ינו] שמואל ויצחק וחיים [בני אב אחינו ומן האלופים והחכמים] והסופרים והתנאים והתלמידים [כי בחמלת אלהינו עלינו] אנו לשלום בגופינו ואף על פי [שהקיפונו צרות] ואפפונו רעות הנה אל ישועתינו אשר לא נתן למוט רגלינו ולא נטשנו.

because it has been preserved in the Genizah with the Gaon's seal on wax attached to it, and hence it is the original one. Had it been sent to another country,[32] only a copy would have been preserved as was so often the case with many other letters and responsa sent to countries beyond Egypt which were copied at Fusṭāṭ during their transmission.

Nehemiah refers to his troubles and worries (no doubt in connection with his feud with Aaron b. Sarjādo), but he was able to hold his own. He complains here (as often subsequently) of the lack of replies from Fusṭāṭ to his numerous letters; only a certain Sa'ad and also Solomon and Ephraim, the sons of 'Alī, responded.[33] Sa'ad is perhaps identical with Sa'īd b. דודק (or דעק) mentioned in the other epistles whereas Solomon b. 'Alī is very likely Solomon b. 'Alī b. טבנאי, Nehemiah's representative (פקיד) in Fusṭāṭ (see infra, p. 78). The remainder of the fragment contains a severe attack on Aaron b. Sarjādo accused of appropriating for himself donations intended for other scholars.[34]

2. Two epistles are dated Kislev 1274 Sel. = 962 C.E., one published by Cowley (*JQR*, XIX, 105–6, from a Bodl. fragment) and the other given below (pp. 78–83). They both supplement each other helping to fill out the lacunae as indicated in the notes to the text. The situation in the Pumbedita–Bagdād school was such that the death of Aaron b. Sarjādo in Elul 960[35] had not yet restored peace because Sherira, the Ab under Aaron (in suc-

[32] Lewin's suggestion (p. 133, note 2) that the letter has been sent to Spain (Barcelona) is unwarranted. The interesting seal, with the words נחמיה גאון בן גאון engraven on the wax, is still attached to the fragment which I have seen among the Genizah fragments in the collection of Mr. Jack Mosseri at Cairo.

[33] Lines 11–12: שצוינו וכתבנו אליכם כמה אגרות ולא ראינו תשובה חוץ מן מחמדינו מרי ורבנא סעד . . . [ומן מרין] ורבנא שלמה בן (read וכן, doubtful in MS.) מרי ורבנא אפרים נצרם אל בני מר' עלי זכ' לב' שכתבו כתב אחד (i. e. a combined letter) תשובה לפנינו.

[34] Lines 14ff.: כלף בן סרגאדו הרע אשר רעותיו מפורסמים ושקרו וכזבו מגולה לכל ולא [רק שנטל שררה לעצמו אלא שגזל] נדבה שהיא באה לחכמים ויותר מזה כי הוא אוכל קדשי היתומים והעניים וכו'.

[35] Sherira's Letter (p. 121): ובתר דשכיב מר רב אהרן בסוף רע"א (i. e. end of Elul 960 C. E.) הדרו מ ק צ ת ה ו ן דרבנן לקמיה דמר רב נחמיה ואנחנא ורבנן נפישי דילנא (i. e. of school of Pumbedita-Bagdād) לא אשוינא עמיה ולא אזלנא לקמיה והוינא ההוא עדנא אב ב"ד ולא קבילנא גאונות עד דשכיב מר רב נחמיה.

cession to his uncle 'Amram, see Mann, הצופה, XI, 148), did not recognize Nehemiah as the legitimate successor to Aaron, no doubt claiming for himself the rightful succession. Moreover even the dignity of Ab could not be given him in Nehemiah's school as his brother, Ḥofni, was holding the office. Yet Sherira did not (or could not) proclaim himself rival Gaon to Nehemiah but remained in opposition as Ab refusing to serve under him (about this period in Sherira's career more is to be said farther on in dealing with Sherira's letters, p. 84 ff.). Nehemiah's brother, Ḥofni Ab, died in the spring of 962 and Sherira could have then functioned as Ab with the assurance of succession to the Gaonate subsequently, and yet no reconciliation was brought about, evidently because the personal animosity had already gone too far. Who succeeded Ḥofni as Ab in Nehemiah's school is unknown. Apparently Ḥofni's son, Samuel, was then too young for the position. He is indeed referred to in our letter as בחור.

Both letters are practically identical in content and style, except that the Bodl. letter is addressed to a community at large (evidently outside Fusṭāṭ because it is only a copy) whereas our letter is sent to an important individual Nissin (=Nissim) b. Benjamin. In both there is the same complaint that his letters are ignored. A year before (i. e. in the fall of 961) he informed those near and far of the news (חדוש) that had occurred after the death of Aaron, viz. that *all* the scholars of the school had taken an oath of allegiance to him. How incorrect this was we learn from Sherira's statement that the majority of the members of Aaron's school refused to acknowledge him. Letters to this effect were sent out by Sherira and his group and hence Nehemiah's missives were ignored, and altogether the outside communities, in bewilderment and also in resentment of this incessant feud at the school, were slow in their donations. Nehemiah is full of invective on כחשון ושבירא (nicknames for Naḥshon and Sherira) whom he had put under the ban; the former is still to be identified. How much these renewed appeals of Nehemiah for support of the school were effective cannot as yet be ascertained.

3. Two more fragments of Nehemiah's letters were published by me (*JQR, N.S.*, VIII, 346–7). The second one (B) certainly belongs to the same time as the previous ones because the names

of his opponents, Naḥshon and Sherira, recur therein with the same admonition that their counter epistles be ignored. The donations to the school should be sent either to the 'sons of Aaron' (as in the Bodl. letter) or to Ṭob Alluf who is identical with the brother of Sa'īd b. דודק (or דעק), mentioned in fragment A (cp. above, p. 76). Fragment A, sent to Fusṭāṭ (also dating between 960–68, the years of Nehemiah's Gaonate after the death of Aaron b. Sarjādo), contains bitter complaints about the way his missives were ignored. Nehemiah doubled on this occasion the usual number of his appeals; no person known to him by name has been left out. Half of this number were despatched to Solomon b. 'Alī b. Ṭabnai (the פקיד of the school in Fusṭāṭ) through one of the sons of Aaron and the other half to Sa'īd b. דודק by his brother the Alluf (viz. Ṭob Alluf). Both Sa'īd and Solomon were no doubt asked to forward the letters to the individuals mentioned therein. Here again the success of this supreme effort is not known.

In all these epistles there are reflected the straitened circumstances under which the school of Pumbedita–Bagdād labored owing to the incessant strife that went on there since the time when Nehemiah broke with Aaron b. Sarjādo. It took Sherira later on a long time until he managed to repair the moral damage that this feud had caused to the academy.

A Letter of Nehemiah Gaon, Dated Kislev (12)74 Sel. = 962 C. E.

[T.-S. 16. 6, very faded.] Address (verso)

[ואל אהובנו וח]שובנו מר ורבנא ניסין יעודדהו יוצרנו [בן מרי ורבנא בינימין]

וישמרהו וינצרהו ויעזרהו [זכרו לברכה].

(Scribble in Arabic and in Hebrew script.)

(Recto)

נח[מיה] הכהן ראש הישיבה שלגולה בן כהן צדק ראש הישיבה שלגולה.

[אל האהו]ב ו[חשו]ב ויקיר וחביב מרי ורבנא ניסן ישמרו איום
ונו[ר]א. ויאמיצו בקרב ברח . . . שמו ייטיבה ויפריחה
ו[יגדיל] שלומו בתדירה. וישרישו בבנים [בני תורה].
ויצליח בכל מיני סחורה[36]. בן מרי ורבנא בינימין זכרו לברכה.
א[פני][37] שלום ונשבי ברכות ואסמי טובות ומ . . . . ותוסף
ישועות [ורחמים א]מיצים מן השמים
יהיו לך יקירנו ולבחור טוב רבֹ מנצור בנך יחייהו רחום וליתר
קרוביך [ואוה]ביך נצח. שא[38] שלום ממנו ומן טובֹי בחורינ[ו
שמו]אל ויצחק וחיי[ם ב]ני אב אחינו ומן אלופי
[וסנהד]רי[39] הישיבה וחכמיה וזקניה. [ואיתניה ובני גאוניה.
וסו]פריה [וכלל] תלמידיה. כי בחמלת אלהינו עלינו. אנו
שלו[ם בגופינו[40]. ואף על פי שתדאב] נשמתינו [עלינו].
[ומאד] תכאב לבבינו. באסיפת אב בית דין ואחינו. רוח יי'י
תניחנו. בשנה שעברה בחדש ניסן כי היה יחיד בדורו והוד
הישיבו[ת][41] ונשתו[מם] עולם עלינו. ו[אחרי]ו שבנו

[36] Likewise in Bodl. (ibid., p. 105, top) read: [וישרישו [ינדיל שלומם ב]תדירה. בבנים] בני תורה. ויצליחו [בכל מיני סחורה].

[37] So also Sa'adyah (above, p. 73, l. 20 of the fragment) in the meaning: (all) kinds of peace (about various meanings of אפן see Ben-Jehuda, *Thesaurus*, I, 352). The next phrase ונשבי ברכות is difficult; נֶשֶׁב is used in the plural (נשבים) in the Mishnah in the meaning of nets, snares (see Talmudic dictionaries), but here the context demands a word denoting treasure or store parrallel to אסמי טובות. Sa'adyah uses the phrase צפוני ברכות (ibid.).

In accordance with the text here read in Bodl. (ll. 1–3): [אסמי שלום ונשבי ברכות ואסמי טובות ומ. . . ו]חוסן (ותוסף :here) ישועות ו[ר]חמים אמיצים מן השמים יהיו לכם יקירנו ולזרעיכם [וליתר קרוביכם ואוהביכם נצח].

[38] Likewise, according to the following, read in Bodl. (ll. 3–4): [שאו שלום ממנו ומן טובי בחורינו שמואל ויצחק וחיים בני אב] אחינו ומן אלופי הדר (=הדרֹ=הדרין, ורבני הישיבה וחכמיה. וזקיניה (rows of school, see Lewin, ibid., Addenda, p. 7 ואיתניה. ובני גאוניה. [וסופריה וכל תלמידיה כי בחמלת אלהינו עלינו. אנו שלום בגופינו. ואף על פי שתדאב נשמתינו עלינו. ומאד תכאב לבבינו. באסיפת אב] בית דין אחינו וכו'.

[39] In Bodl. ומן אלופי הדרֹ ורבני הישיבה; perhaps here read [ומן אלופי [הדרֹ ורב]ני הישיבה.

[40] So in the first letter (above, note 31).

[41] All the lacunae throughout are inserted in accordance with the parallel text in the Bodl. fragment.

אל יוצרנו. וצדקנו משפטיו. והודינו לפניו. על כל מידותיו. ככת[42]
חסד ומשפט אשירה לך [ייי אזמ]רה ומודיעים אנו כי
מי[נ]דת הראש לדרוש] את שלום [אחיו ישר]אל
ולשאל עליהם. ועל [יישוביהם]. ככת[43] שאלו שלום ירושלם ישליו
אוהביך וביותר על שלום [אחיו ורעיו] ככת[44] למען אחי ורעי
אדברה נא שלום בך ותמיד א[נו משא]לים[45]
בשלומך ובשלום אחינו . . . ומברכים אתכם ונוטרים אהבתכם.
ומגידים אחותכם ו[רי]עותכם. למען לא תנ[ש]כחנה ולא
תזחנה. ומעת לעת תצמחנה ותפרחנה. ולקיים מאמר
הכתוב[46] רעך ורע
אביך אל תעזוב והיה ראוי עליכם גם אתם להיזהר בזאת כדי
שלא תסור האהבה מבינינו עד עולם ומרוב אהבתינו לכם
עם עוצ[ם] הב[רי]ת אשר בינינו וביניכם
שאנחנו כותבים אליכם בכל שנה ומקוים ומיחלים מכם שתזכרו
[לנו] האהבה והברית [והידידות] ותזכו[47] בנו ובחכמי הישיבה
ותשלחו לנו ול[הם הנדבות והפסיקות והחומשים]
כאשר היו עושים אבותיכם זכ לב מקדם וגם כעשותכם אתם בימי
הנפטר[48] ויעבור קציר ויכלה קיץ[49] ולא ראינו מכם מאומה
ואיננו יודעים בעבור מה ע[זבתונו] ושכחתונו
והשלכתונו אחרי גוכם ואינכם מחזיקים בברית גאון אבינו נוחו
עדן[50] שכרת את אבותיכם שמה[51] חס ושלום מאסתונו. או
געלה נפשכם אותנו. שאפילו אינכם משיבים

[42] =ככתוב, Ps. 101.1.
[43] Ps. 122.6. [44] Ps. 122.8.
[45] So also in Bodl., but better שואלים.
[46] Prov. 27.10.
[47] Read so in Bodl., l. 10, for בו[יש?].
[48] i. e. the late Gaon Aaron b. Sarjādo.
[49] Cp. Jer. 8.20.
[50] i. e. Kohen Ṣedeḳ, Gaon of Pumbedita-Bagdād.
[51] So also in Bodl. =שמא, perhaps.

על אגרותינו. או שמה[51] יש לכם ספיקה באמיתת שררותינו. ובזקנתינו ובגודל משפ[חתי]נו. ובחכמתינו ויראתינו מי"י הלוא ברחמי שמים כל העם גרורים[52] אחרינו.

ומתנהגים על פינו. וכי אין משיב על דברינו. ולא פוצה פה ומצפצף [כנף לפנינו. אילא] הכל פה אחד לעזרינו. ומשועים[53] להאריך חיינו. כי נשארנו בדורנו זה יתד[54] לראשונים.

ויתד לאחרונים. למה לא תנהגו בנו אחינו כמנהג זולתכם ויותר לפי שהיינו סבורים בכם שתהיו לנו לעזרה ולמחיה כל ימי שנותינו ולא עלתה על לבינו שתכעיסונו

ותעצבונו [כי מר] לנו עזבכם אותנו [בשנים שעברו גם הוקשה לנו כי לא השגחתם בנו] ולולא [כוונתי]נו לזכותכם עם כובד עול החכמים עלינו לא היינו מ[טריחים אתכם]

והיינו מקילים מעליכם ובעבור פרנסת החכמים איננו רשאים ל[הניח לכתוב אלי]כם לבקש מחיתם כי התורה בהם תעמוד וישראל בזכות התורה הן חיין ככת'[54a] כי היא

חייך וארך ימיך [ועוד כי חייבין] אנחנו לגלות אזנכם ולהוכיחכם בכל עת לקיים[55] הוכח לחכם ויאהביך ואומ'[56] טובה תוכחת מגולה מאהבה מסתרת ונאמר[57]

ולמוכיחים ינעם ועליהם תבוא ברכות טוב] על המ[וכיח וע]ל המ[תוכח] ואשתקד כתבנו אליך יקירנו והודענוך החידוש שהיה לנו אחרי הנפטר בחזירת כל

[52] Read so in Bodl., l. 13, instead of גבורים.

[53] Pray (from שָׁוַע).

[54] Read so in Bodl., l. 14, instead of יתר. For the phrase, cp. Yer. Ber. 7d, top: אשרי אדם שזכו לו אבותיו אשרי אדם שיש לו יתד במי להתלות בו, וכי מה היתה יתדתו של ר"א בן עזריה שהיה דור עשירי לעזרא.

[54a] Deut. 30.20.

[55] Prov. 9.8.

[56] Prov. 27.5.

[57] Prov. 24.25.

החכמים אלינו ושבתו[ם] לפנינו ושבועתם לנו והשוותם בגאונותינו עם] עוצם מ[נינם וחרה] לנו [באשר] לא החזרתה התשובה גם החלשתה דעתינו על זאת וײ יצילך

מאונאותינו [עתה יקירנו בבקשה ממך שתיטיב דרכך עמנו ותפול נא תחינתינ[ו] בלבבך ותחסה עלינו ותראה בלחצינו ובאלצינו ורחם על אחיך בני הישיבה

והתבונן בדלותם [וזכה אותם והתנדב לנו ולהם כנדבת רוחך וכטובת עינך גם תכפיל נדבתך תחת] השנים [שעברו והוכיח הקהילות בע[בורם ורצה בעדנו ועשה להם פסיקות חשובות ושלחם בשמינו עם החומשים

הנקבצים אצלכם [ויהיה הכל על ידי בני אהרן שמרם] אל ונחמנו [בפעם הזאת למען נעביר ע[ל כל אש[ר חלף][58] למען תברכם נפשינו עם נפשות רבות ואגרת הפתוחה אשר דרשנו בה

הפסיקה והחומש [הנה שלחנו עמה][59] כתב נידוי על בורות שני הנערים הכלבים העז[ים] כחשון ושבירא הרעים התועים עזור על קריאת[ם] לפני הקהילות והזהיר לעשות ככל ה[60]

הכתוב בהם בלא עיכ[ו]ב ורישול והתרחק] מן המתעים המורדים המנודים ואל תקבל כתבם ואל תפנה אל רהבם ואל תקרא בשמם כי אין טובה עמם ומהר

יקירנו נדבתך והרחיבה וכתוב [לנו אגרותיך ושלחן] לפנינו בחיפזון וכל חפץ וצורך ושאלה אשר יהיה לך שלח לפנינו כדי שנצוה ויקומון כהכין יוצרנו וײ

[58] Bodl., l. 23, has here in addition מן רישולכם, viz. in order that we shall forgive what has passed of your slackness, and then ונשמח ונגיל באחרונה.

[59] In Bodl., l. 24, it is stated that the letter of excommunication was sent through the representative Solomon b. ʻAlī ibn Ṭabnai.

[60] First letter of next line.

יהי בעזרך ויחייה את בנך וירצה פעלך ויהיה בכסלך ויצליח
דרכך ויאזין לשועך ושלומך ושלום בנך ירבה לעד.[61]
כסלו שנת עֹ֗ד[62] ברית שלום.[63]

III. The Letters of Sherira Gaon

The epistles of this great scholar are more numerous. They are seldom dated and only from internal evidence can their time be approximately established. Their structure is more or less uniform. 1) First comes as a superscription the name of the author followed by an indication of the name of the correspondent. Thus: Sherira Gaon, head of the school of the Diaspora (שלגולה, a designation for Pumbedita),[64] to X. the son of X. Usually this correspondent is described in many flattering terms of Paiṭanic phraseology. 2) Then comes a section usually beginning with the word שלום and enumerating the various kinds of happiness that are wished for the correspondent. This section concludes with official greetings from the Gaon, the Allufim and all the members of the school, indicating also that they are all well for which God be thanked; or in time of trouble there would be a corresponding phrase to the effect that "although evils have befallen us," yet God be glorified and praised for all His actions. 3) There follows the substance of the epistle commencing with the word ומודיעים, "and we inform" you. Since 985, when Hai became Ab of the school and brilliantly cooperated with his father, there would usually come towards the end of the letters an addendum emanating from him. After further good wishes the epistles conclude with the phrase ישע רב, may there be great salvation (viz. the Messianic era so ardently hoped for).

61 These 2 words should also be added in Bodl., l. 27, end.

62 The thousand and hundreds of the Sel. era are omitted as well known, hence in reality Kislev (12)74 Sel. = autumn of 962. In Bodl. קֹקֹעֹ֗ד = (1)274.

63 An appropriate phrase of greeting emanating from a Kohen (cp. Num. 25.12). So also his nephew, Samuel Gaon b. Ḥofni (cp. Mann, *JQR*, *N. S.* VIII, 366, and infra, pp. 156, 164, 166).

64 In accordance with the Talmudic statement (R. H. 23b, top): מאי גולה אמר רב יוסף זו פומבדיתא. Cp. also Sherira's *Letter* (p. 82), where the reading is Abbaye instead of R. Joseph.

1. *The letters dating from the period when Sherira as Ab opposed Nehemiah Gaon (960–967–8).* So far only 2 epistles can be assigned with certainty to this period. That many letters were sent out by Sherira and his partisan Naḥshon, is evident from the repeated emphasis of Nehemiah Gaon that they be ignored altogether (above, p. 77). Most of them have been lost. A circular letter to the congregations of Spain and North Africa has been published by Weiss (*Haṣofeh*, X, 159 ff.). Its significance, not realized by the editor, has been pointed out by me (ibid., XI, 147 ff.). The structure of the epistle is similar to the one set forth above (p. 83). In the superscription the identity of the author is fully set forth, viz. Sherira, Ab-Bet-Din of the school, b. Ḥananyah Gaon b. Judah Gaon, to the leaders of the congregations in the above countries. The whole section is written in Paiṭanic style, often rhymed, which the editor did not fully elucidate. Then follows a section beginning with שערי שלום enumerating again in Paiṭanic phraseology the kinds of happiness and success wished by the writer for the person concerned. Added to this are the official greetings from Sherira, his son Hai (ומן האיי בחורנו)[65] and the members of the school who were his camp-followers (ומאדירי הישיבה ואיתניה ואלופיה קרובנו ומהחכמים והסופרים והתלמידים אשר לפנינו). In general they are well and God is praised therefore. Sherira evidently kept up a sort of a rival school with public functions[66]

[65] Hai was born about 939 and was over 99 years old when he died in 1038. See Abraham ibn Daud's ס' סדר הקבלה (in Neub., *Med. Jew. Chron.*, I, 66, bottom) where for והיו ימי חייו ס"ט שנה, the correct variant reading is צ"ט. This is corroborated by the strophes in Samuel ibn Nagdela's elegy on him (in Harkavy, *Studien u. Mitteilungen*, I, 46, ll. 5–6): בכו בכה לרב האיי. אשר היה כלא היה, אשר חיה כמו מאה. וסוף דבר כלא חיה.

As a young man he would frequent the home of Aaron b. Sorjādo as he himself mentions in one of his responsa (*Eshkol*, I, 5): וזכורים אנו כמה שבתות ממר רב אהרן גאון ז"ל שהיינו מתפללין בביתו והוא יושב מן התפלה עד הערב וכו'. In the period of 860–867–8, as a man of over 20, Hai already gave evidence of his great abilities and hence his father could well cite him by name in his epistles. However it was the general custom for a Gaon to introduce his son (or sons) to his correspondents. Thus Sa'adyah in the case of his son Sheerit, Nehemiah in the case of his nephews Samuel, Isaac and Ḥayyim, and Samuel b. Ḥofni in the case of his son Israel.

[66] Ibid., p. 160, l. 6ff.: ובכל פרקים אשר אנחנו קובעים ובכל עצרות (public fasts) אשר אנחנו מקדשים חלה נחלה את פני יי' מעוזינו בעד שארית עמו הנמצאה

at which, he assured his correspondents, their good reputation for support of scholarship was duly commended by him. Then follows the substance of the letter beginning with ומודיעים (ibid. p. 161, l. 25). Unfortunately here the letter breaks off and only a few lines of stylistic generalities are preserved. Probably he set forth therein the reasons for his opposition to Nehemiah and appealed for support of him and his group of scholars. This appeal met however with little success. The next letter to be discussed shows to what pitiable straits he was reduced.

The letter, given below under I (pp. 95–97), evidently belongs to this period, or rather 2 years after Aaron died, hence in 962 (see note 5 to text). It is unfortunately very defective, with beginning and end missing; of the first 2 sections usual in his letters only the end of the second one is preserved followed by the substance of the letter beginning with ומודיעים (l. 5). It is clearly addressed to an important person in Egypt (Fusṭāṭ, see l. 6) who formerly studied in Bagdād during the Gaonate of Ḥananyah, Sherira's father (Gaon for 5½ years from Ṭebet 1249–54 Sel. = 938–43). Sherira was then very intimate with him and his brother, now Alluf at the school. The latter was Sherira's best man at his wedding (ll. 24–6).[67] Sherira appeals to his college friend to aid him in his great distress and complains that he leaves his replies unanswered. When Aaron Gaon lived this person would forward the donations from Egypt accompanying the usual legal

לאסוף נידוחיהם לקבץ פזוריהם . . . (l. 16) ותמיד בכם (r. בכל) קהלה ולהקה זכור שבידכם (r. זכור נזכור שבחכם) בזכרון טוב וספר נספר חכמותיכם ובינתכם ושכלכם ורבים ממידות שבחיכם ושבח אבותיכם וכו'. Sherira refers to his public functions also in other letters (*Saadyana*, 118, ll. 5–6: וקובעים פרקים ואחזים את הגדר שלא ייפרץ; infra, p. 105, where Sherira hopes to resume his פרקים after the troublesome times will be over; infra, p. 108: ובכל פרקינו ועצרותינו). Also Israel b. Samuel b. Ḥofni refers to these meetings (infra, p. 169, fol. 2, r.: ובכל פרק אשר אנחנו קובעים ועצרה אשר אנו מקדשים). Likewise Sa'adyah in his letter of admonition to Egyptian Jewry (דביר, I, 184, ll. 7–8) uses the same expression: ובכל הפרקים אשר קבענו נשאנו תפלה ותחנה לפני יי' צבאות אלינו (= אלהינו) בעד השארית הנמצאת לראות את ענים ולקבץ נדחם וכו'. We see thus that on special occasions public meetings were held under the auspices of the head of the school at which prayers were recited for the Diaspora's welfare and for the hastening of the Messianic age. See further Appendix I (infra, p. 195).

[67] As Sherira died in Tishri 1006 at an advanced age, his wedding was over 60 years previously (before the death of his father in 943).

questions, and the Gaon would give a share of the money to him and his son, i. e. Hai (ll. 10–11). Now he is in distress; nothing reaches him from the donations of Egyptian and North-African communities (l. 23). This epistle eloquently illustrates the conditions under which Sherira then labored owing to the unfortunate dispute. Yet he continued to give jurisdiction (as Ab-Bet-Din) and instruction to the people from morning till evening (ll. 20–21).

2. *The letters dating from 967–8, when Sherira became Gaon, till 985, when his son Hai was appointed Ab.* Sherira assumed the Gaonate at a critical time in the fortunes of the school. Its prestige has dwindled down owing to the incessant disputes. In the early stage of his Gaonate the plaintive theme about lack of support is the keynote of his epistles. Instructive especially in this respect is the letter published in *Saadyana* (pp. 118–121)[68]. It certainly belongs to the period before 985 because Hai is referred to therein as בחורינו (p. 118, line 9) and hence was not yet Ab-Bet-Din. Now it may be assumed that before he reached this dignity he acted for some time as Resh Kallah, and since he is not even styled by this name, the epistle belongs to the early period of his father's Gaonate. From p. 119, l. 16 ff., where the allusion is probably made to Shemaryah b. Elḥanan in Fusṭāṭ (cp. p. 124, bottom), it appears that Shemaryah was already established in the capital of Egypt. Without discussing anew the problem of the 4 captives (cp. my remarks in *JQR, N. S.*, IX, 165–171, and infra, p. 110), it should only be added that the date preferred by me for this event, viz. about 970 (see ibid., p. 169), can now be more exactly fixed as the year 972 when the admiral of the Andalusian navy, 'Abd Allah *ibn Riyāḥin*, actually cruised with his fleet in the Eastern Mediterranean.[69] We may thus date our letter as belonging to a time after 972 when Shemaryah became established in Cairo-Fusṭāṭ as a prominent scholar and as Ab-Bet-Din of the Nagid's court (as shown in *Jews in Egypt*, I, 267, cp. *H.U.C. Annual*, III, 292–3).

[68] Fol. 2 there, is really fol. 1, and vice versa fol. 1 is fol. 2. In this right sequence the epistle has been re-published by Lewin, לקוטים, אגרת רש"ג, XXVII–VIII.

[69] See *Encykl. des Islām*, II, 236, col. 2: "Al-Ḥakam's war with the Fāṭimid al-Mu'izz and his allies, the Idrīsids, ended, after the Fāṭimid gover-

It cannot be definitely ascertained to which country our epistle, the beginning and end of which are missing, has been addressed. Sherira complains that since his correspondents' fathers began to cease sending their questions (with donations) the academy is dwindling down. Several years seem to have passed already. He warns them not to go about with the idea that their own schools will not suffer (בתי מדרשיכם = ולא יישחתון מדרשיכם), if the Babylonian academy goes to ruin. The academy is the fountain head and how can the head be impaired without the body suffering on this account? In appealing for the resumption of sending questions together with donations, he describes poignantly his difficulties in assembling the scholars at each Kallah and conducting these large meetings. Likewise he attends to the progress of the younger students who are periodically examined by him and whom his son Hai diligently gives instruction. Sherira is depriving his own family in order to build up the old seat of learning presided over by his father and grandfather. At the end of the fragment he seems to indicate that Shemaryah was appointed by him, with the consent of all the members of the school, as its representative for the whole West to forward the questions and donations to the school and vice versa to transmit the responsa.[70] My feeling is that this letter was sent to Spain where the tendency was to limit the contact with the Bagdād academy owing to political reasons (infra, p. 111 f.). The process of transmission via Fusṭāṭ was also greatly hindered by the warfare between the Spanish Caliph and the Fāṭimids.

nor Bulukīn had unsuccessfully attacked Ceuta (H. 360 = 971), with the conquest of Tangiers in H. 361 = 972 by 'Abd Allah ibn Riyāḥīn, the Admiral of al-Ḥakam's fleet." This admiral evidently made a subsequent cruise in the Mediterranean to capture boats plying to and from Egypt. It is thus clear that the variants in Ibn Daud's ס' סדר הקבלה (Neub., *Med. Jew. Chr.*, I, 67): אבן דמאחין, א' דמחאן, א' רחמאן, א' דמחאץ are all corruptions of אבן רייאחין!

[70] Ibid., p. 119, l. 16ff.: וכאשר הוכחנוכם באהבה כן הנה היצבנו יד לישר בכל ארץ מבוא השמש בהם כמת (בהסכמת .r) כל חכמיה (ישיבה the feminine ending referring to) את הזקן הרב האדיר והאביר האציל [רבנא שמריה הראש] י[שמרהו] אינו (= אינו = אלהינו) . . . [בן רבינו אלחנן זכרו לברכה]. The lacuna is filled in according to p. 124, bottom. The title הראש is not ראש ישיבה, as Schechter thinks, but either ראש שורת נהרדעאי which Shemaryah held while studying at the Pumbedita-Bagdād school (infra, p. 89), or ראש בית דין (viz. head of the Nagid's court).

In the same tenor is held the defective epistle in *Saadyana* (122–124) again alluding to Shemaryah b. Elḥanan, and likewise the fragment published by me (*JQR*, *N. S.*, IX, 146–147). In the latter fragment we have at the beginning the section commencing with ומודיעים and containing the substance of the letter. Though many years have passed without their questions and donations having arrived, yet the Gaon has constantly in mind those communities addressed. Critical indeed is the situation at the school because the young men of ability are leaving it and there is no increase in the elementary grades, wherein the Mishnah was studied (מדרש המשנה), because the parents do not wish their children subsequently to suffer as scholars who are not supported.

3. *The letters from 985, when Hai became Ab, till the end of Sherira's Gaonate* (*Tishri 1006*). After years of hard financial struggle Sherira succeeded in establishing a great reputation by reason of his outstanding scholarship. Staunch friends he gained in Egypt in Shemaryah b. Elḥanan and in Jacob b. Joseph ibn 'Aubal, and in North-Africa, especially in Ḳairwān, where Jacob b. Nissim and a whole group of scholars duly appreciated the sterling merits of the great Gaon. Certainly Sherira had no more reason to complain of lack of questions as the great number of his responsa testifies. In his work as the leading Rabbinic authority of his age he was brilliantly aided by his eminent son, Hai, who since 985 came to the forefront as a great authority ranking next to his father. Whether the financial support was commensurate with the demands on time and knowledge placed upon father and son to answer the numerous questions on most diverse subjects of Halakhah and Aggadah, doctrines and customs, we are at a loss to gauge. One would for example like to know what donation accompanied the famous questions of Jacob b. Nissim and his learned colleagues in Ḳairwān about the composition of the Talmudic literature and the chronological sequence of the Saboraim and the Geonim—questions which were answered in 987 in the famous responsum going by the name of Sherira's Letter.

While so many responsa of Sherira have been preserved, only a few letters, dating from 985 to 1006, have so far turned up in the Genizah and elsewhere. These are to be discussed herewith seriatim. The long epistle, still defective at beginning and end, given below under II (pp. 98–105), is instructive for the scattering of the Genizah fragments. It consists of 3 fragments of 2 leaves each, fitting into one another and deposited in 3 different libraries (Cambridge University Library, the Bodleian, Oxford, and the British Museum, London)! We have the beginning of the usual second section commencing with שלום and continuing with the official greetings of the academy. Times of political troubles were experienced and the Gaon was grateful to God that "our lives were saved" (fol. 1, r., l. 11 ff.). The correspondent is styled "the mighty Alluf" (l. 6) who and whose brothers were evidently men of great standing, probably in Fusṭāṭ. On receiving a letter from him, the Gaon and the members of the school offered up fervent thanks for the political success of this Alluf whose influence was so beneficial to Jewry at large (cp. fol. 2, recto). This person forwarded a donation from Jacob Alluf b. Joseph (ibn 'Aubal, fol. 2, v. l. 11 ff.). There was some passing misunderstanding between the Gaon and this Alluf but now all worry has gone in this respect (fol. 3, v., l. 2 ff.). From l. 8 ff. it is evident that the epistle was composed by Hai on behalf of his father. There is some obscure allusion to a certain person who wishes to prevent something (fol. 4, r., l. 1 ff.). It seems to have to do with the question of the reopening of the Sura school (see the allusion to 2 leaders, שני רועים, שני מנהגים, l. 15). This Alluf is to send the bequests of X and also of David b. Joseph, his relative, and all the donations of Jacob Alluf b. Joseph who acted as treasurer for the school (fol. 4, v., l. 10 ff.).

This correspondent in his letter to the Gaon praised Shemaryah b. Elḥanan, styled ראש שורת נהרדעאי, for his efforts in bringing about a certain arrangement (תקנה, evidently for the benefit of the school, fol. 5, r., l. 4 ff.). Sherira only adds to this eulogy because he knows more than others of his scholarship, a clear evidence that Shemaryah studied in Bagdād. Because of his merits he became head of the first row of the foremost 3 rows of the school. Also Elḥanan, Shemaryah's son, attended the school and is highly spoken of as giving great promise in scholarship (verso, l. 2 ff.).[70a] His letters and questions were frequently coming to

[70a] About Elḥanan's relations to the Babylonian and Palestinian schools see Appendix II (infra, p. 199).

the school. Elḥanan informed the Gaon of the great honor this Alluf was receiving from the son of the late ruler (fol. 6, r., l. 3 ff.). The Gaon wishes to hear more of such good news concerning his influential correspondent. The latter also commended in his epistle a certain elder Danūn b. Ḥayyim who exerted himself for his coreligionists to ease their burden of taxation and also to help the school (l. 10 ff.).

Finally we have the mention of the political troubles in Bagdād which prevented the school from functioning. When the emergency will pass and the school will resume its activities, then this elder will be publicly commended. Our letter was written in Elul, the usual Kallah month. But this year the Kallah did not assemble and the Gaon was hidden with one student mournfully discussing the tractate of this Kallah season (verso, l. 6 ff.). Where the fragment breaks off the Gaon expresses the hope and conviction that in the following Adar the inaugural day of the Kallah will be right on Rosh Ḥodesh and the public meetings (פרקים) will be joyfully held.

It is difficult to ascertain the causes which necessitated the closing of the school for some time. Perhaps we have to seek them in the disturbed conditions in Bagdād at the beginning of 987 due to the fights between the 2 Būyid brothers Ṣamṣām ad-Daula and Sharīf ad-Daula. The former surrendered to the latter in Ramaḍan 376 H. = Jan.-Febr. 987 C. E. But in Bagdād there broke out a violent battle between the Dailamite and Turkish troops and only after the former, partisans of Ṣamṣām ad-Daula, were overwhelmed was Sharīf ad-Daula acknowledged by the Caliph as Amīr al-Umara. Sharīf died in September 989 and there were subsequent fights between these 2 bodies of troops.[71] The disturbances in February 987 would fit in with the Kallah period of Adar. Owing to the fighting in Bagdād the large Kallah meeting could not be convened and Sherira had to go into hiding as the personal security of the city residents was endangered. It was no special persecution of the Jews but a general time of distress for the whole population.

Who the influential Alluf addressed was is impossible to

[71] See Weil, *Geschichte der Chalifen*, III, 33–4.

ascertain. He had special honor and praise given by the son of the departed ruler in Egypt. The latter allusion is entirely obscure and it would be futile to speculate whether this departed ruler (שליט) was the Fāṭimid Caliph, or the Wezir or another high dignitary. The Caliph al-'Azīz ruled till 996, the Wezir Jacob ibn Killis (a former Jew) died in 990, and the commander-in-chief Jauhar (whom some identify as the Palṭiel of Ahima'aṣ Chronicle fame) departed this life in 991.[72] Any clue about this allusion would help to confirm the date of the troubles in Bagdād from which Sherira and his school suffered. But we must await further information to clarify this point.

The fragment of the letter given below under III (p. 106) has been published elsewhere in a haphazard manner.[73] It is reproduced here again for the sake of completeness. The date is 13. Ab 989 with an addendum by Hai Ab. Evidently the Gaon of Palestine is addressed therein. We have only the conclusion of the letter and hence the contents are unknown. At the beginning of the fragment there is an allusion to some person who is greatly cherished by Sherira as the foremost of his friends. The Gaon of Palestine is requested to give orders to recite the letter (evidently enclosed therewith) in public as was the frequent custom with previous letters sent by Sherira's father and grandfather. In that enclosed letter to be recited it is mentioned expressly that it be done with permission of the local Gaon (as מרא דאתרא, so as to preserve the etiquette). The correspondent is asked to inform Sherira that his request was fulfilled. In that letter evidently it was stated that a number of Palestinian Jews were blessed by the Gaon at a meeting of the school. The Palestinian Gaon is invited to turn to Sherira with a request as occasion would come up. Also Hai greets the Gaon and is ready to serve him.

This letter is of interest for the amicable relations prevailing then between the schools of Bagdād and Jerusalem. The bitterness that was prevalent due to the calendar conflict of 921 had already

[72] See about them Mann, *Jews in Egypt*, I, 16ff.

[73] By Marmorstein, *Z. D. M. G.*, LXVII, 636, note 2, and *REJ*, LXX, 101; see my remarks and corrections ibid., LXXI, 110, and *JQR*, *N. S.*, VII, 475.

passed. These friendly relations continued later on under Hai's Gaonate. The Palestinian scholars even sent questions to Hai, and one of the sons of the Gaon Solomon b. Yehudah (about 1025–51) studied in Bagdād under Hai, though Solomon had sometimes occasion to fret over Hai's growing influence over the Egyptian communities.[74]

Another fragment of a letter by Sherira with an addendum by Hai the Ab was published by Marx (*JQR.*, *N. S.*, I, 101)[75] from a MS. Firkowicz. Where the fragment begins there is an allusion that, together with an epistle sent to R. Jacob החבר (no doubt Jacob b. Nissim of Ḳairwān because he is styled החבר several times),[76] something (some letter or tract) was forwarded to Jacob Alluf b. Joseph ibn 'Aubal, who was the school's representative in Fusṭāṭ and would transmit it to Ḳairwān. Jacob b. Joseph is praised for his interest in the school. In fact he was chosen for this honor (בחרנו בו) only because he formerly studied in Bagdād and was personally acquainted with the scholars. Sherira and his colleagues were grieved at his leaving Bagdād (בצאתו מבבל, l. 5), but his sojourn in Egypt was a great boon for the school because by his exertion certain arrangements (תקנות) had been made (l. 8), viz. to organize on the one hand the receipt of the donations from western countries at Fusṭāṭ for transmission to Bagdād and on the other to forward from there the responsa from the school to the respective correspondents. These תקנות are

[74] See Gaonic Responsa, ed. Harkavy, p. 29, No. 64: שאלה זו באה לפנינו מקץ ימים מעו[טים] מ ה ח כ מ י ם ה ח ב ר י ם שבירושלם. This question arrived in December 1015 (cp. p. 32, top: וכתבו (r. וכתבנו) שאלות הללו בסוף חדש טבת שנת שכ"ז, viz. that the pamphlet of responsa to Ḳabes (p. 27) wherein this statement occurs, was written at the end of Ṭebet 1015). About Solomon b. Yehudah's relations with Hai see Mann, I, 115, 119; II, 126, 133.

[75] Reprinted by Lewin (אגרת, לקוטים, XXXI–XXXII). He heads it מכתב מרב האי גאון but this is incorrect because Hai was still Ab and the letter is really by Sherira with an addendum by the Ab Hai.

[76] See infra p. 107, l. 4, and several times in the responsa (e. g. Responsa, ed. Harkavy, Index). Cp. also Pozn., *Studien*, p. 57, who rightly pointed out the identity of Jacob b. Nissim, though doubtful whether Sherira sent the letter and wondering why an epistle to Jacob b. Nissim should be forwarded to Jacob b. Joseph in Egypt. All this is now clear by reason of the established method of transmission of Gaonic correspondence via Fusṭāṭ.

also referred to in letter II, discussed above, which, if our suggestion be right, dates of February–March 987.

Highly interesting is the addendum of Hai Ab (l. 9 ff.). He states that he "*wrote* (כתבנו, on dictation from his father no doubt) the responsa to the wonderful and previous questions which R. Jacob the Ḥaber (i. e. Jacob b. Nissim) had sent."[77] In addition he *composed* (חברנו) a work in Arabic on the methodology of the Talmud[78], divided into several chapters, which would be a guide even to beginners of the study of the Talmud (ואפילו למגשש). Hai is very pleased with his performance and will forward it subsequently (אחרי זאת, i. e. at the next mail so to say) to the Ḥaber (i. e. Jacob b. Nissim) for whom he had composed it; although Jacob is a great scholar, yet this pamphlet will be of use. Since these arrangements (תקנות), as there is reason to believe, refer to 987, the thought lies near that the wonderful questions of Jacob are nothing else but the questions of 987 about the composition of the Talmudic literature and the chronological sequence of Saboraim and Geonim which culminated in the famous reply of Sherira going by the name of Iggeret. Thus Hai actually wrote this reply on dictation from his father.[79] In this connection Hai

[77] והנה כתבנו תשובות השאלות הנפלאות והמיוקרות אשר כתב מר רב יעקב החבר נט׳ רה׳. וחוץ מהן (i. e. the responsa) הִנֵּה חִבַּרְנוּ אנחנו האיי אב בית דין כתב בלשון ישמעאלים חלוק לכמה שערים בישור דרכי התלמוד ובהלכותיו והליכותיו אשר הוא מורה דרך ואפילו למגשש (one that still gropes about, i. e. a beginner) ברחמי אלהים ויש בו כמה דמיונות מכל שערי סוגיא דשמעתא משרי קְטָרִין (opens things that are fastened together) ופוצה אחידן. והנה אנחנו שולחים אותו (i. e. the tract) להחבר נר׳ אחרי זאת כי בשמו חברנוהו ולו עשינוהו ונותר בו כמעט (i. e. a little remained to complete it) והוא יוצא אליו. ואף על פי כן (כן is to be deleted) כי אדיר גדול הוא ורב מובהק, אלא שגם זאת לשרתה.

[78] Misunderstanding the passage Lewin (ibid. XXXII, note 2) makes this work identical with Hai's ס׳ משפטי שבועות (sic!).

[79] Cp. the heading of the Letter (ed. Lewin, p. 4): שאילתא אילן דשאילו אחנא (r. אחיינון) רחמנא וקימנון נפקו לקדמנא לבבא דמתיבתא לבי דינא דמרנו ורבנו שרירא . . . ורבינו האיי דינא דבאבא . . . ופקידנא ואיקין (=ואיקרין) קדמנא וקמי רבנן דמתיבתא ועיינא (=ועייננא) בהון וקמנא על כל מה דכתיב בהון ופקידנא וכתבו תשובות דילהון כי היכי דאחוו לנא מן שמיא. Hence this questionaire is styled in the usual way as שאלות (in the plural) to which תשובות were sent and therefore the above remark of Hai well applies here that "we wrote the answers of the wonderful questions."

had the happy idea of adding a supplementary composition of his own dealing with the methodology of the Talmud, a subject only touched upon in the Iggeret. It is only to be regretted that this work has not been preserved. But the letter reveals to us Hai at the beginning of his career, 2 years after he became Ab, in which capacity he aided his father for many years lightening the Gaon's labors and ripening himself into the outstanding Rabbinic authority of the first half of the 11th century.

Jacob b. Joseph, as representative of the school in Fusṭāṭ, no doubt received numerous letters from Sherira but only one is so far preserved in a fragment (published by Lewin, אגרת, 135). The first few lines are also found in Gaonic Responsa, ed. Harkavy, p. 270 (No. 549), where therc is a lacuna between fols. 1 and 2 and it is altogether doubtful whether the responsum in fol. 2 has a bearing on the letter at the end of fol. 1. (Lewin, ibid., Addenda, p. 6, haphazardly remarks היא התשובה שראשיתה נדפסה בתשה"ג הרכבי סי' תקמ"ט, but our text contains a letter and not a responsum). The fragment is headed by Sherira Gaon and Hai Ab. Jacob is complimented as גיבור בתורה איתן בחכמה, greetings are sent to him and his son Joseph who (as will be seen farther on, p. 114) was, after his father's death, the representative of both the schools of Sura and Pumbedita. Sherira and all his colleagues report that they are well. After the Hebrew exordium we have only 3 damaged lines of the substance of the epistle written in Arabic.

Finally we give under IV (infra, p. 107) the beginning of a letter by Sherira to Jacob b. Nissim of Ḳairwān who is greatly eulogised. After the usual section beginning with שלום and the official greetings from the school, viz. from the Allufim and mature scholars being all members of the college of 70 (סנהדרים), from the secretaries, Tannaim and students, whose condition is peaceful, we come to the substance of the epistle beginning with ומודיעים. Unfortunately of this section only a few lines are preserved in which Sherira assures Jacob that his name is foremost for praise in the school.

Letters of Sherira Gaon

I.

[T.-S. 16. 3, top and bottom torn, very faded.]

(Recto)

....

....

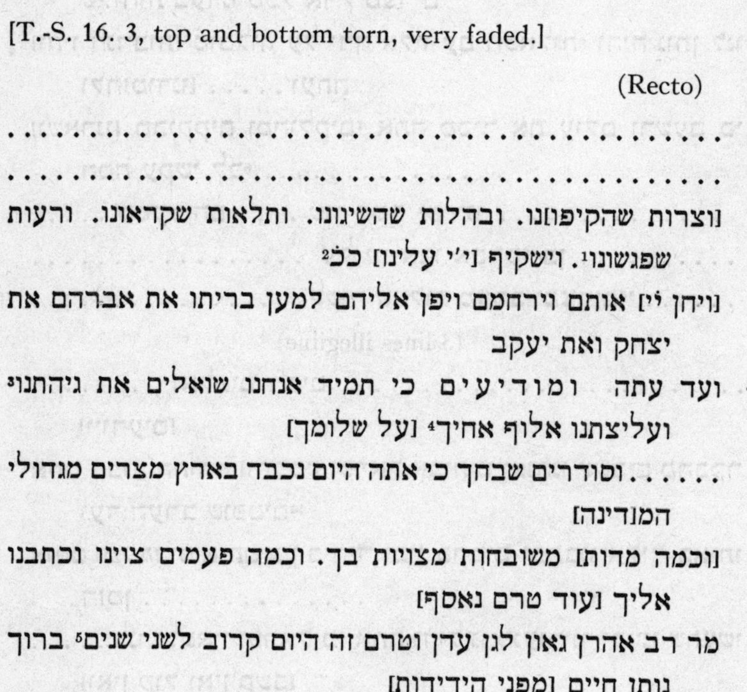

[וצרות שהקיפו]נו. ובהלות שהשיגונו. ותלאות שקראונו. ורעות שפגשונו[1]. וישקיף [י'י עלינו] ככ̇[2]

[ויחן יי] אותם וירחמם ויפן אליהם למען בריתו את אברהם את יצחק ואת יעקב

ועד עתה ומודיעים כי תמיד אנחנו שואלים את גיהתנו[3] ועליצתנו אלוף אחיך[4] [על שלומך]

..... וסודרים שבחך כי אתה היום נכבד בארץ מצרים מגדולי המ[דינה]

[וכמה מדות] משובחות מצויות בך. וכמה פעמים צוינו וכתבנו אליך [עוד טרם נאסף]

מר רב אהרן גאון לגן עדן וטרם זה היום קרוב לשני שנים[5] ברוך נותן חיים [מפני הידידות]

[1] Here perhaps allusion is made to general troubles that befell then Bagdād Jewry and not merely to his private affairs.

[2] 2 Kings 13.23.

[3] From נגה, to shine, here in the meaning of "our light and joy."

[4] Thus the correspondent's brother, the Alluf, was living in Bagdād and Sherira frequently inquired of him about the former's well-being.

[5] From here it appears that Sherira wrote to him about 2 years before at the time when Aaron Gaon died, hence the present epistle was written in 962. But if in l. 7 the lacuna should be וכתבנו אליך [בעת שנאסף] מר רב אהרן, then the second time, nearly 2 years before, took place at some later date and the present epistle dates still later than 962, but certainly before 968, when he assumed the Gaonate, as is evident from the tenor of the letter. However the former alternative is more likely because, after mentioning this letter of 2 years ago, he adds ברוך נותן חיים which expression of thanksgiving would

והברית אשר היתה בינּנו מימי נעורינו . . . .

הלחץ המצוי אצלינו וכשהיה מׄר אהרן גאון קיים היו נדבות שלוחות בעדנו מכל ארץ מצרים

[והיו הנדבות] מובלות על ידך אליו עם השאלות[6] והיה נותן לנו ולח[מודנו] . . . . . ועתה

[נשארנו] מבוקקים ומהולקים[7] אתה מכיר את עולם ורשעם כי המה עקשי לב[8] . . . .

. . . . ממעשיהם . . . . שנו ממך יקירנו . . . .

. . . . על יד אבו אסחק[9] בן . . . .

. . . . לשגר שאלות מערב ומצרים[10] . . . . .

(3 lines illegible)

. . . . ואלפים רבים . . . . . . [ויודעים]

אתם כבוד התורה [וחכמי] ישראל אבותינו ואנחנו יושבים מהבקר ועד הערב שופטים[11]

אותם ומלמדים אותם בין ביחיד ובין ברבים וכתבנו אליך באותו הזמן . . . .

. . . לנו ולשאר ישראל כי אתה גדולינו מנעורינו וקוינו שתעשו [ואין קול ואין קשב]

ולא מענה ולא תשובה ולא זכרון ולא ראינו מנדבת מצרים ומערב פרוטה ושמע [נא יקירנו]

be appropriate for the occasion at the time of the demise of the Gaon Aaron.

6 The correspondent, who had studied at the Bagdād school, was thus subsequently in Egypt the representative (פקיד) of his alma mater.

7 Cp. Is. 24.1.

8 Allusion is evidently made here to his opponents, Nehemiah and his group.

9 =Abraham b. X.

10 Evidently Sherira asked that the legal difficulties from Maghreb and Egypt be sent to him and his section of the school.

11 As was his function as Ab-Bet-Din.

מפני מה מאסת בנו ובדברנו ועברת על[12] רעך ועל רע אביך אל תעזוב כי אתה תדע הא[הבה כשהיית]

בחור בבגדד בימי גאון אבינו זכרו לברכה וכי היית אתה ואחינו אלוף אחיך יעזרהו [אלהינו] . . . .

. . חיר לנו כמו אח והוא שושבינינו ולא ידענו על מה זה געלת בנו נקרא ולא תענה [נבקש ולא]

תשגיח נכתוב ולא תחזור תשובה ואילו פשו העם כהדיוט קל ונבזה[13] כמעשה הזה ו . . . .

יזלזלו בראשיהם ובחכמיהם שומרי משמרת התורה מימי משה ועד ה[יום] ועוזבים . . . .

. . . . אחיך ותשיב אל לבך תדע כי לא כהוגן ולא כראוי אתה עושה עמנו לזה . . . .

אהבתנו וחיבתנו לך וכי אתה נכבד ויקר עמנו עד מאד ועוד כי שמענו כי שיגרוה . . . .

ואויבנו [הנהנים][14] ואנחנו העשוקים אוהביך ואילו ידענו מי המשגר ומי עשה זאת כתבנו [אליו] . . . . .

. . . .

. . . .

. . . . כי רשיותנו . . . .

. . . . ולא . . . .

. . . .

[12] Supply הכתוב, viz. Prov. 27.10. The second ועל should be deleted and for רע read ורע.

[13] Supply לעשות, viz. if the people, such as are common and insignificant, would increase acting like this (to ignore the claims of Jewish scholarship, then) they will (ultimately) despise their leaders and scholars.

[14] Rumor reached Sherira that donations had been sent from Egypt and addressed to the opposing group of Nehemiah. Hence he complains that "our enemies are the ones to benefit and we, your friends, are the wronged ones."

II.

[T.-S. Loan 207, 2 vellum leaves.]

(Fol. 1, recto)

כשפריר[15] נמתח. וברכה כמקור נפתח. והדר כלבוש מלתח[16]. וטוב מלא כל אמתח[17]. ותפנוק[18] עדן דתחתח. עד פרפרת קטנה וכותח. וצדק שלם לא מֻנְתח. בעט ברזל על צור מפותח[19]. וגבורה לחשוב כקש תותח[20]. ושאר הטובות והתשועות וההצלחות תהיינה לאלוף האדיר ולאחיו החשובים והנדיבים ולכל מתי סודו וסיעתו ולכל הנלוים עליו לנצח. ישא אלוף שלום רב ממנו ומן האלופים וזקני סנהדרין[21] וכל חכמי הישיבה והתנאים והסופרים והתלמידים אשר כלם בשפל[22] שוכנים בצל אל ובצלו וְחָיִין במעשיו ובזכר שמו הטוב כי ברחמי יוצרינו שם לנו נפשנו לשלל נודהו ונזמרהו לשמו וברוך

(verso)

הוא. ומודיעים כי הגיעה לפנינו אגרת אלוף יחי לעד החבובה והיקרה וַתֵּרָאֶה לנו כאשר יבקע השחר אחרי מצוק לב מֵאפל וּמֵחשך וינץ עלינו שמו הטוב והנכבד כהנץ החמה ואלתר קודם הפתחה לפנינו קראנו עליה מי זאת הנשקפה

[15] Supply שלום, i. e. peace as expansive as heaven.

[16] Instead of מלתחה (wardrobe, 2 K. 10.22), to suit the rhyme.

[17] Instead of אמתחה (sack), for the same reason.

[18] Pleasure of this world ('the Eden below,' דתחתח=דתחתון, as against גן עדן שלמעלה) including even salad and preserve.

[19] Cp. Job 19.24.

[20] Job 41.21.

[21] The 70 foremost members of the school occupying the 7 rows of ten each (cp. Natan Habbabli's report).

[22] In a low condition.

כמו שחר יפה כלבנה ברה כחמה איומה כנדגלות[23].
אף לא אל השמש הזאת דמינוה כי אם אל שמש
הצדקה ומרפא בכנפיה[24] ובה נעור לבנו כמו מישנה
חיתה רוחנו נתישבה דעתנו יצאנו ונפוש כעגלי
מרבק[25]. וכהקראה לפנינו ויודע לנו שלום אלוף יחי
לעד וסוד אלוה עלי אהלו[26] השתחוינו במסיבנו
לפני אלהים לחכנו עפר ונרבה הודיות ושבח
לפניו על חסדו אשר הוא עושה עמנו בשלום

[Continuation in Bodl. Hebrew e. 44, fol. 80, published by Neubauer, *JQR.*, VI, 222–23. I have procured a rotograph of the fragment and reproduce it here according to the sequence of its lines. See Facsimile I, A and D, infra, pp. 687 and 690.]

(fol. 2 (=Bodl. fol. 80), recto)

אלוף ובהצלחת מעשיו ובתת חנו ובהגבר
ידיו אשר חסדי יי׳ האלה עמנו ועם כל ישר׳[27]
כעל כל אשר גמלנו יי׳ ורב טוב לבית ישראל
אשר גמלם כרחמיו וכרוב חסדיו[28]. קראנו
ונאמרה מאור זה הזרחת לנו אלהינו הגיהו[29]
מהודך נסה עליו אור פניך[30] לא יבא ולא יאסף[31]
כי לאורו נלך חשך[32] ובוא נראה אור. והלכו
גוים לאורו ומלאכים לנגה זרחו[33] מעין זה בקעת
להשקות צמאים לרוות עייפים המשיכהו
מאתך נוזלים מן לבנון לא יכזבו כי מעין ישועה

23 Cant. 6.10.
24 Cp. Mal. 3.20.
25 Ibid.
26 Cp. Job 29.4.
27 =ישראל.
28 Is. 63.7.
29 From נגה, illumine him from Thy splendor.
30 Cp. Ps. 4.7.
31 Cp. Is. 60.20.
32 Cp. Job 29.3. For ובוא r. ובו.
33 Cp. Is. 60.3.

הוא לשואבים נשתלחו מעיניו בנחלים בין הרים יהלכון ישקו כל הקרובים ישברו רחוקים צמאם[34]. עץ חיים זה נטעת בעמך אשר פריו יתן בעתו תנוב למאכל ועלהו

(verso)

לתרופה מאביו אוכל כל רעב תנוב כל עדנים מגד תבואות שמש מגד גרש ירחים מגד ארץ ומלואה[35] ובצלו שוכן כל עיף ורבים ועצומים מחנות מחנות בצל דליותיו תשכנה על יובל ישלח שרשיו ועד נהר הגיע יונקותיו ולא יראה כי יבא חם לחדשיו יבכר ועלהו לא יבל[36]. וכנה אשר נטעה ימינך[37] כורנקי[38] לחכמי דתך גדור גדריה. ועל בן אמצת לך שים עיניך עליו והיה פריו למאכל ועלהו לתרופה. ורבות כאלה בקשנו מלפני אלהינו והוא ברחמיו ישמע ויענה כי הוא ייי אשר לא יבושו קויו. ואשר שלח אלוף יחי לעד הגיע משלחת ידידנו איש סודנו ובעל בריתנו אוהבו החפץ בו השמח באהבתו מחמד עינינו מרי ורבנא יעקב

[Continuation in Or. 5561 B, fols. 9–10, published by Mann, *JQR.*, *N. S.*, VIII, pp. 360–62. See Facsimile I, B and C, infra, pp. 688–689.]

(fol. 3 (=Or. fol. 9), recto)

[וישמ]רהו עו[זרו וישגב]הו ויאמצהו. בן [מרי ור]בנא יוסף [זצ̇]ל[ב̇][39] כאשר כתב אלוף [יחי לע]ד ואכן אין [לנו] לשון להודות מאלוף

[34] Cp. Ps. 104.10–11. [35] Cp. Deut. 33.14–16.

[36] Cp. Jer. 17.8. [37] Cp. Ps. 80.16.

[38] Dining hall (cp. Jastrow, s. v. אכורנקא).

[39] =זכרו לברכה.

. . . . . ולא נדע איך נספר טובו וחסדו
[כי הם נשג]בו מהודאותינו עצמו מספר.
. . . . . . [כ]י לא נוכל. מן השמים יכריזו
. . . . . . ועל . . . . ליך וכן אלהינו
. . . . . יוס[ף] . . . . לנצח נצחים
[ויעלהו] ממ[ע]לה [למעלה וממ]דרגה למדרגה
ואשר הגיד [לנו מן] הגדולות ובצורות
. . . . את אשר
. . . . . . [מ]אור עינינו האל[וף תחיה לעד מן
. . . . אשר בעבורם כתבת אל

(verso)

אל[40] מ֗ר חסן [בן מ֗]ר . . . [יג]וננהו אלהינו ויאמצהו
באותן המלין אשר כ[תב]ת והנה הכר[ענ]ו לכף
זכות והטבנו את נפשנו ועצר המצוק אשר
היה בלבנון[41] מן הדבר הזה פשט[נ]והו וה[ר]וחנוהו
והרחבנוהו ונתישבה דעתינו הס . . . .
את דעתך ירוח לנו כי צר לנו מ[א]ד . . . . .
בקרבנו ואתה אור [ע]ינינו ור[ו]ח אפינו.
ו א נ ו א ב ב י ת [ד י ן[41a] כ [ו] ת ב י ם [ה ד ב ר י ם]
ה א ל ה וכמו אתה [האלוף תחי]ה לעד [עומד]
לנגדנו וכאלו אתה . . . בראש[42] והנה רָוח
לנו כמעט במלין ה[אלה כ]י בהשתוחח נפש[נו]
אותך נשיב אל לבנו על כן אחיל ואת טו[עמך]
הטוב ואת מעשיך הנאים נשובב [ואם][42a]

[40] Repeated from recto.
[41] Read בלבנו.
[41a] Viz. Hai.
[42] The reading is doubtful.
[42a] Perhaps there is a lacuna here between the folios.

(fol. 4(=Or. fol. 10), recto)

הוא דומה לעכב אין העולם מכילנו. ומחמדים אנו לנו מפני טרם זאת כי מאסנו את אבותם לשית עם תלמידינו ויותר [מ]זה אין אנו אומרין אם קרח אם משה[43] [ולולי באה] אגרתך זו אשר נתישבה בה [דעתנו ויש]רה בה נפשנו היינו לומר אם . . . . יך כי האמת עִם אחרים לָך . . . . . . תניחנו ואם לאו אל תאיץ להקניט . . . . . בזכרון תעלולים[44] כי מה אם [מי שאמר וה]יה העולם שיכול יש קניטות [לפניו י]תרומם ויתעלה מזכרון עבודת זרה [כׄכׄ] כׄי קׄצׄר המׄצׄעׄ מׄהשׄתׄרׄעׄ והׄמׄסׄכׄהׄ [צׄרׄהׄ] כׄהׄתכׄנׄסׄ[45] ואמׄ רׄ שמואל ברׄ נחמני אמׄ רׄ [יו]נתן קצר המצע מלהשתורר עליו שניׄ [רועים ו]אמר איך יהיו שני מנהגים ורׄ יו[נתן]

(verso)

כי הוה מאטי האיי קרא הוה באכי והמׄסׄכׄ[הׄ] צׄרׄהׄ כׄהׄתכׄנׄסׄ מי שכתׄ[46] בו כׄונס כׄנד מׄי הׄיׄםׄ תֵעָשה לנו[47] מסכה צרה[48]. אנו איך לא תקנ[נט] דעתנו מכל זאת. אבל אגרת אלוף יחי [לעד] זו הרויחה את דעתנו הרחיבו[ה את נפשנו] . . לו הגדילה השמחה ואין צר[ך] . . . . כי אין כלום כל עיקר ודבר ה . . . .

[43] i. e. whether he be a rebel like Ḳoraḥ or righteous as Moses.

[44] Vexations (cp. Is. 3.5).

[45] Is. 28.20.

[46] =שכתוב, Ps. 33.7.

[47] Read לו.

[48] See Sanh. 103b, Yoma 9b.

לא נחשב הבל וריק ייקנט וב . . . .
לא יתקיים כל עיקר לכן כל . . . .
נקייה ובפשיטות בלי התכנס [ושלח לנו]
הנמצא עדיך בין [מצו]את ר̇ . . . . [ובין]
מצואת מ̇ר דויד בן [מ̇ר] יוסף̇ בן [אבי]
אמך זכרו לברכה ובין כל הנדבנות מן[]
מחמדנו מ̇ר יעקב אלוף̇ בן מ̇ר [יוסף̇ ז̇ל]
ואל תתעכב ואל תירא ב̇רכ̇ות̇ [לר̇אש]

(fol. 5 (=Bodl., fol. 81), recto)

צ̇דיק ופ̇י ר̇שׂ̇ע̇ים יכסה̇ ח̇מס[49]. ברוך יי̇ אתה
וברכתו לך נחלה ומורשה מעתה ועד עולם ויותר
מן הדברים האלה אין אנחנו צריכים תורך נוראות
ימינך ורוח נדיבה תסמכך[50]. ועמדנו על אשר
הזכיר אלוף̇ נט̇ רח̇ משבחו של̇ר̇ב המובהק
אדירנו איתננו רבנו שמריה ר א ש ש ו ר ת נ ה ר ד ע א י[51]
ב י ש י ב ה ש ל נ ו יאמצהו קדושנו ויסעדהו ויעזהו
ויעודדהו בן רבנו אלחנן ז̇ל וכי הוא הראש בתקה[52]
הזאת. אמנם כי כן הוא ואנחנו יודעים בשבחו
יותר מאחרים ומי לנו כמהו ממזרח שמש
וממערב ארי שבחבורה גדול הישיבה ודעתנו
בפלאון[53] חכמותיו וחדרי תבונותיו וקושייו
ופירוקיו ותרביציו[54] וכחו בתורה יותר מדעת
זולתו ולולי כן ל א ש מ נ ו ה ו ל נ ו ל מ ש נ ֶ ה ו ל א

[49] Prov. 11.6.
[50] Cp. Ps. 45.5, 51.14.
[51] About this row see Mann, *JQR, N. S.*, VIII, 352–3.
[52] Read בתקנה.
[53] Read בפלאי.
[54] About the term תרביץ in connection with a school see Brüll, *Jahrbücher*, II, 78ff. But perhaps read here ותירוציו.

(verso)

שתנוהו לראש בשורה גדולה[55] משלש השורות שלישיבה כי שבחו עדינו רב מן הכל. גם הבן היקיר אצילנו*[55] החשוב עלינו מאד מר רב אלחנן חברנו נטׄ רחׄ אשר סמכנוהו בישיבה וכמה שיושבים תחת המקום הקבוע לו. ואמנם כי הוא מוסיף[56] מעת על עת. וכל אגרת אשר תבא מאתו לפנינו טובה מאשר לפניה וכל שאלות שניות טובות מן הראשונות כל זאת עם בחוריו[57]. ובטוחים אנו כי עד אשר יזקין לגבורות[58] יגיע יוסיף ויעדיף על רבים ועצומים ואהבתנו להם אמצת מאד. ומׄר אלחנן נטׄ רחׄ הוא גידולנו וריבוינו ואם יש כמו שיבוש בדעתו שלאלוף נטׄ רחׄ מאשר נראה לנו מדבריו לא מֵעִמָּנו הוא כי משָּׁם וכְלָּה מאהבתם לנו ומרוב

(fol. 6 (=T.-S., fol. 2), recto)

חפצם בנו אשר מבקשים להתיחדנו להם וכן אנחנו מיוחדים להם לכל דבר הוד וסוד והברית אמצת לא נסירנה ולא נפירנה ומׄר אלחנן אור עינינו יחי לעד הוא בְשָׂרֵנוּ באשר נתחדש לאלוף נטׄ רחׄ מן הכבוד והשבח עם בן השליט הנפטר ונחשבנה לו מנחה עריבה ואשכר רצון[58a]. יהי רצון

[55] =דרא קמא, evidently the same as שורת נהרדעאי. Since Hai is writing this as Ab, *the head of the first row was next to him* (מִשְׁנֶה). Hence not מַשְׁנֶה =תנא as Assaf (קובץ של אגרות ר' שמואל בן עלי, 11, note 6) suggests.

*[55] Read אצלינו.

[56] Viz. adds knowledge.

[57] In his youth.

[58] Read ולגבורות.

[58a] For the same phrase, cp. infra, p. 121.

שנתבשר עליך לעולם בשורות טובות ושיחדשו לך מן השמים נסים ונפלאות וטובות וחסדים והוד והדר וכבוד וגדולה מדי התחדש יום ליום יביע אמר ולילה ללילה יחוה דעת[59]. ועל דברת השבח והמהלל אשר ספר אלוף יחי לעד על הזקן הטוב והנכבד מרי ורבנא דנון בן מרי ורבנא חיים נטׄ רחׄ ויהי צור בעזרו ויגן עליו ברוב חסדיו וחנותיו ושמחנו מאד ונפלא הדבר

(verso)

בעינינו והפרטים אשר פרט אשר הוא קם לגדור פרצות אחיו להקל המס ולעזור כושל ומוסר את נפשו לדברים הטובים האלה גם הוא לעזרתה לישיבה להכין חקיה שמחתנו מאד בהם והודינו לאלהינו אשר כן הותיר בעמו והרבינו לו ברכות וכשיעשו מן השמים נסים ותסור הצרה הזאת ונושיב את הישיבה כתקנה ברך נברכהו בקהל רב בסוד ישרים ועדה וי״י ישמע ויענה בו:

וידע אלוף כי בחדש הזה של אלול ימי הכלא[60] היינו מוטלין במרחק עם תלמיד אחד והיינו יושבים בדד ומדדמים[61] במסכתא דכלא בבכי ואנקה. ובטוחים אני כי באדר הזה ברצון אלהינו מראש החדש נשימה יומא דפתאחא[62] ונקבעה הפרקים בטוב לבב [ו]תודה לאל

(Conclusion not preserved.)

[59] Cp. Ps. 19.2.
[60] The Kallah days.
[61] Probably read ומדיימים, from דום, to speak in a low voice.
[62] The opening day of the Kallah.

III.

[MS. Adler Nr. 4009; cp. facsmile in *Catalogue of Hebrew Manuscripts in the Collection of E. N. Adler*, Cambridge, 1921, plate 8.]

ונכבד וחשוב ויקר מאד הוא לפנינו ואין בבעלי בריתנו כו[מ]הו וגם הזכרנוהו. ותובעים אנו בבקשה מן ראש הישׁ[63] יחי לעד שיצוה להיקרא האגרת ברבים כי כן נעשה לאבותינו שם פעמין[64] רבות והנה פירשנו באיג[רתנו] כי ברשות ראש הישׁ נטׄ רחׄ תיקרא. וכן יעשה ואל יאחר ויודיע אותנו כי השלים החפץ וכי נקראה האיגרת נגד כל העם וכי בי[נרכנו] הנקבו[65] בשמות כאשׁ פירשנו. ואם יקרהו חפץ יגיד לנו למען נעמוד בו כחובה אשׁ עלינו. והאלהים יגן בעדו ברוב רחמיו וחסדיו. וגם ממני אני האיי אב בית דין בן ראש הישׁ ישא האדון האיתן ראש הישׁ יחי לעד רבבות שלום. וגם אני [חפץ] בבריתו והוא בגדולת כבודו ידרש. ויצו להודיעני שלומו וכל חפץ וצרך אשׁ לו ולסיעתו למען אעמד במו. ומן השמים יפרשו עליהם יחדו סוכת שלׄ[66]. יגׄ באב שנת אשׁ[67]

[63] =הישיבה. [64] Aram. plural=פעמים.

[65] Those that were mentioned by name; כאשׁ=כאשר.

[66] =שלום.

[67] There follows in the MS. a letter with the heading לר׳ יוסף, viz. by Joseph ibn Abitur to the Palestinian Gaon Samuel Hakkohen b. Joseph (published by Marmorstein, *REJ*, LXX, 101–4, in an incorrect manner; cp. my corrections, ibid., LXXI, 110–12, and *Jews in Egypt*, I, 67ff., for a discussion of the letter).

IV.

[T.-S. Loan 203, 2 leaves of which fol. 1, recto and verso, and fol. 2, recto, top, contain the end of a letter consisting merely of verbiage.]

(Fol. 2, recto, l. 4)

שרירא ראש הישיבה שלגולה
למחמד עינינו ומשא נפשינו. וסגלת
חמדתנו ואיש סודנו. ובעל בריתנו
ושעשועי לבנו. מרי ורבנא יעקב החבר
לנו. הנכבד בישיבתנו. הגדול בסנהדרינו.
האדיר בכלינו[68]. החשוב במקומו כשמש
בחלוניה וככוכבים במסלותם וכירח
באשנבו לממשלת ביום ובלילה יחדו.
ההוד הנטוי על כל חבריו. הצל הפרוש
על כל סביביו. הנהדר המושך מי נזל[69]
לעייפים ומשלח שלולית[70] ימין ושמאל
האילן הגבוה רב שרשים ויפה נוף ומתוק
פרי לכל חך משוש לב כל יודעיו ושמחת
נפש לכל מכיריו ולנו ביותר ולכל בני
הישיבה. יאמצהו קדושנו וינצרהו.
ויסעדהו ויברכהו וירבהו. ויתמכהו

(fol. 2, verso)

ויסמכהו ויעודדהו. ויגברהו ויחיהו
וישמרהו. בן מרי ורבנא נסים זל.
שלום לשום. ותענוק[71] בשׂום. ושעשוע
וססמום[72]. ושבח בפרסום[73]. וטוב אסום.

68 Among our Reshe Kallah (Allufim).

69 Paiṭanic form for מים נוזלים.

70 Pool, rivulet.

71 Read תפנוק, perfumed or spiced delicacy.

72 Probably = Arab. samsam, sesame.

73 Publicity, fame.

שמור וחסום. ממבעה וכרסום[74]. ושאר הטובות והתשועות וההצלחות והברכות תהיינה לך מחמד עינינו ולכל יש לך לנצח. [י]שא אור עינינו שלום רב ממנו ומן האלופים ואיתני הישיבה וסנהדרים כלם יחדו ומן הסופרים ומן התנאים והתלמידים כי ברחמי משגבנו אנחנו שלום ומהללים את שם קדשו יהי מבורך לעולם. ומודיעים כי לבנו עליך מחמד עינינו. יאמצך עזנו. וזכרך מפינו לא ימוש ולא תזח מהגינו[75]. ולא יעדרו זכרוניך מלשוננו. בכל מושבי הישיבה ובכל פרקינו ועצרותינו. ואכן אתה מחמד עינינו. בראש הספורים והחשובים עדינו.

(Continuation of letter missing.)

[74] 'Guarded and shut off from ruin and destruction by man and beasts.' For מבעה cp. B. Ḳ. 3b: מאי מבעה רב אמר מבעה זה אדם ושמואל אמר מבעה זה השן. It seems that the Gaon takes here מבעה in Rab's meaning whereas כרסום, gnawing, refers to animals (cp. Ps. 80.14). But it may be that the expressions מבעה and כרסום are used here Paiṭanically to denote Ishmael and Edom, i. e. Islām and Christianity. Sa'adyah took מבעה to mean a shepherd (cp. Dunāsh b. Labrāṭ, ס' תשובות על רס"ג, ed. Schröter, 1866, p. 3–4, No. 8): ופירש (רס"ג) נבעו מצפוניו (Ob., v. 6) מן לשון המשנה ואמר כי הם ע' מילה (כי הוא מן ע' מלות (r. שלא ימצא דומיהן במקרא (hapaxlegomena) בלתי מלשון המשנה שקורין לרועה מבעה. Now Muḥammad, the founder of Islām, is sometimes referred to in mediaeval Jewish literature as the shepherd (רועה, רועה צאן in a polemical tract published by Mann, *JQR, N. S.* XII, 139, cp. p. 128). Ps. 80.14 יכרסמנה חזיר מיער has long been referred to Rome because the flag of the 10th Roman Legion, stationed in Jerusalem, had the image of a pig (cp. Gen. R. 65.1, Lev. R. 13). Now the expression Edom later on was transferred to Christianity as is well-known.

If this interpretation be correct, we shall have here new metaphors for Islām and Christianity not listed, e. g., by Steinschneider, *Polem. u. apolog. Literatur*, p. 293ff.

[75] From הגה, utterance.

IV. The Letters of Hai Gaon (1004–38)

Since he became Gaon, 2 years before the demise of his father, till 1038 he carried on an extensive correspondence with numerous communities and their leaders. Only a comparatively small number of these epistles to and from the Gaon have been preserved.[1] We propose first to discuss a number of hitherto unpublished letters and subsequently to deal with those already edited.

1. The letter given under I (p. 119–122) is of considerable interest from many points of view. It first establishes the fact that Sherira died in Tishri 1006 because in this letter, dated Elul 14th 1006, he is still referred to as living (l. 24).[2] Our epistle was no doubt sent to Jacob b. Nissim of Ḳairwān. It is regrettable that the beginning is missing. Where it commences we have an interesting passage about Bahlūl b. Joseph, a former correspondent

[1] Elḥanan b. Shemaryah in a letter (cited by Mann II, 41) probably alludes to Hai Gaon in mentioning that a certain person had arrived bearing with him epistles from the Gaon to the Shaikh Abū'l Ma'āli, to Abū Ya'ḳūb (= Joseph) and also other letters (וקד טלע סידי אל . . . שׄצ ומעה כתאב אדוננו גאון נטׄ רח אלי אלשיךְ אבו אלמעלי שׄצ ואלי אבי יעקוב וכתב אכׄר וכו'). For other letters from Hai to Fusṭāṭ cp. ibid. 126, l. 23ff.: כי באו מכתבי רבנו האיי אליכם; 348, ll. 8–9: וגם מכתב אשר מאת ראש ישיבת בבל; 351. See further *JQR*, *N. S.*, XI, 455. Many epistles are alluded to in the fragments discussed here.

[2] The dates of the Gaonates of Sherira and Hai as given by Ibn Daud (ס' סדר הקבלה, in Neub., *Med. Jew. Chr.* I, 67) are confused. More reliance is to be placed on the addition to Sherira's Letter in a MS. Damascus (ibid., p. 189, bottom): ובשנת רצ"ח איסתמיך אדוננו האיי באבות בית דין ובשנת שט"ו נסמך בגאונות. ונפטר אדוננו שרירא בשנת שי"ז כלל שני מלכותו ל"ח. ובשנת שמ"ט נפטר אדוננו האיי בניסן כלל שני מלכותו ל"ד שנה. The date רצ"ח should be רצ"ו, viz. 985, 2 years before Sherira's Letter was written in 987. Hai became Gaon in 1003–4; his father died in Tishri שי"ח (as is evident from our letter), hence שי"ז in the above addendum should be changed accordingly. Altogether Sherira was Gaon from 968–1006, hence 38 years in all, while Hai was Gaon from 1004 till 1038 = 34 years. Since the first 2 years of Hai's Gaonate coincided with the last ones of his father, both together occupied the Gaonate for 70 years (968–1038), the round figure given by Ibn Daud, though his particular dates of their respective tenure of office are wrong. Sherira's demise in Tishri (on the 8th) is corroborated by the fragment given by Mann, *JQR.*, *N. S.*, XI, 419. The correctness of the dates in the Damascus MS. concerning Samuel b. Ḥofni and his son Israel as against Ibn Daud's confusion has also been demonstrated (ibid., p. 410).

of the Pumbedita-Bagdād school, who had ceased to send his questions after changing his allegiance to the Palestinian school (ll. 5 ff.). The last time the Gaon heard of him was in acknowledgement of one pamphlet of responsa sent to him through Shemaryah b. Elḥanan of Fusṭāṭ. A second pamphlet of responsa was left unackowledged. Here we have a characteristic example of the rivalry between the 2 centers of learning in Babylon and in Palestine. How far this reminder had an effect is unknown. But Ṣalaḥ, Bahlūl's son, was subsequently a correspondent of Hai's.[3]

Then Hai Gaon writes about Ḥushiel b. Elḥanan, of whose great scholarship he has heard, and asks his correspondent, Jacob b. Nissim, to urge upon him to send his questions to the school (l. 14 ff.). It establishes the fact that Ḥushiel b. Elḥanan came to Ḳairwān not long before 1006 and that he had no previous connection with the Babylonian schools. This is quite in accordance with his letter to Shemaryah b. Elḥanan (published by Schechter, *JQR.*, XI, 643 ff.) which indicates that he came from a Christian country (probably from Southern Italy), where the influence of the Babylonian Gaonate was not so pronounced owing to the age long connections the Jews of Southern Italy had with the Palestinian school. That there was another Ḥushiel, the father of the famous R. Ḥananel, has been my contention (*JQR.*, *N. S.*, IX, 165 ff.) which has not yet been overthrown by any new evidence. The event of the 4 captives, in which this latter Ḥushiel plays a role together with Shemaryah b. Elḥanan and Moses b. Ḥanokh, can now be fixed in the year 972 (see above, p. 86, note

[3] Cp. Gaonic Responsa, ed. Harkavy, p. 7, where a pamphlet of responsa (Nos. 16–36) is headed: אלות (שאלות .r) מרב בהלול בר יוסף ומר שמואל בר אברהם תאהרתי ומר' אברהם בר יצחק בר אוראי. About Samuel b. Abraham Tahorti see infra, p. 137. Another pamphlet (Nos. 48–58, p. 24) has the heading: מן דרג׳ שאלות מר רב צלח בריה דמר בהלול סנהדרא רבה ורבנן דעימיה מן קירואן דמערבא נפקן לקדמנא. See Harkavy, p. 345, where the argument that Sherira died in 998 is now untenable. Poznański, אנשי קירואן, No. 12, did not realise that Bahlūl b. Joseph was identical with the Bahlūl mentioned in other responsa by Sherira and Hai. Hezekiah b. Samuel Rosh Seder, grandson of Palṭoi Gaon, also corresponded with our Bahlūl (*Geonica*, II, 59). That Hezekiah lived outside Babylon, as Ginzberg argues (p. 54), is hardly likely.

69). Thus this Ḥushiel came to Kairwān about 30 years before Ḥushiel b. Elḥanan who was followed by his son Elḥanan.[4]

Of particular interest are the references to Ḥanokh b. Moses of Cordova (l. 23 ff.). Hai asks his correspondent, Jacob b. Nissim, to exert himself and convince Ḥanokh concerning the "replies of the letters sent to him by our crown the great Gaon, our father, may he live long" (i. e. Sherira). It seems that Ḥanokh refused to reply to them, which indicates that there was real friction between Ḥanokh and the school of Pumbedita–Bagdād. Also Ibn Daud mentions that Hai disliked Ḥanokh because he severed his connections with the school.[5] As Moses, Ḥanokh's father, is not referred to at all, we can deduce therefrom that he was no longer alive then, which is in accordance with the chronology of his coming to Cordova in 972. Moses died still in the lifetime of Ḥisdai ibn Shaprūṭ who was the mainstay of Ḥanokh too. Only after Ḥisdai's death the opposition against Ḥanokh started and a party favored Joseph ibn Abitur instead, but the latter was compelled to go into exile.

The reason of Moses and later on Ḥanokh severing their connection with the academy of Bagdād was probably more political than personal. The 'Omayyad Caliph of Cordova frowned upon too close connections with the hated 'Abbāsid Caliphate. This is reflected by Ibn Daud's remark that the coming of Moses b. Ḥanokh to Cordova and his establishing there a center of Jewish learning pleased the Caliph (viz. al-Ḥakam) "when he heard that the Jews of his realm would not be dependent on their coreligionists in Babylon."[6] Also Ibn Abī Uṣaibia stresses the point that Ḥisdai ibn Shaprūṭ, by his encouragement of local Jewish

[4] All the details about Elḥanan b. Ḥushiel and his position in Ḳairwān, as far as now available, are discussed ibid., p. 160ff., cp. the Addenda, XI, 451.

[5] ס' סדר הקבלה, *l. c.*, 69: ונכנס אבן שטנאש בספינה והלך עד ישיבתו של רב האיי גאון וכמדומה היה שיקבלנו רב האיי שהיה שונא לר' חנוך מפני שארבעה החכמים שהזכרנו כרתו חק הישיבות עד שבאו הישיבות לידי דלדול. Of course this is not correct with regard to all these scholars because Shemaryah b. Elḥanan of Fusṭāṭ was a staunch supporter of Sherira and Hai, but the reference to the friction between Hai and Ḥanokh is now borne out by our letter.

[6] Ibid., p. 68, bottom: ורצה השליש לחזור בו ממכירתו ולא הניחו המלך כי שמח המלך על הדבר שמחה גדולה כששמע שאין היהודים שבמלכותו צריכים לאנשי בבל.

scholarship and by his procuring books from the Orient, made the Andalusian Jews stand spiritually on their own legs and they had no further need to apply to "the Jews of Bagdād" (viz. to the academy of Pumbedita then established in that city).[7] Ḥisdai ibn Shaprūṭ was diplomat enough to know the wishes of his royal master and to orientate the cultural activities of the Jews accordingly. A change in this respect took place only when the 'Omayyad Caliphate became disrupted after 1009. Thus Samuel ibn Nagdela, though Wezir of Granada, was a great admirer of Hai Gaon and must have maintained an intimate correspondence with him through the mediation of their common friend, R. Nissim b. Jacob (b. Nissim) of Ḳairwān. Hai's fame in Andalusia was great indeed in the last period of his Gaonate and his demise in 1038 called forth elegies from Samuel and from the youthful genius Solomon ibn Gabirol.[8]

To return to our letter, Hai received some correspondence from Joseph b. Berakhyah of Ḳairwān and was very pleased with it. He commends him for his scholarship and compliments Jacob b. Nissim for his choice of associates (ll. 25 ff.). After the death of Jacob b. Nissim some time in the winter of 1006–07, thus not long after our letter was written at the end of the summer 1006, Joseph b. Berakhyah succeeded Jacob as the chief representative of both the schools of Sura and Pumbedita.[9] He and his colleagues frequented the school of Jacob b. Nissim even after the latter's death, as is evident from the heading of Hai's responsum dated Adar 1011.[9a] In that school

[7] See the passage cited by Mann, *JQR*, *N. S*, IX, 169, note 163.

[8] Cp. the elegy of Samuel (in Harkavy, *Studien u. Mitteil.*, I, 45–49) and the 3 elegies of Gabirol (in שירי שלמה, ed. Bialik-Rabnitzky, I, 88–90).

[9] Cp. the letter of Samuel b. Ḥofni (published by Mann, *JQR*, *N. S.*, VIII, 365, and see infra, p. 159): וכאשר תשלחום (היינו: הנדבות) יהיו על ידי אדירנו וגבורינו ופקידנו ונאמננו מר רב יוסף החבר הגדול והחכם האדיר יאמצהו מלכנו בן זקיננו מר רב ברכיה זכר צדיק לברכה כי הוא במקום הרב הגדול הגביר והגבור מר רב יע[קב ריש] כלא הנאסף לגן עדן וכי העמדנוהו על עמדו והק[מנ]והו במקומו והצבנוהו על מכונו. About Joseph b. Berakhyah, cp. further Poznański, אנשי קירואן, No. 24.

[9a] See Gaonic Responsa, ed. Harkavy, No. 178: שאילאתא אילן דשדרו מרי ורבנא יוסף בן מרי ורב' ברכיה ורבנן דשכיחין בי מדראשא דמר רב יעקב ראש כלא בר רב נסים נפקו לקדמנא לבאבא דמתיבתא לבי דינא דמרנא ורבנא האיי וכו' בכלא דאדר דשנת אלפא ותלת מאה ועשרין ותרתין וכו'. (1011 C. E.)

Jacob's son, R. Nissim, subsequently figured as the leading scholar.[9b]

Hai enclosed with this letter 2 circular epistles to the West (Maghreb) and requests Jacob to have them copied for distribution to various places (ll. 28–30). Their contents are not stated. He also enclosed responsa to Fez together with 2 circular letters (evidently of the same contents). He asks Jacob to inform him of their arrival (ll. 30–31). Jacob would of course arrange for their being forwarded from Ḳairwān to Fez.

Hai finally asks about the welfare of a close friend of his, Naḥūm the Reader, b. Joseph the great Reader, who then stayed in Ḳairwān. He was Hai's school companion and was now needed in Bagdād as chief Ḥazzān in the large synagogue of the capital. He is to be shown by Jacob this epistle of the Gaon as having his full confidence. This Naḥūm was also a disciple of Samuel b. Ḥofni and corresponded with him from Ḳairwān, as will be discussed farther on (p. 151 ff.) where all the details about him and his father will be summarised.

2. The next dated letter, written half a year later, viz. on the 19th of Adar 1007 (given under II, pp. 123–26), was sent to 2 learned brothers in Fez. The epistle has already been given in excerpt by me (*JQR.*, *N. S.*, XI, 440–442), but it deserves to be edited again in full as far as I could decipher it from the faint rotograph due to the damaged state of the original. The date שי"ה given

Likewise the famous responsum of Hai about mysticism (in טעם זקנים, ed. Ashkenazi, p. 54ff.) was sent in answer to questions by this group of scholars after Jacob b. Nissim's death: על שאלה דשאילו מניה (היינו: מרב האיי) מר רב יוסף בר מר ברכיה ורבנא ותלמידיה דבי מדרשא דמר רב יעקב ראש כלה בר מר נסים על אודות השם וכו'. Jacob is referred to inside the responsum (p. 55a) as already departed. See further Mann, *JQR*, *N. S.*, XI, 449.

[9b] About R. Nissim's school see Mann, *l. c.*: והשיב רבינו האיי גאון ז"ל לבית המדרש שלרבינו נסים ז"ל בלשון הגרית, and Poznański, *l. c.*, p. 41, top. Cp. further infra, p. 329. This school had also the institution of שבתא דריגלא (above, p. 70, note 16) similar to the practice in Babylon where the members of both schools would assemble in honor of the Exilarch on the Sabbath לך לך (Sherira's Letter, ed. Lewin, pp. 91–93; Nathan Habbabli's report, *l. c.*, 78, top). But the time and the nature of this שבתא דריגלא in Ḳairwān at R. Nissim's school is not indicated. Perhaps it was in honor of the Nagid of Ḳairwān Jewry (see note 14). Cp. also infra, p. 329, note 7.

there should be now changed into ש״ח as the rotograph indicates and as the chronology now established from the former letter demands. In Elul 1006 Jacob b. Nissim was still alive. Six months later, in Adar ש״ח (1007), Hai in writing to his Fez correspondents states that the news of Jacob's demise reached him through his friend and representative in Fusṭāṭ Abū'l Faraj Alluf, i. e. Joseph b. Jacob (b. 'Aubal), who succeeded his father to the same title and function.[10] In the address the name of the father of Abraham and Tanḥūm is given by mistake as Tanḥūm but in reality he was called Jacob (as given in the letter, r., l. 4). There is also in the address the indication Fusṭāṭ, viz. that the letter should have as its first destination the capital of Egypt, where it would be handed over to Joseph b. Jacob b. 'Aubal. Then it would be forwarded by Joseph to Fez where Abraham and Tanhūm lived. Their residence in Fez is established by the heading of the responsa emanating from Sherira and from Hai Ab (hence still before 1003–4 when Hai became Gaon).[11] These brothers were evidently the leaders in Fez who would forward questions to the school and receive in due course the responsa. In our epistle there is also a reference to the responsa despatched to them.

Hai informs the 2 brothers of having sent to them a letter through Abū'l Ṭayyib 'Imrān Hallevi b. Hillel enclosing his responsa to 3 questions. There has occurred some mishap and previous responsa were stolen. A few days before, a letter reached Hai from Abū'l Faraj Alluf (i. e. Joseph b. Jacob of Fusṭāṭ) about this matter. Hai asks his correspondents to let him know further details. Abū'l Faraj reported to him the death of Abū Yusuf Jacob (b. Nissim) b. Shahūn which was to him a calamity of the highest order. A memorial service was held for him at the school and at the synagogue. There is an allusion to a sum of 70 Dinārs sent by Khalūf b. Joseph for the school no report of which has

[10] About Joseph's Arabic name Abū'l Faraj, cp. Mann, *JQR*, *N. S.*, VIII, 358.

[11] See the fragment (cited by Mann, *JQR*, *N. S.*, XI, 439): שאילות אילו אשר שאלו מ̇ר̇ אברהם ומ̇ר̇ תנחום בני מ̇ר̇ יעקב ישמרם יוצרם מבני מדינת פאס מלפנינו משער ישיבה שלגולה מבי״ד שלאדונינו שרירא ראש ישיבת גאון יעקב . . . ומבי״ד הגדול שלאדוננו האיי אב בי״ד של ישיבת גאון יעקב וכו'. Cp. also Gaonic Responsa, ed. Assaf (1927), p. 75.

yet reached the Gaon. He requests his correspondents to inquire about the matter. The Gaon seems to have been then in great monetary distress. The maintenance of his family and household depended on his receiving a considerable sum of money. The two brothers should also inquire about what was left by Jacob b. Nissim of the collections for the school. Finally he asks for news about Solomon b. Ḥakim b. Abī שכם and transmits to him his greetings. This Solomon may have been a member of the family of Moses b. Abī שכם quoted in a responsum of Sherira and Hai about the removal of hair from the arm-pits and the pudenda.[12]

3. The fragment given under III (pp. 126–34) is a part of an elaborate letter to Judah Alluf and Rosh Hasseder b. Joseph of Ḳairwān, a frequent correspondent of Sherira and Hai. A part of it has been published by Ginzberg (*Geonica*, II, 278–9), from a Bodl. fragment, who did not realise at first its poetical nature and then gave in *Z. f. H. B.*, XIV, 84–93, a new version of the poetical part which does neither correspond with the text in *Geonica* nor with the original! Another fragment in the Cambridge collection supplies the outer 2 leaves of the Bodleian leaf but the beginning and the end are still missing. We have at first a long poem in rhyme and metre in eulogy of Judah. This poem begins with the heading יהודה מחמדינו שהוא אלוף וראש סידרא and concludes with the same phrase (cp. fol. 2, v., ll. 6–7). Hai shows in this poem the richness of his Hebrew vocabulary, as befitting the author of a dictionary (known as al-Ḥāwi).[13] Judah's father,

[12] Responsa of Solomon ibn Adret, V, No. 21 (cited by Müller, *Mafteaḥ*, p. 227): וכשהיה לפנינו מ' חיים בן עובדיה שאל מלפנינו זאת וכן השבנוהו. אף מ' משה בן אבי שכם וכן השבנו. It would thus appear that Moses b. Abī שכם visited Bagdād just as Ḥayyim b. 'Obadyah did. However in the version of a MS. (given by Kaufmann, *Bet Talmud*, III, 64) the reading after השבנוהו continues differently: ושמח הרבה בתשובתנו ונתקררה דעתו ועשה כן ולא חשש. ואף מ"ר יוסף בן אבי זכריא שאל מלפנינו שאלה זו וכן השבנוהו. But it may be that the passage אף מ' משה וכו' should come in after the second וכן השבנוהו. In Ibn Adret's responsa the sentence from ושמח . . . וכן השבנוהו has been left out due to a scribal error.

Abū Zakariyya is the Arabic Kunya for Judah, hence the Ḳairwān correspondent of Sherira and Hai was Joseph b. Judah, perhaps the father of Judah Alluf and Rosh Hasseder, so much eulogised in Hai's letter to be discussed forthwith.

[13] About Hai's dictionary cp. Steinschneider, *Arab. Liter. d. Juden*, p. 100.

Joseph, is eulogised as "the lord of his people and its leader" (fol. 2, r., l. 3 ff.). It would seem as if he was the Nagid of the Ḳairwān Jews prior to the physician Abraham b. Natan ibn 'Ata who in his turn was succeeded by Jacob b. 'Amram.[14] Hai states that he commenced the poem at noon and finished it in the same day towards evening in spite of his great occupation and worry (fol. 2, r., ll. 17–8). There must have been a special reason for the great compliments heaped upon our Judah by Hai who added that these were only a thousandth part of what he felt towards him (fol. 2, v., l. 8 ff.). The poem was circulated by him throughout Babylon and reached Mosul and Syria and likewise Persia. Greetings are also sent to a certain Dunāsh (but the reading is doubtful), to Isaac, Joseph, Abraham and David.[15] The official salutations from the school are from Hai, Asaf, Rosh Hasseder of the school, Allufim, prominent members, Tannaim, secretaries and disciples who are all well. It is interesting that no Ab is mentioned, the scholar ranking next to the Gaon being this Asaf Rosh Hasseder known from elsewhere.[16] Hai mentions the arrival

[14] About the Nagidate in Ḳairwān see Mann, *JQR, N. S.*, IX, 162–3; XI, 429ff.; *Jews in Egypt*, I, 124, 144; II, 163; above, p. 47, and infra, p. 180.

[15] Should we say that this Dunāsh was Nissim b. Jacob's father-in-law for whom he composed his ס' המעשיות or חבור יפה מהישועה? Cp. about this work Harkavy, חדשים גם ישנים, No. 8 (in *Steinschneider Festschrift*) and Poznański, אנשי קירואן, No. 13.

It is not clear in what relationship the last four persons stood to our Judah Rosh Hasseder. They cannot be his sons since one of them was called Joseph and Judah's father, Joseph, was then still alive. However we hear of a Joseph b. Judah Rosh Hasseder of al-Mahdiyya (near Ḳairwān), who was the author of a tract on the Calendar (*JQR*, XVI, 691: הד"א כתאב אלביאן לחסאב אלעיבור ממא אלפה ר' יוסף בר יהודה ז"ל ראש הסדר אלמהדוי). Also MS. Mosseri, P. 339, contains the beginning of this work with the heading כתאב [אל]ביאן תאליף מרבב יוסף בן יהודה וכו'. But the title ראש הסדר here may refer to Joseph and not to Judah and the author can also be Joseph b. Judah ibn 'Aḳnīn (see Poznański, *JQR*, XVII, 168–70, and cp. also Hirschfeld, 389–90).

[16] Cp. Mann, *JQR, N. S.*, XI, 421 and 436, note 2; *Jews in Egypt*, I, 40, and infra, p. 201. His full name was Asaf b. Beṣalel. In the fragment of 1021 concerning Elḥanan b. Shemaryah Asaf is referred to as departed. Indeed in the list of the dead worthies of the Babylonian schools Asaf is listed as having died before the Gaon Dosa b. Sa'adyah whose demise was in 1017. Hence our present letter, wherein Hai sends greetings also in the name of Asaf Rosh Hasseder, dates some time before 1017.

of 2 letters from Judah which caused him indescribable joy. Where the epistle breaks off we still have the generalities about the great esteem in which Judah is held by the Gaon and his academy. The substance is missing and the hope can only be expressed that the continuation may yet turn up among the Genizah fragments. The occasion must have been an extraordinary one and Judah's endeavors on behalf of the school so outstanding as to merit this effusive eulogy.

4. The letter given under IV (infra, p. 135), dated 19. Shebaṭ 1018, has been published before by me (*JQR.*, *N. S.*, XI, 411–13), but here a better copy is submitted as far as the faint script could be deciphered with the help of a photostat. It is no doubt written to Elḥanan Rosh Hasseder b. Shemaryah of Fusṭāṭ and is a recapitulation of the contents of a previous epistle to him from the Gaon in reply to one by Elḥanan. These contents were as follows. 1) The news of the sale of something and that a certain Abū Daniel of Fez has not written to the Gaon anything about this matter. Whoever may have interfered in the affair by writing to Hai, he will not pay any attention to him, for this person is not trustworthy in the eyes of the Gaon who will repudiate his evidence (ll. 2–4). 2) Elḥanan's letter reached the Exilarch and the Gaon clarified it. This Exilarch is probably Hezekiah whom we find in office in the year 1021 as evident from his epistle, printed by Kamenetzky.[17] 3) The next news concerned the death of Dosa b. Sa'adyah, Gaon of Sura as successor to Samuel b. Ḥofni. Dosa evidently died in the last days of 1017 or in the first ones of 1018. Being already of very advanced age, he occupied the Gaonate only for about 4 years.[18] 4) Further Hai dealt in his former epistle with the evidence concerning an 'Agūnah, apparently as a responsum to a legal question from Fusṭāṭ. She was apparently allowed to remarry.

The purpose of our present epistle is concerning the power of attorney which a Bagdād Jew, Abū'l Ḥasan 'Alī b. Bishr, gave to his brother in Fusṭāṭ, Abū'l Fadhl Joseph b. Bishr, to litigate a claim he was prosecuting in Fusṭāṭ. Elḥanan's cor-

[17] *REJ*, LV, 51–53, see infra, pp. 179–80.

[18] About Dosa see Mann, *JQR*, *N. S.*, XI, 411ff., 424, and cp. infra, p. 153.

respondence concerning this matter reached Hai after his former letter had been written. Hai informs him now that the power of attorney is correct and requests him to exert himself on behalf of this matter because Abū'l Ḥasan is a prominent man in Bagdād and the Gaon has therefore an interest in his case being expedited. Our epistle is evidence of the frequent exchange of correspondence between Hai and Elḥanan.

5. An interesting epistle from Hai some times after Ṭebet 1349 Sel., hence at the beginning of 1038 and a few months before his death in Nisan of this year, to Sahlān b. Abraham, the spiritual leader of the Babylonian community in Fusṭāṭ has been published by Chapira (*Mélanges Israel Lévi*=*REJ*, 1926, 327 ff.). It concerns disputes in that congregation as a result of which Sahlān was assailed in his position by a party formed therein. The Gaon is staunchly on his side and is writing to the powerful dignitary Ḥesed b. Sahl al-Tustari to uphold Sahlān's position. The epistle testifies to the extensive correspondence Hai maintained with Sahlān, with his brother Nehemiah,[19] and with other people in Fusṭāṭ. Some people of the capital of Egypt visited the Gaon in Bagdād and made his personal acquaintance. Such were Sulaimān b. Mubarrak and Ephraim ibn al-'Ani mentioned in this letter. Further correspondents of Hai were Solomon b. Yehudah al-Fāsi, probably identical with the well-known Palestinian Gaon, and Ḥasan al-'Āḳūli. All these people were siding with Sahlān in the trouble he was having with the opposition party in his congregation.[20]

The vigor and mental alertness of Hai, as exhibited in this letter, a few months before his death at the very advanced age of

[19] About another letter of Hai to this Nehemiah, dated Nisan 1037, cp. Mann, *H. U. C. Jubilee Volume*, 258–9.

[20] Chapira's remarks on Sahlān and his father Abraham (ibid., p. 317ff.), which need much rectification, cannot be discussed here in the present connection. It should only be added that my statement (*Jews in Egypt*, I, 98–99) about Abraham being a banker (or money exchanger), which Chapira (*l. c.*, p. 319, bottom) found to lack any proof, is based on the fragment (given in II, 98) wherein we read מׄ ברהון בר סהלאן צ י ר פ א. About Barhūn being another form of Ibrāhīm, cp. Steinschneider, *JQR*, X, 138, whose doubts about this identification no longer hold good. Indeed our Sahlān b. Abraham is addressed in Bodl. 2876[2] as: אדוני ראש כלה בן ברהון החבר נׄעׄ.

99 years, are astonishing. His was a full active life entailing the many duties as president of the school, as spiritual guide of so many communities all over the Diaspora and as scholar and author. For nearly 80 years we can trace his activities, first as a young promising member of the Pumbedita-Bagdād school, then as Ab-Bet-Din, brilliantly aiding his father, and finally as the outstanding Rabbinic authority of the age. The many responsa of his (and they are evidently only a portion of what he actually wrote or dictated) on most diverse subjects are evidence of his comprehensive mastery of the whole field of Jewish lore combined with a fair knowledge of the thought and the sciences prevalent among the Muslim educated classes of Bagdād. The numerous letters he received and answered (and a very small portion of them have been preserved), dealing with communal affairs in several countries of the Diaspora, must have taxed his time and energy to a great extent. He was indeed regarded by his contemporaries as their spiritual father, as his admirer Samuel ibn Nagdela, the famous statesman and scholar of Granada, expressed himself in his elegy on the Gaon:[21] "And though he departed leaving no son (as his successor) . . . he has (spiritual) children all over the dominions of Islām and Christendom!"

Letters of Hai Gaon

I.

[T.-S. 20. 100, paper, top and bottom torn, damaged.]

[ו]חנ[יי]ב . . . .

. . . .

שבחו גדול מלמ[נות] והכמתו . . . .

שלום . . . . האלה אליהם. א . . . . . .

[המ]ה סגלת חמדתנו. ואל אדירנו איתננו מר רב בהלול הרב

נטריה רח[מנא]

[21] Diwān, ed. Harkavy, p. 48, l. 5ff.: ביום הלכו ו א י ן ל ו ב ן. ואם הלך לתחתיה: ולא ילדה תעודתו. ולא חזרה באכסניא: ו ל א ז כ ה ל ב ן ישיב. בכל זדון ובשגיה: י ל ד י ם. ל ו ב כ ל א ר ץ. ע ר ב י ת ו א ד ו מ י ה: אשר גידל עלי תלמוד. וטפח להוריה: וכו'.

וקימ׳[1] בן מר רב יוסף זכ׳ לב׳ יצו אלוף יחי לעד לאמר כי נכספה וגם כלתה

[נפ]שנו לאגרתו ולדבריו הנעימים ומחקריו המופלאים ושתי מחברות ש[ל שאלות]

[קבל]נו מאתו מקץ כמה שנים ותשובות שתיהן יחדו כתבנו ושלחנום אל [מר רב]

שמריה הרב נט׳ רח׳[2] כי על ידו שולחו. המחברת האחת כתב לפנינו כי [הגיעה]

אליו והשנית אחרי א[ש]ר [של]חנוה חדלו אגרותיו כי נספח על חבורת ארץ [הצבי][3]

ול[א י]דענו מ[ה היה לה] יודיענו ההגיעה אליו למען נשקט אם ל[או למען]

נשלח את נסח התשובות עוד שניה וגם אנו תמהין מן מר רב בהלול הרב [נט׳ רח׳][2]

[איך חדל מש]ך השנים האלה מלכתוב ספיקותיו ומחקריו כי זכות [גדולה היא]

[לו וגמולו] מן השמים יבואהו ולכל קרוביו וכל סיעתו הסיעה הקדושה. ו[נשמע]

[אצל]ינו כי יש במקומכם איש גדול בחכמה הר שלתורה[4] בקי בחדר[י הלכה]

מר [ר]ב חושיאל בן מררב אלחנן שמו ינצרהו יוצרו ותמהנו איך [לא שלח]

[1] =וקימיה, preserve him. [2] =נטריה רחמנא

[3] About this designation of the Palestinian academy cp. Mann, *Jews in Egypt*, I, 40, note 1,50, note 2, 54, and several times in vol. II.

[4] About this metaphor "mountain" to designate an authority of learning cp. Gaonic Responsa, ed. Harkavy, No. 51 (about R. Naḥshon Gaon): והר גבוה היה, and No. 257, end, where Sherira compliments Jacob b. Nissim of Ḳairwān (cp. heading before No. 230): ומתוך שאתה תלמיד חבר לנו והר גבוה בתורה גלינו לך את רחישות לבבנו. Cp. further Gaonic Responsa, ed. Assaf, 1927, p. 47, about R. David who arrived at Tortosa on board ship on Sabbath: כי הר גבוה היה. See also Wertheimer, גאון הגאונים, p. 1.

מ[חק]ריו[*4] אל שער הישיבה למען ישתתף
בדקדוקיה כאשר עשו הר[אשונים][*4]
...לח [כדי שנת]חדד [ובשאלו]תיו הנפלאים
ויבינום התלמידים ותרבה [הדעת]
[ואהוב]נו אלוף נט̇ רח̇ ישיאהו מפינו אלפי שלום
ורבבות ברכות ויודיעהו ב[*4]...
..הוא את דבריו [ו]לשמוח באמריו ואם יתאסף[5]
יפשטהו אלוף נט̇ רח̇ כ[י הוא]
[יקיר]נו וסגלת חמדתנו. ויקח אלוף את אגרתו
וישלחהו לפנינו כי זאת [מנחה]
עריבה ואשכר רצון[5a] הוא עמנו כן יעשה וי̇י̇ ישיגהו
כל [מ]שאל [אמן] והנה
תבענו[*4] מן אלוף נט̇ רח̇ שישים את כואנתו[6] לנצח את
מר רב חנוך הרב נט̇ רחמ̇
על תשובות האגרות אשר נכתבו אליו מלפני
נזרנו גאון הגדול אבינו יחילעד
ולא ית[ורפה] ממנו עד יעשה זאת. ושמחנו בדברי
יקירנו מחמדנו מר̇ יוסף בן
מר̇ ברכיה נט̇ רח̇ באמרי נעם הטהורים אשר ידבר והוסיף לקח
בעינינו ונכו...
תבונתו וקראנו עליו לחכם לב יקרא נבון ומתק שפתים יוסיף
לקח[7] ומי יתרע[8] את
אלוף נט̇ רח̇ כי אם כזה ומי חבריו בלתי סגלת העולם. והנה
שלחנו עם זו האגרת

*4 The reading is doubtful.

5 If he (the Alluf) comes together with R. Ḥushiel, let him explain to him the high esteem in which he is held by the Gaon.

5a For the same phrase concerning a letter from Elḥanan b. Shemaryah, see above, p. 104.

6 =כונתו, let him set his aim at convincing R. Ḥanokh.

7 Prov. 16.21.

8 Who associates with the Alluf except a person of this sort?

שתי אגרות פתוחות אל כל המערב יעש כאשר תבענו ממנו לשלוח נסחיהם
אל כמה מקומות. ותשובות שאלות אחינו אנשי פאס המבורכים לייʼ אל חי ושתי
אגרות פתוחות אליהם יודיענו הגעתם. וחמדתנו אהובנו ידידנו מ֗ ר֗ נחום החזן
נט֗ רח֗ בן מ֗ ר֗ יוסף החזן הגדול נוחו עדן יודיענו אלוף [איך] הוא ואת שלומו כי אח
חביב הוּא לנו ועמנו גדל מנעוריו והוא נכבד וגדול בנקהלנו[ו] ומקומנו צריך לו הרבה
כי נאספו הזקנים והוא עכשו המוקדם[8a] על כל החזנים אשר בבבל וכנו[4]* עולה[4]* בכנס[ת]
גדולה בבגדאד ואהוב וכל אשר כתבנו אל אלוף יבי[נט] בו ויעשהו ויגיד לנו שלומו
וכל חפציו ושאלותיו ושלום אלוף וחייו וימיו ירב[ה] לעד יד֗ באלול ש֗יז֗ ישע רב

[There follows after this letter the heading: בקייה֗ שאילות אהל אלפאס והד֗א אלדרג֗ אלד֗. The subject is introduced abruptly: של֗ יוסי שמנכה חצי כסף קידושין חייבת היא להחזיר לו מהם שני כספים וחצי כי כבר נתחייב לה שנים עשר כסף וחצי וכוʼ, which shows that the beginning is missing. From the heading 'the remainder of the questions of the people of Fez' it appears that the responsa were copied on a different sheet or sheets of paper and that the copyist used the bottom of our letter for the continuation for which he had no more space left on the other sheet.

Verso contains a long exposition of the duties of a Jew, especially if he be well-to-do, to bestow of his wealth on the needy. Perhaps it formed the exordium of the previous letter.]

[8a] There seems to have been an office in Bagdād for the leading Ḥazzān to have supervision over all the Ḥazzānim in Irāḳ. Such an official probably held office by authority of the Exilarch.

II.

[T.-S. 12. 829, damaged and very faded; cp. Mann, *JQR.*, *N. S.*, XI, 440–42. See Facsimile II, A and B, infra, pp. 691–92.]

Address (verso)

[למשאי עינינו. ומורשי[9] לב]בנו מרי ורבנא אברהם
[ומרי] ורבנא תנחום ינצרם יוצרם ויגן בעדם ויסעדם
בני מרי ורבנא תנחום[10] זכרו לברכה   פצטאט[11]
ישע רב

There is also an address in Arabic script of which the following words are still legible:

.....الفسطاط الي ابراهيم اخي تنخم ابني [يعقوب] ...
اطال الله بقاهما

(Recto)

[האיי רא]ש הישיבה שלגולה בן שרירא ראש הישיבה שלגולה
[למחמדי רוח]נו. ומשאי עי[נינ]ו. וידידי נפשנו. ומורשי לבבנו.
מרי ורבנא אברהם ומרי ורבנא תנחום החכמים האדירים.
האיתנים החשובים.
.... [ה]גבירים החביבים הסגולים. הידידים הנכבדים
הנחמדים. ינצרם יוצרם ויאמצם. וישמרם ויגוננם. וישגבם
ויעודדם. בני מרי
[ור]בנא יעקב זכרו לברכה. עושה שלום יברך אתכם בשלום.
ויפרש עליכם סכת שלום. ותתענגו על רוב שלום. ויכרת
לכם ברית שלום. ואתם שלום. ובתיכם שלום. וכל אשר לכם
שלום. וידבר לכם שלום. ותשבו בנוה שלום. ויצר לכם שלום
שלום. וישמ[ר]

[9] Thoughts (cp. Job 17.11 and Ben-Jehuda, *Thesaurus*, VI, 2865).

[10] By mistake for יעקב as evident from the body of the letter (l. 4).

[11] The first destination was Fusṭāṭ wherefrom it would be forwarded to Fez where Abraham and Tanḥūm lived.

ל[כם שלום. כי] אחרית לאיש שלום.   שאו שלום ממנו ומן כל חכמי הישיבה כי ברחמי אלהינו אנו שלום ומודים לו.

[ראסלנא]

כתאבנא אליכמא יא מחמדי ע[יני]נו אטאל אללה בקאכמא ולא א[ע]ד מנאכמא ולא אכ̇לאנא מנכמא עלי ידי אבי אלט̇יב מ̇ר̇ עמראן הלוי בן מ̇ר̇

הללו . . . מעה אג̇ובה̈ אלג̇ שאלות. כאנת פי כתא[ב] . . . א אידין ד̇לך קד וצל אליכמא ווקע מוקעה̈ ואלדרג̇ אלד̇י פיה אלשאלות אלאכ̇ר

. . . . פי אל . . . ם ובתה אלסריק. וואפאנא מנד איאם כתאב מחמד עינינו אבי אלפרג̇ אלוף אדאם אללה עזה וד̇כר לנא אנה קד אנפד

[מ]אלה[11]* ואלתמס ג̇ואבהא ומא וצל אליה ד̇לך פאד̇כרא לנא אידכמא [ען] מא תעלמאנה מן ד̇[לך] וד̇כר לנא ופאה̈ א ב י יוסף מרב יעקב אלוף

בן שאהון זכר צדיק לברכה וכאן ד̇לך [עלינא] מציבה̈ מת̇ל אעט̇ם אלמצאיב ואלפג̇איע ומדד מני בעץ̇ מא אבטנתה מן אלחזן עליה רצ̇י

אללה [עליה] וספדת עליה זכרו ל[ברכה] פי [אלמת̇יבה̈] ופי אלג̇מוע ובכת אלג̇מאעה̈ עליה אלהי ישראל ירחמהו ומא אחכן[12] אצף לכמא חיני פאנה

יוצף . . . וורני גרץ . . . [פ]כאן מכה על [מכה] וסל אללה בכת̇רה̈ אלסלאמה וקד כאן פי כתאבה אלד̇י אנפדתמאה אליי ד̇כר ג̇מלה̈

. . . אפצל[11]* אלי . . . לא יצ̇יע[11]* עלי הדה . . . . הי אבו אלפרג̇ אידה אללה כ̇בר ואפאה מן ד̇לך   ואנא אסלכמא

*[11] The reading is doubtful.

[12] Read אמכן.

[א]ן תגדא אלנטר פי הדה אלמעני[11]* אד . . . לא ענה ו . . . מר . . . דכר לי אנה סבעין דינאר אנפדהא ר׳ כלוף בן ר׳ יוסף ז[כרו] לטוב מן

אגמאת ואלי הדא אלגאיה מא ערפנא להא כברא . . . ה יא מח[מ]די עינ[נו] אערפא אתתמאכמא אלי הדה אלמעאני לילא ונה . . . [ולא]

תגפלא ענהא פהדא אכבר מא . . . ה מן אבוא . . . חכי . . . כמא פיה מן אלכתאב מא לא יגיבא ענכמא קדרה לא . . .

. . . ומעולנא ומעול אלמתיבה ואל . . . אללה ועליכמא ולי . . . אלא אבו אלפרג נט רח ואנתמא ועלי אללה[11]* מתכלנא

(verso)

. . . . אסל אללה בה עלי אידיכמא ובאתתמאמכמא פהו כאלדי מן מאתה מאלכמא ולכמא מן אלאגתהאד לנא . . . מה והו מן מאלכ[מא] ומן

. . . . יגעל הדא אל[שי] מן אמרה ו[מ]מאתה ופקכמא אללה לכל מא יחבה וירצאה ואישי ערפתמאה ממא נחב מערפתה

בארהא כאתבאנה בה ווחיאתכמא יא . . . אטאלהא אללה . . . מן אלאצאקה עלי חאל צעבה ואסתהדם שי כתיר מן אלמנאול[11]*

אלתי א . . . . הא ועיאלי ומן יתבעני ואחתגת להא אלי גמלה גאמלה מן אלמוונה אלראתבה[11]* וקד סאלת אבא אלטיב מר׳ עמראן

. . . . אן יכיני[11]* שיא וועד לאן פעל ערפתכמא ומא פעל . . . . בשי פי דלך וממא אנא לייה גמאעה אלריבונין ומן ציק צרדי באלאצאקה קד כררת אלקול

על . . . ה . . . ה באלאהתמאס במא לי קבל אבי יוסף אלוף נוחו עדן ומא נסב אלי אלאג . . . ת מע עלמי אן פי בעץ דלך כפאיה ואנת ולא

בסט אלעדר ותעריפי עלי מן יכון מעוֹלי [פי] אלקירואן וכונה אחק . . . ה . . . כלת והו חסבי ולא תוכֿרא[12a] עני כתאבכמא פי' . . .

א . . . ה וארתאח אליה והו . . . . אללה . . . א מנה ועְרפאני כֿבר מרֿ שלמה בן מֹ רֹ חכים בן אבי שכם נטֿ רחֿ

. . . . ואסלאמה סלאמי ו . . . . . ושלומכם ירבה לעד יטֿ באדר שנת שי"ח ישע רב

III.

[T.-S. Loan 1, 2 vellum leaves, damaged. See Facsimile III, A and B, infra, pp. 693–94.]

(Fol. 1, recto)

[13]אלהיך יזכך וכל נדר בתדורה.
וכל | אמר אשר תגזר יקימהו בגמורה: |
ישגבך בשם קדשו ויענך ביום צרה. |
יברכך בבאך ובצאתך בחזרה:
בטובתו | וברצונו לפקדך ולזכורה.
לחשקה מבלי [צר]ה | ומכל רע ולשמורה:
ומצנים ומפחים ומֵחֵמַה | ומקַרָה.
יחלץ את עצמיך וגלגלת וחשררה[14]: |
ובל תראה חלי נצח ולא מחץ ומָזוֹרה.
מתֹם תֵחי | בלי מכה ולא פצע וחבורה:
ומֵהַדֵם[15] ואֶכֶמת[16] | ומפלגס[17] וממרה.
וחנית בלי בעת[18] ולא נֶכר[19] מצַעֵרה: |

[12a] For תאכֿרא, to delay.

[13] The metre is ---⌣, repeated 4 times in each hemistich. The perpendicular lines indicate the lines of the MS.

[14] The meaning is here that God save you from heavy imposts (גלגלת, poll-tax) and from official tyranny (hence read וּמְשָׂרָרָה).

[15] Evidently in the meaning of torture (dismembering, cp. Jastrow, s. v. הָדַם). Cp. also Arabic 'hadama.'

[16] From אכם, to be black.

[17] From the (terrors of the) sea.

[18] Paiṭanic masc. of בעתה, terror.

[19] Misfortune (Job 31.3).

ואין פגע ואין נגע ואין רעה ואין תגרה.
ואין מזיק | ואין מכלים ואין שטן קתיגורה:
ואין פרץ ואין יוצאת | ואין פחד ומָגוֹרה[20].
ויברך משכנותיך אסמיך ואוצרה: |
ובגרן וביקב ובבית ובִמְגוֹרה[21].
ובחטה וכסמת ובפנג[22] | ובשעורה:
ובתאנה ובזית ותפוח ותימורה.
ובגפן | ובתירוש ובשמן ויצהרה:
ובמעטן ובפיטוס[23] וגם | בגת ובבורה.
ובשרש ובגזע ובבדים ובזמורה: |
ובעשב ובדשא ובירק וחצירה.
יברך את עֲרִיסֶיךָ[24] | והאכר וחוכרה:
ובָצֹנֶה ובמריאים ושור אבוס | וברבורה.
ובעדר ובָשֶׁגר[25] אלפיך ועשתרה:

(verso)

ובסוסים[26] וברכש ובצבים וכרכרה. |
ובספינה כמו הלך בגלי ים ובסערה[27]: |
ובִפְרַקְמַטְ[28] ובתשומה וברכולה | ובסחורה.
והצוֹדָה והשונא והעוין לשוררה[29]: |

[20] Paiṭanic fem. of מגור, fear.

[21] Vocalise ובָמגורה, store house (Ḥaggai 2.19). There is a mark like O on top of this word to indicate evidently the wrong vocalisation.

[22] Ezek. 27.17, taken by some to mean balsam.

[23] Vat (מַעְטָן) and cask, cp. Jastrow s. v.

[24] Read אריסיך, tenants.

[25] Absolute instead of construct שְׁגַר because of metre.

[26] This reading is doubtful as the letters seem to have been written over for correction, but hardly any other word would be suitable in this connection.

[27] i. e. Jonah and Elijah.

[28] For פרקמטיא.

[29] From שורר, insidious watcher (cp. Ps. 56.3 etc.).

יקלֵע בכף קלע והִפְאַמו ופֵארה[30].
ולקללה | ישיתמו בזעם אף ויאורה[31]:
ויכֵמו בשחפת | וקדחת וחרחורה.
ובגרב ובחרס וברתן[32] ובטחורה: |
להדפמו אלהיך ופעמיך להדבירה.
ובתימו יהו | לסחי כמו . . . מנוֹברה:
נטיעתם ליבשה | וקמלה ונזורה.
ענפֵימו לקצֵצה ושרשימו לעקֵרה: |
כתם פרח [ושוש]נה לכרתמו במזמרה.
שלוחותם | לנטשה במו הים ויעזרה[33]:
ללכדמו במו רשת | להפילם במכמורה.
ובצתם לקעקֵע ורעתם לבערה:
וכל עצה למוּלֶך מסְכלת ונבערה.
וכל כלי אשר יוצר | סביביך כאפרורה[34]:
ישימהו כמו קנה מרססת | משְׁברה.
וכל מרעה[35] וחרצְבה מפורדת מפוררה: |
וכל קשר תפתח אגדתו והותרה.
ואלי יענה | קולי ויקשיבה ונעתורה[35a]:
ואתה תעלה רומה | לגבוה עד שמי שפרה.
ראו עמי והביטו | בבהורה[35b] ובאורה:

[30] הפאמו is evidently a Hiph'il denominative from פֵּאָה, may He split them and cut off (cp. Deut. 24.20).

[31] And curse (from ארר).

[32] Name for some disease.

[33] Cp. Isaiah 16.8.

[34] A new Paiṭanic formation from אֵפֶר, dust.

[35] Evidently in the meaning of evil (=Aram. מַרְעִית). For חרצבה (cp. Ps. 73.4) taken in the meaning of suffering, cp. Ben-Jehuda, IV, p. 1781.

[35a] Cp. Prov. 27.6, hence ונעתרה would be better.

[35b] The reading is doubtful.

[ויש]שו בו בכל מדה | משובחה מיותרה.
. . . . יְשַׁכֹּונִי[36] לְבַדֵּה או לשקרה:

[Continuation in MS. Bodl. Heb. d. 47, fol. 3 (cp. *Bodl. Catal.*, II, 2669²), printed by Ginzberg, *Geonica*, II, pp. 278–9; cp. Chajes, *Z. f. H. B.*, XIV (1910), 23–28, Bacher, ibid., 82–4, Ginzberg, ibid., 84–93 (where on pp. 91–3 part of the text is reprinted with vocalisation different from the version in *Geonica*) and 115–17 (including remarks by Brody and Davidson).[37]

The text is given here according to a rotograph which I have obtained. See Facsimile III, C, infra, p. 695.]

(Fol. 2 = Bodl. fol. 3, recto.)

ויגביה מצריך[38] ומעוני [יחסרה].
וביתך להאמן בממשלת . . . [רה][39]:
ולא ישבת עדי נצח כבוד כסאו מנוהרה[40].
ותפרץ ים וצפונה וגם ק[דמה וקדרה][41]:
ואביך גבירנו אדון עמו וסלרה[42].
יחייהו אלינו[43] וכל סברו ומהרה[44]:

[36] Better יְשַׁכּוּנִי, Pi'el of שכך, to appease, here in the meaning to persuade me, entice me to invent or to lie.

[37] Dr. Ginzberg (in *Z. f. H. B.*) has taken liberties with the text by several unwarranted emendations. He should have rather endeavored first to give a more correct version of the fragment.

[38] Thy boundaries.

[39] שררה, as Ginzberg prints, is impossible owing to the metre.

[40] From נהר, to shine. The fem. refers to כבוד used in this gender in Gen. 49.6.

[41] The MS. clearly reads וצפונה which Ginzberg without much ado changes into ותימנה. The southern direction is indicated by וְקָדְרָה suggested by Jer. 49.28 where קדם and קדר are mentioned together.

[42] The best explanation of סלר is by Bacher (*l. c.*) as being a Persian loanword in the meaning of leader (cp. also *JQR.*, *N. S.*, IX, 158, note 141).

[43] =אלהינו.

[44] Read יְמַהֲרָה, i. e. may our God keep him alive and hasten (the fulfilment of) all his hope. Ginzberg's remark is inexplicable to me.

יהי חבלו במנעמו וחלקה לו משופרה.
ולנצח עדי סלה בריתו לא יִנארה:
ויצפן לו להקיצה פעולתו ומשכורה.
ויך צרו בכל עצר בצרעת ממארה:
ולהפילה באר שחת למו תפצה[45] ולמדורה.
ובו יתברכו גוים בתוגרמה וקדרה:
אשר חסדו עלי הכל כאיד עולה וקיטורה[46].
לריח כל שמניהו כמו יורה מקוטרה:
אהלות מר וקנמון וכל אבקה מתומרה.
וטובתו גדולה היא ורבה מלשערה:
ומי יחקר תהלתו ומי ימנה ונספרה.
והוא נותן בלא שאל[47] וגם לבזור להפק[ירה]:
זהב אלף במשקלו בעיניהו כמו גרה.
וככָּרים מאת אלף לפניהו כאיסטרה:
והוא מלך לכל נדיב עלי כסא ובקתדרה[48].
וכלמו לפניהו כאָמָה לא ממירה[49]:
וכל אוָֹה עשה חסד אשר נודע בכל דורה[50]
אשורו אחזה רגלו והוכנה והְשָׂרָה[51]
ונגדו כהתה ידו[52] וגם בושה וחפרה.
הרי כל נחלת יְקָר בכל ארץ מפוזרה:

45 Read תפתה.

46 קיטורה=קטרת, here the longer form is needed for the sake of the metre.

47 Paiṭanic masc. form שְׁאָל for שְׁאֵלָה which would not suit here in the metrical scheme.

48 Read וקתדרה.

49 Like a maid who does not change (the commands of her mistress or master).

50 Perhaps a Paiṭanic fem. is used here for דור. However read perhaps דירה.

51 The last 2 words are not clear in the MS.

52 Referring to the subject of the 2 previous lines, viz. he who desires doing kindness. Ginzberg's emendation ידי is quite unwarranted.

אגודה[53] לי אגודה בו וגם עליו מחֲזרה.
אבל מהם הכנתי[53a] לפי שעה ומ[54] . . . [רה]:
למאלף כְּבַד אחד וממאה כפולרה.[55]
ואמרתי צרפתיה זקקתיה וְנִטְהָרה:
במאזנֶיהָ משוקלת ובשרד מתוארה.
וחוגה היא כבמחוגה וכמגרה מגוררה:
בעת צהר[56] החילתי עדי ערב ונגמָרה.
ונמתקה לפי כדבַש ונמלצה ושוגרה:
ועם עסקי ורב שיחי וכי לבי סחרחרה.
הגיגי בא ואמרי פי כמתנבא וחוברה[57]:

(verso)

. . . שוררה וחס[58] לבי להרהרה.
. . . . לכל חכם וכל סופר ולבלרה[59]
. . . לחקָהָ בעט ברזל ועופרה.
עלי לוח לחרשָׁהָ בצפרן ושמירה[60]:

[53] Evidently for meter's sake Hai would vocalise this word as אֲגוֹדָה (for אֶאֱגוֹדָה), i. e. I will tie together for me a bundle (of strophes) about him, one that goes round (in the form of rhyme) concerning him.

[53a] = הכינותי.

[54] The מ is clearly visible in the MS.

[55] Out of a thousand (things to be said in his honor) one branch and out of a hundred a small coin. For פולרה see Talmudic dictionaries, s. v. פולר.

[56] For צהרים because of metre. At noon I began (this poem), at evening it was completed. The MS. reads clearly החילתי. Where Ginzberg found therein החישתי is a mystery to me.

[57] For חובר, a soothsayer. Hai apologises that with his preoccupations his diction resembles that of a would-be-prophet and soothsayer, i. e. not polished enough.

[58] Can also be וחם. Before שוררה the edge of the MS. is broken off. Where Ginzberg got his line is inexplicable.

[59] For ולבלר, a synonym for scribe (librarius).

[60] Cp. Job 19.24 (here עופרה to suit the ryhme), Jer. 17.1. Here again Ginzberg's emendations are quite unwarranted and likewise in the next line.

[ל]פרשָהָ לפנימו לעינימו כקילורה.
בפיהמו לשומָהָ לערכָהָ כְדִבֵּרה:
לתלף[61] את שעריה בסימנין כמָסורה.
לכל רוּבָה[62] להסדירה כפרשה ואפטרה:
קרא אתָה בכל שבת וכל חדש קרא מקרא.
ותכתב ותשמר לדור אחר ועם נברא:
והנה פה אסַיֵמָה[63] ואחתֹמָה ואצֹרָה.
כהתחלתי[64] בשם הטוב וכן אחתֹם ואומֵרה
יהודה מחמדינו שהוא אלוף וראש סידרא[65]:

ואִלּו אמרנו מאה אמרות כזאת פעם אחת לא הגענו אחת מני אלף מאשר אל לבבינו אבל כאשר חפצנו כן יעשו חבֵרינו ותלמידינו ואוהבינו אשר שם וִילְמדו וילַמדו את זאת ויוציאוה למרחוק יהי רצון שתנחיל עולמות כמנונה[66] ככתֹ להנחיל אהבי יש ואוצרותיהם אמלא. והנה סבבה בבבל כולה בין כל מביניה וכל פקוחי עין לראות ולהגות בה ועד אשור וסוריא הגיעה ועד עילם ופרס וכלם . . . שומעים תמיד שבח ראש סידרא נטֹ רחֹ מפינו ולא זר ולא נכרי בעיניהם כל שבח אשר ישובח כי אם נכוח עדיהם כדבר דבור על אפניו המקום יזכהו להוסיף חסדים ומעשים טובים אשר תהלתם תעמד לעד תלך ותוסיף ופרקליטיו לא ידומו כענין שנֹ ואל תתנו דמי לו עד יכונן ועד ישים את ירוש תהֹ באֹ[67]. ואת זוה[ר]

[61] Evidently a Paiṭanic denominative from תלפיות (Cant. 4.4).

[62] Here in the meaning of young scholar (cp. Ḥullin 20a top: יקבלו הרובין את תשובתן).

[63] So clearly in the MS. and not אסַימה as Ginzberg states.

[64] Evidently Hai vocalised כְּהַתְחַלְתִּי instead of כְּהַתְחָלָתִי which would spoil the metre.

[65] Hence the poem began with this hemistich just as it ended therewith.

[66] This word seems to mean 'as it is counted,' viz. 310 worlds (cp. the last Mishnah of 'Uḳsin based on Prov. 8. 21).

[67] Is. 62.7.

(Fol. 3 = T.-S. fol. 2, recto)

העולם ופרכת ועטוי חן ועטרת צבי וצפירת תפארה ואדר היקר ותפלה זכה ורני פלט וחיי בשרים ומגד ארץ ומלואה ורצון שכני סנה אף גילת ורנן כבוד הלבנון הדר הכרמל והשרון יהיו נא עם כל הברכות והתשועות והתפלות לאדונינו ראש סדרא ולמשושי עינינו ומשאי נפשנו ומאויי עפעפנו מרי ורבנא דנש[*67] יצליחהו אהינו י . . . ה לו וכשריון[*67] . . . . מעוזנו[*67] ומוסד מוסד אשר לא ינתש ולא ינתץ סלה ומרי ורבנא יצחק ומרי ורבנא יוסף ורבי אברהם ורבי דוד השמים . . . . תפלתינו בעדם יישב את . . יעמד שמם וזרעם לפני . . . כאשר השמים החדשים [והארץ ה]חדשה[68] ולכל מתי סודו וכל . . . . . הם ובתיהם וא[והביהם] הנלוים עליהם מעתה ועד עולם: יש א[68a] ראש סידרא ומוריו האיתנים שלום רב ממנו ומן מר רב אסף ראש הסדר שלישיבה ומן האלופים וזקני סנהדרין וכל חכמי הישיבה והתנאים והסופרים והתלמידים כי ברוב חנות יי׳ מגננו אנחנו שלום ומהללים ומברכים ומודים לשמו על פלאיו אשר עשה עמנו ומקוים לשמו כי יעשה ככ׳ אודך לעו׳ כי עש׳ ואק׳ שמ׳ כי טו׳ נג׳ חסי׳[69]. ו מ ו ד י ע י ם כי שתי האגרות המהדרות והמיוקרות והמפוארות הגיעו אלינו שתיהן יחד ונראו לעינינו כשני כוכבי גיה[69a] באפלה וכאשר פתחנום ועמדנו על יפי הדברים והחכמות הכמוסות

*67 The reading is doubtful.

68 Cp. Is. 66.22.

68a Here begins the second paragraph of the letter and on l. 18 the third one (see above, p. 83).

69 Ps. 52.11.

69a Paiṭanic form for נגה.

(verso)

[ו]נהיה כשחר בקוע הולך ואור והבשורות הטובות אשר היו בהן כשמש הזורחת נחשבו. ואלתר נפלנו על פנינו והשתחוינו לפני י׳׳ אלהינו אנחנו וכל חברינו אשר היו סביבינו וכל התלמידים אשר נועדו לפנינו והרבינו הודאות ושבח ליוצרנו אשר לא עזב חסדו ואמתו מעמָנו ומעמֵנו ואשר הותירכם לטובה והשאירכם לברכה. יהי רצון כי כאשר ימצא התירוש באשכל ואמר אל תשחיתהו כי ברכה בו[70] כן יחוס אלינו[71]

ויחמל עליכם וירחם עלינו כי יחוה[72] אתכם לנו וישמרנו ברחמיו מכל מגורות וישיגנו כל משאלותינו בכם ויבשרנו תמיד בכם בשורות טובות ונודה לשמו תמיד על טוביו המתחדשים עדיכם חדשים לבקרים לא יסירון כמוצא מים אשר לא יכזבו מימיו. ואתם תאמרו תמיד ירנו וישמחו חפיצי צדקי. ויאמרו תמיד יגדל י׳׳ החפץ שלום עבדו[73]:

ואנחנו יודעים כי אין אנחנו צריכין לפרוט אל אדירנו ראש סידרא נט׳ רח׳ הרבה בזאת כי אם נרבה דברים כַּיָם ונכבירה מלים כשאון דכיָם לא נגיע לאשר בלבנו וראש סידרא נט׳ רח׳ לא נפלא ממנו. וכלַל כי כשאלת חיים ושלום ותורה לנו כן כמוהם שאלתנו לראש סידרא ולבניו על משכבינו בלילות ובחדרי לבבינו באשמורות ויומם יתר מאד ואין צריך לומר בכל מועד ופרק ועצרת אגודים בתפילתנו. והנם בברכה מברכות יה אשר למדם פינו[67*]

(Here the MS. breaks off and the conclusion is still missing.)

[70] Cp. Is. 65.8.

[71] =אלהינו.

[72] Read יחיה.

[73] Cp. Is. 58.11, Ps. 35.27.

IV.

[T.-S. 10 J. 27[10], brownish paper, damaged and faded; cp. Mann, *JQR.*, *N. S.*, XI, 411–13. See Facsimile IV, infra, p. 696.

The address (verso) is in Arabic script hardly legible but in the middle there are clearly visible in Hebrew script the words האיי גאון.]

(Recto)

ה[איי רא]ס [אלמתיבה֗]

קד נפר כתאבי פי זמנא[74] הדֹא אלי סידי ראש ה[ס]דר אטאל
אללה בקאה גֹואב כתאבה וערפתה פיה כֹבר ביע
אל . . . . הדֹה אליה ואן אבי דניאל אלפאסי נט֗ רח֗ מא
כאתבני פי דֹלך אלאמר בשי וינחל[*74]
. . . . . . מן כאתבני פי הדֹא אלמעני לם אצג אלי קולה לאן
אלנאס[*74] ענדי פי . . . לה ואמנע[*74] שהדה וערפתה אן
כתאבה אד
[וצל אלי ראס אל]גאלות[75] נטרוהי מן שמיא וצפאתה וערפתה
ופאה֗ מר רב דוסא גאון מחסייה זכֹ לברֹ
וערפתה
א . . . . לה מן אלשהאדה֗ פי התרת העגונה אחסן אללה
תופיקה[א] [ו]בעד אן כתבת דֹלך אלכתאב
וצלת מכאתבתה בסבב רגֹל באלפצטאט והו אבו الفضل מֹרֹ
יוסף בן בשר אידה אללה אן אכֹאה אלשיךֹ אבא אלחסן
מֹרֹ עלי בן מֹרֹ
בשר אדאם אללה עזה קד וכלה בטאלב חקוק לה הנאך
ואלאוראכה֗[76] בכֹטה וכתאבה והי צחיחה֗ והדא אלרגֹל
אלמוכל והו אלשיךֹ אבו אלחסן אדאם אללה עזה צדר כביר
בבגדאד מכרם[*74] פי שוכהא[77]. ואנא אסל סידי

[74] Read זמאן. [*74] The reading is doubtful.

[75] Probably the Exilarch Hezekiah is meant here.

[76] =אורכתא, power of attorney.

[77] Read perhaps שיוכֹהא, among the elders of Bagdād.

ראש הסדר אדאם אללה עזה אן יתגדד מעה פי אסתדעא
באו[מ]רה ותחריס אלנטׄר פי אחכאמה
ו. . . . נה ו . . . במכאתבהׄ אלשיךׄ אבי אלחסן אכׄיה במא
ישו[ג]לו פי תקדים אמורה
ו[פי ת]קצי אלי חקוקה ויכאתבני במא יתפצׄל מן דׄלך אן שא
אללה י"ט בשבט שכ"ט ישע רב

(Righthand bottom margin)

. . . .
יפע מן . . . ינפד אליה
והו יכתב אלחסאב וינפדה
[אליה] אן שא אללה

V. Letters to and about Hai Gaon

1. Numerous epistles to him have been alluded to in the data discussed above. The extensive correspondence of the Gaon is made manifest still more in the 3 fragments given here. The first (No. I, pp. 138–40) is from the Babylonian community in Fusṭāṭ. It has been given by me elsewhere in extract but for completeness sake the full text is reproduced. The Babylonian synagogue is stated to go by the name of the Gaon's academy, probably as receiving its jurisdiction and guidance from the school. The letter was certainly written before 1032 because therein Abraham b. Sahlān, the spiritual leader of the congregation, is alluded to as participating in attending to the monetary affairs of the school, viz. the collection of the donations for its upkeep. Abraham was no longer alive in 1032 (Mann, *Jews in Egypt*, II, 101). In our letter it is stated that a preceding epistle to the Gaon contained the excuse for the delay in collecting the donations (חומשים) for the school because of the expenses in completing the building of the synagogue and in ransoming the captives for a large sum. The reference to the synagogue probably concerns its rebuilding after its destruction during the persecutions of al-Ḥakim in 1012–20. Thus the Palestinian synagogue was rebuilt in 1025 (ibid., I, 36, note 1; II, 375). The ransoming of captives (no doubt Jews from Byzantium brought to Alexandria by Saracen pirates)

also falls within the decade of 1020–30 as is evident from the several documents given ibid. (II, 87–93, 344–5, see the discussion of them in I, 87 ff.; infra, p. 366.)

A second letter (No. II, p. 140) from Ḳabes to Joseph b. Jacob b. 'Aubal of Fusṭāṭ, the well-known representative of the Babylonian schools, also reports of the correspondence to and from Hai Gaon from the group of scholars in Ḳabes (North-Africa), headed by Moses b. Samuel ibn Jama' about whom more information will be given farther on (p. 185 f.). Moses acknowledges the receipt of a pamphlet containing the reply (probably from Hai) which Joseph had forwarded (l. 5). He further informs him that Samuel b. Abraham al-Tahorti, another correspondent of the Gaon, had passed Ḳabes in a caravan evidently on his way from Tahort to Fusṭāṭ (where we find him for some time, see ibid., I, 119; II, 132). With him 25 (?) Dinārs were forwarded to Joseph for Hai Gaon and legal questions were written rather hurriedly and given to a non-Jew, a member of the caravan, because Samuel had left beforehand on account of the Sabbath so as to meet the caravan subsequently. Afterwards another more correct copy of the questions was made and Hai is asked to reply to the second copy. If Samuel through Joseph has already in Fusṭāṭ sent off the first copy, the request is made now of Joseph to send on to Hai also the second one. Greetings are sent to Joseph's sons Hillel, Benjamin and Menasse. Likewise Moses b. Samuel ibn Jama' mentions his own sons, Jacob and Abraham, as joining him in their regards for Joseph and his family.

The third epistle (No. III, pp. 142–45), from Nissim b. Jacob, the well-known scholar of Ḳairwān, to our Joseph, is full of concern about the delay of Hai's replies to Nissim. It must have been a very important matter that caused R. Nissim to be so anxious and urgent. Many letters from Hai dated 6 months before had reached Kairwān from Bagdād, including responsa to other people, but none to Nissim, who is surprised at the Gaon's silence. Nissim sent through a certain Abū Naṣr Ṣedaḳah of Palestine (אלשאמי) a question on a very important matter. This he asks Joseph to forward as quickly as possible to Hai. Also a sum of money for the Gaon has been forwarded to Joseph, and Nissim wishes to know all the details about the mode of its dispatch to Bagdād.

Letters to and about Hai Gaon

I.

[T.-S. 16. 318, top and bottom missing. Cp. Mann, *JQR.*, *N. S.*, VII, 478, note 22, XI, 452, note 17. See Facsimile V, infra, p. 697.]

(Recto)

. . . . . [גד]ולה. רב האדר דגל הממשלה. אשר אדרהו נורא עלילה.
. . . . . . מהוללה. מסודרה בשפר ובנואי מכוללה. ובבינה חדה
[ודעה נכונה מסוגל]ה. ובעצה מֵאֱלֹהוּת רום [גבו]לה. ובגבורה להסליל נתיבות נהילהי[1].
. . . . . . ה נכונה נאהלה. וביראת יי׳ שהיא מ[כ]ל [מע]לה. הוא אדונינו ואצעדת[נו].
אור [עיני]נו. וכליל יפיינו. כבוד יקר ה[דרת פ]אר צפירת גדולת סגלת דגלת קדש[ת]
ישישת קשישת[2] מרינו ורבינו האיי גאון כל ישראל ומופת הדור יתמיד אלהינו
הופקותיו[3]. ויתדיר שררותיו. ויוסיף שלטונו אמץ ויעדיף ממשלתו תקף ויפאר
את כל המוני ישראל בארך ימיו בן האדון הגדול אדונינו ומרינו ורבינו שריר[א]
ראש הישיבה שלגולה העתיק בנין] מחצות[4] מצדיקי הרבים ובראש בני עליה
הוא מֵסֵב באסוף אותו כבוד יי׳ במנוחת עדן: נהרי השלום הנטויים

[1] Read נהולה, guided viz. the Jewish community guided by the Torah.

[2] From קשיש, old; קשיש in Aramaic is the same as ישיש in Hebrew.

[3] This seems to be a Hebrew formation modelled after the Arabic تَوْفِيق, success, good luck.

[4] =מחיצות

ברשיון עושהו במרומי עליותיו ימשכו לאדונינו גאוננו ולכל בני בני ישיבתו לעד

ישא אדוננו גאון עם ײ שלום גדול ממנו אנהנו הקהלות המתפללים בכנסת

הבבליים הקרואה על שם ישיבתו כי מודים הם לצור מעוזם אשר הפיקם רצון

בהכניסם אליו והוא בחסדו יפארם במשיכת ימי חלדו עד ביאת הממשלה

הראשונה ממלכת לבת ירושלם[5] קד סבק כתאבנא אלי חצ̇רה̈ גאוננו

יחי לעד עלי ידי מ̇ר עטאף הלוי ש̇צ̇ [ב]ר טוב נ̇ע̇ אעתד̇רנא ען תאכ̇יר תג̇ריד חאל

אלאכ̇מאס בתמאם בנא אלכניסה̈ חמאהא אללה ובמא טרק מן שבויים אשתריו

בג̇מלה̈ כבירה̈ וגיר ד̇לך וד̇כרנא שנ[ו]קנא ותטלענא אלי ורוד כתב חצ̇רתה אג̇להא

אללה היום שלש שנים ולנ[ם] ע[רפ]נא אן ההנא מן יאכ̇ד̇ אלכתב חצ̇רתה אלינא ונחן נסאל

גאוננו אן יסמת במעמד הישיבה באלות נמרצות עלי מן יפעל ד̇לך ויתחול פיה

. . . מנא בפעלה ד̇לך לנפעלה איצ̇א פפי ד̇לך מצלחה̈ כבירה̈. פקד ורד כתאב

גאוננו אלי אדירנו וגדולינו החבר האלוף מרינ̇ ורב̇ אברהם בחיר הישיבה[6] באנה

[אנפד] כתאב אלי אלקהל ולם יצל וקד כנא מתולין עלי אלתדביר פי אעאדה

[5] Cp. Micah 4.8.

[6] Viz. Abraham b. Sahlān who held this title among others (Mann II, 100 and 103).

. . . . . . כנא ד̇לך פלמא כאן פי ראש חדש ניסן משנה זו שהיא

. . . . . . או בעץ̇ אלשיוך̇ אלאחאץ̇ פי ד̇לך פי . . אדירנו בחיר הישיבה

. . . . [ד̇]לך ווצף א[חו]אל אלישיבה ופצ̇אילהא ואג̇תמאע אהלהא פי וקתי

. . . . ל . . . ל . . . . . אלחמשים ולזומהא עלי מא אוג̇בוהא

. . . . לאמה̇ יום שבת ראש חדש ניסן בבית

. . . . ג̇מאעה̇ אלי ד̇לך וערפו̇ מן לם

. . . . ול גמור חמור בברית חזקה

. . . .

(End missing. Verso contains scribble in other handwriting.)

II.

[T.-S. 8 J 28[12], vellum, damaged and torn, cp. Mann, *JQR.*, *N. S.*, VIII, 356–7. See Facsimile VI, infra, p. 698.]

Address (verso)

[לכבוד גדולת] קדושת אהובנו ויקירנו וא[דירנו]
[מר׳ ור׳ יוסף] בן כב׳ גד׳ קד׳ מר׳ ור׳ יע[קב]
[נע׳] בן עובל במדינת מ[צרים]

מני משה ביר׳ שמואל הנודע בן ג̇אמ[ע]
אוהבו ודורש טובו ממדינת קאבס
ישע רב

(Recto)

אכ̇י וסידי וג̇לילי אטאל אללה בקאך ואדואם סלא[מ]תך וציאנתך ורעאיתך [וכל]

אסבאבך ותמם אחואלך ועלא קדרך . . . . . . תבתך ורפע דרג̇תך . . . .

סאמיא ומנזלתך תאבתה̇ . . . ברר . . . נא . . . . ואכ̇וך באיאם אלמנתט̇ר . . . . . .

כתאבי אליך כתבתה פיזך . . . . פיה לל . . . . . . אלמתפ[צלה̇]*[6] . . . . . .

*[6] The reading is doubtful.

וצל אלינא אלדרג אלדׄי אנפדתה גואב כת[אב] . . . לפ . . . . [ע]נדי . . . .

פלא אעדמנא אללה חיאתך ול[א אכׄלא]נא . . . צע . . . . וכאפאך באו . . . . . מכ . . . . [ומנד]

איאם גאז בנא מר רב ש[מואל בי]רׄ אברהם אלמערוף באבן אלתאהרתי

נׄרׄ מע אלקאפלהׄ ואנפדנא [מעה] אלי חצׄרהׄ [סי]ידנא האיי נׄרׄ כׄמסהׄ ו[עשרין][6]* דינאר]

וכתבנא מסאיל ען סרעהׄ [ואנ]פ[ד]נאהא אלי בעץׄ גוים מן אלקאפלהׄ ליוצל [אלי מׄ שמואל]

לאנה סבק אלקאפלהׄ מן גההׄ אלסבת ובעד דׄלך כתבנא נסכהׄ [תׄ]אני[הׄ] . . . .

וסאלנא מן סיידנא האיי נׄרׄ [א]ן יוקע אלגׄואבאת עלי אלתׄאניהׄ וקד מנפ . . . .

פאן כאן יאסידי אנפד מׄ שמואל אלנסכהׄ אלאולהׄ עלי ידיך אחב אן ינ[פד אל]

תׄאניהׄ איצׄא אלי חצׄרהׄ סיידנא האיי נׄרׄ ליתׄיבך אללה דׄלך ואן . . . .

עלמך פתתפצׄל ותע[וו]ל עלי אנׄ . . . . . . ה אלתׄאניהׄ כעואיד ואלג . . . .

פעלת מאנא מר[6]* . . . . . . קד . . . . . . נפסך אלשריפהׄ . . . . סר . . . . . . [מר]

הילל ומר בניומין ומר מנשה] . . . . וולדיי מׄ יעקב ומׄ אברהם וסאיר . .

יכוצׄו גׄמי[ע] . . . . . [א]פצׄ[ל אלסלאם] . . . . ת ען . . . . . .

(Righthand margin)

אחב סלמך אללה אן תוגׄבני בכתבך ותעלאמי בטיב אכׄבארך וחסן אחואלך

לאנת פעלת דׄלך ושוכר אללה עליך ושלום.

III.

[MS. Heb. d. 65, fol. 10; cp. *Bodl. Cat.*, II, col. 381, bottom, where the name of the writer of the letter is wrongly given as Nissim b. Joseph. See Facsimile VII, A and B, infra p. 699.]

(Address, verso; on top there is a line of illegible Arabic script).

סידי ומולאי אלשיך אלג̇ליל אבו אלפרג̇ אטאל אללה בקאה
יוסף בן יעקב בן עובל נ̇ע̇ ואדאם תאיידה ונעמאה
אללה נאצרה וחאפט̇ה
מן נסים ביר̇ יעקב ז̇ק̇ל̇

(Recto)

. . . . . [סידי] ומולאי פי איאמך ואדאם תאיידך ונעמאך ואנסי
פי אג̇לך וחסן לך אלעאקבה̈ פי דינך ודניאך ולא אכ̇לאך
מן אל
. . . . . יג̇ב עליך יאסידי אלתמסך במן תמסך בך ומחאפט̇ה̈ מן
יחאפט̇ ודך ויכרה בעדך ואלקיאס פי אסבאב:
. . . . . ך ואלענאיה̈ באמורהם חסב קצדהם אליך ובקדר מא
תבלגה טאקתך ותרך אלאג̇פאל ואלאחמאל פי חואיג̇הם חתי
. . . פד מן קצדך ומן ולג̇ אליך אסבאבה במן קצד סואך ותחד̇ר
אן יט̇פר בה פהד̇א אלד̇י יליק בך ובאדבך ומייזך
. . לא סיימא וקד תקדם בין אלאבא זכו לב̇[7] מא יוג̇ב אלזיאדה̈
ואלתאכ̇יד̇ וקד אכת̇רת עליך באלסואל ואלרג̇בה̈ פי
עדה̈ כתב אן תג̇הד נפסך פי אלא יט̇פר בנא מן ישנאך ואן תפעל
אלענאיה̈ פי סרעה̈ אלאנפאד ואלחרץ פי ציאנה̈
מא יצל ואלתאכ̇יד̇ פי סרעה̈ אלג̇ואב פמא וג̇דת פיך נשאט אלי
ד̇לך ולעמרי אנך מעד̇ור לכת̇רה̈ אשתג̇אלך באחואל
אלדניא לכן אנמא הי סאעה̈ ואחדה̈ פי חין כ̇רוג̇ אלקאפלה̈ תפרג̇
דהנך אלי מכאתבה̈ מן תכאתבה לא ג̇יר והו אמר

[7] = זכורים לברכה.

קריב ג̇דא וקד עלם יאסידי מא עלי קלבי ומא אנא פיה מן וצול כתב כת̇ירה̈ פי וקתנא הד̇א מן ענד סידנא

האיי נט̇ רח̇ מע אלפיוג̇ תאריכ̇הא ו̇ שהור מן בגדאד ווצל אג̇ובה̈ מסאיל כתבהא ג̇ירנא ונחן פלא ד̇כר לנא

מעהא ולא כתאב ולא ג̇ואבה̈ מסאלה̈ ואלכלאם עלי מא מצ̇י לא פאיד פיה. . . אלאן יאסידי אחב יכן לכלאמי מוצ̇ע

פי נפסך ומוקעא מן קלבך ותג̇ואבני עלי מא אסאלך פיה ותנשט פימ. . . מ. . . . אלי ידינא בך ובקרב . . . . . .

מנך עלי ג̇ירנא. כנת אנפדת אליך מע סידי אבי נצר צדקה אלשאמי אידה אללה כתאב לסידנא האיי [נט̇ רח̇ ופיה]

מסאלה̈ פי מהם עט̇ים כביר סלתה סואלך פי אן תנפדהא מסרע לעל יתפק פיג̇ מתאכ̇ד̇ עליה פי אלג̇וא[ב] . .

איצ̇א מע פיג̇ יכ̇רג̇ מן ענדהם ארג̇י קד פעלת ד̇לך ויצל אליי ג̇ואבה קריב ומ[ע הד̇]ה אנפדת צרה̈[7a] . . . . . .

פיוסט צרה̈ לאבן עלאן עלי ידי אלשיכ̇ אבי עמראן מוסי בן יחיי אלמג̇אני[8] אידה אללה . . . ומסאיל[8a] . ב . . . .

עדה̈ כתב אליך ארג̇ו קד וצלת וקד אכ̇ד̇ת הד̇א ספתג̇ה̈[9] לבגדאד כמא סאלת לך ובעד ד̇לך והד̇ה כת[ב] . . . . .

[7a] A sealed bag of money (evidently containing the donations for the school).

[8] From Majjānah, a place 5 days distance from Ḳairwān (see infra p. 362, note 6).

[8a] Legal questions (to the Gaon Hai).

[9] Money order, cp. Gaonic Responsa, ed. Harkavy, Nos. 423, 548 and 552, and see also Mann, *JQR*, *N. S.*, X, 333–4.

. . . . כרג פי אול שהר שואל מן אלקירואן מר[*9] סלים[*9] אבן אלטנסאוי ומעה כתאב אלי סידנא האיי [נט רח] . . .

. . . . בסרעה[*9] מא בקי ארגי קד וצל גמיע דלך אליך ואנא אסתחלפך [בא]עטם אלא[ימאן] . . . . .

. . . . [תכת]בני מסרע מע פיג אן אתפק כרוגה פי כתאב אלשיך אבי עמראן בתעריפי פי א . . . .

. . . . . . [כתאב]י אלואצל מע צדקה מע אלמסאלה ואן כאן קד וצל אליך אלכתאב אלדי מע אלפיג ואנפד . . .

. . . . ומא אלדי עמלתה פי אמר צרה אלדנאניר והל אנפדתהא ועלי אי טריק אנפדתהא או אכדת . . . . .

ספתגה ווצול גמיע אלכתב ואלמסאיל אלדי קד שרחתהא לך ומא אלדי לם יצל אליך מנהא אחב . . . . . .

דלך וביאנה פי אל . . . ר ואלבחר ואן וצלת אליי כתב לטיפה ומסאיל בעד כרוג אלקאפלה . . . . .

מע פיג או[*9] אתפק[*9] כרוגה ללשיך אבי עמראן בגיר תאכיר וכדלך אדא כתבת לסידנא ה[איי נט רח] . . . . . .

תוכד עליה[*9] אן ינפד גואבי מע פיג יתפק כרוגה מן ענדהם ותעלמה במא עלי קלובנא מן [הא]ל אגובת[ה אלי]

גירנא בסרעה ותאכיר אגובתנא ואעלם יאסידי אני קד סאלת וצמן לי פעלה לא . . . .

ואלמסאיל פי מסרע וקת[*9] ואן יכתב אלדי תצל אליה במצר מע פיג אלי בגדאד בדפעהא ל . . . . .

. . . . . אלטריק ואלסרעה ירגב אליי פי דלך ולם אפעל אד ביננא מן אלודאד ותקדם . . . . . .

מא אוגב אלתמסך[*9] בך ולמא וצלת אלאן[*9] אגובתהם תצל[*9] להם אלטפר ועלת ידהם פאללה אללא יאסידי

לא. ל . . . . גפלה[*9] . . . . עלי אלכתב . . . לה . . . . לה פיהא כתאב . . . ל . . . ותכתב לסידנא ראס אלמתיבה

*9 The reading is doubtful.

(Right hand margin)

.... קד אנפד אלינא כתאב אולא וקד אקסמת עליך אן
תכ̇רג ..... [ג]מיע אלאשיא ולא יזול כתאבי הד̇א[9]* ...
פ' ....

.... מא סאלתך ענה ותביין לגמיעה ביאן חסן ואן כתבת
כת[א]ב אלי אלש[י]ך̇ אבי עמראן פתכתב אליי פי .....
טריק .....

אלשריפה̈[9]* אפצ̇ל אלסלאם ואכ̇ותי ..... אל ....
אל. ל. ואלתלמידים ואל ... ך יסלמו......

VI. Letters of the Geonim of the Sura School after its Reopening

The last period of activity of this ancient seat of learning from its reopening (some time after 987) till some time after 1038 has been discussed by me elsewhere (*JQR.*, *N. S.*, XI, 409 ff., *H. U. C. Jubilee Volume*, 223 ff.) As to the later vicissitudes of this school, see the discussion infra (pp. 212 and 217 ff.). Six scholars in succession are known to have presided over its destinies as Geonim.

1) Ṣemaḥ Ṣedeḳ b. Isaac (b. Palṭoi b. Isaac Ṣemaḥ Gaon b. Palṭoi Gaon).

2) Samuel b. Ḥofni (b. Kohen Ṣedeḳ Gaon).

3) Dosa b. Sa'adyah Gaon.

4) Israel b. Samuel b. Ḥofni.

5) 'Azaryah Hakkohen.

6) Isaac.

Their activities, excluding those of Samuel b. Ḥofni, are on the whole unknown. Also the causes that made for the reopening of the school are still obscure. Only the name of the primary mover in this affair, a celebrated leader by the name of Abraham, has come down to posterity in a number of eulogies (see *Saadyana*, 67 ff.; Mann, *JQR.*, *N. S.*, IX, 153 ff.). We propose to discuss here the letters of these Sura Geonim including a number published here for the first time.

1. ṢEMAḤ ṢEDEḲ B. ISAAC

Only one epistle of his has so far been preserved,[1] extant in a very damaged form, and the conclusions from, it are to be drawn with caution. The Gaon styles himself "head of the schools of Sura" (ראש מתיב[א]תה דסו[רא]) and also sends greetings from "the established academies" (l. 8, ומן הישיבות הנושבות החשובות). The plural used is rather obscure as hitherto only one academy at Sura is known. Ṣemaḥ evidently resided in Bagdād where he expected the arrival of his correspondent Elḥanan b. Shemaryah, who had already reached Mosul, as the Alluf Sahl (the son of Alluf) in Mosul, who acted as the school's representative there, had informed the Gaon Ṣemaḥ. Later on there arrived in Bagdād Solomon, Elḥanan's disciple and attendant, and the Gaon was overjoyed at the approaching visit of Elḥanan. Ṣemaḥ Ṣedeḳ refers to a son of his, Palṭoi, who was no longer alive. The Gaon urged upon Solomon to hasten and fetch Elḥanan, but Solomon explained that Elḥanan was afraid to come to Bagdād on account of governmental reprisal (מחמס המלכות, l. 20). Ṣemaḥ Ṣedeḳ writes to Elḥanan in regret of his non-coming assurring him not to fear. He is ready to go with him to the officials to ensure his safety. The Gaon complains that he has in Bagdād (בבבלה, l. 33) no prominent men to associate with, for the people are corrupt and disobedient. In view of this statement, it seems that his relations with Sherira and Hai were not of the very best. Solomon also reported that Elḥanan's funds were exhausted. Ṣemaḥ Ṣedeḳ regretted that Elḥanan did not inform him before while still in Palestine, as he would have sent somebody to fetch him and would have supplied all his expenses.

It is difficult to ascertain whether this was going to be Elḥanan's first visit to Bagdād because he actually stayed there for some studying under Sherira (as is evident from above, p. 89). Perhaps it was to be a second visit. Whether Elḥanan's fears were personal as hailing from Egypt, a country under the Fāṭimids, the opponents of the 'Abbāsids, or due to the general unrest then prevailing in Bagdād, is not clear. Anyhow Ṣemaḥ Ṣedeḳ had a

[1] Mann, *H. U. C. Jubilee Vol.*, 235ff.; in a more complete form by Chapira, גנזי קדם, III, 1ff., cp. my remarks, *H. U. C. Annual*, III, 309–10.

very high opinion of him and of his prominent father Shemaryah b. Elḥanan. The activities of this Sura Gaon and the length of his tenure of office are all shrouded in obscurity.

2. THE LETTERS OF SAMUEL B. ḤOFNI

The biography of Samuel till he attained the Gaonate is obscure. Above (p. 75 ff.) we have found him as a member of the rival school of his uncle Nehemiah Gaon. His father Ḥofni, Ab of this school, died in 961, and left behind 3 sons Samuel, Isaac and Ḥayyim. Harkavy has found in Samuel's commentary to ויחי a portion of his elegy on the demise of his father Ḥofni (זכרון הגאון רשב"ח וספריו, 7–8). We are altogether in the dark as to the vicissitudes of the members of Nehemiah's school after his demise in 968 when Sherira became the recognized Gaon of the Pumbedita school at Bagdād. We can hardly think that the relations of Samuel and his 2 brothers were very friendly to the new Gaon. Samuel must have felt especially hurt when he was not made Ab in 985 but instead Sherira's son, Hai, occupied this office.

A letter, dated Tammuz 977 (given under I, pp. 155–6), would indicate that Samuel maintained a sort of a school of his own. It concludes with the phrase ברית שלום, appropriate for a Kohen, the same with which his other letters finish, and hence we assign it to him. He appeals for support of himself and the group of scholars attached to him. Like his uncle Nehemiah, he complains of his sending out appeals yearly without effect, and in the meantime he and his associates are starving. The particular complaint in this epistle is about a certain sum donated by a benefactor which Shemaryah b. Elḥanan (or Shemaryah b. Maṣliaḥ, see note 4 to text) forwarded to Sherira, with the result that Samuel's group was left out of it entirely. This seems to be the tenor of the damaged lines (r., ll. 11 ff.). Characteristic is l. 16 where Sherira is styled "one of the scholars who assumed authority" (ושמה בשם אחד החכמים המתכנה בשררות) which would indicate that Samuel and his group never acknowledged Sherira's Gaonate just as Sherira never acknowledged Nehemiah's claim to the office. If this explanation be correct, then we have the fact established, hitherto unknown, that the cleavage in the Pumbedita school, that started with Nehemiah's break with Aaron b. Sarjādo, continued for a considerable time during Sherira's Gaonate. The time to heal the breach arrived when the Sura school was reopened after 987 which afforded the possibility of giving offices to the descendants of former Pumbedita Geonim now in rivalry with Sherira and his son Hai. Ṣemaḥ Ṣedeḳ b. Isaac, a descendant of Palṭoi Gaon, became Gaon of the newly opened school and to it went over Samuel and his group and also Dosa b. Sa'adyah.

The rivalry between Sherira and Samuel came to an end several years before Sherira's demise in 1006 when a modus vivendi was established about the equal division of the donations from abroad, if they had been designated anonymously for the schools. Of this arrangement we learn from two letters of Samuel which require discussion in this connection. The first one is a combination of 2 fragments.[2] It was sent to a Dayyān in Ḳairwān who is highly complimented by Samuel, although he complains of the paucity of this Dayyān's epistles. Even if this correspondent cannot always enclose a donation, his letters are welcome in lieu of gifts and still more so, if they are accompanied by questions requiring responsa. Samuel complains that for many years the donations from the place of residence of his correspondent (i. e. Ḳairwān) were sent to somebody else (viz. Sherira). Now things have changed. He urges upon his correspondent to see to it that his school receives an equal share since the complete agreement, arrived at between him and Sherira before his demise,[3] when Hai married Samuel's daughter, stipulated that any sum donated anonymously for the schools be divided between him and Hai and only specially designated gifts be given to the one without the other being entitled to any claim upon it. Samuel wrote accordingly to Joseph b. Berakhyah of Ḳairwān who was appointed the treasurer of the donations for the schools for the whole dis-

[2] Printed by Margoliouth (*JQR*, XIV, 308–9) and by Lewin (גנזי קדם, II, 20–21); cp. also ibid., III, 76–77, where Lewin combines a third fragment which however is incorrect as will be shown forthwith.

[3] טרם אסיפתו בשנים. Marx's suggestion, which I have accepted before, to read ב' שנים now appears untenable by reason of the next letter (sub II, verso, l. 12) where this agreement is stated to have occurred a considerable time (בזמן מרובה) before Sherira's death.

trict of North-Africa. This position Joseph received in succession to Jacob b. Nissim who died in the winter of 1006–7 (see above, p. 114). Samuel urges his correspondent to admonish Joseph concerning the strict carrying out of this agreement which shows that this correspondent lived also in Ḳairwān. Then Samuel mentions the report that reached him concerning the 150 Dinārs (דרכמונים) which the "departed Rabbi" (i. e. Jacob b. Nissim) sent to Hai (? בשם זולתנו,). Samuel argues that this big sum was no doubt meant for all the scholars of both schools and therefore demands that the Ḳairwān people write to Joseph b. Jacob (b. 'Aubal), the school's representative in Fusṭāṭ, who used to transmit the monies from the West to Bagdād (see above, p. 137), and inform him of the actual purpose of this amount.

The same topic is discussed in the letter given under II (pp. 157–59) evidently sent to some community in Morocco (perhaps Fez) or Spain. At the beginning (as far as preserved) Samuel depicts the poverty of the members of the school. Babylonian Jewry cannot maintain the academy owing to its impoverishment due to the violence and the exactions of the rulers. Hence it is the duty of the outside Jewries to come to the succor of the school. He then alludes to his former epistle (v., l. 11) informing his correspondents of the agreement between him and Sherira and Hai, and continues[4] to give directions as to how the donations should be sent anonymously for the school without mentioning the name of the respective Gaon. The sums should be forwarded to Ḳairwān to Joseph b. Berakhyah, the treasurer in place of the departed Jacob b. Nissim. Samuel emphasizes his standing as a commentator of Bible and Talmud and hence deserving to receive questions from the outside communities with the accompanying donations.

The fragment given under No. III (pp. 160–63) is evidently also by Samuel because it was his method to arrange his remarks

[4] In the fragment added at the end which is clearly the logical continuation. Lewin's attempt (גנזי קדם, III, 76–7) to connect this fragment with the end of the previous letter is impossible, first because of the faulty style (his emendation הנשלחת for הנשלחים makes the sentence still more stilted) and moreover since Joseph b. Berakhyah has been mentioned as the treasurer before, why is there again a full indication of his new office?

under a numerical grouping (see No. II, v., l. 4 ff., and his epistle in *JQR.*, XVIII, 403–5, to Fez). Practically the whole of recto is taken up with a condolence to some person on the death of his son. Only at the end there seems to be the beginning of a new letter. Verso is to an Alluf (evidently in Ḳairwān, perhaps to Joseph b. Berakhyah) thanking him for his endeavors on behalf of the school. He is asked to see that Samuel's letter, officially addressed to the community of Ḳairwān, should be recited in public and also to make copies of his letters and send them to several communities. This person did so before with regard to 2 previous letters of Samuel. Those bore fruit (in the form of donations) and the hope is expressed that now also the response will be satisfactory.

Samuel further mentions the receipt of a letter from Joseph b. Jacob b. ʿAubal (of Fusṭāṭ) wherein it was stated that our correspondent had (evidently in a letter to Joseph) promised to exert himself for the school. The Gaon hopes to see these promises carried out. Owing to the defectiveness of the fragments the prominent persons to whom greetings are extended cannot be ascertained.

From the beginning of the letter, sent to the community of Fez consoling them after an outbreak of riots, which resulted in Jews dying as martyrs, we learn that Samuel presided over a properly organized school. Next to himself he mentions his son Israel, the secretary of the school, then the heads of the Sedarim, the Midrashim and Peraḳim, the heads of the Siyyumim and of the sections, the Allufim and scholars, the sons of the Geonim (viz. of former Geonim, like Dosa b. Saʿadyah, then a member of this school), the judges, the Tannaim, disciples and scribes.[5] It is noteworthy that Samuel mentions no Ab of the school (and neither does Hai, see above, p. 116)[6] but instead in-

[5] P. 404, beginning of fol. 45a: ישאו אחינו שׁ (= שלום) ממנו ומן ישׂ (= ישראל) סופר היש (= הישיבה) המהיר בתורת יי' ומן רא (= ראשי) הסדרים ורא המדרש (= וראשי המדרשים) והפרקים והסיומין והסיעות ומן האלופ והחכמ (= האלופים והחכמים) ובני הגאונים והשופט והתנא והתלמיד והסופ (= והשופטים והתנאים והתלמידים והסופרים).

[6] Should we say that the דיינא דבבא of the Exilarch was also Ab of the school, or should we draw the conclusion that the office of Ab of the school was abolished for this very reason because the דיינא דבבא of the Exilarch

troduces his son Israel as yet only secretary of the academy. "The sons of the Geonim" (i. e. of former Geonim of Sura) occupy a minor position coming only after the Allufim and general scholars. It is evident that Samuel's tendency was to advance his son Israel ahead of the others, and yet a son of a former Gaon, Dosa b. Sa'adyah, succeeded Samuel as Gaon in 1013 whereas Israel b. Samuel had to wait till the office was vacant in 1017 with the demise of Dosa.

Israel also adds his greetings at the end of his father's letter of Elul 1004 (see No. VI, infra p. 165 f.) and likewise at the end of the epistle given here sub No. IV (p. 163 f.).[7] The Nagid Shemaryah b. Maṣliaḥ to whom Samuel wrote (No. V, p. 164 f.) is unknown to me from other data.

Though in his desire to bring his son Israel into prominence Samuel mentions no Ab, yet it seems that the Ab of the school (or of the Exilarch's court?) was his own brother Isaac, as the analysis of the interesting letter, dated Ab 999 from Ḳairwān, by Naḥūm b. Joseph to Samuel reveals (published by Goldziher, *REJ*, L, 182–8). Above (p. 113) we read how Hai inquired about the welfare of the Ḥazzān Naḥūm b. Joseph "the great reader" stating that he cherished him as a schoolfellow and good friend and that he was needed in Bagdād to succeed his father as chief Ḥazzān in the great Bagdād synagogue. The stay of this Naḥūm, known as al-Baradāni the Reader, at Ḳairwān is known from other data discussed by Mann (*JQR.*, *N. S.*, IX, 150–2). He is also referred to in the poems in eulogy of the dignitary instrumental in reopening the Sura school (ibid., pp. 154–5), whence we learn that Naḥūm had three sons, Barukh, Yannai and Solomon. We further hear of his grandsons Joseph and Naḥūm the sons of Yannai. Prominent as Paiṭan was Nahūm's father, Joseph al-

claimed the office of Ab, which led to interference in the affairs of the school by the Exilarch through his spokesman, the דיינא דבבא? For all this, we must await further information. Cp. also infra (p. 216) as to the state of affairs in the Bagdād school in the 12th century.

[7] Sulaimān b. באבשאד, to whom greetings are sent, is perhaps identical with בן באבשד mentioned in Genizah Booklist (see Gottheil, *Jew. Studies in memory of Israel Abrahams*, 156, l. 12, where for באבשר r. באבשד, cp. p. 159, note 76). See further infra, p. 164, note 44b.

Baradāni (see the items from Bodl. listed ibid., p. 155, where the identification of Joseph al-Baradāni with Naḥūm's grandson is to be modified accordingly, and cp. especially the edited Piyyūṭim in Davidson's גנזי שעכטער, III, 51, 92, 95 ff., 116, 128, 129, 131). The liturgical compositions of Naḥūm himself and his third son Solomon are also found in MSS. (Mann, ibid., p. 155).

The purpose of Naḥūm's travels from Bagdād to Ḳairwān and beyond is not clear, but one would not go wrong in assuming that he went on a mission on behalf of both schools. He was a friend of Sherira's and Hai's and also of Samuel b. Ḥofni whose disciple he calls himself in the letter under discussion (at the end of the address: מן נחום בן יוסף תלמידה). In Ab 999 Naḥūm must have already been away from his home for some time. He refers to previous communications to Samuel, the last one of the year before was dispatched from al-Mahdiyya. Samuel's letter to him was forwarded through Abū'l Faraj Benjamin b. Moses b. Aaron (viz. a son of one of the בני אהרן, the friends of Nehemiah, see above, p. 78, and *JQR.*, *N. S.*, VIII, 341–2). The news about conditions in Bagdād and its district (l. 12: ומן אחואל אלבלד) distressed Naḥūm greatly. He refers to a letter by Samuel sent to Abū Zakariyya Judah (i. e. Judah Rosh Hasseder b. Joseph, so eulogised by Hai Gaon, above, p. 115 ff.). Naḥūm's own father, Joseph, was no longer alive (l. 16). He excuses himself for writing in Arabic because he was away and on his return found letters from his children informing him of sad family bereavements. He now writes in haste to catch the caravan. He alludes to his approaching visit to Spain which detains him from starting on his return trip home. He asks Samuel to look after Abū Manṣur (evidently the Arabic name of one of Naḥūm's sons) and encourage him in the study of Mishnah and Talmud and of the sciences. Greetings are sent among others to Isaac Ab-Bet-Din (v. l. 8, ועלי סידי ומר רבנ יצחק אב בית דין) who seems to be identical with Samuel's brother. Indeed Israel b. Samuel refers in 2 letters (given below, pp. 168 and 177–78) to a Joseph "the son of the Ab our uncle" (יוסף בן אב דודנו). How long Isaac lived is unknown, but it seems that in the letter to Fez, wherein Samuel mentions his own son Israel next to himself, the omission of his brother the Ab was due to the fact that Isaac was no longer alive. Whether Dosa b. Sa'adyah succeeded him as Ab is again not certain. Anyhow Dosa succeeded Samuel as Gaon. Only after Dosa's death do the two cousins Israel b. Samuel and Joseph b. Isaac occupy the leading offices in the school, the former as Gaon and the latter as a dignitary of unknown character.

To conclude about Naḥum al-Baradāni. In Elul 1006, when Hai wrote his letter (above, p. 109), Naḥūm was still in Ḳairwān. Ultimately he must have returned to Bagdād. The document (published by Mann, *JQR.*, *N. S.*, IX, 152) concerning the litigation of his grandsons evidently was issued from the Bet-Din of the academy at Bagdād (see l. 1).

3. A LETTER BY DOSA, GAON OF SURA (1013–1017), B. SA'ADYAH GAON

The identification of Dosa as the author of the letter, given infra (p. 166 f.), is based on l. 6 where there is an allusion to the late Gaon Samuel. It cannot emanate from Samuel's son, Israel, as he would have referred to his father in a different manner. Also the conclusion of the epistle would have contained the phrase ברית שלום. Owing to the fact that Hai almost always concluded his epistles with ישע רב, our letter with the ending ושלומך... ירבה לעד cannot be assigned to him. Hence the most likely alternative is to assign the letter to Dosa who is thanking a correspondent for his benefaction. The allusion in the body of the letter to a certain person and to his son is obscure to me. This is so far the only epistle we have from Dosa. Since it is in Arabic we have no criterion of judging his Hebrew style.

4. THE LETTERS OF ISRAEL HAKKOHEN, GAON OF SURA (1017–34), B. SAMUEL B. ḤOFNI

The very existence of this Gaon has only recently been established on the basis of the Genizah data. We find him in correspondence with the Nagid of Ḳairwān, Abraham ibn 'Ata (see Mann, *JQR.*, *N. S.*, XI, 415–6). We give here 2 letters from him, the only ones edited or identified for the first time. The style and structure make a rather pleasant impression. The first one is to a whole community, but its identity is unknown because the beginning is missing. Israel sends greetings in his own name as well as in the names of his cousin Joseph, "the son of the Ab our uncle" (i. e. Isaac b. Ḥofni), the Allufim, other scholars, the sons of the (former) Geonim, the judges, Tannaim, students and scribes of the academy where conditions are peaceful. Prayers are recited for the correspondents at each meeting and assembly of the academy. The section commencing with the phrase ומודיעים contains reflections on God's goodness. Following his father's method (above, p. 149 f.), he groups the aspects of his theme into a unit of ten. Then there follows an appeal for the study of the Torah which study should comprise Bible, Mishnah and Talmud. The knowledge of the Bible alone does not suffice because without Rabbinic tradition it cannot be fully understood. This is evidently directed against the Ḳaraites. He illustrates his contention with examples of the laws concerning the 3 annual pilgrimages to Jerusalem. The extent of this letter and its purpose cannot be ascertained as the end is missing. Perhaps it was a general circular letter on the occasion of his assuming the Gaonate. The trend of his thought can be followed by his emphasizing the need of Rabbinic tradition the home of which was the academy.

The identity of Israel as author of letter No. VIII is established by No. IX (pp. 177–79), dated Ṭebet (1)332 Sel. = 1020–21 and having the conclusion ברית שלום, the same his father employed and before him Nehemiah Gaon as appropriate to a Kohen. Therein too greetings are sent from Joseph, "the son of the Ab our uncle." The letter itself is a complimentary missive to a certain elder Solomon b. X. of Fusṭāṭ (perhaps Solomon b. Sa'adyah, a benefactor also of the Palestinian academy, see Mann, *Jews in Egypt*, II, General Index). Solomon is exhorted to donate to the Sura school and to hand over the amount to Sahlān b. Abraham, the well-known spiritual leader of the Babylonian community at Fusṭāṭ (above, p. 118).

No letters have so far been found emanating from the so-called "last" Geonim of Sura, viz. 'Azaryah Hakkohen (died before 1038) and Isaac (died after 1038). Altogether about their activities nothing more is to be added to the data discussed by me in *JQR.*, *N. S.*, XI, 416 ff. The obscurity that enshrouds the history of the Gaonate in Babylon after Hai's demise in 1038 is not yet entirely dissipated. But some rays of light, which we obtain from the consideration of a number of new data, reveal the continuance of the Gaonate throughout the 11th century and the probability that both schools of Sura and Pumbedita situated in Bagdād existed still as separate entities. This theme, leading up to a consideration of the Gaonate of Bagdād till the end of the 13th century, forms the subject of a lengthy investigation farther on (p. 202 ff.).

Letters of Samuel b. Ḥofni

I.

[Or. 5538 I, cp. the description of this fragment in Margoliouth, *Catalogue of the Hebrew and Samaritan MSS. in the British Museum*, III (1915), pp. 560–61. See Facsimile VIII, infra, pp. 700–01.]

(Recto)

. . . . . ועמדו במחייתם ובסיפוקם ויתנדבו לו[1] בכל זמן נדבותם

. . . . [ולא ה]עלימ[ו] עין ממנו ואתם אחינו יש בינינו ובין הגאונים

[אבותינו ואבותיכם] זכרם ל[בר׳][2] ברית חזקה ואנחנו תמיד נשתע[שע בתורתכם]

. . . . הרבה[*2] ויקרכם ובחכמתכם ובינתכם ורחמנותכם

. . . . שמות החשובים שלנו ברכות רבות שיחולו

[עליכם מאת ע]שה שמים וארץ ובכל שנה ושנה נצוה ויכתבוכם[*2]

[אודות צער]ינו ועשקינו. ונגלה לכם לחצנו ודלותנו. ורוב החובות[*2]

[שעלינו. כדי ש]תרחמונו ותזכונו בנדבותיכם ומתנותיכם וכמ[ו[*2] שהיה]

[מנהגכם] ל[עשות] עם הגאונים אבתינו נוחם עדן ועינינו יצפו משנה

[1] Evidently reference is made here to his grandfather, Kohen Ṣedeḳ, who used to recieve donations from the place of Samuel's correspondents for the upkeep of his school.

[2] =לברכה. [*2] The reading is doubtful.

[לשנה ואנח]נו נרעבים ונכאבים ותוהים ונאנחים מ . . . . בשם זולתנו[3] ולא היה לנו הנ[את] שום[2]* ולא חלק ולא[2]* [נחלה בנדב]ת האיש הישר. בחיי [צ]דקות מוכשר. ובא אחי . . . אדירנו אצול מהדרינו מר רב שמריה ראש קהל ושאל[4] . . . . שנ[2]* ישימהו ייי תפארת בקהלו. ויעצים חילו. וימלא [משאלתו וידענו] חכמתו. וגודל בינתו. ועוצם שבחו. ונדבת רוחו. . . . . . . ושמה[4a] בשם אחד החכמים המתכנה בשררות[5] . . . . [ולק]ח . . . . כל משלחותיכם אליו . . . . מאד ובכינו והורדנו דמעות כמים ונשבר לבנו . . . . . . כל עיקר וכל הזקנים האוהבים שלנו ורבי עם . . . . . ש . . . תם ממנו משלחותיכם ולכן אנחנו צועקים . . . . . זאת ממנו ומן החכמים שלנו ותתנדבו לנו נדבות . . [ות]של[ח]ום עם החומשים שלכם אלינו ובשמנו ותדבר[ו] . . . . . . והשופט והחכם נט̇ רח̇[6] ותרצוהו בעדינו ותחנינוהו . . . ב . . . תינו ולא ימנע חסדו ממנו ולא יעלים עיניו [ויעשה עמנו] כראוי לו וכאשר אנחנו עושים בעבורו תמיד . . . . הגדול בסוחרי מבקר[7] מר̇ יעקב בן מר̇ ברהאן . . . . ועל כל החכמים ותכתבו לפנינו שאלותיכם . . . . ם וימציאם ושלומכם ירבה תמוז שנת רפ"ח[8] ברית שלום

[There are some illegible letters between the last 3 lines. There are also traces of 3 more lines forming a sort of a postcript.]

[3] Viz. to Sherira.

[4] The following eulogies of this Shemaryah would tend to identify him with the well-known Shemaryah b. Elḥanan of Fusṭāṭ. But perhaps Shemaryah b. Maṣliaḥ (see letter V, p. 164) is meant here.

[4a] וְשָׂמָהּ, and assigned it (the donation).

[5] No doubt a reference to Sherira whom Samuel did not then recognise as Gaon (see above, p. 147).

[6] Evidently the Rabbi of the community to which this letter was addressed (presumably Ḳairwān).

[7] This place is unknown to me.

[8] (1)288 Sel. = 977 C. E.

II.

[T.-S. 12. 99, vellum, torn and faded.]

(Recto)

כי הרעב כאיבו גדול ולכן [נדמה למות ולחרב] ואמר[9] הנה עין
י״י אל [יראיו] למ[יחלים] לחס[דו] להציל ממות נפש[ם ו]לחיותם
ברעב
וכתוב[10] ברעב [פדך] ממות [ובמלחמה מידי ח]רב וכל שכן כי
יהיו העניים והרעבים חכמי תורה . . . . יר . . . להחיותם
במתנותם
ולחזקם [ובכ]לכולם ולאמצם בפרנסותם כי העושה באלה ירים
קרן התורה וישא נס תושיה ולו נשבענו לכם אחינו כי
עתים רבות ירעבו מאין מזון ופעמים רבים מצאו קור
באין כסות לחום היינו נשבעים באמת ואין לאל ידינו לחזקם
ולכלכל חוקם בלתי ייחולינו וייחולם לנדבותיכם וקיווינו
וקיווים למתנותיכם כייחול המטר אחרי עצר: ככת'[10a] ויחלו
כמטר לי ופיהם פערו למלקוש כי אנשי בבל[11] נתרוששו
וירדו מנכסיהם ויתרועעו ברוב החמס ועוצם העול
ועתה אחינו זכרו נא אחיכם משכיליכם. והמה ענייכם
ואביוניכם. ושתפום ב[מתנו]תיכם. ושימו להם חלק בלחם
פיכם. כי תברככם [נפשותיהם] ונפשות טפם וטפל[יהם]
ו[תנו להם] במזון קיום ואל [תעלימו מה]ם עין . . . .
. . . . ואלהינו יגמול שכרכם] ויצוה לתת [ברכה]
[במעשה ידיכם] . . . . . ככת'[12] . . . .

. . . .

[9] Ps. 33.18–19. [10] Job 5.20.

[10a] =ככתוב, Job 29.23.

[11] This is an important reference to the impoverishment of Babylonian Jewry which was the ultimate cause of the decay of the Gaonate as the outside donations were never sufficient to maintain the schools entirely (see the discussion infra, p. 202 f.).

[12] A reference to some verse.

(verso)

מביניכם ועינוי . . . . . . [ויזכר]כם ברצון עמו ככת[13] זכרני ברצון עמך ופק[דני בישועתך] . . . או . . . . . בכם לחם לשבוע זכרונם[*13] . . . . שביעו . . . . טי בכם כי יי'י ישביעכם בשלושה מיני שבע. הרא[שון פרנסה] טובה ככת תתן להם ילקוטון תפתח ידך וג[14] והשני כי משב[יע]כם רצון ככת פותח את ידיך ומשביע וג[15] והשלישי כי ישביעכם שמ[חות] ככת תודיעני ארח חיים שבע שמחות וג[16] זכרו [אותנו בנדבותיכם] וחזקו ידינו ואל תזניחונו. ואמצונו ואל תניחונו. ושמחונו ואל תאניחונו.

כאשר צוה אלהינו. חזקו ידים רפות וברכים כשלות תאמצו[17] כי יי' יחזקכם ויאמצכם ככת[18] ואתם חזקו ואל ירפו ידיכם כי יש שכר לפעולתכם וכבר הודענוכם אחינו בכתבינו כי טרם יאסף מרב שרירא גאון לגן עדן בזמן מרובה[19] נקבצו זקני

ישיבתנו עם זקני מקומנו[20] ו[נעשה] שלום בינינו וביניו גם עם גאון בנו[21] חתננו יאמצהו מגננו ו[היינו שלשתנו כאחד ונתחתן [בנו בנ]ו[22] ונשא בתנ[ו] . . . . . [ה]ליכתנו להקב . . . . [והתנ]ינו

[13] Ps. 106.4

[*13] The reading is doubtful.

[14] =ונומר, Ps. 104.28.

[15] Ps. 145.16.

[16] Ps. 16.11.

[17] Is. 35.3.

[18] 2 Chron. 15.7.

[19] See above, p. 148, note 3.

[20] Read מקומו, viz. the elders of Sherira's place (academy). For the designation מקום=ישיבה, see Sherira's letter (*Saadyana*, p. 120).

[21] Hai, who was Gaon at the time this letter was written (after 1006). But at the time of the agreement Hai was still Ab (before 1004).

[22] בָּנוֹ בְּנוֹ. It must have been Hai's second wife since Hai was born in 939 whereas this agreement, followed by Hai's marrying Samuel's daughter, at any rate did not take place before the end of the 10th century. (Cp. also Mann, *H. U. C. Jubilee Volume*, p. 233).

[בי]נינו תנאים[23] כי . . . . הנאסף עלינו . . . . שנים . . . .

[Continuation seems to be in T.-S. 12. 733, *vellum* just as the previous fragment and also having the same number of lines, published by Mann, *JQR.*, *N. S.*, VIII, 365, cp. pp. 362–4.]

[24][בשם הי]שיבה תשלחוה וסתם בלא שם אחד ממנו כי הנשלחת [נד]בה בשמו יקחה לעצמו בהתיר וכאשר תשלחום יהיו על ידי אדירנו וגבורינו[25] ופקידנו ונאמננו מר רב יוסף החבר הגדול והחכם האדיר יאמצהו מלכנו בן זקיננו מר רב ברכיה זכר צדיק לברכה כי הוא במקום הרב הגדול הגביר והגבור מר רב יע[קב ריש] כלא הנאסף לגן עדן וכי העמדנוהו על עמדו והק[מנו]הו במקומו והצבנוהו על מכונו ועתה השמרו נא אחינו בכל [א]ל[ה] והזהרו פן תשלו חלילה לכם מהשתוגג גם מהשאה [וכשת]שלחו נ[דבו]תיכם יהיו עמכם שאילותיכם למען תהיו [כרא]שוניכם הנאספים לגן עדן כי שמותם ושאלותם חקוקות [ו]חרוטות ואכן ידעתם כוחינו בתורת אל ואילותינו בחכמת [ה]מקרא והמשנה והתלמוד וכי פתרנו כמה ספרים מן [המקרא] ופירשנו מס[כת]ות מן המשנה והתלמוד וידענו כי . . . . כם וכי תעשון כן נועילכם כאשר . . . . לכלכל חכמיכם ולפרנס ענייכם . . . . [ככת'[26] השלך על יי' יהבך] והוא יכלכלך . . . . שנת

[23] Some of these conditions are also stated in the Brit. Museum fragment (*JQR*, XIV, 308 = גנזי קדם, II, 20): ויכתבו בינינו תנאים בש[טר] ומהם כי כל הנדבות הבאות בשם כל אחד ממנו יהיו לו לעצמו ואין לאחר עמו ואשר יבא סתם או בשמות חכמי הישיבה יהיו חלוקים חצים לנו והחצי לחתננו.

[24] Thus we have to supply the lacuna at the end of the previous leaf: [וכאשר תשלחו נדבה] בשם הישיבה תשלחוה וכו'.

[25] = וגבירינו.

[26] Ps. 55.23.

III.

[T.-S. 10 G. 58, very damaged, top and bottom missing; cp. Mann, *JQR.*, *N. S.*, XI, 449–50. See Facsimile IX, A and B, infra, pp. 702–03.]

(Recto)

. . . .

. . . . . . תבו . . . . . וטפנו למות ככת'[27] כי . . . . . . [והענין]
השביעי כי נדע שרעות ה[עו]ל[ם] הזה הם . . . .
בו כי חיי צער יחיו בו כי העשיר ירושש ו . . . .
עליהם ככת'[28] כי אם יגדלו את בניהם וג' ואשר יחפ[וץ] שלא יתיסר לא[ו]
בגופו ולא בממונו ולא בבניו הוא חפץ שקר ג[מור כי מי מכל]
הנביאים והצדיקים חיה בלא צער הלא . . . .
והענין השמיני כי חיב ה[מ]תאבל על בניו ועל [בנ]ותיו לקחת מוסר מן]
הנביאים והצדיקים אשר מתו בניהם בחייהם . . . [אהרן]
הכהן הראש אשר מתו בניו בחייו ככת'[29] ותצא אש [מלפני י'י ותאכל אותם וימתו]
לפני י'י] ודמם אהרן ושתק ברצותו משפטי י'י ככת'[30] וידם אהרן וגם דוד ה[מלך]
צם ובכה בעוד הילד חי וכשמת נתנחם כי [ידע כי ילך] אל בנו ובנו לא י[שוב]
אליו ככת'[31] ויאמר [בעוד] הילד חי צמתי ואבכה כי אמרתי מי יודע יחנני י'י וחי
הילד ועתה מת [למה זה אני] צ[ום] האוכל להשיבו עוד אני וג' ואיוב מתו עול[יו]

[27] A verse is quoted here.

[28] Hosea 9.12.

[29] Lev. 10.2.

[30] Ibid. 10.3.

[31] 2 Sam. 12.22–23.

בניו בשעה אחת וקיבל דין יוצרו ככת̇[32] ויאמר ערום יצאתי וג̇ ואחרי כן [אמר[33] גם]

את הטוב נקבל מאת האלהים וג̇ ולכן השיב י׳׳ את שבותו והטיב אחריתו ככת̇[33a]

וי׳׳י שב את שבות איוב בהתפללו ולכן חייב האבל המתאבל על בניו להנחם

[ולהשתדל] להיות כנביאים האלה אשר נתיסרו בבניהם להיות כהם וגם בדבר ר[ב]

[יוחנן למדונו חכמינו שהיו] לו עשרה בנים ומתו בחייו וצידק דין יוצרו[34]. והענין

[התשיעי כי נדע שהמ]ות טוב מחיים וכי אשר המיתו יי׳׳ לטוב לו ככת̇[35] [כי טוב]

[חסדך מחיים שפת]י ישבחונך. והענין העשירי כי אנחנו יודעים שהמתים

[עתידים לחיות כי] י׳׳ מחיה את כלם וכי האב יודע את בניו וישב עמם ככת̇[36]

.... וכאשר ידע ה[אב]ל כל אלה בלבבו או שיודיעו מודיע שור[ש]

[הדברים יחדלו אנח]ותיו ויעברו שאגותיו ככת̇[37] ברוב סרעפי בקרבי תנחומיך

[ישעשעו נפשי]. ענואן[38]. ליקר תפא[רת]

....

32 Job 1.21. 33 Ibid. 2.10. 33a Job 42.10.

34 Cp. Ber. 5b.

35 Ps. 63.4.

36 Perhaps the reference is here to 2 Sam. 12.23: אני הלך אליו.

37 Ps. 94.19.

38 Arabic: heading, viz. here we have the heading (or the beginning) of the following letter.

(Verso)

. . . .

. . . . ה אכן כן הדבר באמונה ומי כמוהו עיקר שמו[רה]

[על זאת ככת׳[39] הל]א תכן לבות הוא יבין הלא אלהים יחקר זאת והזכיר . . . .

. . . . עושה אותה וענות[נות]ו שאינו מחזיק טובה לעצמו מ . . . מ. ה

. . . . והשכר גדול מן הראשון ואין אנו צריכין להגיד לו איך ספרנו

[החידוש אש]ר חדשו ועכשיו סיפור חסדיו וטובותיו כי אין נאה לאמרם בפניו

[אלא כל]ו ש[לא] בפניו מה שלמדונו חכמינו[40] אומרים לאדם מקצת

[שבחו] של[אדם] בפניו וכלו שלא בפניו כדרך שאמר הקב״ה[41] לנח בפניו כי

[אתך י]דעתי צדיק לפני בדור הזה ושלא בפניו [א]מר עליו נח איש צדיק תמים

היה בדרותיו את האלהים התהלך נח. ועתה ישים גדולנו אלוף יחי לעד אלי

לבו לחדש את חסדיו עם חידוש הדבר הזה והאגרת אשר אנו כותבין אל ק[ירואן]

יקראנה בקהל וכאשר כתב כי עשה בראשונה אשר שלח שתי אגרותינו א[ל כמה]

מקומות כן יעשה [עכש]יו יצ[וה לנסחם][42] כי בראשונה נעשו פירות וכי גם אלה יעשו.

והנה באה לפ[ינו אגר]ת מחמדנו ומשוש לבנו ואוה[ב]נו וידידנו מרי ורבנא

[39] Prov. 24.12, Ps. 44.22.

[40] ʻErubin 18b, Gen. R. c. 32.4.

[41] =הקדוש ברוך הוא, Gen. 7.1, 6.9.

[42] To copy them.

יוסף בן מרי ורבנא יעקב אלוף בן עובל יחיהו קדושנו [וישמר]הו ויגוננהו ויהי זכר

אביו לברכה כי הבטיח אלוף יחי לעד בהבטחות יפות אשר אנו מקוים לראותן]

וודאי כי בצדקת אלוף נט׳ רח׳ שמו אלהיו נשוא פנים [מה שלמדונו חכמינו][43]

נשוא פנים שנושאין פנים לדורו בעבורו למעלה כגון ר׳ חנינא בן דוסא ולמטה]

כגון ר׳ אבהו בביתו שלקיסר וכן יתקיים בו לעול[ם] כנכת׳[44] כי שמש ומגן י״י אלה׳ חן וכבוד]

יתן י״י לא ימנע טוב להולכים בתמים . . . . . [ושא נא שלום ממנו למחמד]

עינינו ומשא נפשנו ונכבדנו וחשובנו מרי [ורבנא] . . . . [ישגבהו קדושנו ויעזרהו]

ויתמכהו ויברכהו ומן השמים יבא לו שלום . . . .

בטובה והאלהים יוסיפהו חן וכבוד ויפקד[הו] . . . . [ושא נא שלום ממנו בלי]

קצה ובלי תכלה לזקננו וישישנו וגדולנו האדיר . . . .

הלוי ישגבהו קדושנו ויעזרהו ויתמכהו ויברכהו] . . . .

. . . .

IV.

[MS. Mosseri L. 21, recto, top missing, very damaged. See Facsimile X, infra, p. 704.]

(Recto)

. . . . ויינגדד הנאך מן אמור אלשיוך

. . ן ימסנא אמרהם ומא שיר בה עלינא ויסררנא בה וירשדנא באראה אל . . . . . .

[43] Ḥag. 14a. [44] Ps. 84.12.

אלמבארכה̈ אלסדידה̈ ואן לא יקטע ד̇לך ענא פאנא קד שקינא
וכ̇ד̇נא[44a] פי כתבה אלכתב
וקלובנא מתעלקה̈ במערפה̈ וצולהא ואיצלהא ואלהי ישראל
יסלמהא ו[יסה]ל וצולהא
אלי אצחאבהא ו. . . . . אמור פיהא ויעצ̇דנא בחיוה̈ סידי אלשיך̇
אלג̇ליל ו . . . . . .
עלוה . . וגנא בבקאיה ולא יכ̇להא מן תפצ̇לה וישמיענו בו
שמועות טובות ובשורות יפות. ושלום זקיננו יירב
וליה ישראל הכהן בן גאון יכ̇ץ ג̇ליל חצ̇רתה באפצ̇ל
אלסלאם וסאדתי ואכ̇ותי אולאדה באוכ̇ר אלברכות
אב שנת שי"ט ברית שלום

(Right hand margin)

. . . ושלום רב על גדולנו ונרנו | . . . ו סלימאן אלשיך̇ אלפאצ̇ל
מרי | [ורבנא] . . . בן מרי
ורבנא באבשאד[44b] זקנינו | . . . ד עזהמא

(Verso contains jottings of no connection with recto.)

V.

[T.-S. Loan 169, piece of paper, faint and torn.]

Address (verso)

לגדולנו וגבורנו ונרנו ומאורנו   מצר   בן . . .
מרנא ורבנא שמריה הזקן הגדול   בן זקיננו הגדול מרנא ורבנא
האדיר והנגיד [י]נגידהו מלכנו   מצליח זכר צדיק לברכה

[44a] =ואכ̇ד̇נא.

[44b] The name באבשאד recurs also in the colophons of the Bible Codices of 2. Firkowicz Collection, Nos. 25 and 26 (see Kahle, *Massoreten des Westens*, I, 71): באבשאד הכהן בן דויד בן שלמה בן אברהם בן שהריאר בן אבזון בן בזרגוי. This person was a Ḳaraite in Fusṭāṭ in the first half of the 11th century. Hence in the colophon of a Bible Codex in the Cairo Ḳaraite synagogue (*JQR*, XVII, 636, bottom) read באבשאד for בא בשער which solves the difficulty raised by Bacher (ibid. XVIII, 146). Cp. also above, p. 151, note 7.

(recto)

שמואל הכהן ראש הישיבה שלגולה

בן חפני הראש אב הישיבה שלגולה

בן כהן צדק ראש הישיבה שלגולה

אל גדולנו וגבורנו וגבירנו ונרנו ומאורנו מר רב שמריה החכם ה[אדיר והנגיד]

אדון הנדיבים. ושר המתנדבים. משנה המשנים. ורוזן הרוזנים. יכון [אלהינו] מלכותו

ויסעדה. ולכל ממשלה יועדה. ולמל ..... ה . ואל ...... ויסמכה ואל

........................ל..........................

(No more preserved.)

VI.

[For the sake of completeness, we give here again the British Museum fragment, Or. 5338 II, published by Mann, *JQR.*, *N. S.*, VIII, 364–6. A renewed examination by means of a photostat suggested some better readings. See Facsimile XI, infra, p. 705.]

[מ]עלותינו וטרחם בהנאותינו ויי' ייטיב גמולם וירחיב גבולם

והגיע עו[ם] כתבם נדבת נדיבנו מר' יעקב בן [מר'] מימון ישמרהו

[א]להינו ובירכנוהו ובירכנוכם ברכות אש[ר י]קדמוכם ככת'[45] כי

[ת]קדמנו ברכות טוב תשית לראשו עטרת פז וכבר כתבנו אליו

[כת]ב והוא ב[תוך כתבכם] זה [תג]דילו חסדכם בשלחו אליו[46] ותהיו לנו[47] על

[ה]ברית לנ[ד]רוש הנאותינו [ול]עשות צרכינו ולמלאת חפצינו ותתמידו

אגרותיכם לפנינו בכל עת פנוי בטיביכם ומשאותיכם ומשאלותיכם

[45] Ps. 21.4.

[46] Viz. to the donor Jacob b. Maimūn.

[47] These two words are doubtful.

ובכ[ל] חפציכם כי [אז] נמלאם ואל תחדילו ושלומכם ידידינו יר[בה]

ואני ישראל בן ראש הישיבה משיא אלול שנת שט"ו[48]

את שני גדולינו וש[וא]לינו שלום רב ועצום ברית שלום[49]

VII.

A Letter by Dosa Gaon b. Sa‘adyah Gaon

[MS. Mosseri L 288, vellum, right hand side top torn; verso blank. See Facsimile XII, infra, p. 706.]

(Recto)

.... שמך וא[ר]אד אלפסאד וכא[ן]

.... בא לי וקד שכֿת וטענת פי .....

.... לה אותק ויעלמון בעדי כיף אלצורהֿ

.... א למא יקרב מנה ויזלף לדיה ואנת אדאם

[אללה עזך] פי הדֿה אלאמור במא ישאבה דינך ומחבתך צלאח

... כאן בינך ובין ראס אלמתיבה מררב שמואל נעֿ[50] מודהֿ פאל

.. לא סימא ומא כאן באלדֿי יחב תלם סיאגֿי אלדין ולו

אחקת*[50] בוצול הדֿא אלכתאב אליך אנפדת נסכֿהֿ שרוטנא וקת אצטלחנא

ורקעתה אליי מסאלהֿ פי אמר ולדה הדֿא קבל ופאתה ביומין פלו כאן

אבנה הדֿא כמא יגֿב אן יכון מא גֿאז פי איאמי אן יפסדה אחד בנציב

בל מן יחב אן יוצל אליה שיא אנא אפעלה ומן תגֿאוז דֿלך פקד אפסד

[48] (1)315 Sel. = 1004 C. E.

[49] Num. 25.12, a proper greeting by a Kohen.

[50] =נוחו עדן, the late Gaon Samuel b. Ḥofni.

*[50] The reading is doubtful.

ועליה עון גדול ויסבב עלי נפסה אונאה וחלישות דעת מן שיוך אלריבונין
ורבמא דעו דעא מגׄמלא ואסתחכמו אללה פכאן אצׄר מ . . . א הדׄא אל
שאב והדׄא מא ענדי פי דׄלך ומן עמל שיא פהו אבצר ומא יעמלה
פמע רבה וקד אבתדאת אדאם אללה עזך במא אוגׄב לך אלפצׄל ואסתחקקת
בה אלשכר מן אפתתאח אלמכאתבה̈ פתמם עליה ואלזם תפצׄלך
ולא תקטעה פאני מסרור בך גׄדא מהתם בכל מא תכאתבני וקד
[וצ]לת אלדינרין לא עדמת תפצׄלך אבדא ומודתך ואלאנס בך טוב מאלפי
[זהב ו]כסף[51]: ושלומך מחמדנו ירבה לעד.

Letters of Israel Gaon (b. Samuel b. Ḥofni)

VIII.

[T.-S. Loan 4, six small paper leaves. See Facsimile XIII, A-F, infra, pp. 707–12.]

(Fol. 1, recto)

ויהיה עמם. להעצים שמם. כענין
שכׄ[1] וישב עמי בנוה שלום ובמשׁ
מבטחים ובמנוחות שאננות:
וירחיב גבולם. וישלם גמולם.
וישמע קולם. ויפדם ויגאלם.
ככתׄ[2] הרחיבי מקום אהלך ויריעות
משכנותיך יטו אל תחשכי האריכי
מיתריך ויתדתיך חזקי. וי״י יחזק

[51] Cp. Ps. 119.72.
[1] =שכתוב, Is. 32.18.
[2] Is. 54.2.

ימינכם. ואל תיראו כי הוא עוזרכם.
ככת[3] כי אני י״י אלהיך מחזיק ימינך
האומר לך אל תירא אני עזרתיך
והוא ברחמיו יאזין ברכותינו
לכם. וישמע תחנותינו בעדכם.
ויקשיב תפלותינו בכם. לברך
בתיכם וצאצאיכם. ככ׳[4] כי אצק
מים על צמא ונוזלים על יבשה
אצק רוחי על זרעך וברכתי על
צאצאיך. שלום אמת וברוכה]
אמצת[5] ומדע והשכֵל ותפלה ז[כה]
וחן וחסד ושלות השקט וח[כ]מ[ה]
וגבורה והוד והדר וכשרון והצלה
וכבוד ותפארת ורצון סלה וחמל[ת] אל[הים]

(fol. 1, verso)

וששע[6] שמחות ונעימות נצח
וחוסן ויקר ופדות וישועה.
והצלחת מעשים. ולוית חן
ורוח והצלה וחילוץ עצמות.
והשכלת דרכים ושאר הברכות
יהיו לכם אחינו מאת יוצרנו
ולכל קרוביכם ונלויכם.
שאו שלום ממנו ומן
יוסף בן אב דודנו ומן האלופים
והחכמים השרים והסגנים.
ובני הגאונים והשופטים

[3] Is. 41.13. [4] Is. 44.3.

[5] אֳמָצַת, so also in Sa'adyah's letter (דביר, I, 183, l. 4): ותשועה אמצת.

[6] Read ושובע (cp. Ps. 16.11).

והתנאים והתלמידים
והסופרים כי בעז חנות[7]
אלהינו אנו שוכנים בטח
ושאנן תחת כנפיו נחסה
[ונתלו]נן נודהו ונהללהו ונספרה
[נפל]אותיו ככ׳[8] אספרה שמך
[לאחי] בתוך קהל אהללך.

(fol. 2, recto)

ובכל פרק אשר אנחנו קובעים
ועצרה אשר אנו מקדשים ברוך
נברככם אחינו אדירינו על
שער הישיבה ונגיד מהלליכם
ונזכור שבחכם. יהי רצון מלפני
קדושנו לקיים ברכותינו בכם
להאריך חייכם ושנותיכם ולמלאות
משאלותיכם ולפדותכם מכל צרה.
לקיים בכם מקרא שכתוב[9] ופדויי
י׳׳י ישובון ובאו ציון ברינה ושמחת
עולם על ראשם ששון ושמחה
ישיגו ונסו יגון ואנחה.
ומודיעים כי אלהינו יתרומם
זכרו לעולם טוב מכל הטובים
המטיבים כי רבו טובותיו ועצמ[ו]
חסדיו על ברואיו הסגולים
וביותר על עמו ישראל ככת׳[10] ח[סדי]
י׳׳י אזכיר תהלות י׳׳י כעל כל אש[ר]

[7] From חנן (cp. Ps. 77.10). [8] Ps. 22.23.
[9] Is. 35.10. [10] Is. 63.7.

גמלנו י״י ורב טוב לבית ישרא[ל]
אשר גמלם כרחמיו וכרב חס[דיו]

(fol. 2, verso)

ולכן אנו חייבין להודות לו ככת׳[11]
הודו לי״י כי טוב כי לעולם חסדו
ותחלת טובו וחסדו כי בראנו
חיים מתאוים ומתענגים ככת׳[12]
חיים וחסד עשית עמדי ופקדתך
שמרה רוחי   ובשובנו אל נפשנו
לראות הרכב גופינו וחיבור איברינו
נדע כי בורא חכם בראנו וכאלו
הוא נגד עינינו ככת׳[13] ומבשרי אחזה
אלוה   לפיכך חיבים אנו לדעת
אותו בראיותיו[13a] ותהלותיו וכן כתוב[14]
וידעת היום והשבות אל לבבך
כי י״י הוא האלהים וג׳   ואם לא
נדעהו איכה נעבדהו ונאמין
בדברי שלוחיו הבאים אלינו
הלא כן כתוב[15] ונדעה נרדפה
לדעת את י״י וג׳ וכה הבטיח
לעתיד שלא יצטרכו אחד לחבירו
ללמוד ממנו חכמת דעתו כי
כולם ידעו אתו ככת׳[16] ולא ילמדו

[11] Ps. 106.1, 118.1, 29.
[12] Job 10.12.
[13] Job 19.26.
[13a] By his manifestations and attributes (cp. fol. 3, r., l. 8).
[14] Dt. 4.39.
[15] Hosea 6.3.
[16] Jer. 31.33.

(fol. 3, recto)

עוד איש את רעהו ואיש את אחיו לאמר דעו את י״י כי כלם ידעו אתי וג׳ וטוב י״י אדנינו ואם רַב הוא מלפרטו אמנם נזכור מקצת לפי אילותנו. והם עשרה פנים האופן הראשון אור השכינה וכן כתוב[17] ויאמר אני אעביר כל טובי על פניך וג׳ ויש שאמרו[18] שהם תהלותיו הנזכרים בשלוש עשרה מדות שלימד לקראתו[19] בהם ולהתחנן לפניו בדבריהם ככת̇[20] ויעבר י״י על פניו ויקרא י״י י״י אל רחום וחנון וג׳

והאופן השני רחמיו על הבריונ[ת] ככת̇[21] טוב י״י לכל̇ ורחמיו על כל מעשנ[יו]

והשלישי בנין בית המקדש ככת̇[22] הטיבה ברצונך את ציון תבנה חומות ירושלם. והרביעי לשבת בבית י״י ולגור באהלו ככת̇[23] אך טוב וחסד ירדפוני כל ימי חיי ושבתי בבית י״י לארך ימים.

(fol. 3, verso)

והחמישי בהציל את יראיו מאויביהם ככת̇[24] חֹנה מלאך י״י סביב ליראיו

[17] Ex. 33.19.

[18] Cp. R. H. 17b: ברית כרותה לי״ג מדות שאינן חוזרות ריקם and the Gaonic views cited in Manhig, ed. Berlin, 48a. Cp. also Poznański, לקוטים מן ספר מגלת סתרים לר׳ נסים, p. 48.

[19] Read לקראו.

[20] Exod. 34.6.

[21] Ps. 145.9.

[22] Ps. 51.20.

[23] Ps. 23.6.

[24] Ps. 34.8, 9.

ויחלצם טעמו וראו כי טוב י״י אשרי הגבר יחסה בו׳. והששי כלכול ברואיו ופרנסתם ככת׳[25] כפירים רשו ורעֵבו ודרשי י״י לא יחסרו כל טוב. והשביעי ענות קרואיו אשר יקראוהו באמת ככת׳[26] ענני י״י כי טוב חסדך כרב רחמיך פנה אלי. והשמיני בעשות אותות ונפלאות ככת׳[27] עשה עמי אות לטובה וג׳.

והתשיעי בקיבול השבים אליו הנכנעים לפניו ככת׳[28] חטאות נעורי ופשעי אל תזכר כחסדך זכר לי אתה למען טובך י״י טוב וישר י״י על כן יורה חטאים בדרך. והעשירי טוב העולם הבא ושכר הצדיקים ככת׳[29] לולא האמנתי לראות בטוב י״י בארץ חיים. וכת׳[30] מה רַב טובך

(fol. 4, recto)

אשר צפנת ליראיך פעלת לחוסים בך נגד בני אדם. לפיכך חיב האדם לעסוק בתורה וללמוד ולדעת את י״י בראוי לו[31] כי בכן יגדל טובו וחסדו עליו ויבהיק זיוו שכך אמרנו[32]

[25] Ps. 34.11. [26] Ps. 69.17.

[27] Ps. 86.17. [28] Ps. 25.7, 8.

[29] Ps. 27.13. [30] Ps. 31.20.

[31] In what is manifest to him (cp. note 13a).

[32] Uses this phrase when quoting a Talmudic passage (cp. fol. 5, r., l. 3; v., l. 2); this manner of citation is frequent in the Gaonic writings. Our passage is in Ḥag. 12b.

אמׄ רׄ שמעון בן לקיש כל העוסק בתורה בלילה הקׄבׄהׄ מושך עליו חוט שלחסד ביום שנׄ[33] יומם יצוה י׳׳י חסדו ובלילה שירו עמי תפלה לאל חיי מה טעם יומם יצוה י׳׳י חסדו מישום דבלילה שירה עמי ואיכא דאמרי׳ אמׄ רׄ שמעון בן לקיש כל העוסק בתורה בעולם הזה שדומה ללילה הקׄבׄהׄ מבהיק[34] זיוו לעולם הבא שדומה ליום שנׄ יומם יצוה י׳׳י חס[דו] ובלילה שירה עמי וגׄ וחיב הל[מד] תורה להיות יראת י׳׳י נגד פניו ולגור מחרונו ולשמור חקותיו ולעשות רצונו ומצוותיו כי בכן יצליח וישכ[יל] בכל דרכיו ככתׄ[35] ובכל מעשה אשר הח[ל]

(fol. 4, verso)

בעבודת בית האלהים ובתורה ובמצוה לדרש לאלהיו בכל לבבו עשה והצליח וכן אמרו רבותינו[36] אמׄ רׄ יהושע בן לוי כל העוסק בתורה נכסיו מצליחין דבר זה כתוב בתורה שנוי בנביאים משלש בכתובים כתׄ בתׄ[37] ושמרתם את דברי הברית הזאת ועשיתם אתם למען תשכילו את כל אשר

33 =שנאמר, Ps. 42.9.

34 Our text has מושך עליו חוט של חסד as above.

35 2 Chr. 31.21.

36 'A. Z. 19b (cp. MS. Munich in דקדוקי סופרים a. l.).

37 =כתוב בתורה, Dt. 29.8.

תעשון שנוי בנביאים[38] לא ימוש ספר התורה הזה מפיך והגית בו יומם ולילה למען תשמר לעשות ככל הכתוב בו כי אָז תצליח את דרכיך ואז תשכיל   משולש בכתובים[39] והיה כעץ שתול על פלגי מים אשר פריו יתן בעִתו [ו]עלהו לא יבול וכל אשר יעשה יצ̇

(fol. 5, recto)

ואף על פי שהלמד מתחיל לקראת[40] בתורה חיב לשנות במשנה ובתלמוד ואחרי כֵן לסבור ולחקור שכך אמרנו[41] אמ̇ ראבא ליגמר איניש והדר ליסבַר [42] כי אם בתורת יי׳ חפצו ובתורתו יהגה יומם ולילה. ואל יסמוך על המקרא לבד כי יש בפירוש כל דבר כמה פנים והרבה פעמים שוים[43] זה כנגד זה. ובשוב האדם אל דברי רבותינו אשר העתיקום[44] בפתרון כל מצוה ומצוה לבאר אי זה אופן הוא הרצוי לא[45] ידע חפץ בוראו לעשותו. כ[י רק]

[38] Josh. 1.8. [39] Ps. 1.3.

[40] Read לקרא.

[41] 'A. Z. 19a (and so also in MS. Munich, see ד"ס).

[42] Insert שנאמר=שנ׳, Ps. 1.2.

[43] Read שונים, different.

[44] In the meaning of handing down as a tradition (cp. also verso, l. 1, fol. 6, r., l. 4). So also Sa'adyah in his Sepher Haggalui (*Saadyana*, p. 5, ll. 6–7: ויאספו כל מלה אשר העתיקו מני קדם) and Ibn Ezra in his Bible commentary (e. g. Introd. to Pent. commentary, where מעתיקי הדת mean the Rabbinic authorities).

[45] The sense rather demands אז for לא.

השמע[46] הוא העיקר ולכן ינחלו ה[חכמים] באמת בהיותם רבים ועצומים כ[בוד] ויקר ככתֹ[47] אשר חכמים יגידו ולא כ[חד]ו מאבותם להם לבדם נתנה הארץ ולא עבר זר בתוכם. הלא תד[עו כי] כאשר אמר אלהינו[48] שלוש פעמ[י]ם בשנה יראה כל [זכ]ורך

(fol. 5, verso)

והיה הדבר הזה כלל העתיקו רבותינו בפירושו מה ששנינו[49] הכל חיבים בראייה חוץ מחרש שוטה וקטן טומטום ואונדרגנוס[50] נשים ועבדים שאין משוחררין החיגר והסומה[51] החולה והזקן וכל שאינו יכול לעמוד[52] ברגליו.

ולכן הוציאו רוב הנזכרים מן הכלל ההוא מפני שלא באו תחתיו טמטום ואונדרגנוס[50] ונשים וגם מקצת הנזכרים[53] [י]צאו ממנו בראיות השכל [ו]תחלתם השוטה כי כבר ידענו שאינו חיב במצוות לא בחג ולא בזולתו כל זמן שהוא בשטיותו וגם החולה והזקן שאין בה[ם]

[46] =שמועה, tradition.

[47] Job 15.17, 18.

[48] Exod. 23.17; 34.23; Dt. 16.16.

[49] Ḥag. 1.1.

[50] Read ואנדרוגנוס.

[51] =והסומא.

[52] Read לעלות (cp. fol. 6, r., l. 7).

[53] Read הזכרים.

יכולת כי לא חייב יוצרנו לעשות
יתר מן היכולת ולא ה[יכול]ת
כולה [ב]זאת ידענו שיצא[ו] אילו

(fol. 6, recto)

בראיות השׂכל והנשארים
בראיות השֵׁמע[46] נודעו. ולולי
דבריהם אשר ידענו אמתם
וכי מפי הנביאים הועתקו
היה החרש וה[קט]ן והעבדים
והחיגר והסומה ומי שאינו
יכול לעלות ברגליו חייבים
כולם בראייה ובאים תחת
המקרא הזה ו[אלא] כשהוציאום
והגידו שאינן [חייבין] ידענו שהמקרא
בכל מצוותיו [צר]יך [לי]מוד ולימוד
פתרון כל מצוה ומ[צוה]. וכן בס[דר]
קרבנות שכת[וב] בה[54] וסמך ידו [על]
רא[ש הקר]בנ[ות יצ]או רבים ש[אינם]
חיבין [לסמוך ש]כך אמרו[55] הכו[ל]
[סומ]כיון חוץ מח]רש שוטה ו[קטן]
[וסו]מה [ו]עובד כוכבים והע[בד והשליח ו[האשה]
ור . . . . ואף על פי [שישנן]
כל[לות ב]מקצת המצוות [חיב לבדוק]

(fol. 6, verso)

היש על הכלל ההוא תנוי[56] או פרט
שאם יש תנוי חיב לעשות לפיהו
ולכן כשאמרו[57] כל מצות עשה

[54] Read בו.

[55] Men. 9.8.

[56] =תנאי.

[57] Ḳidd. 1.7.

שהזמן גרמה[58] אנשים חיבים
ונשים פטורות. [הוצ]יאו תנוי על
הכלל הזה ואמרו[59] הרי מצה
ושמחה והקהל דמצות עשה[60]
שהזמן גרמה ונשים חיבות.
לפיכך אמׄ[61] [רׄ] יוחנן אין למידין
מן הכללות [ואפילו] במקום שנׄ[62]
בהן חוץ. ולא [א]מר שלא ללמד
[מ]הם כל [עק]ר אילא שאם יראה
[הכל]ל יחפש ויבד[וק] היש ראיה
[לה]וציא ממנו . . . . [ז]ולת . . . מוצא
אמרם חוץ ו . . . . ה
. . . אחריה ואם . . . . . . לפ[ני]
[הכ]לל ההוא ור . . . . . . [וז]ה
[ש]שנינו[63] בכל מע[רבין ומשתתפים]
[חוץ מן המ]ים ומן המ[לח] . . . שינו

(Here the MS. breaks off.)

IX.

[MS. Mosseri L. 8, paper, very faded.]

Letter addressed (recto, l. 2) to מרי ורבנא שלמה . . . בן מרי ורבנא (continuation on l. 3 illegible).

4 . . . . ישא חשובנו וגדולנו שלום ממנו ומן יוסף בן
[א ב]

[58] גְרָמָה, fem. suffix referring to מצות עשה, is better than the usual reading גרמא which introduces an Aramaic noun into a purely Hebrew phrase.

[59] Ḳidd. 34a top.

[60] Viz. each of them is a מצות עשה which time causes (or, in other words, is dependent on the occasion).

[61] =אמר, ibidem. [62] =שנאמר. [63] 'Erubin 3.1.

[דודנו ומן האלופים והחכמים השרים והסגנים ובני הגאונים והשופטים והתנאים והתלמידים]

[והסופרים]

(Lines 5–7 illegible.)

לקיים[64] הן יראת יי׳ היא חכמה וסור מרע בינה וכת׳[65] וענוים ירשו ארץ והתענגו על רב

שלום ושמענו שמעך יקירנו בשכלך ובינתך וענותך ויראת יי׳ אשר בך ושמחנו

להיות בעם יי׳ כמוך דומה לתמר אשר פורח ויפריא ככת̇[66] צדיק כתמר יפרח כארז בלבנון

ישגה ובירכנוך [במעמד כל] הישיבה והגדנו מהלליך וספרנו שבחך כראוי לכבודך

כעין שכתוב[67] אמרו צדיק כי טוב כי פרי מעלליהם יאכלו יהי רצון לקיים ברכותינו

בך לשימם לוית חן לראשו̇ך] ולעטרת פז ככת̇[68] תקדמנו ברכות טוב תשית לראשו עטרת

פז וחפצנו להיות בינינו ובינך אהבה מחוזקת וברית מאושר ולכן הקדמנו האגרת

הזאת והקבלנו פניך בברכותינו ומשכנו אהבתך אלינו וכאשר כרתנו לך ברית כן

עשה גם אתה עמנו וכרת לנו ברית להיות ידך עמנו ולהסגל בנו להיות מגדולי

אוהבינו ומחשובי ידידינו...... ואם ייטב בעיניך ויכשר בפניך להתנדב ולעשות

חסד עמנו ולהיטיב לנו עשה [כפי יכלך] וקח טוב וקנה שכר גדול ויהיה על ידי חשובנו

[64] Job 28.28. [65] Ps. 37.11.
[66] Ps. 92.13. [67] Is. 3.10.
[68] Ps. 21.4.

[וגדולנו] מרי ורבנא סהלאן המומחה ברבי אברהם המומחה האוהב בן האוהב יברכם אל
כי הגיד כבודך ויקרך וצנ[יעות] לכתך ואהבתך ל[עש]ות חסד והוא עומד במקומנו שמה
להשתדל בתועלותינו ולהתעסיק בקיבוץ [הנ]אותינו .... והתמיד כתביך לפנינו בטוביך
ומשאותיך ובכל חפציך וצרכיך ומהר ואל תאחר כי כן ייטיב ייי לך מטובו
הצפון ליראיו ככת׳[68a] מה רב טובך אשר צפנת ליראיך פעלת לחסים בך נגד
בני אדם ויצק ברכ[ותיו] עליך ועל זרעך ככת׳[69] כי אצק מים על צמא ונוזלים
על יבשה אצק רוחי על זרעך [וברכתי] על צאצאיך וכן יהי רצון ושלומך ירב
טבת שנת שלב׳[70] ברית שלום

VII. The Letters of Hezekiah, Exilarch and Head of the Pumbedita-Bagdād School

Hezekiah was the 4th generation after David b. Zakkai and became Exilarch some time before 1021. After 1038 he was also appointed head of the school as successor of Hai. The report of Ibn Daud that he only functioned 2 years in this combined office of Exilarch-Gaon is now proved to be untenable (see infra, p. 204).

Here our task is to deal only with his letters. Such are mentioned as having been sent to Elijah Hakkohen b. Abraham, an important Rabbi in some Mesopotamian community (Mann, משרת ראש הגולה, p. 22). A formula of a letter written in Nisan 1021,

[68a] Ps. 31.20.
[69] Is. 44.3.
[70] (1)332 Sel. = 1020–1 C. E.

to a certain elder, has been edited by Kamenetzky (*REJ.*, LV, 51–53). It contains nothing specific except the name of Hezekiah's דיינא דבבא, Abraham.[1]

The 2 letters given here (pp. 181–184) contain matters more substantial. The first, the beginning of which is missing, was written in Ab 1040. The concluding phrase ישועה is also used by Daniel b. 'Azaryah and still before him by Sa'adyah (see above, p. 74, note 28). That it emanates from Hezekiah is not only evident from the next letter, which has his title, but chiefly from the contents. It is a powerful admonition to the Babylonian section in Fusṭāṭ to uphold the authority of its Rabbi Sahlān Alluf b. Abraham who met with much opposition. Now we have found that Hai Gaon shortly before his death (in 1038) was compelled to uphold Sahlān's authority (above, p. 118), and Hezekiah's letter 2 years later shows that the internal conflict within that community was not yet settled. Hai was to write to the powerful Ḥesed b. Sahl al-Tustari on behalf of Sahlān, and this Ḥesed is evidently alluded to in our epistle (fol. 1, r., l. 3 ff.). Hezekiah urges the Fusṭāṭ congregation to obey Sahlān's ruling and states that he is giving him his full support (fol. 1, r., l. 18 ff.). He further mentions that letters came from Fusṭāṭ about the dues for the school (חומשים=אלאכמאס, fol. 1, v., l. 6)[1a] and in this connection he mentions that his cousin (בן דודנו, l. 10) sent him some information. It is unknown who this person, who evidently then stayed in Fusṭāṭ, was. He further informs the congregation that all legal questions should be sent through Sahlān. The congregation should further continue to pray for the Shaikh Abū Naṣr (i. e. our Ḥesed b. Sahl, fol. 2, r., l. 4 ff.) because of his sterling value and merit and obey him without murmur.

No. II is the commencement of a letter from Hezekiah to the Nagid of Ḳairwān Jacob b. 'Amram (cp. above, p. 116). Unfortunately only the exordium has been preserved.

[1] 'The heads of the two academies' referred to there (p. 52, l. 23) are not Hai and Samuel b. Ḥofni (as Kamenetzky remarks, note 14) but, as we now know, Hai and Israel b. Samuel b. Ḥofni.

[1a] Cp. also above in the letter from Fusṭāṭ to Hai (p. 139, l. 17).

LETTERS OF HEZEKIAH, EXILARCH AND GAON

I.

[T.-S. Loan 40; 2 paper leaves.]

(Fol. 1, recto)

. . . [לם] נצרף תפציל מא גׄרי אלא אנא נתק באן אלאמר אנתהי . . . מא יעוד בגׄמאל צאחבנא ואנתטׄאם אמורה וקד כׄץ רב אלעאלמין יתברך שמו הדׄא אלשיךׄ אל[גׄליל] באלפצׄאיל אלעטׄימהׄ ואלמחאמד אלכרימהׄ . . . . אלשיוךׄ אלמתקדמין פסאד כל ואחד מנהם כמא וזארהׄ מנהם פאגׄתמעת פיה דׄאך לרצׄא טריקתה וסלאמהׄ ניתה ומעלום קול אלאולין[2] מגלגלין זכות על ידי זכוי[3]. פאן אללה יעד אלאכׄיאר לל . . . . ויופקהם ללמכארם כמא יעד אלאשראר לל . . . עת ואלי דׄלך אשא[ר] אלחכים בקולה[4] כל פעל י״י למענהו חתי אלאוקאת ואלאמ[א]כן תגׄרי איצׄא הדׄא אלמגׄרי כמא קאלו[5] עת מזומנת לטובה עת מזומנת לפורענות. וקד ראית א[ס]תכׄאר אלנבי בתרתיבה ללבש[ו]רות אלחסני בקולה[6] רוח י״י אלהים עלי יען משח י״י אותי לבשר ענוים וגׄ ואללה נסל אן ידים לגׄמאעת בה בללנא ולכאפהׄ אלאמהׄ אלגׄמאל בה וישלם גמולו יפה ונעים. ויתן לו חן וחסד וידועים. וכל אשר יעשה יצליח ואל כל אשר יפנה ישכיל. ונחן עניד אלוצאהׄ לגׄמאע[הׄ] . . . בטאעהׄ צאחבנא מ רׄ ס ה ל א ן ה א ל ו ף [נט] ר חׄ ואלאנתהי אלי קולה ותדבירה כי דבריו דברינו ואין להמרות על פיו וכל אשר יורה ממנו מבורך לפנינו ואשר ימרה על פיו ויקללנו גם אנחנו נצוה

[2] Sabb. 32a and frequently.
[3] =זכאי.
[4] Prov. 16.4.
[5] Sanh. 102a.
[6] Is. 61.1.

(verso)

לנדותו לפיכך חוסו על עצמיכם ובחרו בחיים ויי׳ ינחילכם חיי שני עולמים. ולסנא נסתחסן . . . ריד מע אתׄבתכם עלי אטראחנא אלא למחלכם [ומו]צׄעכם ולאן אלעין אליכם ואלקלב ענדכם ונרגו אן [תס]תאנפון מא יליק בכם. ואעלמו אן כאנת אלכתב תרד אלי חצׄרתנא בדׄכר אלאכׄמאס ולא נעלם מא הי וכנא נטׄן אנהא רסום עליכם פי . . . לכם כמא ילזמכם לנא פנטארנא עליכם וא . . . מאכׄודׄין בכפאיתנא וכפאיהׄ מן יתבענא מן אלחכמים חתי ערפנא מן גהׄה [בן] דודנו נטׄ רחׄ אנהא מאכׄודׄהׄ ממא ינ[ת]צל ללעניים אלוארדין [א]לי אלבלד . . . ועלי . . . דׄלך וכר[הנ]א אכׄדׄ שי קד אכׄרגׄ לל . . . פ . . . וקד . . . ר להם וקד ראינא אדׄאלהׄ דׄלך פאן סהל עלי אלגמאעהׄ אלתזאם ידאעונהא בה מן אלנדבה מן אמואלהם כגירהם פדׄאך אלדׄי יליק בהם והם אנמא יוצלין [אלי] חיי שעה ויצלון בדׄלך אלי חיי עולם ושכרנא להם יתגׄד וברכותינו להם יתוספו ומא . . . כף פמא נכׄלף אלגמאעהׄ א . . . בל נדו[ן][*6] . . . פר עלי חמל אתׄקאל אלגמאעהׄ וכׄלפה . . . ונקים במהמאתהם ומא יערץׄ מן שאילאתה[6a] פי דאעונא בדׄלך ויקירנו מרׄ סהלאן האלוף נטׄ [רחׄ]

(fol. 2, recto)

יחמל אלי חצׄרתנא חקוק אלפירסות[7] ומעשה בית דין ויכתב אלי חצׄרתנא פי כל וקת באכׄבאר

*6 The reading is doubtful.

6a Legal questions requiring responsa from Hezekiah and his school.

7 This word seems to be corrupt and is unintelligible to me.

אלגמאעה̈ וגמיע מא ערץ̇ וען אלאחכאם וגירהא ולא תכ̇לון אלשיך̇ אלג̇ליל בובא[8] נצר ואדאם[9] אללה תאיידה מן אלדעא ואד̇כרוה באלברכות פי כנאיסכם דאימא כי האלהים הקימו ויתנהו לברית עם לאור גוים לפקוח עינים עוורות להוציא ממסגר אסיר מבית כלא יושבי חשך[10] ויי' יחזקהו ויאמצהו ויברכהו כצנה רצון תעטרנו. ואכ̇לצו קלובכם פי טאעה̈ לרחמו ושימו מצוותיו על לבכם ואד̇כרו אן ט[עו]ת א[ב]ותינו הי אלתי כ̇רבת אלמקדש ושתתת אלשמל[11] ועונותינו אנחנו מעכבת[12] את הקץ ולא תגתרו באל מהלה̈ אד̇א עאלת פאנה אד̇א שא אן ינתקם מי יקום בחרון אפו ומי יעמוד בהראותו[13] פאגתנמו אלתובה̈ מהמא תמכן דרשו יי' בהמצאו קראוהו בהיותו קרוב[14] ויי' ימול את לבבכם למען שמו להודיע את גבורתו ושלומכם אחינו ירבה לעד נכתב בחדש אב שנת אלף ושלש מאות וחמשים ואחת[15] ישועה

II.

(verso)

מן יחזקיהו ראש גליות כל ישראל
בן דויד בן יחזקיהו ראש גליות כל ישראל.
אל אדירנו ואצילנו הנגיד מרי ורבנא

[8] Read אבו. [9] Read אדאם. [10] Cp. Is. 42.6–7.
[11] Cp. Yoma 9b: מקדש שני . . . מפני מה חרב מפני שהיתה בו שנאת חנם.
[12] =מעכבות. [13] Cp. Nahum 1.6, Mal. 3.2.
[14] Is. 55.6 [15] 1351 Sel. = 1040 C. E.

יעקב ראש מערכות ישראל אשר הוקם למו
על בגלותם וניתן למו סתר מצר יצרם אור עול[16]
לנוס אליו ועמוד ברזל
להישען עליו וחומת נחושת לשגבם
לגדור פרצות ולחזק הסייג
ולחבב התורה על לומדיה בכבוד שהוא חולק
להם במתנותיו הרחבות ובשלחנות שהוא
עורך לקרוביהם. ובלחמו הערוך על שולחנות
רחוקיהם. ומלבושי פאר שהוא מלבישם שש
ומשי ורקמה יונקיהם יינקו חל[בו] ועולליהם מתגדלים
מתפנוקיו ובחוריהם זכרו בפיהם כיין וישישיהם
באהבתו שוגים ומתפארים וזקניהם מתפללים
על חייו יאריכם צור עולמים ויוסיף ימים על ימיו
ושנותיו כמו דור ודור וירים ידו על צריו ויכרתו
כל איביו ומשל בגוים רבים ובו לא ימשולו ועליו
יטה חסד לפני המלך ויועציו ושריו וגבוריו
וגדל בבית המלך כבלשן[17] ושמעו הולך בכל
המדינות כי האיש[18] [19]מר ורבנא עמרם
זכרו לברכה ולתחיה שלום באין קץ

(Here the MS. breaks off.)

VIII. Anonymous Letters from Babylonian Geonim

We give here 3 anonymous letters that evidently emanate from Babylonian Geonim or members of the schools.

No. I (pp. 188–90) is apparently a private letter by a Gaon, hence there are no official greetings from the academy. It is addressed to a scholar who is styled הרב; whether Shemaryah b. Elḥanan

[16] =עולם. For יצרם read יצרו.
[17] =Mordecai (cp. Ezra 2.2, Neh. 7.7, and Men. 65a, top).
[18] Cp. Esther 9.4.
[19] Supply here בן or בר.

is meant is subject to doubt. The writer refers to his troubles and the demise of his children and complains that his letters are kept unanswered. Knowing this Rabbi and his group to be busy with the study of the Torah, he is all the more eager to receive letters from them on learned questions and to enjoy in addition their good style. The present letter is to introduce a certain Na'man b. Moses b. Salmon with the request to befriend him because of his learning and the standing of his late father. Na'man entrusted his son to the care of the writer. The Rabbi, referred to, has helped the writer before by sponsoring his request. The donation from the elders of the *Babylonian congregation in Ḳairwān* (we hear of such a congregation for the first time here) has arrived through a certain Shemaryah, the representative of the writer. The Rabbi, the writer is sure, will explain to his congregation the pressing need of help for "the captivity" (evidently some people were imprisoned). A certain Isaac b. Salmon arrived praising the people whom this Rabbi served for their kindness to him. The writer is pleased at it because Isaac is a respected man and of good family.

Perhaps this Rabbi should be sought in Ḳairwān but any identification must remain speculative till the beginning of the letter will turn up among the Genizah fragments.

No. II (pp. 190–93) has been published by Weiss (הצופה לחכמת ישראל, V, 14–15) in a defective manner. In reproducing it here we have tried to correct his version as much as possible without a facsimile of the original. Weiss has altogether misunderstood the nature of the letter and has been looking far afield for a Jacob b. Moses, to whom the letter was addressed, even going to Narbonne for a namesake. There is no doubt that this person was Jacob b. Moses b. Samuel ibn Jama' of Ḳābes (North-Africa), a correspondent of Hai Gaon. Moses b. Samuel, Jacob's father, was a prominent scholar who sent his questions to this Gaon.[1] He had 2 learned sons, Abraham and Jacob, the former sending questions in the name of his father then already old.[2] Hai com-

[1] Cp. Gaonic Responsa, ed. Harkavy, Nos. 59–67, with the heading (p. 27) and the conclusion (pp. 31–33); No. 369, end (p. 185, bottom).

[2] Ibid., p. 167, heading of No. 336: שאילאתא אילין דשדר מ' ר' אברהם בר רב משה בר נאמע ממדינת קאבס באתר מערבא משם סאבא חשיבא מנהגא מ' ר' משה רבה בר מ' ר' נאמע.

pliments Abraham greatly together with his aged father and his brother (i. e. our Jacob).[3] Jacob too sent questions to Hai (see ibid., the heading of No. 315 and the end of No. 328). Moses is also the author of the letter to Joseph b. Jacob ibn 'Aubal (above, p. 140). The Ibn Jama' family continued to be prominent in Ḳābes for a long time. Thus in the 12th century we have the Dayyān Samuel b. Jacob Ab-Bet-Din, the author of the work on Sheḥitah (excerpts from which were given by Steinschneider, *J. Z.*, vols. I–IV) and of addenda to R. Natan's 'Arukh (published by Buber, *Graetz Jubelschrift*, Hebrew part, 1 ff.).[4] Abraham ibn Ezra eulogised him and his three sons Jacob, Judah and Moses (*Diwān*, ed. D. Kahana, II, 31 ff., cp. p. 41).

Having established the identity of our Jacob b. Moses (ibn Jama'), a correspondent of Hai's, let us analyse the letter sent to him. The style is certainly Gaonic as is evident from the structure including the characteristic divisions beginning respectively with שא שלום רב, שלום and ומודיעים (see above, p. 83). That it is by Hai, I am not yet prepared to say because the writer does not mention in his greetings also the members of his school. The writer rather seems to have been a lone figure and complains of having no companions, his only consolation being his few disciples (l. 20–21). He adds that, in view of the paucity of Talmudic scholarship, he decided to write a commentary on the Talmud in accordance with the traditions of his teachers. The real purpose of the letter is to introduce a certain Abraham b. Solomon who deserves help and encouragement.

Finally we give under No. III (p. 194) a fragment of a letter emphasizing the need of communal leaders. The grouping of this theme of leadership in a numerical scheme reminds one of the method of Samuel b. Ḥofni and of his son Israel (see above, pp. 149–50, 154). Perhaps this fragment is actually from a letter of theirs.

[3] See the conclusion of No. 344 (p. 172): ואתה יקירינו אהובינו החביב עלינו מ' אברהם הח' בר מר רב משה הרב . . . והזקן הרב אביך ייטיב אלהיו אחריתו יראהו משאלותיו כלם. וגם אהובינו אחיך החכם האדיר יהי מקורו ברוך וכו'. Cp. also Lewin, גנזי קדם, II, 21.

[4] Cp. also above, p. 64, note 4.

In conclusion, for the sake of completeness, other anonymous epistles, already published, should be mentioned.

a) A letter, evidently sent to Spain, tells of the poverty of the schools at Bagdād. Appeals for donations are made, these to be sent to the representative Saul b. Joseph in Ḳairwān who will forward them to Merwān b. Abraham al-Maghribi, who settled in Bagdād and has become the treasurer of the dues for the school. For the edition and discussion of this letter see Mann, *Hebrew Union College Jubilee Volume*, 249–52.

b) Another epistle, evidently to Ḥisdai ibn Shaprūṭ of Cordova, informing him of the honor of Rosh Kallah bestowed upon him, has been edited and discussed by Mann, ibid., 252–57.

c) A third anonymous letter from a writer, who presided over some school and met with religious persecution, is given ibid., pp. 261–2.

d) Finally we have the highly interesting letter of 953 (*JQR*, XVIII, 401–403) the identity of whose authorship is still subject to doubts (see my remarks ibid., pp. 229–30, and *H. U. C. Annual*, III, 309–10). This letter casts a lurid light on conditions at the Pumbedita school under Aaron b. Sarjādo.

The correspondence of the Babylonian Geonim, discussed in the above pages, are replete with valuable information about conditions in the schools, the personal relations, the rivalry and jealousies prevailing between the various members of the academies, and the intercourse with the outside communities and their spiritual leaders. As a red thread running through all of them is the appalling need of the schools for outside help owing to the impoverishment of Babylonian Jewry, which ultimately led to the downfall of the ancient seats of learning in Babylon and not the opening of new centers in the countries of the Diaspora as the well-known account of Ibn Daud would make us believe (see infra, p. 202 f.). These letters are only a very small portion of what issued from the schools throughout the Gaonic period. The more of them are discovered and edited, the fuller will our knowledge of this obscure period become.

Anonymous Letters from Babylonian Geonim

I.

[T.-S. 12. 146, vellum, top and bottom missing.]

(Recto)

. . . .

מאצלכם בעדכם וכשאשמע שלום אדוננו הרב ושלומ[כם וגוד]ל תפארתכם א[שמח]

ואשיש ואעלוז בעלץ ואשבח לצור על ככה המקי[1] יגדיל את כבודכם למעלה ויוסיף על

כבודכם ועל גדולתכם ויניב בטוב שיבתכם ויתמיד לכם החיים והשלום. ומודיע

כי בחסדי משגבנו וחמלת חוננו אנו שרוים בטח הודיה לגומל חייבים טובות ואף לפי[2]

שצרות הקיפונו. ורעות אפפונו. ופטירת ילדים תכפונו. רחמיו לא עזבונו. [וח]סדיו לא

נטשונו. יתברך על כל ברכה ותהלה. וכמה כתבים כתבנו אליכם ותשובה מכם

לא ראינו ובידוע שעסקיכם מרובים בהגיון תושיה. ובגרסון[3] עמקי פליליה. ועל זאת

רוחנו משתאפת ונפשנו משתוקקת מאד מאד להשתעשע בחרוזי כתביכם ובנעימות

לשונכם ובמתיקות תשובתכם. האל יאמצכם יברך מעשה ידיכם יותירכם לטובה

יתמוך אתכם ויעודדכם ויקיים בכם מקרא שכתי[4] ייי אלהי אבותיכם יוסף עליכם ככם וג׳

[1] =המקום.

[2] =על פי.

[3] Paiṭanic formation from גרס (to study).

[4] Deut. 1.11.

ומוביל מכתבי זה עדיכם מר נעמן בר̇ משה בן שלמון נ̇נ̇[5] בבקשה מכ[ם]

שתסייעוהו כפי יכלכם בעסקיו ותעשו עמו כווסתכם[5a] הנאה ומנהגכם המונא[ה]

ביען שהיה אביו ימצ̇ רחמ̇[6] זקן דורנו וחשוב קהלינו ואוהבנו ואהובנו ו[באמת]

ראוי לכבדו לכבוד אביו ולהטפל בצרכיו שהוא תל̇ חכ̇[7] ולא עוד אלא ש[חמודו]

מסרו בידי והוא כאחד מבניי. הילכך אחיי גם אציליי אבקשה מכם ש[תתנהגו עמו]

כבן כדי שיבוא אצלינו והוא משבח מהללכם ונעימותכם. ועמדנו על[

הגמול הטוב שגמלנו אדוננו הרב יגדל למעלה בהלצת ישרו בכתביו הנ[חמדים]

הישיבה דכ̇ ובר̇[8] והגיעה הנדבה שנתנדבו זקני בבל במדינת קירואן

אלינו על ידי ר̇ שמריה הזקן שלוחנו והנותר הנם מוכן[9] לשגרו [ואדוננו יציע]

לפניהם אמתת דברינו בעד השביה האל המשלם גמול טוב ישל[ם]

גמולהו וינצרהו ויאשרהו ויראהו מ[חלציו כמותו] . . . .

תורה ומאל [המשאל] . . . .

. . . .

5 =נוח נפש.

5a As your good habit (for נֶסֶת in this meaning, cp. Mann, *Jews in Egypt*, II, Hebrew Index and Glossary, s. v.).

6 =ימצא רחמים.

7 =תלמיד חכם.

8 The dots evidently indicate that these 3 words should be deleted.

9 Read מוכנים.

(Right hand margin)

ובבוא מר יצחק בר שלמון סיפר מהללי שבחיכם וגודל
תפארתכם
ושפרת גמולכם לו ושמחתי ועלזו כליותי יען שהוא בן טובים
ומבעלי בתים.
ומשכורתכם תהי שלמה מעם צור ישראל ושלומכם יירב הרב

II.

ליקרת הוד הדר אדירנו וגבירנו[9a] אהל התורה. משכן מדורה[10].
גבירה וגבורה[11]. מר רב יעקב רב השכל וגם
המשרה. הנוחל חכמת צנועים[11a]. אמון שעשועים[12]. מהורים דעת
אלהים יודעים. מקודשים בקדושת ארון[12a] תוך קלעים.
אמרות טהורות מביעים. מכסף מזוקק צרוף שבעים. ותבונות
כמעיינות נובעים. נקיים מכל מום ורשעים. אין
פרץ לתועים. ואין יצאת למתעים[13]. גורלם חלק טוב ונעים. חמדת
שמות מי[ודעים]. אמ[רות כ]זיקות דנור מופיעים.
מזומנים לכת שלישית ברקיעים[14]. אמת . . . ם בין השועים הללו
הידועים . . . . לתורת אל ותלמידיו . . . [עים]. ומדרשות
ומדרשות[15] בראשי הישיבות הנטועים. והעמיד תלמידים
מפ[ורסמים וידועים]. בתורה וביראה שבוע

[9a] Probably so for אדירנו כבירנו in the printed text.

[10] The fem. suffix refers to תורה (so also Weiss).

[11] So also in Samuel b. Ḥofni's letter (above, p. 159, 2nd fragment, l. 5: הגביר והגבור).

[11a] Cp. Ḳidd. 71a (so Weiss).

[12] Cp. Prov. 8.30 applied to the Torah.

[12a] For אדון in the printed text.

[13] Cp. Ber. 17b top (so Weiss).

[14] Cp. Ḥag. 14b, and the responsum (in תה"ג מתוך הגניזה, ed. Assaf, p. 77, l. 18): ויזכה אותך לראות פני מלך בהראותו עם כת שלישית. See also Assaf's note 2.

[15] Repeated in MS.

שבעים[16]. מאורם כמנורת זהב בגביעים[17]. מוסר רב מקשיבים
ושומעים. ובהדר או[רם] מוסיפים ולא גורעים. בלשונם[18]
מרפא כל פצעים. מחיה וגם יראה . . . . . . ידועים. יקרים . . .
[עים]. בן מרנא ורבנא משה מופת
הדור סיני ועוקר הרים אשר זיו כבוד[19] בית יי׳ [עליו הו]חק חמדת
ישראל. [מלא] ברכת אל. אשר בשמאלה מעשרת ומברכת[20].
ובימינה ימים מארכת[21]. בהוד הדר לבניהם המ[ה תפארת][22].
ובניהם למו כותרת ועטרת. יהי רצון שוכני סנה לכונן
אשוריהם.
למלא משאלותיהם. להקים על סלע רגליהם. להודיעם אורח
חיים שובע שמחות את פניו נעימות בימינו נצח[23]. ש ל ו ם
משמי
מעל[24]. וברכה בכל פועל. והצלחה בבנין[25] אל פעל. ומרפא
למזור צרי ותעל. וריחוק כל רעל. ודיחוי רע בליעל. עם
שאר
כל הברכות וההצלחות והתשועות תהיינה לך ולכל יש לך סלה.
שא ש ל ו ם ר ב ממנו ומכל הנלוים [על]נו. כי[26] ברחמי
משגבנו שלום לנו. ומודים בכל לב לאלינו[27]. שמו לעולם מכבדים
ככת̇[28] אודה י׳י אלהי בכל לבבי ואכבדה שמך לעולם.
ו מ ו ד י ע י ם[29]

[16] שְׂבָעִים.

[17] Instead of נוביעים in the printed text.

[18] Instead of בלשונך in the printed text.

[19] In the printed text ככד.

[20] Probably so instead of בכבוד ת in the printed text.

[21] Cp. Prov. 3.16.

[22] Cp. Prov. 17.6.

[23] Cp. Ps. 16.11.

[24] Thus the rhyme demands instead of מעלה in the printed text.

[25] Evidently vocalise בְּבָנִין.

[26] Thus to be inserted.

[27] =לאלהינו.

[28] Ps. 86.12.

[29] Instead of ומדיעים in the printed text.

כי תורת אלהינו היא מקור חיים מסירה מחזיקיה ממוקשי מות
ככת̇[30] תורת חכם מקור חיים לסור ממוקשי מות. והמצוה גם
היא שומרתו ככת̇[31] שומר מצוה שומר נפשו. ובהיות התורה
והמצוה על גביהן ובה בכל[32] כמוך אשר נתת תורת אמת
מלבושך. והמצוה אדרת עטייתך. והיראה צניף לראשך. אשרי
הוריך פקדוך חקרוך למדוך[33]. ואשרי רואיך הנושאים
והנותנים
עמך בדברי תורה תמיד שמתוך דבריך נמשך [חוט של חסד][34].
והיינו חפצים להיות בכמוך ובכיוצא בך[35] מוחברים ביחד
כי לא נעלם ממך
נכבדנו מקום רבותינו וזקינינו הנאמנים . . . הדר . . . ידוע
ומפורסם וכבר עב . . . ל . . . א ואנחנו עמהם במשקלנו
הידוע.
ועכשיו נותרנו בלי חבר בחסד ואמת מכריע[36]. ולולי שאנחנו
מתנחמים במקצת הת[למידים שלנו][37] יזכו בתורה וביראה
ואנו שמחים בהם כשמחת אדם בבנו חמודות ובעובר אמו[38] [היינו
באים לידי][39] מידה [או חברו]תא או מיתותא[40]. גם ראינו
בעלי התלמוד מתמעטים ומתגברים בעלי לשון עול בלשונם[41]
ואין עומד בפרץ לפיכך מלאנו לבנו לפרש התלמוד ונעשה
[בו]

30 Prov. 13.14. 31 Prov. 19.16.

32 This text is evidently corrupt. In the absence of the original one can only surmise some correction. For ובה בכל probably read ובאשכול (=באיש שהכל בו, cp. Soṭah 47b bottom); for גביהן we would expect על גבי היראה.

33 Instead of (בי) במדיך in the printed text.

34 Weiss inserts [מיץ חמאה] but the above insertion is obviously better being based on Ḥag. 12b.

35 Instead of כמוך וכיוצא בך in the printed text, or read עם כמוך וכיוצא בך.

36 Viz. as God ordained (based on Ber. 60b bottom).

37 Thus the lacuna in the printed text is to be reconstructed.

38 In the printed text העובר אמו which is evidently corrupt.

39 Weiss's insertion [היינו מתאוים] is impossible.

40 Ta'an. 23a, bottom. 41 An allusion to the Ḳaraites?

כפי מה שקיבלנו מרבותינו זכׄ לבׄ[42] מהם מה שמסרנו לתלמידינו
ומהם מה[43] שלא מסר[נו להם והבקש]ה ממך שתסייעינו
בתפילה
על זה שיספיק הקבׄהׄ [על ידינו וכן] יהי רצון[44] ואודות כתבנו זה
אליך אחינו הנכבד מרבים עסק מרׄ ורבׄ
אברהם נטׄ רחׄ ואחיׄ[45] בן מרׄ ורׄ שלמה זכׄ לברׄ[46] המוביל כתׄב זה
אליך להודיעך כי הוא איש ישר איש[47] כשר באורחותיו.
תמים בדבריו[48].
לא ראינו בו עולה אמנם ראינו בו טובות מרובות והוא בן
תורה והוצרכנו להודיעך כדי שתזכה בו להיות לו מליץ
יושר
ותורהו מה לעשות ותהיה לו לפה דלא כל ימים מזדמן כזה
והחוטף[49] שזכה אשרו והמתעצל מתנחם אחרי כן ואינו
משיג
[ואין אנו מזהירים אלא מזכירים] ופחות מזה לאיש רב נבון וחכם
כמוך דורש שלומך ושלום כל אנשי[50] ביתך ובני עמך . . .
כ״ד[51]

. . . .

[42] =זכרם לברכה. The printed text has ובלב which is no doubt a misreading of זכׄ לבׄ.

[43] Thus for . . . מי שלא מפי in the printed text.

[44] Thus for the impossible חוה׳ם רצון in the printed text.

[45] =נטריה רחמנא ואחיה for the impossible שיח׳ ואחי׳ in the printed text.

[46] Thus for the impossible ומלבד in the printed text.

[47] For עש (sic!) in the printed text.

[48] To suit the rhyme, for בדרכו in the printed text.

[49] Viz. he who eagerly snatches up the מצוה (cp. Num. R. ch. 20.16: אוכלסין שיצאו מאותן שהיו חוטפות ומחבבות את המצות).

[50] For אנש in the printed text.

[51] So in the printed text which is impossible as the Geonim did not use this phrase כה דברי at the end of their letters. It may denote the date (24th) of the month when the letter was written.

III.

[H. U. C. Genizah Collection, No. 17, small vellum leaf.]

(Recto)

שרי המלך הגבורים ואני התחזקתי ביד
י״י אלהי עלי ואקבצה מישראל [ר]אשים
לעלות עמי[52]: ולמה נקרא כל אחד
מן הראשים ראש לחמשה ענינים הענין
הראשון כי הוא דומה לראש[53] לגוף וקהלותיו
ומקהלותיו אשר[54] ראש עליהם דומים
לאיבריו לשרתו בכל סְבָרָיו[55] וללכת אחריו
אל כל אשר יפנה ככת֗[56] בלכתם אל ארבעת

(verso)

רבעיהם ילכו לא [יס]בו בלכתם כי המקום
אשר [יפנ]ה הראש אחריו ילכו לא יסבו
בלכתם: והענין השני כי כמו שראש בן
אדם המשכיל צפה וספון דעת וחכמה
ואפון בכל אופני חכמה כן ראשי הקהלות
ונגידי המקהלות אשר באמת נקרא ראש[57]
הוא הראוי להיות משכיל ככת֗ו[58] משכיל
על דבר ימצא טוב ובוטח ביי׳ אשריו
והענין השלישי כי הראש הוא הוד קהילותיו
והדר[59]

[52] Ezra 7.28.
[53] Read כראש.
[54] Supply הוא.
[55] Thoughts, intentions.
[56] Ezek. 10.11.
[57] Viz. each of them.
[58] Prov. 16.20.
[59] Clavis of the next leaf which is missing.

Appendix I (to page 84, note 66).

THE SPECIAL MEETINGS OF THE SCHOOLS

In addition to the Kallah meetings there were occasions for assemblies convened by the heads of the schools or the Exilarchs at which the public at large was present. Several Geonim, like Sa'adyah, Sherira, Hai and Israel b. Samuel b. Ḥofni, refer to these meetings by the designations of פרק and עצרה. Also the later Bagdād Gaon, Zekharyah b. Berakhel, in a letter of Adar II, 1194, speaks of such an assembly (in Assaf, אגרות ר' שמואל בן עלי, 75: ועתה בבואנו אל מחוז חפצנו (viz. after our return to Bagdād) קבענו פרק בעזרה (r. ב ע צ ר ה) וברכנום ברכה אדורה וכו'). See further infra, p. 201, note 9 (end), with regard to the meetings of Elḥanan b. Shemaryah.

The meetings, as everything connected with the schools, had a religious character and prayers were recited for the welfare of communities at large or individual patrons of the academy. The whole procedure goes back to the Talmudic times. In R. H. 35a we read: א"ר אלעזר לעולם יסדיר אדם תפלתו ואחר כך יתפלל. א"ר אבא מסתברא מילתיה דר' אלעזר בברכות של ר"ה ושל יום הכיפורים ושל פ ר ק י ם אבל דכל השנה לא. Rashi takes פרקים to denote the Festivals (מועדות), but in reality all special occasions like public fasts and public assemblies are meant by this term. A special feature of them were the sermons of the Rabbis held either in the synagogue or house of study (cp. the passages of דרש ב פ ר ק א, cited by Bacher, *Exeget. Terminologie*, II, 164). Hence the sermons themselves also went by the name of פרק. In Babylon the Sabbath לך לך, set aside annually for honoring the Exilarch (cp. Sherira's Letter, ed. Lewin, 90–91), was the occasion for such a meeting with special sermons. Cp. Ber. 30a, bottom: מרימר ומר זוטרא הוו מכנפי בי עשרה בשבתא דרגלא ומצלו והדר נפקי לפרקא, viz. they went to hear the sermons delivered on the occasion. Likewise the stay of the Exilarch at Hagrunya was the cause for calling a special popular meeting on the Sabbath (Yoma 78a: ריש גלותא איקלע להגרוניא לבי רב נתן, רפרם וכולהו רבנן אתו לפירקא, רבינא לא אתא). Rashi explains לפירקא as דרשה דר"ג, but there were probably other speeches and sermons in his honor. Similar assemblies must have taken place when a president of the school or another prominent leader visited a community. Thus in 'Erubin 36b a prominent scholar (חכם)

is one who could summon a general assembly in a community in order to address the congregation (מותיב פירקי, cp. Rashi's comment: לדרוש ברבים). As the ceremonial developed in course of time, when a prominent representative of the schools visited a community, he was received with great pomp. His arrival at the synagogue, usually for his sermon on the Sabbath or on a special day set aside for it, was made the occasion for popular expression of the esteem in which he was held. The audience was called to attention by the summons from the Ḥazzān "Hear ye what so and so has to expound" and after the sermon Ḳaddish (the Talmudic יהא שמיה רבא דאגדתא, Soṭah 49a, cp. Mann, *H. U. C. Annual*, IV, 275 ff.) was recited. See the interesting description in Samuel b. 'Alī's letter of Tammuz, 1191, to Aleppo introducing his son-in-law, Zekharyah b. Berakhel, who was on a pastoral tour on behalf of the Bagdād school (in Assaf, *l. c.*, 48–9): ונתנו לו רשות לדין ולהורות ולהתיר בכורות ולדרוש תורה ברבים ו ל ק ב ו ע פ ר ק י ם ולהעמיד מתורגמין ולומר קודם מדרשו (=דרשתו) ש מ ע ו מ א י ד ס ב ר ה ואחר מדרשו קידוש השם ולצאת ולבוא בראש . . . ועל הקהלות ברוכים יהיו כאשר ישמעו בבואו אליהם שיצאו לקראתו ולקדמהו בסבר פנים יפות ויכנס בעם רב בכבוד. וכאשר יבוא אל בית הכנסת יקראו לפניו וישב בכבוד במושב הדור ומצעות נאות כראוי לאבות בתי דינין וכסת אחריו. This ceremonial (repeated also in the circular letter to the communities of Upper Mesopotamia and Syria, ibid., p. 56) probably goes back to earlier times as it developed in Babylon in connection with the schools and also with the Exilarchate.

There were in Babylon occasions for both schools to meet in full strength, either on Sabbath לך לך to honor the Exilarch, or to install a new Exilarch,[1] or for some other special purposes. At such פרקים, Sherira explains, there took place the coming together of Rab and Samuel (Letter, p. 81: ולפרקין הוו חזו רב ושמואל אהדדי) and of R. Huna and R. Judah b. Ezekiel (p. 84: והוה מתחזי ליה לרב הונא לפרקים). R. Ashi's prestige caused the שבתא דרגלא in honor of the Exilarch to be celebrated at Sura, and this would bring annually the Pumbedita scholars to this city for a common meeting (pp. 91–92). After the founding of Bagdād as the

[1] Cp. Natan Habbabli's account (in Neub., *Med. Jew. Chronicles*, II, 83–84).

capital of the ‘Abbāsid Caliphate these larger meetings were evidently held there since the Exilarchs took up their residence at the seat of the government. In addition each school would hold special meetings, called פרק and עצרה, with prayers and sermons or addresses as the occasion would require. As a result there developed special titles bestowed both at the schools and as honorary ones given to prominent people elsewhere.

Originally a recognized scholar (חכם), who had the right to summon a meeting and address it (קובע פרקים, מותיב פירקי), was a ראש פירקא, viz. as sitting at the head of such an assembly. As such a function required the art of public speaking, and, even if the actual address was delivered by means of a Meturgeman, the art of Aggadic presentation of a theme was a prerequisite, there seems to have developed a sort of specialisation for a group of people (perhaps the former רבנן דאגדתא) to be the leaders of such assemblies. These became known as רישי פירקא. This process of development we see in evidence in Palestine in the 6th century. The notorious Novella 146 of Justinian of 553, regulating the service of the synagogue and especially forbidding the Rabbinic interpretation of scripture (Deuterōsis), mentions the archipherekitai =רישי פירקא. We should not draw the conclusion from the order of sequence in this edict, viz. first archipherekitai, then ‘elders’ (presbuteroi) and finally teachers (didaskaloi), that the Rēshē Pirḳē were the most respected scholars of the time, as Graetz (*Gesch. der Juden*, V., 4th ed., 19) does. For all we know the ‘elders’ (presbuteroi) were the Talmudic זקנים[2] and the ‘teachers’ (didaskaloi) the Talmudic חכמים who were the real authorities on Jewish law by which Jewish life was guided. But since the Novella chiefly concerned the synagogue service, naturally the preachers, known as רישי פירקא, figure prominently therein. Of Mar Zuṭra, the posthumous son of the executed Babylonian Exilarch Mar Zuṭra, it is reported that he was brought to Palestine where, as he grew up, he first became ריש פירקא and subsequently head of the school of Tiberias as ראש סנהדרין, which shows that the real Rabbinic authorities were not the archipherekitai but the members of the school.[3]

[2] Cp. e. g. זקן ויושב בישיבה (Yoma 28b) and several other passages.

[3] Cp. Mann I, 58, note 1.

Likewise in Babylon there were ראשי פירקי in connection with the schools who certainly were of lower rank than the Geonim and the leading Allufim. Indeed they are only mentioned by the later Geonim such as Sherira and Samuel b. Ḥofni,[4] but we may assume that such title-holders existed in Babylon in earlier times just as in Palestine, viz. scholars or communal leaders, skilled in the art of public speaking or of homiletic interpretation of sermonic themes, who figured at the special meetings of the schools (פרקים) as Rēshē Pirḳē assisting the Exilarchs and the Geonim. Eppenstein (*Beiträge z. Gesch. u. Literatur im geon. Zeitalter*, 18–19) has thus failed to realize this whole process in explaining the ראשי פירקי or ראשי הפרקין, mentioned by Sherira and Samuel b. Ḥofni, to denote scholars who worked through a chapter (פרק) of a Talmudic tractate as against the ראשי הסדרים who mastered a whole section (סדר) of the Talmud.[5] In all these titles we have reminiscences of the older times in Babylon. Originally the head of the school, before Rab and Samuel, was only ראש סידרא or רישא דרבנן (Sherira's Letter, pp. 78 and 80). Then, when the Babylonian academies gained in prestige so that their presidents became known as ריש מתיבתא or ראש ישיבה, the title Rosh Hasseder was given to minor officials in the school and also as honorary degree to outside scholars. Likewise the title ראש בי רבנן was held in the school by some members (perhaps the ראשי המדרשים, ראשי מדרשי mentioned by Samuel b. Ḥofni) and was bestowed on sages, e. g., of Ḳairwān and Egypt (see infra, p. 206). The same happened with the title Alluf

[4] Curiously enough the only occasions, when Sherira and Samuel b. Ḥofni give a full list of the dignitaries of their respective schools, are in letters to Fez. Sherira together with Hai in replying to legal questions of certain Fez people, who were forcibly removed to Ashīr (cp. Epstein, *Jb. d. jüd.-liter. Ges.*, VII, 254–5, and Mann, *JQR*, *N. S.*, VII, 484, XI, 438--39), send greetings in their own names and on behalf of the following dignitaries: ומן ראשי כלי וראשי מדרשי וראשי פרקי ומן רבנן דדרא רבא ומן רבנן דסיומי ומן רבנן תנאי ומן כל מתיבתא. This responsum (or responsa) was written in Adar 987.

Samuel b. Ḥofni, in condoling with the Fez community about a persecution that overtook them (*JQR*, XVIII, 403–5), mentions these dignitaries and others in a somewhat different form (above, p. 150, note 5).

[5] The very fact that Sherira mentions the ראשי פרקי before the scholars of 'the first row' shows that the former were familiar with more than a mere chapter of a tractate!

(= Resh Kallah), the bearer of which had a purely internal function in connection with the semi-annual meetings of the school, which title was held by so many outside patrons and savants. Finally the same applies to the title ראש הפרק (ריש פירקא), originally denoting a scholar who could summon a special assembly (פרק) and address it, which was given to such members of the school who by reason of oratorical or homiletic gifts would figure at such meetings. Subsequently a learned Ḥazzān, who combined with his vocal powers the art of preaching (דרשן), would be honored by the Geonim with the title of Rosh Happereḳ (see Mann, I, 269–70). The old names were retained, though their connotations underwent a process of change in the course of the centuries.

Appendix II.

ELḤANAN B. SHEMARYAH OF FUSṬĀṬ AND HIS RELATIONS WITH THE SCHOOLS OF BABYLON AND PALESTINE

Like his more prominent father, Elḥanan was held in high respect by Sherira and Hai on the one hand and by the presidents of the reopened Sura school, Ṣemaḥ Ṣedeḳ and his successor Samuel b. Ḥofni, on the other (above, pp. 89, 104, 117, 135–6, 146–7). He studied in Bagdād and came into personal contact with the leading scholars there. After his return to Egypt he would send legal questions to Sherira, Hai and Samuel b. Ḥofni.[6] The title ראש הסדר was probably bestowed upon him by Hai Gaon (see Elḥanan's letters in Mann, II, 38–9; *JQR.*, *N. S.*, VIII, 344, where he styles himself as ראש הסדר שלכל ישראל, cp. also Mann I, 38, note 1, and 39–40). A fragment of a letter from the Palestinian congregation of Fusṭāṭ to Elḥanan (Mann II, 341) also gives evidence of the high esteem he was held in locally.

And yet the Gaon Solomon b. Yehudah of Palestine had a poor opinion of him. In a letter to Ephraim b. Shemaryah, the Ḥaber of the Palestinian congregation of Fusṭāṭ, Solomon expresses himself sharply about Elḥanan and evidently also about

[6] Cp. Gaonic Responsa, ed. Harkavy, pp. 2 and 147, *Geonica,* II, 59, *Ginze Ḳedem,* IV, 35, bottom.

his father Shemaryah (Mann, I, 110–11; II, 121, 347–48). The cause of this resentment is only vaguely discernible, but it seems to have had to do with a change of attitude on the part of Elḥanan towards the Palestinian academy. For a time he evidently was a member of this school holding even the title of 'Sixth' with the expectation of advancing to the rank of 'Third.' This is indicated in T.-S. Loan 18, a long strip of paper, concerning a lawsuit, which has the following heading: שמריה אב בית דין שלכל ישראל בירבי אלחנן הראש. אלחנן השושי המעותד לשלישי בירבי.
Whether he ever advanced to the rank of 'Third' is not known, but it is evident that there arose some conflict between him and the Palestinian academy which caused him to sever his connections with this school. For several years after his father's death he went by the Babylonian title of Rosh Hasseder but not by any Palestinian one forsaking even the one already held by him, viz. הששי. In this connection the fragment, published by Kamenetzky (*REJ.*, LV, 49–51) has to be reconsidered. I had occasion to consult it in Heidelberg (listed under Papyri, No. 910) and could establish some different readings.[7] The fragment is evidently the end of a letter the beginning of which is missing. Where it commences there is a reference to an Alluf Judah b. Abraham. Then the writer continues to express his astonishment at Elḥanan b. Shemaryah for writing to the Palestinian Gaon not to make any innovation in the school till he would appoint him (Elḥanan) as Ab (ותמה אני ממר אלחנן בר שמריה כי בא ממנו כתב אל שער הישיבה הגיד בו כי שלח כתב אל מרנו גאון צבי יחי לעד הזהירו לבל יחדש דבר עד אשר יקבנו בשם אבות). Now this passage could be interpreted that Elḥanan asked that he be confirmed in the office of Ab-Bet-Din in Fusṭāṭ held by his father (אב בית דין שלכל ישראל). But in view of the above heading one could argue that Elḥanan had attained the dignity of 'Third' at the Palestinian school and now asked for advancement as Ab. The matter cannot at present be decided for lack of further material. Anyhow Elḥanan was disappointed

[7] L. 1, after שלגולה insert בר אברהם; l. 2, for ראש הסדר more likely בר שמריה; l. 4, for לו r. בו; l. 8, the filling in of the lacuna [בעיבור וקידוש] is certainly not borne out by the marks in the MS, more likely [בדבר זה]; l. 10 ידע is crossed out to be deleted; l. 13, for קרא r. קבע. l. 30, for בטוב טיבו r. ברוב טובו.

in either ambition and his relations with the Palestinian Gaonate were strained.

But interesting and rather strange it is that the writer of the above letter, dated Adar 1021, is evidently a member of Hai's school and yet sides with the Palestinian Gaon against Elḥanan. The epistle is written to some Alluf (probably in Ḳairwān)[8] whom he requests to inform some of his friends of the true situation as he saw it. Elḥanan's unfavorable reputation is known in Aleppo, Damascus, Fusṭāṭ and Palestine. The writer adds a piece of gossip about Elḥanan's stay in Bagdād when Asaf Rosh Hasseder (b. Beṣalel, above, p. 116) visited him and found him to be a superficial student of the Talmud.[9] However this opinion of him is contradicted by the view of Sherira and Hai of his great promise in scholarship (above, pp. 89–90). Of course our letter of 1021 may reflect a later change of attitude towards Elḥanan even within the circle of Hai's school. Only further material will clarify the obscurities concerning the career of our Elḥanan and the likes and dislikes he was subject to in its pursuit.

[8] Poznański (ibid. p. 245) thought this Alluf to have been identical with Yehudah Alluf and Rosh Hasseder b. Joseph of Ḳairwān (see above, p. 115) on the basis of l. 1., but this is now untenable because there the reading is בר אברהם. Moreover this Alluf Yehudah (b. Abraham) was a resident member of the Pumbedita-Bagdād school (אלוף בישיבה שלגולה). But in l. 27, ובקשתי מאלוף האדיר נט̇ להעמיד על הטורים האלה מקצת רעיו, another person is evidently meant. My assumption that the latter lived in Ḳairwān is only based on the reference in l. 11 to Aleppo, Damascus, Fusṭāṭ (צוען) and Palestine where Elḥanan's "deeds are famous" (for their notoriety). Had the recipient of the letter lived himself in Fusṭāṭ, he would not have had to be reminded by the writer of Elḥanan's carryings on there. But any further identification is at present impossible.

[9] L. 25: ובימים מועטים השלימו גירוס מנומר (גירוס מנומר, a patchy, striped study, is apparently another way of saying לא ירד לעמקם של הדברים). Interesting is also the reference to Elḥanan's claim of being entitled to call a public meeting to be addressed by him (l. 13 וגם נם כי ק ב ע פ ר ק) and that a certain Barhūn (=Abraham, perhaps Abraham b. Sahlān) helped him (l. 14–15, וכי ברהון עמד על ראש בהגדה ושבועה). For ושבועה probably read וקדושה, viz. this Abraham assisted him in reciting the Ḳaddish after the sermon (see above, p. 196). Elḥanan further insisted that in all the above mentioned places only he knew how to conduct such meetings and to manage a school (ll. 15–17): כי כל יושבי האדמות ההמה לא ידעו מ נ ה ג ה פ ר ק י ם קל וחומר מנהג הישיבה. The writer is indignant at this conceit of Elḥanan whose knowledge was only superficial.

2.

THE BABYLONIAN GAONATE FROM THE DEATH OF HAI TILL THE CLOSE OF THE 13TH CENTURY AND ITS RELATIONS WITH THE EXILARCHATE

Introduction

The Babylonian Gaonate did not come to an end with the demise of Hai Gaon (in 1038 C. E.) as is the prevalent theory in our history books. This erroneous assumption is all due to Abraham ibn Daud, several of whose incorrect data concerning the so-called Gaonic period have long been taken for granted only finally to be discarded in recent times by the new light which the Genizah finds have shed on the obscurities of this period. And among those discarded notions the view of the end of the Gaonate soon after 1038 is to be singled out here. The Gaonate continued to wield great influence on the Jewries of the Orient extending to Syria and to Egypt and it is therefore entirely erroneous to speak of the end of the so-called Gaonic period with the death of Hai. As regards the Orient it continued down to the end of the 13th century. Only in Spain and in other European countries the rise of centers of learning was bound to result in a diminution of the influence of the Babylonian academies. This process started already in the middle of the 10th century. Sherira and Hai, owing to their own eminent abilities, still had a great reputation in the West, but their successors were overshadowed by the learning of the scholars of Spain and France. Maimonides in Egypt revealed the bias of Hispano-Jewish intellectual superiority against Babylonian learning, as represented in the Bagdād school by the Gaon Samuel b. 'Alī and his disciples, and this disparagement may have ultimately reduced the influence of the Babylonian Gaonate in Egypt and perhaps in Syria (e. g. in Aleppo where Maimonides' disciple Joseph ibn 'Aḳnīn resided). But among the numerous congregations in Babylon, Persia and the adjoining territories, the Gaonate had still a great sustaining power just as the Exilarchate continued to hold its sway. The ultimate decline of both these factors in Oriental Jewry is to be sought in the general political and economic conditions obtaining especially since the Mongol invasion leading down to the overthrow of the 'Abbāsid Caliphate in 1258 C. E. The subsequent events till the exploits of Tamerlane (died 1405) completed the reduction of these countries to shambles and at the same time the ruin also of the local Jewries.[1] Dazzled by the brilliance of the literary productions of Spanish Jewry on the one hand and faced by lack of sufficient data concerning the full life of Oriental Jewry since the 11th century on the other hand, Jewish historiography was apt to depict the decay of the Babylonian Gaonate with the death of Hai as concurrent with a decisive shifting of the spiritual center of Jewry from the East to the West, and Jewish history since then became chiefly a record of the vicissitudes of European Jewry. But as new data are more and more made available a revision of this onesided attitude is necessary. The 11th, 12th and 13th centuries are still a period of considerable intellectual activity in the Orient in the field of Rabbinics, poetry, Biblical exegesis and other branches of Jewish and general learning. And the Bagdād schools still wielded their influence on the Oriental communities in maintaining the tradition of Rabbinic Judaism.

In the time of Hai the two ancient academies, formerly situated in Sura and Pumbedita respectively, continued to function in Bagdād; the latter, over which Hai presided, having been removed to the capital of the Caliphate in 890 whereas the former was reopened there about a century later after having closed its doors in Sura about 45 years before.[1a] We know now that Isaac, Gaon of the Sura-Bagdād school, outlived Hai[2] and we have as yet no definite information that after Isaac's death this school was

[1] Already Samuel b. Ḥofni states in one of his letters that the impoverished condition of Babylonian Jewry made it impossible for them to support the schools (above, p. 157) and the economic condition became worse as time went on.

[1a] About the residence in Bagdād of Ṣemaḥ Ṣedeḳ, the first Gaon of the reopened Sura academy, see above, p. 146, and about the residence there of his successor, Samuel b. Ḥofni, see infra, p. 390.

[2] See the list drawn up by a certain Israel, a member of the Pumbedita-Bagdād school, published by Mann, *JQR, N. S.*, XI, 419.

closed again for ever. As to the Pumbedita-Bagdād school the very fact that the writer of the list referred to speaks of this academy as 'ours' (דילן) even after Hai's death would indicate that it continued to function also after 1038. Indeed Abraham ibn Daud knows of the Gaonate of Hezekiah Exilarch in succession to Hai and he limits his tenure of office to two years. However this figure has been shown to be impossible and the correction to substitute 20 for 2 ('כ for 'ב) has been suggested thus bringing us down to 1058.[3] But even with this correction the statement of Ibn Daud that after Hezekiah's tenure of office as Gaon the schools in Bagdād ceased to function[4] is to be challenged.

Owing to the lack of sufficient data the obscurity surrounding this phase of the history of the Babylonian Gaonate is indeed great. Yet a letter from North-Africa (either from Ḳairwān or al-Mahdiyya) sent to Fusṭāṭ which we present here (infra, pp. 244–48) may throw some light on this obscure problem. Unfortunately it is very damaged and hence the conclusions to be drawn from it are not as certain as we should have liked them to be. The letter certainly dates after 1056 as is evident from the reference to Joseph ibn Nagdela of Granada and his late father Samuel ibn Nagdela (verso, lines 7–8). The latter's demise took place in 1056.[5] Indeed the epistle seems to allude to the troubles in North-Africa which resulted in the plunder of Ḳairwān in 1057.[6] Now shortly before the date of this epistle R. Ḥananel

[3] See for the latest discussion of this point Mann, *Livre d'hommage . . . Poznański*, Hebrew part, 22–23.

[4] ס' סדר הקבלה (ed. Neubauer, *Med. Jew. Chronicles*, I, 67). ואחר חזקיהו ראש ישיבה וראש גלות פסקו ישיבות וגאונים.

[5] Ibn Daud's date (*l. c.*, p. 73) דתתטו should be corrected into דתחטו as Mr. David Sassoon, on the basis of his complete copy of Samuel's Diwān, claims the date 1056 to be the correct one (see his pamphlet *The Newly Discovered Diwan of the Vizier Samuel Hannaghid*, p. 3), though his remarks present some difficulty since Nisan 4815 is not 1056 but 1055. However Samuel was still alive in Tishri 4816 (ibid., p. 15), or in other words in the fall of 1055. Let us hope that the expected edition of this Diwān will clarify this point. Cp. also infra, p. 630, note 1.

[6] About the warfare in North-Africa due to the invasion of Beduin tribes from Egypt see Müller, *Islam im Morgen-u. Abendland*, II, 628–9. Cp. also Poznański, אנשי קירואן, p. 8. His assumption, that after the plunder of Ḳairwān

(b. Ḥushiel) died. During his lifetime he held the title of 'Rosh be-Rabbanan', bestowed upon him by the Babylonian Gaonate, and was in charge of the donations for the schools that used to be collected in North-Africa and all over the Maghreb. After his death R. Nissim (b. Jacob) succeeded him to this title and to the same duties towards the upkeep of the schools.

The corresponding passage in our letter (recto, l. 20, margin and verso, l. 1–5) reads, "I do inform you that there arrived a letter from our master, the head of the school, may God prolong his power (authority), to the people (viz. the Jewish community) of Ḳairwān in condolence for (the demise of) our teacher Ḥananel. Therein he (the Gaon) referred to our teacher Nissim expressing great gratitude to him. He named him Rosh bē-Rabbanan (a title held before by R. Ḥananel) and handed over to him the supervision (over the donations) in the remainder of the Maghreb." The writer goes on to suggest that the Gaon (evidently to be informed accordingly by the representative of the Babylonian school in Fusṭāṭ (פקיד הישיבה) to whom apparently this letter was addressed) ought to write again to the congregation (of Ḳairwān) and express his sympathy for the calamity that befell them, their exile from their district and their homes and the destruction of their synagogue. At the same time the Gaon should urge the collection of the deposits belonging to 'the schools" (in the plural) and a strong Ḥerem should be issued concerning this matter. Evidently owing to the upheaval in consequence of the plunder of Ḳairwān and other cities and the flight of the population certain sums, designated for the upkeep of the schools and deposited with certain people, were being withheld by those to whom they had been entrusted.

Now it could be argued that the title of Rosh bē-Rabbanan,[7]

in Nov. 1057 the Jewish community there ceased to exist, is not borne out by our letter.

[7] This title was held, as far as known, by Ḥushiel b. Elḥanan and his son Elḥanan in Ḳairwān (see Mann, *JQR, N. S.*, IX, 161, XI, 452, and infra, p. 333), and by Ḥananel by inference from the fact that R. Nissim succeeded him to this title. R. Nissim also held the title ראש הסדר (infra, p. 467). In Egypt we have such title-holders in Abraham b. Natan and Isaac b. Samuel Hassephardi and the latter's son Yehoseph (Mann, II, 202 bottom, 228 (בי

held by R. Ḥananel and now given to R. Nissim, was a Palestinian title and hence the Gaon referred to was the head of the Palestinian academy. However the then living Gaon in the Holy Land was Daniel b. 'Azaryah (1051–62) who was a member of the Exilarchic family of Babylon and is always referred to as הנשיא in addition to his official title of ראש ישיבת גאון יעקב.[8] Moreover that the title Rosh bē-Rabbanan was a Babylonian one can be inferred from the fact that Jacob b. 'Alī, the representative of the Bagdād Gaon Samuel b. 'Alī, is also the bearer of it.[9] The assumption is therefore justified that the Gaon, mentioned in our letter written in about 1057 or afterwards, was the head of the Bagdād school. By the same reasoning that he is not also called Exilarch his identity with Hezekiah, who occupied the Gaonate after Hai, has to be rejected. Perhaps this Gaon was none else but מרנא ישראל, the author of the list mentioned before (note 2). Anyhow we have at this time in Bagdād a ראס אלמתיבה maintaining close connections with the Ḳairwān community and with its eminent scholars, the late R. Ḥananel and the still living R. Nissim. The latter, just as his father Jacob, was a great friend of Hai and

רבנן = ראש בי רבנן), 232, bottom, 310, note 2). Abraham b. Natan, who lived at the end of 11th and beginning of 12th centuries, held both titles of ריש בי רבנן וראש הסדר (ibid. 202, bottom) just as R. Nissim in Ḳairwān. As Rosh Hasseder was a title bestowed by the Babylonian schools (see Mann I, 279) so also was Resh bē Rabbanan. The fact that Abraham b. Natan went by these titles testifies also to the continued existence of the school in Bagdād which bestowed them upon him. A corresponding lower title to Resh bē Rabbanan was צורבא מרבנן (see infra, note 9).

[8] See Mann II, 189, bottom, 218, l. 15, 219–21, 362; *Hebrew Union College Annual*, III, 287; infra, p. 234, note 72.

[9] See Mann II, 310, 312, and especially the letter of Samuel b. 'Alī (in Assaf, קובץ של אגרות ר' שמואל בן עלי ובני דורו, Jerusalem 1930, p. 97, l. 9). Previously he has been styled by the same Gaon as צורבא מרבנן in addition to his function as Dayyān (ibid., p. 39, l. 17; p. 43, l. 16; p. 45, l. 20). Both titles clearly were Babylonian titles as Jacob b. 'Alī was Samuel b. 'Alī's disciple and travelled about in 'Irāḳ and Persia on behalf of the Bagdād school. The title צורבא מרבנן was evidently lower than ראש בי רבנן. And yet the famous Nagid of Egypt Meborakh held the former title and likewise his grandfather and namesake (see Mann II, 100, bottom, 257), and curiously enough also Maimonides is styled so (ibid. I, 222, note 2, l. 16). Also a Samuel ראש בי רבנן in Bagdād is mentioned by El'azar Habbabli (infra, p. 282, l. 32).

he continued in his loyalty towards the Pumbedita-Bagdād school even after the great Gaon's death. In 1057 he must have been already of an advanced age and we are uninformed about the length of his life subsequently. The reference to the 'schools' (ישיבות), the donations for which were entrusted to R. Nissim, would indicate that both the Sura and Pumbedita academies still functioned then in Bagdād.

Unfortunately we hear nothing more of Israel who may have been the Gaon of the Pumbedita-Bagdād school at this time. In about 1070 we have a Spanish scholar, Isaac b. Moses, as head of this academy, according to Ibn Daud who however adds hardly any information as to his activities.[10] In 1090 we have another reference to "the scholars of Sura and Pumbedita," viz. the members of the two schools situated in Bagdād.[11] Meager information indeed, but enough to justify the conclusion of the continuance of the Bagdād seats of learning throughout the 11th

[10] ס' סדר הקבלה, *l. c.*, 75, where something is missing (see Poznański, *REJ*, LXV, 314): וכך היה מכונה אלחבר ר' יצחק בר' משה הידוע בן סכרי מן קהל דיניאה (Denia) כי פעמים נקרא חבר ופעמים נקרא רב ולא היה חבר לאלו ולא עצר כח בימיהם והלך מדיניאה לארץ מזרח ונקרא שם גאון והושב על כסא רב האיי ז"ל. Ibn Daud adds caustically: ולפי דרכנו למדנו שלא נשאר שם ושאר לתלמוד בכל ארץ שנער, a remark that should be taken with caution as it seems to have been the tendency in Spain to overrate the local Jewish scholarship at the expense of that of the Orient. Spanish Jewry gloried in the fact that it became self-supporting intellectually and especially independent of the center in Babylon, an attitude that seems to have grown up in the times of Ḥisdai ibn Shaprūṭ (see above, p. 111 f.). There was a political motive then behind this attitude in the glorious times of the caliphates of Abderraḥmān and his son Ḥakam who, as 'Omayyads, cordially hated the 'Abbāsids who lorded in the Orient. Thus there is the interesting report of Ibn 'Uṣaibia about Ḥisdai procuring books for the Andalusian Jews so as to make them independent of "the legal decisions of the Jews of Bagdād" (viz. of the Geonim and their schools, see Mann, *JQR., N. S.*, IX, 169, note 163). This claim of intellectual superiority of Spanish Jewry was widely spread. Maimonides too brought with him to Egypt this consciousness and thus thought very little of the learning cultivated in the Bagdād school and in other Oriental cities.

About the claim of Spanish Jewry excelling in poetry over the rest of the Diaspora, see infra, p. 263 f.

[11] Ebyatar Hakkohen in about 1090 speaks of חכמי התורה . . . [מחס]יה ופום בדיתא and also mentions Hezekiah the Exilarch concerning whom anon (Mann, II, 228). The date of about 1090 is justified from the reference in this letter to the death of a certain person in Tebeṭ 1401 Sel. (=December 1089 C. E.).

century. Whether these two schools continued to function separately or there was a merger at some date in the 11th century, is a matter of speculation till more data are brought to light (but see infra, pp. 212, 217). The Bagdād Gaonate emerges in the 12th century, after the obscurity that surrounds it in the 11th since Hai's demise in 1038, as a strong factor in the life of Oriental Jewry continuing till the end of the 13th century.

The Exilarchate in Bagdād, too, continued to function throughout the 11th century again emerging in the 12th as a force frequently competing with the Gaonate. Hezekiah, of the family of David b. Zakkai, functioned as Exilarch already in 1021 and was in office quite a considerable time. There is reason to believe that he was succeeded by his son David who in his turn had a successor in Hezekiah II (mentioned in about 1090), probably David's son.[12] Then comes an Exilarch David II, probably the son of Hezekiah II, already in the first half of the 12th century, succeeded by his son Ḥisdai and by his grandson Daniel about both of whom we have more information from the travel accounts of Benjamin of Tudela and Petaḥyah of Ratisbon and from other sources.[13] The relations between the Exilarchate and the Gaonate

[12] For the latest discussion see Mann, *Livre d'hommage . . . Poznański*, Hebrew part, 21–23.

[13] The hitherto missing link between Hezekiah II and Ḥisdai can now be supplied from the fragment, published by Assaf (גנזי קדם, IV, 63–64), containing a sort of a formula of a proclamation by the Exilarch. It began with verses in honor of the royal family of David and then continued with the summons to listen to the behest of the Exilarch (שמעו מאי דסברה ואציתו למאי דאמרה מרותא בר מרותא ריש גלותה בר ריש גלותא רבא דעמיה וכו'). The nature of the proclamation is not known because of the defectiveness of the fragment. The Exilarch in question is Ḥisdai, styled after many complimentary appellations, הנשיא הגדול ראש גליות כל ישראל b. David הנשיא הגדול ראש ג' כ' י'. This introductory phrase שמעו מאי דסברה וכו' was used in the Babylonian schools in connection with the sermons or discourses of the Geonim and other members of the school, as Assaf has rightly pointed out (p. 63, and קובץ של אגרות שמואל בן עלי, p. 10). Hence in the Fusṭāṭ *Babylonian* congregation, where Sahlān b. Abraham was Rabbi holding also the title *Alluf from the Babylonian school*, the Ḥazzān would call the assembly to attention before Sahlān's sermon with the phrase: שמעו מאי סברה רבינו סגן הישיבה ריש כלה החבר למימר קדם בְּחַאֲיֵי וצִיבוּרֵי (see Mann, II, 104, top).

However in our case it need not be the Exilarch's installation sermon (as Assaf thinks) but an important proclamation by the then reigning Exilarch

in the 11th century are obscure. The action of Hezekiah I in occupying both offices after Hai's death in 1038 must have certainly called forth a great deal of friction. It was the first time in the history of the Babylonian Gaonate that such a situation existed. How long Hezekiah managed to be both Exilarch and Gaon[14] is unknown. Who knows whether the denunciation to the authorities from which he suffered, according to Ibn Daud's report, had not something to do with the concentration of so much power in one person. It meant subordinating the school completely to the will of the Exilarch; there must have been dissatisfaction on the part of the leading members of the school and some influential Jewish grandees in Bagdād probably sided with them against the Exilarch. Such intervention happened before, e. g., in the affairs of 'Uḳba with Kohen Ṣedeḳ and of David b. Zakkai with Sa'adyah. Hezekiah I must have been a man of some Rabbinic learning[15] to be able to aspire to the dignity of president of the school, especially after a man of the calibre of Hai, but still more must he have been a powerful figure to be able to attain his ambition. In the latter respect he was a true descendant of the powerful David b. Zakkai.

Ḥisdai b. David. But the fact that the phrase is Babylonian makes it evident that we deal here with a Babylonian Exilarch and hence the identification with Ḥisdai, the Bagdād Exilarch mentioned by Benjamin of Tudela, is most likely. His father David was also a full-fledged Exilarch as the numerous titles testify. Also the chronology fits in as well as the genealogy, viz. Hezekiah I—David I,—Hezekiah II—David II and then Ḥisdai followed by his son Daniel.

[14] In reality he is never mentioned by the title of Gaon but only by that of Exilarch. Cp. his responsum (cited by Judah b. Barzillai in his ס' השטרות, ed. Halberstam, p. 87, cp. also Pozn., *Babyl. Geon.*, p. 1): לאחר שנפטר רבי' האיי גאון זצ"ל לבית עולמו בגן עדן נשאל חזקיהו נ ש י א י ש ר א ל בהלכה זו וכו'. Also his letter, following immediately the one of Ab 1040 (above, p. 183), begins with the heading מן יחזקיהו ראש גליות כל ישראל just as in the epistle of Nisan 1021 when Hai was still alive (*RÉJ*, LV, 54). As we have only the information of Ibn Daud that he succeeded Hai (ס' סדר הקבלה, *l. c.*, 67: אבל בני ישיבת רב האיי הקימו חזקיהו ר"ג . . . והושיבוהו על כסא רב האיי ז"ל) and in view of Ibn Daud's proven unreliability about the history of the Gaonate, we should be inclined to be skeptical even about this item till we have more certain data. In the case of Daniel b. 'Azaryah, who was actually Gaon of Palestine, the appellation נשיא וגאון is employed so frequently (see note 8).

[15] Cp. the responsum cited in note 14.

After some time the Gaonate again became separated from the person of the Exilarch. Unfortunately we have no information whatever about the course of events and have only been able to infer from the letter discussed above that in about 1057 the Gaon of Bagdād was not identical with the Exilarch. When we come to the 12th century we know more of both Gaonate and Exilarchate and their mutual relationship. Since 1914, when Poznański dealt with this phase of our history in his *Babylonische Geonim im nachgaonäischen Zeitalter*, the most valuable addition of new material has been presented recently by S. Assaf.[16] However, Assaf's conclusions need rectification on several points, and altogether he has not endeavored to reconstruct the larger aspect of the problem. On the basis of some additional material from El'azar Habbabli's Diwān[17] we shall discuss first the chronology of the Bagdād Gaonate in the 12th and 13th centuries and then the relations between the Gaonate and the Exilarchate. In this connection some remarks will be added about the Gaonates in Damascus and in Fusṭāṭ.

I.

The Chronology of the Bagdād Gaonate (12–13th Centuries)

An Abraham Gaon, eulogized in a poem by Isaac b. Abraham ibn Ezra, whom Poznański (*l. c.*, p. 11) placed as the first of the Bagdād Geonim in the 12th century, should be definitely removed from this group. Already in my *Jews in Egypt* (I, 224) I suggested the identity of this Abraham with the Gaon Abraham b. Mazhīr whom I then placed as successor to Maṣliaḥ Hakkohen as Gaon of Egypt. He now turns out to have been really Gaon in Damascus (see infra, p. 250). But that Isaac b. Abraham ibn Ezra wrote his poem for Abraham b. Mazhīr I was able to convince myself when in the spring of 1927, while in Cairo, I was able for a brief

[16] קובץ של אגרות ר׳ שמואל בן עלי ובני דורו, Jerusalem 1930 (reprint from תרביץ I, Nos. 1–3).

[17] Cp. the extracts given infra, p. 569 ff.

while to consult Isaac's Diwān in the possession of Mr. Ezra Silvera (formerly of Aleppo).[18] Isaac b. Abraham ibn Ezra on his way to Bagdād, where we find him in 1143, naturally touched Damascus and there he became acquainted with the local Gaon Abraham b. Mazhīr.

1. The first Gaon of Bagdād in the period under discussion was *'Alī Hallevi I*, the father of Samuel b. 'Alī. As to the data discussed by Pozn. (*l. c.*, 12–15) it should be remarked that the affair of David Alroy and his Messianic movement should be placed at the time of the Second Crusade (1146–47).[19] Prior to this movement David Alroy studied in Bagdād under the Exilarch Ḥisdai and under 'Alī, styled by Benjamin of Tudela ראש הישיבה גאון יעקב. 'Alī's reputation as a scholar must have been considerable because the leading scholars of Aleppo, including the prominent R. Barukh b. Isaac, sent their legal questions to him.[20] The fact that R. Barukh corresponded with 'Alī indicates that the latter's activity as Gaon should be placed earlier in the first half of the 12th century than hitherto assumed. R. Barukh functioned in Aleppo already in 1083 and we can trace him till some time after 1119 when 'Obadyah the Proselyte decided to leave Aleppo for other Jewish communities and obtained a letter of introduction from R. Barukh.[21] In view of this length of service R. Barukh's

[18] When will this unique and important Diwān be made accessible? It has been in private possession already for about 30 years and the owner does neither edit it himself nor let others copy it. About the few specimens of Isaac's poetry, see Harkavy, חדשים גם ישנים, No. 7, pp. 47–50; Brody *Z.f. H.B.*, III, 124–26; Brody-Albrecht, שער השיר, pp. 159–62; Brody-Wiener, מבחר השירה העברית, 209–10.

[19] For the latest discussion of this Messianic movement see Mann, התקופה, XXIV, 341–49; cp. also *RÉJ*, LXXXIX, 257–58.

[20] Thus his son Samuel b. 'Alī informs us in a letter of his, dated Tammuz 1191 (in Assaf, *l. c.*, 48, ll. 21–22): ואגרות החכמים הגדולים אשר היו ביניכם ושאלותיהם היו באות לפני אדונינו אבינו עלי ראש הישיבה זצ"ל כגון רבנו ברוך זצ"ל ורבנא יוסף ורבנא שת וזולתם שאגרותיהם ושאלותיהם מצויות באוצרנו. About Barukh b. Isaac, the leading Rabbi in Aleppo, see Mann התקופה, *l. c.* 352–4, and infra, p. 392. We find him there already in 1083. J. N. Epstein's attempt (תרביץ I, No. 4, 27ff.) at identifying this Barukh with the Talmud commentator Barukh b. Samuel of southern Italy (מארץ יון) is not to be considered as successful. But the matter cannot be discussed here at length.

[21] See especially Mann, *RÉJ*, LXXXIX, p. 247ff.

span of life hardly extended, say, beyond 1130 C. E. Of 'Alī's genealogy and life story we have no information whatever. Whom he succeeded as Gaon of apparently the Pumbedita-Bagdād school is also unknown. Between him and Isaac b. Moses of Denia (in about 1070) there certainly was one occupant (and perhaps more) of the presidency of the school. Whether the Sura-Bagdād school functioned in 'Alī's time is not stated, but it is significant that in Benjamin of Tudela's account of the affair of David Alroy it is related that the Sultan of Persia requested the Caliph of Bagdād to order the Exilarch and *the heads* of the schools (לדבר עם ראש הגולה ועם ראשי הישיבות) to induce David Alroy to put a stop to his Messianic movement (as Pozn., *l. c.*, 14–15 has rightly pointed out). Should we thus assume that there were then two Geonim of both schools in office? Poznański speaks in a general way of 'other schools' in Bagdād (see infra, p. 215 ff.) but 'the heads of the schools' called in by the Caliph together with the Exilarch in an official capacity naturally can only be the Geonim of these two schools. However the names of the Sura Geonim of that period are entirely unknown and until more material is available their whole existence must remain problematic (see also infra, p. 217).

2. 'Alī's successor was *Solomon* whom we find in office in Adar 1152[22]. In a letter to some Oriental community a case of disobedience to the Gaon and his school is sternly suppressed. A certain Aaron b. Merayot started the disobedience and was joined by Kahlāf the teacher (his full name being Shealtiel

[22] See his long letter in Assaf, *l. c.*, 78–82. I had occasion to consult this MS. in Leningrad, and there are a number of corrections to be made in Assaf's text. (Cp. also the corrections in תרביץ, I, No. 4, 146–47). P. 80, l. 23, the MS. actually reads אובל (as Epstein rightly emended); l. 24, for מחבל r. מסבל; verso, l. 8, for ו . . r. שמו; p. 81, l. 16, for נפשו r. נפשנו; l. 26, for ובמענו r. וכמעט; l. 28, for [וראוי לאנשי] r. [וחדשנו אתו]; l. 29, for להרצות r. להרדות and for עמנו r. עמו; l. 30, for ולחקור r. ולחתוך; p. 82, top, for לה [ונדב[ה r. ונדב[ת הקה]לה; fol. 26a, l. 1, for ע. . . r. בצע and for במרוצה לעלות אלינו וכו' r. באמונה לשלוח אלינו דבר שנה בשנה; l. 6, for 'מ נא . . . א r. אבומר נֿעֿ (viz. Abū 'Alī's father was Abumar, both Shoḥeṭim); l. 11 for ויטמננו r. וישאננו (from שאנן). In the next item (No. 28), also by Solomon Gaon, in the heading for בעיֿץ יכתא r. בעֿץ כתֿא (=כתאב). The end reads in the MS. והנשאר פרסי, viz. the remainder of Solomon's letter was in Persian and hence not reproduced by the copyist of the MS.

Khalāf המלמד (=al-Mu'allim) b. David המלמד) in the capacity of Ḥazzān and secretary. The ban was imposed upon both of them. The Gaon's representative in this district was Daniel holding the title Alluf from the academy. Now Khalāf is willing to submit again to the ruling of the Gaon and the ban is lifted from him on condition that he accepts the ruling of this Daniel Alluf. When this Khalāf visits the smaller communities to decide their lawsuits, he has to be mindful of the dues of the academy and to forward faithfully year by year the amount collected to the Gaon. This Khalāf is also permitted to supervise the ritual slaughtering and to install as Shoḥeṭ Abū 'Alī who succeeds his father Abumar. This letter illustrates the authority of the school over the congregations and also their organization as regulated by the school. Certain dues and donations went to the academy. Then there was a graduate of the school with the title Alluf who was Ab-Bet-Din of the district. Certain dues for lawsuits went to this scholar and his court.[23] In addition there were smaller officials, like Khalāf the teacher, entitled to decide lawsuits in outlying districts, to issue legal documents and to supervise the Sheḥiṭah, but all this under the authority of the Ab-Bet-Din of the district, Daniel Alluf in our case, and through him under the supreme authority of the Gaon and his academy.[24] This letter thus well supplements our information of the communal organization in Babylon and surrounding countries under the Gaonate as known for example from the account of Natan Habbabli.[25]

The beginning of another letter by Solomon, sent in condolence to a certain al-Ṣafī (pure, true friend) in Hamadān (Persia) has also been preserved (Assaf, *l. c.*, 82–3), but the substance of the epistle being in Persian, it was not incorporated by the copyist. Nothing further is known of the life and activities of this Gaon

[23] P. 81, bottom: ואל ישכח (היינו: כלף) את בריתו כל ימי חייו לשמור את חוק בית דין ואת האבידין (=ה א ב ב י ת ד י ן) מדי חדש בחדש ושבת בשבתו . . . ולכתוב מעשה בית דין אחרי קחת חוקיהם הקצובים לבית דין. The Ab-Bet-Din is Daniel Alluf.

[24] P. 82, l. 2ff.: שלא לצעוד על מדרגת ההוראה לחרוץ אסור ומותר חייב וזכאי כי אם על ודאי שאין בו ספק אשר למדו מפי תלמידנו דניאל אלוף המעתיק שמועה מפינו . . . ובקימו התנאים האלה (היינו: כלף) נתנו לו (היינו: לכלף) רשות לעשות פשרות בין העם וכו'. Assaf (p. 18) erroneously refers the last sentence to Daniel Alluf.

[25] See Mann, *JQR*, *N. S.*, X, 337–40.

Solomon. He is not the son of a Samuel, as Assaf (*l. c.*, p. 59 and cp. p. 5) thinks, because the MS. there reads ע ז ר י ה . . . ביר׳ שמואל and not שלמה b. Samuel! This 'Azaryah, who was Samuel b. 'Alī's son-in-law, will be discussed later on. The length of tenure of office of Solomon as Gaon is unknown. Under him served Samuel b. 'Alī who received from him his ordination and was designated to occupy the Gaonate held by his father 'Alī prior to Solomon's regime.[26]

3. The best known and evidently most eminent of the Bagdād Geonim was *Samuel b. 'Alī (I)*. The family name seems to have been Ibn al-Dastūr.[27] His activities have been described in detail by Poznański, *l. c.*, 15–36, 54–61, and additional material has been given by Mann (הצופה לחכמת ישראל, VI, 104 ff., *H. U. C. Annual*, III, 295, note 137) and now especially by Assaf (*l. c.* 37–57, 67–70, 72–74, 84–97).[28] We find Samuel in office in the fall of 1164. The last available letter of his is dated Tishri (1)505 Sel. = autumn 1193 (Assaf, *l. c.*, 89, top) whereas in Adar II of the same Sel. year (= March 1194) already his son-in-law Zekharyah b. Berakhel heads the school (Assaf, *l. c.*, 76 and 78). Hence Samuel's demise took place between these two dates. Samuel reveals himself in these letters as an energetic champion of the needs of the school keeping up an extensive correspondence with the congregations in Babylon and Persia on the one hand and with those of Syria on the other. His influence reached also to Egypt as the fragments found in the Fusṭāṭ Genizah testify. When the needs of the school were pressing, prominent members of the school would be sent out to visit the various communities to exhort the people to be generous towards the seat of learning.

[26] Samuel b. 'Alī in his letter of Adar I, 1191, states (Assaf, *l. c.*, p. 69, ll. 22ff.): ומפני זה [באנו] להודיעכם כי מיום שבתנו בישיבה. ומעת עלות גורלנו להתיצב ב[ראש מושב] מני ים רחבה. ב ס מ י כ ת מרנו ורבנו גאוננו שלמה ראש ישיבת גאון יע[קב ו]זולתו מן הראשים וכו׳; Job 11.9 is taken in 'Erubin 21a to refer to the Torah (cp. Mann, *JQR*, *N. S.*, IX, 159, l. 5, and XI, 450, bottom). About the question of Semikhah see infra, p. 229 ff.

[27] About this name see Mann, II, 140, note 5.

[28] There are many corrections to be made in the texts as edited by Assaf. Some of them will be given infra. Cp. also the corrections in תרביץ, I, No. 4, 146–7.

Such a representative was Jacob the Dayyān (styled צורבא מרבנן and later on ראש בי רבנן) b. 'Alī who travelled about in Persia in the years 1185–86 (ibid., pp. 39, 40, 41, 43, 45, 97). Jacob ultimately seems to have settled in Fusṭāṭ where his son Joseph Rosh Hasseder composed (in 1211) a commentary on the Hafṭarot (chiefly a compilation from earlier exegetes) and essayed other literary tasks also of a mere second hand nature.[29]

About the organization of the school under Samuel b. 'Alī confusion seems to have been created by Benjamin of Tudela in speaking of 10 academies in Bagdād.[30] Evidently as an outsider he mistook the functions assigned to the ten leading members of the school (including the Gaon) to be identical with activities of separate Yeshibot. Samuel b. 'Alī always speaks of "the school" in the singular and in extending greetings to his correspondents he frequently associates with himself his brother Ḥananyah, styled סגן הישיבה, who, according to Benjamin, was supposed to have been the head of the second Yeshibah.[31] We know now that in

[29] About this Joseph Rosh Hasseder b. Jacob (b. 'Alī) cp. Mann, II, 310–313, *H. U. C. Annual*, III, 297–8; Ginzberg, גנזי שעכטער, II, 403–14.

Jacob is also mentioned in Or. 5536 (see Margol., *Catal.*, III, 560, col. 2) which contains letters and decisions by Samuel b. 'Alī (marked ט' and י' of the corresponding collections of items emanating from the Bet-Din of the school, משער הישיבה יכון סלה). A certain student, 'Ezra b. Menasse the Ḥazzān, had slandered Jacob whereupon the Bet-Din of the school decided to expel the culprit from the college. The date of number 8, of which only the end is preserved, is given: מן סנה כ̇מס וסב̇עין [וארב]ע מאיה̈ (Sel. = 1164 C. E.; Margoliouth's date A. H. 575 = 1179–80 is incorrect). Then we have item 9: ט'. משער הישיבה יכון סלה. אנהי אלי בית דין הגדול שלישיבה יכון סלה א[ן] אלתלמיד עזרא בן אלחזאן מנשה .סי אלארב . . . ק תלמידנו נכבדנו החכם הנבון מ̇ו̇ר יעקב [ה]דיין [צורב]א מרבנן . . . פאסתחק עזרא אלמד̇כור בפעלתה הד̇ה לאבעאד משער הישיבה . . . ואללה תעאלי ישוב לב עוברי על ר[צו]נו לעשות רצונו ושלום על כל ישראל. הא̇ לנו א̇ למושעות (Ps. 68.21) .אבתצ"ב (=אמן במהרה תבנה ציון בימינו). But more likely read אב תצ"ב and hence the date of this affair is Ab (1)492 Sel. = 1181 C. E. which fits in very well with the chronology of our Jacob b. 'Alī.

The expelled student appealed again to the school for re-admission but was not successful. Item 10 begins: י'. משער הישיבה יכון סלה. קד חבררת מכאתבאת אלתלמיד עזרא בן המלמד מ̇ מנשה נ̇ע וכו'.

[30] *Itinerary*, ed. Adler, 38–39; cp. Pozn., *l. c.*, 15ff., who accepts Benjamin's account without much criticism (see p. 19).

[31] The title סגן הישיבה of Samuel's brother, Ḥananyah (Assaf, pp. 37, 42, 47, 50, 68, 85, 95, and also in הצופה לחכמת ישראל, VI, 108, where I wrongly sur-

addition to the סגן הישיבה there was also an Ab-Bet-Din under Samuel b. ʻAlī, viz. Zekharyah b. Berakhel, his son-in-law.[32] Hence we have 10 leading members of the school excluding the Gaon, and this number corresponds to that given by Natan the Babylonian, viz. 7 Allufim, the heads of the rows, and the 3 Ḥaberim, who seem to have formed the Bet-Din of the school and hence the Ab-Bet-Din was one of them.[33] Thus we find in the time of Benjamin of Tudela's visit to Bagdād (12th century) the same number of the leading figures of the school as in the time of Natan Habbabli (10th century). Only these ten scholars next to the Gaon have now different titles. The title Alluf (=Resh Kallah) was given so frequently to people outside the school that it no longer befitted the resident leading members.[34] The formerly leading Alluf, head of the first row, seems now to be called סגן הישיבה. Other titles mentioned by Benjamin are יסוד הישיבה (held by Daniel, probably b. Elʻazar who later became סגן הישיבה and finally Gaon),[35] Ḥaber (a reminiscence of the 3 Ḥaberim in Natan Habbabli's time), Rosh Hasseder, סוד הישיבה, פאר החברים and בעל הסיום.[36] Some of these titles we know from the times of Samuel

mised (note 5) that Daniel סגן הישיבה was meant), has become corrupted in Benjamin's Itinerary as סגן הלוים.

The title סגן הישיבה was also held by Daniel, probably b. Elʻazar b. Hibat Allah, after Samuel's death (Pozn., *l. c.*, 65, 69, 70). He may have been the third in rank (יסוד הישיבה) mentioned by Benjamin of Tudela.

A Rabba סגן הישיבה is mentioned by Elʻazar Habbabli in the time of the Bagdād Gaon Isaac b. Shuwwaikh (Pozn., *l. c.*, 45 and 61). The son of the Gaon ʻAlī (II), Zekharyah, is also styled so (Pozn., *l. c.*, 72).

[32] As rightly pointed out by Assaf (*l. c.*, p. 12). For a Samuel Ab-Bet-Din, see Selections from Elʻazar Habbabli's Diwān (infra, p. 278).

[33] Cp. Mann I, 273.

[34] The list of Allufim given by Pozn., ענינים שונים הנוגעים לתקופת הגאונים, 50ff., can now be considerably increased. Indeed it seems that the honorary degree of Alluf, given to scholars and benefactors who never studied in the Babylonian academies, was also given to a graduate who qualified as Dayyān and held an important communal position, this title corresponding to the title Ḥaber (החבר בסנהדרין גדולה) of the graduates of the Palestinian school.

[35] See note 31.

[36] About several of these titles see Mann I, 277–279. The function of בעל הסיום reminds one of רבנן דסיומי of the earlier period (cp. Lewin, אוצר הגאונים I, p. 128).

b. Ḥofni and Hai and hence the development of the change in the appellation of the leading members of the school is to be traced already to the beginning of the 11th century. In Samuel b. ʿAlī's time (as no doubt also before) they had certain duties of teaching groups of students and hence Benjamin of Tudela, as a visitor from Spain and unfamiliar with the internal organization of the academy, conceived the idea of 10 Yeshibot whereas in reality there was one central college (called by Benjamin himself הישיבה הגדולה) under the presidency of Samuel b. ʿAlī who alone held the official title of ראש הישיבה and Gaon. It was necessary to expatiate on this point in order to remove the confusion which Benjamin's account has wrought.

Now Samuel b. ʿAlī presided over the school that was formerly the Pumbedita academy transferred to Bagdād in 890. What about the Sura school reopened in Bagdād under Ṣemaḥ Ṣedeḳ (after 987)? We have been able to trace the two schools throughout the 11th century and also in 1146–7 during the Messianic agitation of David Alroy (above, pp. 207, 212). Now the Gaon Zekharyah b. Berakhel in his letter of Adar II, (1)505 Sel. (1194 C. E.) actually speaks of *"the gates of both academies,"*[37] which can only refer to those going by the name of Sura and Pumbedita.[38] We have thus to assume the existence of both academies right down to the end of the 12th century and even beyond, and that both were headed by Geonim. Only thus can we explain the appearance of a Gaon ʿAzaryah b. Samuel in the lifetime of Samue b. ʿAlī who was ʿAzaryah's father-in-law.

Elʿazar Habbabli in his Diwān mentions twice this ʿAzaryah as Gaon in elegies composed on the death of the daughter of Samuel b. ʿAlī. When this lady died her father Samuel was no longer alive nor ʿAzaryah, evidently her husband.[39] Pozn. (*l. c.*,

[37] Assaf, *l. c.*, 75, ll. 18–19: ועתה בבואנו אל מחוז חפצנו קבענו פ ר ק ב ע צ ר ה (so in MS. and not בעזרה as Assaf prints; about this phrase see above, p. 84, note 66). וברכנום ברכה אדורה. ערוכה בכל ושמורה. זאת להם תמיד מ ש ע ר י (so in MS.) ש ת י ה י ש י ב ו ת.

[38] The phrase שתי ישיבות occurs so frequently in the Gaonic Responsa. We hear also of an Alluf of both schools (אלוף שתי ישיבות, Mann, I, 167, II, 193, top).

[39] Pozn., *l. c.*, 65, ll. 37ff.: עד לקחה (היינו: התמותה) את חמודו נַחֲתָנוֹ ותלמידו... ראש הישיבה עזריהו גאון יעקב וכו'; p. 66, l. 39ff.: וגם לקחה גאון יעקב עזריה אשר כל דברות

35–6), not being able to fit in this 'Azaryah in his chronology of the Bagdād Geonim, begs the question by suggesting that he was designated to succeed Samuel b. 'Alī but he died in his lifetime and hence El'azar Habbabli in a complimentary manner styled him Gaon. Assaf (*l. c.*, p. 7–8) on the other hand is ready to substitute for עזריה as a copyist's mistake the name זכריה, viz. Zekharyah who too was Samuel's son-in-law and from whom we have actually letters with the heading of Gaon. But so we have a long letter from 'Azaryah in the very collection published by Assaf (*l. c.*, 59–66) which he erroneously attributed to Solomon the predecessor of Samuel b. 'Alī (see above, p. 214). I had occasion to consult this MS. while in Leningrad (May 1927) and read therein twice עזריה instead of שלמה.[40] 'Azaryah had the misfortune of losing his only son, Samuel, a young man of 20 giving promise by his learning of succeeding his father.[41] Thus we have an 'Azaryah b. Samuel who actually was Gaon and cannot be fitted in the chronology unless we assume that he was the Gaon of the formerly Sura-Bagdād school as a contemporary of Samuel b. 'Alī. The contacts between the two Geonim must have been cordial owing to their relationship as father-in-law and son-in-

פיהו חמודות וכו'. The phraseology shows that he died after Samuel (see infra, note 42). However he was Gaon still in Samuel's life time.

[40] The copyist's heading reads (p. 59): נסכ֗ה כתאב כתבה מרנו [ורבנו אדוננו וגאוננו] עזריה ראש הישיבה שלגולה ביר֗ שמואל הרב הגדול זצ"ל וכו'. The letter itself begins with the superscription: עזריה ראש הישיבה שלגולה ביר֗ שמואל הרב הגדול זצ"ל. While the designation ישיבת גאון יעקב was applied equally to both schools, the term ישיבה שלגולה was originally used only as regards Pumbedita on the basis of the statement in R. H. 23b top where גולה is identified with Pumbedita (cp. also Sherira's Letter, ed. Lewin, 82, and the anonymous account concerning the superiority of Sura over Pumbedita, (אלה המעלות in Neub., *Med. Jew. Chr.*, II, 77): הלך רבה בר נחמני ועשה ישיבה בפומבדיתא . . . והיתה י ש י ב ת ג ו ל ה). Thus Sherira and Hai and their ancestors are called ראש ישיבה שלגולה (see e. g. Gaonic Responsa, ed. Harkavy, p. 215). However in course of time, and especially in the 12th century, with both schools removed from their original localities already for ages (890 in the case of Pumbedita and after 987 in the case of Sura), the designation ישיבת גולה stood alike for both schools as against the Palestinian school (ישיבת ארץ הצבי) which even in the 12th century continued to exist in Damascus. Cp. the letter of Samuel b. 'Alī to Damascus (Assaf, p. 67, l. 19): אשר לישיבת ארץ הצבי נחולים ועל פי ישיבת הגולה מתנהלים.

[41] Assaf, *l. c.*, p. 60, ll. 8–9: שמואל אשר גדל בישראל לעטות הדרנו. לרשת מ צ ב נ ו (so in MS.) ו מ ש ר ת נ ו.

law. There was established a modus vivendi as regards the income from the communities and from the donations. We have here a parallel to the situation at the end of the 10th century when Hai married Samuel b. Ḥofni's daughter and peace was established between the Sura and Pumbedita schools as regards the assignment of the donations (see above, p. 148). In learning Samuel b. Alī was no doubt superior and he became famous as the exponent of the Babylonian Rabbinic lore in the 12th century whereas the presidents of the other existing school were almost forgotten by posterity just as several of the Geonim of Samuel's school before and after him have only in recent times been rescued from oblivion. The rivalry between the Gaonate and the Exilarchate during Samuel's regime will be discussed infra (p. 229 ff.).

4. After the death of Samuel b. 'Alī between Tishri 1193 and Adar II, 1194, another son-in-law of his succeeded him to the presidency of the Pumbedita-Bagdād school viz. *Zekharyah b. Berakhel.*[42] He was a native of Aleppo and was known there for

[42] The point of Samuel having 2 sons-in-law is complicated by the statement of Petaḥyah of Ratisbon that the Gaon had only one daughter who knew Bible and Talmud and would even lecture to the students on Bible through a latticed window (סבוב, ed. Grünhut, p. 10; cp. Pozn., *l. c.*, 35–36, and Assaf, *l. c.*, 7–8). But there is really no difficulty if we assume that Petaḥyah refers to Samuel's unmarried daughter who later on became the wife of Zekharyah b. Berakhel of Aleppo. As a young learned girl in her father's home she became famous for her knowledge and actually helped her father in instructing the younger students in Bible (והיא מלמדת הקרייה (=מקרא) לבחורים והיא סגורה בבניין דרך חלון אחד והתלמידים בחוץ למטה ואינם רואין אותה). Petaḥyah mentions her activity as an item of curiosity. But as for the other daughter, married to 'Azaryah b. Samuel and living elsewhere in Bagdād, Petaḥyah had no reason to mention her in his altogether sketchy and far from complete travel account.

The 3 elegies of El'azar Habbabli on the daughter of Samuel b. 'Alī (Pozn., *l. c.*, 62–64, 64–66) are too vague to indicate whether the first or the second daughter are meant. It was his custom to enumerate on such an occasion the dead members of the family concerned. If the departed lady was the wife of 'Azaryah, we ought to have expected on p. 65, ll. 37–8, a reference to him as her husband but no conclusive argument can be deduced from this fact owing to the exigencies of the metre. Thus she may have well been 'Azaryah's wife. However Poznański's deduction (36, top) from l. 11 of p. 65 that she died on the same day as Samuel is altogether unwarranted. The poet in a general manner depicts the misdeeds of Death causing sometimes the demise of father and *son* on the same day as against the Biblical prohibition of killing even an animal

his scholarship and would send legal questions to Samuel b. ʿAlī who had a high opinion of him. The Gaon seems to have invited him to Bagdād, a match with his daughter ensued and he was made Ab-Bet-Din of the school designated to succeed later on to the Gaonate. Three important letters concerning him we have from the Gaon, one of Adar I, (1)502 Sel. (1191) sent to the Gaon and the school of Damascus (Assaf, *l. c.*, 67–70),[43] another of Sivan of the same year in the form of a circular letter to several congregations in Upper Mesopotamia and Syria[44] and a third of Tammuz of the same year to Aleppo, the home town of Zekharyah.[45] The latter two epistles were for the occasion of a pastoral tour undertaken by Zekharyah to these districts to collect donations for the school.

and its offspring on the same day (Lev. 22.27): מנע אלהים זבוח שה ביום את בנו איך הורגה (the fem. refers here to תמותה) איש ואביהו רוצחת. Now had the poet wished to allude to the death of Samuel and his daughter on one day, the metre would have perfectly well allowed him to say ב ת ו א ב י ה and not איש ואביהו!

[43] This letter will be discussed more fully infra (p. 252 f.) in connection with the Damascus Gaonate. We give here the following corrections of the text as printed by Assaf. P. 67, l. 15, read קהלות[נו]; ll. 23–24, for בינה המקים . . . מאורינו r. ב[עולם ב ן] ההקים . . . מאורים וכו', hence Abraham was the son of Ezra!; l. 25, for נהלאות r. להנחות; l. 26, for כושלות r. כושלים, and ועל יד[ו עומד] מחזיק הבדק; p. 68, l. 10, for כתחלה r. בתחלה; p. 69, l. 13, for לה[שיב] r. להודיעו; l. 22, for ברורנו r. ברורה; ll. 23–24, see above, note 26; fol. 19b, l. 1, for ותבונה r. ותעודה; l. 2, for רצי[נו] r. בא[נו]; p. 70, l. 8, for ויבחר בישיבה r. ו נ ת ח ת[ן ב ב ת נ ו]; l. 9, for בחכ' r. בהל' (=בהלכה); l. 10, read מן הה[נא כט] אדנ' יר' ה' (=אדננו ירחמהו ה') בידה אלכר' (=אלכרימה), viz. the whole letter was written by Zekharyah on instruction of the Gaon Samuel (p. 67, top), but ll. 11–14, from אדירנו to אחריתו, were in the Gaon's own handwriting since it would not have been appropriate for Zekharyah to refer to himself with all the titles as הרב המומחה החכם המופלא; in l. 14 after אחריתו, where Assaf has dots between the lines, the MS. reads אלי ההנא, viz. up to here extends the handwriting of the Gaon Samuel the remainder being continued by Zekharyah; l. 17, for ננהגתם r. ניהגתם; l. 25, read במתק לשון [ובנעים] קול ששון.

[44] *L. c.*, pp. 49–57. The letter begins with an alphabetic exordium, hence in l. 6 for דבר read זכר; l. 17, read ועיניהם הנבונים (the עיני העדה are frequently mentioned); l. 24, for ארכות r. ערבות; p. 57, l. 10, for ואלפראס r. ואלפרנאס (=פרנסים)!

[45] *L. c.*, 45–49; p. 46, l. 18, for ויעדו r. perhaps ויענדו; p. 48, l. 19, for עד עתה r. נודעתם; fol. 11b, l. 1, for אליהם r. אלי רהבם; l. 2, for בינה ותורה r. בינה יתירה; p. 49, top, for מתורגמן r. מתורגמין; l. 16 שראיים = שראויים; l. 22, for ולכבוד r. ולכבודו (viz. Zekharyah's honor) and thereupon follows the blessing אלהי ישראל יזכה אתכם וכו'.

There are two letters by Zekharyah, dated Adar II, 1194, in the capacity of Gaon (Assaf, *l. c.*, 74–78).[45a] His period of office seems to have been very short because in Iyyar 1201 we find already Daniel b. El'azar b. Hibat Allah (=Netanel) in office, and before him there was an occupant of the dignity by the name of El'azar b. Hillel b. Fahd (see infra, p. 222).[46] Zekharyah, while still in Aleppo, corresponded with Maimonides who had a rather poor opinion of him. He also wrote some poetry which al-Ḥarizi disparages though acknowledging his Talmudic scholarship.[47] Thus we have conflicting views about him from his contemporaries according to their predilections, Samuel b. 'Alī holding him in high regard, a regard that was mutual, Maimonides disliking both and Ḥarizi criticizing his poetry according to his general low opinion of the whole output of Hebrew poetry outside of Spain (see infra, p. 263 f.).

[45a] The following corrections should be made in Assaf's text. P. 74, in the heading for אולפהא r. אלפהא; p. 75, l. 1, for הבחורים r. הבחונים; l. 10, for בעזרה r. בעצרה (=בעצרת, assembly); l. 19, for משער r. משערי; p. 76, l. 9, for ב[ס]ברה וב[ענ]וה r. כ[ת]ורה וכ[מצ]וה; l. 10, for בבערכם r. כבערכם and for [בחג שמור]ים ומצה r. [כהקריבכם מרור]ים ומצה; p. 78, end of letter, for סכ"ו r. ס"ט (=סימן טוב)!

Also the letter (pp. 72–74), the beginning of which is missing, would seem to be by our Zekharyah because the ending (p. 74), which Assaf gives as תשרי תק"ב יום ישועה, is far from certain. For יום probably r. ס"ט and also ישועה looks more like ישע רב, hence the same ending as on p. 78! The date תק"ב should be a later one תק"ו. Whether the Alluf Daniel mentioned in this letter is the same as the one dealt with in the letter of the Gaon Solomon in 1152 (pp. 81–82) is doubtful owing to the interval of more than 40 years between the two epistles.

[46] It is significant that in the edict of the Caliph al-Nāṣir, dated May 15 1209, confirming the Gaonate of Daniel b. El'azar (Pozn., *l. c.*, 37–39) there are mentioned his immediate predecessors El'azar b. Hillel and ibn al-Dastūr (Samuel b. 'Alī), עאדה̈ אלדארג̈ אלמשאר אליה (viz. El'azar b. Hillel) חית̇ כאן אבן אלדסתור ראס מת̇יבה̈ but Zekharyah is omitted. Assaf (p. 9) explains the omission to have been due to the shortness of his tenure of office, but this explanation is not satisfactory in view of the care with which official documents were usually drawn up. Who knows whether Zekharyah was not in reality the Gaon of the other Bagdād school in succession to his brother-in-law 'Azaryah b. Samuel whereas the direct successor of Samuel b. 'Alī was El'azar b. Hillel?

[47] Cp. the data discussed by Assaf, 6–7, and 9. In Ḥarizi's Taḥkemoni (Maḳama 18, ed. Lagarde, p. 94) וממשוררי מזרח הקדמונים הרב שמריה וראש הישיבה זכריה, by הקדמונים not 'the ancients' are meant because Zekharyah Gaon was practically Ḥarizi's contemporary, but the phrase denotes the Easterns (viz. further East than Damascus and Aleppo mentioned earlier in this Maḳama).

5. From the next Bagdād Gaon (possibly the direct successor of Samuel b. ʿAlī), *Elʿazar b. Hillel b. Fahd*, we possess now an incomplete letter describing his troubles as head of the school.[48] His election met with much opposition. He admits himself that only a section of the Bagdād leaders decided to bring about his appointment which he himself was hesitant of accepting. Soon after his entering upon the duties of head of the school his enemies slandered him to the Caliph who as a result of the slander ordered his arrest. Forewarned by a friend, the Gaon had to go into hiding and two other people (evidently his assistants) were arrested instead. For their release 200 Dinārs were demanded. This document reveals a dark side of the internal jealousies prevalent in Bagdād Jewry. The outcome of this affair is not given owing to the unfortunate defectiveness of the fragment. But it is to be concluded with certainty that he ultimately succeeded in appeasing the Caliph and was allowed to continue in his office because in the Caliph's edict of 1209 (see note 46) he is mentioned as the late Gaon whom Daniel b. Elʿazar succeeded. This Daniel apparently was סגן הישיבה under Elʿazar b. Hillel (and probably rival Gaon subsequently). He is evidently the person referred to by Elʿazar Habbabli in his poems (see note 31).

6. We are more informed about the Gaonate of *Daniel b. Elʿazar b. Hibat Allah.*[48a] Several letters of his testify to his con-

[48] MS. Adler, No. 4011, 2 leaves the first of which is in Arabic. There is a lacuna between fols. 1 and 2. Marmorstein (*RÉJ*, LXX, 107) has drawn attention to this fragment but as usual with him has edited it incorrectly. Recto, which Marmorstein omitted altogether, shows that Elʿazar was at the head of a regular academy. He sends greetings (l. 10) ... ומשער ישיבת (11) הצדק הנצבת ... (15) בעוז יו"י (thus is the Divine name spelt throughout the letters יוי representing the same numerical value of 26 as יהוה) ... ומהשרים והראשים (16) שלמשמעתה סרים בלבבות ברות. ומהחכמים והתלמידים שמלחמת (17) ההויות לוחמים עודרי ה ש ו ר ו ת. ומהזקנים והישישים רבי הישיבה (18) המתפללים על חייה בכל רגעים . . . Verso, which Marmorstein edited, l. 3, for מר' ור' r. מר רב; l. 4, for ומפילי מכמורות r. ויעשו לי מכמורות; l. 5, for להזקני r. להזיקני and for כגונב r. גנב; l. 7, for מהשרים r. השרים; l. 10, for והעם יעשוני . . . r. והעם . . . עשני ויחשיקוני בזה ואומר לפני יו"י; l. 13 for אזני r. עיני and for איש ברוך י"י r. איש ישר ברוך יו"י; l. 14, for ושבתי r. ישבתי; l. 15, for וכהחבאי r. ובהחבאי; l. 19, for ולא שקץ חטאתי r. ולא שקץ ענות [עני] חטאתי וכו'; l. 20, for כי . . . r. כי אמת (supply after אמת the word עשית, cp. Neh. 9.33).

[48a] Marmorstein's peculiar suggestion (in *RÉJ*, LXX, 107–08) of identifying our Daniel's grandfather Hibat-Allah with the apostate Abū'l Barakāt

nections with various communities and personalities. The first dated letter, as far as known, is of Iyyar 1512 Sel. (=1201 C. E.), sent to the congregations of Wāsiṭ and Baṣra.[49] The epistle deals with the position of the beadle at the old Jewish shrine in Babylon known as "the synagogue of Ezra."[50] A certain Abū'l Ḥasan was the occupant of the post and he obtained in his lifetime written assurances from the Gaon Samuel b. 'Alī and from the Exilarch David that his son Abū Manṣur would succeed him. The latter used to help his father in his duties and after his death produced these documents[51] before the Gaon Daniel b. El'azar who too in our letter reconfirms his office and gives notice to the above-mentioned communities not to disturb this arrangement. The conclusion of one of these documents produced, dated Iyyar 1197 C. E., has

Hibat-Allah (see Steinschneider, *Arab. Lit.*, 182–86) does not deserve to be seriously considered. He even becomes, according to Marmorstein, a Gaon in spite of his apostacy!

[49] Published by Leveen, *JQR*, *N. S.*, XVI, 396–97, where the identity has been obscured. It is the second letter that is by our Daniel and not the first one. The first epistle concludes ושלום רב יופרש על אהלי כלל עמו בית (and then on one line) ישראל נצח. אייר תקח. ישועה. האל לנו אל למושעות. Then there is space more than the usual amount between the lines. (The above information I have received from Mr. Leveen in his reply (Jan. 15, 1929) to my inquiry). The second letter has as the heading the Gaon's name and title דניאל ראש הישיבה שלגולה בירבי אלעזר החסיד וצ"ל (exactly as the letter in Assaf, *l. c.*, p. 30, where the lacuna should read accordingly). Then follows the indication of the congregations addressed, viz. those of Wāsiṭ and Baṣra and their surroundings. The concluding motto from Ps. 62.9, אלהים מחסה לנו סלה, is also found in the other letter emanating from Daniel.

The first epistle, dated Iyyar (1)508 Sel. (=1197 C. E.) has the concluding motto from Ps. 68.21 usually used by Samuel b. 'Alī. However he was then no longer alive and moreover the phrase ישועה was used by members of the Davidic family (like Daniel b. 'Azaryah of Palestine, see Mann, II, Hebrew Index, s. v.; Hezekiah Exilarch (above, p. 183) and the Bagdād Exilarch in his letter of 1161, infra, p. 230). Hence it is more likely that this letter emanates from the then ruling Exilarch David who is mentioned in our very epistle of the GaonDavid b. El'azar (see infra, note 51).

[50] About the synagogue near the supposed tomb of Ezra, mentioned by Benjamin of Tudela, Petaḥyah of Ratisbon and Judah al-Ḥarizi, see Obermeyer, *Die Landschaft Babylonien*, 323–25.

[51] ובידה כתאב אדוננו ה ר ב ש ל נ ו גאוננו שמואל הלוי ראש ישיבה שלגולה זצ"ל וכתאב נשיאנו דויד ראש גלויות כל ישראל ירום הודו. Samuel b. 'Alī is called 'our master' showing that Daniel studied under him at the academy.

also been preserved. It evidently is the one issued by the Exilarch David already after the death of Samuel b. 'Alī. This Exilarch is to be regarded as the son of Samuel of Mosul, who succeeded to the Exilarchate of Bagdād after the childless demise of the Exilarch Daniel b. Ḥisdai (see infra, p. 228 f.).

Other letters from Daniel b. El'azar have been edited by Assaf (*l. c.*, 30–36, 98–122).[52] They are dated from 1. Adar 1516 Sel. (=1205 C. E.) to Tishri 1520 Sel. (=1208 C. E.). Several are written in Nisan or Tishri containing good wishes for the Festivals, a gentle reminder of the needs of the school, because as a rule the individuals or the congregations addressed would reply expressing thanks for the good wishes and enclosing at the same time donations. Other letters deal with communal affairs such as the case of a Ḥazzān of former evil repute but now a penitent and of good conduct, the question being raised whether he be allowed to act as Reader during the solemn days of New Year and Yom Kippur. In a reply, dated Elul 1208, the Gaon decides in the affirmative (pp. 35–36). Then there was the case of a Dayyān in Wāsiṭ, Abū Yasir b. Tobias, whom the Gaon opposed as unfit for the position. Aiding this Dayyān in opposition to the Gaon was a certain Neṣaḥ (נצח) al-Ifranjī (viz. from a Christian Western–European country, pp. 110–12, 118–22).

All these letters date before Daniel's official confirmation as Gaon by the Caliph issued on May 15, 1209. This interesting edict has been given by Poznański in the original Arabic with a translation by Goldziher (*l. c.*, 37–39, cp. 10–11). The edict states that Daniel applied to be recognized as 'head of the school' in

[52] A number of corrections should be made in the texts as edited by Assaf. P. 31, l. 7, for ירים r. נרים; p. 32, l. 23, for ע . . . r. [מט]ע as the alphabetical scheme of the exordium demands; p. 34, No. 5, l. 1, for וב . . . r. [וב]נעם י״י]; l. 9, for [ה]פקיד . . . r. [היקר וה]פקיד and for טיב read טוב (the name Ṭob is known from the earlier Gaonic letters); p. 35, top, r. עליהם [ויהי]; p. 101, bottom, the date אתקי״ח reads in MS. אתקי״ז (1206); p. 102, top, r. בן אל[צראתי], as on p. 100; l. 15, הליל can also be read חליל; p. 104, No. 6, l. 1, for שבע r. שובע; p. 106, l. 18, for נאמן המלכות r. ומשען המלכות; verso, l. 1, for וצור r. ועוד and for מאוה r. תאוה; p. 108, l. 1, for אלאכרם r. אלמכרם; l. 2, for ותכלף r. מוֹר כלף; p. 109, l. 6, for שקר r. שבר; p. 111, verso, l. 2, for עזר[א] r. עזריה; p. 112, top, for יקוה הישיבה r. יקיר הישיבה; No. 11, l. 1, r. אבו מנצור [אלי אל[רייס; l. 2 for המצפה r. הנדבה; p. 114, No. 12, for לרייס r. אלרייס.

place of the late El'azar b. Hillel b. Fahd and, after information had been obtained from the Jews as to Daniel's good qualities and proper conduct, the Caliph al-Nāṣir (1180–1235) granted the petition. The Gaon is to be distinguished by a special dress of his rank and the communities in Bagdād and the whole of 'Irāḳ together with their judges (Dayyanim) are to be subject to his decisions. It is rather strange that there should have been such a long delay since 1201 in his confirmation as Gaon.[53] The suggestion lies near that it should be connected with the opposition against El'azar b. Hillel b. Fahd. The latter's election was much opposed and it led to his denunciation. Daniel b. El'azar may have been elected as a rival Gaon (as was so often the case in Babylon), but as long as El'azar b. Hillel lived he could not be confirmed officially because El'azar had been previously recognized by the Caliph. Only after El'azar's death (evidently in 1209) Daniel received the official confirmation. How long after 1209 he continued in sole possession of the Gaonate is not known, but in 1221 there is already mentioned his successor Isaac b. Israel ibn Shuwwaikh (see Pozn., *l. c.*, 42).

7. The Bagdād Geonim of the 13th century besides Daniel b. El'azar and Isaac ibn Shuwwaikh were the following, according to Poznański, Daniel Hakkohen b. Abū'l Rabi'a, then 'Alī (II) and finally Samuel b. Daniel Hakkohen. This list has to be supplemented by two more names. Between Isaac ibn Shuwwaikh and Daniel Hakkohen there has to come in the Gaon Isaac Hakkohen b. al-Awāni. Indeed Pozn. (*l. c.*, pp. 45–6) knew of an Isaac b. al-Awāni from Ḥarizi's disparaging remark about him and again of an Isaac Hakkohen Gaon from three items in El'azar Hababli's Diwān (p. 67) who thought well of him. But he hesitated to identify the two and thus treated of them separately finding

[53] Assaf (p. 9, note 1), who overlooked the material about El'azar b. Hillel discussed above and also Daniel's letter of 1201, even doubts whether the letter of Nisan 1206 (pp. 30–32) is by our Daniel in spite of the ending אלהים מחסה לנו סלה! That the heading דניאל ראש הישיבה וכו', belongs to this letter we have seen above (note 49). Assaf could not understand how Daniel should have been Gaon for several years prior to the Caliph's confirmation. And yet he himself edited still earlier letters of Adar I, 1205 (pp. 100 and 104), and in both of them greetings are extended from the school (משער הישיבה) over which Daniel presided! Our explanation given in the text seems to solve this difficulty.

it altogether difficult where to place the Gaon Isaac Hakkohen in the chronology. Now El'azar Habbabli has actually an elegy on the death of "the head of the school *Isaac Hakkohen b. al-Awāni*" (see infra, p. 298, No. 47) praising him for his piety and scholarship. Since Ḥarizi mentions this Isaac b. al-Awāni immediately after Isaac ibn al-Shuwwaikh[54] we would have to place him as successor of the latter. As El'azar Habbabli refers to him as Gaon at the time of his demise, there is no reason to assume with Poznański (p. 45) that he retired from his office during his lifetime.[55] Perhaps Isaac b. al-Awāni was the Gaon of the formerly Sura school so that there would be no need to crowd him into the congested chronology of the Pumbedita-Bagdād school.

The second name to be inserted is between 'Alī (II) and Samuel b. Daniel Hakkohen. El'azar Habbabli also composed a poem on the occasion of the marriage of this Samuel with the daughter of the Gaon Isaac Hallevi b. 'Alī (infra, p. 273, No. 10). It is doubtful whether this Isaac Hallevi was the son of 'Alī Hallevi (II) because in our heading Isaac Hallevi's father is not styled 'head of the school'.[56] Moreover El'azar Habbabli in his poems in honor of 'Alī II mentions only two living sons, viz. Zekharyah and Joshu'a (see Pozn., *l. c.*, 49–50). Now Isaac Hallevi, being the father-in-law of Samuel b. Daniel, was naturally older than the latter and should thus be a contemporary of Daniel Hakkohen, Samuel's father. This Isaac Hallevi may of course have been Gaon after 'Alī (II) and was succeeded by his son-in-

[54] Taḥkemoni, Maḳama 18 (ed. Lagarde, 94): ומבחר משורריהם ר' יצחק בר ישראל ראש הישיבה . . . ו א ח ר י ו החזיק ר' יצחק בן אלאואני. הוא מאד עשיר אבל שירו דל ועני. והוא קנה באלף זהובים הישיבה וזולתו ירכיבנה. ואשה יארש ואיש אחר ישכיבנה. והוא מחבר שירים מנופצים בשחת בלי. ונשחת הכלי. ואם ישאל שואל איזה השיר הנמאס למשכילים. ויאמר ה' הנה הוא נחבא אל הכלים. The biting poem on the spoilt vessel and the muse being hidden among the vessels is due, as Kaufmann (*Z. f. H. B.*, II, 188) so well pointed out, to Isaac's name al-Awāni (al-awān meaning vessels). Brody (*l. c.*, 157–59) and Kaufmann have both shown how unjustified Ḥarizi's criticism of Isaac's poetry was.

[55] Poznański's surmise is based on Ḥarizi's phrase וזולתו ירכיבנה, but this is only a wish of Ḥarizi's in his nasty temper, viz. "somebody else will occupy the Gaonate instead", exactly as Ḥarizi goes on to hope that his bride will be unfaithful to him.

[56] However neither is Samuel's father, Daniel b. Abū'l Rabi'a, given his due title of Gaon.

law Samuel Hakkohen whose father Daniel occupied the office before ʻAlī (II). However the chronology is here also congested and again recourse may be taken to the former Sura school in Bagdād over which Isaac Hallevi really presided.

To sum up what has become evident from the previous remarks, we have to keep in mind the two former academies of Pumbedita and Sura, both established in Bagdād, in order to arrange the chronology of the Geonim, so far known of the 12th and 13th centuries, accordingly. A tentative list may thus be construed.

12th Century

Pumbedita-Bagdād School	*Sura-Bagdād School*
1) ʻAlī (I)	1) Unknown
2) Solomon	2) Unknown
3) Samuel b. ʻAlī	3) ʻAzaryah b. Samuel (younger contemporary)
4) Elʻazar b. Hillel b. Fahd	4) Zekharyah b. Berakhel, (doubtful, may have succeeded Samuel b. ʻAlī).

13th Century

5) Daniel b. Elʻazar b. Hibat Allah	5) Unknown
6) Isaac b. Israel al-Shuwwaikh	6) Isaac Hakkohen b. al-Awāni
7) Daniel Hakkohen b. Abū'l Rabiʻa	7) Isaac Hallevi b. ʻAlī
8) ʻAlī (II)	8) Unknown
9) Samuel Hakkohen b. Daniel	9) Unknown

The Gaonate like the Exilarchate survived the crisis of the Mongol conquest of Bagdād in 1258. An Exilarch Samuel was treated well by the conquerors[57] and he probably used his influence to uphold the other important factor in Babylonian Jewry,

[57] Cp. infra, p. 229.

viz. the Gaonate. Samuel Hakkohen was still Gaon in Tishri 1288 C. E. His motto chosen from Psalms was ויהי י״י משגב לדך (Ps. 9.10) placed at the head of his letters and followed by his name and title. He mentions, in the only two epistles preserved from him, his two sons Ḥananel Hakkohen and Aaron Hakkohen in addition to the disciples and members of the school.[58] Whether one of his sons was able to maintain the office after Samuel's death is entirely unknown. Here again we must await further information to dissipate the complete obscurity before which we are placed.

II.

The Rivalry Between the Exilarchate and the Gaonate in Bagdād in the 12th Century

Above (pp. 208 ff.) the chronology of the Exilarchs in Bagdād was traced throughout the 11th century right into the 12th. The outstanding Exilarchs in the latter century were Ḥisdai b. David, who was in office in 1146–47 during the Messianic movement of David Alroy, and his son Daniel whom Benjamin of Tudela saw while in Bagdād and who died a year before Petaḥyah of Ratisbon arrived at the capital of the 'Abbāsid Caliphate.[59] Daniel died childless and after a division of opinion among the Bagdād communal leaders about his successor, the choice being between the two counsins David and Samuel, of the Exilarchic family of

[58] Kobak's *Jeschurun*, Hebrew part, VII, 76–80. In the first letter to the scholars of 'Akko and David Nagid (p. 76, bottom) he writes: ואנחנו ושני בנינו חננאל ואהרן הכהנים משרתיו והתלמידים ובני הישיבה שואלים בשלומו וכו' and in the second letter (p. 80, top) we read: וכקרוא הספר במקהלות אנשי כולי עלמא וכל התלמידים והחכמים ובני הישיבה אימה חשיכה (r. וחשיכה) גדולה נפלה עליהם וכו'. The expression כולי עלמא for Bagdād = Babylon is based on Gen. 11.8–9. Cp. Gen. R. 38, 8 התכנסו כל אוה״ע לראות איזו בקעה מחזקת להם and 38, 16. Samuel's concluding phrase at the end of his letters was ברית שלום (cp. Num. 25.12), appropriate for a Kohen (the same was used by Nehemiah Gaon, Samuel b. Ḥofni, his son Israel and other priestly dignitaries).

[59] About the Bagdād Exilarchs in the 12th century cp. Pozn., *l. c.*, 115ff., and Mann, *Livre d'hommage . . . Poznański*, Hebrew part, 23–25, on which the above remarks are based supplemented by the additional material now available.

Mosul, the latter seems to have won out. His period of office is not clearly defined but in 1197 we find already a new Exilarch David, probably Samuel's son, who is also mentioned as living in 1201 (above, p. 223, note 51). Again we are uninformed as to the length of his tenure of office after 1201. But when the Mongols conquered Bagdād in 1258, before which event both the Exilarchate and the Gaonate suffered from the extortions of the last 'Abbāsid Caliph al-Musta'ṣim, the Exilarch in office was Samuel who was well treated by the conquerors.[60] One does not go wrong in regarding this Samuel (II) as the son of David and the grandson of Samuel (I) formerly of Mosul.

Whenever powerful personalities happened at the same time to be Exilarch and Gaon respectively, there was bound to be a clash of interests between them. Such was the case, e. g., with Uḳba and Kohen Ṣedeḳ and David b. Zakkai and Sa'adyah. The same phenomenon we observe in the case of the Gaon Samuel b. 'Alī and the Exilarch Daniel. Both tried to exert their influence even on Jewries beyond Babylon. The former was successful in Syria where, in the capital of Damascus, there was established a Gaonate that was bolstered up by Samuel. The latter wielded an influence in Egypt where the Gaonate in Fusṭāṭ found it necessary to seek the support of the Babylonian Exilarch against the rival claims of the Damascus school. One of the chief points of contention was the problem of *Semikhah* (*Ordination*). The whole problem in its historical development and actuality cannot be discussed here and has to be reserved for another occasion.[61] Here only the phase concerning the argument between the Exilarchate and the Gaonate is dealt with. The right of Semikhah was claimed and practiced by the school of Palestine all along till its extinction with the First Crusade. Now in the 12th century the Exilarch of Bagdād denied this right to be exercised by the contemporary Gaon Samuel b. 'Alī whereas the latter claimed on the other hand that the only restriction applicable to the head of the Babylonian school concerned cases of fines

[60] See Mann, *l. c.*, 24–25, and *RÉJ*, LXXXII, 373–74.

[61] For the latest discussion see Bornstein, משפט הסמיכה וקורותיה (in *Hattekufah*, IV, 394–426, which requires amplification and modification on many points.

(דיני קנסות) which alone were the privilege of those ordained in Palestine. In all other respects ordination could be effected in Babylon.

The point at issue in 1161 were the rival claims of the Damascus and the Fusṭāṭ Gaonates which will be discussed separately farther on. The former regarded itself as an heir to the defunct Palestinian Gaonate and in addition one of its Geonim, Ezra b. Abraham (b. Mazhīr), received ordination from Samuel b. 'Alī.[62] Through this ordination coupled with the supposed taking over of the rights of the Palestinian school, the Damascus Gaon would have liked the Egyptian Jews (or at least the *Palestinian congregations in Fusṭāṭ and Alexandria*) to acknowledge his spiritual leadership and through him that of his superior, the Gaon of Bagdād. Donations and dues formerly sent to the Palestinian school would thus go to that of Damascus and a share probably to the Bagdād school. Now there was a Gaonate in Fusṭāṭ too which called in the aid of the Babylonian Exilarch against the above claims of the Damascus Gaon. The occasion arose when Netanel Hallevi had to succeed his father Moses Hallevi in Fusṭāṭ as head of the local school. A highly interesting letter, dated Tishri 1161, by the Exilarch (no doubt Daniel b. Ḥisdai of Bagdād) has now been edited by Assaf (125–134).[63] That a Baby-

[62] As Petaḥyah of Ratisbon (סבוב, ed. Grünhut, 28) reports: וראש ישיבה ר' עזרא מלא תורה כי ס מ כ ו רבי שמואל ראש ישיבה בבבל . . .

[63] This letter in its present form is the result of a remarkable combination of 3 Genizah fragments, MS. Adler 4011 published by me (*H. U. C. Annual*, III, 293–94), T.-S. 8 J 2 edited by Schechter, *Saadyana*, 107–111 (hitherto regarded to have emanated from David b. Daniel b. 'Azaryah of Megillat Ebyatar notoriety) and MS. Antonin 1131 published for the first time by Assaf.

A number of corrections in the text should be added here. P. 125, fol.1, recto, between lines 8–9, there is missing in my edition a line due to the printer's mistake. These lines should read: והבשן בתוקף אמונותיו. והיה אמונת עתותיו. חוסן ישועותיו. ודעת חכמותיו. יראת יי' היא אוצרותיו וכו'; fol. 3, recto, l. 15, read as in MS. בין מלך על הארץ לאלהים. ובין עד האלהים the former (the king on earth for God's sake) being the Exilarch (see p. 132: ובאהבת מלככם) and the latter, the chief judge of the Egyptian Jewry, being the new Gaon Netanel (for the phrase עד האלהים, cp. Exod. 22.8; Assaf did not comment at all on this difficult line); fol. 3, verso, l.7, for נקראים r. הנקראים; p. 127, top, for דורותיכם r. דורותיהם; verso, l. 6, for אלא read as in MS. אילא; p. 128, top, for ידע r. ודע; in T.-S., l. 2,

lonian Exilarch is the author of the epistle is evident especially from his reference to the ruling Caliph al-Mustanjid billāh (1160–70) under whose kind protection the writer is living and hence none else but Daniel b. Ḥisdai can be this person.

The Exilarch upon the request of Netanel confirms his appointment as head of the school. At an assembly of elders and other people in Bagdād he bestowed this title upon Netanel and now he lets it be known that Netanel is president of the supreme Jewish court in Egypt having the right to establish law courts in every district and to command obedience to his behest.[64] To counteract the claims of the Damascus Gaonate the Exilarch argues that Semikhah ceased with Daniel b. 'Azaryah, Gaon of Palestine (1051–62), who was also of Davidic descent. The writer does not recognize the authority of Daniel's successors, the priestly Geonim Elijah and Ebyatar, and still less of the latter's brother Solomon Hakkohen, the founder of the school at Ḥadrak later on transferred to Damascus.[65] Although he concedes that Semikhah can only be in Palestine (after Sanh. 14a)

for [שתנו] r. [נכון]; p. 129, the Arabic lines cannot now be taken to refer to the Fāṭimid Caliph because the Exilarch writes from Babylon, for אלמחדסה r. אלמקדסה̈; indeed for אל מסתוגדה r. אלמסתנגדה̈ באללה referring to the then ruling Caliph in Bagdād al-Mustanjid billāh ("Who asks for assistance from God," 1160–1170)!; p. 133, fol. 2, recto, l. 10, for למנון r. לחנון; l. 13, for יושע r. יושיב; p. 134, l. 17, for לרפאת r. לרפאות את.

[64] P. 125: ושמנו המצנפת. והפאר העודפת. על ראש קצינינו אחינו ראש הישיבה שלגולה וקראנוהו בשם קדוש במעמד שרינו וגבירינו וכל הקהל עונים אמן. כי בארשת שפתינו ס מ כ נ ו ה ו. וכאשר בלבבינו תמכנוהו. והוד והדר עטרנוהו. ומהוד המלוכה האפדנוהו. למען ישמעו כל עדת בני ישראל והוא ב י ת ד י ן ה ג ד ו ל בכל מדינות ארץ מצרים ובכל הארצות יורה וידין ויקבע בתי דינין בכל פלך ופלך וכל החכמים ושרי לאומים ויתר עם קדש ישמעו אליו ויאזינו למילוליו ויתנו לו יד באמת ובישרת לבב.

Although the Exilarch uses the phrase "we have ordained him", this is only a matter of stylistic flourish because he forthwith argues that Semikhah no longer exists. He uses again the expression Semikhah in a similar manner on p. 126: ולמי כל חמדתינו הלא לשלשלת החכמה והיופי (viz. Netanel) שאין בסמיכתה מום ולא דופי.

[65] P. 126: והלא ידוע וגלוי כי ח ב ל ה ס מ י כ ה נרתק מכמה שנים מעת אסיפת אדונינו נשיאנו דניאל ראש ישיבת גאות יעקב זק"ל והכהנים הנקראים אחריו (viz. merely called Geonim after him) נהגו קלות ראש באורחותם ודחקו את השעה ולא הבינו לאחריתם ותהי זאת להם לפוקה ואין להרהר אחרי מעשיהם ימצאו מנוחה בבית מלונם וכו'. Here we have a reconstruction of the events after David b. 'Azaryah's death from the point of view of a member of the Exilarchic family from which Daniel also had sprung

he adds that since the exile of the Sanhedrin from Tiberias (evidently in the time of the last Patriarchs) nobody has the right there to intercalate a year or to change the rules of calendation.[66] Here again is a disapproval of the claims of the Palestinian Geonim to fix the calendar,[67] but this is only in the nature of an historical retrospect because we have no reason to assume that the Damascus Gaonate in the 12th century still presumed to exercise this right.

The Exilarch goes on to refer to his studies of the Torah having gone through several times "four sections" of the Talmud, viz. Zera'im, Mo'ed, Nashim and Neziḳin; the sections Ḳodashim and Ṭoharot were usually not studied because (except Ḥullin and Niddah) they had no practical value. He also mentions his distress owing to political troubles in the country as a result of which he became impoverished even having to sell his clothes. He and his family are in great need and in addition there is much internal strife in the (Bagdād) community liable to bring about revenge and fierce wrath, an allusion to his conflict with the Gaon Samuel b. 'Alī.[68] Yet he admits of his good standing with the ruling Caliph Yūsuf al-Mustanjid whose rule is beneficial

up. Evidently the action of Daniel's son, David, in setting himself up in Fusṭāṭ in rivalry to Ebyatar Hakkohen is here by implication approved of.

66 P. 127: ואחרי גלות סנהדרין גדולה מטיבריה והיא היתה הגלות העשירית לא נשאר רשות לכל ישראל ולא אפילו לנשיא הדור ויחיד הזמן לעבר שנים ולא לשנות מחקי העבור הקבועים על פי ארבעה שערים והתוקע בשבת ואפילו בבית הועד מחלל הוא את השבת וענשו מרובה. Did ever such a case of blowing the Shofar on Sabbath happen during the period of the Palestinian Gaonate?

67 Well-known is the case of Aaron b. Meir in his dispute with Sa'adyah and the Babylonian authorities (920). Also Ebyatar Hakkohen in his Megillah claimed the same right and although he was ready to abide by the rules of calendation as based on "the four principles" (ארבעה שערים), yet the actual sanctification of the year had still to be done by the head of the Palestinian school (see *Saadyana*, p. 102). He actually records how his father Elijah Hakkohen visited Ḥaifa in 1083 to "sanctify the year" and at the same time to reaffirm the succession to the Gaonate (p. 88–89: ובשנת מותו הלך לחיפה לקדש את השנה ויחדש את הגאונות ואת הסמיכה בחיפה בבית הוועד).

68 Assaf, p. 128, bottom: אבל עוצם החלואות (r. התלאות) הכחיד כחינו. וירושש עיר מבצרנו. עד כי אזלה פרוטה מן הכיס ומכרנו את בגדינו. ולא נשאר לנו זולתי חצרותינו. והננו ואת אשר נלוים אלינו. בדוחק גדול וצר ומצוק מצאונו עד למאד ורבה משטמה בקרב עדת איומה. להעיר נקם ולהעלות חמה.

to the Jews.[69] This important passage concerning the straitened circumstances of the Exilarch Daniel in October 1161 is in flat contradiction to the account of Benjamin of Tudela describing him to have been very wealthy.[70] If Graetz's contention be right that Benjamin did not start his journey before 1165 (*Gesch. d. Juden*, VI, 4th ed., 394), then we have to assume that by a favorable turn of circumstances the Exilarch recouped his fortune in the interval between the date of our letter and Benjamin's visit to Bagdād.

After this personal digression the writer returns to the theme of his letter referring to "the superior school which we have established," which shows that the Exilarch had a learned institution of his own in Bagdād in opposition to the one presided over by Samuel b. 'Alī. The latter is perhaps meant in the phrase "and he who goes astray will (ultimately) know his place and God's honor will be revealed."[71] He then turns his displeasure against

[69] Ibid., p. 129, top: ואף גם זאת בהיותנו בארצות עליזות הטה אלהינו עלינו חסדו בעיני אלמואקף אלמוק[ו]דסה̈ אלעלייה̈ אלאמאמייה̈ אלנבוייה̈ אלזכייה̈ . . . אלמסתנגדה̈ באללה יתמיד מעוזינו ממשלתה . . . הלא אנו וכלל איומתינו בצל מנעמי מלכותה לא נתן למוט רגלינו בימיה והחובה עלינו ועל כל ישראל להתמיד השאלה והעיתור בעד ממלכתה וכו'. Goldziher (*JQR*, XV, 73), on the assumption that our letter was by David b. Daniel b. 'Azaryah in Fusṭāṭ (between 1080–84)—an assumption legitimately held by all of us till the new material has proven that our epistle dated from October 1161 C. E., —has naturally endeavored to explain the above allusion to the Caliph as meaning the temporary Fāṭimid ruler of Egypt al-Mustanṣir billāh (1036–1094). Hence he emended אלעלייה into אלעלויה̈ as meaning the 'Alīd dynasty (Fāṭima being the wife of 'Alī, Mohammed's son-in-law) and אל מסתונגדה באללה into אלמסתנצרה̈ באללה. But in the light of the true origin of our letter from the Exilarch in Babylon, the reference can only be to the ruling Caliph in Bagdād. Hence אלעלייה can only mean here "the superior, sublime" and the obvious emendation of אל מסתונגדה באללה is אלמסתנגדה̈ באללה because the 'Abbāsid Caliph then was Yūsuf al-Mustanjid billāh. Assaf (p. 129, note 1) had thus no idea of the historical construction of our letter by simply quoting Goldziher's remarks which are now no longer tenable.

[70] *Itinerary*, ed. Adler, p. 41, after describing at length the exalted position of the Exilarch Daniel, he adds: והאיש עשיר גדול וחכם בפסוק (Bible) ובתלמוד ואוכלים על שלחנו רבים מישראל בכל יום.

[71] Ibid., p. 129: ולהפיק משמי מטל זממינו בהדרת הישיבה המעולה. אשר הצבנוה במאמר נורא עלילה. לאחוז בכנפי הארץ וינערו רשעים ממנה ואשר הולך שולל הוא ידע את מקומו ונגלה כבוד יי'י ויבינו הכל כי יש אלהים שופטים בארץ למלאת הדין משפט יתמכו כבוד ענוים. ואיה מחרפי מערכות עליון? הלא רוח יי'י נוססה בהם ואינימו ככל

the Damascus Gaon and his claim of having authority in Egypt. This authority belongs to himself as the Exilarch. Since the times of his ancestors the school of Palestine had no right over Egypt for this country just as Babylon is outside the Holy Land (חוצה לארץ).[72] Only because Daniel b. 'Azaryah combined in himself the dignities of both Gaon and Nasi, the Egyptian communities came under his authority. With his demise the right returned to the Babylonian Exilarchate represented by "the respected school" in Fusṭāṭ. Playing up to local patriotism he reminds his

יקפצון וכראש שבולת יקצצון. It seems that the school mentioned here as situated in Bagdād was in opposition to Samuel b 'Alī's school. Who knows whether the former Sura school is not referred to here over which the Exilarchs always had great influence? If so, then later on, after Daniel's death when Samuel b. 'Alī won the ascendancy, a modus vivendi was established with this school when its Gaon 'Azaryah b. Samuel became Samuel's son-in-law. However, it must be admitted, that the above interpretation is problematic and that "the superior school which we established" may mean the one in Fusṭāṭ over which Netanel Hallevi, confirmed by our Exilarch, presided. Cp. the sentence on p. 130: והישיבה החשובה. אשר ממים חיים שאובה. הנה קבועה ביניהם (viz. among the Jews of Fusṭāṭ, צוען, as the context clearly shows). However there is the difficulty in the phrase "which we have established" since the school in Egypt was already established during the time of Maṣliaḥ Hakkohen (1127–38) and Netanel Hallevi succeeded in his turn his father Moses Hallevi. For further discussion of this problem, see infra, p. 255 ff.

[72] Ibid., p. 129, bottom: ועתה איך יתהלל חוגר כמפתח אשר ארש לו את נאות יעקב? (evidently the Damascus Gaon is meant who claimed for himself "the habitations of Jacob" (i. e. Palestine, cp. Lam. 2.2), viz. the rights of the Palestinian Gaonate) ונדע באמת כי בדבר אשר זדו עליהם. הלא להם לדעת כי כסא יסודותינו בהררי קדש. לא יסור שבט ממנה עד כי נצדק קדש. ורשותה (viz. of the Exilarchate) פושטת על כל ארץ צבי וסוריה ומימי אבותינו הקדמונים לא היה לישיבת צבי בארץ מצרים חלק ומנת כי מצרים חוצה לארץ כבבל חשובה. ולמען כי היה אדונינו נשיאנו דניאל גאון ונשיא (Daniel b. 'Azaryah) בדורו כרבנו הקדוש עברו קהלותיה (היינו: קהלות מצרים) תחת מסורת בריתו. ואחריו המסיגים גבול ראשונים הנאמנים . . . נתיבותיהם בעיקוש מצינים וכו'. The claim, that only during Daniel b. 'Azaryah's time the school of Palestine had influence over Egyptian Jewry, is of course historically untrue, as the numerous Genizah letters, e. g. of Solomon b. Yehudah, Daniel's predecessor, and of other Palestinian Geonim, show. As for the other argument that the Babylonian Exilarchs, because of their descent from King David (כי כסא יסודתינו בהררי קדש), have rights over Palestine, Syria and Egypt, one could advance the counter arguments put forward over 75 years before by Ebyatar Hakkohen (*Saadyana*, p. 92, and cp. Mann I, 189). But our passage is characteristic for the sweeping ambitions of our Exilarch Daniel b. Ḥisdai to rule over the whole of Jewry as ראש גליות כל ישראל.

readers of the story of Jacob and his sons in the country of the Nile and of the birth there of no less a person than Moses.[72a] And in conclusion he appeals to Egyptian Jewry to send him the donations due to the Exilarchate.[73] By his taking sides with the Gaon of the Fusṭāṭ school, Netanel, against the claims of the Damascus Gaonate he evidently hoped to benefit materially as a recognition for his stand just as Samuel b. 'Alī must have hoped to benefit for his school through extending his influence indirectly by the instrumentality of the Damsacus Gaon whom he had ordained.

Such is the construction of this interesting letter revealing the cross-currents of the ambitions of Gaon and Exilarch in Bagdād and their making use of the rivalry between the Damascus and the Fusṭāṭ Gaonates to further their own interests.[74] For a time Daniel wielded some authority in Egypt owing to the disturbed communal situation there after the death of the Nagid Samuel b. Ḥananyah (about 1159). Netanel Hallevi although called שר השרים by Benjamin of Tudela, a title usually held by the Nagid, was really no occupant of this office but, as head of the

[72a] Ibid., p. 131: הלא ארץ מצרים חוצה לארץ ותם (Jacob) ונזיר אחיו (Joseph,) שבטי (r. ושבטי) חמד גרו בה ואשר ידעו יי'י פנים אל פנים (Moses) בה נולד (cp. Deut. 33.16).

[73] Ibid., p. 133, top: האזינו ושמעו קולנו. הקשיבו ושמרו מצותינו. ותנו יד לאלהינו ולכסא יסודתינו. והחובה הקבועה עליכם (viz. the dues for the upkeep of the Exilarch-ate) מימי אבותיכם. ואתם קבעתם אותנו. ולא שלחתם אותה אל מושבינו. שלמו ונדרו להובילה כמצותה לפנינו. When writing this letter the Exilarch did not know the individual names of the Fusṭāṭ leaders because he had only a request from Netanel Hallevi to support his Gaonate (p. 125: אשר בהגיע הדבר אל מושבינו זחל זחלנו. ומשפטי אלהינו קבלנו. ועל משמרתינו עמדנו. לשום לו תקוה ואחרית). Hence he excuses himself and promises later on to bestow upon these leaders titles as was the custom of the Exilarchs and Nesiim such as חדות הנשיאות, דגל הנשיאות etc. (see Mann, I, 272, top). The corresponding passage reads (p. 133): ואחינו אבירינו. שרי עדתינו. ידינונו לכף זכות כי לא ידענו גדוליהם ושמות שריהם וכנוייהם לא נתבארו לנו. ועוד מעט (supply והגיע מכתב אל) פיאורם וכתר ראשם להכתירם בשם הטוב וכו'.

[74] Assaf had no idea of the whole subject. He identifies (p. 124) the writer with an Exilarch Daniel in Fusṭāṭ. But this person should now be identified with our very Daniel b. Ḥisdai of Bagdād (see infra, p. 395). It shows that the Exilarch was able for a time to establish his authority in Fusṭāṭ so that legal documents were stated to have been issued under his jurisdiction (probably by the *Babylonian* community of Fusṭāṭ).

school and by authority of the Exilarch Daniel, was in charge of the supreme Jewish court in the country of the Nile (בית דין הגדול) and had the supervision of the Dayyanim and other communal offices in the various communities.[75] In fact Netanel seems to have been the official Dayyān al-Yahūd next in office to the Nagid called Raīs al-Yahūd (see Mann, I, 266–67; *H. U. C. Annual*, III, 292–3). The Exilarch's influence on Egyptian Jewry probably gained in strength since Nureddin of Aleppo began to interfere in the Fāṭimid dominion by sending his general Shirḳūh with an army to Egypt (1164). Nureddin acknowledged the suzerainty of the Caliph of Bagdād and, when Saladin succeeded Shirḳūh as actual master of Egypt, pressed him to change the Khuṭbah in the mosques so as to substitute the name of the 'Abbāsid Caliph for that of the Fāṭimid Caliph. Saladin finally complied with this command in 1171 shortly before the death of the last Fāṭimid Caliph al-Ādhid.[76] With the formal acknowledgement of the Bagdād Caliph in Egypt naturally the Babylonian Exilarch could use his influence in Bagdād to further his claims of recognition there. And to a certain extent the Exilarchate must have succeeded in this endeavor. Maimonides in his letter to Joseph ibn 'Aḳnīn describes how an epistle of the Exilarch (viz. Samuel, the successor of Daniel b. Ḥisdai) was read with great ceremony in Fusṭāṭ the whole assembly including himseld standing at the recital.[77] This is evidence of the high respect the Exilarch was held in there and the explanation is to be found in the underlying political situation since the end of the Fāṭimid Caliphate. Saladin throughout his reign acknowledged the overlordship of the Bagdād Caliph.

[75] See note 64, and cp. Benjamin of Tudela's *Itinerary* (ed. Adler, p. 63): וביניהם נתנאל שר השרים ראש הישיבה והוא ראש לכל הקהלות של מצרים להקים רבנים וחזנים והוא משרת פני המלך הגדול היושב בארמון צוען המדינה.

[76] See Wüstenfeld, *Gesch. der Faṭimiden Chalifen*, 330ff. 350; *Weil*, *Gesch. der Chalifen*, III, 334–35.

[77] Cp. the Arabic original given by Pozn., *l. c.*, 60: ואמא מא טאלבת מני מן מכאתבה ראס אלגלות פקד כאתבנא וצלני כתאבה וקראתה פי דארי ו א נ א ו א ק ף וכאן פי אלדאר כל מן פי מצר מגדול ועד קטן אן כאן בהם מעלה וכאן פי סכות ו כ ל ה ם ו ק ו ף ל ו ק ו פ י וכאן יומא עטים לי וכאן קאריה ר' שמואל המלמד וגמיע שיוך אלגמאעה ען ימינה ויסארה עלי דכה. Cp. Pozn., p. 33, and infra, p. 241 f.

What counter argument to the above letter of October 1161 from the Exilarch Daniel, the Gaon Samuel b. 'Alī advanced is not known. The same MS. contains after this epistle the heading: "A copy of a letter from the head of the school Samuel which reached (Fusṭāṭ?) through (a certain) Samuel". On it there was the seal of the Gaon Ezra (of Damascus) who then stayed in Aleppo. The date is either Tammuz 1172 or Tammuz 1175.[78] There follows a poem with the acrostic עזרא testifying to the trustworthiness of the bearer of the letter which unfortunately is missing as the MS. breaks off. Its contents are of course unknown. Here we are already at the time when Daniel b. Ḥisdai was no longer alive and a new Exilarch, Samuel of Mosul, succeeded him after an interregnum.[79] With this Exilarch Samuel b. 'Alī also came into conflict. During the time of the interregnum Samuel b. 'Alī probably made use of the opportunity to strengthen the Gaonate at the expense of the Exilarchate and to obtain dues and donations from communities that formerly sent these to the Exilarch. When the next incumbent of the Exilarchic office, Samuel of Mosul, established himself in Bagdād he probably tried to regain the prestige built up by his influential predecessor, and friction with the Gaon was bound to spring up. That the conflict was a long drawn one is evident from Samuel's important letter of Sivan 1191 to the congregations of Upper Mesopotamia and Syria when his son-in-law Zekharyah b. Berakhel was sent on a pastoral tour on behalf of the school.[80] The latter is portrayed as the throne of the Torah in direct succession from Moses. He who opposes the authority of the school is opposing God and Moses his messenger.[81] Taking a side thrust at the appellation

[78] Assaf., *l. c.*, 134.

[79] Daniel died childless a year before Petaḥyah of Ratisbon visited Bagdād, hence in about 1174 C. E. Some time must have elapsed till Samuel obtained the office in preference to his cousin David. In 1175, when Petaḥyah was there, there was no agreement yet between the partisans of the two candidates. In 1197 we hear already of another Exilarch David (probably the son of Samuel) Hence the latter's period as Exilarch falls between 1175–97 approximately (see above, p. 229).

[80] Assaf, 49–57, cp. above, note 44.

[81] P. 51: מנצב הישיבה הו כסא התורה אלנאיב ען משה רבנו עֹהֹ פי כל זמאן וזמאן . . .

of the Exilarch as "king of the Jews",[82] Samuel draws attention to the displeasure of God when Samuel the Prophet presented the wishes of the Israelites to have a king (I Sam. c. 8). Anyhow in the Diaspora the Jews have no king and only need the guidance of their teachers and scholars.[83] Even king David relied on the advice of the scholars according to the Aggadah (Ber. 3b).

Then comes the crucial part of the letter which shows that Samuel b. 'Alī had refused to acknowledge the new Exilarch at least morally, because actually he had to bow to the force majeure since the Exilarch was recognized by the Caliph. The Exilarch is accused of ignorance in matters Jewish. He prevailed by the aid of money and the government authorities, but "he who is the *ordained one* of the generation" (viz. the Gaon) did not approve of him. While the Gaon is universally recognized, the scholars and the pious did not agree to the other's Exilarchate. Many who joined him did so under compulsion.[84] The Exilarch is accused of trying to deprive the school of its rightful income, the dues and the donations, which are an obligation in Israel in place of the former Half Sheḳel for the upkeep of the Temple. Hence the Gaon is sending out his son-in-law Zekharyah b. Berakhel on a pastoral tour to Upper Mesopotamia and to Syria to collect these dues and bespeaks for him an honorable reception as due to Zekharyah's standing as Ab-Bet-Din of the school.

פאלישיבה מנצב משה רבנו ובהא יתם דין ישראל וכל מכ֗אלף עליהא פקד כ֗אלף עלי רב אלתורה אלתי הי מנצבהא וכ֗אלף עלי משה רבנו עָהָ אלד֗י הו כרסיה.

[82] Cp. the letter of the Exilarch Daniel b. Ḥisdai (Assaf, p. 132): ונירו לכם ניר בשמירת חוקי אלהינו ומשפטיו ובאהבת מ ל כ כ ם. See also above, note 63. About other data wherein the Exilarch is called "our king" (מלכנו), cp. Mann, II, 208–09.

[83] Pp. 52–3: ותעלמון אן ישראל למאטלבו (r. למא טלבו) מלך פי זמאן שמואל מא חל בהם מן אלסכ֗ט . . . ופי איאם אלגלות ליס להם מ ל ך ולא חרב ולא מעני מן אלצ֗רוראת אלי אלמלך ואנמא יחתאג֗ון אלי מן ירשדהם ויבצרהם ויערפהם לואזם דינהם ויפצל חכומאתהם ויפתיהם.

[84] Pp. 53–4: כסף (r. פכיף) יג֗וז אן יקבל ממן ידעי אלאנתסאב אליה מע כון אלכ֗לק יערפה באנה לא קרא ולא שנה ולא שימש (היינו: חכמים) בל תקוא באלמאל ואליד אלסלטאניה֗ ולם יואפק עליה א ל ד֗ י ה ו ס מ ו ך פ י ע צ ר ה וישראל בכל העולם כלמתהם מתפקה֗ עלי ישיבתו ואלחכמים ואהל אלדין לם יואפקו עלי ג֗אלותיתה וכת֗יר ממן תבעה מכרהא וגיר ד֗לך ממא לעל קד אנתהי אלי עלם אצחאבנא כת֗יר מנה. סהל (r. פהל) יחל לאחד מן ישראל אן יואפק עליה או ימיל עליה וחאלתה הד֗ה וכו'?

We can better understand the situation, if we bear in mind that the Exilarch Samuel was formerly of Mosul and hence was held in honor by the surrounding communities. He thus could compete successfully with the demands of the Gaonate on the communities of Upper Mesopotamia.[85] As for Syria there was in Damascus the local Gaon who was ordained by Samuel b. ʻAlī and thus sided with his master. Then there was in Aleppo a prominent scholar, Zekharyah b. Berakhel, who came to Bagdād attracted by the Gaon. The Exilarch's party tried to win him over to their side but he refused, as Samuel b. ʻAlī triumphantly reports, and became intimately connected with the Gaon by ties of relationship marrying the Gaon's daughter and advancing to the dignity of Ab-Bet-Din.[86] Through him Samuel b. ʻAlī figured on strengthening his influence in Syria because Zekharyah was a native evidently of Aleppo and was known there for his scholarship. And in the summer of 1191 we find our Zekharyah touring Upper Mesopotamia and Syria on behalf of the school.

Interesting is the recurrence of the Ordination question at this stage of the conflict. Samuel b. ʻAlī regarded himself as the "ordained one" (סמוך) of his age and as such ordained his son-in-law Zekharyah as Ab-Bet-Din with the understanding of his succession to the Gaonate later on. But the legitimacy of Ordination outside

[85] To upper Mesopotamia (al-Jazīrah) belonged ar-Raḳḳah, Ruha (Edessa), Sarūj, and Ḥarran mentioned in our letter (cp. Le Strange, *Lands of Eastern Caliphate*, 101ff., and see Map facing p. 87). To Mosul itself we have no letter from Samuel b. ʻAlī. There the Exilarch's prestige was of course strong. The congregation of Irbil (the old Arbela, ארבאל), near Mosul, also seems to have defaulted the Gaon as is evident from his plaintive letter of October 1093 (Assaf, pp. 84–89, see especially, pp. 87–88).

[86] Assaf, p. 48: וכאשר שבה תשובתנו אליו מיהר לבוא לפנינו. ויסיתוהו אנשי תוך ומרמה. (viz. the Exilarch's followers) להטותו מבתי ועד וחכמה. ולהפרד מהישיבה ולהיות בכללם. ולא שמע בקולם. ולא נטה אליהם (אלי רהבם r.) ולא ניסת ב כ ס פ ם ו ז ה ב ם. והבליהם. ויט מעליהם. ונכלל בחכמי התורה. ונתן לכסאה (היינו: הישיבה שהיא כסא התורה) כיבוד (כבוד r.) ומורא. וכאשר בא לפנינו ראינו בו בינה ותורה (בינה יתירה r.) . . . נאה למשרה וראוי למצב הישיבה. וכאשר ראינו בו המדות החמודות הנכבדות האלו . . . ס מ כ נ ו ה ו אב בית דין שלישיבה ונתַנו לו רשות לדין וכו'. Cp. the corresponding passage in Samuel's letter to the Gaon of Damascus (ibid., p. 70, and see above, p. 220, note 43).

Palestine was challenged, as we have seen above, by the Exilarch Daniel b. Ḥisdai and no doubt by his successor Samuel of Mosul. In announcing this ordination of Zekharyah to the Gaon of Damascus, Abraham b. ʿEzra, Samuel b. ʿAlī found it necessary to refute the argument as to the illegitimacy of Ordination outside the Holy Land. Since Rab and Samuel the practice was for the heads of the schools to ordain their future successors. The rule of no Semikhah outside Palestine applied only to the settling of cases of fines (דיני קנסות). Otherwise every Gaon received approbation from his predecessor. Samuel mentions that he possessed responsa or letters from Hai and other Geonim in corroboration of this practice. Samuel himself was ordained by the Gaon Solomon before him.[87]

How much truth there was in the Gaon's accusation of the Exilarch Samuel's ignorance, venality of office and depriving the school of its legitimate income we cannot say till we have material emanating from the Exilarch's side on this matter. So far we have only a onesided picture of the actual situation with its rights and wrongs. Into this conflict of interests between Gaonate and Exilarchate Maimonides was drawn when defending his theories against the strictures of Samuel b. ʿAlī. Joseph ibn ʿAḳnīn, Maimonides' favorite disciple, visited Bagdād possibly on several occasions (he was there in the year 1192). Whatever the actual

[87] Assaf, pp. 67–70, (cp. above, p. 220, note 43). The passage pertaining to our theme is on p. 69: ולא ימשו (=ימישו) ראשי הדורות כל אחד ואחד מהם בוחר מי שהוא ראוי לישיבה וקוראו ומסכים עליו וסומכו. ואם יאמר האומר (viz. the Exilarch) כי אין סמיכה בחוצה לארץ יש לאל מלים להשיב[ו (להודיעו r.) ולהרגיעו כי האמור אין סמיכה בחוצה לארץ הני מילי לדון דיני קנסות אבל לדיני הודאות והלואות יש סמיכה. יש (ויש r.) על עקר זה ראיות לא תכילם אגרת זו אך הגדנו לכם עיקר ויסוד לבנות עליו . . . והמעיד על היסוד הזה אשר יסדנוהו מנהג ראשי הישיבה בבבל מימי רבנו רב ועד היום הזה כל אחד ואחד ככתוב בזכרוניו ואגרותיו כי אין ראש אלא מי שמקבל רשותו וגדולתו מהראש שהיה לפניו. והנה דברי רבנו האיי וזולתו מן הגאונים בחרט (=בכתב) ידם בענין הזה כדברים האלה ועדיכם עדיכם הגאונים ודבריהם הנכונים. ולא חרטנו (=כתבנו) אליכם כאלה אלא שלא תשימו לב לזולת מה שחקקנו לכם בחרט ברורנו (ברורה r.) וכו׳. Sherira in his Letter indeed uses several times the expression סמך in connection with appointments at the schools (cp. ed. Lewin, p. 117: ולבסוף אסכימו למסמך למר רב נתן אלוף; p. 120: ובתריה אסתמיך מר רב אהרן . . . ומר רב מבשר גאון סמכיה בדרא רבא במתיבתא p. 121: ובשנת רע״ט אסתמיכינא בגאונות וסמכונהו להאיי בננו באבות ב״ד). Cp. also above, p. 104.

remarks of Samuel b. ʻAlī and of his son-in-law Zekharyah may have been about the disputed theories of Maimonides concerning the resurrection of the dead and other matters, the Gaon's opponents no doubt magnified their disparaging nature to Joseph ibn ʻAḳnīn while in Bagdād. The latter was naturally wrought up and promptly informed his master thereof and the sage of Fusṭāṭ in his reply to his disciple gave vent to his displeasure.[88] The self-importance of Samuel b. ʻAlī is bitingly ridiculed and likewise his claim of the high standing of the school. Of Zekharyah[89] Maimonides has a still lower opinion. Although Zekharyah wrote to Maimonides from Bagdād with due respect, as the latter himself admitted, and also Samuel b. ʻAlī followed with another epistle, Maimonides purposely delayed answering them in order that they should not boast of his correspondence. He satirizes the mutual admiration of both writers, Zekharyah praising the Gaon and vice versa. But Maimonides held the Exilarch in high respect.[90] He corresponded with him and one of the Exilarch's replies was read in Maimonides' house with great ceremony with all the leaders of the community, including Maimonides himself, standing as a

[88] See Goldberg's rendering of this letter (in זכרונות סי' ב', ברכת אברהם) which can now be checked by the original Arabic given by Pozn., *l. c.*, 56–61, cp. his discussion p. 30ff.

[89] No doubt Zekharyah b. Berakhel, originally of Aleppo but now in Bagdād, as this passage clearly shows (Pozn., *l. c.*, 58): (viz. of Zekharyah) וגרץ̇ כתאבה כאן תעט̇ים ראס אלמתיבה ואנה (the Gaon) ואחד אלעצר ואנה הו (Zekharyah) ראמוה פי בגדאד אן יקדמוה פלמא סמע כלאמה וראה (viz. saw the Gaon) עלם אנה לא יחל מקאומתה. See also Assaf, p. 6–7.

[90] The passage ודכר אן כל ת'ח מנעזל ען הדא ראס אלגלות כארהא לה should read ודכר אן כל ת'ח מנעזל מן הדא וואן ראס אלגלות כארה לה, as Goldziher rightly suggested (Pozn., *l. c.*, 32, note 3), so that there is no disparagement whatever of the Exilarch. Hence Poznański's interpretation that Maimonides recommended a new Exilarch (pp. 33–34) is not tenable. His El'azar Exilarch never existed (see Mann, *Livre d'hommage . . . Poznański*, Hebrew part, pp. 23–4). There is no cogent evidence that the Exilarch Samuel of Mosul, who occupied the office in Bagdād since some time after 1175, was then dead and that a new Exilarch arose (1190) of whom Samuel b. ʻAlī did not approve (as Assaf, p. 26–27 construes the course of events). The struggle between Samuel b. ʻAlī and the Exilarch Samuel was a long drawn one as evident from our discussion of the data. Of a new Exilarch, David (probably Samuel's son), we hear first in 1197 (see above, p. 223–4).

sign of respect. Yet Maimonides, to do him justice, on realizing the conflict between Exilarch and Gaon wished to withdraw from it. He apologized for his writing to the Exilarch because he knew not of the controversy.[91] He also strongly advised Joseph ibn 'Aḳnīn not to set himself up in Bagdād in opposition to Samuel b. 'Alī out of respect for his age if not for his scholarship. Evidently the Exilarch would have wished Joseph to settle in Bagdād as a sort of rival head of a school under his authority. Maimonides strongly urges upon Joseph not to entertain this proposal.[92]

As to the legal side of the problem of Semikhah Maimonides in his Mishnah commentary, written long before our present dispute, recognizes this right only to the Gaon of Palestine and yet the nominees of the Babylonian Exilarch can function both in Palestine and in the Diaspora. The former must be an outstanding scholar whereas the latter need not be one, but by reason of his royal descent has the full authority[92a]—a more favorable opinion

[91] There is some obscure allusion to a case of a Geṭ due to which the Gaon was ready to pounce upon the Exilarch and bring about his downfall, were it not for the aid given to the latter by Joseph ibn 'Aḳnīn (Pozn., *l. c.*, p. 59): אן לולא אנת לכאן ראס אלגליות בין ידיה כפרוג פי מכאלב הדאה ואנה כאן ישנע עליך אמר וגירה ויפתרסה א ל נ ט, perhaps for אלנט r. אלכט, the signature, viz. a certain undertaking on the part of the Exilarch to abide by the Gaon's decisions.

[92] See the passage in Goldberg's rendering (this part is not given in the original by Poznański except for one line on p. 31, note 2): ואמנם מה שזכרת מהליכתך לבגדד כבר נתתי לך רשיון על זה שתפתח מדרש ותלמד ותורה לאחרים עם שמירת החבור (יד החזקה) אך יראתי כי תמשוך עליך רעות עמהם תמיד ולא תבא לתכלית כי אם לרעות. וכן אחרי אשר תעמיס עליך חובה ללמד תמעט במסחר ואני לא איעצך שתקח מהם דבר כי טוב בעיני דרהם אחד שתרויח מאריגה או מחייטות או מנגרות משתרויח מ ר ש ו ת ר א ש ה ג ו ל ה. This school (בית מדרש=מדרש) was thus to be by authority of the Exilarch from whom Joseph would obtain his income. The Exilarch, not having succeeded in obtaining Zekharyah b. Berakhel of Aleppo, now turned to another Aleppo scholar, Joseph ibn 'Aḳnīn. (Pozńanski speaks vaguely of a licence from the Exilarch).

[92a] Commentary to Sanh. 1.3: סמיכת הזקנים היא מנוי הדיינין . . . ואין אנו צריכין סמיכה בידים אבל האיש אשר ראוי למנותו יאמרו לו הבי"ד הממנים אותו: „אתה רבי פלוני ס מ ו ך אתה ורשאי אתה שתדין דיני קנסות". ובזה יהיה האיש ההוא סמוך והוא נקרא אלהים וידין כל הדינין ודבר זה לא יהיה כי אם בא"י ואמרו ז"ל אין סמיכה בחו"ל אבל צריך שיהיה הממונה (הממנה .r) ואותו שרוצין למנותו כולה (כולם .r) בא"י . . . ויראה לי כי כשתהיה הסכמה מכל החכמים והתלמידים להקדים עליהם איש מן הישיבה וישימו אותו לראש ו ב ל ב ד ש י ה א

about the Exilarch's rights than that which Samuel b. 'Alī was ready to acknowledge.

Of the relations between Gaonate and Exilarchate after Samuel b. 'Alī we have hardly any information. Only we find the Gaon Daniel b. El'azar in 1201 mentioning his contemporary Exilarch David with respect (see above, p. 223, note 51). Altogether the 13th century is shrouded in obscurity with regard to the activities of the school and of the political heads of the Babylonian Jewry. The Exilarch Samuel (II), who played a role in Bagdād after the Mongol conquest of the 'Abbāsid capital in 1258, is only once mentioned in our available sources. During the agitation of Solomon Petit in 'Akko against Maimonides' writings we hear of the Exilarchs of Damascus and Mosul and of the Gaon of Bagdād, Samuel Hakkohen, having been approached by David Maimuni to oppose Solomon Petit (1187–88, see infra, p. 421, and cp. above, p. 228). The contemporary Bagdād Exilarch, whether Samuel II or his successor, does not figure at all in this affair. But it would be hazardous to draw any conclusion as to the standing of the contemporary Exilarch because he may have been also asked to intervene, only his reply has not been preserved. Till more information is available no opinion can be ventured on this phase of the history of Oriental Jewry.

ז ה ב א"י כמו שזכרנו הנה האיש ההוא תתקיים לו הישיבה ויהיה ס מ ו ך ויסמוך הוא אחר כן מי שירצה וכו'.

As regards a licence (רשות) to act as judge, apart from Semikhah, the rights of the Exilarch are more extensive than those of the Palestinian Gaon. See commentary to Bekhorot 4.4: ונשאר עלינו לברר מי הוא הנותן רשות ולמי ראוי לתת רשות שיועילנו. ואומר שהנותן רשות הוא ר"ג הממונה בבבל ואין צריך להיות חכם. וראש ישיבה ממונה בא"י אבל (r. אבל ראש ישיבה ממונה בא"י) ראוי שיהא גדול בחכמת התורה מאד עד שלא ימצא גדול ממנו בשום פנים בא"י בזמן שממנין אותו. ואם הדיין הזה נקט רשות מר"י בא"י אותו הרשות מועיל לא"י בלבד ואינו מועיל בחו"ל. ואם נקט רשות מראש הגולה הרי הוא המועיל (r. מועיל) בכל מקום בא"י ובחו"ל לפי שדינו של ר א ש ג ל ו ת ע ל כ ל י ש ר א ל כדינה של מלכות שאונסת ומכרחת . . . הלא תראה שאין אנו חוששים לחכמתו אלא ליחוסו וממנים אותו בהסכמת אנשי מקומו בלבד וכו'. Cp. further his Mishneh Torah, ה' סנהדרין, c. 4, where the whole matter of סמיכה and רשות is recapitulated, and see also Abraham Maimuni's remarks, in connection with the dispute between Joseph b. Gershom and the Nasi Hodayah (cp. infra, p. 398 ff.), in Ḳobeṣ, I, No. 250, and in *Guttmann Festschrift*, 218 ff.

Appendix (to pages 204–07).

[MS. Mosseri (Cairo), L. 135, paper, very torn and damaged. See Facsimile XIV, A and B, infra, pp. 713–14.]

(Recto)

. . . .

. . . . ממן הם אשפק עכה* אכת̇ר מנא

. . . . [אלא]כ̇יאר אלנאס ואג̇לאהם אסל אללה יג̇עלהא
אימן סאע[דה̇] .

. . . . ץ̇ פאחב תהני עני מולאי אלשיך̇ אלג̇ליל
צהרך[1] ומא ל . . . .

. . . . קד . . הך̇ אל[א]כ̇יאר אלנאס פיג̇ב תעתקד
אן לם ימו . . . .

. . . מן ה . . . . ל אן לא תכ̇אלפהם ואן ת[ע]מל מא ישירו . . . . .

. . . ן אשפק מנא . . . . . ת[ע]תקד פי מולאי צהרך באעתקאדך
פי ואלדך[2] נע̇ . . . .

ו . . . [א]ללה . . . . . [ו]אלד ועלי ולדה ובדלך תג̇על סידתי
חמאתך[3] כמת̇ל[ה]א . . . .

ו . . . . ואללה א[ס]ל ואליה ארג̇ב ילהמך ללכ̇יר ואלתופיק
ויג̇עלה אימן אתצאל ויג̇מע ב . . .

. . . . דיאר ואמא הדה̇ אלדיאר קד שא אללה הלאכהא והלאך
מן בהא נסל אללה יחסן . . . .

* The reading is doubtful.

[1] Either son-in-law or brother-in-law of the recipient of this epistle. The latter evidently lived in Fusṭāṭ and is perhaps identical with Nahrai b. Nissim who had an extensive correspondence with coreligionists in North-Africa, Sicily and Spain (see Mann, I, 204–07, II, 240–48; *H. U. C. Annual*, III, 290). Many more letters to and from Nahrai are to be found among the Genizah fragments.

[2] Here this person's late father is referred to.

[3] Probably read חמאמתך, your beautiful wife.

וינט̇ר אלינא ברחמתה כי באו מים עד נפש טבענו ביון מצולה ואין מעמד באנו במעמ[קי]
מים ושבולת שטפתנו[4] ואנא מנתצ̇ר[5] כתאב יצול אלי[6] מן סקליה̈[7] ותצל אליך כתבי ....
ואעט̇ם אלאשיא תק[ר]ב* ענד חואיג̇ באלמ[ה]דיה̈[8] ב . . . . וב . . . ן דרה'[9] ואל ....
עלינא אלאצאטיל[10] מן אלמהדיה̈ אחיל בינא ובינהא רגע* אלצרף אליום ....
אלדינ'[11] קיראט ד̇הב ואמ[א] . . . כמא שא אללה ד̇כרת יא ולדי מא עאמלך בה סידי פתחל . . . .
אב[ו] זכריא אלטב[יב][12] .... אחסן ..... ג̇זאה ......
סלאמי ומא לי קלב . . . אן אכתב אליה לאן לו ג̇רי עלי אלג̇באל מא ג̇רי עלינא להלכת אף [שכני]
בתי חומר אשר בעפר יסודם וגו'[13] [ו]ד̇כרת אן אוג̇ה לך מקאטע ורדאת מא יג̇ה̈* אלמתאע ......
ג̇ר[ן]* לה לא גאל ולא רכיץ ואקרב . . . קה פיהא יח̇ דראע תסוא דינ' ונצף תסוא ....
ולו כאנת צאלחה̈ אש[ן] יכ̇רג̇הא ואינא יוצלהא כתב נוג̇הו ללמהדיה̈ מא ירג̇ע ....
אן סלם אלי שהר לאן פי ו . . . צח גדר דרכי בגזית נתיבותי עוה[14] ואעלמך אן וצל כתאב

[4] Cp. Ps. 69.2–3. The reference is here to the troubles in Ḳairwān and all over North-Africa.

[5] =מנתט̇ר. [6] Read אליי. [7] Sicily.

[8] Al-Mahdiya near Ḳairwān.

[9] Probably =דרהם.

[10] =אלאסאטיל, plur. of אסטול.

[11] =אלדינאר.

[12] Abū Zakariya (=Yehudah) the physician.

[13] Cp. Job 4.19. Here again the allusion is to the troubles in Ḳairwān.

[14] Lam. 3.9.

(right hand margin)

סידנא ראס|אלמתיבה אדאם אללה|עזה לאהל
אלקירואן באלעזא | פי רבנו חננאל זצ״ל[15]
ופיה דכר|
רבינו נסים ושכרה אלשכר אלעטים | וסמאה
ראש בי רבנן ואטלק ל[ה]|אלנטר פי סאיר
אלמגרב|
[ו]ואפק וצול אלכתאב מא גרנ[י] | . . . . א ען* יולי פתכל | . . .

(The remainder of the margin is missing.)

(verso)

אדאם אללה עזה[16] יכתב ללגמאעה ויעזיהם פי מא גרי עליהם
וגלאהם ת[ם]*
מן בלדהם וכרוגהם מן דיארהם וצארת חארתהם ואלמקדש
אלגליל[17] כל עובר
עליה ישום וישרוק על כל מכותיה[18] וינבההם עלי גמע מא ענד
אלנאס מן אלודאי[ע]

[15] R. Ḥananel was still alive in 1053 as is evident from the remark in his commentary to 'A. Z. 9a: כמו שנתינו זו שהיא שנת ד' אלפים ותתי״ג לעולם כשתסיר מהם ג' תמ״ח נשארו בידך אלף ושל״ה (ושס״ה .r) למלכות יון. However the corrections of the revisor in the Romm edition of the Talmud, Wilna, note 3: תת״ג . . . ושנ״ה are also possible because the corruption of שנ״ה into של״ה is paleographically more likely than of שס״ה into של״ה. But our letter, referring as it does, to the time of the destruction of Ḳairwān in 1057, also points to the death of R. Ḥananel shortly before this event and therefore the former reading of 1053 should be preferred. (Berliner, מגדל חננאל, VIII, and Poznański, אנשי קירואן, p. 20, did not at all occupy themselves with the difficulty of the contradicting dates of A. M. and Sel. given in the above passage).

[16] Evidently referring to the Gaon mentioned in the margin.

[17] The synagogue (מקדש in the meanning of מקדש מעט (Ezek. 11.16) which, according to the Aggadah (Meg. 29a), denotes the synagogues and the houses of study).

[18] Cp. Jer. 19.8, 49.17, 50.13.

ללישיבות[19] ואן יחרם פי ד̇לך חרם שריר לה עלו אלראי וכתאב אלג̇מאעה̈ תצל לחצ̇ר[תה]

באלאעתד̇אר אן אמכנת תו[כ]תב אליה תשרח לה ד̇לך אפעל וארג̇ו אנך אצרפת לי . . . .

צרף גייד ואנא נעלם אני ננתפע באקבאלך ג̇עלך אללה מקבל מסעוד ולא אכ̇לא . . . . . .

תופיק וצלו אצחאבנא אלאנדלסיין ללמהדיה̈ ואחכו אן יהוסף ולד אלנגיד ז[צ̇ל][20]

. . . ה ואעלא מנזלה וג̇מיע אצחאבנא אלד̇י פי עמל בן חבוס[21] אלמתוליין באל[גראנטה̈] . . .

ואעלי וג̇מ[י]ע אל[א]הל בכ̇יר . . . בן יהודה אלד̇י תואלד לה תופי ולך טול אלבקא . . . .

ולדהא חסן אללה בלגתהם[22] אעלמתך ד̇לך . . . נפסך . . . אלסלם[23] ג̇מיע אלאה . . . . . .

אלס . . . . לי באלמהדיה̈ ובני עמי[24] ובניהם בכ̇יר יכ̇צוך אלסלאם ודאוד בן בע . . . . . .

מוסי . . . . . תו . . . . ר בניה אסלך תבולג סידי אברהם סלמה אללה אלסלם[23] וג̇מלה̈ מ[א] . . . . . .

. . . . אלכתאב וסידי אבי אלסרור אלסלם[23] וכתבי ת[צל] . . . . . .

. . . ורוה מו . . . . . . אברהם בן אלסכני . . . . אפצ̇ל סלם . . . תת . . . .

. . . . אללה . . . . . . ולעל נג̇ד אכתב אליה וקד ד . . . . . .

. . . . א ערפתה ענה אנה אל . . . .

[19] In the plural (cp. above, p. 207).

[20] Joseph b. Samuel ibn Nagdela.

[21] Viz. Bādīs ibn Ḥabbūs, king of Granada.

[22] This word is in Arabic script.

[23] Read אלסלאם.

[24] The writer's uncle.

............ה ודעא לה [ו]ל[ס]איר אלתלמידים אלדין
בנאלמהדיה* .....

............וסידי ר̇ ישועה בית [דין][25] אפצ̇ל אלסלם
וס[יד]י ר̇ אלחנן* ....

........א וולדה אלסלם וכל מן סאל עני אלסלם ועקב שלום

[25] If this be correct, then this R. Yeshu'ah is probably identical with Yeshu'ah Hakkohen b. Joseph, Dayyān of Alexandria, who actually corresponded with Nahrai b. Nissim (Mann, II, 240), and thus the above suggestion (note 1) to identify the recipient of our letter with Nahrai would be strengthened.

3.

THE GAONATE AT DAMASCUS IN THE 12TH CENTURY

Above (p. 230) we had occasion to introduce this Gaonate as it was involved in the conflict of interests between the Bagdād Gaon Samuel b. 'Alī and the Exilarch Daniel b. Ḥisdai. Here it is intended to summarise the data at present available about the school established in the capital of Syria and to fix the chronology of the successive Damascus Geonim.[1]

The Palestinian Gaon, Elijah b. Solomon Hakkohen, two years before his demise in the fall of 1083, fixed the succession of the first three ranking dignitaries of the school, viz. his elder son Ebyatar to become Gaon, his second son Solomon to become Ab and Ṣadoḳ b. Joshiah Ab to be 'Third.' This arrangement was reaffirmed in the year of the Gaon's death. Then came the serious conflict between the Nasi David b. Daniel b. 'Azaryah and Ebyatar Hakkohen which seriously hampered the activities of the Palestinian school then established in Tyre. In 1093 Solomon Hakkohen Ab had to leave Tyre after his brother, the Gaon Ebyatar, had been ousted from the school still earlier.[2] In Megillat Ebyatar it is described vaguely that "Solomon set his face towards the inheritance of Asher and the congregation of Naftali", viz. to upper Galilee.[3] While we find Ebyatar established in Tripolis

[1] My remarks in *Jews in Egypt* I, 224–26, and II, 295, about the identification of the Damascus Geonim are now to be modified in the light of the new data discussed here. Cp. further Assaf, *l. c.*, 14–15, who in spite of his command of the new data confused the chronology of these Geonim.

[2] See Mann, I, 187ff.

[3] *Saadyana*, 91, l. 25: ובשנת אֿתֿדֿ (=1193) חזרה צור לתקוה. . . וירדפו אחרי אב (= אב הישיבה) להרגו ויצילהו י״י מידם . . . ויסתירהו לחפשו. וידכאו את ביתו ואת מגרשו. וישם פניו אל נחלת השר (r. אָשֵׁר) בחוסר כושר. וקהל נ פ ת ל י המתאשר. Perhaps the congregation of Tiberias is meant because it is identified with the Biblical רקת which belonged to the territory of the tribe of Naphtali (cp. Josh. 19.35 and Meg. 5b, 6a).

(Ṭarābulus ash-Shām) during the 1st Crusade, Solomon, who may have resided till the arrival of the Crusaders in Tiberias or Safed, took refuge in Damascus. In 1116 we find him at the head of a sort of a school in Ḥadrak (חדרך), a locality near Damascus.[4] In his work Solomon was aided by his son Maṣliaḥ destined to succeed him.[5] The vicissitudes of this school under Solomon are very obscure and also the reason why his son Maṣliaḥ left Syria and became Gaon in Fusṭāṭ (evidently after Solomon's death) where he functioned during 1127–38.

The school of Ḥadrak found its continuation in Damascus. The first Damascus Gaon we hear of was *Abraham b. Mazhīr*. Isaac b. Abraham ibn 'Ezra, while on his way to Bagdād where we find him in 1143, stayed for some time in the capital of Syria and came into contact with this Gaon. A poem in his honor is found in the still unpublished Diwān of this luckless only son of Abraham ibn 'Ezra (see above, p. 210f.). Abraham b. Mazhīr seems to have been connected with the family of Solomon Hakkohen and Maṣliaḥ.[6] One may perhaps venture to suggest that Abraham was a son-in-law of Solomon Hakkohen. When Maṣliaḥ left Syria to settle in Fusṭāṭ (1127), Abraham, influential in Damascus, continued there his father-in-law's school. His father Mazhīr is styled השר הגדול יסוד הישיבה. Abraham was certainly in office in 1138 when Maṣliaḥ died because the latter's will, which contained some disposition about his belongings in Damsacus, was submitted to the court of the Gaon Abraham.[7]

[4] Mann, II, 233–4. The address of this letter reads משער הישיבה הנשגב בשם יי' צבאות. משגב לנו אלהי יעקב סלה. ישע מעוזינו מבטחינו לעולם ועד. The last phrase was his motto also at the end of his epistle.

[5] Maṣliaḥ was evidently a student of the Palestinian school in Tyre. He is mentioned as 'Fourth' and as 'destined to be Gaon': הרביעי (בישיבה) המעותד לישיבה (Mann II, 234).

[6] Samuel b. 'Alī in his letter of Adar I, 1191, to the community of Damascus styles the local Gaon Abraham (II), the grandson of Abraham b. Mazhīr, as: שורש הגאונים האיתנים הבא מחמת משפחת הכהנים האיתנים (Assaf, *l. c.*, 67, l. 22) which seems to be a reference to the priestly family of Palestinian Geonim from which Solomon Hakkohen had sprung up.

[7] Cp. the letter from Natan b. Samuel to a person in Fusṭāṭ (Mann, II, 277–79). My interpretation of this epistle (I, 225–26) has now to be modified in so far as the writer Natan was then in Damascus and was closely

Although he is styled "the great Gaon", we know nothing of his scholarship. His successor was his son *'Ezra* who was ordained by Samuel b. 'Alī. Benjamin of Tudela and Samuel b. 'Alī call him "the head of the school of Palestine." This designation, we can now understand, is due to the fact that the Damascus school was the continuation of Solomon Hakkohen's school at Ḥadrak.[8] Solomon Hakkohen, after the death of his brother Ebyatar, probably regarded himself as the legitimate Gaon of Palestine, although, on account of the political situation in Palestine held by the Crusaders, his school had to be situated in Syria. 'Ezra found the title of "Gaon of Palestine" convenient to claim through it authority over the Egyptian communities and thus demand dues and donations and thus indirectly benefiting Samuel b. 'Alī who had ordained him. But these claims were opposed by the Fusṭāṭ Gaonate, of which anon, aided by the Bagdād Exilarch Daniel b. Ḥisdai as described in detail above (p. 230ff.). Benjamin of Tudela mentions the officers of the school, viz. 'Ezra as Gaon, his brother Sar Shalom as Ab-Bet-Din and Joseph as "fifth of the school" (החמישי בישיבה). Bearing in mind the organization of the Palestinian school where the chief issues were decided by Gaon, Ab and

connected with the school of Abraham b. Mazhīr whom he styles הכוכב המנהיר אשר עלה והאיר על בני גילו . . . אדונינו גאונינו אברהם ראש ישיבת יעקב אשר אהב סלה בן אדונינו מזהיר השר הגדול יסוד הישיבה . . . Natan assures his correspondent in Fusṭāṭ that he constantly makes mention in the circles of the school of the services the Fusṭāṭ dignitary was rendering it (p. 278: מודיע להדרתו כי בכל יום ויום אני משתדל לספר שבחו ומבאר קצה (r. קצת) מהלליו ורוב אהבתו. ועוצם שירותו למושב הישיבה הקדושה. ושמה נרשם ונחקק בפינקסי ישיבתה לפארו ולאמצו ולקרוא בשמו ולגדלו לפני קהלות הקודש). Natan then requests his correspondent to interest himself in the case of the last will of Maṣliaḥ Gaon (בעסק הצואה הנזכרת לפני מושב אדונינו הגאון יכון כסאו (viz. Abraham b. Mazhīr) אשר צוה אותה אדונינו מצליח הכהן גאון בן גאונים ז"ל בעסק מה שיעשה אחר מותו על עזבוניו ומה שיניח אחריו).

Some time after the date of this epistle Natan b. Samuel moved to Fusṭāṭ where he became secretary to the famous Nagid Samuel b. Ḥananyah. See his letter, dated Marḥeshwān 1453 Sel. = 1141 C. E., to the Gaon Abraham b. Mazhīr (Mann, I, 224–25).

[8] *Itinerary* (ed. Adler, 31): ושם (בדמשק) ראש הישיבה של ארץ ישראל ושמו ר' עזריה (r. עזרא according to one variant). ואחיו שר שלום אב בית דין. ור' יוסף החמשי בישיבה. ר' מצליח ראש הסדר הדרשן. ור' מאיר פאר החברים. ור' יוסף בן אלפלאת יסוד הישיבה. Samuel b. 'Alī (*l. c.*, 76, bottom): מרנו ורבנו עזרא ראש ישיבת ארץ הצבי.

'Third',[9] there is no doubt that for החמישי בישיבה we should read השלישי בישיבה[9a]. In addition there are mentioned other dignitaries who held titles connected with the school, viz. Maṣliaḥ Rosh Hasseder who was the preacher, Meir פאר החברים and Joseph b. פלאת אל[9b] styled יסוד הישיבה. The title Rosh Hasseder was Babylonian in origin[10] and Maṣliaḥ may quite well have obtained it from Samuel b. 'Alī. But perhaps the Damascus Gaonate, influenced by the Babylonian school, introduced some titles that were prevalent there. But its basic organization was modelled after the old Palestinian school with Gaon, Ab and Third at the head. Whether there were functionaries called Fourth, Fifth, Sixth, and Seventh respectively as in Palestine is not known.

Of 'Ezra's correspondence as Gaon only a small item has been preserved testifying to the genuineness of an epistle that arrived from Samuel b. 'Alī. It is dated Tammuz 1172 or 1175 at Aleppo where he then stayed.[11] But there must have been a considerable correspondence between him and Samuel b. 'Alī and also letters by him sent to Egypt. But all this has been lost.[12] His scholarly activities are also shrouded in obscurity. In 1191 we find already his son *Abraham* (II) established as Gaon in Damascus aided by the Ab Sar Shalom (evidently his uncle) and Mazhīr the Third.[13] This we learn from the letter of Samuel b. 'Alī informing the Damascus community of the appointment of Zekharyah b. Berakkel as Ab of the Bagdād school and at the same time appealing for monetary support for this school.[14] This letter testifies

[9] See Mann, I, 273.

[9a] A title Samuel b. 'Alī mentions indeed in his letter.

[9b] About this scholar, whose real name seems to have been Joseph b. Palṭoi, cp. Mann, II, 296–7.

[10] Mann, I, 279, and above, p. 198.

[11] Assaf (*l. c.*, 134). His signature is עזרא עניא זעירא ראש ישיבת גאון יעקב ברבי אברהם ראש ישיבת גאון יעקב זצ"ל. His motto at the end of his epistles was evidently: עזרת המעוז. לנו תעוז.

[12] Only one fragment, very damaged, of a letter to him has been preserved (Mann, II, 295).

[13] The former 'Third' Joseph must have departed this life in the meanwhile and Mazhīr (a member of the Gaon's family) succeeded him.

[14] Assaf, *l. c.*, 67–70, cp. above, p. 220, note 43, for the corrected text as given here. The Damascus community is addressed (p. 67, l. 16ff.): הקהל הקדוש

to the dependence of the local Damascus school on the more ancient seat of learning of Babylon. A curious phenomenon of a school, supposedly the continuation of the Palestinian academy and organized after its model and yet guided intellectually and orientated *politically* by the energetic Samuel b. 'Alī, Gaon of Bagdād.

Abraham's activities are again entirely obscure. Also the school of Damascus disappears from our records. Ḥarizi, who visited Damascus about 1215, mentions the local Exilarch Joshiah b. Jesse but not the head of the school. On the other hand he met in Safed a luckless scholar by the name of Ṣadoḳ whom he styles the son of ראשי ישיבות גאון יעקב. His ancestors were also heads of the school but this Ṣadoḳ experienced many troubles and after assuming the title of Gaon was removed from his office and had to go into exile.[15] The thought lies near to connect him with the

היושבים ובערי[ם] דמשק חדרך ... אשר לישיבת ארץ הצבי נחולים ועל פי ישיבת הגולה (school of Bagdād) מתנהלים ... בהיות בראשם איש חי רב פעלים ... שורש הגאונים האיתנים הבא מחמת משפחת הכהנים האיתנים מורנו ורבנו אברהם ראש ישיבת גאון יעקב המישר בעין חכמתו אורח שכל בנועלם בן ההקים בישראל שתילים מאירים כמאורים הגדולים ... מרנו ורבנו עזרא ראש ישיבת ארץ הצבי ההנהיג בעודו מקהלות ישורון בשובה ונחת ופדע כושלים משחת. It is evident that when this letter was written 'Ezra was no longer alive but his son Abraham (II) was functioning as Gaon. Assaf (p. 15) has misunderstood the whole passage and thus makes 'Ezra to have been the last Damascus Gaon.

Samuel b. 'Alī goes on to enumerate the two assistants of Abraham II, viz. the Ab and the Third (p. 68, top): יעל ידו (viz. of Abraham) [עומד] מחזיק הבדק. באמונה וצדק. להסיר כל חדק. רבנו שר שלום אב בית דין של [י]שיבת[ו] ... רבנו מזהיר השלישי בחבורת הצדק וכו'.

In appealing for monetary support from the Damascus community Samuel b. 'Alī continues (p. 70, l. 16ff.): ... ומימי אבותיכם על פי הישיבות ניהגתם ולא נעלם מכם אחינו הדוחק אשר דחוקנ[ו] ... והחובות אשר רבו עלינו בהלוך רכילים ומלשינים ועזות [מ]צח ונדב[ו]תכם אחינו היתה לנו למעוז.

[15] See Mann, II, 295–6. As against Kaminka's text of Taḥkemoni (p. 354), where Ṣadoḳ is himself styled Gaon, ed. Lagarde, p. 168 reads: צדוק הצדיק בן ראשי ישיבות גאון יעקב. אבותיו היו ראשי ישיבות וכו'. Yet Ḥarizi himself goes on to say: והורד מכסאו אחרי מלך. והורק מכלי אל כלי ובגולה הלך. This Ṣadoḳ seems also to be referred to in a responsum by Maimonides (Mann, ibid.). My suggested dating there of this responsum as being 1177 or 1178 has to be changed since we find still in 1191 the Gaon Abraham (II) in Damascus. Maimonides mentions the wording of the Ḥerem issued against honoring this Ṣadoḳ and other dignitaries (Ḳobeṣ I, 29d): אבל אם היתה השבועה כמו ששאלו ממני מקצתכם וכתבו נוסח

Damascus Gaonate. He may have been a son of Abraham (II) and for some unknown reason he lost his position. With his exile the school probably ceased to exist or was continued in some manner by the local Exilarch.

This in outline, as far as our meagre sources now allow, is the history of the Damascus Gaonate lasting for about a century. The attempt to continue the Palestinian academy in Syria was not a lasting success. Its influence was on a small scale and the scholarship of its Geonim does not seem to have commanded wide recognition. But we must reserve a final judgment till more material is available concerning this Gaonate. As it is, the above sketch is only possible as a result of recent finds of new data which, let us hope, will be still augmented to a considerable degree.

החרם ואמרו שכך החרימו על מי שיחזור מהיום ההוא והלאה ישמע לאדם רשות לא בטבה ולא זכר ולא תסמיה לא עלי ספר תורה ולא על פי כתב ולא עלי שום מן הברכות עד אתקפ"ח שנה זהו הנוסח ששלחו לי. The Arabic here is evidently corrupt and can be corrected by Bodl. 2670[2k] (*Cat.* II, 71, top): ישמע לאדם רשות כצובה (r. בצובה) ולא כ̇טבה̈ ולא דבר (r. ד̇כר) ולא תסמיה̈ לא עלי ספר תורה ולא פי כתאב ולא עלי שי מן אלברכות עד א̇ת̇ק̇פ̇א̇ שנה זהו הנוסח ששלחו לי [by another hand: מאסכנדרייא של מצרים]. Cp. also infra, note 30.

The time limit of the Ḥerem was to be till 1581 Sel. (1270 C. E.) but we have no means of ascertaining when the Ḥerem started. This Ṣadoḳ is referred to by Maimonides as בן פלוני הגאון ראש ישיבת ארץ הצבי וכו' (ibid., 30a). If the question came from Alexandria, Ṣadoḳ then in his wanderings from Damascus reached Alexandria, where he also met with trouble, and later on was found by Ḥarizi in Safed.

4.

THE GAONATE AT FUSṬAṬ IN THE 12TH CENTURY

As a counterpart to the Damascus Gaonate we have to discuss in the light of the new data the Gaonate at Fusṭāṭ. The hitherto prevalent idea that David b. Daniel b. ʻAzaryah started a school in Fusṭāṭ, in opposition to the Palestinian one under Ebyatar Hakkohen,[16] has now to be discarded since the fragment *in Saadyana* (pp. 107–111) is proven not to have emanated from him but from the Bagdād Exilarch Daniel b. Ḥisdai (above, p. 230). The first Gaon of Egypt was *Maṣliaḥ Hakkohen* who, for some unknown reason, decided to leave Ḥadrak and settle in Fusṭāṭ where his activities continued for 11 years (1127–38).[17] He is always referred to as ראש ישיבת גאון יעקב and never as ראש ישיבת ארץ הצבי, although he could have easily claimed to continue the tradition of this school through his father who was actually Ab of the Palestinian academy.[18] But it may be that he was satisfied in leaving the Ḥadrak-Damascus school, actually founded by his father and going by the name of ישיבת ארץ הצבי, because of the cordial relations

[16] Mann, I, 190–92, 219, 220. The Yeshibah of Joshuʻa b. Dosa (Mann, II, 272, l. 24) is too vague an affair to be considered in this connection.

[17] See Mann, I, 220ff., II, 274–77, 382; Yellin, *Ḳiryat Sepher*, II, 294–5; Halper, *Descriptive Catalogue*, p. 181, Nos. 342–43; Weiss, הצופה לחכמת ישראל, V, 4-11, whose remarks on and edition of the texts require several corrections.

His letters began with Ps. 124.8 followed by his name, title and genealogy: מן מצליח הכהן ראש ישיבת גאון יעקב החוסה בשם יו' אלהיו מגן הוא לכל החוסים בו. ביר' שלמה הכהן ר' י' ג' י'. בן אליהו הכהן ר' י' ג' י'. נין שלמה הכהן ר' י' ג' י'. נזע יהוסף הכהן בית דין כהן צדק. נכד אהרן הכהן הראש קדוש יו'. His motto at the end of his epistles was: עזרת מגינינו הבטחתינו לעד (Mann, II, 275; Weiss, *l. c.*, 6–7).

[18] An allusion to the Palestinian school, supposedly represented by his own academy, may be found in the letter of Iyyar 1132 (Weiss, p. 6, l. 12): ומשער הישיבה קרית מלך רב. The phrase קרית מלך רב in Ps. 48.3 means of course Jerusalem but here it may be a stylistic reference to Fusṭāṭ-Cairo (whence our letter was actually despatched) as the capital of the Caliph. Anyhow besides this allusion he does not seem to have emphasized the parent school of Palestine.

he had with Abraham b. Mazhīr who evidently was related to him, perhaps as his brother-in-law (above, p. 250). Of the organization of Maṣliaḥ's school in Fusṭāṭ we have no information but it may be surmised that he had as colleagues an Ab and a 'Third', although their names are unknown.[19]

The next Gaon we hear of in Fusṭāṭ was *Moses Hallevi b. Netanel* the '*Sixth*' (הששי בחבורה).[20] It is probable that Netanel was a member of the Palestinian school under its last Gaon Ebyatar. With its cessation as a result of the 1st Crusade Netanel found refuge and scope in Egypt. His son Moses Hallevi may have been Ab under Maṣliaḥ Hakkohen and succeeded him on his demise in 1138. He had two sons, Netanel and Sar Shalom, who succeeded him in turn. The latter signed his letters as ראש ישיבת גאון יעקב and ראש ישיבת ארץ הצבי by which two titles he also mentions his father Moses.[21] However the second appellation may have been an afterthought as a counter claim to the Damascus Gaonate. Just as the latter could claim its origin from the erewhile Palestinian school by reason of Solomon Hakkohen, so the former could do it by reason of Maṣliaḥ Hakkohen who was associated with his father's school in Ḥadrak. Sar Shalom also calls his father 'the descendant of Geonim' (נין הגאונים), but it is difficult to find out of which Gaonic family his grandfather Netanel had sprung up, certainly not of a Palestinian Gaonic family since there was none there of Levitic origin.[22] But perhaps from the maternal side Moses Hallevi was the offspring of previous Geonim. Of Moses' activities in Fusṭāṭ as Gaon very little is known. It is possible that Judah Hallevi while in Egypt met him and wrote a eulogistic poem in his honor. If the poem is really by Judah

[19] In the above letter (Weiss, p. 6, l. 13–14) Maṣliaḥ speaks in a general way of the members of his school as: שרי הקדש אדירי התורה. ותלמידיה וחבריה סופריה ושאר ס מ ו כ י ה. Did he too continue the prerogative of Semikhah as in the Palestinian school?

[20] Mann, I, 234, II, 294–95. My suggestion that Moses Hallevi was Gaon in Damascus has now to be discarded.

[21] See Mann, II, 294, 298–99.

[22] We know of the Ben-Meir family claiming descent from R. Judah the Patriarch, the priestly family of Joseph and Samuel and the other priestly family of Solomon, Elijah and Ebyatar. Solomon b. Yehudah was neither Kohen nor Levi and Daniel b. 'Azaryah was of the Exilarchic family in Babylon.

Hallevi, then it would seem as if Moses' reputation as scholar reached Babylon in the East and Spain in the West.[23] However this poem may really be by Joseph ibn 'Aḳnīn in honor of his great master Moses Maimonides to whom the above eulogy certainly fits better. Anyhow of Moses Hallevi's scholarship we have no record. Natan b. Samuel, who corresponded with Abraham b. Mazhīr (above, note 7) and with whom Judah Hallevi actually came into contact, is styled Kātib (secretary) of the Nagid Samuel b. Ḥananyah and also secretary of the school (סופר הישיבה), but this school was more likely that of the Nagid and not that of Moses Hallevi, although the latter's period of activity coincided with that of the Nagid Samuel[24].

Next comes his son *Netanel Hallevi* of whom we hear in the decade between 1160–1170.[25] His appointment as Gaon was the occasion for the interesting letter by the Bagdād Exilarch Daniel b. Ḥisdai in October 1161 opposing the claims of the Damascus Gaonate to have jurisdiction over the Egyptian communities by reason of its being the supposed heir to the Palestinian school (as described above in full, pp. 230 ff.). This Netanel is called by the Exilarch ראש ישיבה של גולה just as the Bagdād school was known. Under this title Netanel actually figures in legal documents issued at Fusṭāṭ in 1164.[26] It would seem from a portion of the Exilarch's letter as if he purposely established this title for Netanel in Egypt to free the Egyptian communities from any obligation to the Palestinian school, now represented by the Gaonate of Damascus, since in the Exilarch's opinion Egypt was חוצה לארץ just as Babylon and hence its school was also ישיבה של גולה. All this was a political move on the part of the Exilarch in opposition to Samuel b. 'Alī who ordained the Gaon of Damascus, 'Ezra b. Abraham b. Mazhīr.

Netanel's brother and successor, *Sar Shalom Hallevi*, went one step further and simply called himself ראש ישיבת ארץ הצבי

[23] See Mann I, 234, note 3.

[24] See Mann I, 225, note 1; II, 286.

[25] See the data collected by Mann II, 293–4. A new letter to him is given as an Appendix (infra, pp. 259–62).

[26] Mann, II, 293, Nos. c and d, and so also in the letter given in the Appendix (infra, p. 261).

giving the same title also to his father who was Gaon in Fusṭāṭ before Netanel in succession to Maṣliaḥ Hakkohen. The latter never went by this name, although he certainly had a far better claim to the title than Moses and his son Sar Shalom. This Gaon's period of tenure of office we have traced between 1170–1188.[27] With Sar Shalom the Fusṭāṭ Gaonate apparently comes to an end as we hear subsequently of no other person by this title. In the 13th century and beyond the Negidim of the Maimunian family were called ראש ישיבתה של תורה which may be regarded as a relic of the Gaonate. The Egyptian Geonim also commanded no wide recognition for their learning and their whole school was only of local significance. Altogether this juggling of titles must have struck a keen outsider, not familiar with the old traditions connected with them, as grotesque and childish. In the light of the cross currents of ambitions for prestige and influence, as revealed by the data now available, we can fully understand the sarcastic remarks of Maimonides in his Mishnah Commentary, completed in 1168 in Fusṭāṭ when he was a newcomer to the country.[28] "Do not be misled in all these matters, which I have included here, (by) the titles known in Palestine and in Egypt. Some are called 'Head of the School' and others 'Ab-Bet-Din' and a distinction is made between ראש ישיבת גאון יעקב and ראש ישיבה של גולה. Unknown people are addressed as Rosh Yeshibah or by some other title. All these things are only mere flavoring of a name.[29] People go by such appellations and hereditary distinctions. I have already seen in Palestine people called Ḥaberim and in other places there are such called Rosh Yeshibah and yet do not measure up to a student of one day's standing!" Later on, with more familiarity with actual conditions as they developed historically in the Oriental countries, Maimonides was no longer so sarcastic. In the responsum, mentioned above (note 15) with regard to the titles of Ṣadoḳ, Maimonides decided that Ṣadoḳ be given all the honorary appellations by which he and his

[27] Mann, II, 294; cp. the letters from and to him, ibid., 298–301, and see I, 237–38.

[28] To Bekhorot 4.4, cited by Mann, I, 239, note 1; ארץ המערב there is to be taken as Egypt in juxtaposition to ארץ ישראל.

[29] פטומי שמא בעלמא, cp. B. M. 66a: פטומי מילי בעלמא הוא.

ancestors were used to be known.[30] Conditions brought about the disappearance of both the Damascus and the Fusṭāṭ Gaonates towards the end of the 12th century. There only remained the Bagdād Gaonate functioning till towards the end of the 13th century when it too disappears from the annals of Jewish History as far as preserved to posterity.

Appendix

A LETTER TO THE GAON NETANEL HALLEVI

The epistle given here emanates from a person who signs himself "the son of אלנזר," no doubt identical with one of the sons of Natan b. Samuel and very likely this son being Meborakh whom we find as Dayyān in Fusṭāṭ. One document of his, dated 1164, is issued under authority of our very Gaon Netanel Hallevi.[31] In our letter too the writer is an obedient nominee of the Gaon claiming to follow always the behest of his superior. The subject of the letter concerns again the question of titles. A certain Abū'l

[30] *Ḳobeṣ* I, 30a, top: ואף לפי נוסח זה שכתבו אם אירע דבר לזה השר הנכבד רב צדוק ש"צ להזכיר שמו ושם אבותיו נ"ע כגון שישא אשה או יולד לו בן זכר או יעלה לקרוא בתורה מברכין אותו ומקלסין אותו כראו ילכבודו ומזכירין אותו בכל מיני כנויים שירצה ושם אבותיו הקדושים וצ"ל ואומרין בן פלוני הגאון ראש ישיבת ארץ הצבי וכו' ואין בזה שום אסור על כל הנשבעין ששמעו דברים אלו. וכן אם נתן דבר לצדקה וברכוהו ברבים כדרך שמברכין כל מתנדב מזכירין שמו בכל כנוייו ושם אבותיהן (r. אבותיו) בכל כנוייהן ואין בזה חשש איסור. אבל אם לא יארע שם (r. שום) דבר אלא יזכירו שמו ושם אבותיו ברבים בשבתות או במועדים ויבקשו עליהם רחמים כדרך שהיו עושין מקודם לראשי גליות או לשאר השרים הרי אותם הנשבעים שלא ישמעו לא בטבה ולא זכר (r. כֿטבהֿ ולא דֿכר) ולא תסמיהֿ אסור להם לשמוע. To prevent quarrels, Maimonides goodnaturedly would tolerate such high sounding titles, although he at heart despised them. Also his son, Abraham Maimuni, pokes fun at calling persons by the title al-Raīs although they have never held any government or other office (*Ḳobeṣ* I, 50b): כמו שיאמרו היום בלשון הישמעאלים למי שהוא בן שר או ממשפחת השררה שר אף על פי שלא נתמנה מימיו על שום מנוי קוראין לו ר י י ס כלומר בשם אביו. וידוע הוא אצל בעלי השכל שרוב אלו הכנויים שמכנים לאדם זהו לשון הבאי ופטומי מילי בעלמא ובקיאי הדעת ממעטין מהם ושונאין אותם אבל אוהבי הגדולה הרודפים אחר השררה ומעלתם מרבים בהם ואוהבים אותם שהם גדולתם. About the profusion of titles, see also Mann, I, 280.

[31] See the data collected in Mann, I, 227, note 1; II, 293. Meborakh's father Natan b. Samuel, the secretary of the Nagid Samuel b. Ḥananyah, was known as אלנזר = נזר החברים (Mann I, 225, note 1). Meborakh's brother Yehoseph, called נזר השרים אמין אלמלך, was also an influential figure in Fusṭāṭ (see Mann I, 227, note 1, 267; II, 280, and infra, p. 449).

Faraj Hakkohen b. Fatūḥ was indignant that the title Ḥaber, given to his late father Fatūḥ, was omitted apparently in a legal document (perhaps a Ketubah) and the blame was laid on our Meborakh who evidently drew it up. Abū'l Faraj went with his complaint to the Raīs Abū'l Mukārim, evidently the brother of the Gaon Netanel (and hence this was the Arabic name of the later Gaon Sar Shalom Hallevi), who denied that his brother (i. e. the Gaon Netanel) had any knowledge of this slight to the memory of a dead person and attributed the fault to ibn al-נזר (our Meborakh) and his brother (either Sa'adyah or Yehoseph). Naturally Abū'l Faraj went and took Meborakh to task. Now the writer points out to the Gaon that all his official actions are first approved of by Netanel and hence the responsibility is his and not as Abū'l Mukārim insinuated to the aggrieved person. Meborakh reports that there is the case of another Ketubah involving Abū'l Fadhl b. Abū'l Baḳa al- 'Ajamī (the Persian), whose wedding is to take place on the following Sunday, and suggests that the same procedure be followed in his case (viz. not to mention the title Ḥaber). He adds that after what happened in the case of the wedding on Tuesday (evidently our letter was written between Tuesday and Sunday of the following week), probably referring to the affair of Abū'l Faraj, he will not again allow any rank to be mentioned in a Ketubah lest the rumor should be renewed among people that he was discriminating in this matter.

The above letter reveals the social conditions within the Fusṭāṭ community in the middle of the 12th century and the sensibilities of people with regard to titles and honorable appellations in which they gloried. The Exilarch and the other Nesiim as well as the Geonim fully made use of this human weakness of vain glory and would bestow all sorts of titles on persons expecting monetary support for their institutions as a reward.[32] There developed a sort of 'trade in honors' as a means of arousing the generosity of the would-be supporters of the schools and of other communal establishments. Therein lies perhaps the justification

[32] Cp. the many titles listed and discussed in Mann, I, 252–80. The many legal documents found in the Genizah teem with such honorable appellations.

for all these honors as they served useful purposes in the life of Jewry of those days.

[Antonin Collection, Leningrad, No. 1154, paper.][33]

(Recto)

ממלוך הדרת יקרת צפירנת תפארתן כבוד גדולת קדושת מרנו ורבנו אדוננו גאוננו נתנאל הלוי רכב ישראל ופרשיו ארי התורה יחיד הדור ראש הישיבה של [גו]לה יכונן אלהינו כסא גאונותה[34] ויצליח בכל מפעל ויסב לב כל ישראל אליה. יקבל אלארץ̇ בין ידי מג̇לסהא אלסאמי וינהי אנה סמע מן אלנאס מן אללום מא לא לה חד בס[ב]ב ואלד אלשיך̇ אבו אלפרג̇ אל כהן בן פתוח נ"ע וד̇לך אן אלרג̇ל אג̇תמע במולאי אלרייס אבו אלמכארם חפצה[35] אללה ולאם אלממלוך ענדה וקאל לה הד̇א אלאטראח ליס הו בי בל מא פעל ד̇לך אלא פי חק אל מותא וד̇לך אן אבי נעתה אדוננו גאוננו בחבר מן פ̇[36] סנה̈ והד̇א אמר משהור מעלום כיף̇ חתי אסקטתו[37] ד̇לך ענה פכאן ג̇ואב מולאי אלרייס אבו אלמכארם ש̇צ̇ לה הד̇א ג̇מיעא פעל בן אלנזר ואלא אכ̇י[38] מא ענדה מן הד̇א כ̇בר וקד עמל בן אלנזר ואכ̇וה ולג̇דה מא עמלה מא אנכר אחד עליה ד̇לך באן עמל איצ̇א ללאכ̇ר חבר פג̇א אלרג̇ל אליי וחדת̇ני חדית̇ה וקאל אלד̇נב לך אנת אלד̇י אטרחת בחקי ובחק ואלדיי

[33] I had before me only a copy made by the late Dr. Harkavy. Some necessary corrections of it are indicated in the following notes. I have also supplied the diacritical marks.

[34] The feminine suffixes throughout refer to הדרת יקרת וכו' (l. 1).

[35] For חפט̇ה.

[36] This must be a mistake and rather ה' should be read because 'our lord and Gaon' (viz. Netanel, see also ll. 2 and 18) could not have bestowed the title Ḥaber on Abū'l Faraj's father 80 years before.

[37] Read אסקט הו.

[38] My brother, viz. the Gaon.

והדרת אדוננו גאוננו תעלם ותתחקק אן ענדהא[38a]
מנד כרס[39] בין ידיהא לם יעמל קט כבירה̈ ולא צגירה̈
אלא באמרהא ובאד̇נהא ובעד משאורתהא
גיר ד̇לך אן כתובה עבדהא אלשיך̇ אבו אלפצ̇ל
בן אלשיך̇ אבו אלבקא אלעג̇מי נ"ע ותקדסה[40] יום אלאחד
פמהמא אמרת בה פי חק אלמד̇כור תאמר בה
לימת̇לה כ̇אדמהא

(margin)

פבעד מא ג̇רי פי חק צאחב תקדיס יום אלג' מא יעוד אלממלוך
יכ̇לי לאחד פי אלכתובה
מכאן[41] לאלא יעוד חדית̇ בין אלנאס כמא ג̇רי לגירה אנהא
כ̇אדמהא ד̇לך ושלום יקרה יגדל לעד

(verso)

ממלוכהא
ולד אלנזור

[38a] Read עבדהא.
[39] Read כ̇דם, served.
[40] Read ותקדיסה.
[41] In the meaning of 'rank', though מכאנה̈ is the usual expression.

5.
EL'AZAR B. JACOB HABBABLI

This poet is the last one in Babylon who has produced a considerable number of poems forming a Diwān of an extensive size. His period of activity falls chiefly in the first half of the 13th century whereas in the second half of this century flourished Joseph b. Tanḥūm Yerushalmi in Egypt (see infra, pp. 435 ff.). These two poets seem to close the classical period of Neo-Hebrew poetry in the Orient of whose origin and development we have no adequate account yet. The Genizah has preserved a goodly number of compositions of these Oriental poets from the end of the 10th century and onwards, but owing to the fragmentary character of these finds only occasionally do we learn the names of these poets. Their fate was to have fallen into oblivion while the productions of the Spanish poets were more known to European Jewry and hence handed down to posterity. And then there was the tendency of the Spanish poets to characterise the output of Andalusia as superior to that of the rest of the Diaspora. Indeed there was good reason to glory in the poetry of a Samuel ibn Nagdela, Solomon ibn Gabirol, Moses ibn Ezra, Judah Hallevi and a host of others. But we in modern times need not take this opinion for granted. Exactly as there is the vaunted superiority of Spain even in Halakhic studies after the establishment of the school in Cordova by Moses b. Enoch, a tendency we can detect in Abraham ibn Daud's Sepher Seder Haḳḳabalah (see above, p. 207, note 10) and also in Maimonides' disparagement of his contemporaries in Egypt, Syria and Babylon, so we have evidence of the emphasis that Spain was the home of the best productions in Hebrew poetry. Moses ibn 'Ezra devotes a whole chapter of his Kitāb al-Muḥādhara al-Muḏākara to this theme,[1] and especially Judah

[1] Cp. Halper's translation (שירת ישראל, 1924, pp. 62–80): התשובה על השאלה החמישית. מדוע יש יתרון לבני הגולה שבספרד בחבור שירים ומאמרי מליצה ואגרות בעברית על בני הגולה? By the way, the passage concerning Ḥisdai ibn Shaprūṭ's inviting

al-Ḥarizi in his Taḥkemoni belittles all the Oriental poets whom he met or heard of during his wanderings in the East.[2] That the latter was not always justified in his criticism, which seems to have been biased by his impecunious condition as a globe trotter expecting everywhere monetary assistance by reason of his literary wit and brilliance, has already been noticed before.[3]

In rectification of this claim of superiority the modern task is first to make available the output of Oriental poetry and investigate it thoroughly, and then intrinsically compare it with the poetical productions of Spain in order to come to an independent opinion on this matter and not merely adopting the views of the Spanish poets themselves as final. Even the question of the introduction of the meter by Dunāsh b. Labrāṭ is not yet settled. The part of the Diwān by a Syrian or Egyptian poet towards the end of the 10th century and the beginning of the 11th, rescued from the Genizah, seems to show that the meter was developed in the Orient and that Dunāsh was only the first to have introduced it in Spain.[4] The numerous specimens of poetical productions in honor of Egyptian celebrities of the 11th to 13th centuries, evidently composed by local writers, that have so far been published from among the Genizah finds,[5] reveal to us a familiarity with the technique and the phraseology of verse that should command our appreciation and should compel us to revise our views as to the traditional claim of Spain as the classical country of

to Andalusia men of knowledge "from Syria and Babylon" (p. 63, bottom, ואסף אליו את אנשי המדע מסוריא ובבל) should really read "from Palestine and Babylon." The Arabic original שאם was used by the Jews of those days to denote Palestine as already Bacher (*JQR*, XVIII, 564–5) has pointed out and as so many Genizah finds testify. Moses ibn Ezra (p. 49, top) himself mentions Tiberias as being in the land of Shām which Halper wrongly translates as בארץ סוריא!

[2] Maḳamas 3 (cp. ed. Lagarde, p. 22: . . . כי שירות בני ספרד חזקות וערבות ומשורריהם כזכרים וכל משוררי עולם כנקבות), 18, 46, and occasionally in 50 (pp. 188, top, 197–98).

[3] Cp. Brody, *Z.f. H.B.*, II, 157–59; Kaufmann, ibid., 188–89; Poznański, *l. c.*, 43.

[4] Mann, II, 14–21, cp. I, 22–26.

[5] See Davidson, גנזי שעכטער, III, (cp. my remarks in *Journal of Sem. Languages*, XLVI (1930), 275ff.) and his articles in *JQR.*, *N. S.*, I–II, IV; Mann, II, General Index, s. v. Elegies, Poems.

mediaeval Hebrew poetry. This mere touching upon an important problem is only by way of prefatory remarks on the present theme concerning El'azar Habbabli a number of extracts from whose Diwān are given here.

El'azar b. Jacob Habbabli seems to have been a sort of a house poet to several important families in Bagdād including the presidents of the local school. Events of joy and of sorrow in the lives of these families were the occasions for employing his muse. He no doubt received an honorarium for his poems. It was the custom in well-to-do Jewish homes to have a poet perpetuate in verse the birth of a child, the circumcision of a boy, a betrothal, a wedding or a sad event such as death.[6] There were poets whose living consisted of employment of this sort. On their part they were on the lookout for some opportune occasion in the careers of their patrons in order to honor them with the fruit of their muse in the expectation of being handsomely compensated. And indeed when the compensation was not handsome enough, some poets did not hesitate to change their former eulogies into abuse and vilification.[7] Bearing the impecunious condition of so many poets

[6] The Jews followed therein the custom of their Muslim neighbours. Of Ḥisdai ibn Shaprūṭ it is reported that when his mother died he hastened on foot to his Hebrew secretary, the stylist Menaḥem b. Sarūḳ, at midnight to request him to compose an elegy in Hebrew for her. When he found Menaḥem already at work on this elegy before he had been asked, he promised him his lifelong gratitude for this act of loyalty to his family. See the passage in the famous letter of Menaḥem to Ḥisdai (published by Luzzatto, בית האוצר, reprinted in Stern, *Liber Responsionum*, XXXII, bottom): אחרי זאת זכור נא אדוני ליל תמרורים אשר בו נאספה גבירתי יולדתך ירחמנה עושה. כה יעשה לי אלהים וכה יוסיף מחרונך אם לא כחצות לילה רגלי באת אליו ל ת ק ן סַ פָּ ד ולהכריז נהי. מצאתני ואני כותב ונזהרתי טרם תזהירני ויהי כי ראית כה נשבעת באל עליון: שמורה זאת תהיה לך כל הימים!. Menaḥem also composed an elegy on the death of Isaac, Ḥisdai's father: הלא כה קראני בהאסף אדוני אביך כוננת (read כוננתי as in בית האוצר) רב ספד וחקותי דברי קינות אשר קוננו כל ישראל דבר יום ביומו כל ימי האבל.

[7] Cp., e. g., the indignation of the anonymous poet (cp. note 4) at the Wezīr Menasseh b. Ibrāhīm al-Ḳazzāz (Mann, II, 16–17) and at the person who sent a cheese as remuneration for his poem (p. 20, No. XV, cp. p. 380). See especially Ḥarizi's Taḥkemoni (ed. Lagarde, pp. 187–8, Nos. 17, 19–20, 22–23, 25–26, 29–30; p. 189, No. 41; p. 190, No. 45, No. 46 (ועשיתי על אנשים הללתים בשירים ולא הביטו דרכם ולא ידעו מהלכם), No. 51; p. 191, No. 56; p. 192, No. 63; p. 193, Nos. 70 and 78; p. 194, No. 79; p. 195, Nos. 85 and 88; p. 196,

in mind, their eulogies and their abuse have to be taken cum grano salis. There was also rivalry between the hungry adepts of the muse, and their criticism of each other also has to be taken with caution.[8] Added to this we have to keep in mind the general Oriental manner of stylistic exaggeration which evidenced itself especially in poetry. Hence the shrewd characterization of Aristotle became familiar that "the best part of poetry is its falsehood" (מיטב השיר כזבו).[9] Considering the number of people in Babylon eulogized in an extravagant manner by El'azar Habbabli in his Diwān, Bagdād and other cities of 'Irāk must have had an oversupply of worthy and eminent people in the first half of the 13th century. But Ḥarizi, living on his wits during his wanderings that carried him to the East, has a rather poor opinion of the cultural level of the Jews of Bagdād and of other Oriental cities.[10] The truth should be sought midway between the eulogies of El'azar Habbabli and the condemnation of Ḥarizi. Anyhow El'azar Habbabli's Diwān testifies to a familiar knowledge of Hebrew among many Jews in Babylon who would receive these poems and would feel honored by them, frequently rewarding the poet for his verses.

The Diwān of El'azar Habbabli, acquired by Mr. E. N. Adler at Aleppo in 1898, is unfortunately not yet edited. But several scholars have made use of its data, expecially Poznański in his *Babyl. Geonim* (cp. p. 8 ff., 61–77).[11] This MS. is incomplete and

Nos. 95 and 96; p. 201, No. 122, No 128: לאחד מן הנדיבים והוא ראש לנבלים ושבחתי לאיש נבל באשור (Mosul). בשיר כזב אשר אין בו נכונה. ונדר לי נדרים הם כשירים. מלאים שוא ואין בהם אמונה).

[8] Gabirol is also conscious of his own superiority over the other poets (cp., e. g., ed. Bialik, I, 95ff.: ושירנו כילודי אמנה ושיריהם כמו ילדי זנונים (p. 99); pp. 157–58). Especially Ḥarizi gave vent to his spleen about other poets in his Taḥkemoni, Maḳamas 18, 46 and 50.

[9] See Dukes, נחל קדומים, II, 54ff.

[10] Taḥkemoni, Maḳamas 24, 46 and 50 (ed. Lagarde, p. 190, top: ועשיתי על בני עדינה. אשר היו בימי קדם פאר כל מדינה. ועתה נותרו למשל ולשנינה. אנשי עדינה נבזים ושפלים. מבחר המונם דומן לאשפה. וכו').

[11] Cp. the bibliography on El'azar Habbabli by E. N. Adler (*Livre d'hommage . . . Poznański*, 24) to which there should be added Brody's edition of the poems on the family Ibn Karām (הצופה לחכמת ישראל, VI, 123–133). The fragment published by Davidson (גנזי שעכטער, III, 229–242) as possibly being a part of this Diwān is very problematic as regards the identification (cp.

for a future edition MS. Firkowicz, 2. Hebrew Collection, No. 210–1, will have to be utilized. The latter MS. contains a portion of this Diwān in a different arrangement. Substantial extracts from MS. Firkowicz are given here for the purpose of adding to our knowledge of the notabilities in Babylon in the first half of the 13th century. My aim was not to edit this MS. because it would have had to be done in conjunction with MS. Adler to which I had no access. Two data were used above (p. 226) in connection with the discussion of the Bagdād Gaonate. Some additional remarks are due here on some of the personalities mentioned in our manuscript (cp. also the notes). It is very difficult on the basis of the brief indications to obtain a definite identification of the personalities mentioned in the poems. Moreover there are several namesakes which complicate matters. But a number of families can be regarded as outstanding in Bagdād Jewry and elsewhere, even after discounting the extravagant praise of our poet.

A prominent figure was Daniel Hakkohen, styled 'Izz ad-Daula (dignity of the state), b. Isaac (or Jacob). He was the son-in-law of Yeshu'ah Abū'l Faraj b. Berakhel.[12] The elegy on the latter's death (No. 21) eulogizes Daniel as נגיד עם האלהים and introduces other respected people connected with this family. To Daniel Hakkohen our poet devotes two other poems (Nos. 9 and 26). From the designation נגיד עם אל it is evident that he is also meant in No. 41 where a son of his, Aaron, is mentioned in addition.

Mann, *JSL.*, XLVI, 280–81). But the epigrams (pp. 213–17, cp. Davidson's remarks, p. 201) are evidently by El'azar. Similar to items 8–9 in rivalry to other poets, cp. No. 9 in our extracts.

[12] Cp. Adler, *JQR*, XI, 684, and Steinschneider, XII, 202, No. 512b, where the Hebrew name of 'Izz-ad-Daula is wrongly given as Samuel (see also ibid., p. 205, No. 600). From MS. Adler it appears that Daniel's Arabic name was Abū'l Ma'āli. Daniel's father-in-law, Yeshu'ah b. Berakhel, seems to have been connected with a Gaon's family because the heading of the elegy on him (No. 21) has the indication מכאן גאון בית יעקב (מכאן=rank, see above, p 262, note 41). Should we say that he was a brother of the Gaon Zekharyah b. Berakhel? However there would have been some indication to this relationship in the poem proper.

Much praise is bestowed upon Joseph b. al-Barḳūli of Wāsiṭ (between Bagdād and Baṣra, Nos. 3–5, 33–36) who seems to have been a high government official (see note 85). The al-Barḳūli family is also represented by Samuel, to whom Ḥarizi dedicated in Bagdād his Taḥkemoni, evidently a brother of Joseph. Their father was Meborakh Abū Manṣūr b. al-Barḳūli holding the title נאמן המלכות (=Amīn al-Mulk).[13]

An important official was Mordecai b. al-Ḥarabiyya who, after some trouble, was restored to his office of Keeper of the Mint.[14] To him evidently refers poem No. 46. Whether Isaac b. Mordecai, styled Muhaḏḏib ad-Daula (the repairer of the state) b. al-Māsha'īri, was a son of this Mordecai is doubtful. Anyhow this Isaac, to whom No. 50 was dedicated on the occasion of the circumcision of his son 'Obadyah, was evidently an influential notable. Isaac's eldest son was El'azar (l. 3) and in No. 54, f, we have a poem in honor of him where he is styled al-Raīs Amīn ad-Daula b. Manṣūr b. al-Māsha'īri. We thus learn that Isaac's Arabic name was Manṣūr.[15]

Another official eulogised is Moses Najm ad-Daula (the star of the realm) b. Abū'l Sa'ūd (No. 49) who lived in the time of the Gaon 'Alī (II). Another dignitary bearing the title Najm ad-Daula was Samuel Abū'l-Barakāt al-Ṣilhi (a place above Wāsiṭ, No. 44). Just as Mordecai b. al-Ḥarabiyya was the keeper of the mint so we have another Jew Samuel, called Shams ad-Daula (sun of the state), b. Kurrātha holding this office. He is greatly eulogised in No. 11 for his protection of his coreligionists. From his designation as נגיד עם אל it is evident that he is also meant in No. 27.

We are too meagerly informed about the life of the Jews in Babylon in the first half of the 13th century. But the titular names of the above mentioned notables, in addition to several

[13] Cp. the letters from the Gaon Daniel b. El'azar (in Assaf, *l. c.*, pp. 112–14; the heading of No. 11 there should read אבו מנצור בן אלברקולי [אלי אל]רייס).

[14] Cp. החלוץ, III, 153, and IV, 66; *JQR*, XII, 129, No. 218e.

[15] Steinschneider, *l. c.*, 118, No. 22, has the reading Abū Manṣūr (and so also Adler, *l. c.*, 683) and hence El'azar's Arabic name was Abū Manṣur. But אבו can be a misreading of אבן. Anyhow this El'azar was a member of this family.

others referred to in the notes to the extracts from El'azar's Diwān, testify to the high offices which several Jews held in the closing period of the 'Abbāsid Caliphate.

SELECTIONS FROM THE DIWĀN OF EL'AZAR HABBABLI

[MS. Firkowicz, 2. Hebrew Collection, No. 210–1, 51 leaves. Where 'וכו is placed at the end of a line, it indicates that one or more of the subsequent lines in the MS. have been omitted here. The lines are numbered according to the text given here in extract.

The corresponding numbers in MS. Adler of this Diwān can now be ascertained by consulting Dr. Davidson's אוצר השירה והפיוט, vols. I–III.]

1.

(Fol. 1, recto, contains the conclusion of a poem.)[1]

— — ⌣ — | — — — ⌣ — | — — — ||

וירדפו שבעת בני עש אחר   כימה[2] אסרוה בחבלי נומה
אמרו למשה הגבוה [מן]   שחק ויתר מעדנות כימה
כי הוא אשר עלה והוריד משפ־   טי[3] אל והוא נודע ונכר שמה וכו'
חשך בצאתו מעדינה[4] תארה[5]   ותעדה רעד ובגדי אימה וכו'
ככה השמני צבי הודו יום[6]   רכב כרובי נור והלך רומה

2.

ולה פי שכץ באלאסכנדריה[7]

— — ⌣ — | — ⌣ — | — — — ⌣ — | — — ||

עורה כבודי והעיר את חליליך
ופרוט נעים שירך על פי נבליך

[1] This is evidently an elegy on a late personality (Moses) of Bagdād.

[2] Cp. Job 38.31–32.

[3] Vocalize מִשְׁפָּטַי, poetic license for מִשְׁפְּטֵי.

[4] Bagdād.   [5] Vocalize תָּאֳרָה.

[6] MS. ביום which spoils the metre.

[7] By him (El'azar Habbabli) about a person (i. e. 'Obadyah, l. 3) in Alexandria.

שיר נחמד חברו ראש כל משורר ענק[8]
על גרגרות מחמד כוכבי זבוליך
מנחה שלוחה לעובדיה אשר העביד
אותך לעולם ואת כל מהלליך וכו׳

(There are also mentioned ʿObadyah's 2 sons without name and a daughter Leah.)

3.

(Fol. 1, verso, bottom, has the heading: ולה פי אלרייס ר׳ יוסף בן אלברקולי. There follows one faded line. There is a lacuna between fols. 1 and 2. Lines 1–3 of fol. 2, recto, contain the end of a poem. Then we have the following item.)

4.

ולה פי ר׳ יוסף בן אלברקול[י][9]

– – ˘ – – | – ˘ – – | – – ||

אל נא תדמו נוף ותחפנחס לתוך[10] ולא יוסף[11] לזה יוסף
כי איך יהי נותן כלוקח או איך יהי זורה כמו אוסף
יוסף בהון השביר למצרים בר[12] ולשוברים זה יתנה כסף

[8] Here the metre is faulty.

[9] Our Joseph lived in Wāsiṭ. He is probably the brother of Samuel b. al-Barḳūli to whom Judah al-Ḥarizi dedicated his Taḥkemoni. Samuel evidently lived in Bagdād (ed. Lagarde, p. 9, ll. 15–17: הנביר המעלה רבי שמואל בן אלברקולי זצ״ל. מצרים (Fusṭāṭ) תתאוה להיות מדרך אדמתו, ודמשק מנוחתו, וצובה (Aleppo) תקנא בשמועתו, ואשור (Mosul) תעיד גדולתו, ועדינה תתפאר כי היא אמתו, viz. Bagdād boasts that she is subservient to him, hence he resided there). In ll. 31–32 his two brothers Joseph and Ezra are mentioned (ושני אחיו השר הנכבד רבי יוסף והשר הנחמד רבי עזרא). Steinschneider (H. B. XX, 134) places this Samuel in Damascus whereas in *Hebr. Übers.*, 851, his residence is given as having been in Egypt. Both statements are unwarranted. Samuel and his two brothers are also referred to in Maḳama 46 describing the Jewry of Bagdād and Wāsiṭ (תוך, p. 176, bottom).

[10] Wāsiṭ, "the middle city," cp. Le Strange, *The Lands of the Eastern Caliphate*, 39ff.

[11] Joseph of old.

[12] Cp. Gen. 42.6.

5.

ופי אלמדׄכור[13]

|| — — | — ◡ — — — | — ◡ — —

אל נא ידמוהו ליוסף כי   יוסף בהון השביר וזה חנם
אותו בעקבה העביד[13a] עמים   ולזה באהבה רצעו אזנם

(There follows a poem of 3 lines with the heading: ופי בעץׄ אלחתנים.)

6.

ולה בדיהא̄ סאעהׄ דרגׄ ולדה אבו אלסעאדאת יעקב[14]

|| — — ◡ | — — — ◡ | — — — ◡

למות יעקב בני דמעי כצולה   עלַי לחיי ולבתי אמולה
ואש תוקד בצלעותי ועשן   באפי יעלה יומם ולילה
היש מכאוב כמכאובי ובי נ־   געה יד אל וסלדתי בחילה[15]

(fol. 2, verso)

שעו מני ובבכי אמרר   וארד אל בני אבל שאולה

7.

ולה מרתׄיהׄ פי ראש הישיבה יצחק בן אלשויךׄ זצ"ל[16]

(=No. 214 of MS. Adler, printed by Poznański, *l. c.*, 75–77, where the heading is: ולה ענד ופאהׄ ראס אלמתׄיבהׄ יצחק בן אלשויךׄ זצ"ל. The last line of fol. 2, verso = l. 16 of ed. Poznański. There is a lacuna between fols. 2 and 3.)

[13] Concerning the afore-mentioned (Joseph b. al-Barḳūli).

[13a] Better עָבְדוּ.

[14] An extemporary dirge at the time when his son Abū'l Sa'ādāt Jacob died childless.

[15] Cp. Job 6.10.

[16] A dirge on the death of the Gaon Isaac b. al-Shuwwaikh.

8.

(Fol. 3, recto, commences with the end of the following poem.)

|| – – | – – – – ⏑ | – – – ⏑

ויום אקביל פני הודו בבבל   לאל שדי אשלם הנדרים
ואיך אצא לחפשי מחסדיו   וטובו יעבידני לדורים
יחי לעד ויתנשא ויחיו   בני ביתו גדולים עם צעירים
ומוסדי דור ודור מהם יקומם   לעולמי עד ויבנה הנצורים
והם אל יועצי ארץ כשרים   וטפסרים ולגבירים גבירים וכו'

9.

ולה פי שכץ רד עליה פי שערה ותנזל פי

אכ̇רה ימדח אלרייס עז אלדולה בן אבי יעקב[17]

|| – ⏑ – – | – – ⏑ | – – – ⏑

זמן החיה בני סכלות והחרים   בני שכל והשכינם קברים
ואישים מהרו צחות לדבר   בחבלי מותה[18] שמם אסורים
ונותרתי נביא חכמות לבדי   ובלעדי נביאי השקרים
כקורא יגנבו שירים ויעשום   תפלים מבלי טעם יקרים
ולא עשו לנפשם רב בחכמת   לשון קדש ולא קנו חברים
ומפי סופרים אמרו חכמים   הוי למד ולא מפי ספרים
ואיכה אל תכונת שיר יבואון   והמה מלשון קודש כזרים
וכל יהיר וזד תרץ לשונו   ורצה להיות שופט בשירים

(fol. 3, verso)

ואולם כי חכמים הם להרע   ואמורים[19] ודעתם כחמורים
ומצנפתם כארץ על בלימה   וראשיהם כמו דעתם חסרים

[17] Concerning a man who criticized our poet in his verse. Our poem ends with a eulogy on 'Izz ad-Daula b. Abū Yaḳūb. In l. 16 this dignitary is called Daniel b. Jacob whereas Abū Yaḳub is usually = Ishāḳ. Either read here יעקב for אבו יעקב or in l. 16 בנו י צ ח ק. Our Daniel was a Kohen (l. 17). See also infra, No. 26.

[18] Vocalise מֻוּתָה.

[19] Probably read וְאָמוּדִים (for וַאֲמוּדִים on account of metre), viz. they are esteemed.

ושיבה זרקה בהם וסכלות   בלבותם קשורה כנערים
וכמעט אזכרה אותם בשמות   ואכתוב תועבותם על ספרים
ואכן אשמרה את הברית ל־   אבי רוזנים ושר שרים וחורים
לדניאל בנו יעקב יחיד דור   אשר החיה לכל החי ומטרים
נגיד עם אל ובן אהרן קדוש אל   ונכד לובשי תמים ואורים
יחי לעד ויתנשא ויגדל   וכסאו יהיהנכון לדורים

10.

ולה פי רא הישי שמואל בן דניאל הכהן בן אבי אלרביע זצ"ל למא תזוג באבנה רא הישי יצחק הלוי בן עלי ז"ל[20]

|| – – ⏑ | – – – ⏑ | – – – ⏑

הֲקול ששון וקול שמחה ושירים   וקול כנור יעורר השחרים
ואם קול מצהלות חפות חתנים   ושושבינים בבית משתה נערים[21]
וכו'

(The poem is incomplete at the bottom of fol. 3, verso, and there is a lacuna between fols. 3 and 4. Fol. 4, recto, has a new poem, with the heading ולה איצֿא, in eulogy of a certain person who built a synagogue (אשר הכין לאל לבו ומקדש מעט כונן ביד האל ובנה). This poem ends on fol. 4, verso, top, followed by No. 11.)

11.

לה פי אלרייס שמס אלדולה בן כראתה[22]

|| – – ⏑ | – – – ⏑ | – – – ⏑

להר המור וגבעת הלבונה   מקור התום ומעין האמונה
נגיד עם אל וגם מלכם שמואל   אשר אין קץ בשנ[כ]לו לתבונה

[20] Concerning the Gaon Samuel b. Daniel Hakkohen (ibn Abū'l Rabi'a) when he married the daughter of the Gaon Isaac Hallevi b. 'Alī.

[21] Probably read נעורים, plural of Niph. participle of עור.

[22] Concerning the dignitary Shams ad-Daulaḥ b. Kurrātha. He was the keeper of the mint (נאטר דאר אלצֿרב, cp. Steinschneider, *JQR*, XII, 132, No. 288b). From l. 2 we learn that his Hebrew name was Samuel.

כרוב ממשח אשר לבו לדת אל   כמו ארון ועיניו לאמונה
גביר רעה בעז שבטי ישורון   והרביצם במרבצת שמנה
גביר לו יאתה משרה ואחר   בלות היה לעם קדוש לעדנה[23]
ויום יום על זמן היו מלינים   עדי משל וחשך התלונה
גביר לולי יהי עוזר לעם אל   עליהם כתבו מנדה ושטנה[24]
גביר הרס מעון און ועמל   ובתי האמת יסד ובנה[25]
גביר מכר לשכלו תאוותיו   ובין משך בכוס עינו וקנה[26]
ואל שרי הזמן העניק יקרו   כשמש תעניק אור ללבנה
גביר עטו[27] בכפיו יעשה כ־   עשות רמח ביד גבור וצנה
בלבו נמצאו לבין מקורות   ובלעדיו עלי לבם מגנה
גביר ידיו כמו עב טל בקציר   ואור פניו כשמש או כלבנה
ידמו מושלים כפיו לעבות   וכחרף לבד תמטיר[28] ענגה

(The poem is evidently incomplete here at bottom of fol. 4, verso, and there is a lacuna between fols. 4 and 5, although the poem on fol. 5, recto, has the same metre and rhyme.)

12.

[מרתׄיה][29]

||——⏑|———⏑|———⏑

תמה איך הזמן הבלו יסיתם   ועל לבם ישו יום יום מגנה
והמה ידרשו חיים בגופם   ולנפשות לבד חיים למקנה
ולו חכמו שאול[30] עזבו ועלו   במעלות האמת לשמי מעונה

[23] Cp. Gen. 18.12.

[24] Cp. Ezra 4.6, 13, where מנדה means land-tax, but here מנדה is taken as a synonym of hatred (cp. Is. 66.5).

[25] Here there seems to be a reference to his having caused the destruction of the assembly places of heretics (Ḳaraites?) whereas he helped to build synagogues and houses of study styled here "the houses of truth."

[26] Cp. Prov. 23.31.

[27] Referring to his profession as a government secretary (Kātib).

[28] Better ימטיר referring to חרף.

[29] A dirge (for a Bagdād lady).

[30] This earthly abode.

כבת נדיב אשר גברה בשם טוב   עלי שרות ובנות[31] ע ד י נ ה
אשר מיום ילדוה בחיק ה׳   אמונה ועדן היתה אמונה
אשר היו בני ביתה יתומים   ובו רבצו במרבצות שמנ[ו]ה
יהי חלקה בעדן גן אלהים   ונשמתה בטוב שדי דשנה
ינחם אל לבב איש התהלות   י ש ו ע ה[32] ואבי החכמה ובינה
פאר [חכמ]ה וכותרת תהלה   כליל משרה ונזר הכהנה
אשר נמשח בשמן הוד ובגדי   יקר לבש כמ[ו מ]דיו שמונה[33]
יחי לו מחמד לבו ע ז ר י ה[34]   ואותו יעטור רצון כצנה
ולב משכיל נבון לחש ש מ ו א ל   והמכתיר בכתר התבונה
ירא אל אשר [לבש] צדקה   וגם אזר חלציו באמונה
ולב ד[ו ד א]ביר הדר וכבוד   אשר אין קץ בשכלו לתבונה
אשר [שם] לוית חן בראשו   וממנו היות יתד ופנה
וי ש ר א ל נדיב [לב אי]ש חמודות   אשר שם טוב כבר לקח וקנה
אשר . . . . ומטר נדבות   ומועצתו כמו חרב שנונה
ולב[35] חמדת יקר פ י נ ח ס [נדיב לב]   אשר [הוא] כשושנה [בכנה]

(fol. 5, verso)

אשר פיהו לשיר מכתם כנבל   ושפתותיו כחליל תהמינה
ולב התם והישר ש מ ו א ל   אשר [דעתו לאל שדי] נכונה
ולב עמה ומשפחתה אשר נ׳   שאו קינים [וביום מותה כיענה]
ולב עם אל בבנין בית אריאל   בראש [הרים וי]שוב אליו שכינה

[31] Here the metre is faulty. Probably insert ארץ.

[32] Yeshu'ah Hakkohen (l. 9) was probably the lady's husband, but perhaps her father (hence בת נדיב, l. 4).

[33] Viz. the High Priest (cp. M. Yoma 7.5).

[34] Yeshu'ah's son (cp. the frequent phrase חמוד for son).

[35] From here to the end the lines are identical with those printed by Steinschneider in *He-Ḥaluṣ*, III, 153 (No. 280). The lacunae here have been filled in accordingly.

13.

ולה איצֿא מרתֿיהֿ[36]

– – ⏑ – | – – ⏑ – | – – ⏑ – ||

שמש שמחות לערוב איך פנתה היום ושמש האנ[נ]חות עלתה וכו'
(fol. 6, recto, l. 5)
שואל ללבי איך ככנור יהמה עלי ועיני איך ולמה בכתה
דע כי ל ד נ י א ל נדיב לב בכתה עיני ונפשי כהמות ים המתה
ישכן בעדן גן עדי עת קץ ושם עין בעין תחזה שקותה
נחם ל א ל ע ז ר צבי חמדה אשר בינה ילדתהו ועצה רבתה
ופנה ל ע ו ב ד י ה ואל י פ ת ואל א ה ר ן אשר נפשם עדי חן עדתה
לבב ס ע ד י ה ו חתנם גם בנו יראה כמו לבו ונפשו אותה
ולבב עדת קדש בפסג ארמנות ציון[37] ועל תלה כמאז נבנתה

14.

(fol. 6, recto and verso)

ולה מרתֿיהֿ פי זוגֿהֿ אלשיךֿ אבי גאלב אלכסאר[38]

⏑ – – – | ⏑ – – – | ⏑ – – ||

אדמה בגדה בבני בריתה ומדתה להמית כל ודתה וכו'
למות בת ילדה בן שעשועים ובן אוני קראתו במותה[39]
ינחם אל לבב נ צ ח[39a] ירא אל אשר נפשו לאל כרתה בריתה
נדיב לב אשר ידו תחלק לכל עני ואביון מתנתה
ולב מ ש ה בנו חמדת לבבו אשר פניו כשמש בעלתה
ייהו אלהינו ואחיו ונפשם צור ימלא תאותה

[36] Another elegy in honor of a certain Daniel.

[37] Cp. Ps. 48.14.

[38] An elegy on the wife of the elder Neṣaḥ Abū Ghalib, the retailer of goods (retail merchant). The lady died at childbirth (l. 2).

[39] Cp. Gen. 35.18.

[39a] For this name cp. in Assaf (*l. c.*, 111, 121): נצח אלאפרני, in Wāsiṭ.

15.

(fol. 6, verso—7, verso)

ולה איצא מרתׄיהׄ[40]

|| – – ⏑ – | – – – ⏑ – | – – – ⏑

עדי אן תברחו מחץ תמותה ועל מצח אנוש דתה חרותה וכו'
ואשרי איש אשר הרס בתבל ונפש יסדה בגן[41] ובנתה
כאיש יושר ותום יפת אשר גדלה נפשו ביראת אל ורבתה וכו'
ינחם אל לאביתר ונפשו חדה אחרי אשר כהתה וכהתה
ויסיר דאגת לבו בבן חן ככל שבחרה נפשו ורצתה
ואלעזר ישר דרך אשר נטתה נפשו למ[צות] אל ופנתה וכו'
ונחם אל מנחם איש תבונות אשר סירו לאורח שפותה
אשר מקדש מעט[42] בנה והחיה צדקה אחרי היותה [בלותה]
אשר הורה בדרכי אל נבונים ונפש שובבה שובב[43] וזנתה
יחי לעד ויפרוץ על שמאל מ- נהר שיחור ועד תבוא כרתה
ואלעזר בנו יפרח כגפן אשר בה פרחה נצה ועלתה
ומשפחתו ובית אביו ונפש למותו נשברה גם נהיתה
ובת ציון ינחם אל בגואל ויצור צור ויבעל בעלתה[44]

16.

ולה מרתׄיהׄ

|| – – – | – ⏑ – – – | – ⏑ – – –

האין לילדי הזמן מוכיח ישקיט חרון אפם וגם יניח וכו'

The poem is incomplete at the bottom of fol. 7, recto, and no name is mentioned. There is a lacuna between fols. 7, verso, and 8, recto. The latter commences with the last 2 lines of a poem:

[40] Another elegy for a certain Yefet (l. 3).
[41] Viz. in Gan 'Eden.
[42] Viz. a synagogue.
[43] He brought back (to the right path). Cp. Is. 58.12, Jer. 50.19, Ps. 23.3.
[44] Vocalize בְּעָלָתָהּ, for the fem. בְּעָלָהּ, owing to the necessities of rhyme and metre. For the phrase cp. Is. 62.4–5.

‿ — — — | ‿ — — — | ‿ — — — ||

ותמצא ידך אל אויביך ויבנה ממך האל נצורים
בעוד רוח אל ארץ תרחף וירוצו ברום גלגל ואורים

17.

ולה איצׂא[45]

‿ — — — | ‿ — — — | ‿ — — — ||

1.4 צבי ריחו כמור או שם סעדיה אשר נכתר בארבעה כתרים
גביר הבין בכל חכמה ומדע ובלתו כחמור נושא ספרים
יחיד הדור בתורת הנדבות ורעיוניו לדת אומן מקורים וכו'

18.

(fols. 8, verso–9, recto)

ולה מרתׂיהׂ חיתׂ תופת עמהׂ רבׂ שמואל אב בית דין[46]

‿ — — — | ‿ — — — | ‿ — — — ||

עלמות אחזו מידי עלמות וגם שלחו וקראו לחכמות
תמהרנה שאת נהי קינה חגורות שק בכל קצוי אדמות

Condolence is expressed to this Samuel styled ראש המדברים and also to the physician ʻObadyah.

וגם נחם לעובדיה חכם לב צבי כל רופאי עמים ואמות

19.

(fol. 9, recto and verso)

ולה איצׂא מרתׂיהׂ

(Condolence to several people on the death of a lady.)

‿ — — — | ‿ — — — | ‿ — — — ||

ינחם אל לבב איש בין שמואל אשר רוה בטל כפיו אדמות
אחי בינה ונין סגני כהונה אשר [הרים]לאל שדי תרומות

[45] A eulogy in honor of a scholar Saʻadyah.

[46] An elegy when the paternal aunt of Samuel Ab-Bet-Din died.

ויוחנן מקור דעה וחכמה ....

וסופר באמת מהיר ומזהיר ....

ולב עזרא בנו מטע תהלה ....

צבי חמדה אשר בינה ועצה   עלי לוח לב[בו גם] רשומות

ולב יפת צבי חן איש חמודות ....

(There follows one more line on fol. 9, verso. The poem is evidently incomplete and there is a lacuna between fols. 9 and 10. The end of an elegy follows on fol. 10, recto = No. 177 of MS. Adler, cp. Poznański, *l. c.*, p. 71. The last 2 lines, not given by Poznański, read:

ופנה ברצון לעובדיה אבי   כל חכם לבב ויפנה בכל דבר ויצליח

ושאר קרוביו ומשפחתו ואמו   ואת אחיו תגדל ותשמיח ותפריח

The next item, with the heading ולה מרת̇יה̈, extending on fol. 10, recto, and verso, is equal to No. 179 of MS. Adler, given in extract by Poznański, *l. c.*, 71–72. It begins with the line:

|| – – ⏑ | – – – ⏑ | – – – ⏑

זמן יבגד באנשי האמונות   ויוריד אל שאול בנים ובנות וכו'

The poem is incomplete at the bottom of fol. 10, verso, and there is a lacuna between fols. 10 and 11.)

20.

(fol. 11, recto and verso)

ולה איצ̇א מרת̇יה̈[46a]

– – ⏑ | – – – ⏑ | – – – ⏑

זמן יפקוד עלי אנשי אמונות   ויהפוך את זמיריהם לקינות וכו'

ינחם אל לבב השר מבורך   אשר רקח שמו צדים ופנות

גביר עומד לנס עמים וישרו   כעמודים ושכלו כמכונות וכו'.

[46a] An elegy for a departed lady, evidently the wife of Meborakh (l. 2). See also infra, No. 52.

ולב חמדת יקר והוד ש ל מ ה   אשר לו שם בערים עם מדינות
ולב התם והישר ש מ ו א ל   ישר דרך ירא אל איש חמודות[46b]
ו ר ב נ ס י ם אשר גלה עמוקות   ופענח בדת אמון עמוקות וכו׳
וככה לב נדיב לבב ס ע ד י ה   אשר ידיו נהרות ועינות
ו ד נ י א ל שתיל משרה אשר לו   יקר והוד בעין בנים ובנות
ולב יתר קרוביהם ועמם   אשר נשאו במותה קול כתנות[47]

21.

(fol. 11b)

ולה מרתֿיה פ י א ל ש י ך א ב ו א ל פ ר ג ב ן ב ר כ א ל[48]

(On the margin we have the indication: מכאן גאון בית יעקב.)

⏑ — — — | ⏑ — — — | ⏑ — — — ||

זמן בגד באנשי התהלות   והפך את נכון ימים ולילות
ולכד לאנוש מעבר תמותה   בעד תבל ועלה בה מסלות
יקוו לעלות על במתי עב   ומחר ירדו עמקי מחלות
ואיך יחיו ומארבע יסודות   כבדות חוללם האל וקלות[49]
תמה איך ישגו בשאול דרכיו   ועל ילדי אנוש חוזר חלילות

(fol. 12, recto)

ואיך ישגו באהבתה וישגו   ולהם כל זמן תסיג גבולות
ומדתה להחליא או להחלים   והמה ידרשו בעדה תעלות

[46b] Cp. also No. 25.

[47] Instead of כתנים on account of the rhyme.

[48] An elegy on the elder Abū'l Faraj b. Berakhel. From l. 13 it is evident that his Hebrew name was Yeshu'ah. The marginal note may refer either to Yeshu'ah or to his father Berakhel; מכאן (for מכאנה, above, p. 262, note 41) in the meaning of rank. Yeshu'ah was apparently related to a Gaon of Bagdād.

[49] Viz. man like other mundane beings has been created from the four elements earth and water, fire and air, the former two being the heavy ones whereas the latter two are light. Cp., e. g., Maimonides, משנה תורה, ה׳ יסודי התורה, 4א: ארבעה גופים הללו שהם אש ורוח מים וארץ הם יסודות כל הנבראים למטה מן הרקיע . . . 4ב . . . טבע האש חם ויבש והוא קל מכלם, והרוח חם ולח, והמים קרים ולחיים. והארץ יבשה וקרה, והיא כבידה מכולם והמים קלים ממנה . . . והרוח קל מן המים . . . והאש קל מן הרוח.

ויד תפתח לכל סכל ובפני   בני שכל דלתיה נעולות
שאולים בה ועל הבלה מריבים   כהלחם כלבים על נבלות
בעת השבעה תשקור ותסמוך   שבועתה בדברי מהתלות
והמה קוראים בה על אדמות   שמותיהם ובידיהם שאולות[50]
ולו חכמו עזבו אדמה   ועלו רום בלי סלם ומעלות
כאיש התום והיושר ישועה   ירא האל וחמדת התהלות
אשר הואיל לישר את דרכיו   ואחר אל בכל לבו למלאת
יהי חלקו בעדן גן ויצאו   לעמתו כרובי חן המולות
יתומותיו ינחם אל בחיי   כרוב ממשח ומוסד הגדולות
כדניאל[51] נגיד עם האלהים   אשר פניו בהוד שדי כלולות
גביר כפיו כשטף לנדבות   ועשר אצבעותיו כתעלות
גביר שם טוב כלוית חן בראשו   ועליו מהדר מלכות שמלות
ומתתו כנבכי ים ומתת   נדיבי הזמן כלם כגולות
ואם אומר פרוט מקצת שבחיו   ולכתוב מתהלותיו כללות
דיו ייבש וקלומוסים יסוסון[52]   ותקצרנה ואם ארכו מגלות
וכגביר הוד ומטע המלוכה   אשר כל הגדולות לו נקלות

(fol. 12, verso)

נגיד עם אל ושר שרים יחזקאל   אשר לו נתכנו ביקר עלילות
ויראה[52a] הגביר יוסף כחפצו   וידרוך במתי עוז בנעולות[53]
ואדרת יקר יפת גביר הוד   אשר זכרו קציעות ואהלות
אשר פניו כמו שמש נדבות   ומהם מלאה הארץ תהלות

[50] For שאולים (referring to שמותיהם) on account of rhyme.

[51] Daniel Hakkohen 'Izz ad-Daula (above, p. 267), Yeshu'ah's son-in-law.

[52] Read perhaps יסיסון (similar to Arab. سيّس, to be worm-eaten, cp. סָס, Is. 51.8). I can find no parallel to the use of this verb in Hebrew literature.

[52a] Read בגביר, viz. may Ezekiel see (realized) in Joseph (his son) as is his desire. That Joseph was Ezekiel's son is evident from No. 54a. For the same names as here, see No. 27.

[53] Viz. ברגלים נעולות.

גביר משרה והוד פינחס אשר אל   אפיקי ים שתי ידיו משולות
גביר ירש שררה מאבותיו   ואורות מהדר פניו אצולות
ונין העוז והישיבה שמואל   אשר פניו כירח מהלות
יזכהו אלהים לעלות כס   ישיבה והמון צריו לכלות
מקור חכמה ובין ראש בי רבנן   שמואל מעמיד על קו תהלות
נבון לחש אשר מושב יקר לו   בבין חכמי זמן נודע ומעלות
וחמדת היקר יפת צבי הוד   נדיב לבב ורוח רב פעולות
אחי שכל אשר מחשב לבבו   וזמותיו בשמן תום בלולות
נדיב לבב יקר רוח שמואל   אשר ידיו כעב טל או מצולות
אשר רקח בטוב זכרו קצוות   והגיה באור פניו אפלות
ינחם אל לבב אחיו ובניו   נדיבי לב ועיני הקהלות
אשר קרע סגור לבם במותו   ושם דמעם עלי לחים כצולות
ולב השר יהוסף איש נדבות   אשר מליו כמו בצוף טבולות
צבי חמדה וילד הנסיכים   והחורים ואנשי הגדולות

(fol. 13, recto)

שאר עמו אשר מצאו תלאות   ונפשותם להאספו אבלות
ולב ציון בבנין בית אריאל   והעלות בעדו חטאת ועולות

22.

(fol. 13, recto and verso)

אלאֿואני ולה מרתֿיה פי אלרייס אבו אלפרג הלוי בן אבי אסחק[54]

|| — — ⏑ | — — — ⏑ | — — — ⏑

זמן יבגד בשרי התהלות   וימצא על נדיבי עם עלילות וכו'
כשר היקר ישועה[54a]   אשר לו מעלות בתבל מעולות וכו'

[54] An elegy on the dignitary (Raīs) Abū'l Faraj b. Abū Ishāḳ (=Abraham) al-Awāni. From l. 3 it appears that his Hebrew name was Yeshu'ah. Cp. Steinschneider, *JQR*, XII, p. 117, No. 12b. Since our Yeshu'ah was a Levite he was not related to the Gaon Isaac Hakkohen b. al-Awāni (above, p. 226).

[54a] The metre is faulty. In the second hemistich בתבל is corrected in the margin into בזבול which restores there the metre.

ינחם אל לבב השר מבורך אשר פניו כאור בקר מהלות וכו'
וככה לב גביר היקר שמואל אשר לבו לשום שכל כגלות וכו'
ולב ילד יקר יצחק צבי הוד אשר נחל יקר והוד נחלות
ולב ציון בבניה ויחיש לגולים על ידי צמח[55] גאלות

23.

(fol. 13, verso,–14, recto)

ולה איצֿא

— — ◡ | — — — ◡ | — — — ◡

ראו רעים ביראת אל ידועים עליהם יעביר משקה גביעים
אשר פיהם חלקים מחמאות ומדותם בתום לבב טבועים
בראשיתם גביר משרה סעדיה אשר אזני בני יום[56] לו רצועים
ושר שלום גביר הדר וכבוד אשר דשאו בטל כפיו סלעים
ואהרן ראש בני אהרן גביר חן וציץ נזר נדיבי לב ושועים
ומשה הגביר איש התהלות בפתו כל עניים שבעים
וגם יוסף גביר חן איש חמודות יפה תאר יפה מראה ונעים
יסוכך אל באברתו עליהם ובטוב יפקדמו לרגעים
ויחיו הם וילדיהם לעולם ויזהירו כזהר הרקיעים

24.

(fol. 14, recto and verso)

ולה תהניהֿ פי אלרייס שמס אלדולהֿ אבו אלחסין
אבן אבי אלרביע פי טֿהר ולדה סדיד אלדולהֿ
אבו מנצור יל[57]

(This poem is equal to No. 194 (197) of MS. Adler, printed in extract by Poznański, *l. c.*, 73–74. After l. 16, where Poznański's extract ends, there is a reference to Sa'adyah's two sons.)

[55] Viz. the Messiah.

[56] The vicissitudes of time (cp. Mann, II, 267, note 2a).

[57] = יחי לעד; a poem of congratulation to the elder Shams ad-Daula Abū al-Ḥusain ibn Abū'l Rabi'a on the occasion of the birth of his boy Sadīd ad-Daula Abū Manṣūr.

25.

(fol. 14, verso–15, recto)

ולה מרתֿיהֿ פי אבנהֿ אלחכים שעיב רחמֿ אל תעֿ[58]

|| — — ⏑ | — — — ⏑ | — — — ⏑

יריבוני ברוב בכיי עלי בת   במותה קרעה לבי קרעים וכו'
ינחם אל לבב התם ש מ ו א ל   ישר דרך וחמדת הצנועים
גביר נודע בזכר טוב כהוריו   אשר בטוב וחסד ידועים
ולבו יחבוש לעד ב[חיי]   גביר נ ס י ם תמים חכמות ודעים
וכו'

26.

(fol. 15, recto and verso)

ולה איצֿא פי אלריים [עז אלדו]להֿ בן אבי יעקב[59]

|| — — ⏑ | — — — — ⏑ | — — — ⏑

צבי חמדה יפה תאר ונעים   [אשר פ]ניו כזהר הרקיעים וכו'
ואין מרפא למחלתי לבד כי   ב ד נ י א ל תמים שכל ודעים
נגיד עם אל אשר תוכו כברו   ובזממיו עצי חיים נטועים וכו'
שלחו אל לחבוש נשברי לב   והורות את נבוכי לב ותועים

(The next item on fol. 15, verso, has the heading [ולה] איצֿא תמגיד and is identical with No. 203 of MS. Adler, printed by Brody, *Z. f. H. B.*, IV, 27. Of this poem only 3 lines are found on fol. 15, verso, and there is a lacuna between fols. 15 and 16.)

27.

(Fol. 16, recto and verso, contains the end of the elegy, found in MS. Adler No. 203 (206) and given in extract by Poznański, *l. c.*, 74–75. We give here the continuation from l. 21 of the poem of which Poznański gave only 3 lines).

|| — — ⏑ | — — — — ⏑ | — — — ⏑

ינחם אל לבב השר ש מ ו א ל   נגיד עם אל וכתר הנציבים

[58] =רחמהא אללה תעאלי. An elegy on the daughter of the physician Shu'aib. Cp. Steinschneider, *l. c.*, p. 209, No. 721. From l. 3 it appears that her father's Hebrew name was Samuel.

[59] Cp. above, note 17.

פאר [דורו] . . . .   אשר חקים בצור לבו כתובים
. . . . עדת אמון . . . . . .   לשון קדש וחכמת הערבים
וכ[כ]ה יחבוש לב רב י ה ו ד ה   בילדי חן שתילי הא . . . . . וכו׳

(fol. 16, verso)

ולב השר והטפסר י ח ז ק א ל   אשר מצוף . . . . . ערבים
סעיף משרה מטע המלוכה   ומוציא מרבב שכלו שביבים
ושר היקר י ה ו ס ף איש חמודות   יפלח את כבד צרים ואויבים
ולב י פ ת גביר משרה אשר מד־   ברי פיהו כצוף או יין ענבים וכו׳
ולב יצחק גביר [מש]רה חכם לב   צעיר ימים ו[עצותיו] כשבים וכו׳
וככה לב גביר משרה ש ל מ ה   אשר מליו כמו שירי עגבים וכו׳
ולב השר ס ע ד י ה ו גביר חן   אשר הטיב לכל רעים וטובים וכו׳
ולב חכם ונבון ראש י ש ו ע ה   אשר ידיו בעת מתן כעבים וכו׳
ולב פ ינחס שתיל משרה וחכמה   אשר האיר באור פניו ערבים וכו׳
ונין העוז והישיבה ש מ ו א ל   אשר חבש בחייו הלבבים
ימלא את מקום אבותיו ולב אר־   הביו גילות ולב אויבים[60] עצבים

(Here ends fol. 16, verso. The poem seems to be incomplete and there is a lacuna between fols. 16 and 17. The latter contains an elegy the beginning of which is missing.)

28.

(fol. 17, recto and verso)

|| – – ‿ | – – – – ‿ | – – – ‿

שעו מני מנחמי לא אליכם   . . . . וכו׳
והפך את ימי חופה ימי און   ו[אבל ב]מקום שירים עגבים וכו׳
ינחם האלהים לב ע ז ר י ה   גביר שרים ותפארת נדיבים
אשר נעלה עלי כל שר וקצין   ועל אישים בשם מלכות נקובים
וכו׳
יחיה לו סעיף משרה ומלכות   א ל י ע ז ר אשר יאיר ערבים וכו׳
ולב אחיו א ל ע ז ר ינחם   ואש לבו יכב כמטר רביבים

[60] Or אויביו.

ועובדיה ידבר על לבב[ו] בנחמות כרחב ים רחבים
ואת יוסף יגדיל[61] האלהים וגם יסעד ברוב ימיו לבבים
ודניאל פאר היקר ינחם בנחומים מדבבים וטובים
ואביתר אבי עצה ומוסר יכבה מחדר לבו שביבים
ויעזור אל לבב עזרא צבי חן וגם ירתום לעזרתו רכבים
וגם לב מחמד לבות שמואל ינחם אל ורוחו העצבים
ואלעזר בנו יחיה ויגדל במזרחים שמו ובמערבים
ויסעוד את לבב פינחס צבי הוד ותוגותיו לריק יהיו חשובים
ולב עמך בבנין [ה]ר אריאל ויקריבו לך דם עם חלבים

(Fol. 17, verso, contains a poem with the heading: ולה פי אלרייס מעתמד אלדולה̈ בן כרם, printed by Brody from MS. Adler in הצופה לחכמת ישראל, VI, 124–5. The next item on the last line of fol. 17, verso, has the heading: ולה מרת̇יה̈ פי רבנו אברהם בן הרב רבנו משה בן מימון ז"ל printed partly from Maḥzor Aleppo (cp. Brody, *Z. f. H. B.*, IV, 24, note 1). Fol. 18, recto, is very faded and it is doubtful whether we have thereon the continuation of this elegy on Abraham Maimuni. It rather seems that there is really a lacuna between fols. 17 and 18. At the bottom of fol. 18, recto, there seems to be a superscription of a new elegy which however is illegible. We give here the continuation on fol. 18, verso–19, recto.)

29.

[מרת̇יה̈][62]

|| — — — | — ⌣ — | — ⌣ — —

רשת תמותה על יקום נמשכת תמיד וכסיר הזמן נהפכת
יום [הלכ]ה ירה . . . . [בת מ]שרה[63] עם פאר ממלכת
דרך נכוחה אחזה רגלה ובני[64] תיבות צדקה היתה הולכת וכו'
אנא אלהים דברה על לב גביר משה כפיר גוים אביר מערכת

[61] Read יְגַדֵּל.

[62] An elegy for a lady.

[63] Poetic license turning a Sheva quiescent into a moving one. For עם read עמה to restore the metre.

[64] From here onwards the metre of the first hemistich is throughout — ⌣ — — | — ⌣ — — | — ⌣ — —.

ה ר ב אשר אמרת שפתו כושלים תקים וברך כורעה תומכת וכו׳
ולב נדיב הדור ושוע הזמן עזרא אשר כפו כעב שופכת וכו׳
ולב יראאל אהרן התם אשר בינת לבבו כקרב עורכת
ושאר קרוביה ומשפחתה אשר נפש למיתתה באון נחרכת
שרי עדינה וחכמיה אשר בם נושעה עדה ומתברכת

30.

(fol. 19, recto and verso)

ולה איצׂא מרתׂיה̈[65]

|| — — — ◡ | — — — ◡ | — — ◡ — —

עד אן חמת הזמן בנו מהפכת
ידה בכל יום ולא שוקטה ושוכבת
אם אומרה מחרת תקל אזי כבדה
או אומרה תעבור רגע ונמשכת
חמדת מלכים אליעזר אשר היתה
אברת חסדיו כמו שפריר ופרכת וכו׳

(The poem is incomplete at the bottom of fol. 19, verso, and there is a lacuna between fols. 19 and 20.)

31.

(fol. 20, recto and verso)

[מרתׂיה̈][66]

| — ◡ — | — ◡ — — | — ◡ — | — ◡ — —
— — | — ◡ — — | — ◡ — | — ◡ — —

נגה אהה נאסף נגהו וכבה מאור
כוכב והוסר פאר סהר בשמים

[65] An elegy for a certain Eli'ezer (l. 3).

[66] An elegy. The beginning is missing. The poet introduced in his composition the seven planets and 12 signs of the Zodiac. Where the poem now begins (l. 1) he mentions the planets נגה (Venus), כוכב (Mercury) and סהר (=לבנה, Moon). Probably in the previous lines the other planets were enumerated. The signs of the Zodiac are mentioned in their usual order (ll. 2–5).

טלה בשחת בלי הוטל ושור שרשו
שרשו[67] ונתן תאומים בנחשתים
נפרט ונשרט בשר סרטן וארי[68] בעז
נטרף והגרו בתולות על חלצים
התעותו מאזנים אז ונכרת זנב
עקרב וקשת דרוכה אך ברגלים
שסף ושסע גדי עם גר[69] ודלל דלי
עם ים עדי נתפשו דגים בידים
ועש[70] כבגד אכלו עש[71] וכימה כמו
רמה ונחשב כסיל ככסיל שפתים
על מות עטרת צבי והוד והדר א ב י־
נ ד ב ירא אל טהור לבב ועינים
בו יפגעו מלאכי אל עם כרוביו בפ־
מליא ויקרב ויתחבר למחנים[72] וכו׳
נחם אלהים לבב ע ז ר א שתיל חן אשר
זכרו כקנה וקנמון לאפים
ישיש וישמח ב א ל ע ז ר חמודו ויתֿ
נשא וירום עדי יגע בשמים
ולבב ש מ ו א ל נשוא פנים ונהדר תנ־
חם אל ותהפך שחור לילו לצהרים
ולבב נגיד עם אלהינו י ה ו ס ף ישי־
מהו ב ב ב ל[73] כמו יוסף במצרים וכו׳

[67] שָׁרֳשׁוֹ שָׁרְשׁוֹ.

[68] Read ואריה to restore the metre.

[69] גָּר, dweller, viz. the owner of the גדי. But perhaps read מזל=גָּד (cp. Is. 65.11, Gen. 30.11).

[70] Here he mentions the three stars עש, כסיל and כימה (cp. Job 9.9) usually taken to mean the Bear, Orion and the Pleiades.

[71] Cp. Job 13.28.

[72] Cp. Gen. 32.3.

[73] In Bagdād.

ולבב פאר כל גביר יצחק עטרת צבי
ושתיל מלוכה אשר שתול עלי מים וכו'
יראה בחייו לבנימן ילדים ככל
תאות לבבו וכמנשה ואפרים וכו'
גם דבר על לבב השר עזריה אשר
לו פעמן חן ורימון הוד בשולים[74] וכו'
ולבב המודו אליעזר צבי חן יפה
תאר חזק לב .... ומתנים וכו'
תחת אבותיו יהיו בניו בתבל ישי־
תמו לשרים בבבל עם ספרוים
ושאר קרוביו ומשפחתו אשר
אבלו עדי יעלה קולם באזנים
חכמי עדינה ושריה תגדל ותש־
מיעם בהר קדשך שיר על מצלתים

32.

(fol. 20, verso)

ולה איצ̇א מרת̇יה

— — ◡ — — | ◡ — — — — | ◡ — — — —

אש התלאה בלב יקדה ונשקת   לבי תפוצץ וכליותי מפרקת וכו'

(Three more lines follow on fol. 20, verso; there is a lacuna between fols. 20 and 21. The latter, recto, contains an Arabic introduction, the beginning of which is missing, to the following section containing couplets arranged according to the Alphabet. This introduction is followed by a Hebrew rhetorical preface. On fol. 21, verso, last line but one, there begins the section of letter 'א (חרף אלאלף). The couplets are in the form of Moses ibn Ezra's *Tarshish* and extend till fol. 23, verso (with a lacuna between fols. 22 and 23), where letter 'ז is reached. There is again a lacuna between fols. 23 and 24.

[74] Cp. Exod. 28.33–34.

Fol. 24 (which has on top the siglum יבֹ, i. e. the 12th quire of the MS.) contains riddles on Adam, Noaḥ, Isaac, Jacob, Levi, Dan, Lemekh, Gad and Abner. Herewith as examples the first two riddles.)

ולה לגז פי אדם[75]

— — ⏑ — | — — — ⏑ — | — — — ||

מה אב אשר הוא אם וארבעה יתרוצצו תמיד בתוך קרבו[76]
לו שם כשם אדם ועיר[77] ושמו ידו בקרב כל ויד כל בו

פי נח[78]

— — ⏑ — | — — — ⏑ — | — — — ||

מה לך[79] אחי תיגע נפשך למצא אשר בקשו יגעי כח
קח נא יהושע ואליו חברה שני כנעו תמצאה בם נח[80]

(There is a lacuna between fols. 24 and 25.)

33.

(fol. 25, recto)

ואליה[81]

— — ⏑ — | — — — ⏑ — | — — ⏑ — ||

יוסף אשר יספו תהלותיו עדי נחלק במעלתו קצת המשוררים
יש אומרים יוסף עלי בן יעקב יוסף[82] ונראה לי דבר יש אומרים

[75] A riddle (لغز = לגז) concerning Adam.

[76] Viz. inside the word אדם there is the letter ד׳ = four.

[77] Cp. Josh. 3.16.

[78] (A riddle) concerning Noah.

[79] The metre is faulty here. Probably insert הָכִי, thus: מה לך הכי |אחי תי|נע נפשך וכו׳.

[80] The meaning of this riddle is not clear to me.

[81] 'And to him', viz. this strophe is in honor of Joseph mentioned before (in the lacuna). Probably Joseph ibn al-Barḳūli of Wāsiṭ is meant (see above, p. 270, note 9).

[82] Viz. that this Joseph is 'above' (superior to) the Biblical Joseph b. Jacob. Cp. also Nos. 4–5 where this superiority is stressed.

34.

וכתב אליה בעד ספרה מן בגדאד[83]

–|–––⏑–⏑–––|–––

היום גביר היקר ימים בהאריכם

חוק אהבה ימחו בכתב אמת נרשם[84]

נסע לנסעך לבי אל מחוז חפצך

ובעודך שמה עיני ולבי שם

35.

ולה למא כאן אדעי עליה בעץ̇ אלמתמחלין באלכד̇ב

וכאן יוסף אלמד̇כור יערף ד̇לך פעט̇ם אלוסואס עליה חתי

ראי פי נומה כאנה קד חצ̇ר אלדיואן אלעאלי ותבת תמחל

ד̇לך אלשכ̇ץ וכתב אלי יוסף אלמד̇כור הד̇א אלאביאת צורה̇[85]

––⏑–|–––|––⏑–|––

5 בך בטחה נפשי ביום עלי הואיל וטפל אויבי שקרו

ואחזה בחלום והן שלח על ידך לי יוצרו עזרו

עדותך שלחה ותתקים ויהי חלום נכון וזה שברו

[83] And he (the poet) wrote to him (Joseph) after he departed from Bagdād (probably to return to Wāsiṭ.)

[84] Viz. this day (of your departure) is marked in true writing (cp. Dan. 10.21) for a time when the length of days will obliterate the law (covenant) of love (friendship).

[85] 'By him (the poet), when some intriguer spread falsehood (slander) against him (Joseph) and the above mentioned Joseph was aware of this and the stigmas increased against him. Thereupon he (the poet) had a dream as if he entered the High Diwān (the council chamber of the Caliph) and proved the intrigue of that person (the slanderer). He then wrote to the above-mentioned Joseph these lines'.

36.

ולה מא כתב אליה וקת מא אנפד לה מן מחאסבה̈
בינהמא ג̇ דנא̇[86] וד̇ אוקין אלמנאם אלד̇י רא̇ה[87]

– – – – | – ◡ – – – | – ◡ – – | – ◡ – | – ◡ – – | – ◡ – –

יוסף שיר[88] אחיו אשר אלות[89] חס־ דיו בכרו לנו בד אשכל[90] חדש
הואיל והתקדש בכל ענין עדי שם משקלותיו משקלות הקדש

37.

(fol. 25, verso)

ולה[91]

|| – – – ◡ – – – | – – – ◡ – –

הואל זמן ושמע עצה ואל תפרע ובפוך יקר היטיב עין לבך וקרע
ועלי גרון השר יצחק דביר זהב שים כי ביצחק יקרא לך זרע

(There follow till fol. 27, verso, several such small poems. Some of the headings are: ולה פי ר׳ עזרא בן אלתקה̈ חין עץ̇ אלכלב בקדמה[92] (fol. 27, recto), ולה אלי בעץ̇ אכ̇ואנה[93] (verso), ולה איצ̇א (in honor of השר יהוסף), ולה פי שכ̇ץ ג̇אהל וכאן ידע באלחכים.[94] There is a lacuna between fols. 27 and 28.

On fol. 28, recto, there is a poem, with the heading ולה פי רא הישי[95] יצחק אלשויך̇ זצ״ל ענד זמנה[96] which is equal to No. 104 of MS. Adler, published by Poznański, *l. c.*, 68. There follow 4 more couplets on fol. 28, recto.)

[86] =דנאניר.

[87] This poem was in connection with the letter the poet sent Joseph acknowledging the receipt of his accounts including 3 Dinārs and 4 ounces (of certain goods) as a gift for the dream which the poet saw (see previous note).

[88] שְׁיָר. [89] אֲלוֹת. [90] Read ואשכול.

[91] By the poet (in honor of a certain Isaac).

[92] Concerning Ezra b. al-Thiḳa when a dog bit his foot. Cp. also Steinschneider, *l. c.*, 210, No. 771b. Another poem in his honor is given infra sub No. 53. Cp. also note 135.

[93] To one of his friends.

[94] Concerning an ignoramus who proclaimed himself to be a physician.

[95] =ראש הישיבה.

[96] Concerning the Gaon Isaac al-Shuwwaikh during his chronic disease (being crippled).

38.

(fol. 28, verso)

ולה אלי רבֿ אברהם בן רבֿ משה בן מימון זצ"ל[97]

|| – – | – ⌣ – – | – ⌣ – –

לולי שלחך אל נביא חכמות ספו ואבדו מאנוש זכרם[98]
ואשר[99] דרשום בלתך יגעו כי לך לבדך אצלו אורם
ויאמרו אחר אשר נלאו לדרוש ולא מצאו קצת שברם
איך יכרתו לנו ברית חכמות איכה והם בעלי ברית אברם[100]

39.

ואיצא אליה

|| – – | – ⌣ – – | – ⌣ – –

יום נהרות בין נשאו דכים ויהימו גליו ומשברם
לא יכלו חכמי זמן לעבור רק פגרו ויעבור אברם[101]

40.

ואליה איצא

|| – ⌣ – – | – – | – ⌣ – –

אל נא תריבוני בכרוב יקר אין ראש למהלליו או אחרית
כי איך ברית רהביו[102] אפר והן כרת יוי[103] את אברם ברית[104]

(There follow other poems, one with the heading[105] ולה פי שכץ אסמה עלי and several (fol. 30, recto and verso) in honor of Joseph

[97] The next three items are in honor of Abraham Maimuni, Nagid of Egypt (1205–37 C. E.).

[98] For זכרן, (referring to חכמות) on account of the rhyme. But throughout the poem the noun is taken as masculine.

[99] Vocalize וַאֲשֶׁר. [100] Cp. Gen. 14.13. [101] Cp. Gen. 12.6.

[102] רָהְבָּיו (cp. Ps. 90.10). The question כי איך means here 'for certainly' (like הֲכִי in mediaeval Hebrew poetry).

[103] =אֲדֹנָי to complete the metre.

[104] Cp. Gen. 15.18.

[105] Concerning a man named 'Alī.

b. al-Barḳūli. There is a lacuna between fols. 30 and 31. The latter contains several items in honor of the Gaon ʻAlī. The first one has the heading:[106] ולה פי ראס אלמתׄיבהׄ עלי זצ״ל למא אבל מן מרצה; it is equal to No. 55 of MS. Adler, published by Poznański, *l. c.*, p. 67–68. Between fols. 31 and 32 there is a lacuna. Fol. 32, recto, begins with the end of an elegy for a lady. Condolence is extended to *Meborakh* and *Ezeḳiel*.

Then there follows another elegy (ולה איצׄא [מרתׄיהׄ]) the first line of which reads: על מות מקור . . . אשר לבות למותו כמעיל נקרעו. Condolence is expressed to גביר עזרא and his 2 sons, to *Samuel*, *Yoḥanan* and his son *Ezra* (see above, No. 19), *Yefet* and *Daniel*. This poem ends on fol. 32, verso.

On fol. 33, recto and verso, we have another elegy with the heading:[107] ולה מרתׄיהׄ פי בנת אלמעיד. No names are mentioned and the poem is incomplete. Between fols. 33 and 34 there is a lacuna.)

41.

(fol. 34, recto)

(End of a poem on the occasion of a ceremony of circumcision. The following persons are complimented therein.)

|| – – ⏑ | – – – ⏑ | – – – ⏑

ודניאל נגיד עם אל ומלכם   אשר ידיו לרוב מתן כבדות וכו'
ויראה את בנו אהרן כחפצו   והחכמות בלבו צמודות
ולב השר שמואל איש תהלות   אשר עצות עלי ראשו ענודות וכו'
ויראה את חמוד לבו יחזקאל   כמו יתאו והוגה בתעודות וכו'
ואברהם ירא אל איש תהלות   וצור מעוז יהי לו עם מצודות
ומשפחתם אשר גילת ורנן[108]   ושמחת לב לצבאותם פקודות

On fol. 34 we have a poem with the heading: ולה תהניהׄ פי אלשיך אבי אלרצׄא בן עקיבה.[109] In l. 1 the first hemistich is in Hebrew and

[106] Concerning the Gaon ʻAlī when he recovered from his sickness.

[107] Steinschneider, *l. c.*, 123, No. 128d, and 198, No. 366b, seems to have read in MS. Adler אלמעיר.

[108] Cp. Is. 35.2.

[109] A poem of praise (or congratulation) to the elder Moses Abū'l Ridha b. ʻAḳiba (cp. Steinschneider, *l. c.*, 123, No. 128c).

the second one in Arabic while in l. 2 the order is reversed, and so on. Abū'l Ridha is called in the poem גביר משה while his 2 sons were *Jacob* and *Joseph* (יהוסף).

There follow several poems with such bilingual structure on fols. 34 and 35. One has the heading: ולה קלב הדה אלאביאת.[110]

On fol. 36, recto, we have the end of an elegy with condolence extended to *Daniel*, *Moses*, *Pinḥas* and *Samuel* (נין הגאונים).

42.

(fol. 36, recto and verso)

ולה תהניה̈ פי בית בן קנתאנה̈ פי ולד ג̇א להם[111]

|| — — — | — ⌣ — — — | — ⌣ — —

כוכבי תהלות מזבול זרחו   היום ושושני יקר פרחו וכו'
יחיה וכזקנו באפרים יהי[112]   נכבד ואויביו על שאול ישחו וכו'
מיזה כאפרים נדיב לבב אשר   עבי חסדיו על יקום סרחו
חמדת צבי והוד ישועה איש אשר   באל ובו ילדי עני בטחו וכו'
ובכן לאל עזר נדיב רוח אשר   ידו לים כסף ופז צלחו וכו'

43.

(fols. 36, verso–37, recto)

ולה איצ̇א

|| — ⌣ — — | — ⌣ — — | — ⌣ — —

כוכבי תהלות ברקיעים זרחו
ודמי ענבים בגביעים קרחו וכו'
ריחם כמור או שם גביר משה אשר
עמו לחברה כוכבי אור זרחו וכו'

[110] Transposition of these stanzas. In this poem the first line is entirely in Arabic while the second one is in Hebrew, and so on.

[111] A poem of congratulation to the family of ibn Ḳintana on the occasion of the birth of a child whose grandfather was a certain Ephraim (l. 3).

[112] Here and in the following lines the Sheva Mobile in יְהִי and אשר is ignored.

44.

(There follows another poem on fol. 37, recto, with the heading ולה איצא, and then on fol. 37, verso, bottom):

ולה איצא פי נגם אלדולה אבו אלברכאת אלצלחי[113]

|| — — ⏑ | — — — — ⏑ | — — ⏑

שמואל הגביר חמדת נפשים   ונין שרים ונכד הקדושים
יקר רוח טהור עין טהר לב   והטוב עם אלהים וא[נ]שים וכו'

(The poem is incomplete and there is a lacuna between fols. 37 and 38.)

45.

(fol. 38, recto and verso)

[מרתִׄיהׄ][114]

(The beginning is missing.)

|| — — ⏑ | — — — ⏑ | — — — ⏑

שפתים אדומות מפנינים
ושנים כעדר הקצובות
ודמעתי לפירודה כים או
כיד השר שמואל איש נדבות וכו'
ואיך אדאג לרעות הזמן איך
ולי יום יום ידי השר מטיבות
וסופר עד מאד מהיר במלכות
בני גמ[ר][115] וחוש[ב מחשבות וכו'

[113] A poem concerning Najm ad-Daula (the star of the realm) Abū'l Barakāt al-Ṣilḥi (near Wāsiṭ). His Hebrew name was Samuel (l. 1).

[114] An elegy for a lady, probably the wife of Samuel (l. 2), a government secretary (Kātib, l. 4). His son was Tobias, a promising student (l. 5).

[115] Cp. Gen. 10.2 where גמר is mentioned as one of the sons of Yefet. Sa'adyah in his Pentateuch translation (ed. Derenbourg, p. 17) identifies גמר with תרך, Turks. Here מלכות בני גמר refers to the Seljūḳs (also Turks) who de facto ruled in the 'Abbāsid Caliphate of Bagdād in the time of our poet El'azar Habbabli.

וטוביה בנו יראה כחפצו
ותאותו בראש חכמי ישיבות וכו׳
והמדת היקר עזרא צבי חן
ושעשועי[116] ילודי חן ואבות וכו׳
ושר שורין יקר יוסף אשר מ־
חמאות פי[117] ולבתו קרבות
וכותרת יקר ועוז ישועה
אשר ידיו כגשמי הנדבות וכו׳
ואלעזר צבי חן איש חמודות
ולוקט מתבונותיו תנובות וכו׳
יחיה לו שני בניו לעולם
ויורמו במישרי נתיבות וכו׳

46.

ולה איצׄא

|| — — ⏑ | — — — ⏑ | — — — ⏑

לך שר מרדכי כסא שררה — לך יאות ונזר ועטרה
ובך יתפארו משרה ומלכות — וממשלה גדלה[118] עם גבורה וכו׳

(The poem is incomplete and there is a lacuna between fols. 38 and 39. The latter contains an elegy on the mother of David which is the same as printed by Steinschneider, החלוץ, III, 150–151 (No. 281). There follows on fol. 39, verso, another elegy (ולה מרתׄיׄה) the first line of which reads:

|| — — ⏑ | — — — ⏑ | — — — ⏑

עדי אן הזמן תשיא אנשים — בהבלי שוא לצודד הנפשים

The poem is incomplete and there is a lacuna between fols. 39 and 40. The latter contains (on recto) the end of another elegy wherein condolence is expressed to *Sa'adyah*, *'Amram*, *Samuel* and *Jacob*.)

[116] Probably read ושעשועיו referring to 'Ezra's children.
[117] Read פיו.   [118] Read גְּדוּלָה.

47.

(fol. 40, recto and verso)

ולה מרת֗יה֗ פי ראש הישיבה יצחק הכהן בן אלאואני[119]

|| – – ⏑ | – – – ⏑ | – – – ⏑

זמן פרש בעד תבל מצודיו	להתנכל ולצוד את ילדיו וכו'
ולא יועיל ביום דין הון ועשר	ולא יציל לאיש כי אם חסדיו
כיצחק כהננו ראש ישיבת	גאון בית יעקב ונגידנגידיו
אשר עלה בסלם תום שמי רום	והיו כוכבי היקר נדודיו
ושרה על בני חכמה והמה	ברוב שכלו ומיטב מעבדיו[120]
וכאחותו אשר שלחה ימין תום	וארתה מעצי חיים מגדיו
אשר היתה בעודנה כאם אל	יתומי עם מחוננת שרידיו

(The poem is incomplete and there is a lacuna between fols. 40 and 41. The latter (recto) commences with the end of a poem to a certain person.

There follows another piece of 4 lines with the heading ולה פי נג֗ם אלדולה֗ בן אבי אלסעוד.[121] The person celebrated is called *Moses* as is also evident from the next two numbers.)

48.

(fol. 41, recto and verso)

ולה איצ֗א רחמה אללה עליה[122]

|| – – | – ⏑ – – | – ⏑ – –

זה באמת יעצר בעד עמו	ותהיה משרה עלי שכמו וכו'
יחיה וסימן טוב עלי עמו	יהיה ועל אביו ועל אמו

[119] An elegy on the Gaon (of Bagdād) Isaac Hakkohen ibn al-Awāni.

[120] The metre demands this construction which otherwise should be והמה ברוב שכלו ממיטב עבדיו.

[121] Concerning Najm ad-Daula b. Abū'l Sa'ūd. Cp. Steinschneider, *l. c.*, 199, No. 411b.

[122] When our Diwān was collected this dignitary Moses was no longer among the living. The poem was evidently composed on the occasion of the birth of a son to Moses (see l. 2).

מ ש ה כרוב ממשח אשר הוחק   ספר יקר על פיו וחותמו
השר אשר בחר אלהים בו   ואב לכל מלך ושר שמו
תחת כנפיו יחסו רוזנים   ובני יקר ועוז בצל נעמו וכו'
השר אשר היה לרוב אחיו   רצוי ודורש טוב לכל עמו
ועלי ג א ו ן ב י ת י ע ק ב ע ל י   רוקח פני תבל ורום בשמו
מנאמו עלף[123] לצוארו   נטפי בדלח כענק לשמו
ושני כרובי עז[124] עלי כסאו   ישבו עלי פניו ובמקומו וכו'

(The poem seems to end at the bottom of fol. 41, verso. There is a lacuna between fols. 41 and 42. The latter commences with the end of a poem and then there follows (fol. 42, recto and verso) another one given under next number.)

49.

ולה ימדח אלשיך אלאגאל אלצדר נגם אלדולה בן אבי אלסעוד[124a]

⏑ – – – | ⏑ – – – | ⏑ – – – ||

יפת מראה ילדיה אדמים   ופניה ושמש רום תאומים
וקולעת אלי לבות בעין   כחץ שחוט וגם קוסם קסמים
ורוק פיה כמו חמאה וצוף   או כיין רקח מעורב בבשמים
וטומנת לכל לב פח אהבות   ופורשת לכל נפש חרמים
וטורי פז בלחייה ועגילים   באזניה ועל אפה נזמים
ולה חן חן . . . . מצבאות   ומגורי ארי פחד ואימים וכו'
ומימיה כשמן מר דרור או   כשם מ ש ה נגיד כל היקומים
פאר שרים וטפסרים וחורים   ויחיד לא עממוהו סתומים[125] וכו'

[123] Cp. Cant. 5.14.

[124] The two sons of the Gaon 'Alī II (cp. Poznański, *Babyl. Geonim*, p. 49).

[124a] A poem of praise for the most respected elder, the chief, Najm ad-Daula b. Abū'l Sa'ūd.

[125] Cp. Ezek. 28.3.

50.

(fol. 42, verso)

ולה פי אלצאחב מהד͘ב אלדולה͘ בןאלמאשעירי

תהניה͘[126]

|| — — ⏑ | — — — ⏑ — — — ⏑

לך יצחק חבלים בנעימים
ולך שם טוב כמו ראשי בשמים וכו'
והתפאר בילד[127] חן וחסד
עלי כל שר ונכבד ביקומים
באלעזר צבי חמדה צבי הוד
אשר זכרו כריח מור וסמים
וככה באליעזר נדיב לב
אשר פניו כקשורי לשמים
ועובדיה אשר נמול כהיום
אשר פניו ושמש רום תאומים
יהי לו דם ברית נחשב בעין אל
כדם חטאת ועולות ואשמים וכו'

(The poem seems to end at the bottom of fol. 42, verso, but there is a lacuna between fols. 42 and 43. The latter (on verso) contains the end of an elegy wherein condolence in expressed to *Yefet*, *Pinḥas*, *Aaron*, השר כנניהו, השר שריה and נשיאנו [נחמי]ה[128]. There follow several small poems and there is a lacuna between fols. 43 and 44. The latter commences with the end of a complimentary composition.

[126] A poem of congratulation to the master, Muhaḍḍib ad-Daula (the upright of the realm) b. al-Māsha'īri. His Hebrew name was Isaac and that of his father Mordecai (cp. Poznański, *l. c.*, 70, note 5). The poem was written on the occasion of the circumcision of Isaac's third boy 'Obadyah (l. 5). The first two sons were El'azar and Eli'ezer (ll. 3–4). About El'azar cp. infra, No. 54f.

[127] Better בילדי.

[128] Evidently a member of the Exilarchic family. Cp. also the other poems of our Diwān (ed. Poznański, *l. c.*, p. 65, bottom, and 66, l. 58).

There follows an elegy (ולה מרתִֿיהֿ) for a lady the first line of which begins: מות אשר החזיק בכנף מעילנו לא יטשנו ואם הרבה חללינו. The poem is incomplete and there is a lacuna between fols. 44 and 45.)

51.

(Fol. 45, recto, begins with the end of a complimentary poem on the occasion of the festivals. There follows another one for such an occasion with the following heading):—

ולה פי שר שלום אלרייס אבי אלעלא בן אלנטאר[129]

|| — — | — ⏑ — — — | — ⏑ — — —

אמרו לשר שלום עלה ושלם וחיה עלי אף צר עדי עולם וכו'

(Greetings are extended to his sons *El'azar*, *Yeshu'ah* and *Pinḥas.*)

52.

(fol. 45, verso–46, recto)

ולה מרתִֿיהֿ[130]

| — ⏑ — — | — ⏑ — — | — ⏑ — —

| — — — | — ⏑ — — | — ⏑ — —

איכה תמותה תאמרו הוללות
איכה ובין קדש וחול מבדלת וכו'
גזלה צבי חמדה מבורך איש אשר
כפיו כעב מטרת סגור[131] נוזלת וכו'
האל ינחם את לבב עלי גאון
יעקב אשר לבו כלב קהלת

[129] A poem in honor of Sar Shalom (the dignitary) Abū'l 'Ala b. al-נטאר (read perhaps נאטר, the keeper, and hence a government official). But Steinschneider (*l. c.*, 202, No. 482) lists from MS. Adler an Abū'l 'Ala b. al-'Aṭṭār (the perfumer) and hence perhaps here too read אלעטאר for אלנטאר.

[130] An elegy on the death of a certain Meborakh, perhaps the person mentioned in No. 20.

[131] Money (cp. Job 28.15).

ר א ש ה י ש י ב ה המרוה את פני
תבל ימי[132] ידיו כמו שבלת
ופנה ל א ל ע ז ר נגיד עם אל ושר
משרה אשר ידו לים נמשלת
ולבב בנו י ו ס ף צבי כבוד אשר
ריחו כריח חלבנה ושחלת[133] וכו׳
ככה ל א ב י ת ר חתנו איש אשר
גפן חסדיו סורחה גומלת וכו׳
גם את בנו ש ת[133a] נחמה האל ומ־
לא בו לבית אביו לעד משלת[134] וכו׳

53.

(fol. 46, recto and verso)

ולה פי ר׳ עזרא בן אלתקה[135]

⏑ — — — | ⏑ — — — | ⏑ — — — ||

צביה קדחה בלב רשפים ונפשות אוהבים שרפה בגופים
ומשכה קשתות גבות וירתה בחין עפעף קרבי הגופים
בשורי תארה אכהה כשמש תשוה את פני רואה שזופים
לאטה תהלוך הלוך וטפוף מעכסת ברגלי נאפופים
ושדים כאשכולות וקומה כמו תמר ותנוד כענפים
לחייה שני אורים גדולים ותלתלי קוצתה[136] נשפים
ותמשך קוצתה בלחיה כמשך הנחשים השרפים

[132] Read בְּמוֹ

[133] Cp. Exod. 30.34.

[133a] For this name cp. רבנא שת of Aleppo (Assaf, *l. c.*, 48).

[134] Read מַמְשֶׁלֶת.

[135] In honor of 'Ezra b. al-Thiḳa (probably תִּקַּת אלדולה, trust of the realm). See above, note 92.

[136] קְוֻצָּתָהּ (cp. Cant. 5.11).

כאלו לחיה מרר ואדם[137] יצרה הצור ובה ממור נטפים
ושניה שני טורי בדלח ומתחת לשונה חן וצופים
יפת מראה והיא נאוה כתרצה[138] וטובת חן והיא בעלת כשפים
לבבי גנבה מני בנסעה כרחל גנבה את התרפים[139]
לבלתי אדעה דרכה וארדוף ועל כן הם [140] מבוהלים דחופים
ומיום נדדה נדדה שנתי ורעיוני ביד יגון טרופים
ויגעתי לבקש את לבבי[141] בכל בקעה ושן סלע וכפים
ולא נמצא לבד היום בענדי בזכר הגביר עזרא צניפים
גביר נתן זמנו לו רבבות ביום נתן לאלופיו אלפים [142]
יצו האל הברכה באסמיו והיו כל שעריו מאליפים[143]
והמאות אשר נענש[144] ישובון לאוצרו רבבות ואלפים
ויראה מחמד לבו שמואל וכל כבוד וחכמה בו אסופים

(Here ends fol. 46, verso. The poem seems to be incomplete and there is a lacuna between fols. 46 and 47.)

54.

a) Fol. 47, recto and verso contains the end of a poem in honor of גבירנו חנניהו wherein also his sons are greeted. There are further mentioned *Ezekiel* (ובם ישמח לבב השר יחזקאל[145] נגיד עם אל ושר שרים ורוזנים וכו') and evidently his son *Joseph* (יחי לו הגביר יוסף וכו'),[146] then *Solomon*, *Pinḥas*, *Ephraim*, *Joseph* (יהוסף) and *David*.

b) On fol. 47, verso, there follows an elegy (ולה מרת֗יה֗) the first line of which reads: זמנים נתנו ארבם בקרבם והכרת פניהם ענתה בם. It is incomplete and there is a lacuna between fols. 47 and 48.

[137] Read וְאֶרֶס (poison) keeping up the metaphor of the snakes.

[138] Cp. Cant. 6.4. [139] Cp. Genes. 31.19.

[140] The plural refers to רעיוני in next line.

[141] Viz. the desire of my heart.

[142] Cp. 1 Sam. 18.7. [143] Cp. Ps. 144.13.

[144] Evidently 'Ezra suffered a monetary loss by an imposition from the government.

[145] He is mentioned also in No. 21, l. 24, and No. 27, l. 5.

[146] See above, note 52a.

c) On fol. 48, recto and verso, we have another elegy for a certain Sa'adyah (על מות סעדיהו בחיר האל אשר דעתו בחשב היקר נאפדת). Condolence is expressed to *Joshua*, *Isaiah* (twice mentioned and hence perhaps 2 different persons), *Israel* and *Moses*.

d) On fol. 48, verso, there follows another elegy with the heading:—

ולה מרתֿיהֿ פי אל[רייס] . . . . . [בן אבי] אלרביע

הנבכי ים ואם מימי דמעות . . . . אש . . . צלעות

The poem is incomplete and there is a lacuna between fols. 48 and 49.

e) There follows on fol. 49, recto and verso, another poem with the heading:

תהניהֿ ולה איֿצא אלי אלרייס . . . . . .

There are mentioned *Samuel*, *Ezekiel*, *Abraham* and *Joseph* (יהוסף).

f) On fol. 49, verso—50, recto, there follows another composition:

ולה תהניהֿ פי אלרייס אמין אלדולהֿ בן מנצור בן אלמאשעירי פי אלחנוכה[147]

◡— — —|◡— — —|◡— — —||

באלעזר גביר חן שר תהלות

[ופ]ארו בנות ימים ולילות

פאר משרה ונאמן המלוכה[148]

אשר לו יאתו כל הגדולות וכו'

ומעלתו ירושה מאבותיו [149]

ומעלת כל בני מעלה שאולות וכו'

[147] A poem of praise for the dignitary Amīn ad-Daula (the faithful of the realm) b. Manṣūr b. al-Māsha'īri on the occasion of the feast of Ḥanukkah. His Hebrew name was El'azar. He is evidently the son of Isaac Muhaḏḏib ad-Daula (No. 50 where the eldest son El'azar is mentioned). We thus learn that Isaac's Arabic name was Manṣūr.

[148] An allusion to his title אמין אלדולהֿ.

[149] Viz. his father Isaac and grandfather Mordecai were all state dignitaries.

פאר משרה נין ראשי ישיבות
זכריהו אשר ידיו כגולות וכו'

There is also mentioned השר יהושע.[149a]

g) Fol. 50, verso, contains another eulogy: ולה איצׄא תהניה. It is faded and incomplete and there is a lacuna between fols. 50 and 51.

h) On fol. 51, recto, we have the end of an elegy. Condolence is expressed to *Isaac*, *Sar Shalom* (who perhaps was a Dayyān), *Joseph* the physician (רופא נאמן), *Daniel* and *Moses*.

i) Finally we have another elegy (fol. 51, recto and verso):

ולה מרתׄיה פי אלמעלם אלעזר בן כלינאת[150]

— — ⏑ | — — — ⏑ | — — — ⏑

עדי אן הזמן תפרע פרעות
בבניך ותשביעם ב[דמ]עות וכו'
כאלעזר ישר דרך ותמים
אשר תורות בצור לבו נטועות וכו'

Condolence is expressed to *Menaḥem* and *Ephraim*. The elegy seems to be incomplete at the bottom of fol. 51, verso, with which the MS. breaks off.

[149a] Zekharyah and Joshu'a were the sons of the Gaon 'Alī II, (see Pozn., *l. c.*, 49–50, 72–3).

[150] An elegy on the scholar (אלמעלם, Hebrew המלמד) El'azar b. כלינאת.

SECTION III

PALESTINIAN AFFAIRS IN THE 11th CENTURY

PALESTINIAN AFFAIRS IN THE 11TH CENTURY

THE proximity of Palestine to Egypt and the close contacts of the Jewries of these two countries naturally brought about a frequent exchange of correspondence on diverse topics between the communal and spiritual leaders. While the letters from Egypt to Palestine have mostly been lost, owing to the vicissitudes that passed over Palestinian Jewry especially since the coming of the Crusaders, the epistles from the Holy Land to Egypt, and in particular to Fusṭāṭ, have been preserved in considerable numbers in the famous Genizah of one of the Fusṭāṭ synagogues. Chiefly on the basis of this correspondence I have attempted to reconstruct the life of the Jewish center in the Holy Land in the 10th and 11th centuries in my work "The Jews in Egypt and in Palestine under the Fāṭimid Caliphs" (cp. also the supplement in *H. U. C. Annual*, III, 257 ff.). The fact that the material has by far not yet been exhausted has been explicitly pointed out (I, 5–6, cp. *Annual*, III, 257). The present section (III) as well as the following one (IV) are in reality further supplements to this subject. The new material, as it is made available, necessitates a revision of numerous conclusions hitherto arrived at and also renders our knowledge of the actual conditions of Jewish life in these countries more intimate and colorful. Every worker in this field of research must be prepared to submit his theories to constant correction and change in order to do justice to the goal of scientific truth.

1.

SOME ADDITIONAL LETTERS FROM SOLOMON B. YEHUDAH, GAON OF PALESTINE (c. 1025–1051)

The Genizah has preserved from no other Palestinian Gaon so many epistles as from Solomon b. Yehudah. Besides the two letters published by Schechter[1] and by Poznański (*REJ*, XLVIII, 172–73) over 50 are edited either in extenso or in extract in my *Jews in Egypt and Palestine* (and also in *H. U. C. Annual*, III, 269 ff.) in addition to several more that are merely cited. These letters show the extensive correspondence kept up by this Gaon with the outside communities, especially with those of Egypt. The personality of Solomon and his expressive Hebrew style are made manifest in them. More letters follow in this and in the next chapters thus supplementing the topics that were discussed in connection with those epistles edited previously.[2]

1. *The conflict with the Ḳaraites in Jerusalem* (ibid., I, 134–141; II, 152–57).

The fragment given under I (infra, p. 315 f.) clearly emanates from this Gaon. It reveals how it came about that members of the school, the two priestly brothers Joseph and Elijah, the sons of the late Gaon Solomon (as we now learn), were arrested for declaring a Ḥerem against the Ḳaraites with regard to the prohibition of eating meat together with milk (בשר בחלב). On Hosha'na Rabba the assembled crowd of pilgrims accused the Gaon of having been bribed by the Ḳaraites not to include this item in a Ḥerem. Solomon refused at all to pronounce any ban on that occasion for fear of government reprisal although this

[1] *Saadyana*, pp. 111–13, cp. my corrections in *Jews in Egypt*, I, 126, note 1.

[2] An additional epistle by Solomon has been published by Gottheil-Worrell, *Fragments from the Cairo Genizah in the Freer Collection*, 1927, 26–31. The facsimile (plate VIII) reveals that the editors have misread the leaf in numerous places including the very signature of the author, and that their translation and comments also leave very much to be desired. We discuss this letter in some detail infra under No. 4.

was an old custom. His plea as well as that of the 'Third' of the school had no effect. He announced the fixing of the calendar for the following year according to Rabbinic calendation but refused any further action against the sectaries. However, to pacify the crowd, the two priestly Ḥaberim together with Solomon's son, Abraham, did declare the Ḥerem making it appear as if the item of בשר בחלב was included. After the ceremony before the Gaon reached his home, soldiers of the governor of Ramlah appeared and evidently arrested the Ḥaberim. Solomon's son seems to have gotten free probably by intervention of his father. Here the fragment breaks off. These Ḥaberim were taken as prisoners to Damascus and there harsh conditions were to be imposed upon them before regaining their freedom as described in connection with the other fragments. The whole subject will be discussed comprehensively in volume II of our *Texts and Studies*, in the sketch of the Ḳaraite center in Palestine.

2. The fragment, given under II (infra, pp. 317–20), evidently is in connection with the mission of Solomon's son, Abraham, to Fusṭāṭ on behalf of the Rabbanite community of Jerusalem groaning under a heavy burden of debts which led to the arrest of a number of people (cp. I, 120 ff.; II, 136 ff.). In l. 3 there is an allusion to his son's leaving Jerusalem on his mission. The prisoners sent an appeal to Ḥesed al-Tustari and to other elders to help them in their need. The debt amounted to more than 900 Dīnars. Solomon mentions that the Ḳaraites too were hard-pressed and, in spite of their having been assisted by their fellow-sectaries in Fusṭāṭ, they still owed 800 Dīnars. The letter is probably sent to Ephraim b. Shemaryah who is urged to make peace with his opponent Abraham the Ḥaber (l. 32), probably Abraham b. Sahlān. The Gaon alludes to his former visit to Egypt and how on his return he was made Reader of the Jerusalem congregation. Two years have passed and his services went entirely unrewarded owing to the great distress prevailing in the Holy City.

The quarrel between Ephraim and Abraham assumed a wider aspect by the latter accepting the title Alluf from Hai's academy. Abraham was the head of the Babylonian synagogue in Fusṭāṭ but he also kept up correspondence with the Palestinian academy from which he held the title Ḥaber. The letters given in II, 124–129, should now be interpreted in connection with this dispute between these two important figures in the capital of Egypt. In our letter, just as in the one given in II, 136–38, Solomon strongly urges Ephraim to forgive and bring about peace in the community. Ultimately the conflict subsided and after the death of Abraham (in 1032) his son Sahlān, who succeeded him, maintained cordial relations with the Gaon.

3. The third letter (infra, pp. 320–22) is from Solomon to Sahlān acknowledging the receipt of a bequest of 10 Dīnars for the Jerusalem poor. Evidently the same bequest is also acknowledged in a letter from Solomon to Ephraim b. Shemaryah (II, 146–47).

Interesting are the remarks of the Gaon about the Aggadot (l. 19 ff.). He reveals therein the same rationalistic tendency as maintained by the Babylonian Geonim like Sherira and Hai and also Samuel b. Ḥofni. Solomon points out that most of the Aggadot cannot be regarded as interpreting the verses correctly and if he, e.g., would now give such interpretations, he would not be heeded by the hearers whose tastes have changed. In Jerusalem evidently, where there was a strong Ḳaraite center, there was then a tendency for the Peshaṭ rather than the homiletic way of the Aggadic interpretation. The whole subject of the rationalism prevalent in the Gaonic period will be dealt with in another connection.

4. The letter, cited in note 2, is clearly by Solomon as the signature should be deciphered שלמה הצׄ (=הצעיר) ברׄ יהודה נׄעׄ. It is addressed to Jacob b. Joseph, who was no Gaon but had the title מעותד, probably מעותד לחבורה (cp. Mann, I, 278, top; II, 313, No. 3), viz. a candidate for the degree of Ḥaber (cp. also l. 2 of this letter המעותד לשם בגאון יעקב, designated for a title by the Gaon of the school). He cannot be identical with the scholar of Aleppo, formerly of Fusṭāṭ (I, 37–8, II, 174, note 1; *H. U. C. Annual*, III, 263–5) because the latter's father Joseph was Ab-Bet-Din of the school whereas in this letter he is only styled as החסיד. Our Jacob, a resident of Jerusalem, went to Fusṭāṭ for certain purposes. On this occasion he was entrusted by Solomon b. Khalāf al-Barḳi to arrange in Fusṭāṭ the latter's affairs with

his wife who refused to follow her husband to Jerusalem. The affair resulted in a divorce. Solomon b. Yehudah expected his friend Jacob to return by Pentecost, then by Tish'ah be-Ab and finally for the festivals in Tishri. He expresses the pious wish that this delay be for good and that his friend rejoin him soon (l. 28: והנה נתאחרת צור ישימהו לטובה ויקרב ההכלל עמך).

There follow a discreet allusion to the collapse of the Mosque al-Aḳsa and the prayerful wish that 'a permanent building' be soon erected in its stead (viz. the Jewish Temple at the Messianic age). This is the evident meaning of ll. 29–30: והמקום ההדור הבנוי עליו נפל ביום י"ז לחודש אוב וה[ו]א יום אחד בשעה העשירית ביום יהי רצון שיבנה בנין מקויים. This event brings us to the year 407 H. (1016 C. E.) when during an earthquake the dome of the Mosque collapsed.[3] The date given here, Sunday 17th of Ab, does not correspond with our present calculation according to which Ab of 4776 A. M. commenced on a Monday (July 9th)[4] and hence the 17th was on a Wednesday (July 25th). But י"ז may be a lapsus calami for י"ד. Another alternative is that there is some inexplicable flaw in our calculation of the calendar of bygone ages. Such a difference of 3 days we find also in the Fusṭāṭ document dated Wednesday, Kislev 11th, 1062 Sel. (750 C. E., *JQR*, XVII, 428), whereas according to our calculation Kislev of 4511 A. M. began on a Thursday and hence the 11th was on a Sunday.[4a] Anyhow there is no reason to doubt that the allusion here is to the above event which must have made a great impression on the minds of the Jerusalem Jews and hence Solomon even recorded the hour (4 p. m.) when the dome collapsed. To the Jews as well as the Christians it must have been a significant omen, especially since it happened during the reign of al-Ḥakim who ordered the destruction of synagogues and churches all over the Fāṭimid empire (see I, 32 ff.). The dating of our letter in 1016 makes it evident that Solomon wrote this letter before he became Gaon and indeed in our epistle he

[3] Cp. Le Strange, *Palestine under the Moslems*, 101, and R. Hartmann, *Der Felsendom in Jerusalem u. seine Geschichte*, 1909, p. 43.

[4] Cp. the table in Mahler's *Handbuch d. jüd. Chronologie*, p. 557.

[4a] See Bornstein's discussion of this point in התקופה, XIV–XV, 371–2.

signs הצעיר without the accompanying title ראש הישיבה.[5] The presidency of the school was occupied then by Joshiah (see I, 72)[6] who was succeeded (in about 1020) by Solomon Hakkohen b. Joseph. Solomon b. Yehudah did not become Gaon till about 1025.

The above correct interpretation of this letter[7] disposes of the fanciful speculations of Dinaburg (ציון, III (1929), 67 ff.) who has imaginatively reared a synagogue on the Temple mount (next to the Mosque al-Aḳsa!) which synagogue was destroyed by orders of al-Ḥakim in 1018. The writer of our letter becomes

[5] Cp. his usual signature (or שלמה הצ׳ ראש ישיבת גאון יעקב (ראש הישיבה in Mann II, 65, 112, 115, 122, 125, 128, 135, 148, 151, 152, 155, 162, 167, 186; infra, pp. 320, 322, 340. Only in II, 131, l. 3, he signs as here הצ׳ but the address (p. 129) clearly indicates that he was already Gaon then.

[6] To the letters from Joshiah (given in Mann, II, 66–72) there should be added T.-S. Loan 44, very damaged and faint, containing an epistle to Ephraim b. Shemaryah of Fusṭāṭ. It establishes the fact (discussed in vol. I, 100, note 1) that Ephraim was ordained as Ḥaber at the Palestinian school during the presidency of Joshiah Gaon. The address (verso) reads:

[לכנק מר׳ אפרים המומ[חה] מפינו בן רב שמריה המלמד
[ישמרהו אלהינו ויעזרה[ו] החסיד נ״ע

(There follow 2 faint lines of Arabic script).

The letter itself is found on recto: (1) יאשיהו ראש ישיבת גאון יעקב בירבי[ם] (2) שלום אביעה. וברכות ארגיענ[ה] . . . (3) בכל שעה. ואורה וישועה. אול אהובנו רב אפרים החב[ר] (4) המומחה מפינו אנו בית דנין הגדול בשער הישיב[ה] . . . (5) והחרידות הנכונה. המזומן . . . [כת בני[ו] (6) עוננה. והמתחזק באמתו . . . (7) כחנית וצינה. תינצל מכל . . . ובן רב[נ] (8) שמריה המלמד החסיד נ[ע] . . . (9) גאון הישיבה באמת ואה . . . [והכתב] (10) הכתוב בלשון הקודש אשר א. . . (11) והכתב אשר הוא בלשון הנגרי[ת] . . . (12) מרור׳ טוביה החבר בסנהדרין גדול[ה] . . . (13) [ול]קח מן הכתבים ולא בא . . . (14) . . . והלו . . . מו . . . (verso) . . . (2) בתשובה על כל עינין . . . (3) [נק]רובה גם לא נעלם ממנו ה . . . (4) . . . ול מחיתה לו והוא אשר ה . . . (5) גידלו והלך למקום שנגלה בו . . . (6) [ה]ודענוך הכול ושלומך יגדל . . . רק בעיני[ך] (7) תביט ושלומת רשעים תראה . . . (8) הראשון . . .

By the כת בני עוננה the Ḳaraites are meant represented in Jerusalem by their Nasi, a descendant of ʿAnan. Joshiah came into conflict with these sectaries as is evident from the letter given in II, 66–69. Tobias the Ḥaber figures later on as 'Third' under Solomon b. Yehudah (see infra, p. 324 ff.).

[7] I see now that Sukenik (ציון, IV, 159–60) rightly drew attention to the event of 1016 without however realizing that the author of the letter was not Solomon Hakkohen but Solomon b. Yehudah. Dinaburg in his rejoinder still fails to comprehend the discreet allusion in the phrase יהי רצון שיבנה בנין מקויים, viz. that instead of the Mosque this site be occupied by the Jewish Temple as a result of the appearance of the Messiah.

the Gaon Solomon Hakkohen and his correspondent Jacob b. Joseph Ab-Bet-Din while the phrase המקום ההדור הבנוי עליו נ פ ל denotes just the *destruction* of this synagogue! All these statements are of course unwarranted just as numerous other ones with which Dinaburg's long paper (pp. 54–87) is teeming and which cannot be refuted here in detail.

I.

[T.-S. Loan 11, paper, top and bottom missing, verso blank.]

(Recto)

. . . .

כמו אלה . . . . רבים מעם הארץ [מח]רחרים ריב ויה[ני יום] הושענא ויעלו העם כמנהגם אל ה[ר ה]זיתים [והמשמיצים][1] אומרים לעם האיש הזה[2] נתנו לו הקראים זהובים [כדי שלא] תזכר בשר בחלב סתם ויבטיחם על זה [וע]תה התקב[צו ואמרו] לו אל תשנה מנהגינו ואם ימאן אל תשמעו לו והקה[ילו עליו] קהלה ויהי אחרי הפתרון[3] ואדבר אל העם דברי רכות בעב[ור] הנדבה הנשלכת על השמלה[4] והנה איש נודב כי אם מעט במספר והם אשר באו להתפלל והרוב אשר עלו לחרחר ריב משמיצים מאריכים פה מרחיבים לשון מעיזים פנים אומרים לי אתה אומר בפתרונותיך אני מקבל[5] כאחד מכם כאשר קבלתי[6] ה[קבלה] והמנהגות אל תשנה מנהג הראשונים ואם תשנה כולם ילכ[ו] ויהיו קראים וידברו דברים אשר לא [כן ויהי] כראותי כי אין

[1] The slanderers (cp. *Jews in Egypt*, II, 426, s. v. שמץ).

[2] Viz. the Gaon Solomon b. Yehudah.

[3] After the sermon based on some Scriptural interpretation.

[4] Evidently there was spread out a cloth on Mount Olivet near where the Gaon sat and the pilgrims would place therein their donations for the school.

[5] From קבלה, tradition, viz. I am as good an adherent of Rabbinic tradition as you.

[6] The 'ת is doubtful in MS. and can also be read as 'מ, but the sense demands as above. But perhaps read קבלנו.

שומע ואין מאזין ואעמוד מעל הכסא[7] ואומרה הנה רשותכם בידכם עשו כאשר תרצו וגם רבינו השלישי שמׄ צוׄ[8] דבר באזניהם לאמר זאת אינה מצוה להריב עליה מה לנו ולמחלוקת ולא שמעו איליו[9] ותרב מריבת העם בהר עד מאד ויבואו זקנים עם השר אשר על העיר[10] ויאמרו עלה והכריז סדרי מועדי י׳[ני][11] ואעלה ואכריז כמנה[ג] ויאמר[ו] החרים[11a] ואומרה כבר יצא מפי כי

אני לא אחרים ויעמדו שני האחים החברים יש אלׄ[12] ובני[13] עמהם ויחרימו ויפיסו את העם ב[דבר]ים דימו[14] להם כי זכרו בשר בחלב וירדו מן ההר עוד לא [באתי] בביתי עד אשר באו חילי השליט על הארץ[15] המכונה [מ]עתז אלדולהׄ יש אלׄ[16] ואלכה והנה אצלו אשר ....

....

[7] This shows that a chair was placed for the Gaon on the mount during the long service on Hosha'na Rabba.

[8] =שמרו צורו. This 'Third' is evidently Tobias b. Daniel (see infra, p. 324 ff.).

[10] The prefect of Jerusalem.

[9] Read אליו.

[11] On the other hand we find Ben Meir sending his son to announce the calendar on the 'fourth month' (either Tammuz or Ṭebet, cp. Bornstein in Sokolow's ס׳ היובל, 74, note 2, and Epstein, *Haggoren*, V, 138, note 1). But this may have been a special occasion. Ben Meir refers to הכרזות תלמידינו בהר הזתים סדרי מועדות, but whether this refers to a previous proclamation on Hosha'na Rabba (as Malter, *Saadia Gaon*, p. 81, note 168, thinks) is still doubtful. On the other hand the declaration of a leap year was made in Ab of the previous year. T.-S. Box F 8 contains 2 large vellum sheets of explanations to B. Batra and Sanhedrin. On fol. 2, verso, we have the following comment to Sanh. 12[a]: ובקשו לקבוע נציב אחד. בקשו לעבר זאת ה[ש]נה חדש אחד ומתי קובעין אותו בחדש אב וכך המנהג עד הנה שבחדש החמשי מעבירין את השנה.

[11a] = החרם, Imperative.

[12] ישמרם אלהים, i. e. Joseph Hakkohen and Elijah Hakkohen, the sons of the late Gaon Solomon Hakkohen.

[13] Evidently Abraham, the son of Solomon b. Yehudah.

[14] Pretended to them that they included the item of בשר בחלב in the Ḥerem.

[15] Evidently the governor of Filasṭīn situated in Ramlah.

[16] = ישמרו אלהים. His title was Mu'tazz ad-Daula, the Illustrious (one) of the State.

II.

[T.-S. Loan 43, torn and damaged.]

(Recto)

משמים.................................. טובה ואסעם כי הגיד.............. ואחרי צאתו מעיר הקודש הקשו בעלי.......... [ה]לוים והערבים ונתפשו הנשאר והציר להם.......... ושאלו לכתוב מכתב על פיהם מבית הכלא ונתנו בו כיר[16a] ידיהם ונשלח עלי ידי פקיד הזקן הגביר אבו נצר[17] יהי אל עזרו ועמו מכתבים רבים ואחד מהם אליך על אודות הזקנים אלדסאתרהֹ[18] כי לא תעלה ארוכה לדבר כי אם באשר אצלם כי [ה]חוב גדול יותר מתשע מאות זהוב מאין יכולת לפרעו המן הגרן או מן היקב הנה אחינו הקראין אחרי כל אשר [נ]שלח אליהם מצוען[19] נשאר עליהם שמונה מאות זהוב ואם הם ככה אנחנו מה נאמר אבל יושבי צלע[20] השליכו כל יהבם על הנשיאים[21] יהי אל עזרם וכת הרבנים משיאים לי יד לאמר אנחנו גמלנוך טובה ולא הכללנוך עמנו[21a] כאשר עשו כת הק[ראים]

[16a] Handwriting (see Mann, II, Hebrew Index and Glossary, s. v.)

[17] i. e. Ḥesed b. Sahl al-Tustari.

[18] Also mentioned in Solomon's other letters (II, 155, No. 57, l. 10, and 140, l. 30).

[19] Fusṭāṭ

[20] The Ḳaraites living in the quarter of Jerusalem identified with צלע האלף היבוסי (see I, p. 275). To the passages cited there, there should be added the statement of Sahl b. Yeruḥam in his commentary to Lamentations (1. Hebrew Firkowicz Collection in Leningrad, No. 560). In dealing with the murder of Zekharyah b. Yehoyada' in the Temple (cp. 2 Chron. 24.26–27) in connection with Lam. 2.20 (אם יהרג במקדש אדני כהן ונביא) Salman remarks: והדא זכריה עׄ אלסׄ (= עליה אלסלאם) מדפון פי אלקדס אלשריף פי סמרתקהֹ אלדֹי הי צלע האלף היבוסי והי אליום תערף הארהֹ אלמשארקהֹ עלי מא דֹכרה מברך בן נתן בן ניסן נעׄ לאן הדֹא מברך י׳ אל (= ירחמהו אלהים) פי בעץׄ אלקינות קאל: ואבכה מול קבר זכריה בן יהוידע. אשר קברו בצלע האלף נודע.

[21] About these Ḳaraite Nesiim see volume II of our *Texts and Studies*.

[21a] Viz. we exempted you from paying the impost.

לנשיא[ים] לכן יקירנו ראוי לך להתחזק עמהם והזכיר לי אברהם[22]
. . . [החו]קים[22*] אשר היו לאדוננו גאון ולאב נוחם עדן[23] לשאול אותך
. . . .
בעדה[24] ואני אודיעך את דרכי אני אחרי שובי מארץ מצרים
בשנה אשר נכנסתי אליה פתוני הירושלמים והושיבוני חזן
[בי]רוש[25] כי אמרו לי את[ה] איש מעביר עתותיך בדבר מועט[26]
[מיום] בואך ועתה אל תצריכנו לאיש אחר וקבלתי מהם והייתי
מעביר עתותי פעם במלא ופעם בחסר עד הימים האלה היום שתי
שנים[27] [ל]א נתנו לי הירושלמיים שוה פרוטה כי לא נמצא בידם דבר
. . . בהם כדי לעמוד בספקם ובאה השנה הזאת וגילת[27a] כל נסתר
ונצרכתי למכור הנותר בבית כי ראיתיה מתחלתה קשה
ו. . . . . . . מקוה כי תעבור ואנחנו בחיים כי הי[תה] הצרה עד
מאד וברוך גומל טובוות ל[חיבים[28] ועתה אהוב אני איש אין
דרכי לזה לק[ח]ת דבר שיש [בו] ריח אסור ו[א]ם . . . תדע כי הדבר
הזה אלי מות[ר] . . . . . תביעות . . . . . . וכשר בעיני הזקנים
עשה אותו בטובו[תך] ואם וחס ושלום יש שם דבר שיש

[22] Probably Solomon's son, Abraham, who is referred to in l. 3 as having gone from Jerusalem to Egypt on behalf of these prisoners.

*[22] The reading is doubtful.

[23] The late Gaon is evidently Solomon Hakkohen, but the late Ab is unknown to me, unless we identify him with X. b. Yoḥai (infra, p. 323).

[24] If the reading החקים be correct (l. 16), then we should read here בעדם.

[25] = בירושלם.

[26] Evidently in the meaning of being satisfied with a small livelihood.

[27] Read שנים.

[27a] =וגלתה, revealed.

[28] Cp. the well-known ברכת הגומל.

(verso)

[בו רי]ח אסור אל ת[שלח] וא[שר תעשה] בדבר שכרך מהאל וגלוי לאל כי לו היתה
. . . . משגה ח[נס] ושלום לא הכלמ[תי] ואתה חכם ונבון ואני שואל ממך
[להשי]ת בינך ובין ר׳ אברהם החבר של[ו]ם ויסבול כל אחד מכם את חבירו
[כי לא] כימים הראשונים הימים האלה כי לפני כן הייתם ברשות עצמכם ועתה
[הלא את]ם ברשות אל וברשות ישראל[28a] ולא יכשר לכם להדמות כי אם ליראי
[שמו ו]ללכת בדרך טובים ואורחות צדיקים לשמור ואל יהיה בינ[יכם]
[מחלוק]ת[29] כי המחלוקת מביאה לידי חרוף להשמיץ כל אחד לחבירו
[ואף אם אתה] שומע הדבה לא תשוב ומה יש יכולת להשיב לבעל הדין ביום
[הדין כי] לא ידע האדם את עתו לא חשב הנאסף[30] כי יומו [י]בא מה
. . . . היה מדמה כי ישב בר]אש[31] וכי השעה תעמד לו
. . . . . דוקן[22]* לו ואיה א[פו]א תקותו ותקותו מי ישורנה[32] וכמו כן

[28a] The reference is here to a change in the former arrangement of the spiritual leaders of the two Fusṭāṭ congregations administering justice each separately. Now they had to hold a combined Bet-Din (cp. also Mann, II, 143, ll. 17–20, 145, l. 10). For a document of 1022 signed by both Abraham b. Sahlān and Ephraim b. Shemaryah, see ibid., II, 97, No. 1.

[29] The reading is doubtful; if correct, then read תהיה for יהיה.

[30] Evidently the late Ab (see note 23) who thought that one day he would succeed Solomon as Gaon (היה מדמה כי ישב בראש).

[31] Viz. בראש הישיבה.

[32] Cp. Job 17.15.

. . . [של]מה הכהן גאון נעׄ . . . וא . . . לא כן דומה וגם הכ[ות]ב[33]
לא ידע מתי

[תבא עתו והמ]שאל מהאל להנהיג בחסדו לעשות הטוב והישר
בעיניו וגם אתה

[תשתדל ו]תרדוף אחרי השלום וכאומר[34] בקש שלום ורדפהו
ושלומך

[ושלום כל נלויך יר]בה נצח

שלמ[ה] הצׄ[35] ראש הישיבה ברבי יהודה נׄנׄ

[There follows, in reversed side, a postscript in different ink but by the same hand, very faint, dealing with some ,lawsuit. There is mentioned therein a certain R. Tobias, perhaps identical with the 'Third' of the school.]

III.

[T.-S. Loan 14, paper; verso contains the address in Arabic script which is illegible.]

(Recto)

ליקר פאר כגקׄ מרׄ ורׄ סהלאן ה[מעוטר ב]ארבעה כינוי שלכבוד[36]

יהי צור עזרו וצל סתרו. ויעטר[ו[37] וינצ]רו. ויתן לו תאות לבו
וסברו[38].

ויעמיד ממנו מקים שמו וזכרו. [בן כבׄ גדׄ] קדׄ מרׄ ורׄ אברהם
החבר נעׄ

שלום שלום תשמענה אזניו. ומלך ביופיו תראינה עיניו. וימלא

[33] i.e. Solomon b. Yehudah, the writer of this epistle.

[34] Ps. 34.15. [35] =הצעיר.

[36] Sahlān had several honorary titles: Ḥaber, Alluf, Rosh Hasseder, סגן הישיבה and חמדת הנשיאות (see Mann, II, 102–3). At the time when our letter was written he held only four of these titles. In another letter Solomon addresses him as הנקוב בשבעה כינויין (ibid., II, 80, note 10) but the other two titles are as yet unknown. Cp. also Chapira, *RÉJ*, LXXXII, p. 326.

[37] Cp. Ps. 5.13.

[38] Hope.

בטוב ימיו ושניו. [גע][38a] מכתבו המיוקר. רשום בכבוד ויקר. עם הדיוקני[39] אשר בעשרה זהובים בשם העניים אשר צוה מ אבר[הם] בן נחום טוליטלי[40] ימצא רחמים הם אשר היו מופקדים ביד מר ורב מבורך הזקן הנכבד השולחני שצ בן מור דויד נע והוא[41] שמרו צור קבלם מידו ונתנם לכך הזקן האביר מור חסד יהי צור עזרו בן מר ישר נו[42] עדן וכתב בהן דיוקני למר פצל הזקן בן דניאל נע[42a] וקבלתים מידו ונתתי אותם לפרנסי העניים בירושלם וחלקום לעניים כמנהג[נם] והזכרנו את הנאסף מר אברהם במנוחה[42b] ואת אשר נתעסקו בהם[43] עד אשר הגיעו לידי העניים בברכות ותפלות שיהי רצון[44] בהם ובכל צאצאיהם והוא[44a] שמ צור בראש יען כי יגע וכאשר צוה להיות האחד[45] לכך מר רב עלי הכהן החזן שצ כן נעשה. ואשר שאל לשאול את השלישי[46] על אודות מדרש שיר השירים לכתוב לו מן הדודאים ולכה דודי[47] והפירוש ההוזכר בו הוא קרוב לאשר

38a =הגיע (for this erroneous use of the Ḳal, cp. Mann, II, Hebrew Index and Glossary, s.v.).

39 Consignment of money (cp. Mann, II, 415, s. v.).

40 Of Toledo (Spain).

41 Viz. Sahlān took the money from Meborakh and handed it over to Ḥesed who sent an assignation to Fadhl b. Daniel.

42 =נוחו.

42a Fadhl b. Daniel was Parnās of the Jerusalem community (cp. II, p. 146, No. 51, l. 7ff.).

42b Similar to the אשכבתא (השכבה) in the Babylonian school (infra, p. 414, note 10).

43 Viz. the amount of 10 Dinārs (l. 6).

44 Supply שתחולנה.

44a Viz. Sahlān b. Abraham to whom our letter is written.

45 Evidently the meaning is that one Dinār of this amount be given to ʻAlī Hakkohen the Ḥazzān (cp. infra, p. 346).

46 i.e. Tobias b. Daniel.

47 The order of the verses is misplaced here (Cant. 7. 14,12).

במדרש חזית[47a] ואני אין דרכי לשאול ממנו כי אין דרכו להשאיל

ולא נכחד ממנו כי רוב האגדות דעות הן לא יוכל אדם לאמר כי האמור בהן הוא פירושיהם[48] אשר עליהם נאמרו ואיש כמו אנ[י][*48] בעת הזאת אם ידרוש לא ישמעו לו כמו לכה דודי נצא השדה נראה אם פרחה הגפן אלו בעלי מקרא פתח הסמדר אלו בעלי משנה

הנצו הרמונים אלו בעלי תלמוד[49] ופירוש הדודאים דודאי לא[ה] ורחל וכו׳[50] פירושין שלא ייערבו לשומעיהם הודעתיה[51] ומי שיש בו בינה יכול לדרוש בהם[52] זולתי הנאמר ושלומו ושלום מֹרֹ סעדיה אלוף[53] ירבה נצח שלמה הצעֹ[54] ראש ישיבת גאון יעקב ברבי.

[47a] The former Midrash, a copy of which was in the possession of the 'Third', was evidently different from our Midrash known as מדרש חזית because of its beginning with the verse in Prov. 22.29. Since we have no actual quotations here from this other Midrash, we cannot ascertain its identity, whether it be the one published by Grünhut from a Genizah MS. dated 1147 (Jerusalem, 1897) or the other version (published by Schechter, *JQR*, vols. VI–VIII, and by Buber, מדרש זוטא). In this connection attention should be drawn to Brit. Mus. Or. 5554 A, fol. 12, which contains apparently the end of a version of a Midrash to Canticles. The fragment (recto; verso is blank) reads as follows: שלתורה שנתחזקה לה בירושלם מחשמונים והילך עד שעת חרבן מיכאן ואילך ברח דודי ודמה לך לצבי וגו׳ על הרי בשמים (שה״ש ח׳ י״ד) אילו שתי הישיבות שריחן נודף מסוף העולם ועד סופו והינו דאמרינן בבבל היכא בי כנישתא דהוצל בי כנישתא דשף ויתיב בנהרדעא וכול׳ (מגלה כ״ט, ע״א) וללמדך שנסתלקה לה שכינה מירושלם ושרתה לה בבבל היא דכתֹ חולי וגוחי בת ציון וגֹ (מיכה ד׳, י׳), ומן תמן את אמֹ ברח דודי וגֹ כנסת ישראל היא שאומרת לפני המקום רבונו של עולם מה לך לטלטל שריות שכינתך ממקום למקום שאני שרויה בו: כלך למקום שריות הראשונות כתֹ ברח דודי ודמה לך לצבי: יכול לחוצה לארץ תלֹ לומֹ על הרי בשמים שהן כלל לבשמים שבעולם ואי זה זה בית המקדש שכתֹ הר ציון ירכתי צפון וגֹ (תהלים מ״ח, ג׳).
This Midrash glorifying the two schools (of Sura and Pumbedita) was probably written in Babylon during the Gaonic period.

[48] Better would be פירושי המקראות. [*48] The 'א is doubtful.

[49] See 'Erubin 21b, bottom.

[50] This Aggadah I could not locate.

[51] Read הודעתיהו, viz. I let you know my view on the Aggadot.

[52] Viz. can interpret the verses without taking recourse to the Aggadot.

[53] Sa'adyah Alluf was the uncle of Sahlān (Mann I, p. 99). His full name was Sa'adyah b. Ephraim.

[54] = הצעיר.

2.
THE AFFAIR OF NATAN B. ABRAHAM AS RIVAL GAON OF PALESTINE TO SOLOMON B. YEHUDAH.

About the antecedents and the personality of Natan b. Abraham we are now in a better position to obtain definite information by means of new fragments which supplement and elucidate the obscurities of the former data (as collected and discussed for the first time in *Jews in Egypt and in Palestine*, I, 141–51; II, 159–74, 352–54; *H. U. C. Annual*, III, 273–76).

Natan was the nephew of the Ab of the Palestinian school (בן אחות בן יוחיי אב) whose first name has not been preserved. Natan was also a student of the school and when he had to leave for North Africa, presumably Ḳairwān, to attend to his father's inheritance some time before the end of 1011 C. E., Samuel the 'Third' b. Hosha'na recommended him highly to Shemaryah b. Elḥanan of Fusṭāṭ. Natan's father was evidently also a scholar as Samuel refers to him as רבנא אברהם בן שאול and seems to have died in North Africa (i. e. Ḳairwān?) at the time when his son Natan was a student in Palestine. It is unknown whether this Abraham b. Saul was a Palestinian and for what purpose he visited the West. Anyhow at his demise he left there belongings warranting his son Natan to make the long trip from Palestine via Egypt. His master, Samuel the 'Third,' gave him a letter of introduction to Shemaryah b. Elḥanan who was to help this young and untried student on his way from Egypt to the West. Samuel already then regarded him as a promising student worthy of support.[1]

[1] The corresponding passage in Samuel's letter (ibid., II, 24, l. 16 ff.) reads: כתבנו להודיע רבינו (r. לרבינו) כי בימים האלה נשמעה שמועת רבנא אברהם בן שאול כי נפטר, ימצא רחמים וחיי לרבינו שבק, ושם בלבו ר' נתן בנו לצאת בשביל עזבונותיו שלא יאבדו, ופייסנוהו למנות שליח ולא יטריח הוא על עצמו כי חסנו עליו מיגיעות הארחות, ולא הוטבה נפשו בשליח. והוא ילד זך תמים גידול טהרתנו. ודיגול תורתנו. וכל יום מוסיף לקח ויש בו תמימות ובריריות ולא ניסה במה שהושדר לו. ותובעים אנו מרבינו שישים עליו עין ויורהו דרך הטוב המועילתו ויבינהו וישכילהו ויפארהו במכתביו ואגרותיו. אל מקהלותיו ואל סיעותיו. השותים בצמאה מדברותיו. ואל ריעיו ואוהביו גמיאי הטפותיו. כי כל מה שיעשה עמו עמנו הוא עשוי.

It may be taken for granted that Shemaryah befriended this young student and helped him to reach his destination where, after attending to his father's belongings, he remained for several years studying under the great Rabbinic authority R. Ḥushiel at Ḳairwān. The death of his uncle, the Ab of the Palestinian school (who stayed for some time in Egypt where he departed this life), caused our Natan to return to Egypt evidently with the view of claiming another inheritance, viz. the office of his uncle. In Fusṭāṭ he was able to obtain powerful support in order subsequently to proceed to Palestine and sustain his claim. By right of advancement, the office of Ab belonged to Tobias the 'Third' b. Daniel the Ḥaber and indeed there was such an agreement between the late Ab, X. b. Yoḥai, and Tobias that in case Solomon b. Yehudah, the aged Gaon, died, both contracting parties would advance to the offices of Gaon and Ab respectively. But Tobias was an inferior scholar compared to Natan who devoted several years of study under Ḥushiel. Natan obtained strong support in Cairo-Fusṭāṭ and when he came to Palestine, accompanied by influential people, Tobias was peaceably persuaded to make way for Natan who became Ab.

Soon Natan and the veteran Solomon b. Yehudah were involved in a severe conflict. Solomon indicates (in the new letter, l. 15 ff.) that the condition imposed upon Natan was to have no authority in the school itself (רשות בחבורה) but merely to bear the name of Ab. This evidently irked Natan, who resided in Ramlah, whereas the school proper with the Gaon at its head was in Jerusalem. Upon hearing of the independent actions of Natan in Ramlah, Solomon proceeded there together with Elijah the 'Sixth' (i. e. Elijah Hakkohen b. Solomon, the later Gaon of Palestine in succession to Daniel b. 'Azaryah) who was to settle there as the Gaon's representative. The matter came to a head at the synagogue during the Sabbath morning service. Solomon had his party and Natan his, and the two sections were eager for a fight. Fearing the consequences of such a physical encounter

This passage is now clarified by the statement in the letter of Solomon b. Yehudah (infra, p. 338, l. 7 ff.): כי בשנה הזאת בא אל ארץ ישראל מן המערב נתן בן אברהם בן אחות בן יוחיי אב הלך מקדם אל מערב מבקש ירושת אביו וישב שם שנים הרבה יושב פני רבֿ חושיאל הרב ללמוד תורה. My remarks (ibid., I, 27) are to be rectified accordingly.

with the inevitable interference on the part of the governor of the city, Solomon left this synagogue for another house of worship. Thereupon Natan proclaimed himself ראש הישיבה (or as Solomon bitingly remarks, l. 24, ראש תועבה). As a counterblast Solomon at the other synagogue ordered the scrolls of the Torah to be taken out and formally excommunicated Natan b. Abraham and his chief partisans, viz. 1) the son of the 'Third', 2) his cousin, 3) Maṣliaḥ his disciple, 4) the sons of Shawi'a and 5) 'Omar the physician.

The first follower in this list is perhaps the son of Tobias the 'Third,' viz. Solomon b. Tobias mentioned in Bodl. 2878.4 as one of the signatories of a document (שלמה ביר׳ טוביה השלישי בחבורה זצ״ל), which shows, by the way, that this Tobias, who had to make way for Natan as Ab, died as 'Third' and never advanced higher in the school. If this identification be correct, are we entitled to conclude that there was a tacit agreement between Natan and Tobias that the latter become Natan's Ab when he would attain the Gaonate and hence Tobias' son, Solomon, supported him officially while his father kept in the background waiting for the outcome of the affair?[2] The second follower in the list was evidently the son of the late Ab, X. b. Yoḥai, Natan's uncle. Natan's disciple, Maṣliaḥ, is perhaps identical with מצליח ברבי שמואל, a signatory of a document issued at Fusṭāṭ in 1041 (Bodl. 2876.30, cp. 2806.10). The other persons are not known from elsewhere. They were evidently residents of Ramlah.

Thus a rival Gaonate was created in Ramlah on a Saturday morning. Naturally each side began to send out letters to Egypt and elsewhere for support. In the light of the above account[3] let us enumerate the epistles of both parties as far as they are preserved.

[2] But this 'son of the Third' may also be identified with Abraham b. Samuel the 3rd b. Hosha'na. Since Samuel was the master of our Natan, it may be that his son Abraham later sided with Natan when he proclaimed himself Gaon. Abraham the Ḥaber b. Samuel the 3rd signs a Geṭ at Ramlah dated 1026 (see ibid., II, p. 25, bottom). From MS. Adler 4007 (see Catalogue, p. 100) we learn that Abraham at one time held the dignity of 4th, perhaps after Elijah Hakkohen advanced to the office of 3rd.

[3] It modifies my remarks in *Jews in Egypt*, I, 141 ff.

The following items emanate from the veteran Gaon Solomon b. Yehudah.

1. To Sahlān b. Abraham of Fusṭāṭ (given in *Jews in Egypt*, II, 159–161) before the conflict began. Solomon still had a good opinion of Natan. He describes how Natan was appointed Ab. Solomon was persuaded before the arrival of Natan to make an agreement with Tobias that he would succeed the late Ab, but afterwards Tobias gave way because he realized that he could not measure up with Natan. When the Ab, X. b. Yoḥai, was sick in Egypt (Fusṭāṭ) Tobias declared himself as entirely fit for the office about to be vacant (this is evidently the meaning of ll. 4 ff.). When subsequently news came of Natan's leaving Ḳairwān for Egypt (l. 8 ff.: ועת אשר שמעו כי יצא) there was a covenant concluded at the school that Natan be called neither ראש (i. e. ראש בית דין=Ab) nor Gaon. Evidently an agitation continued on his behalf owing to his scholarship and in view of the very advanced age of Solomon b. Yehudah. At the memorial service for the late Ab Solomon publicly declared that Tobias the 'Third' would succeed to the vacant office (ll. 10–11). All this was upset after the arrival of Natan to Jerusalem in the company of prominent elders from Fusṭāṭ, among them the dignitary (השר) Meborakh b. 'Alī b. Ezra (cp. ibid., II, p. 153, where he is styled Meborakh Abū'l Fadhl b. 'Alī).[4] Tobias quickly realized his inferiority when it was pointed out to him (l. 13 ff.: הנה המקום פנוי לך, אם יאמר לך מלא מקום הנאמר בתפלה על הקהל ובדברי תורה ואתה לא נסית הלא נהיה לבוז). This casts a lurid light upon the internal conditions in the school where the high offices became subject to claims of seniority and not of actual fitness. Thus Natan was appointed and the Gaon had to take up a neutral attitude since his candidate Tobias withdrew his claim. Solomon remarks that Natan was better than pictured before (l. 30).

Tobias was a cousin of the brothers Joseph and Elijah Hakkohen, the sons of the late Gaon Solomon Hakkohen (see ibid., II, 148: ובני אחות אמו); thus Tobias's father, Daniel the Ḥaber,

[4] Perhaps he was one of the signatories of the Ketubah listed in Bodl. 2873.39 where read הכהן (for זרעה) מברך בן עלי֗ בן עזרא; the co-signatory David b. Shekhanyah belongs to this time.

and Solomon Gaon married sisters, the brother of these ladies being a certain Menasseh Hakkohen.

2. In another short letter to Sahlān Solomon reiterates briefly how Natan peacefully became Ab alluding to his former letter on the subject, viz. No. 1 (cp. ibid., p. 165, II, l. 2 ff.: כבר ביארתי לאהוב איך היה השלום וכו').

3. To Solomon, the physician, b. 'Alī (given below, pp. 337–40, under No. I) which relates fully how Natan brought about the conflict resulting in the rival Gaonate and announces the ban on Natan. Solomon b. Yehudah urges that no letters from Natan be accepted.

4. To Ephraim b. Shemaryah of Fusṭāṭ (ibid., II, 161–2) at the height of the quarrel and full of invectives. Solomon has also no good word to say about the late Ab, Natan's uncle, against whom also Ephraim had a grudge because his own rival in Fusṭāṭ was given the title Ḥaber by this very Ab (cp. ibid., II, 146–8, and especially ll. 23–33). Natan was going about seeking help from the Jerusalem Ḳaraites (cp. ll. 14–15 and l. 24). Solomon bitingly expresses his chagrin that Tobias had not courage enough to insist upon his claim (ll. 17–18: ונפלתי בין שנים צדיק הרבה ונשתומם. ורשע הרבה ימיתו אל ויעמם.). The Gaon is asking Ephraim to procure copies of a letter of his, addressed to the Fusṭāṭ congregation, and forward them to the West (i. e. Ḳairwān) in order to make known how a former student of R. Ḥushiel was conducting himself (l. 26 ff.: ואני שואל ממך שתתן הכתב אשר שלחתי אל הקהל אל המשוש (=משוש הישיבה) לא נסחם (read לנסחם) לשלחם אל המערב).

5. Another letter to Ephraim b. Shemaryah (ibid., II, 162–3) where there is an allusion to the 'rebel' (l. 22). It seems that the influential Ḥesed (Abū Naṣr) b. Sahl al Tustari was called upon to intervene in the matter.

6. A third letter to our Ephraim (*H. U. C. Annual*, III, 274–5) where allusion is made to a reply that arrived from this Ḥesed and the other elders. Solomon has some grudge against Ḥesed and does not wish to appeal to him (this is also evident from No. 5). There is an allusion (l. 21 ff.) to the closing of a synagogue due to Natan and his followers. Evidently the synagogue wherein Solomon excommunicated Natan and his partisans was closed by order of the government. In the whole epistle

Solomon is despondent over the situation and leaves it resignedly to the Divine will, if the time has arrived for his laying down the office of Gaon.

7. An obscure, because mutilated, letter (ibid., II, 165–6) but no doubt emanating from Solomon. Here is again an allusion to the closing of the synagogue (l. 20).

8. A letter from a partisan of Solomon, Shemaryah b. Maṣliaḥ, to the Nagid of Egypt we have ibid., II, 352–54. The Nagid is taken to task for supporting Natan having sent 2 epistles to a certain elder Abū'l Ḳasim בן אלאדוה̇ to lend his influence with the government officials to the usurper's side. Shemaryah reports in the name of Natan that he left the West (Ḳairwān) with this very purpose of proclaiming himself Gaon (r., l. 6: וכן גם כי ממערב יצא לו בזאת העצה). This Nagid's name is still unknown (the identification given there, p. 352, is now untenable).[5] Maṣliaḥ mentions that Natan's followers succeeded in obtaining from the authorities the decree forbidding the mention of Solomon's name at prayers in the synagogue.

9. With both sides trying to win superior support Solomon seems to have had the better of his opponent. On instructions from the Caliph and the Wezir the governor at Ramlah took sides with Solomon and through him the commander of Jerusalem followed suit. The Gaon in a letter (ibid., II, 166–7) to Fusṭāṭ expresses his triumph. He still refers to Natan in an angry mood (ll. 22 ff.). Allusion is made to a letter from his son, Abraham, to the same correspondent wherein the new development of the situation is fully described (l. 9).

In what way the government helped Solomon is not stated. Anyhow the other party realized the realities of the situation and finally peace was established between Solomon and Natan, the latter returning to his former dignity of Ab. Before describing the peace agreement let us discuss the letters that emanated from Natan prior to and during the short period of his rival Gaonate.

1. A letter sent to a Babylonian scholar, Meborakh, b. David, then staying in Ḳairwān (given infra, pp. 340–42, under No. II).

[5] See *H. U. C. Annual*, III, 287, bottom.

The epistle was evidently written from Egypt prior to his going to Palestine to become Ab, hence Natan attaches no title to his name. Natan and Meborakh were evidently well befriended. The former was very glad to learn from the latter's epistle to him that in Ḳairwān an important physician, Abraham b. 'Alī, was befriending him. Natan in his reply sends his greetings to Abraham and also to a certain Ḥananyah[6] whom he must have known from his long stay in Ḳairwān.

This Meborakh b. David while in Ḳairwān came into contact with R. Nissim b. Jacob and his school.[7] Also the letter from Yehudah Hassofer b. 'Alī (Bodl. 2805.14) was no doubt sent to our Meborakh while in Ḳairwān because greetings are expressed therein to Abraham the physician (ותן שלום לאדוני מרי ורבנא אברהם הרופא זקננו וחשובנו בן כג"ק מרנא ורבנא עלי נ"נ).[8]

2. A letter from Natan to his disciple Netanel b. Revaḥ of Fusṭāṭ (ibid., II, 169–70), evidently sent from his journey to Palestine. We learn that originally Natan's intention was not at all to become connected with the Palestinian school. He had some capital, which he had brought from Ḳairwān, and evidently entrusted it to certain people in order that he should be able to live from its income and devote himself to study and teaching (cp. l. 3 ff.). But his capital was lost and he was deprived of everything, even his family was retained in Fusṭāṭ, apparently till he would pay up the debts. He was proceeding via Damietta whence he would take a boat to the coast of Palestine, evidently the land route was then dangerous. There is an obscure reference to his father-in-law and his business dealings with a certain

[6] A Ḥananyah b. Berakhyah in Ḳairwān (listed by Pozn., אנשי קירואן, p. 13) is really non-existent (see Mann, *JQR*, *N. S.*, XI, 451).

[7] See Pozn., *l. c.* pp. 35–36. The stay of Meborakh b. David in Ḳairwān, as now proven by our letter, disposes of Albeck's remarks in his edition of ס' האשכול, pp. 73–74, note 4. R. Nissim mentioned is no doubt Nissim b. Jacob. Interesting is that in R. Nissim's school there was also a שבתא דריגלא as in the Babylonian schools. Should we say that the Nagid of Ḳairwān celebrated this Sabbath just as the Exilarchs in Babylon did? See also above, p. 69, note 16, and p. 113, note 9[b].

[8] Judah in a postscript mentions also Abū 'Imrān (=Musa) b. Yaḥya al-Raḳḳi who then stayed in Ḳairwān (וקד גׄעלת רקעה̈ דרג̇ כתאבך מתפצ̇ל תרפעהא לסידי אבי עמרן בן יחיי אלרקי).

Christian. We infer thus that only after impoverishment Natan decided to make practical use of his scholarship and claim the office of Ab in the school of Palestine.

3. A letter of greeting to the same person, dated Tammuz 1039 C. E. (ibid., II, 167–8), wherein Natan styles himself already ראש ישיבת גאון יעקב. His disciple and friend was given the honorific title עזר הישיבה. Natan sends greetings from the members of his school (ומכל בני ישיבתנו).

4. Another epistle of greeting of the same date (ibid., II, 168–9) to some follower whose friendly attitude towards the new Gaon was commended in an epistle from Meborakh 'the head of the communities' (evidently identical with Meborakh b.'Alī, cited above, p. 326).

5. An epistle to a follower styled ידיד הישיבה (ibid. II, 170–71) which included other letters to Mebasser b. Jesse 'head of the congregations and נאמן הישיבה'. The community, where these persons lived, had as its Rabbi a disciple of Natan's, Abraham the Ḥaber b. Shelah. The new Gaon describes how his partisans in Ramlah appealed to the governor repudiating the activities of a certain Revaḥ and his relatives in compelling the whole community to acknowledge Solomon as Gaon. The appeal met with success in so far as 'the synagogue of the Palestinians' in Ramlah was assigned to Natan and his party where he was officially called Gaon and where he was giving his sermons. Also a nominee of his was appointed for the Kosher meat market. There is an obscure allusion to the 'Sixth' (viz. Elijah Hakkohen whom Solomon b. Yehudah established in Ramlah as his own representative).

6. An Arabic letter to his disciple Berakhah b. Revaḥ (probably a brother of Netanel) who held the honorific title רצוי הישיבה (ibid., II, 172–3). There is a reference to the West (אלגרב, probably Ḳairwān) which ought to be informed of the deceit of a certain 'boy,' X. b. Meir (probably a descendant of the Gaonic family of Ben Meir), who had written from Egypt against Natan and who was therefore excommunicated. Natan goes on to describe with joy the news that reached him from Damascus how he was proclaimed Gaon there and with what great rejoicing the reading of Megillat Esther was celebrated at his school in Ramlah

(or Jerusalem?) in the presence of Rabbanites and Ḳaraites. The Babylonian synagogue in Ramlah was empty, the Palestinian synagogue had only about 20 worshippers and with Solomon b. Yehudah (called al-Fāsi, cp. above, p. 118) only 10 people remained.

7. The beginning of a letter to Peraḥ (Peraḥyah) b. Muammil (מומל) styled Rosh Happereḳ (ibid., II, p. 173). Fragments of other epistles to Solomon b. Natan and his son Abū Sa'ad and to 'Amram b. Yefet we have ibid., II, 174, note 3, and *H. U. C. Annual*, III, 275. Peraḥ b. Muammil and others sent a deposition of evidence to Natan as head of the school. Another document issued from Natan's court is given infra, pp. 343–45, under No. III. This document is further evidence of the trade carried on by Jews between Egypt, North Africa and Sicily (cp. also infra, p. 359).

8. Finally we have a letter from Natan, dated Marḥeshwan 1042, referring to the peace established after the long dispute (ibid., II, 174.). Since he had to renounce his assumed title of Gaon, he no longer sends greetings from the members of his school but from himself, his son Abraham, and those attached to us (מכל הנלוים אלינו).

The nature of this settlement has been preserved in an important fragment (published by Gottheil-Worrell, *Fragments from the Cairo Genizah in the Freer Collection*, 1927, pp. 196 ff.).[9] Natan had to renounce all titles of Gaon or head of the school and to undertake not to do anything in matters pertaining to the school except by agreement with the Gaon Solomon, Tobias the Third, Joseph Hakkohen the Fourth and his brother Elijah Hakkohen the Fifth. Natan evidently stayed on in Ramlah and yet there remained also the nominee of Solomon, Joseph Hakkohen the Fourth, as judge of the community and superintendant of the Kosher meat market. Lawsuits brought before Joseph cannot be referred to anybody else except to the Gaon.[10] If

[9] There are a number of corrections to be made in the printed text. In l. 1, for אשמעו r. אשמעה; l. 9 read ואלסוק, the Kosher meat market, mentioned before in the letters; l. 17 for הרביע r. הרביעי; l. 18 for עלמא r. עלי מא; l. 22 for חסד r. יוסד. For other corrections see infra, p. 332. Also the translation has to be corrected in several places as evident from the summary given here.

[10] L. 10 ff: active and not passive as stated in) ואי כצמין חצרו בין ידיה וחכם

Natan will become Gaon (viz. after Solomon's demise), the other dignitaries from Third to Sixth will advance in their order to the higher rank, thus the 'Third' as Ab, and so on. All the nominees of Solomon[11] are to retain their standing which presupposes that Natan's appointments during his rival Gaonate were set at naught. Natan was allowed to settle lawsuits in Ramlah as Ab-Bet-Din but, before accepting a case, he had to investigate whether it had not been brought beforehand to Joseph Hakkohen the Fourth. The agreement was drawn up on Hosha'na Rabba (the day of the great assembly at Jerusalem when many pilgrims were present) 1041 at Jerusalem.

The list of signatories has been incorrectly printed. A comparison with the facsimile shows that the lines (verso, 2 ff.) should read:

אליהו החמישי בחבורה בן שלמה גא[12] טוביה השלישי בחבורה
ברבי דניאל החבר נע̇

נתן אב בית דין של כל ישראל בי'[13] שלמה הצ̇[14] ראש ישיבת גאון
יעקב ברבי

יחזקיה הנשיא בן שלמה הנשיא בן דויד הנשיא נ̇נ[14a] יוסף הכהן
השופט והדאין בר של' ג̇[15]

מבורך בן עלון בן משה נ̇נ

Whereas when the conflict began Elijah Hakkohen was 'Sixth' we find him here as 'Fifth.' It seems that in the meanwhile the Fourth died and there is reason to believe that he was Solomon's son, Abraham (see ibid., II, 115–16, and cp. p. 58).

למן יחצ̇ר באלרמלה מעה ממן (in the meaning of "not") בינהם מא (note 18 there תקדם ד̇כרה אן ינקול אלחכם סוא אלרייס ראש ישיבה. The translation of the line is incorrect.

[11] L. 14: אצחאב אדוננו שלמה גאון, i.e. the judges and other communal officers like Ḥazzanim, Shoḥeṭim and supervisors (נאמנים) of the markets.

[12] =גאון.

[13] =בירבי, viz. the son of R. (Abraham).

[14] =הצעיר.

[14a] About this Ḳaraite Nasi see vol. II of our *Texts and Studies*.

[15] =שלמה גאון, viz. Joseph Hakkohen judge and Dayyān at Ramlāh (and also holding the dignity of 4th at the school).

Thus some time before the date of the agreement Joseph Hakkohen advanced from 5th to 4th and his brother Elijah moved on from 6th to 5th. Natan b. Abraham evidently died before Solomon's demise in 1051 and also Tobias died when still 3rd and hence by 1051 Joseph was Ab and his brother Elijah was 3rd.[16] Their expectations of further advancement were checked when Daniel b. 'Azaryah became Gaon.

The above agreement was drawn up at the beginning of 1353 Sel. (fall of 1041). Throughout the year 1352 Sel. (1040–41 C. E.) Natan still styled himself Gaon and ראש ישיבה. This fact establishes the identity of the author of a work cited in a colophon of MS. Adler 4012 (fol. 2, verso) which has been the subject of recent discussion.[17] It reads:

תצניף מר̇ ור̇ נתן גאון ממא נקלה ען אבאה̈
הישיבות הקדושים וען מעלמה חושיאל ריש
בי רבנן זצ̇ל̇ נסך̇ במצר סנה̈ אלף̇ ש̇נ̇ב̇ לשטרות

That this Natan Gaon (and there is no other one by this name)[18] is identical with our Natan b. Abraham is obvious from

[16] See *Jews in Egypt*, II, 65 and 347.

[17] See Marx, *Livre d'hommage . . . Poznański*, 76 ff., where the other references are given. I have seen this colophon in London only hurriedly on a dark morning in winter 1917 and hence my version in *JQR, N. S.*, XI, 452, was subject to rectification. I accept Marx's correction וען or ומן for בן which fully establishes the meaning of the sentence. On the other hand Marx still has the year שי"ב (1000–1), which is now impossible since Ḥushiel is referred to as departed whereas in Hai's letter of Elul שי"ו (1006) he is mentioned as evidently having only recently arrived in Ḳairwān (above, p. 110). Moreover in 1000–1 our Natan was still a youth. Hence there is no doubt that for שי"ב we should read שנ'ב (1040–41) which fits in perfectly with the time of Natan's rival Gaonate.

I suggested this emendation to Dr. Marx and asked him to re-examine the MS. (now at the Jewish Theological Seminary, New York) in order to ascertain whether the 'י was really not a 'נ with the bottom faded so as to appear as 'י. In a letter, dated February 18, 1929, Dr. Marx fully confirmed my surmise and hence the date שנ'ב is now clearly established.

There is no need to refer further point by point to Marx's remarks as the discussion here disposes of many of his conclusions and suggestions.

[18] See the passages collected by Poznański (*Babyl. Geon. im nachgäon, Zeitalter*, p. 109), wherein a Natan Gaon is cited who, however, was only

the fact that Ḥushiel is referred to as his teacher. The "fathers of the schools" are probably the Palestinian Geonim (and not the Babylonian ones, as Marx states) because we have no record of Natan ever having attended the Babylonian schools whereas we have found him as a student of the Palestinian school prior to his going to Ḳairwān. His work was copied in Fusṭāṭ in 1040–41 and hence he is still called Gaon. But when the work was actually composed is not stated. At any rate after his stay in Ḳairwān. Also the nature of the work is still problematic.

Fols. 1, recto and verso, and fol. 2, recto, contain a part of an Arabic Bustanai account. They form the outer leaves of Or. 5552 (published by Margoliouth, *JQR*, XIV, 304–5).[19] There can be no doubt that fol. 2, recto, of MS. Adler is the continuation of Or. 5552 (קרב אללה פרג̈ אמתה וליס בבעיד בקאה̈ הד̈ה אל | מודה̈ אלסלאפה̈). Now this Bustanai account finishes on fol. 2, recto, of MS. Adler (תם אלכתב, perhaps the plural is the copyist's lapsus calami for אל כתאב, but Natan's work may have contained other items besides the account concerning Bustanai). It is thus natural to assume that the above colophon on fol. 2, verso, refers to this account and that its author was our Natan b. Abraham.

Tykocinski (דביר, I, 152 ff.) in discussing the parts of this Bustanai account, as known from the publications of Margoliouth and Worman, was led to date this account as late as the 13th century. There is no need to refute his remarks here in detail as he has overlooked or was unaware of the more recent Genizah material. The only difficulty lies in the statement of this account that Bustanai had no other children except from the Persian princess whereas the Babylonian Geonim in their responsa clearly state that he had sons from a Jewish wife. Now since our Natan has received his information from the Palestinian Geonim and also from Ḥushiel, who had no connections with Babylon (as evident from Hai's letter, above, p. 110), it is quite easy to explain how this discrepancy could arise. In the 10th century and before, the Palestinian Geonim had much trouble with the Ḳaraites led by

designated as Gaon of Sura (before Sa'adyah) but never assumed the office
owing to his premature death. He was Natan Alluf, the uncle of Sherira Gaon.
Cf. also Mann, *H. U. C. Jubilee Volume*, 224.

[19] Cp. also the fragment published by Worman, *JQR*, XX, 212–15.

their Nesiim, the descendants of ʻAnan, and also with the Bagdād Exilarch during the struggle about the fixing of the calendar of 921.[20] It was therefore a part of particular bias to discredit both the Bagdād Exilarchs and the Ḳaraite Nesiim at the same time by making them to be the descendants of a non-Jewess. The Gaonic family of Ben-Meir, tracing its descent from Judah Hannasi (and hence from the Davidic family also), may have had a personal interest, in addition, to enhance its own purity of descent as against the Ḳaraite Nesiim and the Babylonian Exilarchs. This derogatory version about Bustanai was thus current in the Palestinian school and also Ḥushiel, hailing evidently from Southern Italy which had of yore close connections with the Palestinian school, had a knowledge of it. These Bustanai stories were subsequently incorporated in Natan's account as stated in the colophon.[21]

Natan must have regretted ever having composed it because during his rival Gaonate he had to seek the help of the Ḳaraites and of their Nesiim (cp. above, p. 327). Who knows whether his

[20] For the details cp. *Jews in Egypt*, I, 49 ff., and 57, 59 ff., and especially vol. II of our *Texts and Studies*.

[21] But it should be pointed out that the Palestinian Gaon Joshiah (1015), in attacking a Ḳaraite member of the Exilarchic family, states that Bustanai had 5 children two of whom were legitimate (ibid. II, 67, l. 24 ff: אחר דורות הרבה נמשך וחדל (r. וחזר) חתן ששך (i.e. Bustanai marrying a daughter of king of Babylon) (viz. the person attacked descended לשיאורו אחר שבעה עשר דורות מבת מלכים מקורו ואיך מדורות חמשה. בני ערלה ובושה. שניים מהם ירשו from this princess) (see the explanation on p. 68) קדושה. וזה מהם נעשה באושה.

It is interesting that in the above Bustanai report Bustanai's descendants from the non-Jewess are stated to have been ʻAnan, Boʻaz and the descendants of Zakkai (viz. the descendants of David b. Zakkai and Joshiah b. Zakkai, cp. Mann, *Livre d'hommage ... du Poznański*, Hebrew part, p. 19 ff.): פכ̇רג̇ מן נסלה ענן וסאיר (read perhaps סייד=סאיד) בעז ובני זכאי רוס ג̇ואלית בגדאד. But in the lampoon of Khalāf b. Sarjādo against Saʻadyah the 'sons of Boʻaz' are the descendants of the non-Jewess whereas David b. Zakkai, with whom Khalāf sided, was by implication of pure descent from the Jewish wife of Bustanai (cp. Harkavy, *Studien u. Mitteilungen*, V, 227, l. 8 ff.): ויתחברו אליו (אל סעדיה) זקן פסילות...וכסיל חרשים וילדי זונה הם בני בעז בהודאתם ובני השפחות. Thus partisan bias could at will disqualify a member of the Bustanai family by impugning his descent from the non-Jewish wife of Bustanai. (About the identity of Boʻaz see my remarks ibid., II, p. 68, and especially vol. II of our *Texts and Studies*).

account was not purposely copied in Fusṭāṭ in 1040–41 to show to the Ḳaraites in Egypt and in Palestine what this Gaon thought of the legitimacy of 'Anan and his descendants? It is also significant that in the agreement of Hosha'na Rabba 1041, which deprived Natan of his title Gaon, the Ḳaraite Nasi was one of the participants (see above, p. 332). It may be deduced that the Ḳaraite leaders changed their attitude towards Natan and began siding with Solomon after his Bustanai account, evidently written before his arrival in Palestine, was made public through this very copy discussed here.

Having established the time of Natan Gaon, the author of this account, his identification with Natan the Babylonian, the author of the famous account about the Exilarchate and the Gaonate in Babylon (as Marx does), is out of question. First there is the difference in names, the former being Natan b. Abraham, while the second is cited as נתן הכהן בר יצחק הבבלי. Then there is the difference of time, our Natan belonging to the first half of the 11th century whereas Natan the Babylonian clearly lived in the 10th century. There is a further negative consideration in view of our Natan's account ending with the Bustanai story whereas we would have expected it rather to deal towards the end with the more recent events, at least with the Sa'adyah-David b. Zakkai conflict (not to speak of the later history during the second half of the 10th and the beginning of the 11th centuries). Hence we have no right at all to assume that Natan the Babylonian dealt at all with the Bustanai story. His aim was rather to relate the events in Babylon in his own time and in that of just a generation before. Thus the Neṭira account (published by Harkavy, חנ"י, II, No. 5) is very likely a part of Natan's original Arabic narrative because through it the reader was to understand the power of Neṭira in successfully opposing the Exilarch 'Uḳba which story is explicitly reported as emanating from Natan the Babylonian. But the Arabic Bustanai account, as now accessible in part in the Genizah fragments, had as its author in all probability Natan b. Abraham, a Palestinian scholar who also studied in Ḳairwān but who hardly had any direct connections with the Babylonian schools and whose acquaintance with contemporary conditions in Bagdād were based merely on hearsay (e. g. through information of his friend Meborakh b. David the Babylonian). Of these accounts of course the one by Natan the Babylonian is by far the more important and further finds of parts of its Arabic original among the Genizah leaves would greatly increase our knowledge of conditions in Bagdād Jewry in the 10th century.

I.

[T.-S. 16.261, paper, between glass.]

Address (verso)

לזקנינו וחשובנו כ֗ק מ֗ר ורב֗[1] שלמה הרופא   בן מר רב עלי נב֗ע֗[2]
הזקן הנכבד ישמרו צור. ומכל רע יהי נצור.   ישע רב

(Recto)

השלומות התמימות המקוימות. הרשומות החתומות. ליקירנו וזקנינו
וחשובנו כב֗ קד֗ מ֗ר ורב֗ שלמה הזקן הרופא החכם והנבון העשוי[3] נחת
רוח במבצר סינים[4] האוהב בעלי תורה ומכבדם ישמרו צור. ומכל רע
יהי נצור. בן מר רב עלי נוחו בעדן גן. שא זקיננו. שלום רב ממנו. ומן
חמודנו[5]. ומן החברים אשר לפנינו. כי לשלום אנו חונים וברוך הטוב[6] ובכל

[1] =כבוד קדושת מרנא ורבנא. [2] =נשמתו בגן עדן. [3] Supply להיות.

[4] This locality is obscure. Sa'adyah in his Pent. translation takes Gen. 10.17 ואת הסיני to mean the people of Tripoli (ואלטראבלסיין), whether Ṭarābulus ash-Sham (in Syria) or Tripoli on the North–African coast is not clear. However Is. 49.12 מארץ סינים he translates מן בלד סין, meaning evidently China. Yet Ḳimḥi, a. l., remarks: ופירש רב סעדיה ז״ל אטרא בלפוון (אטרא בלפוון is no doubt a corruption of אלטראבלסיון). Should we say that Ḳimḥi read so in Sa'adyah's Is. translation or that he took it from the Pent. translation (cp. Derenbourg, *Oeuvres Complêtes de R. Saadia*, III, p. 76, note 2)?

Perhaps Assuan is meant here (cp. Ezek. 29.10; 30.6 ממגדל סונה). At any rate this community must have been beyond Fusṭāṭ where the letter was copied in the process of transmission and hence it was found in the Genizah.

[5] i.e. Abraham b. Solomon b. Yehudah.

[6] i.e. the good (God).

עת אנו זוכרים אותך ופורטים טובותיך ונדבותיך ומתפללים עליך צור
ישמע ויענה. ומודיעים לך יקירנו שצ׳[7] כי בשנה הזאת בא אל ארץ ישר[א]ל
מן המערב נתן בן אברהם בן אחות בן יוחיי אב הלך מקדם אל מערב
מבקש ירושת אביו וישב שם שנים הרבה יושב פני רב׳[8] חושיאל הרב
ללמוד תורה ודמינו כי התורה יסרתו. והתבונה הודיעתו. והנה הוא לא לקח
מוסר ולא שמר חכמה ויהי בעת בואו אל עיר הקודש הקבלנוהו וכבדנוהו
ויקרנוהו[9] וקראנוהו ראש[10] לישראל דמינו כי ילך בדרך היושר ויתהלך
עם העם לאט ויהי בעת רדתו אל חולת המחוז[11] הלך עמהם בדרך גאוה
וגסות וגבהות והתחיל משים עצמו עיקר וזולתו[12] טפל והתני[13] היה עליו
שלא יהיה לו רשות בחבורה ואשר נתננו לו מקום משרפו[14] בלבד להיות
נקרא בשם זה ולתת בו כיר[15] ידו וכאשר ראו זקני רמלה רוע דרכיו אז כתבנ[ו]
אלינו כי האיש אשר כניתה בשם ונתתה לו מקצת פשט ידו על הכל

[7] =שמרך צורנו. [8] =רבנא.

[9] This is a misstatement as Solomon originally was opposed to him and had to consent to his appointment because Tobias the 3rd relinquished his claim.

[10] =ראש בית דין=Ab.

[11] i.e. Ramlah, the capital of Filasṭīn (raml in Arabic = חול, sand). Cp. also *Jews in Egypt*, I, 139).

[12] i.e. Solomon. [13] = והתנאי. [14] Maternal uncle.

[15] Signature (cp. ibid., II, 418, s. v.).

ועתה מהרה רדה אז ירדנו אל רמלה ולקחנו עמנו ר̇ אליה הששי[16] ליישב[17]
אותו ברמלה ויהי כאשר ראה כי ירדנו קבץ סביבותיו אנשים רקים ופוחזים
שכר אותם בכספים ומלבוש ומאכל ומשתה ויהי ביום שבת באו הזקנים
ושאלונו לרדת אל בית הכנסת ויהי אחרי בואנו אל הכנסת ירד הוא ונקבצו
הנה העם כל אחד מהם מבקש לריב את חברו ואטריח על עצמי ואל[כה]
מבית הכנסת ולולי כן היה העם מריבים והשלטון פושט את ידו עליהם
ו[יהי] אחרי צאתנו קמו שכיריו וגם הוא ויתפלל על עצמו ראש תועבה[18] ונתכנה
בשם גאונות ולא ירא אלהים וכאשר נתאמת הדבר לפננו ואנו בכנסת האחר[ת]
הוצאנו ספרי תורות ונדינוהו בשמו נתן בן אברהם וכל עוזריו ו[סומכיו]
והם בן השלישי ובן דודו ומצליח תלמידו ובני שויע ועמאר הרופא ונדינו
כל מי שיקראו בשם שררות וכל מי שיקרא לו כתב יד וקרינו עליו ארור
מסיג גבול רעיהו[19] ואשר היה הודענו בקוצר עתה זקנינו אתה סגולתינו
ואהובנו הזהר והזהיר לבל לקראות לו כתב אם יבא אליכם כי כתביו [חקקי]

[16] i.e. Elijah Hakkohen b. Solomon Gaon. He signs as 6th in a document drawn up in 1037 C. E. (ibid., II, 64–5).

[17] Better להושיב.

[18] Sarcastic pun on ראש ישיבה.

[19] Deut. 27.17.

און וכתבי עמל ותאמר לחזן לנדותו אם יכשר והנה כתבנו פתיח[20]
קטון
אל הקהל לנדותו ויבוא כתבך אלינו בכל הנעשה ואם יהיה צורך
או חשש[ות][21]

(right hand margin)

תודיענו. צורנו קדושנו ישמע
תפלתינו בעדך ובעד כל [והנלוים עליך]
ויראנו מחלציך כמותך וירבה
כמוך בי[ש]ראל ושלומך
ושלום כל מתי סודך ושלום
כל הקהל ירבה.

ישע רב

שלמה הצׄ[22] ראש ישיבת גאון יעקב
בירבי

[There is some scribble on the top of recto and also some liturgical compositions in different handwriting on verso. Evidently the blank space on verso was utilized by some person for copying the compositions.]

II.

[T.-S. 8.3, vellum.]

Address (verso)

ליקר רום השר אחי החכמ[ה] וה[בינה מרנא]
[ורבנ]א מבורך החכם והנבון] בר [מרׄ] דויד
החסיד נ[עׄ]
[מדורש שלומו ושו]חר טובו ביׄר אברהם זׄל
קירואן בעזרת האל[23].

[20] =פתיחתא, formula of ban (cp. the wording in *JQR*, *N. S.*, IV, 26, No. III).

[21] Read חשחות, need, from חשח (cp. Ezra 7.20). See Mann, II, 417, s. v.

[22] = הצעיר.

[23] (To) Ḳairwān, (it will reach) with God's help.

(Recto)

שלום בכל אברים. וישו[עה] . . . . וברכות בלי מצרים. וכלל כל המחמדים להרים.

לכבוד יקירנו כבירנו גדולי[נו] . . . . . השר המכובד. והידיד הנכבד. אשר לא יערכנו

זהב ורב פנינים לא יס[ל]ה [בכתם אופיר. וב]שוהם יקר וספיר[24]. הוא כבׄ גדׄו קדׄו מרׄ [ור]בנא

מבורך אשר לשונו בתלמודו . . . . [רך]. ובין בבינו לא יֶערך. וי . . . .

[מפ]רך. משנאו יוצמת ויופרך[25]. והוא מחכמת אל יבורך. בן מר רב דויד החסיד נׄעׄ

ישא יקרנ׳[26] ובבת אישוננו שלום רב עד בלי ירח ממנו דורשי טובתו ושו[נאיו]

שלומו כי ברחמי מעוזנו אנו שלום מודים לו על רוב מעשיו ואם אין ערוך לנפלאות

חסדיו וכעני׳ שנ׳[27] רבות עשית וגו׳ ומודיעים כי נכספה וגם כלתה נפשנו לראות פני יקי׳[26]

הנחמדים והנעימים השקולים כ[ראות] בני אים[28] וכי בהגיע כתבו היקר. הרצוף כל מיני

יקר. השקיט הנפש מתשוקתה. ושיכך להבת דליקתה. ונתננו שבח ליוצרנו על כי החיש

תעל למחל[29] וזור[30] למזור ורטיה לטריה באשר הזכיר יקירׄ כי הקים לו האֵל מליץ יושר

[24] Cp. Job 28.16–17.

[25] From פרך, hard labor.

[26] =יקירנו.

[27] =וכענין שנאמר, Ps. 40.6.

[28] =אלהים, cp. Gen. 33.10, hence read here פני for בני.

[29] Paiṭanic masculines of תעלה and מחלה.

[30] A noun formed from זור (cp. Is. 1.6). רטיה, plaster, is Talmudic while טריה=מכה טריה (Is. 1.6).

להשיב נפש ולכלכל שיבה הוא זקננו חשובנו מר רב אברהם הרופא נטֿ רֿ והרח[ניב]

בזכר שבחו וטוב מפעלו עמך ואמנם שמגלגלים זכות על ידי זכאי ומבלי ספק כי

חביבה מצוה בשעתה ושעת הדחק שאני ואדהכי והכי נפקא מינה לחיי שעה[31] ואפעלפי

שהבטיח[32] כי לא יעזוב את חסידיו אבל אשרי הזוכים עמך והעושים ומעשים כי

מצוה גדולה עשו ולמעלה מעולה עלו תכתב להם לצדקה. והזכרת כי איכא מאן דחזי

למיהוי סניגור ונעשה קטיגור[33] ולא אנס[34] לך שדרכן שלתלמידי חכֿ[35] להיות עלובים ולא עולבים

שומעין חרפתם ואין משיבים ועם זאת הא אמרי רבנן[36] האי צורבא מרבנן קודשׁ ברֿ הוא תבע יקריה

(right hand margin)

ומאת צור נשאל להצליחך בכל אודותיך

ולמלאת שאילתך להמציאך ייחול ליבך[37]

...................ך

הגדול ....

ושלום זקננו [חשובנו מר רב אברהם]

הרופא ירבה ואל [ידל ושלום זקננו מר]

רֿ חנניה ירב.

ישע רב[38].

[31] Familiar Talmudic phrases.

[32] viz. in Ps. 37.28.

[33] Viz. somebody in Ḳairwān who ought to have helped Mehorakh b. David but instead opposed him.

[34] Probably read יאנס, let not (this) oppress (trouble) you.

[35] =חכמים, cp. Sabbath 88b.

[36] Cp. Ber. 19a, top.

[37] Cp. Ber. 16b in the prayer of R. ‘El‘azar.

[38] Here Natan still uses this concluding phrase but later on he consistently used ישע יקרב evidently to differentiate himself from Solomon b. Yehudah who employed throughout the phrase ישע רב.

III

[MS. Mosseri, Cairo, L 101, very damaged and faint. See Facsimile XV, A and B, infra, p. 715.]

(Recto)

[חצ̇רו אלי בית דין הגדול] שלאדונינו נתן ראש ישיבת גאון יעקב נט̇ רח̇ כ̇לף [ב]ן מוסי אלברקי

[וסלמאן בן דאוד בן שמ]עון וטאלב כ̇לף הד̇א לסלמאן הד̇א בעדל אלניל[39] ד̇כר אנה אנפדה ג̇ אעד[אל]

.... ועדלין ניל אלי סקליה̈[40] עלי ידי דאוד בן עזרון ואן מן הדה אלג̇מלה̈ עד[ל] ....

.... סה[לאן] בן יהושע אלטראבלסי[41] אלסאכן בסקליה̈ ואן עדל ניל מנהא ....

...... אלמקים בסקליה̈ ואן[*41] גא[*41] [אל]מרכב אלד̇י כאן פיה אלעדל אלניל אלמפר[ד] .....

.... הד̇א במדינה̈ [אל]מהדיה̈[42] ואן סלמאן בן דאוד בן שמעון הד̇א קבצ̇ה מן אל

.... פיה פסאלנא סלמאן הד̇א ען מא ד̇כר כ̇צמה פקאל אני כנת בסקליה̈ חתי

.... סהלאן ...... עדל מחמול אליה מן כ̇לף הד̇א ד̇כר אנה ח[צ]ל באלמהדיה̈ ואן

... אבו יעקב בן אלשאמה̈ ניאבה ען סהלאן הד̇א פאג̇בת..... לה ת̇ם אחצ̇ר [אבי]

יעקב אליי מע סהלאן וכתב לי כתאב אלי בן בני[ה] באן יסלם אלעדל אליי ואמרני אבי יעקב

[39] A bundle of indigo-plant.

[40] Sicily.

[41] Evidently of Tripoli in North Africa, now residing in Sicily.

[*41] The reading is doubtful.

[42] Al-Mahdiya near Ḳairwān.

בן אלשאמ[ה] באן ארפע אלעדל אלי סהלאן ה[דׄ]א ואן אמו . . .

אלמהדיה̈ . . כתאב אבי יעקב בן אלשאמה̈ ללבניה בן כׄלפון . . . באלת[סלי]ם אליי . . .

אלכתאב אנה[41]* מכאן אבי יעקב בן אלשאמה̈ ואכׄרג . . . . . . מכתוב עליה רב . . . .

סלם וכלת לכׄלף בן מוסי מרסולה אלי סהלאן בן יהושע אלי ס[קלי]ה̈ פבעת אלעדל

פצח בי[41]* אלמבאע מן אל[עדל] נׄ דינר ובקי מן אלעדל קטעה̈ ניל . . . .

ענד בן אלמגאני[43] באלקירואן ואשת[רית] סׄ זק זית בהדא אלמאל ולם יבק מ[ן] אלגׄמלה̈ סוא

תׄקׄ דרהם הי באקיה̈ ענד מוסי בן ברהון בספאקס[44] תׄם אחצׄר אלי בית דין בניה בן כׄלפון

וקאל וצל אליי אבו יעקב בן אלשאמה̈ מן סקליה̈ עלי ידי סלמאן הדׄא ואמר בפתח

מכׄזנה ותסלים אלעדל אלי סלמאן הדׄא תׄם אחצׄר סלמאן הדׄא שאהדין והם יעקב בן

כׄלף אלאנדלסי וששון בן אברהם שהדוא בוצול הדׄה אלסׄ זק זית אלמשתרי מן . . . . . .

הדׄא אלניל אלי סהלאן במדינת סקליה̈ ואן סהלאן הדׄא תנאזע מע סלמאן פי . . . מא תולאה[41]*

מן הדׄא אלזית ופי גׄמלה̈ אלכלאם גׄרי מא תוגׄב אן אשהדנא עלי נפסה אן הדׄא אלעדל אל

. . . . . ניל אלמשתרא מנה הדׄא אלזית אלמר . . . לכׄל[ף] . . . . .

. . . . . כׄלף בן מוסי הדׄא [מ]ע סלמאן . . . .

[43] Viz. the father of this person in Ḳairwān originated from Majjāna (מגאנה̈). See infra, p. 362, note 6.

[44] Safāḳis (Sfax) south of Ḳairwān.

(verso)

אלתֿק אלדֿי אעתרף אנהא . . . ענדה מן תֿמן הדֿא אלעדל אלדֿי לכֿלף . . . . . ואנה יכתב

כתאב אלי בן אלמגאני יאמרה בתסלים אלרזמהֿ אלניל אל . . . ראני אלבאקיהֿ מן אלעדל אלמדֿכור לכֿלף הדֿא

ויתברא . . . הא ועלי . . . ה יגֿיב כֿט אבי יעקב בן אלשאמהֿ או באלשאהדֿ[ין] ישהדו באקראר ה . . .

אנה ענד . . . אטלק לה קבץֿ אלעדל אנה אמרה בתסלימה אלי סהלאן וכתב פי [אד]ר שנת

אשנֿאֿ לשטרות במצרים . . . . רֿ נתנאל

[ה]חבר ביר֗ ישו[ע]ה ור֗ . . . . . ביר֗ ריוח[41]*

ונח]ברו אלעזר בן שמואל

ואקני מנהמא גֿמיעא באלרצֿא בגֿמיע

מא תקדם שרחה

3.

LETTERS PERTAINING TO PALESTINE IN THE 11TH CENTURY

The Fāṭimid sway over Palestine was very unstable during the 11th century and the country suffered from revolts and invasions. Especially notable events were the revolt of 1024–9 (Mann I, 158 ff.), the invasion of the Seljūḳs in 1071 (ibid., 186 and 192, *H. U. C. Annual*, III, 288–9) and the coming of the Crusaders in 1099 (ibid., 198–200).[1] The three letters given here illustrate further the trials of the impoverished Palestinian Jewry in consequence of the disturbed conditions.

1. No. I has been given in excerpt in vol. II, 222–23, but deserves to be reproduced in full. It is addressed to Ebyatar Hakkohen, then 4th (later on Gaon) of the Palestinian school, b. Elijah Gaon. Its date is evidently during the Seljūḳ invasion of 1071. Ebyatar then stayed in Fusṭāṭ, probably to seek help for the school, whither our letter was sent to him. The writer was ʿAlī Hakkohen b. Ezekiel the Reader, the data concerning whom are given in II, 223. He was in dire straits in Jerusalem and also intended to go to Fusṭāṭ but was delayed by the news of fear and famine. In his distress he wrote several letters to the Nagid (viz. Yehudah b. Saʿadyah) and to his brother, styled Alluf and Ḥaber (viz. Meborakh b. Saʿadyah, the later famous Nagid), in Fusṭāṭ hoping to receive some support from them in order to live through the critical time. ʿAlī could not even visit other Palestinian communities like Tyre which was shut up. Altogether even the journey from Jerusalem to Ramlah was perilous and all roads in a state of insecurity. Evil reports arrived from all sides.

ʿAlī requests Ebyatar to write from Fusṭāṭ to Milij to the former's son-in-law, Hibah (=Natan) b. Israīl, to urge him

[1] About the general political situation cp. R. Hartmann, *Palästina unter den Arabern*, 1915, p. 34 ff.

to return to his wife and children whom he has left in Jerusalem in great distress.[1a] They were starving together with ʻAlī who could not support them. Hibah failed altogether to support his family. He also wishes to inform this Hibah through Ebyatar that if he sends cotton (or flax) via Jaffa the governor there would confiscate the goods to hand them over to the general of the Fāṭimid army (בעל המחנות), fighting the Seljūḳs, whereas through Ashḳelon the import was possible. This direction shows that the return from Egypt to Palestine by land was dangerous and only the coastline of Palestine, still in the hands of the Fāṭimids, could be reached by boat. The central government yet held sway over Ashḳelon, Jaffa, and of course Tyre which was then strongly fortified.

Greetings are sent to the Nagid and his brother and to their mother, and also to the priestly Parnās styled נאמן הישיבה (viz. ʻAlī Hakkohen b. Yaḥya).[2] There is a cryptic allusion (ll. 31–32)

[1a] About the material affairs of another Hibah al-Maṣri b. Israīl, cp Mann, II, 355.

[2] Cp. about this Parnās of the Fusṭāṭ (Palestinian) community I, 192, note 1. His father's Arabic name Yaḥya corresponded to the Hebrew חיים. We give here additional data concerning this Parnās. Bodl. 2878.37 contains the following letter to him.

(1) שלום וישועה . . . (3) . . . עלי הכהן הפרנס הנאמן . . . (4) ביר׳ חיים הכהן המומ[חה]
תנצב׳ה. הגיע כתבו הנעים באומץ שעשועים. במתק דבריו להטעים . . . (7) . . . וכי אנו בזו
העת נשארנו רקים מכל (8) עד אין לנו נחמה אלא בקיומו. ובשמענו בכל עת שקטו ושלומו.
(9) ונתקיים בנו מקרא שכתו׳ (Ps. 88.9) הרחקת מיודעי ממני שתני תועבות למו (10) כלא ולא
אצא והקׄ ברוך הוא יעשה למען שמו. ויסיר חמת זעמו ויכונן אולמו. (11) אודיע שמרו צורו כי
אמר אבי כי היה עם כלל הנכסים אשר היו (12) מופקדים לו אצל יפת בר כלב שמנה ספרי
נביאים אינם מגיהות (13) ולא בדוקות הם. היה שמרו צורו (viz. ʻAlī) לקחם מאצל שפחת יפת
בר כלב (14) ושלחם על יד מגיע הפיתק הזה מר׳ עלי בר יפת ואין עליו (viz on ʻAlī) מסכנתם
(15) כלום כי אנו צריכים לביאתם ולא נחשוב אותם אלא דורון שלח (16) אלינו מאיתו (r. מאתו)
ואם לאו יודיעני מה היה להם ואל יאחר ממנו כתבו שעה (17) אחת בשקטו ושלומו וצרכיו כי
עינינו אל הדרך לדעת (18) שלומו. ושלומו ושלום חמודו וכל נלויהם יועצם לעד נצח סלה.
ישע רב (19) מודה חסדיו נתן הכהן המומחה ביר׳ מבורך סׄטׄ.

Natan Hakkohen was Dayyān in Ashḳelon (see II, 202). Another letter from him to ʻAlī Hakkohen b. Ḥayyim is listed in Bodl. 2876.65 wherein he states: 'In my last letter to you I mentioned among other things that the Exilarch (ראש גולה) had written to the reader Abraham (מר אברהם החזן ש״צ) as to his duties. The Ḥazzān afterwards came to me about it, with the elders of the congregation, and affirmed his devotion to his work and to the orders of the Exilarch'.

Our ʻAlī Hakkohen b. Yaḥya (=Ḥayyim) is also a signatory of a docu-

to a conspirator in Tyre who was overthrown (whether against the government or against the school is impossible to ascertain). Ebyatar is requested to write about the success of his affairs in Fusṭāṭ. 'Alī transmits greetings to Ebyatar on his own behalf and that of his brother as well as of Abū'l Ṭayyīb and the latter's brother (apparently 'Alī's two sons). The epistle was written on the 27th since the counting of the 'Omer, hence 3 weeks after Passover. The Arabic style is stilted and also the orthography is faulty.

2. No. II is a letter of introduction by Abraham, styling himself Ab-Bet-Din שלכל ישראל, b. Isaac (the great, רובה) who held the title Alluf from both the Sura and the Pumbedita academies. The writer as well as several of his congregants were captured and suffered pitifully. He was ultimately ransomed and thus signs (l. 37) "who was freed from captivity." The present letter is an appeal for support for the bearers Joshu'a b. 'Alī b. Tobias and his companion David b. Samuel, formerly well-to-do but now reduced to begging. They evidently went to Fusṭāṭ to obtain support in their need.

It is altogether doubtful whether our letter emanates from a Palestinian scholar. It may rather belong to a Rabbi of some Syrian city, Damascus or Aleppo. Also the occasion that brought about this captivity is unknown to me nor can I identify the two persons for whom this letter of introduction was written. In appearance the MS. dates from the early part of the 11th century.

3. No. III, defective at beginning and end, is evidently from a prominent leader of an important community. Acting with great energy he collected a sum of 5000 Dīnars (=about $30,000) for ransoming captive Palestinian Jews. The sum sufficed for the release of about 200 people but the number of the unfortunate ones was still greater. In graphic Biblical style, chiefly a conglomeration of Scriptural verses, the ruin that befell Palestine is depicted. The writer alludes to many captives that returned

ment dated 1093 (see Halper, *Descriptive Catalogue of Genizah Fragments in Philadelphia*, No. 340).

Where the Exilarch referred to in the above letter resided is difficult to ascertain. Should we say that the Bagdād Exilarch wielded some influence in Palestine and Egypt at the end of the 11th century? About the problem of the Exilarchate in Egypt see infra, p. 394 ff.

from a Christian country (evidently Byzantium) where they were ransomed by their coreligionists. Passing through the city, where the writer lived, they had to be maintained and cared for by the local Jewry. The letter is in reply to an inquiry of a prominent Jew in Fusṭāṭ (complimented as נשף חשקנו, l. 52) who asked concerning the fate of the Jewry in the districts of Mosul and Babylon (l. 51–2). These Jewries were saved.

There too one is at a loss clearly to ascertain the occasion of this great ruin that befell Palestine. A surmise can only be offered that the letter emanates from Damascus or Aleppo and that the writer was an Exilarch.[3] Hence the allusion to the Davidic family (l. 57 ff.). The writer was expectant of the Messianic age near at hand (ll. 44 and 55 ff.). Should we connect the events with the coming of the Crusaders and that many Palestinian Jews were sold into slavery to Byzantium whence they returned after regaining their freedom via Aleppo or Damascus? However the paucity of the material at our disposal precludes any definite conclusion. Only further Genizah finds can enable us to solve the obscurity of the events under discussion.

[3] About the Exilarchic families of Damascus and Aleppo see Mann, *Livre d'hommage . . . Posnański*, Hebrew part, pp. 28–30.

I.

[T.-S. 13 J 15.23; cp. Mann, *Jews in Egypt*, II, 222–3. See Facsimile XVI, infra, p. 716.]

(Recto)

רבות שלומות מרובבים. ואלפי ברכות מאולפים. ומאות טובות
ניאותים[1]. ועשרות שמחות מעושרים. לאביר בתורה. ברכות לו
להחבירה. ונזר להכתירה. לכבוד גדולת קדושת מרינו ורבינו אביתר
הכהן הרביעי בחבורה. אשר חכמתו צבורה. והיא כאבן יקרה. לעיני

[1] The parallel to the other items of the first 2 lines (myriads, thousands and tens) demands here the reading מאותים, a peculiar Paiṭanic participle formed from מאה.

כל להאירה. אשר אהבתו קשורה. אסורה. לא מותרה. לא חלפה ולא

נתמרה. ישמע צור בעדו כל עתירה. ויצילו מכל צרה. נין[2] כבוד גדולת

מרינו ורבינו נזרינו וכתרינו ועטרת ראשינו אדונינו אליהו הכהן

ראש ישיבת גאון יעקב דגל עם י״י נטריה רחמנא נין כ̇ב̇ גד̇ קד̇ מר̇

ורבינו אדונינו שלמה ראש ישיבת גאון יעקב ז̇צ̇ל̇ קד נפדת כותבי

לחצ̇רת סידנא אלראיס אלרביעי נ̇ט̇ ר̇ח̇ עידה̈ יום יג̇י פג̇ואב ארגו יכון

ד̇אליך לכ̇יר וסלאמה̈ וקד שרחת מא ענדי מן אלוחשה̈ פי ג̇מיע כותבי

אללה יאנס בבקאה̈ ויסתג̇יב מני צאליח מא אדעוה תבע כל צלאה̈

וקד ערף̇ סידנא סבב תאכ̇רי ען אלד̇כול אלי מצר ללאכ̇באר אלת̇י כל יום

תצל מן הפחד והרעב צור ברחמיו ישקיף̇ על עולמו וקד סאלת פי ג̇מיע

כותבי אלמכאטבה̈ לסידנא אלנגיד נ̇ט̇ ר̇ח̇ ולמולאי אלחבר אלוף̇ הבינות

חכם הישיבה ש̇צ̇ לעל יחצל שי אג̇יז בה וקת לאן קד אגגלקת[3] מן אלכ̇רוג̇

אלא מוצ̇יע צור סגורה לא יוכל אדם לצאת מירושלם אל רמלה וכל הדרכים

בחזקת סכנה וקד תבת̇ וליוצא ולבא אין שלום[4] והשמועות מכל צד ופינה

רעות ואסאל חצ̇רתה אלג̇לילה̈ אלמכאתבה̈ אלי מליג̇[5] אלא הבה̈ צהרי בן אסראיל

[2] =בן here and so also in l. 8. [3] Read אתגלקת.
[4] Zach. 8.10. [5] Milij (in Egypt).

ואן ילטוף פי אמא רג̇ועה אלא אולאדה יוד̇י קד תרכהום סנתין בלא שי וקד

בקיו הום וואלדתהום האלכין ענדי וקילה ומא בקי פיה אנא לשי מן קילה

וצ̇יקת יד וט̇עף חאל וחאל וסידנא עאריף בחאלי ולה הד̇ה אלמודה̈ לם

ינפד אליהום דרהם לא אקל ולא אכת̇ר ומא כאן אלאמל פי הד̇א לו אנהום

מא הום אולאדה וסידנא נט̇ רח̇ לא יתרוך מג̇הוד פי הד̇א חתא יפעלה וקד

סאלת חצ̇רתה אלג̇לילה̈ באן ישתרי לי מן מצר מניף[6] תינכאר ג̇יר בלוג̇י ותכון

צוחבתה תצל ויעלם הבה̈ צהרי אן תצל לה כתאן יכון וצולה בה אלא עסקלאן

ויטלע בה מן עסקלאן לאן כל מן וצל בשי אלא יאפא יקח אותו השליש אשר ביפו

ויתן אותו לבעל המחנות כ̇צצת חצ̇רת סידנא אלראיס אלרביעי נט̇ רח̇ באתם אסלאם

ואסאל יכ̇וץ חצ̇רת סידנא אלנגיד נט̇ רח̇ באתם אסלאם ועלי סאדתי אולאדה שצ̇

אתם אסלאם ועלי מולאי אלחבר אלמעולה חכם הישיבה אלוף הבינות שצ̇ אתם

אסלאם ועלי סידי אלכהן אלפרנאס נאמן הישיבה וולדה אתם אסלאם ואשר בצור

אשר קשר לא נשאר לו עוזיר והפילו צורו ואסאל חצ̇רתה אלג̇לילה̈ יערפני בכתאבה

[6] Dual of מןّ, a weight of 2 roṭls. The kind of goods indicated by תינכאר is unknown to me.

בגמיע אלכבארה ומא יכון מן אמורה ואן יכון לה מקאם ועבדה אבו אטיב[7] ואכוה
יכוצו חצרתה באתם אסלאם ו אכי יכוץ חצרתה אלגלילה באתם אסלאם וגמיע
אלאוהבים יכוצו חצרתה באתם אסלאם ולם יתגיר אחד ען אלמחבה נכתב בזכ
לעומר עבדה עלי הכהן בר יחזקאל החזן נבע

II.

[T.-S. Loan 49, vellum, torn and faint. See Facsimile XVII, infra, p. 717.]

(Recto)

אל רבי הע[דה] ואצילי הצבור . . . .
ואחר לשארם. כולם לפי פאירם . . . . מבחרם.
שלום אהבה ברכה רחמים והשקט מבטחה. א נ[שי]
הַמְּבֵר. נוטרי בַר ונוֹצְרֵי שֵׁבַח . . . כַבֵד שטחה. ל[שרי]
ישראל אשר בכל גרות גלות פיאר ביחוד מקומות מושבותם.
האהובים. במעשים טובים. הבָרִים. בהקבלת[8] העוברים.
הרחומים. ברצון רחמים. ההדורים. בהיישרת מהדורים.
המעוטרים. במצוות נוטרים. אבינו שבשמים יאמר לנטור
אתכם. וליטור שורריכם. ולהפיל מִגוֹבַה המתגבר לְשַׁבֵּר.
. . . . . סבר. להתאשר מכל מְדַבֵּר. ככ[9] ואשרו אתכם כה
[כי תהיו אתם ארץ] ח וג כבשורת רבינו[10] בתורה אשריך יש מי כמוך
[עם נ ביי ודויד] המלך כהשכילו אשרי שאל יעקב[11] וכ בת[12]

[7] For אלטיב, hence Abū'l Ṭayyīb.

[8] Better בקבלה, by receiving hospitably wayfarers.

[9] =ככתוב, Mal. 3.12.

[10] i.e. Moses, Deut. 33.29.

[11] Ps. 146.5.

[12] =וכתוב בתריה, viz. Ps. 146.6.

[השו]מר אמת לעולם. ואף לפי׳. . . . [ל]עתיד הו או[13] [מוציא] אסורים [בכושרות וכבשורת זכריה שו]בו לבצרון אסירי [הת]ק ג ה מ מ א ל[14] אף על פי׳. . . . . . . נפלאות שהוא גומל בחסדו בכל זמן כי שומ[ר] . . . . . ולא יחרש עד . . . . . . עשותם כי גואל חזק הו[א יתבר]ך שמו לעולם: . . . . . שומע אנקת אסורים[15] ל[קרוא לה]ם פקח קוח ולהדריר[16] השבואים. ואוי לנו כי גרמו עונ[ותינו] . . . עֲנוֹתֵינו ונדדנו בגזרת שביה שהיא קשה מכל הקודמות בפסוק[17] דכולהי שכיחי ביה מוות וחרב ורעב וראינו החרב כי נגעה עד הנפש והרבה רעבנו וכפשע בינינו ובין המוות ובחרנו בו מחיים במה שֶׁקְרָאָנוּ[18] וראינו גם בחבירינו כי הזהב עָם וכתם הטוב נִשְׁנָה ואבני [פז] [ברא]ש כל חוצות תשתפכנה[19]. ואֵילוּ יהושע בן עלי נח נפש בן טוביה אֱמון היה עלי תולע. וחבק אשפתות[20] כי בגוים נבלע. ובשבי נצלע. וכן חבירו דוד בן שמואל. והרי הן משועממים בתמ[הון] לבב. וצרכו לסבב. בגיא דבבי[21]. ואין לו[22] עזר נובב. ונצטרכו לגבב[23].

לבת שבב. עתה אחינו ישראל חוסו חמלו עליהם ורחמום לפרנסם לנהלם ממקום למקום ב . . . [ה]ונכם וב . . . . שכר לפעולותיכם הרבות הטובות ברב פעלים תזכו להחשב . . . . . . ותזכו ונזכה לחנינה המחוכה וברוממות הרחמים ולחזות [בנועם]

[13] =אומר, Ps. 68.7; הו is the Arabic form for הוא.

[14] Zach. 9.12.

[15] Cp. Ps. 102.21, Is. 61.1.

[16] To free (from דְרוֹר).

[17] Cp. Jer. 15.2 and Baba Batra 8b: שבי קשה מכולן דכולהו איתנהו ביה.

[18] What befell us.

[19] Cp. Lam. 4.1.

[20] Cp. ibid., 5.5.

[21] Enemy (from Aram. דבבא).

[22] Read להם.

[23] To collect (charity, from Aramaic גְבַב) from the Jewish people (?) called בת שובבה (Jer. 31.21). But perhaps non-Jews are meant since the phrase is also used concerning Ammon (Jer. 49.4).

יי׳ ולבקר בהיכל המשוכלל. ביסוד חידוש יופי מכלל. וכל יש
הקדושים בכלל. בישועה קרובה ובגאולה שלימה אמן.
ושלום כבודכם יגדל וירום ונשא וגבה מאד
אברהם אב בית דין שלכל ישראל בירבי יצחק[24] רובה אלוף
שתי ישיבו[ת] שלגולה[25]
המודרר משביה ובצור [בוטח][26]
ינחם מושב שלומכם.
נזכה לחזות סבר פניכם.

III.

[T.-S. Loan 28, paper, damaged and torn.]

(Fol. 1, recto)

קבלם ות. . . יה וקול דייקם השחית
בשרות[יה עד כלו]תם ויבוא אליה כמבוא
[צר ואויב] עיר מבוקעה ואיש כלי מ̇
מ[שחיתו ביד]ו[27] ויהי כהכותם על הקן זקנים
[לא חשכו ועל] נערים לא חמלו וילכדו
[ילדים וטפים] אשר טיפחום אבותם וריבום[28]
[ונשותיהם הלבושות] רקמה ובנותיהם הצנועות
[והכשרות אשר] מלאות כמזרק כזויות
[מזבח מחט]בות[29] ועינם רואות וימכרום
[לעבדים ולש]פחות ואין לאל ידם ויאספו
את [עמל] בתיהם ואת יגיע כפיהם אוסף

[24] The reading is doubtful and can also be מנחם though יצחק is more likely.

[25] i.e. holding the title Alluf from both the Sura and the Pumbedita academies. Thus Jacob b. ʿAubal held the same title (Mann, II, 193, top, cp. I, 167).

[26] This reading is quite uncertain; for ובצור also ובצער can be read and hence instead of בוטח another more appropriate verb like חונה should follow.

[27] Cp. Ezek. 26.8–10, Jer. 5.10, Ezek. 9.1.

[28] Cp. Lam. 2.22.

[29] Cp. Zech. 9.15, Ps. 144.12.

[הארבה ו]ה[ח]סיל כמשק גבים שוקקהו[30] וישעוהו
[כאשר יעטה] הרועה את בגדו[31] ויציגום כלי
[ריק ויב]לעם[32] [כתנין] וימלאו כרשם מעדניהם
ויאכלום וי[צי]לום ומבתיהם המלאים כל טוב

(verso)

הוציאום וידם על ראשם [כי] מאס י״י בׄ
במבטחם ולא הצליחו[33] [והכה] את הׄ
הבתים הגדולים רסיסים והבת[ים הקטנים]
בקיעים[34] ויסחבום מהם בראש [מקרח וב]כתף
מרוטה ובידים גדודות[35] כי אמ[ר י״י שלח]
מעל פני ויצאו ויאמרו א[נה נצא והקו]ל
מפוצצת ואומרת אשר [למות למות ואשר]
לחרב לחרב ואשר לרעב [לרעב ואשר]
לשבי לשבי[36] והיה כל רוא[יהם יתנודדו]
לאמר שודדו בני ארץ הצבי[37] . . . . ו
והם בוכים על עצמם ונושאים ב[ני]הם
קינה ואומרים בושנו וכסתה פנינו כלמה
כי היינו משסה לשוסינו ובזה לבוזזינו
והגלת חמדתינו כלה הגפ[ן] שלו[מים][38] וגם
אנחנו בכינו הרבה בכ[י]ה לקשה יומם

(fol. 2, recto)

[וגדלה צעקתנו על כו]בד יגונם וקראנו עליהם
[בכל רחובות מ]ספד ובכל חוצות אמרנו הו הו
[כי רעה יצאה] מאת י״י לשער ארץ הצבי
[וכששמענו] אנחנו וכל בני קהלינו כי נשבה
[השביה מעסקנו] חדלנו והעמדנו על נפשנו

30 Cp. Is. 33.4.
31 Cp. Jer. 43.12.
32 Read ויבלעום and cp. Jer. 51.34.
33 Cp. Jer. 2.27.
34 Cp. Amos 6.11.
35 Cp. Ezek. 29.18.
36 Cp. Jer. 15.1–2.
37 Palestine.
38 Cp. Jer. 13.19.

[לקבץ ולאס]וף הון רב וחיל גדול לגאול [את אחינו מידי] שוביהם ונגבה מאת חנננו [השם ומכ]ל הסרים אל משמעתינו [ומכל אנשי] קהלותינו כחמשת אלפים [דינר זהב] סגור[39] ונפדה בהם כמאתים ואף על פי שלא היו למדי לגאול כל השביה ועודנו מתאמצים לפדותם [מ]תחזקנ[י]ם לגאלם ובטוחים אנו על גו[א]ל חזק י״י צבאות שמו כי תרום הגאולה על יד [אחינו] עתה הבאים מהשבי יום יום מכל ג[בולות]

(verso)

ארץ אדום ומשעריה א[שר נשבו בארץ] הצבי נחזיק בהם וכל מערומי[הם נכסה] ונלבישם וננעלם ונאכילם ונש[תה אותם] וננהלם לאט במישרים לכל כו[של ומן] השמים יסכימו על ידינו להס[פיק להם] ולעשות כתורה וכמצוה [ועל אודות אשור][40] ובבל אשר שאל נשף חש[קנו כמעט] רגע היתה תחנה מאלהינו [לתת לנו] שארית בארץ ולהחיות [לנו לפליטה] גדולה[41] כל שכן באלו הימים [אשר ירים] אלהינו קרן הגולה וחידוש המלוכה [ויש]מיע מ[כ]ל קצה הארץ הנה מלך ה[מל]ך לבית [דוד] מלכ[נו צמח] שמו וישב ומשל על [כסאו][42] [למען י״י] אשר [נ]אמן ולמען חסדי דוד [הנא]מנים[43] כי אחרי ימים רבים אשר

(The fragment breaks off here.)

[39] Cp. I Kings 6.20.
[40] Mosul.
[41] Cp. Ezra 9.8, Gen. 45.7.
[42] Cp. Zech. 6.12–13.
[43] Cp. Is. 49.7, 55.3.

SECTION IV

EGYPTIAN AFFAIRS AND PERSONALITIES
(10th—15th CENTURIES)

1.

LEGAL DOCUMENTS OF THE 10TH CENTURY

ONLY a few documents of this century have been preserved in the Genizah. One, dated 979 C. E. at Fusṭāṭ, was cited in *Jews in Egypt*, I, 99, note 1. Ephraim b. Ṣadoḳ, who signs this document, figures also in another one (T.-S. 12.19, vellum, damaged with date missing). The signatories are אפרים בר צדוק and שר שלום בן יצחק. The document is followed by a testatum (קיום) of the Bet-Din signed by שמריה בירבי אלחנן, the famous Rabbi of Fusṭāṭ. A testatum of Shemaryah's court, dated 1002 C. E., is also cited by Schechter, *JQR*, XI, 646, note 2.

Another early document, drawn up at Damietta in 989 C. E., is given in II, 69, note 1. A Ketubah of 990 from Barḳah in North-Africa has been recently published by Assaf, ס' השטרות לרה"ג, pp. 53–55.

We reproduce here three more such documents of 967, 978 and 982, C. E., respectively. The first two are of especial interest as reflecting the business relations between Fusṭāṭ and Ḳairwān. In 967 Isaac b. Abraham of Maghreb borrowed in Fusṭāṭ 600 pieces of silver from David Hakkohen b. Solomon promising to repay his debt in Ḳairwān which city David was evidently to visit for business purposes. In 978 this Isaac b. Abraham was already dead but in the intervening years he continued his business transactions with Fusṭāṭ. On the last occasion of his stay in the capital of Egypt he left with Ḳimoi b. al-Ḥasan two containers of indigo-dye which were subsequently after his demise forwarded to Ḳairwān where they were duly received by the legally appointed guardians of his belongings, Judah b. Ḳiyūma and X. b. Isaac al-Majjāni.

The document, drawn up at Ḳairwān in 978, gives us the names of the members of the local Bet-Din.

The third document of 982 evidently emanates from the Bet-Din of the Babylonian community in Fusṭāṭ because the first signatory (apparently the Ab-Bet-Din), David Alluf b.

Yotam Alluf, held a title from the Babylonian school just as his father did. The case deals with a marriage settlement, the husband agreeing to settle on his wife as her Ketubah over 150 Dinārs of which amount the lady's father undertook to supply 100 Dinārs. Actually he advanced only 20 whereas the remaining 80 are contracted in our document as a debt to his son-in-law.

I.

[T.-S. 12.515, vellum. See Facsimile XVIII, infra, p. 718.]

(Recto)

זכרון עדות שהיתה בפנינו בחמישי בשבת בשנים עשר יום לחדש סיון

שנת אלף ומאתים ושבעים ושמונה שנים למיניין שאנו רגילין למנות בו[1]

בפוסטאט מצרים שעל נילוס נהר מושבה איך יצחק בן אברהם המערבי

אמר לפנינו היו עלי עדים וקנו ממני מעכשיו וכתבו וחתמו עלי בכל

לשון שלזכות ותנו לו לדויד הכהן בן שלמה שאני מודה בפניכם בלב

שלם ובדעת שלימה בלא אנוס ובלא טועה שנטלתי וקיבלתי ממנו שש

מאות כסף הידועים נקאר[2] מעשה בדולח והם עלי בהלואה ובה[ר]שאה

שאפרע אותם לו במדינת קירואן ואיני מעכבו ואיני משרפו[3] ואיני מֹ

[1] Viz. 1278 Sel. = 967 C. E.

[2] Plural of نقّرة, molten silver, ingot.

[3] Read מסרבו. This interchange of פ' and ב' recalls the spelling הבקר for הפקר in the Palestinian Talmud. Also the Gaon Solomon b. Yehudah writes להבקיר for להפקיר (see Mann II, 161, note 5). Cp. also infra, p. 430, note 7.

מונעו ואיני דוחיהו מעת לעת כי אם אשלמם לו שלימים ומשולמים במדינת קירואן בעת יתבעם ממני בלא עיכוב ובלא שירוף[3a] ובלא אחור ובלא נד]חיה מיום ליום [וע]ל אודותם שיעבדתי אני יצחק בן [אבר]הם כל נ[כס]ין שימצא[ו] לי תחת כל השמים לדויד כהן זה בן

שלמה בין בים בין ביבשה בין במדבר בין ביישוב בין בבית בין בשדה בין מטלטלי בין מקרקעי בין כל ממון שיהיה לו[*3] עם כל בני אדם שיהיו ערבאין ואחראין תחת ידו ותחת ידי יורשיו אחריו עד שישתלם ממני אני יצחק הכספים הללו הוא או יורשיו אחריו וכי

נאמן יהיה עלי בדיבורו כשני עדים נאמנים מאודות הכספים הללו שהם עלי חוב קיים וכי יש לי אני יצחק בן אברהם עם דויד זה כהן בן שלמה שנים עשר מן גוזיה[**3] בתוך משואותיו שלדויד זה לא . . . . ע לו השש מאות כספים הידועים נקאר צריפת . . . . [כ]ל מודעין ותנאין ומודעין שלמודעין . . . . [יצחק] בן אברהם וכל שעתיד למסו[ר] . . . . [יור]שיו בכל לשונות שא . . . . [ע]לי אני י[צחק בן אברהם] . . . .

II.

[T.-S. 12.468. See Facsimile XIX, infra, p. 719.]

(Recto)

בא לפנינו אנו בית דין אברהם בר כביר ומסר כן ואמר כי יצחק בר אברהם[4]

נֹּנ הניח עזבון אצל קימוי בר אלחסן במצרים והיא פרקמטיה ולאחר

[3a] Read סירוב. [*3] Read לי.

[**3] Probably = Arabic 'Juziyyah', special small bundles.

[4] This Isaac b. Abraham is evidently identical with Isaac b. Abraham of Maghreb in the preceding document of the year 967.

פטירת יצחק זה הגיע לכאן מאצלו[4a] ממצרים פרקמטיא על יד ר̇ נסים

[ב]ר זכריה הניכר באלמחארה הוא אסטיס דמתקרי ניל שאמי[5] שני נודות

[דמ]תקרין ג̇ראבין משקלם קנטאר ועשרים ליטרא בנודותיו והגיעו לכאן

. . . [ו]קבלום אפוטרופין[5a] של ר̇ יצחק הנפטר והם ר̇ יהודה בר קיומה

[ור̇] . . . בר יצחק מג̇אני[6] ומבקש אני מבית דין עתה שישלח אחרי

[שני אפוטרו]פין אילו וישאלם על טענותיי אם אמת הם יכתוב לי כתב

[כדי לשגרהו למצרים ל]ר̇ קימוי לזכרון עדות שלא יקומו עליו היורשים לאחר

. . . [מ]י הרשא[7] אותך למתן שלנו לאחר וכשומענו אנו בית דין

[את דבריו ש]כהוגן שאל שלחנו אחרי ר̇ יהודה בר קיומה ור̇

[. . . בר יצחק מגאני] וקיימו אפטרפסותם בפנינו פעם אחרת ושאלנו

[אותם] . . . . [וא]מרו הין כשמסר קיבלנו על ידי ר̇ נסים בר זכריה

. . . . . . [שני נו]די ניל משקלם קנטאר ועשרים ליטרא קבלנום

. . . . ם באוצר ר̇ יצחק הנפטר עם כל עזבונותיו והכל

. . . . [וכשנתקיי]מה הודאת אפוטרופין אילו בפנינו צוינו לכתוב

[4a] Viz. from Ḳimoi b. al-Ḥasan.

[5] Syrian Indigo-dye.

[5a] Read אפוטרופסין (and likewise in lines 8 and 16).

[6] The father of this person, living in Ḳairwān, originated from Majjāna, a distance of 5 days' journey from Ḳairwān. Cp. also the Gaonic responsum (ed. Assaf, תה"ג מתוך הגניזה, p. 23, No. 69): ראובן מן בני קירואן הוה ליה חנואתא ודרתא במיגנה. See also above, p. 143, where R. Nissim mentions Abū ʿImrān Musa b. Yaḥya al-Majjāni, and p. 344, note 43.

[7] Read הרשה.

[לאברהם בר כביר זכרון עדות] כדי לשגרהו למצרים לר׳ קימוי בר אלחסן

. . . . אן להיות בידו לזכות ולזכרון עדות ויהא מתג[8]

[ובפי כל מי שטוען עליו מכ]ח יורשי יצחק בשלישי בשבת בעשתי עשר יום

[לחדש] . . . [בשנת ארב]עת אלפים ושבע מאות ושלשים ושמונה לבריית

[העולם][9] . . . . . בקירואן מחוזא רבא שבאפריקה וחתמנו

. . . [דו]יד בר אברהם שמואל בר חיון משה בר יוסף

. . . . [של]מה כהן בר נסים

. . . . [ב]ר יצחק

III.

[T.-S. 16.142, vellum. See Facsimile XX, infra, p. 720.]

(Recto)

[ז]כרון עדות שהיתה בפנינו בששי בשבת בעשרים ותשעה לחדש סיון שנת אלף ומאתים ותשעים

ושלש למי[נין ש]אנו ר[גי]לין למנות בו[10] בפסטאט מצרים [דעל נילוס ה]נהר מושבה איך יעקב בר [יוסף] בר

מוניח אמר לפנינו הו[יו ע]לי עדים וקנו ממני מעכשיו וכ[תבו וחתמו] בכל לשון שלזכות ותנו לו ליו[סף] הכהן

חתני בר אברהם הניכר אלמזוק מחמת שרציתי ברצון נפ[שי ובלא] אנוס ובלא שוגה ובלא טועה ובלא

[מו]כרח כי אם בלב שלם ודעת שלימה אני מודה לפניכם כי כן התניתי ביני ובין יוסף זה שיכתוב על

[8] Literally 'a bridle,' here in the meaning of a restraint against the arguments of Isaac's heirs.

[9] 977–8 C. E.

[10] 1293 Sel. =982 C. E.

[עצ]מו בכתובת אש[תו] גאליה[11] בתי בנדוניא שלה כלי זהב וכלי מלבוש ותשמישי בית במאה וחמשים

[ו] . . . ה זהובים כמ[נה]ג כתובות המדינה הזאת וקיבלתי על עצמי שאתן לו מאה זהובים טובים

[שקולים] במ[טבע ש]ל . . . ש . . . שאין בהם חסר[ון] ונתתי לו מאילו המאה זהובים עשרים זהובים ונשאר לו

[סך שמ]ונים [זהובים א]חריהם עלי ככל ה[הלוא]ות והחובות יען על תני[12] זה קבל לכתוב על עצמו הנדוניא

. . . . גאליה ועל זה . . . ו וכל זמן שתבא[*12] לידי השמונים זהובים הללו אתנם

[לו] . . . . מעת לעת [ואם חס ו]שלום ותקרב יום פטירתי מן העולם ולא נישתלם

. . . . שלו ר . . . . . . מעזבונותי בלא שבועה יען כי הם כחוב וכהלואה

. . . . . . ות השמו[נים הזה]בים האלה עלי אני יעקב ועל יורשי אחרי ועל כל שפר

[ארג נכסיי] שימצאו לי ת[חת] כל השמים בין בים ובין ביבשה בין בבית בין בשדה

[בין מטלטלי בין מקרקעי ואפ]ילו מן הטלית שעל כתיפי שלא כאסמכות ולא כטופסי השטרים

[אלא כתוקף כל החובות ו]ההלואות וככל תקנת חכמים ותנאי בית דין . . . . שאי איפשר

. . . . [ובטל ל]פנינו כל מודעין ותנ[אין] ומודעין שלמודעין [עד סוף כל] מודעין שמסר

. . . . . כמות[**12] שאמרו חכמים [ש]בוטלין בהם מודעין ותנ[אי]ן מהיום הזה ועד לעולם

[11] About this name cp. Steinschneider, *JQR*, X,514, No. 107.

[12] =תנאי, condition.

*12 Read שיבואו.

**12 The reading is doubtful.

[וקנינו מיעקב בר י]וסף בר מוניח ליוסף זה הכהן חתנו בר
אברהם בבלי הכשר לקנות בו [בכל]

[הכתוב למעלה שריר וקיים] . . . . . . ק[ב]ל תלויים ביני חאטי[13]
מקוימים דויד אלוף ביׄר [י]וׄתם אלוף

. . . . חסן בר פשאט[14] חסן הכהן [בר] . . . .

. . . . בר תׄאבת . . . .

[13] Here is indicated that the word קבל and another one (in the lacuna) are to be found between the lines and are verified.

[14] A Solomon b. פשאט is the signatory of a document of 1016 C. E. (Mann, I, 38, note 1).

2.

A FURTHER DOCUMENT CONCERNING THE RANSOMING OF BYZANTINE CAPTIVE JEWS IN EGYPT

The occasions for ransoming their unfortunate brethren of Byzantium, who fell captive into the hands of Saracen pirates in the Mediterranean, were frequent in the annals of the Alexandrian and Fusṭāṭ Jewries in the 11th century. To the data discussed and presented in *Jews in Egypt*, I, 87–94, II, 87–93, 344–5, we add here another document emanating from the two Alexandrian congregations, headed by the Dayyān Joseph Hakkohen (the father of Yeshu'ah who wrote some of the other epistles), to the Palestinian community in Fusṭāṭ headed by its well-known Ḥaber Ephraim b. Shemaryah. The topic is the pressing problem of redeeming captives. After the settlement of the affair of the 4 captives, who had been brought from Barḳah (cp. also II, 88, l. 16), the Alexandrian Jews had to collect money for a new captive. Altogether 20 Dinārs were collected locally, which sum the captor accepted as the first instalment for the ransom of his victim. The full sum required, viz. 33⅓ Dinārs, was subsequently forwarded from the wealthy Fusṭāṭ Jewry. This captive was sent home and there remained still 15 Dinārs in the possession of the Alexandrian community. Before Passover three more captives were brought, among them a woman. They were allowed to spend Passover with their coreligionists but after the Holidays the captor dragged them back to servitude because the Alexandrian Jews delayed their ransom since they were busy collecting money for the mission of Abraham, son of the Gaon Solomon b. Yehudah, who arrived at Alexandria. Abraham's stay in Fusṭāṭ in Kislev 1026 C. E. is evident from the document cited in II, 97–8 (cp. I, 120). Probably a few months later, after Passover 1027, Abraham came to Alexandria to collect money for Palestinian needs. Yet the Alexandrian Jews could not bear to see the captives treated cruelly and hence gave the captor the 15 Dinārs as a deposit and stood surety for the remaining 85 needed for the full ransom. They appeal now to the Fusṭāṭ Jews to send them this sum because the Arab captor constantly sends his underlings demanding the payment of the debt. A special messenger was despatched to Fusṭāṭ to carry our letter and he had to be paid 1½ Dinārs for his services. The following year 1028 was especially trying on account of the large number of new captives that were landed at Alexandria as the letter of Kislev 1028, written by Joseph's son, Yeshu'ah, well testifies (*JQR*, XIX, 250–54, cp. the analysis in my *Jews in Egypt*, I, 88–90). The number of captives enumerated in this letter is eighteen.

[T.-S. 24.29.]

Address (verso)

לקדושת אחינו. אנשי שלומנו. הקהל הקדוש
המתפללים בכניסת הירושלמים ש[ב]מצר[ים]
ובראשם כגק מר ור[1] אפרים החבר
בסנ גדול[2] בן מ[3] שמריה זל ולת[4]
ישע רב

יברכם מאמץ ברוכים.
[וי]עודדם מתמך מכים.
[ויע]ליצם סועד נכים.
ויפדם לבל יהון פרוכים[5].
ברית שלום[6].

[1] =כבוד גדולת קדושת מרנא ורבנא.

[2] =בסנהדרין גדולה.

[3] =מרנא.

[4] =זכרו לברכה ולתחייה.

[5] From פרך, hard labor.

[6] The same concluding phrases ישע רב ברית שלום are also to be found in the letter of Yeshu'ah b. Joseph Hakkohen (of Kislev 1028 C. E.), printed in *JQR*, XIX, 254 (cp. Mann, I, 88).

(Recto)

[After an exordium of seven lines in fourfold rhymed verse there follows the indication of the people to whom the letter is directed.]

ובפרט הקהל הק[דוש] המתפללים [ב]כניסת הירושלמים
ובראשם כֹגֹק מרנא ורבנ[א]
אפרים החבר בסנ̇ גד̇ החכם והנבון העומד לגדור פרצות וכו׳

[There follow seven more lines of stylistic verbiage.]

(l. 9 of prose)

. . . . שאו אחינו. אנשי שלומנו.
אנ[ש]י גאולתנו. שלום עצום כחלל שלעולם ממנו יוסף הכהן
הדיין . . . . . .
ומכלל שתי הקהלות הקדושות. אשר בנא אמון[7] מאוששות[8]. ובשתי
הכניסיות
מתפללות וכו׳

[There follow nine more lines of verbiage.]

(l. 20)

. . . . ומודיעים אנו לכבודכם כי הלכו מכתבים
אליכם בימי החרף עם שלוחנו שמו [יה]ודה בן חיאן הודיעכם
במו[אתיית השבוי]
אחר הארבעה האתויים מארץ ברקה[9] [והצ]טרכנו לדמיו ובעת
הליכת השליח ה[איץ]
אדון שלשבוי בתביעתו[10] שנגזרה תענית צבור ועש[ינו] יו[ם] ביטול
מלאכה . . . .
הכרזנו . . . נביא נדבה לפדיון השבוי הזה [וכל איש] אשר נשאו
לבו הביאו דבר מזהב ומכס[ף]

[7] Alexandria.

[8] Are founded, established (from אשש, cp. Ben-Jehuda, *Thesaurus*, I, p. 435).

[9] Barḳah (on the North-African coast).

[10] Supply עד.

וכן הנשים עד אשר נתקבץ שמנה עשר זהוב[ים וגם] מהמערבים[11] שני זהובים

נהיה הכלל עשרים לקחם אדנו שלשבוי ונשאר עלינו ש[לש]ה עשר זהובים בא השליח

ועמו כתב דיוקנא[12] בשם ר׳ יהודה המלמד בן יצחק נֿעֿ בשלשה ושלשים זהובים עמדנו

[עמ]ו עד שלקח הזהובים ופרענו לבעל השבוי שלשה עשר זהובים נשאר מהן עשרים

באו ימי הליכת הספינות וביקש השבוי לשוב אל ארצו שקלנו לבעל השער [שלה]ים[13]

שני זהובים וחצי וקנינו לו כסות בשני זהובים וחצי ונשארו עמו חמשה ע[ו]ל מחית[ו]

והלך השבוי אל ארצו לחיים ולשלום. [ובתו]ך הדברים האלה באו שלש[ה] שבו[יים א]שר

[הז]כרנו ביאתם שני אנשים ואשה והנה אין בקהל כח לעמוד בדמיהם . . . . ל לו מא[ת]

זהובים[14] והם לאחד מהערביאים שמו מקה בן גאבר הנודע לחר רב[14*] מן בְּנִי קְדַּר

וכבואם אלינו ראינום בצער גדול מיגיעת הדרך וכריתת . . ב[ג]דים . . . . את פניהם[14**]

מאת אדונם והיו בתוכנו כל ימי חג הפסח ולא יכלנו לעשות [חוץ מ]המזו[נ]ות לפי שהיו

[11] From Jews of Maghreb living in Alexandria (or visiting there for business purposes).

[12] Consignment of money.

[13] Commander of the port (of Alexandria). About a Jew holding this position for about 15 years, cp. Mann, II, 274.

[14] A hundred Dinārs were needed for their ransom at the rate of 33⅓ Dinārs per person.

[*14] The reading of these two words is doubtful. Perhaps they form one word taken from the Arabic 'ḥarrab' in the meaning of a violent man.

[**14] The reading is doubtful.

הקהל משתדלים בצרכיו של כגֹקֹ מרֹ ורֹ אברהם החבר בן
אנדו]ננו גאון נטרוהי מן שמיא[15]
ולאחר הפסח בא אדונם לבקש ממונם ולא מצא ולקחם בפרו[ך]
והוציאם אל אוהליו בזעף
לאחר כן שלחנו שלוחים ודברנו על לבו עד שהשיבם אלינו
ונתננו לו [חמש] עשר ז[ה]ובים
שהיו עמנו וערבנו על חמשה ושמנים זהובים עד חמשה עשר ימים
בחדש סיון.
ולא נעלם מכם ענינו ודלות קהלנו העני הזה המשוך מכל צד
הרצוץ מכל [פנ]ה אשר
המס כבד עליו מכל מקום ולו היה בקהל כח או אֱיָל לא היו
מקפידים ולא מצריכים אתכם
לשוה פר[ו]גט]ה אחת: עתה אחינו אנשי שלומנו הוצרכנו לשכור
השלוח הזה נושא
[מכתבינ]ו אליכם ואל כלל הקהלות. שתי הכתות המהוללות.
ישמרם מגננו בזהוב וחצי
מ[פני הצער מ]זה הערבי אשר בכל יום שלוחיו הולכים ובאים
אלינו ואין לנו צד שנפנה
אליו כי אם אל יי׳ אלהינו ואל חסדכם. על זאת אל דמי לכם
אחיכם. ואל תִּשָׁלו ואל
נא תחרישו ותשקוטו ואל תתנו פוגה לכם על כאב אחיכם האנוש
ועתה הראינו לדעת
ולנ[ירָ]א ולזחול מעלילות אלהינו פו[ל]אים כי מי דמה או מי העלה
על לב אם לעת כזאת יהיו
אלה ש[ו]בוים ב[מצוק ובמצו]ר . . . . . שהיו אדנים לנשיאיהם[14]**
ושרים בבתיהם וכן דאוג נדאג

. . . .

[15] Abraham b. Solomon b. Yehudah.

3.

FURTHER DOCUMENTS BEARING ON ABŪ SA'AD ABRAHAM AND ABŪ NAṢR ḤESED, THE SONS OF SAHL AL-TUSTARI

The importance of these two brothers in Cairo in the first half of the 11th century has been dicsussed in my *Jews in Egypt* (I, 73, 76–83, 119–22 and in the corresponding fragments edited in vol. II). Their prestige becomes the more evident the more the Genizah fragments are made available. Hai Gaon corresponded with Ḥesed and likewise the Exilarch Hezekiah of Bagdād urged the Babylonian community in Fusṭāṭ to obey the commands of this communal leader (see above, pp. 118 and 180). Herewith 3 more documents are edited and a fourth one, already published, brought into its proper setting—they all increase our knowledge of the activities and contacts of this al-Tustari family.

The first fragment (No. I) establishes the fact that Sahl had 3 sons, viz. the above-mentioned Abraham and Ḥesed and a third one Abū'l Manṣūr Aaron. This explains the name Harūn which Maḳrizi confusedly gave to Abū Naṣr whose real name was Ḥesed (= Fadhl) whereas his brother Abū'l Manṣūr was Aaron (= Harūn).[1] Our fragment is a document written after Ḥesed's death. Therein a certain Khalāf b. Aaron, whose family originated from Ramlah (Palestine), testifies to have received from Aaron b. Sahl and from the heirs of the late Ḥesed b. Sahl a deposit which Khalāf's late father, Aaron, had entrusted to the care of Ḥesed. Aaron b. Sahl evidently acted as guardian of Ḥesed's heirs and managed the business of his late brother. The document is of interest from the legal side as giving us a specimen of a deed of settlement of a claim. We notice a developed legal phraseology safeguarding the payer against any possible new claim on the part of the payee. Our document has

[1] See the passages cited by Wüstenfeld, *Gesch. d. Faṭimiden-Chalifen*, p. 227.

also a testatum of the Bet-Din of the Babylonian congregation in Fusṭāṭ headed by Sahlān b. Abraham.

This legal phraseology is still further developed in No. II, being a Ḳaraite document wherein Yeshu'ah b. Abraham renounced all claims he had on Sa'īd b. Israel al-Tustari. The latter belonged to this family being the brother of Sahl (Yāshar) al-Tustari, the father of the above-mentioned 3 brothers. His full name was Abū Sahl Sa'īd (= Sa'adyah, I, 122, note 1). In the complimentary poem (II, 76, top) he is described as a scholar in Bible and Jewish law (סעדיה המבונן זקן תורה ופרושים ודינים ופתרונות חמודות מזהובים ופקודים משמחים והגונים). The Ḳaraite character of this document is probably due to the fact that the declarant Yeshu'ah was a Ḳaraite and should not be taken as evidence that the family al-Tustari belonged to this sect (see my remarks in II, 376–78). But this problem is connected with the next item.

No. III is a letter from Tobias to Abū Surūr Peraḥ b. Mumal. The latter is known from his connection with Natan b. Abraham, the rival Gaon of Palestine to Solomon b. Yehudah (see II, 173–4). The writer styles himself האבל (in the address) and also העובד (l. 5). The first designation (cp. also המתאבל, l. 5) could be explained by reason of his having sustained a loss in his family (see ll. 17–18), but the expression העובד and the whole tenor of lines 5–6 indicate that he was one of the Abele Ṣion in Jerusalem. Now there is known a Ḳaraite author and translator of Byzantium, Tobias b. Moses, called העובד and המעתיק הבקי (see the latest summary of the data about him by Poznański, אוצר ישראל, V, 12–14). He is placed in the second half of the 11th century, but if he be the author of our present letter and of another one to be discussed forthwith, then his time has to be advanced into the first half of this century. Elijah Bashiazi informs us that Tobias went to Jerusalem to study under the famous Ḳaraite scholar Yeshu'ah b. Yehudah (Abū'l Faraj Furḳān) and that there he translated Yeshu'ah's works from Arabic into Hebrew which he subsequently brought to Constantinople where he evidently lived till the end of his life.[2] In our letter there seems to be a reference to another

[2] אגרת גיד הנשה preceding his אדרת אליהו, ed. Gozlow, 1835. This appendix has no pagination but our passage is on fol. 1d: הלא תראה שאנשי דורו בקוסנדינא אשר היו בימים הקדמונים היו נמשכים בפסקי החכם רבי' ישועה, וכן בענין העריות. וזה מזמן

great Ḳaraite authority in Jerusalem, Abūl Faraj Harūn (l. 22, הזקן אבו אלפרג׳ אהרן ש״צ), known as המדקדק הירושלמי, who was older than Yeshu'ah and was one of the latter's masters.

Internal evidence seems to indicate that the writer of our letter was Tobias of Constantinople. There is evidently in l. 11 a Greek word (וסונגילאת), though its meaning is obscure to me. He was a stranger and was about to leave Jerusalem to return to his native land (ll. 31–32). His evident quotation of an Aggadah (l. 14) does not militate against his being a Ḳaraite because from Tobias' writings it appears that he was familiar with Rabbinic literature. Moreover in writing to Peraḥ b. Mumal, a Rabbanite scholar in Fusṭāṭ, he was apt to use Rabbinic quotations. Our letter is in reply to Peraḥ's epistle, wherein there was some allusion to the fear entertained in Egypt concerning certain enemies (l. 9). Perhaps the revolt in Palestine in 1024–29 is referred to which also threatened Egypt. Tobias lived in great distress in Jerusalem. He complains that nobody befriended him except Abū'l Faraj Aaron who occasionally inquires about his welfare. As a particular grievance he mentions that money was sent by Abū Naṣr Ḥesed (al-Tustari) and likewise by a certain Abū 'Alī Yephet b. Abraham for distribution among the poor (including of course the Abele Ṣion) and that he was left out entirely. He asks Peraḥ to send him a certain sum he holds for his account (l. 30) because he wishes to return to his home abroad.

That he left Jerusalem and stayed over a year in Egypt is evident from a letter to Abraham b. Sahl al-Tustari (edited by Gottheil-Worrell, *l. c.*, 142–148).[3] Tobias reminds Abraham that he has not come to Egypt to ask from the elders for his

שהלך רבי׳ טוביא המעתיק אצל רבי׳ ישועה ולמד עמו והעתיק ספריו מלשון הערבי ללשון הקדש והביאם בקוסדינא כפי מה שידוע זה בספרו בספר יהי מאורות.

[3] The text has been faultily edited and the translation and several notes are altogether impossible. There is nothing missing between the two parts which originally formed one sheet of paper, though the letter is incomplete at the end. The writer was Tobias (p. 144, l. 21, cp. also the acrostic on p. 142, lines 6–10, where l. 9 ought to precede l. 8 as is evident from the facsimile by the indications of the letters א and ב between the lines). The following corrected readings are given here. P. 142, l. 5, for בו לכת r. בהלכת; l. 6, for מצאר r. מצאוי, and for בת חן r. בתחן, in prayer (=בתחנה); l. 14, for יקל r. ידל; l. 16, for יתהוללו r.

maintenance but to serve Abraham in some employment in which he remained for a year. Apparently he did some copying of books for him. From the handwriting we can see that he was a professional scribe. He complains that his salary was very meagre and that he and his family (3 souls in all) had a very hard struggle to live.[4] Now he heard that Abraham was angry with him. He beseeches his patron to help him leave the country by procuring for him a safe conduct. Tobias on his first arrival from his native land (a Christian country, see ibid., p. 148, l. 24) at Damiette (בחנס, p. 148, l. 19) was put in prison but was released by the intervention of Abraham. Then Tobias had money and could offer bribery but now he is destitute. Tobias assures Abraham that he will spread his fame for his good deeds in all the congregations of the land of Edom (viz. Byzantium) and will see to it that in the synagogues a blessing be recited for Abraham on every Monday and Thursday (viz. after the reading from the Torah).

It is thus evident that Tobias on his journey to Palestine first landed at Damiette where he was arrested as a Byzantine subject. Abraham aided his release and also Tobias' bribery helped. He stayed for some time in Jerusalem where he was reduced to hard straits. Finally he set out on his return home via Egypt where actually he stayed for a whole year (whether in Fusṭāṭ or in Alexandria is not clear). He was employed by Abraham during this time but finally his patron tired of him. As a last favor he asks for a safe conduct to leave the country. As Abraham was assassinated in 1048, we have a terminus ad quem for the return of our Tobias home.

If our identification of this Tobias with the Ḳaraite scholar of Constantinople be correct, we should have further evidence of the interest of Abraham and Ḥesed al-Tustari in the Ḳaraites.

יתחוללו, and for מבֿ r. כבֿ; l. 18, for תחא r. תהא, and after נחוייה r. [במחיצות]; p. 144, l. 19, בננת חיים is impossible because of the rhyme; l. 24, for אודות r. אודותיי; p. 146, l. 1, for שאתכרכר r. שאתכלכל, and for אחר r. אדוני; l. 7, after אלפרג r. היבה, Hibah = Natan; l. 15 for שעשה r. שיעשה; p. 148, l. 19, for הייתי היום r. הייתי אמות (exactly as in No. III, l. 20).

[4] In the former letter there is a reference to his only daughter and to a certain woman accused of misconduct.

However this does not point to their Ḳaraite allegiance but rather to their general generosity towards all needy Jews, especially if they be pious and learned. It should be added that the reference to an Abraham משנה למלך, belonging to the family known as אלדסאחרה which was headed by Yashar b. Ḥesed b. Yashar (II, 376), is also found in other Ḳaraite Memorial Lists (cp. MS. Firkowicz, 2. Hebrew-Arabic Collection, Nos. 2969, 2970, 2971 and 2976). There is some confusion in these lists because our Abraham al-Tustari was really b. Sahl (ישר) b. Israel whereas there he is supposed to be b. Yashar (=Sahl) b. Ḥesed (= Fadhl) b. Yashar. Moreover the colophons, with the altered dates which place Abraham al-Tustari משנה למלך במצרים in 790 and in 847 C. E. (see I, 79–80) and which I suggested to belong really to the 11th century (847, e. g., to be 1047), can hardly refer to our Abraham al-Tustari because the original second date must have been 946 as shown by Kahle (*Massoreten des Westens*, 1927, 60–63). We cannot fathom out the skill of Firkowicz in changing or correcting colophons. Nor can we ascertain fully the veracity of the Memorial Lists. But Abraham al-Tustari's position in the reign of al-Mustanṣīr till his assassination in 1048 is now borne out by the many claims on his generosity and his political intervention on behalf of individual Jews and of whole communities, both Rabbanite and Ḳaraite, as the Genizah documents testify. In this noble work he was aided by his brother Abū Naṣr Ḥesed. Their father and uncles also seem to have been prominent figures in Fusṭāṭ-Cairo. We append here at the end a genealogical table of this important family.

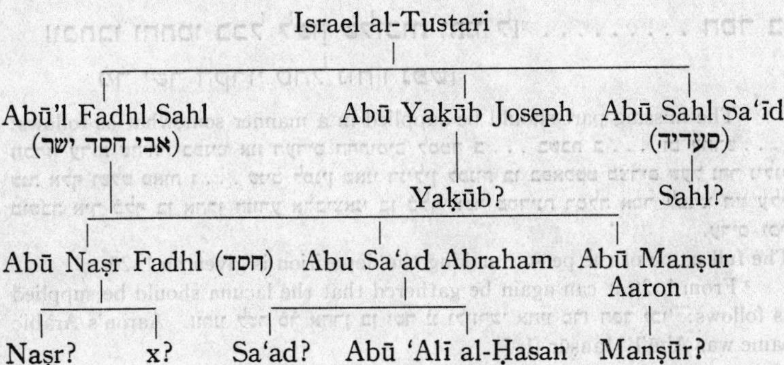

Since Yashar (Sahl) had the Kunya Abū'l Fadhl and his eldest son was Fadhl (חסד), I presume that the Kunyas of his brothers also denote the names of their eldest sons, thus Joseph had a son Jacob and Sa'adyah a son Sahl (ישר), perhaps born after the death of his brother Yashar. The same is presumed about the Kunyas of Yashar's three sons, thus Ḥesed had a son Naṣr, Abraham a son Sa'ad and Aaron a son by the name of Manṣūr (= פנחס?). Now there is mentioned a person המשכיל משה (?) בן השר חסד (I, 79, note 1), but owing to his Ḳaraite affiliation he should not be taken as a son of our Ḥesed. Hence the second son of Ḥesed listed in the above table is altogether problematic. That he had more than one child is apparent from the expression "the heirs of Ḥesed" (No. I, l. 20).

With regard to Abraham's children there is mentioned a son of his Abū 'Alī al-Ḥasan who was twice Wezir during 1063–4 (see I, 78, note 2). A brother of his, Sa'ad, is doubtful.

Whether Sahl b. Aaron and his son Abū Ṭayyīb 'Alvān b. Sahl, who helped the Jerusalem community (II, 185, cp. I, 162), are members of this family, so that, e. g., Sahl was the son of Abū Manṣūr Aaron, is of course problematic.

I.

[T.-S. 16.145. See Facsimile XXI, infra, p. 721.]

(Recto)

. . . .

.... [אמר לפנינו היו עלי] עדים[1] וקנו [ממני מעכשיו]

[וכתבו וחתמו בכל לשון שלזכות ותנו ל][2] .... חסד בן

מׄר ישר הקרוי סהל נוח[ו נפש]

[1] The missing part should be supplied in a manner somewhat as follows: [זכרון עדות שהיתה בפנינו אנו העדים החתומים למטה ב... בשבת ב... יום לחדש.... שנת אלף ושלש מאות ו... שנים למנין שאנו רגילין למנות בו בפאסטט מצרים שעל נהר נילוס מושבה איך כׄלף בן אהרן הנודע אלביצאני בן כׄלף אשר ממדינת רמלה אמר לפנינו היו עלי] עדים וכו'.
The full name of the person making the deposition is given on l. 20.

[2] From l. 20 it can again be gathered that the lacuna should be supplied as follows: [ותנו לשר מׄר אהרן בן ישר נׄנׄ וליורשי אחיו מרׄ] חסד וכו'. Aaron's Arabic name was Abū'l Manṣūr (l. 7).

.........ם מחמת שאני מודה בפניכם הודאה גמורה

[וברצון נפשי] ......תי וגמר דעתי בלא אונס ולא טעות ולא חולי ולא פיתוי כי אם בלב שלם ובנפש חפצה ובגוף בריא

ובדעת נכונה ונקיה שנטלתי וקיבלתי מיד אהרן הנזכר שלשים ותשעה זהובים[3] ושני שלישי זהוב טובים שקולים הדורים

ממטבע היוצא והוא כלל הראוי לי מעזבון אבי אהרן שהניח אצל פצל[4] בן סהל הנזכר ויצאו הזהובים האילו מיד אבו אלמנצור זה

ומרשותו ומחזקתו ונעשו ברשותי ובחזקתי ובידי ולא נשאר לי מהם מאומה ולפיכך פיציתי וביריתי[5] את אבו אלמנצור ואת [יורשי אחיו]

חסד הנאסף .... מכל טענה ותביעה שבעולם וכתבתי להם שטר פיצוי זה להיותו מוחזק בידיהם ובידי יורשיהם

[אחריה]ם ממני ומיורשי אחרי כי אחרי שנטלתי השלשים ותשעה זהובים והשני שלישי זהוב לא נשאר לי ולא לאדם בעולם מחמתי

[ושלא מחמתי] מחמת אבי אהרן הנזכר שום כלום תביעה ובקשה מכל צד ומכל פינה לא אצל אהרן זה ולא אצל אחיו ולא אצל יורשיהם ולא אצל קרוביהם

[ולא] אצל משר[תיהם] לא זהב לא כסף לא נחשת לא בדיל לא עופרת לא מקרקעין לא מטלטלין לא סחורות לא פרקמטיאות לא דיוקני[6]

[3] Dinārs.

[4] Fadhl is the Arabic equivalent for Ḥesed. His Kunya was Abū Naṣr. Cp. Bodl. 2878.15: אבו נצר אלפצ̇ל בן סהל אלתסתרי. In T.-S. Box K 6 there is to be found a letter with the following address (verso): חצ̇רה̈ מולאי אלשיך̇ אלפאצ̇ל אבו נצר אלפצ̇ל בן סהל אלדסתרי אג̇לה אללה מן מעתקד מחבתה יהודה בן יוסף ב̇ן אלהגי אלאנדלסי אלפסטאט אן שא אללה.

[5] Cleaned; more correct ובירֵרתי.

[6] Consignment of money.

. . . . [ל]א תמצית חשבון לא ירושה לא נחלה לא עזבון לא כל דבר שנקרא ושנהגה ושיש לו שם וחניכה וכן נמי לא חרם

[לא שבועה] לא אלה לא גזירה לא אפיל[ו] חרם סתם ומחלתי להם מחילה גמורה מעתה כל טענה ותביעה שבעולם וכל שבועה וגלגול וכל ערעור

. . . . מחילה שאין לה חזרה ואין לה הפרה וסילקתי ידי ורשותי ורשות הבאים מכוחי מתביעתם סילוק גמור וכל הקם לעורר עליהם

[מחמת] פיצוי זה בין מחמתי בין שלא מחמתי עלי להצילם מהם ולשלם להם כל מה שיגיע אליהם מחמתם מדבר הפסד וחסרון וכל כתב היוצא מחמת

ידי כל אדם בעולם כדי לבטל פיצוי זה שקר וכזב ותרמית אין למדין מהן ואין עושין בהן דין לא בדיני ישראל ולא בנימוסי עממים וכל מודעין ותנאין

ומודעין שלמודעין ומודעין היוצאין מתוך מודעין עד סוף כל מודעין שמסרתי ושמסרו לי אחרים ושעתיד אני למסור על שטר פיצוי זה כולם בטלים

ומבוטלים בפניכם מעכשיו בכל לשון שמבטלין בהם חכמים מודעין ותנאין וקיבלתי עלי אני כ̇לף בן אהרן אחריות שטר פיצוי זה כחוזק וכחומר כל שטארי

מחזקי מעליי . . . . . ועל ירתאי בתראי דלא להשנאה כדתקינו רבנן ונהגין בעלמא מן יומא דנן ולעלם דלא כאסמכתא ודלא כטופסא דש[טרי]

וקנינא מן כ̇לף דנן בן אהרן הנדע אלביצאני[*6] בן כ̇לף אשר ממדינת רמלה לשר מ̇ר̇ אהרן זה בן ישר נ̇נ̇ וליורשי אחיו השר מ̇ר̇ חסד בן ישר בכל הכתוב ומפו[רש]

*6 The reading is doubtful.

למעלה בכלי הכשר לקנות בו שריר וקיים הנאסף סתם לא זה
אצל זה בפניכם זה תלוי ביני חאטי[7] וקיימין סעדיה בר
אפרים החבר
מבורך בן סעיד דאוד בר משה נ̇נ̇ שלמה בר עלי נ̇נ̇
[יצחק ב]ן מומל יהודה ב[ר שמואל]
שמואל ב[ר נחום נ̇נ̇]

איתקיים שטר אביזאריה[8] דנן קדמנא בבי דינא
דנוסחיה ושהדוהי כתיבין לעילא וקיומיה
מיניה וביה לתתא בכתב ידי שהדי אילין דאשהידו ביה ואינון
סעדיה בר אפרים
החבר מבורך בן סעיד דאוד בר משה נ̇נ̇ שלמה בר עלי נ̇נ̇ יצחק בן
מומל יהודה בר
שמואל ושמואל בר נחום נ̇נ̇[9] דחתימין בחתמות ידיהון וסימניהון
ומדמחזקא קדמנא בבי דינא שהדותיהן [דתרי מנהון]
[ואינון סעדיה בר אפרים הח]בר ומבורך בן סעיד אישרנוהי
וקיימנוהי להדין שטר פיצוי ותירצנוהי כדחזי

הח̇ סג̇ חמ̇ הח̇ בח̇ ז̇ל
סהלאן ראש הסדר בר אברהם ראש הסדר[10]
הא̇ היש̇ הנש̇ הא̇ היש̇ הה̇

שמואל בר אברהם נ̇נ̇ נתן הלוי בר ישועה זלע̇[11]

[7] Here there is the indication that 8 words are to be found between the lines (8, 13, 10, 16, 18, 20) and are valid.

[8] The Aramaic form of this document is found in Hai Gaon's Sepher Ha-Sheṭarot (cp. Harkavy, הפסגה, III, 49–50, and now in ed. Assaf, 1930, p. 22).

[9] Of these signatories Sa'adyah b. Ephraim was the uncle of Sahlān b. Abraham (cp. Mann, II, sub Index) while Meborakh b. Sa'īd is probably the later Nagid Meborakh b. Sa'adyah.

[10] Sahlān's titles were: החבר האלוף סגן הישיבה חמדת הנשיאות while his late father Abraham (hence here זלה̇ה̇ = זכרונו לחיי העולם הבא) went by the titles: החבר האלוף בחיר הישיבה. See Mann, II, 102–3. Sahlān had also a fifth title ראש הסדר. Cp. also above, p. 320, note 36..

[11] About Natan Hallevi b. Yeshu'ah cp. Mann, II, 103, note 1, and 245.

II.

[T.-S. 16.160. See Facsimile XXII, infra, p. 722.]

(Recto)

[זכרון עדות שהיתה] לפנינו אנחנו העדים החתומים למטה בכתב הזה
. . . . שהוא יום תשעה לחדש אב משנת אלף ושלש
[מאות] . . . . [וש]מנה שנים למספר יונים[12] בארץ מצרים במדינת פסטאט
כן היה כי ב[א י]שועה בן אברהם ויתודה ויאמר לפנינו היו עלי עדים וקנו
ממני וכתבו וחתמו [ע]לי בכל לשון שלזכות על כל מה שאני מודה לפניכם
ואני לא אנוס ולא מו[כרח ו]לא טועה ולא שכור כי אם בתם לבי וגמר דעתי
ורצוני וחפצי ותאות נפשי אני מודה לפניכם כי נקיתי ופטרתי אני ישועה בן
אברהם לסעיד בן ישראל אלתסתרי[13] מכל דבר בעולם ומכל דרישה ובקשה
וחקי[ר]ה ומכל ת[ב]יעה ותואנה ומכל דין ומשפט בין בדיני ישראל ואם בדיני
הגויים ופטרתי אות[ו] מכל אלה ושבועה ואחרמה ואכרזה סתם ופרוש ואין לי עליו
לא מ[שכון ולא] הלואה ולא עבוט ולא עזבון ולא ערבון ולא משכון ולא ערְבָה

[12] The date 13[.]8 Sel. corresponds to 10[.]7 C. E.

[13] Sa'īd b. Israel al-Tustari is probably identical with the uncle of the famous grandee Abraham b. Sahl al-Tustari (see Mann I, 122, note 1).

ולא פקדון ולא אבדה ולא דבר לשמירה ולא קנין ולא מכירה ולא סחורה ולא

חבורה ולא שכירה ולא לקיחה ולא נתינה ואין לי עמו ולא אצלו ולא ברשותו

ולא תחת ידו לא כסף ולא זהב ולא נחשת ולא ברזל ולא בדיל ולא עופרת ולא זכוכית

[ו]לא חרש ולא [כ]לי עצים משוחים ולא כלי זהב וכסף ולא כלי נחשת ולא כל בגדי מלבוש

[ולא] . . . . . ולא פשתים [ולא ש]ש ולא ארגמן ולא משכבות ולא מצעות ולא מסכים ולא

[אבנים י]קרות ולא מרגליות ולא רכוש ולא מקנה ולא ארץ ולא שדה זרע

. . . . . [ול]א כרמים ולא גנות ולא פרדסים ולא אילנות ולא פרות ולא תבואה

. . . . . [ול]א חטים ולא שעורים ולא פול ועדשים ולא כל מיני זרע ולא בהמה ולא

. . . . . ולא נחלה ולא ירושה ולא עבד ולא אמה ולא . . . . ולא בקר ולא סוסים ולא

[חמורים ו]לא גמלים ולא מרכבות ולא אניות ולא בתים ולא חצרות ולא עצים ולא

[אב]נים ולא כל מאכל ומשקה לא יין ולא שמן ולא דבש ולא רקות ולא בשמים

[ול]א שמנים מרקחים ולא ספרים ולא פתרנות[14] ולא כתבות ולא חשבנות ולא דברים

[אחרים] ולא מצה ומריבה ולא ערעור ולא ביני ובינו מעשה ולא כל דבר בעולם אשר יעשו

[14] Commentaries on the Bible. כתבות are evidently in the meaning of general writings.

[ב]ני אדם בין איש וחבירו אם בים ואם ביבשה ואין לנו עליו קנץ[15] נקניץ בו ואין
לא[דם] בעולם לדין עמו או להשפט עמו משמי אני ישוע[ה בן] אברהם אם בחיי או לאחר
[מיתתי מחמ]תי ומקרובי ומיורשי ולא להם לבקש ממנו דבר בגללי וכל כתב ושטה
[שאוציא אני י]שועה בן אברהם או יוציאו קרובי ויורשי הוא בטל ומ[בוטל] בלי
[ו]הועלה וחיב על כל בתי דינים והשפטים שלא ישמ[עו] ולא . . . . . .
[יאזינו ולא ישגי]חו בו כי הוא שקר וכזב אחרי שכתבתי אני ישועה [בן] אברהם
[לסעיד בן ישראל אל]תסתרי הכתב הזה והוא כתב אביזארה ושטר נקיון להיות
[לזכות ולראיה בידו] על כל מי אשר יבקש ממנו דבר או יתאונן אתו או יצטדק
[אתו וכשמענו אנח]נו העדים את דברי ישועה בן אברהם הזה אשר
[הגיד לפנינו] . . . . . וקנינו מן ישועה בן אברהם בקנין שמים וא[רץ][16]
. . . . [בש]טר [ה]זה ועל רצונו בנקיון הזה אחרי שקראנ[ו]
[לפניו] . . . . והוא שמע והתודה בב[ר]ית . . . . .
. . . . [ומ]ה שהיה לפנינו כתבנו [ו]חתמנו . . . .
. . . . לראינ[ה] . . . .
. . . .

[15] Proof, argument (from Job 18.2). About the use of קנץ in this meaning by the early Rabbanite and Ḳaraite authors, cp. Pinsker, ל״ק, 166.

[16] About this phrase in Ḳaraite legal documents in connection with a קנין, see vol. II of our *Texts and Studies*.

III.

[T.-S. 12.347, faint and damaged.]

Address (verso)

[לכ] גד קד מרׄ[17] אבוסרור פרח היקר
[החכם והנבון] בן רבׄ מומל הזקן ירׄאׄ[18]
במצרים שלום[*18]

ממני טוביה האבל [הדורש] שלומך
מן עיר הקדש תבנה ות[כונן]

(recto)

שלומות רבות וישועות עצומות. ובשורות נאומות. ושנים נע[ימות].
וברכות רשומות. מיודע תעלומות. לאדׄ[19] ומרי כבׄ גד ק[דושת]
הדרת יקרת תפארת עטרת מרׄורׄ הזקן היקר הח[כם וה]נבון הידוע [אבוסרור]
פרח האלהים ישׄ[20] ויעזרהו וינצרהו. בן כבׄ קדׄ [מ]רׄורׄ הזקן מ[ומל ירׄ אׄ]
ממני אני טוביה העובד התו[למ]יד ה . . . המת[אבל] . . . .
ובעד שבר כל ישׄ ועל ציון וירושׄ האלהים ינחמנו ככתׄ כאיש אשר אמו[ ]
תנחמנו כן אנכי אנחמכם ובירוש תנוחמו[21]: [ו]מדׄיע אל הזק[ן]
היקר כי באה אלי כתבך הנאה והיקרה ושמחתי בו . . . .
וכי אתם מן פחד האויבים ביראה גדולה ברוך י״י אלהינו אשר . .
מעמו כי היה הוא יודע כי יעבור על זאת האמה השפלה . . . . . .
וסונגילאת[22] שאם יבוא[23] לנו צרה נשוב אליהם[24] ונקח . . . .

[17] =לכבוד גדלת קדשת מרנא. [18] =ירחמהו אלהים.

[*18] The reading is doubtful.

[19] =לאדוני. There is a blank in the MS. after this word.

[20] =ישמרהו. [21] Is. 66.13.

[22] The meaning of this word is obscure to me.

[23] Read תבוא.

[24] It is not clear to whom the plural suffix refers. Read perhaps אליו, viz. to God.

נפשנו כי לא נאבד ותחלתם[25] ואף גם זאת בהיותם בארץ [איביהם וג' מקוה]

יש וג' מקוה יש' מושיעו בעת צרה וג'[26] בכל צרתם [לא צר ומלאך פניו וג']27

מלמד שאמ' החכמ' זכ' לב'[28] שבכל . . . .

במקרא. ואשרי שיבטח בו וא[שרי החוסה בו] . . . .

כי לא כתבתי לך עד עתה חי נפשך וחי נפשי . . . .

לא עשיתי זה אלא מדאגה גדולה כי שבר גדול . . . .

את נפשי בבית המת אני ואין איש יסור לשאול לשל[ומי]

ואין איש מנחם ולולי רחמי שדי ובאו אנשים . . . .

בדברים טובים הייתי אמות. וכל שכן כי . . . .

ואפילו גרה אחת לא יתנו לי ואני כרתי את נפשי מן העולם ואות[ר][18]* . . . .

בעולם ולולי כי הזקן אבו אלפרג' אהרן שצ' ישלח אחת לעתים וישאל [לשלומי]

לא הייתי אדע טוב או רע. וכל שכן כי באו לזקן אבונצר חסד באלה הימים

דרכמונים ופיזרום לכל איש וכן לאבועלי יפת בן אברהם יר' אל ופיזרו גם אלה

ולא נתנו לי אפילו שעורה אחת. ולא הם זכרו אותי בשאר האנשים ולא ב[ועד]

הקינות שעשיתי עליו[29] וברוך יי' ואם הם הניחוני ולא זכרו לי האלהים [לא]

[25] This is evidently corrupt for תוחלתם, but here again this plur. suffix is obscure and תוחלתנו would fit in better, viz. our hope as expressed in the following verses.

[26] Lev. 26.44, Jer. 17.13, 14.8. [27] Is. 63.9.

[28] =שאמרו החכמים זכרם לברכה. Probably there follows here the well-known Aggadic statement in connection with Is. 63.9 that God takes part in the suffering of Israel (cp. Exod. R. 2.7).

[29] Evidently the writer composed dirges on the death of Abraham, the father of Abū 'Alī Yefet.

יעזוב את יראיו כי אם יכלכלם ברחמיו כי מי אני עתה ומה . . . .
מערב עד ערב לא יחסיר לי הקבֿה מן פת חרבה שאוכל . . . . . .
מזימותיו. אבל לא חפצו בברכה ותרחק מהם . . . .
תחפוץ שאותן הכספים שלך שהם לך עלי ושגר . . . .
אצלך ואל תאחר בזה אדוני כי אני חפץ לצאת אחר[30] . . . .
והנמהר אולי ישיבני יי׳ אל ביתי ואל נחלת אבותי כי . . . . . .
וכל שכן כאב הבת היחידה לא תזוז מלבי . . . .

(righthand margin)

יומם ולילה. ומי היה יתן | והיתה תמות ולא היתה עם | האשה המנאפת. |
ואם תראה לזקן אבו עלי | תין[*30] תתן לו שלום | בחסדך וגם תשאל | לשלום ביתו |
ותכתוב לי שלומם. | ושלום אדוני | הזקן הישר ירבה | לעד אמן.

[30] Evidently our Tobias wanted to leave Jerusalem after the Festivals (as the lacuna seems to indicate) and return to his home (l. 32).

[*30] The reading is doubtful. Better נָתַן.

4.

MOSES B. JOSEPH IBN KASHKĪL

This learned Spanish Jew of the second half of the 11th century deserves to be rescued from the obscurity in which the past has enshrouded him. His was the lot of a wanderer. We find him in Sicily, then in Egypt, again he turns up in al-Mahdiyya (near Ḳairwān) and finally in 'Akko where he resided for some time and where he died. A man of the world, he was employed in a diplomatic capacity by the last Muslim Amīr of Sicily, Aḥmad, styled Ṣamṣām ad-Daula (sword of the realm). He was well versed in Judaism combining with it a thorough knowledge of philosophy and the sciences. And yet he was conservative in his religious views and strenuously opposed the rationalism of a man like the Gaon Samuel b. Ḥofni.

In our modern literature he was for the first and only time mentioned by Harkavy in 1880.[1] In my *Jews in Egypt and in Palestine under the Fāṭimid Caliphs* (II, 239–40) there is published an interesting letter, probably from the Dayyān of Alexandria to 'Alī b. 'Amram, the Ḥaber of the Palestinian congregation in Fusṭāṭ,[2] wherein a Spanish Jew, Moses b. Joseph, who is about

[1] זכרון הגאון רב שמואל בן חפני וספריו, p. 53, bottom: וזה עתה מצאתי בפ' שמואל בערבית כ"י פ"ב (= פטרסבורג) ממחבר לא נודע שמו, כי מצא בעיר עכו מאמר אחד באריכות מחכם ספרדי אהד ששמו ר' משה בן יוסף בן כַּשְׁכִּיל (שחברו בשנת דתתל"ט=1079 בעיר אלמהדיה באפריקא ומת בעכו), אשר בו יתוכח באורך עם בן חפני ועם הרס"ג בענין בעלת אוב, כי לדעתו כל הדברים אמתים בפשיטותם, ויקרא: "יא רבי שמואל בן חפני מי יגלה עפר מעיניך חתי ארפך גמיע דלך" (אי ר' שמואל בן חפני! מי יגלה עפר מעיניך ואודיעך את כל זאת!).

[2] About 'Alī b. 'Amram see Mann, *Jews in Egypt*, II, General Index, s. v.; *Hebrew Union College Annual*, III, 283–4, 285–8. A few more data are added here. Just as 'Alī corresponded with the Nagid Joseph ibn Nagdela of Granada so he did with Joseph's more illustrious father Samuel ibn Nagdela (hence before 1056). T.-S. Loan 178 contains a verbose letter from 'Alī to Samuel who is styled: נגיד הגולה. נשיא עם סגולה ראש הסדר הגדול (hence Samuel had the title ראש הסדר bestowed upon him by the Babylonian academy). 'Alī asks for support and mentions: אשר בכל בכל שבת ומועד בצאת (r. בהוצאת) הספרים (scrolls of the Torah) בהתפללם על אדוננו דניאל הנשיא והגאון יחי לעד (Daniel b.

to visit the capital of Egypt, is introduced. Moses arrived in the company of the ambassador of the Sicilian king, Ṣamṣām ad-Daula, and remained on board ship till the report of his arrival reached the writer of the letter. This was shortly before the New Year. He invited Moses to stay with him over the Festival and was greatly impressed by his guest's versatility in Bible, Talmud and the sciences. The writer urges 'Alī to receive this Moses with due respect, pointing out that he is in need of no support and that he is on the contrary "one of those who give and not of those who take" (from others).[3] As shown in vol. I (pp. 202–04), our epistle probably dates from before 1061. Ṣamṣām ad-Daula was involved in a civil war and was driven out from his capital Palermo. This civil war led to the calling in of the Normans in 1061 with whose coming the Muhammedans ceased to rule for ever in Sicily, although 30 years had to pass until the final conquest was accomplished. The hard pressed king evidently sent an embassy to the Fāṭimid court of Cairo to obtain help and our Moses was a member of this embassy, not in the usual capacity of interpreter for which there was no need in this case since Arabic was the common language for the Muslims in Sicily and in Egypt, but rather to influence some Jewish courtiers in Cairo that the request be granted. The Jews of Sicily were evidently keenly interested in their country remaining under Muhammedan rule for fear of persecution under Christian masters.

Joseph and) אשנה התפלה עליך נגיד הגולה ועל חמודיך ('Azaryah, Gaon of Palestine
החכמים. האלהים ישמע ויענה כל תפילה ותחינה (תפלה ותחנה .r) בעדכם וכן יהי (Elyasaf
רצון. Ms. Antonin, No. 460, vellum, contains a Ketubah, dated 5. Nisan, 1376 Sel. (=1065 C. E.) at Fusṭāṭ, and signed by: ,[נעֿ] בר יוסף [מבורך] and [ישר]אל
יוסף בן אלעזר השופט נעֿ, עלי החבר ביר ע[מר]ם בר אברה[ם].

[3] Lines 3ff.: הקדמתי פני אדירי החבר בשתי שורות הודיע (=להודיע) כבודו כי בא אל ארצנו איש אחד מארץ ספרד עם שלוחו של מלך צמצאם אלדולה מאי צקליה שמו כג״ק מרו״ר משה בר׳ יוסף הספרדי ש״צ ועמד בספינות עד שאצל עלי שמעו. הלכתי ושאלתיהו לרדת מן הספינה לעשות אצלנו יום הזכרון וענה שאלתי וירד עמי ועמד אצלנו חמשה ימים. וחפשתי חדריו והנה הם מלאים כרמון חכמות ובינות והדעת אשר בו מכריעות (מכריעה .r) את כולם ויראת שמים וענוה יתירה. ואם אבקש דבר מהמקרא והמשנה והתלמוד וחכמות חיצונים אמצאהו מכל חכמה מלא. אלהינו ירבה בבני גילו כמותו. וקבעה (ונקבעה .r) בלבי אהבה יתירה ונקשרה ידידותו בנפשי. וציירתיהו שתי (בשתי .r) שורות הללו לפני אדירי החבר המעולה להודיעהו מעלתו מן החכמה ויראת שמים כדי לכבדהו וליקרהו. ואינו צריך למתנת בשר ודם ולא להצטייד בהנאותם והוא מן הנותנים ולא מן הלוקחים.

When our Moses came from Spain to Sicily and what his occupation prior to this diplomatic employment was are entirely unknown. The diplomatic mission must have ended in failure and anyhow Sicily was lost to the Muhammedans. The further whereabouts of our Moses were unknown to me till I had the occasion of consulting the above-mentioned MS., cited by Harkavy, when the identity of our Moses b. Joseph with his namesake Moses b. Joseph ibn Kashkīl was revealed to me, an identity which is strengthened by other data. MS. Firkowicz, 2. Hebrew-Arabic Collection, No. 3362, contains 77 leaves of the commentary on 1. Samuel by Isaac b. Samuel the Spaniard, an important Dayyān in Fusṭāṭ at the end of the 11th and the beginning of the 12th century.[4] Isaac evidently commented on the whole of the Earlier Prophets.[4a] A portion of his commentary on 2. Samuel is found in Brit. Mus. Or. 2388 [5]

[4] About this scholar see Mann, II, General Index, s. v.; *Hebrew Union College Annual*, III, 290. MS. Antonin, No. 856, vellum, contains a Ketubah, dated Sivan 1420 Sel. (1109 C. E.) at Fusṭāṭ. The bridegroom was Ḥalfon b. Tamim and the signatories were:

מנשה הכהן בר יעקב הכהן סׄטׄ   יוסף ביר̇ סעדיה נׄעׄ אברהם בר משה ביר̇ מצליח זׄצׄלׄ
עובדיה ביר̇ אהרן זׄצׄלׄ   אלעזר הלוי
עמרם בר יאיר השופט   בר אברהם סׄטׄ

At the bottom we have the testatum of the Bet Din:

בפנינו אנו בית דין חתמו אלו העדים
אברהם בר שמעיה החבר נׄבׄתׄוׄיׄאׄ נין שׄ גׄ (= שמעיה גאון) נׄעׄ
יצחק בר שמואל הספרדי זׄכׄ לחׄ הׄעׄהׄבׄ

Abraham b. Shema'yah and Isaac b. Samuel are also the signatories of the document of Ab 1427 Sel. (1116 C. E.) published by Gottheil-Worrell, *Fragments from the Cairo Genizah in the Freer Collection*, pp. 2–6. The third signatory there is יפת בר יהודה נׄנׄ and not יפת ברי דוד as printed there. (There are several other corrections to be made in the text there and especially in the translation and notes).

[4a] Cited by Jacob Rosh bē Rabbanan as תפסיר ארבעה̈ אלאול לרבינו יצחק אלכנזי (Mann II, 310, see especially note 2).

[5] See Margoliouth, *JQR*, X, 385–403, and *Cat. of Hebrew and Samaritan MSS. in the British Museum*, I, pp. 125–128, where numerous extracts are given. Margoliouth's identification of the author with the Fusṭāṭ Dayyān is no doubt correct against Steinschneider's later dating (cp. *Arab. Liter.*, p. 247) as will be borne out by the details of Samuel's visit to Palestine and Syria discussed forthwith.

and a comparison with the Firkowicz MS. establishes the identity of both as the work of one and the same author. In both of them there are citations of earlier authorities, the latest in time being Judah ibn Bala'am. In the Firkowicz MS. there is also a reference to the author's commentary on Joshua just as in the Brit. Mus. MS. there are references to the same commentary and also to the one on Judges.[6]

We give here the extract from the Firkowicz MS. bearing on our Moses b. Joseph ibn Kashkīl. In discussing the story of the witch of 'En Dor (1 Sam. c. 28) the author cites various opinions of earlier authorities. The rationalistic explanation of Samuel b. Ḥofni, denying the literalness of the story to the effect that Samuel appeared alive to Saul, has called forth a great deal of criticism on the part of those more conservatively minded. Our passage begins after a lacuna with an account of a third theory on this event (probably citing before the views of Sa'adyah and Samuel b. Ḥofni).[7]

אלת̇אלת̇[8]. הו תעליק ט̇פרת בה ואנא באלשאם פי מדינה̈ עכא והו מנסוב אלי רג̇ל פאצ̇ל מן אהל אנדלס יסמא רבנו משה בן כַּשְׁכִּיל רצ̇י אללה ענה סכן בעכא ומאת בהא. וכאן לה תעלק כביר ואטלאע ואפר פי אלעלום אלפלספיא וכאן מסתצ̇לע פי אלעבראני ואללגה̈. והד̇א נץ מא וג̇דת לה פי ד̇לך.

The treatise of Moses extends over 13 pages in the MS. It begins: קאל משה בן יוסף and discusses the above Biblical story. Samuel b. Ḥofni is severely criticized.

ואמא ר̇ שמואל בן חפני גפר אללה לה פאבטל ג̇מיע עבאראת אלפצל וגלט ג̇מיע אלחכמים זכ̇ לב̇ פי מא פסרוה מן ד̇לך ופי מא ביינוא פי אלמשנה ואלתוספה ואלתלמוד מן צנאעאת

[6] Margol., *l. c.*, 400.

[7] The quire is marked כ̇, the 20th one of the complete MS. of this commentary.

[8] Viz. the third opinion (אלמד̇הב אלת̇אלת̇, mentioned at the end of our passage).

אוב וידעוני וגירהא. וג̇לב פי תגליטהם עשרה̈ אצול[9] כלהא מבניא
עלי אעדול ען אלעבאראת אלתי נקלוה אלאנביא ע̇ אלסל[10]
ואלחכמים זכ̇ לבר̇. וקצד אזאלתהא מן אן תכון קצה̈ שאול ושמואל
הנביא הרמתי עליה אלסלאם מע אשת בעלת אוב כאנת פי עין דור
צחיחה̈ וג̇עלהא קצה̈ לשמואל–בן חפני א ל ד̇ י כ א ן ב ב ג ד א ד
ר א ס מ ת̇ י ב ה̈[11] מע בעלת אוב אסתנבטהא לנפסה. יקול אלהי
ישראל יתברך לעד. אשר לא צויתי ולא דברתי ולא עלתה על
לבי[12]. ואן אכ̇ד̇ת פי אפסאד ג̇מיע כלאמה אחתאג̇ אלי נקלה כלה
ואקאמה̈ אלאדלא עליה עלי אן ליס יחתאג̇ פי הד̇ה אלקצה̈ אלי
שי מנה. ולי אשגאל תמעני ען מת̇ל הד̇א אלפצ̇ול. ולכן אד̇כר
אלאצל אלאול. ואביין ג̇פלתה פיה וצ̇עף נט̇רה פי עלם אלכלאם
אלד̇י הו צנאעתה אלמד̇כור בהא ואד̇א וקף אלנאט̇ר עלי כת̇רה̈
זהקאתה פי אליסיר אסתדל בד̇לך עלי באקי אלאצול אלתסעה̈
ולא אשגל נפסי פי אלרד עליה פי אלתאוילאת אלכ̇ארג̇ה̈ ען מקאצד
אלאנביא ע̇ אס̇ לטולה.

At the end of the treatise we have the following colophon:

תם אלקול בפצ̇ל אלהי ישר̇ יתרומם כרוממותיו וכאן תמאמה
יום אלאת̇נין אלת̇אני עשר מן ניסן שנת ארבעת אלפים ושמונה מאות
ושלשים ותשעה ליצירה באלמהדיה̈.

The commentator Isaac b. Samuel excuses himself for inserting the whole treatise because in his opinion the author spoke excellently and then goes on to quote Judah ibn Bala'am's stricture of Samuel b. Ḥofni.

[9] Cp. also the passage edited by Ginzberg (גנזי שעכטער, I, 304, ll. 31 ff.): וסול רבנו שמואל בן חפני ז"ל ען קצה̈ בעלת אוב והל אחייא אללה שמואל פי ד̇לך אלמקאם ואג̇אב ען ד̇לך בג̇ואב מתסע אנה לם יחייה ואנמא בעלת אוב לבסת עלי שאול וקדם פי אלג̇ואב ע ש ר ה̈ א צ ו ל ובעד ד̇לך נזל עלי גרץ̇ אלסואל וג̇על פיה ג̇ מסאיל וכו'.

[10] =עליהם אלסלאם.

[11] About Samuel's residence in Bagdād as Gaon of Sura, see above, p. 203,

[12] Jer. 19.5.

אלי הנא כלאמה זכ̇ר לבר̇. ולקד אטאל ואסהב לכנה אג̇אד. הד̇א הו אול אלמד̇הב אלת̇אלת̇. וו̇גדת בעד ד̇לך לר̇ יהודה בן בלעם זכ̇ר לבר̇ פי̇ נכת אלארבעה ועשרין אלתי לה יקול אעלם ען שמואל בן חפני הכהן גאון זכ̇ר לבר̇ ינכר אן יכון שמואל אחיי[13] וכו'.

Isaac b. Samuel had a high opinion of our Moses testifying to his great attachment to and ample information of the branches of philosophy and also to his thorough knowledge of Hebrew and philology. He evidently had more information about him than is evident from his treatise on the story of the witch of 'En Dor. As a resident of Fusṭāṭ, Isaac heard about Moses' stay there not so many years previously when he accompanied the ambassador of the Amīr of Sicily. The length of Moses' sojourn in Egypt is so far unknown. It is to be presumed that after some time he returned to Sicily together with the embassy to report to his master. With the coming of the Normans in 1061 Moses evidently left the country for North-Africa. At al-Mahdiya he composed this tract in the spring of 1079. Subsequently he emigrated to the Holy Land becoming a resident of 'Akko where he finished his earthly life at an age and at a date that are unknown.

A discussion of Samuel b. Ḥofni's rationalistic views, attacked by our Moses in one case, would be out of place here and is reserved for another occasion. There only remains to mention a few data bearing on the visit of Isaac b. Samuel to Palestine during which he was also at 'Akko where he found our Moses' treatise. An Egyptian poet gave expression of his regard for Isaac when he started on his trip wishing soon to behold him again.[13a] Then there is a letter from Abū Zubair Ṣedaḳah al-

[13] See this passage from Judah ibn Bala'am's commentary on I Samuel as given by Harkavy, *l. c.*, p. 14, note 20.

[13a] גנזי שעכטער, III, ed. Davidson, p. 301, No. 13 bearing the superscription: וכנת קד ודעת רבנו יצחק הרב הגדול יאריך אלהינו ימיו בטוב ושנותיו בנעימים ענד ספרה אלי אלשאם פקלת הד̇ה אלאביאת. לאט משכה גמליך ערבי, הלא עמך כבר נמשך לבבי. לפירוד רב אשר אחיה בצלו, גבור קדוש כמלאך אל ונביא. הכי לו נכספה נפשי וכלתה, וסר או[ני] ותעה מחשבי. (Davidson's suggestion אזני is inexplicable to me) לעת אזכור דבריו הערבים, אשר לי נחמדו מכל זהבי . . . והנני ליום בואו מצפה, כמו גואל אלי ציון ל[והביא].

Maghribi, living in Jerusalem, to Nahrai b. Nissim of Fusṭāṭ (where he was an important figure in the second half of the 11th century)[14] asking for news of the safe return of R. Isaac the Spaniard (styled רבינו), viz. from his journey to Palestine. The writer no doubt knew him from Fusṭāṭ and met him again in Jerusalem. He held him in great affection.[15] Finally there is Isaac's own reference in his commentary to Kings to his trip as far as Aleppo and to his having received on his journey a letter from R. Barukh, 'the great Rabbi of Aleppo.'[16] This R. Barukh (b. Isaac) is now known as the important spiritual head of the Aleppo Jewry at the time of the First Crusade.[17] These scattered

By the title הרב הגדול he is also addressed in the letter sent to him by Ebyatar Hakkohen, Gaon of Palestine, in Tammuz 1091 C. E. (Mann II, p. 228, cp. I, 192).

[14] About Nahrai b. Nissim cp. Mann, II, General Index, s. v.

[15] Gottheil-Worrell, *l. c.*, p. 126, ll. 12–15: ואן סמע לר' יצחק אלאנדלסי חרסה אללה כֿבר בוצולה יכתב אליי בפצֿלה פאני מעלק אלקלב אליה. אללה יסמעני ענה כֿיר. ויערפני בפצֿלה אן כאן וצל רבינו יחי לעד (viz. our very Isaac; the editors (note 91) have misunderstood the meaning) למצר. אללה תעאלה יגֿעלה פי חיז אלסלאמה.

It is interesting to note that the writer of this letter had among other items copies in his own handwriting of the responsa of Samuel b. Ḥofni on the stories of the witch of 'En Dor, Balaam's ass and the serpent in Paradise, all of which he explained in a rationalistic manner. P. 124, l. 4: והי ה̇ כראריס פיהא מסאיל בכֿט ידי לרבנו שמואל פי אשת בעלת אב (r. אוב) ואלאתון ואלנחש ומסאיל כתֿירה̈ וכראסה̈ פיהא כ[תאב] איכה (see facsimile there) וכו'.

About Samuel b. Ḥofni's views, only vaguely known, on the matter of Balaam's ass and the serpent cp. Harkavy, *l. c.*, p. 12, note 15.

[16] See Steinschneider, *H. B.*, XX, pp. 10–11. Unfortunately he did not give the corresponding passage, found in Abraham b. Solomon's Collectanea on the Prophets (Bodl. 2488), in the original. However this passage is now cited by J. N. Epstein from a MS. Jerusalem as follows (תרביץ, I, No. 4, p. 32): וקאל ר' יצחק הנע ועִוָה (מלכים ב' י"ח ל"ד) קיל אנהא אסמא מואצֿע ואנא למא סאפרת אלי חלב אול וצולי אלי אלשאם ווצלת אלי מערת אלנעמאן כאתבני רבינו ברוך הרב הגדול ז"ל מן חלב יקול לי בלגה̈ אלתלמוד מְטַת בְשוֹרְתָא דמְטָא לֵיה מָר לְאַנְאַנָא דְהֵנַע פעלמת מן קולה אן הֵנַע הי מערת אלנעמאן.

About Ma'arrah an-Nu'mān, a populous city in the 11th and 12th centuries, 2 days' journey to Ḥalab (Aleppo), see Le Strange, *Palestine under the Moslems*, 495–97.

[17] Epstein's identification of R. Barukh with R. Barukh b. Samuel of Southern Italy (מארץ יון) is unacceptable. The leading Rabbi of Aleppo of that time was R. Barukh b. Isaac as numerous other data show (see Mann, התקופה, XXIV, 352–54, and cp. also above, p. 211, note 20).

data supplement each other and establish the fact beyond any doubt that Isaac b. Samuel Ha-Sefaradi, who functioned as Dayyān in Fusṭāṭ at the end of the 11th and the beginning of the 12th century, was the author of the commentaries to Joshua-Kings. This trip to Palestine and Syria occurred before 1098 because in that year Nahrai b. Nissim was no longer alive (see Mann, II, 247). While in 'Akko he found Moses b. Joseph ibn Kashkīl's treatise (the author was then no longer alive) which was discussed above.

5.

THE RABBANITE EXILARCHS IN EGYPT

1. The problem of the establishment of the office of Exilarch in some countries outside Babylon towards the end of the Gaonic period has recently been discussed by me.[1] But as is the case with obscure problems based on scattered and fragmentary Genizah material, new data as they are coming to light supplement and modify views and conclusions that are but of recent date. The new material on the Exilarchate in Babylon has been discussed above (pp. 208 ff.). The Ḳaraite Nesiim of Palestine, who were involved in the affairs of the local Rabbanites as well as those resident in the country of the Nile, will be dealt with in vol. II of our *Texts and Studies*. The Rabbanites in the Holy Land had evidently no Exilarchs, the only exception being Daniel b. ʿAzaryah who, although a member of the Davidic family, figured chiefly as Gaon of the Jerusalem school (1051–62 C. E.). In this section the question of the Exilarchate in Egypt is taken up in connection with some additional material bearing on some of the occupants of this office.

From the Fāṭimid regime (969) to the conquest of the country by the Turks (1517) Egyptian Jewry was strongly organized under the Nagid who was the chief of Rabbanites, Ḳaraites and Samaritans alike, recognized by the government as Raīs al-Yahūd. There was thus no hope for the establishment of an Exilarchate as a political factor in Jewish life as was the case in Babylon.[2] Now and then a member of the Exilarchic family would visit the country, chiefly to collect money for private or communal purposes, but his stay would be of a temporary nature.[3] The document of 1055 C. E., referring to an Exilarch in

[1] משרת ראש הגולה בבבל והסתעפותה בסוף תקופת הגאונים (*Livre d'hommage a la mémoire du Dr. Samuel Poznański*, 1927, Hebrew part, 18–32).

[2] About the erroneous report of R. David b. Zimra, followed by Sambari, that the first Nagid in Egypt was a member of the Exilarchic family of Bagdād see Mann, I, 251f.

[3] Thus David b. Hezekiah visited Palestine and Egypt (ibid. I, 112–13,

Fūsṭāṭ,[4] probably deals with a Ḳaraite Nasi (infra, vol. II). Likewise the Exilarch Ḥisdai, who confirmed the election of a new Nagid, probably was also the Ḳaraite Nasi of this name, though the dating of this document (as suggested by me to refer to the Nagidate of Yehudah b. Sa'adyah in about 1062) is now subject to doubt.[5] The only exceptional case in the 11th century was the attempt of David b. Daniel (b. 'Azaryah) to establish an Exilarchate in Egypt.[6] But he soon came into conflict with the occupant of the Nagidate, the eminent Meborakh b. Sa'adyah, and ultimately Meborakh had the upper hand. David's Exilarchate came to nought but his vicissitudes subsequently are still unknown.

In the second half of the 12th century we hear of an Exilarch Daniel under whose authority documents were issued in Fusṭāṭ (1164–65 C. E.).[7] But this Daniel probably was the contemporary Exilarch of Bagdād whose authority was recognized by the Babylonian community in Fusṭāṭ. The same Exilarch evidently confirmed in 1161 C. E. the appointment of Netanel Hallevi b. Moses as Gaon of the academy of Egypt (see above, pp. 230 ff.). The influence exerted by the Bagdād Exilarch on Egyptian Jewry was, in addition to political reasons, probably due to the fact that since the death of the famous Nagid, Samuel b. Ḥananyah, in 1159 the communal organization was much disrupted owing to internal conflict and the Nagidate did not function fully

II, 122–4, 347) and Joseph b. Hezekiah (II, 145, note 7). About the activities of a bogus Nasi, who visited Egypt, Palestine and Syria, cp. ibid. I, 172–4, II, 205–6.

[4] *Hebrew Union College Annual*, III, 279.

[5] *JQR*, IX, 717–18, and cp. Mann, I, 253–54; משרת ראש הגולה, 31. For further discussion see vol. II of our *Texts and Studies*.

[6] Mann, I, 187ff. David's activity in Fusṭāṭ as Exilarch lasted from 1082–94 C. E. The fragment in *Saadyana* XL, on the basis of which it has been assumed that he also wished to establish a Gaonate in Egypt (Mann, I, 190–91), has now turned out to be a later document and has no bearing on the conflict of David with Ebyatar Gaon (see above, p. 255).

[7] Mann, II, 209; Bodl. 2821.1,l: "fragment, mostly illegible, of a bill of divorce, at the beginning (there) is the name of אדוננו נשיאנו מלכנו דניאל הנשיא הגדול"; Halper, *Descriptive Catalogue of Genizah Fragments in Philadelphia*, 1924, pp. 182–3. The date there should be 1164 and not 1163.

till the time of Abraham Maimuni who assumed this dignity in 1205.[8]

2. It is only in the time of Maimonides that we find in Fusṭāṭ an established Exilarch, viz. Judah b. Joshiah b. Solomon, who countersigned responsa of Maimonides.[9] According to

[8] Cp. Mann, I, 234–36.

[9] Cp. Epstein in *Moses b. Maimon*, II, 53, notes 4–6, who cites a passage from Bodl. 2359, No. 143. This responsum is now printed from another MS. by Isaac Badhab (כי ביצחק: קובץ תורת משה, Jerusalem, 1929, pp. 17–21). Maimonides' responsum is given there as No. 23, and then in No. 24b we have the Nasi's testatum: הדין שחרץ הרב הגדול רבינו ומורינו משה קצין עם רב. ממזרח שמש עד מערב. בן רבינו מימון זצ"ל הוא אמת ואין אדם שיוכל להשיב על דבריו כי נכוחים הם למבין וישרים למוצאי דעת ואין לסמוך על משענת קנה הרצוץ ולהניח דברי אמת ולפנות אל רהבים ושטי כזב. וכתב יהודה הנשיא נשיא גליות כל ישראל. בן יאשיה הנשיא נשיא גליות כל ישראל. בן שלמה הנשיא נשיא כל גליות (r. גליות כל) ישראל נאם (r. נין) הגבר הוקם על נמשיח אלהי ישראל [as in Bodl. ונעים זמירות ישראל זכר צדיקים וקדושים לברכה ושלום.

No. 25 contains a responsum by the Dayyān Solomon b. Zakkai in agreement with Maimonides' decision. לאשר נשאל (r. נשאלה) במושב הנשיאות של אדונינו נשיאנו נשיא כל ישראל אביר התעודה. מלך העדה. רב יהודה. הרב. בעל (r. על) אנשי מזרח ומערב. ירום הודו. ויגדל כבודו. עד ביאת מורה צדק השאלה הנזכרת למעלה והשיב עליה מורינו. אור עינינו. משה הרב הגדול פטיש החזק אור העולם ופלאו. ממזרח שמש עד מבואו. ירבה אלקינו תורתו. ויגדיל וירומם מעלתו. וכתב . . . ואין לדון אחר רבינו יחי לעד הואיל וכל דבריו הם באמת ובתמים אין בהם נפתל ועקש והרוצה ליחנק יתלה באילן גדול ורבינו ממולא אופני מזימות ומעיני החכמה ומי יערוך דברו לנגדו. ומי יתגדר לצידו. כי כל טהרותיו מעשה חכמה היא (sentence evidently corrupt) ומלאת חושב דברי חכמים וחדותם אלקינו יחייהו ויאמצהו אמן נצח סלה. וכתב שלמה בר זכאי ז"ל.

Finally we have in No. 26 the opinion of Peraḥyah b. Joseph on this matter: לאשר בא (r. באה) במושב הנשיאות של אדונינו יהודא נשיא גליות כל ישראל שאלה על ראובן . . . ונזרה עלי הדרת הנשיאות תרומם שאכתוב מה שיראה בדין זה ועשיתי כדי לקיים מאמרו לא מהיותי ראוי לדון ולהורות ואין אני כמכריע ולא מורה לפני רבותי . . .

Solomon b. Zakkai is a signatory of a document in 1188 (Mann, II, 294, bottom), perhaps identical with the scholar of Alexandria mentioned by Sambari (Neubauer, I, 133, top; Mann, II, 317, No. 6). A Peraḥyah b. Joseph signed a responsum together with the Exilarch Solomon b. Jesse who flourished in 1244 (Mann, II, 209). But here a scholar, who lived earlier, is evidently the author of the responsum No. 26. Perhaps he was the Dayyān of Maḥala (Sambari, *l. c.* ר' פרחייא בר' יוסי (r. יוסף) דיין אלמוחלה (r. אלמחלה), Mann, II, 317, bottom).

About the Exilarch Judah see further Sambari (*l. c.*, p. 116): כפי מה שראיתי בספר שאלות ותשובות להרמב"ם ז"ל כתיבת ישן נושן וחתומים בה הרמב"ם ושני ר ב נ י ם ע מ ו מ מ צ ר י ם וכתיבת יד הנשיא מסכים עמהם בזה הסדר: וכתב משה (Maimonides). וקפת על האדֹה אלפמויי (r. אלפתוי) ואנא מואפק עליה צדוק בר ששון. אנא מוואפק עלי גֹמיע דלקי (r. דֹלך) וקאלילא (r. וקאילא) בה שמואל הלוי ברבי סעדיה. הבנתי בזו השאלה והיא

Sambari he was a resident of Damascus. When he settled in Fusṭāṭ is not known. His father Joshiah and grandfather Solomon were presumably Exilarchs in Damascus but so far we have no information of their activities in the capital of Syria. What the nature and the extent of the authority wielded by Judah in Fusṭāṭ and in other Egyptian communities were is also obscure. It is very doubtful whether his office of Nasi was at all recognized by the government. Judah may merely have exerted moral influence by reason of his Davidic descent and his own personality as a scholar. For his living he was probably dependent on the benevolence of individuals and communities. He would occasionally visit various communities and expect to be treated with the honor due to him as a Nasi. Of course he would beforehand announce his arrival in a letter sent to the local Dayyān whose task was to address his congregation and urge upon it to receive the distinguished guest with proper honors.

This mode of procedure is vividly illustrated by the letter given under I. A leader of some Egyptian community in writing to the Nasi Judah apologizes for his delay in replying to the Nasi's epistle wherein he evidently expressed his intention of paying a visit to this congregation. The writer mentions that the distinguished scholar Meir of France[10] had greatly commended

כתורה וכהלכה ואין לזוז ממנה וכתב יאודה הנשיא נשיא גליות כל ישראל בן יאשיהו הנביא זצוק"ל (r. הנשיא).

Cp. also p. 133 where Sambari states that he hailed from Damascus (והיה מתושבי דמשק).

[10] R. Meir (b. Barukh) of France came to Fusṭāṭ still in the lifetime of Maimonides. Cp. his letter to Samuel ibn Tibbon, Ḳobeṣ, II, 27a, column 1, bottom, which passage reads according to Bodl. 859 (Neubauer, *Cat.* I, p. 176, bottom): וכן כשבא אצלנו ר' מאיר החכם היקר שהיה למד אצל ר' אברהם הרב הגדול שבפוסקיירש ואצל ר' יעקב הרב ז"ל ואצל ראב"ע.

Thus our Meir was a student of Abraham b. David of Posquières, of Jacob Tam of Ramerupt and also of Ibn Ezra during his stay in France. He told Maimonides of Judah ibn Tibbon's activities as a translator of grammatical and philosophical works (גם הוא ספר לי אודות החכם הנכבד אביך זצ"ל והודיע לי כל הספרים שהעתיק מספרי הדקדוק ומספרי החכמות). Meir must have stayed some time in Egypt. In Fusṭāṭ he met the Nasi Judah and was very much impressed by him. He travelled about in Egypt and in our letter we find him in the community whence it was despatched. Subsequently he and his brother Joseph set-the Nasi to the local Jewry and that he himself had prepared them for the coming of Judah. All the local scholars are ready to head the delegation that would go forth to meet the visitor. A second letter from the Nasi, sent from Alexandria (where he evidently stayed for some time in connection with his pastoral tour), was the signal for completing all the preparations for his reception. Of the local leaders there is mentioned by name Netanel the physician. In this manner the Nasi Judah would visit the various communities in Egypt and exert what moral and spiritual influence he was capable of, expecting at the same time some monetary assistance.

3. While Judah Nasi made a very good impression upon the French scholar Meir b. Barukh, another French Rabbi, Joseph b. Gershom, while Dayyān in Alexandria had a serious conflict with a visiting Nasi Hodayah b. Jesse who hailed from Damascus.[10a] This irascible Nasi came to Egypt for some purpose (probably to collect money). He visited Fusṭāṭ, where the Nagid Abraham

tled in Jerusalem as leaders of the French Jews who established there a community after the reconquest by Saladin. See Ḥarizi's Taḥkemoni, Maḳama 46 (ed. Lagarde 167, bottom): ומשם (ממצרים) נסעתי אל ירושלים. ונפתחו לי השמים. ואראה מראות אלהים. ויפגעו בי מלאכי אלהים. הם חסידי עליון. הבאים מארץ צרפת לשכון בציון. ובראשם הרב החסיד ר' יוסף בן הרב רבי ברוך. יהי לאלהיו ברוך. ואחיו החכם ר' מאיר. בנר שכלו חשכים מאיר.

In *Catalogue Adler*, p. 59 (No. 4025), there is listed an Arabic work of Maḳamat similar to Ḥarizi's Taḥkemoni and therein Joseph b. Barukh and his brother Meir b. Barukh מארץ אלאפראנג (France) are mentioned. A son of Joseph was perhaps Moses, the author of comments on Num. c. 31 (on the number of the Midianite captives).

These comments are to be found on a long leaf of paper (T.-S., Box C 6) which concludes with the colophon: ולפי מה שפירשנו עולה יפה אני משה בר׳ כבוד החכם מרנא יוסף רו׳ תֿבֿעֿ (=רוחו תנוח בגן עדן) צרפתי. Of these two learned brothers Abraham Maimuni speaks in his מלחמות ה' (in Ḳobeṣ, III, 16c): ושמענו על הרב ר' יוסף ז"ל ואחיו ר' מאיר ז"ל שכשהעתיק ר' יהודה ן' אל חריזי ז"ל גם הוא ספר מורה הנבוכים ללשון הקודש הבינו בו ושמחו בעניניו אע"פ שהיתה העתקתו משובשת ומקולקלת וצוו שלא לגלותו לכל בני מדרשם לאשר לא היו אצלם כדי להבין הסודות והרמזים שבו.

Judah al-Ḥarizi evidently showed them his translation of the Moreh during his stay in Jerusalem.

Cp. also Krauss, *RÉJ*, LXXXII, 346, whose remarks need rectification.

[10a] See the interesting responsa in Ḳobeṣ, I, Nos. 250–51, and especially Simonsen, *Festschrift J. Guttmann*, 217–24. Cp. further Mann I, 175–6, II, 370–73.

Maimuni received him well, and then stayed for a long time in Alexandria.[11] There he came into contact with Joseph b. Gershom and at first thought well of him. But when Joseph was appointed by the Nagid as third Dayyān of the community, the Nasi was bitter about it, probably because he wished to derive an income from the local Jews by reason of his learning and ancestry, and now this French Rabbi, who was easily his equal in learning, would compete with him.[12] In his temper this Nasi denounced all French Jews as heretics because they believed in anthropomorphism and declared a ban on anybody helping a Jew coming from a Christian country.[13] Hodayah was in monetary straits and was ready to bargain for a high price in attending to a communal matter. The Alexandrian Jews had imposed upon themselves a certain obligation by means of a Ḥerem but, as this obligation was impractical and led to the breaking of the Ḥerem, there was an urgent need of revoking this institution in order to

[11] See Abraham Maimuni's responsa (ed. Simonsen, *l. c.*, 221): אבל זה הנשיא הנכבד הנזכר השם יקים סוכת ביתו, ממשפחה גדולה נין מלכים ונכד נביאים שלשלת יחוס (r. יחוסו). והוא בעצמו אדם זקן ויש לו שמועה בארצו ונתגדל בין חכמים. ומפני זה עשיתי בכבודו כפי דרכי ומנהגי בדרך ארץ וגמילות חסדים ואמרתי אולי שיצא מן הארץ הזאת בשלום וכבוד כאשר יצאו רבים ונכבדים לפניו. וכאשר ארכו לו הימים בנא אמון וכו'.

[12] Ibid. p. 222: והאמת שאני יודע שהוא התחיל להקפיד בך ובאנשי צרפת כולם כמה הקפדות ובעבור שאתה צרפתי. כתבו הגיע לי מנא אמון בזה מעת שהסכימו עליך (viz. the Alexandrian Jewry) להיות דיין ומאחר שהיה אוהב אותך ומשבח אותך נהפך לך לאויב בעבור שנקבעת דיין וכו'.

[13] Letter of complaint of Joseph to Abraham Maimuni (*l. c.*, 219, bottom): וקרא אותי ממזר וקלל אבותי החכמים לאחר מיתתם בלשון ארור בן ארור וקרא לכל בני צרפת מינים וכופרים ועושים לבורא גוף דמות וצורה ומספר אחרי מיטתן של תלמידי חכמים והחרים כל מי שיהנה מנכסיו לא רומי ולא צרפתי וכו' (רומי = Rūmi, from Rūm, Byzantium or any Christian country). Hodayah Nasi here demagogically played up to the passion of the Egyptian Jews who were then incensed about the agitation in the Provence against Maimonides' writings led by Solomon b. Abraham of Montpellier. Abraham Maimuni's responsum is dated 13. Adar, 1545 Sel. (1234 C. E., ibid., p. 223, bottom), when the anti-Maimunian conflict was at its height in the Provence. The designation of heretic for one holding an anthropomorphistic view of the Deity is of course based on Maimonides' statement (משנה תורה, ה' תשובה, 3.7): חמשה הן הנקראים מינים . . . והאומר שיש שם רבון אחד אבל שהוא גוף ובעל תמונה.

Well-known is Abraham b. David's comment (השגת הראב"ד): ולמה קרא לזה מין וכמה גדולים וטובים ממנו הלכו בזו המחשבה לפי מה שראו במקראות ויותר ממה שראו בדברי האגדות המשבשות את הדעות.

safeguard the general sanctity of the ban subscribed to by oaths.[14] The Nasi when requested to revoke the Ḥerem asked 10 Dinārs as a fee but was offered only 8. To put a stop to this disgraceful bargaining Joseph b. Gershom rightly denounced any giving of money for a religious exercise of authority to which a scholar was by duty bound.[15] Abraham Maimuni of course approved of the courageous stand taken by the Dayyān Joseph[16] but naturally the relations between Joseph and the Nasi became still more strained.

This whole correspondence sheds a lurid light on the pretensions and the acts of some of the so-called Nesiim who attempted to lord it over the communities by reason of their descent from the revered Davidic family. Abraham Maimuni disposes thoroughly of these pretensions denying the Nesiim any legal rights, except the Exilarchs in Babylon, and yet he throughout treats the Davidic family with great respect.[17] The

[14] Such cases are discussed in the Gaonic responsa (שערי תשובה, Nos. 33, 139 and 339; ed. Musafia, Lyck, No. 41; הלכות פסוקות, No. 116). Cp. Mann, *JQR*, *N. S.*, X, 365.

[15] Joseph's letter (*l. c.*, 220): נם בקש מבני נא אמון עשרה דינרים מצרי כדי להתיר חרם אחר שהחרימו על עצמם והביאו לו מהם שמונה דינרים ונשבע שלא יתיר החרם בפחות מן העשרה. והיו רוב העם עוברים על החרם ושם שמים מתחלל על תביעתו של ממון כדי להתירה (להתירו .r). גם הונד לי כי נשבעו שלא יחזרו ליתן לו מאומה. בשביל זה עמדתי וקנאתי ליוצרי ואמרתי על (=אל) ראשי העדה לאנשים ולנשים כל מי שירצה ליתן לנשיא הנזכר דרך נדבה הן רב הן מעט ברוך יהיה ואני מחזיק לו טובה בדבר, א ך ב ש ב י ל ה ת ר ת ה ח ר ם א ל ת ת נ ו מ א ו מ ה כ י ל א ת מ כ ר ה ד ת ל ע י נ י נ ו. ואחרי שנתמנינו על פי אדוננו נגידנו הרב רבנו אברהם להיות בית דין אני וחברי על הקהל עניני העיר מוטלים עלינו. וחטאתם על צווארינו. ונסיר מכשול ונמנה במנין. ונתיר הענין. וכו'.

[16] Abraham Maimuni's responsum (*l. c.*, p. 224): על ענין התרת החרם לא ידעתי מה טענה בזה. הואיל והתר לדבר מצוה ולהציל העם מן העונש שהיו עוברים על החרם כאשר שמענו מפי אחרים אנשים נאמנים (כדין or הטוב והישר supply) עשיתם. ומכשול מבין ישראל סלקתם. ועל אודות הממון שפסקו לו אם הוא נדבה וצדקה או ארוחה ינתן . . . ואם הממון תַּפְסוּק שכר על התרת החרם אוי לדור שישמע בו בין ישראל שילקח שכר על הדינים וכו'.

[17] See the corresponding responsum in Ḳobeṣ, I, No. 250: שאלה ילמדנו רבינו אם כל הנשיאים הנקראים בשם זה בזמן הזה דינם כמו נשיא הכתוב בתורה או הנזכר בתלמוד או לא. כי לפי עניות דעתי אין הפרש ביניהם לשאר העם כי אם הממונה ראש הגולה. . . תשובה. ודאי אין קרוי במשנה ובתלמוד ובשאר דברי רז"ל נשיא אלא ראש ישיבה הסמוך בארץ ישראל שהוא ראש לסנהדרין או מלך. ולפי שראשי גליות שבבבל במקום מלכים הם עומדים . . . על כן יקרא ראש הגולה נשיא . . . אבל אלו זרע אדוננו דוד ע"ה אין אנו קוראין אותם נשיאים מפני שכולם ראשי גליות או ראשי ישיבות אלא הואיל והם מזרע המלוכה והמלך נשיא נקראו נשיאים כמו שיאמרו היום בלשון הישמעאלית למי שהוא בן שר או ממשפחת השררה אף על פי שלא

further vicissitudes of our Hodayah are obscure. The fragment of a letter to him (given under II) testifies to his appeals for monetary help which he sent out to Egyptian communities. A reference is made to his brother who visited the community from which our epistle has been sent. Probably he acted as a representative for Hodayah. He is probably identical with Solomon Nasi b. Jesse whom we find in Fusṭāṭ in 1244 C. E., about 10 years after the above correspondence concerning the conflict with Joseph b. Gershom (cp. the data collected about this Solomon in Mann, II, 209–10, and see I, 175–6).

4. The document given under III, dated Adar (1)522 Sel. (= 1211 C. E.), and written by Daniel the Babylonian b. Sa'adyah, also refers to a Nasi for whom a collection of money was made. The thought lies near to identify the writer with the critic of Maimonides' Mishneh Torah and Sepher Hammiṣvot. These criticisms were sent to Abraham Maimuni who was constrained to reply to them in defence of his father's views.[18]

נתמנה מימיו על שום מנוי קוראין לו ריי"ס (Raïs) כלומר בשם אביו. וידוע הוא אצל בעלי השכל שרוב אלו הכנויים שמכנים לאדם זהו לשון הבאי ופטומי מילי בעלמא ובקיאי הדעת ממעטים מהם (בהם .r) ושונאים אותם אבל אוהבי הגדולה הרודפים אחר השררה מרבים בהם ואוהבים אותם שהם גדולתם ומעלתם ... אבל מי שהוא מזרע אדוננו דוד ע"ה ואינו לא ראש גולה ולא ראש ישיבה אינו קרוי נשיא אלא כנויי בעלמא לפי שהוא מזרע המלוכה דאנו קוראים לקטנים שבהם נשיאים בייחוסם וכו'.

Referring to his father's comment in his Mishnah commentary (to Bekhorot 4.4) Abraham Maimuni defines the rights of the Babylonian Exilarch: והואיל וראש גולה אין אנו צריכין במנויו להיותו חכם בחכמת התורה אלא לייחוסו בהסכמת אנשי מקומו שהם בני בבל שיסכימו עליו להיות רה"ג . . . ודאי צריכין אנו להתנות במנויו עם יחוסו יראתו ואהבתו לצדק וכניעתו למשפטי התורה ושילך על פי הוראת החכמים ואסור להסכים עליו ולקבל אותו אם לא יהיה כך. ואין מנויו להיות דן משפטי התורה בין ישראל שלא ידינו אלא החכמים במשפטי התורה שנשלמו בהן תנאי הדיינין . . . אבל מנויו להיות במקום מלך זכר למלכות בגלות ולהיותו נותן רשות לדיינים הדנים בין ישראל כדי שיהיו פטורין מן התשלומין אם יטעו בשקול הדעת וכו'.

The Nagid further accepts Joseph's contention that there can be only one Exilarch at a time, viz. the one in Babylon: ולענין שני ראשי גליות בדור אחד לא עלה על דעת אדם דהכי קיימא לן דבר אחר בדור ולא שני דברים בדור (Sanh. 8a) ומפני זה דין נשיא של יחוס שלא נתמנה להיות רה"ג או ראש הישיבה בזמן הסמיכה שנפסקה (supply זה) כמה שנים דינו כשאר בני ישראל ואין שום הפרש ביניהם. ואם הוא חכם דינו ונדויו כשאר החכמים ואם הוא תלמיד הרי הוא כשאר התלמידים ואין לנדויו מעלה כלל מפני הייחוס אלא אם כן יהיה ראש גולה בלבד ויעשה מן הדין של תורה וכו'.

[18] See ברכת אברהם, ed. Goldberg, 1859, and מעשה נסים, ed. Goldberg, 1866.

This identification is not only borne out by the identity of the names and by the time of our letter but also by the same verse (Ps. 27.1) used as the conclusions of the epistle (l. 55) and of the criticisms of Sepher Hammiṣvot (מעשה נסים, p. 104), viz. יי' אורי וישעי. Now Abraham Maimuni relates (in 1235 C. E.) that Daniel, a disciple of the Bagdād Gaon Samuel b. 'Alī, settled in Damascus and from there sent him the above-mentioned criticisms which were duly refuted by him (1213 C. E.). Some years subsequently Joseph ibn 'Aḳnīn informed Abraham Maimuni from Aleppo that Daniel had composed a commentary on Ḳohelet wherein he attacked Maimonides and the earlier Geonim (probably those following the rationalistic method like Sa'adyah and Samuel b. Ḥofni). Joseph in his indignation asked the Nagid to excommunicate Daniel, but Abraham in his gentleness of spirit refused to accede to this request. Abraham Maimuni gives Daniel credit for his correct theories about the unity of God and other dogmas of Judaism, except that he differed from Maimonides about demons and other such smaller matters. He also reports that Daniel was an eloquent preacher in Damascus and that his sermons had an effect in improving the morals of the people. However Joseph ibn 'Aḳnīn and other zealous admirers of Maimonides were not satisfied with this peaceful reply of Maimonides' own son but sent word to the Exilarch of Bagdād, David, who promptly issued the Ḥerem against that worthy scholar. Daniel had to recant his views before the ban was lifted from him. Subsequently he became ill and died in Damascus.[19]

Daniel's criticisms were sent in 1. Adar 1524 Sel. (1213 C. E., cp. מעשה נסים, p. 104) and Abraham's reply was despatched in Ab of the same year (ibid., p. 107, bottom: אב יה (= יהפך) לששון אֿתֿקֿכֿבֿ (r. אֿתֿקֿכֿד) ושלום). Cp. also Poznański, *Babyl. Geonim*, p. 16, note 3.

[19] מלחמות ה' (in Ḳobeṣ, III, 16d): והמעשה שהיה הוא כי תלמיד אחד מתלמידי רבינו שמואל ראש הישיבה שבבבל ז"ל דניאל הבבלי שמו בא מבבל (Bagdād) לדמשק. וחבר קושיות וספקות על הלכות מחבור הצדיק אבא מארי זצ"ל ומספר המצות ושלח אותם אלי וכתבתי לו פירוקים מכמה שנים. ואחר אשר שלחתים לו בשנים אחרות (r. אחדות) בא אלי כתב ושליח מתלמיד נכבד חכם גדול היה תלמיד הצדיק אבא מארי זצ"ל שמו ר' יוסף ב"ר יהודה ב"ר שמעון ז"ל. בצובה היתה ישיבתו אחר פרידתו מרבו הצדיק אבא מארי זצ"ל והוא שחבר אבא מארי זצ"ל בעבורו ספר מורה הנבוכים על שמו. ורב נכבד היה בכל ארץ ישראל (ארם צובה because belonged once to King David) בחכמת התורה ובשאר החכמות. בא אלי השליח מצדו ועמו כתבים כתוב בהם שדניאל הנזכר חבר פירוש לספר קהלת ונכר מדבריו שהרים

Our letter of 1211 evidently came from Damascus where Daniel settled probably some time after the death of his master Samuel b. ‘Alī (died in 1193–4 C. E., above, p. 214). The causes that led to his moving from Bagdād to Damascus are unknown. We have no reason to assume that he had occupied before any official position in the Bagdād school.[20] In Damascus he seems to have enjoyed a reputation as a scholar and preacher. The critical Judah al-Ḥarizi on his visit to this city was impressed by his learning.[21] Besides his writings referred to above Daniel was also the author of a work in Arabic called תקוים which probably was also of a polemical nature (see Pozn., *REJ*, XXXIII, 308–11). This polemical character of his literary activity, focussed especially against the views of Maimonides, ultimately made him a victim of the overzealousness of Joseph ibn ‘Aḳnīn and his associates in Aleppo. Who knows whether the Ḥerem hurled against him and his humble recantation did not undermine his health and led to his death (as one can read between the lines of Abraham Maimuni's account)?

לשונו בצדיק אבא מארי זצ״ל וגם בגאונים הראשונים ז״ל אבל בדבריו הוא כמורה חצי לשונו לתומו לא זכר אדם בשמו. ובקש ממני הרב ר׳ יוסף הנזכר ואחרים עמו שאנדה אותו בשם ואחרימו ולכבוד הצדיק אבא מרי זצ״ל משכתי ידי ממנו והשבתי להם כי אני כבעל דינו והוא כשונא לנו ולא אדין אותו לכבודי ולא לכבוד בית אבא זלה״ה שמא יהא בדבר חלול השם יתברך יותר . . . ועוד שאמונתו בייחוד השם יתברך ושאר עקרי התורה אמונה מתוקנת היתה ולא חלק עליו אלא בענין השדים וכיוצא בהם. ועוד שאני שמעתי עליו שהוא דורש ברבים דברי תורה ומושך לבם ליראה ולעבודה ומחזיר חטאים בעלי תשובה . . . וכשהגיע כתב תשובתי לידם שלחו לראש הגולה אדונינו דוד יצ״ו ונדה אותו ונשאר בנדויו עד שחזר בתשובה והדר ביה מההיא דעתא ונשתטח לפניהם והתירו לו ואחר כך חלה וסגר יומו בדמשק. זהו הענין ומעשה שהיה כן היה:

The Exilarch David may have been the one of Mosul whom Ḥarizi saw on his visit to this city in about 1216 (Taḥkemoni, Maḳama 46, ed. Lagarde, p. 176): ושם ראיתי אדוננו דויד ראש הגולה היהודיה. ובן אחותו הודיה. אין להם שני בבני זמניהם. ואין מי יעשה כמעשיהם. ותקצר לשוני לספר קצת מדותיהם (cp. also Mann, משרת רה״ג, *l. c.*, 23–24). But more likely the Exilarch of Bagdād is meant (see above, p. 223 f.).

[20] Poznański (*Babylon. Geon.*, 16–17) rightly rejects the identification of our Daniel with the presiding officer of the so-called third academy in Bagdād cited by Benjamin of Tudela (cp. about these so-called schools above, p. 215 ff.).

[21] Taḥkemoni, Maḳama 46 (in MS. Günzburg cited by Senior Sachs, מעשה נסים, XVI, and in MS. British Mus. cited by Kaminka in his ed. of Taḥkemoni, p. 509): ושם (בדמשק) ראיתי החכם הגדול דניאל הבבלי הוא מעין המתגבר ובחכמתו ארזים משבר. וחילים יגבר.

To return now to the subject matter of our letter. Where the epistle commences (it is defective at the top) there is an allusion to a Nasi who was stranded in a certain community. It is doubtful whether the Nasi Joshiah b. Jesse is meant here because he seems to have been a regular resident of Damascus and was held in much respect as we may gather from Ḥarizi's description of him.[22] But perhaps his needs caused him to travel about, or it may be that even in Damascus his position was not so splendid as Ḥarizi's poetic effusion would seem to make it. The addressee had some influence in the city where the Nasi stayed (ll. 5–6). There is a reference to a certain physician (al-Ḥakīm, l. 12). Daniel sends greetings to several people in Fusṭāṭ which seems to indicate that he visited this community. Perhaps our very letter is sent not from Damascus but from some place in Egypt. Only in 1213 we find Daniel settled in Damascus. However in Abraham Maimuni's account there is no reference at all to Daniel's stay in Fusṭāṭ or in any other Egyptian locality.

Of the persons mentioned in our letter only some could be identified with some likelihood but these are sufficient to show that they were living in Fusṭāṭ. The letter also contains some details about the copying of certain works which was done for Daniel.

I.

[T.-S. Loan 20, 2 paper leaves.]

Address (fol. 2, verso)

אל שער יקרת צפירת תפארת מרינו ורבנו אדונינו נשיאנו נשיא
גליות כל יש[1] אביר התעודה. מלך העדה. רבנו יהוד[2] הנשיא הרב. על
כל בני מזרח ומערב. אשר המשרה על שכמו לבד. היקר הנכבד.

[22] Ibid. (ed. Lagarde, 168): ושם הנשיא ר' יאשיה בן ישי נשיא גליות כל ישראל כתר הנכבדים. ובעל המעשים הנחמדים. אוסף המדות הטובות. ובכל תבל מדובר בו נכבדות.

Still more eulogies Ḥarizi heaped upon him especially in Maḳama 1 forming a sort of dedication of the work (pp. 13–15).

[1] =ישראל. [2] =יהודה.

בר מרינו ורבינו יאשיהו נשיא גליות כל יש מנוחתו כבוד נין ידידיה[3] היושב על כסא יי׳ למלך ניכד הגבר הוקם על משיח אלהי יעקׄ ונעים זמירות ישׄ[4] ינשא אלהים נשיאותו ותיכון לעד משרתו אמן.

(fol. 1, recto)

על פי נתעכבתי[5] והתאחרתי מלהשיב. ותדמה כי אינני על דבריך מקשיב. חלילה לי׳

חלילה מחדול עמך מלעזוב[6]. ותומת שררותך אעזב. אם לזרע דויד אכזב[7].

ועתה כבואך אל עמי. יודיעוך נאמי[8]. כי בכל עת ובכל שעה הייתי מחבה

מפלליך[9]. ומסדר יופי מפעליך. אשר שמעתי. והעמדתי עדים להאמין

אמרתי[10]. ר׳ מאיר הרב הצרפתי. שׄצׄ כי הוא אשר נטע בלבי גן אהבתיך

והשקהו. עד אשר הרוהו. והוא המאריך לשון בשבחיך כפי תורתו המרובה.

וכפי דעתו הנכונה הרחבה. וכפי ענותו ויראתו אשר לא קצובה. ולאשר

מדבר על הדרתו תועה. יפגיעהו רעה. ודבר אליו קשה ונצח בלשונו

תצחו[11] ירבה אלהי כמותו בחכמׄ[12] ויגדל גבולו בתלמידים ובראותי מה הוא

[3] Viz. Solomon one of whose names was also Yedidyah (cp. 2 Sam. 12.24–25 and Ḳohel. R. 1.2). Here Judah's grandfather was actually a Solomon.

[4] David (cp. 2 Sam. 23.1). [5] =אף על פי שנתעכבתי.

[6] Cp. Exod. 23.5. [7] Cp. Ps. 89.36.

[8] When you come to my people (viz. my congregation), they will acquaint you with my speech (statements about you).

[9] I caused your decisions to be liked.

[10] אֲמַרְתִּי. [11] Read ינצח. [12] =בחכמים.

עושה תמיד לעם למרחוק נשאתי דעי. וחספתי זרועי. להודיע לקהל
מה הראוי לחלוק לך מן הכבוד ולנטות אחריך. לעבור ולצקת את עמודיך
ולחזק את ידיך. בעבור חכמתך וגדולתך ובעבור אבותיך הטהורים קדושים
אשר בארץ המה וג׳[13] אשר בזכותם אנו חיים בין לבאים. העוברים ובאים.

[Continues to expatiate on the importance of the Davidic family.]

כזה וכזה דברתי. (bottom line)

(fol. 1, verso)

וכפי כוחי חיברתי. על[14] אשר החזרתי. את כל הקהל לב אחד. לנטות אחריך ולהתאחד.
ובכל יום ויום שואלין מני מתי יבוא. ונצא לקראת רכבו. ובפני ר׳ מאיר שׂצ׳ שאלו מני
עצה להבין חובי[15]. ולדעת מה יש את לבי. מה׳[16] לאענם אני אצא לקראתו. ואכבדהו
כראוי לאבותיו ולתורתו. ואם תשמעו מני ככה תעשו כולכם ותהיו בו שמחים
וששים. וכל חפציו עושים. ויענו זקניהם ויאמרו עצתך לא ניפרע. וכל אשר
דברת נעשה ונשמע. וכבר הסכמנו כולנו החכמ׳ והדיינין והתלמידים ושאר הקהל
הברוכים לצאת לקראתך ולכבדך כפי כוחינו. ונשים ביי׳ מבטחינו. ובעת אשר

[13] =וגומר, Ps. 16.3.

[14] Read עד.

[15] =חֻבִּי (cp. Job 31.33).

[16] =מהרתי. For the incorrect form לאענם read לענותם.

הגיע אלי הכתב השני מנא אמון[17] קיבלתי אותו במהללי. ועגדתיהו עטרות לי. ויהי
דברו לי מדבש ערב. ושמחתי בו כמוצא שלל רב. ומיד קראתי מכתבך אל ריעינו
ומיודעינו. ר׳ נתנאל צמיד זרועינו. הרופא הגדול. המעוז המגדול. והודעתי
ענייניו. וביארתי כל מצפוניו. והרבתי על הדברים כהנה וכהנה עד אשר הפכתי
לבו לאהבתך ויתן יד לעבדך. והנה כתבו יגיע אליך. ואומר אליו ואל קצת הזקנים
אין ראוי להיות נתארח אצל אחד מהעם. כי הזהב לא יועם[18]. אבל ראוי
שתהיה לו מנוחה. וחצר פתוחה. לדורשו בה כל זקני המוני. וכל מבקשי יי׳.
ולא נחנו ולא שקטנו. עד אשר היכינו. חצר במקהלם. קרובה לבתי כנסיות אלהים
יציב גבולם. כל זה היה בליל ששי בעת שהגיע הכתב וממחרת ביום השבת
קיבצתי כל הזקנים והדיינים ורוב הקהל ודרשתי להם. והודעתים מה ראוי לחלוק
לזרעו של דויד ומה משפט כל חולק עליהם. והרביתי הדברים והארכתי. וראיות
ערכתי. ואמרתי להם הנה שם אותי פה אליכם. אם יש את נפשכם. לכבדו כראוי לו
אני אכתוב לו וישיב דבריכם. ואם לא הוא ישוב לדרכו ויענו כולם
ויאמרו חלילה חלילה לא ניראה ריקם וכפי כוחנו נוביא[19] לו שי. חלק לנו בדוד ונחלה

[17] Alexandria. [18] Cp. Lam. 4.1. [19] Read נוביל.

לנו בבן יישי. והנה כולם מצפים מתי ידרוך הכוכב בארזינו[20].
וישגיח מחלונינו.
ויציץ מחרכנו. ובקרבך אל המדינה תשלח שלוח להודיענו. עד
אשר נצא להקביל
פני הדרתך. אלהים ייטיב אחריתך מראשיתך. ותעמוד תמיד
על [מ]כו[נ]נך. ושלומך

(fol. 2, recto)

ושלום התלמיד היקר הנכבד ר׳ שמואל ושלום
כל הנלוים אליו ירבה ויגדל מעלה מעלה.

(A marginal scribble reads here אל יי׳ מן הגלגל (cp. Judges 2.1) which has no connection whatever with the letter.)

II.

[T.-S. 20.15.]

The letter after much verbiage gives the name of the addressee:

הודיה ה[נשי]א נשיא גליות כל ישראל ... בר כ̇ב̇ק̇ מ̇ו̇ר̇ ישי נשיא גליות כל ישראל בגן עדן עם אבותיו המלכים הקדושים יהי חבלו ...

The writer after fulsome flattery proceeds to state:

קול בשורה נשמע בארצינו. כי זה הרוכב[20a] משקיף עלינו. מגיה חשכינו. ויגל לבינו. וכהגיע אגרותיו החטובים. היקרים הטובים ... ואל אלהים הוא יודע כי מעת הכתבים הגיעו ולקטתי מפניניו. וידעתי סוף ענינו. שמתי מגמתינו להשלים חפצו. ולכבוש לפי[20b] י׳ ארצו. ולהודיע לקהל מה ראוי לחלוק לך מן הכבוד ... ולחזק את ידיך ... וכשהגיע אחיך אדונינו השר הגדול ... חזק ידינו. והגביר כחנו. והאמינו העם לדברינו. והסכימו כל הקהל לב אחד לנטות

[20] Read בארצינו.

[20a] Read הכרוב.

[20b] Read לפני יי׳, cp. Num. 32.22.

אחריך ולהתאחד וישמעו אלינו ויאמרו לא נראה ריקם וכפי כוחנו נוביל שי וחלק לנו בדוד ונחלה [בב]ן ישי. . . וכפי השגת ידינו עשינו. לא כפי מעלת נסיכנו. וכו׳

III.

[T.-S. 24.41, paper, top torn; verso contains a Midrashic passage.]

(Recto)

. . . . רים עד . . . . לרפאת[*20] בחמת . . . . . . [ל]כבוד הנשיא שישנו אצלם ונשאר בדד יושב כל אילו הימים ואין מי שפונה אליו ואפ̇י[21] כמה שהיו עושין בתחלה לא עשו שכל מה[22] שהיה עושה לא היה עושה אלא מתוך יראתו ממך שאתה מבין עניניהם ואתה יוד[ע ש]אלף [ת]נאין עם סוחר אחד לא יספיקו ולפי שיש מבטלין לא נתקיימו דברו וכן שנו[23] אותן המאתים שנדרו לדמי בית המדרש אמ̇[24] שליחיהן שאין בידו[*20] רשות[*20] . . . אצל הרב ידו[*20] לכך[*20] . . . את דבריו ויאמר שאינו רשאי לשנות ואני אומר ודא[ני] אין בידו רשות לזכות בדבר זכות אלא הקב״ה הוא מזכה מי שהוא חפץ . . . לא בא אלחכים[24a] . . . ם ואפ̇י אם יצא[*20] אני יודע שהם מתעסקין בנשיא י[היה][24b] להם פנאי שיעשו טובה ואני אומר מתוך שהתריסו בדבר ולא רצו לעשות כמה שעשו אחרים טוב הוא להניחם ושלא לאמר להם בדבר שמא אינן [רוצ]ין ואע״פ[25]

*20 The reading is doubtful.

21 =ואפילו.

22 Read מי.

23 שָׁנּוּ, changed.

24 =אמר. For שליחיהן. read שליחם.

24a The physician (al-Ḥakīm).

24b Read perhaps [ו]אין.

25 =ואף על פי.

שחוב הצבור . . . . הוא שיגבה . . . . שהגיע זמן השקלים וימנו הכל מי שנתן ומי שלא נתן מתחלה והוא דוחה את הדברים ואומ׳[26] שאילו אומרים ואינן עושין ומתוך שהיה זה האיש[27] במדינה לא יכולתי להתעסק בדבר יותר שלא יעלה על דעתו שאני מבטל על ידו ואודיע להדרתו שדברתי עמו בשביל עשרים הכסף שאמ׳ לי כבודו ואמ׳ אני לא אמרתי אלא כדי ליקח אותם מן הרופה[28] ועתה איני יכול מתוך שנתמעטה יותר מדאי ואותו המועט אנחנו צריכין לו בשביל כבוד הנשיא ומחלה אני פני הדרתו להוביל שלומותי להדרת אדוני הרב רבנו מאיר[29] מאיר עיני הגולה יגדל כבודו שכל רגע ורגע אני מתאנח על פרידתו . . . . הדרתו ושלום בנו הנחמד יגדל ושלום החכם הנהדר רב׳ חננאל[30] ור׳ שלמה אחיו הם ובניהם יגדל לעד ושלום הרב רב׳ אברהם[31] תשגה [אחרי]תו והעניו החכם המפואר ר׳ יוסף ובנו ירבה לנצח ושלום החכם העניו רב׳ יצחק הנעים ירבה לעד ושלום החכם ר׳ שמריה ושלום החכם ר׳ דויד והחכם ר׳ יחזקאל יגדל לעד ושלום אדוני הרב ר׳ יחיאל החכם המרובה[32] ובנו יבורכו לעד ושלום כלל החכמים וכלל התלמידים אשר לעבודת יוצרם נצמדים. ובחסדיו נסעדים. ומתורת פיו לא נפרדים. שמלפניו

[26] =ואומר.

[27] Is this person the physician mentioned in I. 12?

[28] The reading is doubtful. Probably read הקופה, the charity box of the community.

[29] Evidently Meir b. Barukh of France, who was in Egypt some time prior to his settling in Jerusalem.

[30] Perhaps the recipient of the letter from Mishael b. 'Uzziel (edited by Horovitz, *Z.f.H.B.*, IV, 155–58, cp. Pozn., ibid. p. 186).

[31] Perhaps Abraham Maimuni is meant although he is not called by his title of Nagid.

[32] Evidently Yeḥiel b. Elyaḳim, a respected contemporary Dayyān in Fusṭāṭ (see Mann, I, 239–41; II, 301ff.; *Hebrew Union College Annual*, III, 298).

יהיו שלומותיהם תמידים.   ותלמיד אחד משלנו יש אצלכם ושמו ר׳ יפת תשא שלומותיו אליו ובחסדיך תשא שלומותי אל השר הנכבד ר׳ אליה השם יהיה בעזרו וכן תשא שלומותי אל הדרת החכם המכובד רב׳ כלב הכהן וכן אל השר ר׳ סעדיה בן הימיני ולבניו ור׳ אליה שמאלכסנדריה ישא שלום ממני. ועדיין לא הגיד לי אדוני על עניני הכתיבה שום דבר אם כתבו או לא כתבו ומה שהם כותבין יכתבו בכל דף ודף כפי התנאי שהתנה עמהם ואין צורך לרבות את השיטות ולקחת כפי חשבון אלא על פי התנאי יהיו השטות בלא תוספת ולא גרעון וכבר הגדתי להדרתו שלקחתי מיד שושן ח׳ כספים חוץ מאותן ה׳ שלקח הוא ואותו ר׳ אלעזר התלמיד בעל הכספים שלח לי שהרשה את אדוני הרב כדי לתבוע אותו בשאר הכספים ומה שנשתייר בידו שלשים ושנים כסף כשיתבענו תקח את השלשים מידו עם השלשים שעמך ותגיד לי כמה נכתב עד עתה ואם יש לכבודך שום צווי שתצוה לעבדך לעשותו אל תאחר שאני שלם בעבודתך השם ירבה כבודך ויעזרך ויסעדך ויעודדך ויהיה לך צנה וסוחרה וירבה שלומך לנצח וכן יהי רצון אדר תקכ״ב יי׳ אורי ויש[33] עבד אהבתו דניאל הבבלי ביר׳ סעדיה זצ״ל

(margin, righthand corner)

ובעל הבית הכהן ר׳ יהודה משתחוה להדרת אדוני ובנו מנשק ידיו ומנשק יד כלל הרבנים והחכמים ומשתחוה להם.

[33] Ps. 27.1.

6.

ANAṬOLI B. JOSEPH, A CONTEMPORARY OF MAIMONIDES.

A contemporary of Maimonides in Egypt was Anaṭoli b. Joseph, evidently a scholar from Lunel who settled in Alexandria where he became Dayyān. He corresponded with Maimonides and the latter appreciated his residence in Egypt as it meant an increase of scholarship and spiritual influence in the country of the Nile. Anaṭoli kept up a correspondence with acquaintances in Sicily (he probably visited the country on his trip from Lunel to Alexandria) and thus received a legal question from the community of Siracusa concerning which he asked the opinion of Maimonides. Abraham Maimuni also was on friendly terms with this Dayyān of Alexandria.[1]

Anaṭoli is also known as a liturgical writer. Indeed he seems to have been a poet and a stylist. MS. Firkowicz, 2. Hebrew Collection No. 72[1], contains 29 leaves of a collection of letters and poems most of which are by or to our Anaṭoli. One item has the heading: ובעתֿ ר' שמואל הנפוסי לר' אנטולי ז"ל למא ספר אלי מ ס י נ י הדה אלאביאת. Thus Samuel of the district of Nafūsa (in Tripolis)[2] sent him a poem when the former travelled to מסיני.[3] Evidently Samuel visited Alexandria and made the acquaintance of Anaṭoli. Another item has the heading: ולה (viz. Anaṭoli) איצֿא בעתֿ אלי אלמעלם סנבאטי נעֿ. This scholar of

[1] Cp. Mann, I, 247–8; II, 324–26; *Hebrew Union College Annual*, III, 298. Cp. also Halper, התקופה, XVIII, 209, for some data on Anaṭoli cited from MS. Simonsen containing a collection of Maimonides' responsa.

[2] Jebel Nafūsa (הר נפוסה) had an extensive Jewish population since early times. See the data collected by Poznański, *REJ*, LXV, 42, and J. N. Epstein, *M.G.W.J.*, LX, 112–13.

[3] The nearest identification of this place would of course be Messina in Sicily. However a colophon in Bodl. 286, dated Iyyar 1452 C. E., mentions a city מסין in Jebel Nafūsa (בעיר מיסין שבהרי נפוסה) and hence it is more likely that our Samuel Nafūsi travelled to this place which may have been his home town.

Sunbāṭ[4] (in Egypt) is styled in the poem מרנו ורבנו שבתי ראש מקהלות ישראל. There is also to be found in the collection a letter from Samuel b. הרב רבנא מנחם זצ"ל.[5] A third heading reads: וכתב ר' אנטולי אלי שכך כאטבה בשער פאתר, thus this person addressed Anaṭoli by a poem appropriated from another poet (viz. the poem was not this person's own composition) and Anaṭoli wrote to him accordingly. There are several compositions exchanged between a scholar Elyaḳim and Anaṭoli. The former travelled to Palermo, the capital of Sicily, from which city he sent a poem to Anaṭoli as the following heading shows: ממא בעת אלחכם ר' אליקים אלי ר' אנטולי ז"ל ענד מגיה אלי פ ל י ר נ ו[6] הדה אלאביאת.

MS. Firkowicz, 2. Hebrew Collection No. 72[3], also seems to be a part of the Diwān of Anaṭoli. One poem is addressed to אלרייס אלגליל רב יעקב הלוי אלמערוף בן אלרביב[7]. There are several pieces of stylistic letters exchanged between Anaṭoli and Samuel of Nafūsa. One piece has the heading וכתב אליה רבי שמואל אלנפוסי חין דכולה ללמדינה, thus Samuel wrote to Anaṭoli when he (the latter) entered the city (perhaps Alexandria).[8] Anaṭoli's reply is indicated by the heading: פאגאבה אנטולי בהדא אלאביאת.

Finally MS. Firkowicz, 2. Hebrew Collection No. 105[8], contains 2 leaves of stylistic letters which seemingly belong to Anaṭoli's Diwān. One letter has the heading: ולמא נפטר אלרב רבינו דוד הלבן ז"ל במצרים ארסל אלי ר' חייא אלי דמשק הדא אלכתאב ליעלומה בדלך ל... יעמל לה השכבה. R. David is probably one of the French scholars who left France to settle in Palestine. They visited Cairo where the Nagid Abraham Maimuni, a younger contemporary of Anaṭoli, received them cordially.[9] Whether David died so soon after his arrival in

[4] About this city see Mann, II, General Index, s. v.

[5] This Menaḥem is perhaps the Dayyān of Fusṭāṭ in the time of Abraham Maimuni. Ḥarizi greatly eulogized him (Taḥkemoni, ed. Kaminka, pp. 352 and 395; cp. also Mann, I, 247, note 1).

[6] For פלירמו which is the usual spelling.

[7] About the family name al-Rabīb cp. Steinschneider, *JQR*, XI, 609, No. 690.

[8] But it may refer to Samuel Nafūsi when he arrived at מסין (see note 3). Thus Samuel sent him as a parting gift a poem when he started his journey home and then wrote to him on his arrival.

[9] Cp. the passage in Abraham's מלחמות ה' (Ḳobeṣ, III, 16c): וכשהגיעו חכמי צרפת

Egypt or whether he left for Palestine and also visited Damascus, where he met the local scholar R. Ḥiyya, and only during a subsequent visit to Egypt passed away is unknown. Anyhow R. Ḥiyya knew of him and Anaṭoli informed R. Ḥiyya of the sad news so that he should hold a memorial service (השכבה)[10] for the departed scholar.

אל הארץ הזאת הרב הגדול ר' יוסף ז"ל... ור' דוד הרב הנכבד וחכמים אחרים ז"ל כמה וכמה ראינו שהיו בעלי חכמה וסברא ובינה ויראה ושמחנו בהם ושמחו בנו ועשינו בכבודם כפי חובתנו.

Whether this David 'the White' is identical with one of the Tosafists (see Zunz, *Zur Gesch. u. Liter.*, p. 48) cannot be ascertained. The nickname 'the White' was also held by the Tosafist Isaac the brother of Petaḥyah of Ratisbon (סבוב, beginning: אחיו של רבינו יצחק הלבן בעל התוספות, and also end; cp. ed. Grünhut, p. 37, note 3). Indeed we have a הר' דוד בר' אברהם הלבן בן ר' יהודה מקוצי, the author of the philosophico-Ḳabbalistic work ס' מסורת הברית (see Gross, *Gallia Judaica*, 559), but he lived, according to Gross, in the second half of the 13th century at the earliest.

[10] The term השכבה, Aram. אשכבתא, is already to be found in a responsum of R. Naṭronai, Gaon of Sura (שערי צדק, 20b, No. 12): וכך מנהג ההספד נשיא שנפטר וכן שונאי חכמים (שונאיהם של ישראל, cp. evidently a euphemism) בין גדולים ובין קטנים אם נפטר בניסן או באייר או בסיון או בתמוז או באב או באלול מספידין אותו בישיבה שבאלול (viz. at the Kallah meeting) ולישיבה (r. ובישיבה) של אדר ושם הספד (ההספד .r) השני [נקרא] אשכבתא ושוב אין רשות להזכירו לישיבה (r. בישיבה) אחרת של אילול שעבר עליו יותר משנה... ואם נפטר בניסן ויש בשנה הבאה אדר ואדר מספידין אותו ומשכבין (r. ומשכיבין) אותו לישיבה (r. בישיבה) של אלול.

We learn thus that there were 2 kinds of memorial services for prominent people, the first one was called הספד whereas the second one, still within the year of the demise, was called השכבה, viz., as the Hiph'il noun and verb indicate, to pray that the dead should rest in his grave in peace (cp. the phrase ינוח על משכבו taken from Is. 57.2). Cp. further the Gaonic responsum (no doubt by Hai Gaon) cited by Naḥmanides (תורת האדם, ed. Warsaw 1876, 22a, top): לגאון. והספד נוהגים בישיבה להספיד לפני המטה לשאר תלמידים, אבל חכם ואלוף וגאון מכניסין אותו לבית המדרש... ולזמן ישיבה (viz. at the Kallah meeting) סופדין אותו כל ישראל הקרובים והרחוקים לפי כבודו בחדש אדר ואלול... ולתכלית שנים עשר חדש משכיבים אותו ומבקרין אותו.

(The conclusion of this responsum, as cited by Meiri (see Schorr, החלוץ, VI, 66, note 1, end), reads: ולתכלית חודש משכיבים אותו בביה"כ בישיבה. No doubt before חודש the number י"ב should be inserted).

Cp. further the letter from 'Alī b. 'Amram of Fusṭāṭ to Joseph ibn Nagdela of Granada informing him of the memorial services held in Fusṭāṭ for his departed father Samuel ibn Nagdela (Mann, *Hebrew Union College Annual*, III, 287): פי וצול אלשמועה הרעה באסיפת האדון נגיד ישראל נוחו עדן פי השכבות עמלתהא לה פי גמע ספדנים ומקוננים.

In Palestine the term for השכבה seems to have been מנוחה (see above, p. 321, note 42b).

The above data testify to the scholarly and literary connections of our worthy Dayyān of Alexandria and of his interest in poetry and stylistic writing. A fuller appreciation of him will only be obtained when his literary remains will be made available in extenso.

7.

THE EGYPTIAN NEGIDIM OF THE FAMILY OF MOSES MAIMONIDES

Maimonides himself apparently never occupied the office of Nagid.[1] When he arrived in Egypt (in 1165) and for several years afterwards in the reign of Saladin Egyptian Jewry was headed by a Nagid, called Sar Shalom and Zuṭṭa, who was very unpopular.[2] Maimonides soon had occasion to come into conflict with this Nagid as Abraham Maimuni reports.[3] As a Spanish Jew used to a uniform liturgy, based on 'Amram Gaon's Siddur, Maimonides objected in Fusṭāṭ to the many differences in the rituals of the synagogues, especially those of the Palestinian and the Babylonian communities. He wished to bring about uniformity but he was stopped in this design by the Nagid Sar Shalom. In this respect the action of this Nagid was probably justified because it paid due consideration to old established traditions going back to several centuries. The growth of these two communities, recruited from immigrants from Babylon and Palestine respectively, evidently started soon after the founding of Fusṭāṭ as the capital of Muhammedan Egypt (641 C. E.). But Maimonides, as an outsider, had no proper regard for this

[1] Cp. Mann, I, 242, note 2, 262.

[2] Ibid., 234–36.

[3] Cp. the interesting passage from Abraham Maimuni's Kifāya (published by Dr. Büchler, *JQR*, V, 421): ועינינו ראו ולא זר פי הדׄה אלבלד אלתי נחן פיהא מדינהׄ מצר כניסתאן משהורתאן אחדאהמא תערף באלעראקיין אלמנהג פיהא פי אלצלאהׄ ואלקראהׄ פי ספר תורה כמנהג בני הגלות כולם ותׄאניתהמא תערף באלשאמיין כאן להא מנהג מכׄאלפא לכל. אחד יקרי פי הדׄה פי ספר תורה פרשה (Annual Cycle) ופי הדׄה סדר (Triennial Cycle) ויקף פי הדׄה פי אלקדושה ויגלס פי הדׄה פי אלקדושה וגיר דׄלך מן אלאכׄתלאף פי גׄואיאת כתׄירהׄ וכאן אבא מארי זצ״ל ינכר דׄלך ושר אלאשראר וגירה אקצׄי לה אלסכות. וגירה מן תלמידי חכמים יציח ויסתגית (ויסתגני .r) מן דׄלך ואין לאל ידם.

The whole tone shows that Maimonides like his son disliked the Palestinian ritual because the rest of the Diaspora followed the Babylonian one.

שר אלאשראר, the evil of all evil, is a pun on the official title of the Nagid שר השרים (cp. Kaufmann, *M.G.W.J.*, XLI, 462)

historical development and his policy of uniformity would have probably led to a great deal of local conflict about customs (מנהגים)—a conflict that certainly would not have been worth while.[4] And indeed his son Abraham, although Nagid, could only re-echo his father's disapproval but took no steps to abolish these differences by ordering the Palestinian synagogue to give up its time-honored ritual and simply adopt the Babylonian one. He must have realized that such a procedure would have led to much friction. Thus in 1211 the ritual of the Palestinian synagogue was formally reconfirmed, the only compromise with the Babylonian custom being that the Pentateuch was recited also in the annual cycle from ordinary copies whereas the official reading from the Scroll continued in the triennial cycle.[5]

The Nagid Zuṭṭa (Sar Shalom), though right in the above case, was otherwise much hated for his regime. Four years after Zuṭṭa's occupancy of the Nagidate under Saladin (either from 1169–73 or more likely from 1171–75) Maimonides intervened with the authorities against the abuses of the Nagid whose final overthrow was brought about later through the exertion of Maimonides' colleague on the Bet-Din of Fusṭāṭ, Isaac b. Sason. With the removal of Zuṭṭa the office of Nagid was apparently vacant for several years. Nowhere is Maimonides himself called by the official title of שר השרים or נגיד הנגידים in spite of all the eulogies that were usually heaped upon him.[6] He wielded great influence on Egyptian Jewry by reason of his scholarly eminence and as a court-physician and he may have held some such office in Fusṭāṭ as ראש הקהלות and hence he is referred to as al-Raīs (ראש הראשים, הראש, אלרייס).[7] But in the numerous Genizah

[4] Kaufmann in his discussion of this episode (*l. c.*, 461–3) is not fair to the much-maligned Nagid.

[5] Cp. Mann, I, 221–3, *Hebrew Union College Annual*, II, 283, IV, 288–9.

[6] See the many eulogies, e. g., in the fragment published by Friedlaender, *H. Cohen-Festschrift*, 261.

[7] About the title ראש הקהלות cp. Mann, I, 258. The letter of congratulation to him on the occasion of his assuming an office of leadership (אלריאסה̈, published by Friedlaender, *l. c.*, 261–3) may well refer to this dignity of ראש הקהלות, viz. of Fusṭāṭ-Cairo. The fact of his having to attend to communal affairs seems to be alluded to in his famous letter to Samuel ibn Tibbon (Ḳobeṣ, II 28c): סוף דבר לא יוכל אחד מישראל לדבר לי או להתחבר ולהתבודד עמי זולת יום השבת, אז יבואו כל הקהל או רובם אחר התפלה, אנהיג הצבור במה שיעשה כל ימי השבוע.

documents he is not given the title of Nagid by which his son and later descendants are styled. Probably had Maimonides exerted himself he could have attained the Nagidate. But considering his extensive medical practice, his fragile health and his occupation with his great literary enterprises, he deemed it advisable not to shoulder upon himself the larger burden of Nagid over all the Egyptian communities. Or there may have been other reasons of which we are not aware now. But just as it is manifest that Maimonides himself was not Nagid, so likewise it seems that after the overthrow of Zuṭṭa there was no other holder of the office till Abraham Maimuni (1205).

Beginning with the latter, the office was an inheritance of the Maimunian family for 5 generations from father to son, for over two centuries. We are somewhat informed about the activities of Abraham and of his son David but very little indeed about those of their descendants. Their chronology is also not entirely fixed. In addition to the data given in *Jews in Egypt* (I, 248, II, 326–32, 382),[8] in supplementing those discussed by Brann and Steinschneider,[9] some further material is collected here about the Negidim of the Maimunian family without, however, intending to present here their full biographies.

Nothing new is added here about Abraham Maimuni, a full appreciation of whose life and work will only be possible after his chief opus, the Kifāya, will be fully edited.[10] His son, David, became Nagid in Ab 1238 at the tender age of 16, an eloquent testimony to the reverence in which the memories of Maimonides and his son were held.[10a] David lived a long life of 88 years

[8] Cp. also *Hebrew Union College Annual*, III, 298, 304.

[9] *M. G.W.J.*, XLIV, 14–24, 138–40; XLV, 129–37; *Arab. Liter.*, 224–25.

[10] To Eppenstein's biography (*Abraham Maimuni*: *Sein Leben u. seine Schriften*, 1914, cp. Poznański's review, *Z.f.H.B.*, 1916, 9–11) there is now to be added, besides the needed fuller appreciation of the material available before, the treatise by S. Rosenblatt, *The High Ways of Perfection of Abraham Maimonides*, 1927.

[10a] According to Jaffe (Hebrew Graetz, V, 405) David was born in December 1212 and died in August 1292. Hence he was 25 years old when he became Nagid. However besides Sambari's data we have now also the items in MS. Or. 5549 (see Mann, II, 328) which confirm the date of 1222 for his year of birth.

(d. 1300) and thus for 62 years the affairs of Egyptian Jewry were entrusted to his care. Owing to his advanced age his son Abraham was acting Nagid towards the end of David's life. Abraham as Nagid is mentioned side by side with his father David in a document of 1292. About this prolonged period of activity (1238–1300) we have but meagre information. David is styled ראש ישיבתה שלתורה (a title which was held also by his descendants) but the functions and scope of this school and its president are very obscure. It is also not stated that David was by profession a physician like his father and grandfather, but it may be assumed that this was the case because usually the Nagid would wield more influence at the court if he combined with his office the prestige of a court physician. However it is very doubtful whether at the age of 16, when he became Nagid, he had already become expert in medicine.[11]

David's career as Nagid seems to have been a checkered one. He was once involved in a great crisis which necessitated the collection of funds on his behalf by the Jews in Spain. Solomon ibn Adret, the eminent Rabbi of Barcelona, was instrumental in bringing monetary succor to the Nagid.[12] The story of this crisis is not recorded and it is difficult to establish the course of events. It seems that David had to leave Egypt for a considerable time and find refuge in 'Akko, the last stronghold of the Crusaders, hence outside of the jurisdiction of the Egyptian Sultan. While there he also put an end to the agitation against Maimonides' writings started by Solomon Petit. However the primary reason for his stay in 'Akko was not this affair but the insecurity of his position in Cairo due to Jewish traducers. After the

[11] His interest in medicine is evidenced from a prescription of his grandfather recorded by him (see Steinschneider, *M.G.W.J.*, XLV, 131).

[12] Samson b. Meir, a disciple of R. Solomon, mentions in his letter to Abba Mari of Montpellier (מנחת קנאות, No. 67, p. 138): כמו שהייתי שליח מצוה כשהלכתי לקשטילא ולנבארה וליתר הקהלות על ענין השר הנגיד בן בנו מהשר הגדול ר' משה. וקבצתי לו עם כתב רבינו (היינו רשב"א) כה' אלפים נודיניסי כסף.

For נודיניסי probably read נוביניסי, novenes (cp. Zunz, *Zur Gesch. u. Liter.*, pp. 553–4). On account of this help David maintained of course cordial relations with the Barcelona Rabbi. Cp. Ibn Adret's letter to Jacob b. Makhir (ibid., No. 40, p. 88): ואין בכל בית הרב והנגיד בן בנו חכים ואהוב ובעל ברית כמוני וצא ושאול (r. ושאל) לעוברי ימים וינידו לך (see also Harkavy, חדשים גם ישנים, X, p. 30).

difficulties were removed he returned to Cairo in about 1289 where he spent the last decade of his life.[13]

David was very friendly with the eminent scholar Tanḥum Yerushalmi and his son Joseph who was a gifted poet. The latter indeed was a sort of house poet of the Nagid's family. The occasion of the Nagid's return from ʻAkko was the cause for several poetical compositions by Joseph.[14] In a letter to David there is a discreet, albeit picturesque, allusion to conditions in Cairo-Fusṭāṭ during the absence of the Nagid.[15] A number of Jews, stubborn and rebellious (סוררים ומורים, evidently the above-mentioned מלשינים), carried on their nefarious doings in the ʻtwo cities' Cairo-Fusṭāṭ. The number of years David was

[13] Graetz (*Geschichte*, VII, 4th ed., 147–8) connects the crisis of David with the intolerant policy of the Sultan Kila'un (1277–90) against the employment of Jews and Christians in the administrative offices of the government. But this order was issued in Shabān 689 H. (August-September 1290) when David was already back in Cairo. Graetz himself alludes to the report of Abraham Zacuto about the denunciation of David by Jewish traducers, but this report evidently refers to the time when David was away in ʻAkko. It reads (יוחסין, ed. Filipowski 219b): ובימי הרשב'א היה (r. היו) ר' אברהם ור' שלמה בני הנגיד ר' דוד בן בנו של הרמב"ם ז"ל. והיה הנגיד ר' דוד מתפלל במערת הלל ושמאי ויצאו מים קרים ואז החרים למלשינים. וביום ההוא מתו ת"ק מלשינים בארץ מצרים, ולשני חדשים להלן נשיהם ובניהם נעקרו מן העולם. The traditional burial place of Hillel and Shammai was in Galilee (in Meron according to Benjamin of Tudela, ed. Adler, 30, top; cp. Petaḥyah's סבוב, ed. Grünhut, p. 30, and other accounts of travellers collected in Luncz's המעמר, III, pp. 32, bottom, 38, 52, 76, top, 83, top, etc.). It is only natural that David while in ʻAkko made a visit to this cave. The reference to the Malshinim rather indicates that David's troubles were due to disgruntled Jews in Egypt and not to the policy of the government. On account of these slanders he had to leave for ʻAkko to be outside the power of the authorities and remained here for several years (cp. the data given from the Diwān of Joseph b. Tanḥum Yerushalmi, infra, p. 439 ff.). Graetz's construction (p. 166) has thus to be modified.

[14] See the items cited infra, p. 439 ff.

[15] Published by Brody, קבץ על יד, 1893, section מטמוני מסתרים, p. 18: ואפשר נספר לפני אדוננו. כי נדודכם החריד רעיוננו. ויעזבנו נָסים ממוקש למוקש. ואין דורש ואין מבקש. וכל איש במדבר אולתו תועה. כצאן אשר אין להם רועה. כי נסעת ותעזבנו ללצון. ולא הודעת על מי נטשת מעט הצאן. הבריזה (r. הבריאה) ברזה תבעט. וכבוד הכבודה בעיני הנקלה ימעט. ויצאו האילים המתחבאים מפחד הארי. וינגחו נחשלי הצאן בחרי. וירבו בשתי הערים (Fusṭāṭ and Cairo) השוררים והמורים. אך כמוך לא ישים לבו לאלה הדברים. כי כל משכיל יודע שהמעלה הגדולה היום לשמש. אחרי אשר ערבה אמש. ומעת שם אדוננו מגמתו למצרים. הוכו כלם . . . ברבים וכו'.

away in 'Akko is not stated. Joseph uses the vague figure מדה̈ סנין or סנין עדה̈. The document of the Ḥerem against Solomon Petit issued by the Nasi of Damascus, dated Tammuz 5047 A. M. (= 1287), was evidently sent to David while in 'Akko because it is stated there that all the writings of a critical nature against Maimonides' doctrines should be handed over to the Nagid or to his sons within 3 days which can only refer to the writings found in 'Akko, the center of the opposition.[16] The letter of the Bagdād Gaon, Samuel Hakkohen b. Daniel, dated Tishri 1600 Sel. (= September, 1288 C. E.) was evidently also sent to David while in 'Akko.[17] By Passover 1289 David seems to have been back in Cairo and on account of his resumption of the Nagidate Joseph b. Tanḥum composed a Piyyuṭ for the 7th day of the Festival wherein he alluded to this event (infra, p. 440). His son Abraham, who was with him in 'Akko, married some time before the following festival of Tabernacles and Joseph celebrated this event also in a poem (ibidem). The return of David to his office was also the occasion for another poem whose author was also probably our Joseph b. Tanḥum. There

[16] See כרם חמד, III, 169ff. Cp. the corresponding passage p. 170, bottom: כל מי שיש בידו כתב או העתקה או הסכמה או אגרת חתומה . . . יתחייב להוציאם מרשותו ומיכלתו וימסרם הם והעתקותיהם ביד הנגיד רבנו דוד ש"צ בן הנגיד רבינו אברהם ז"ל או ביד אחד מבני הנגיד (supply הממונה) תחתיו לקבלם ימסרם תוך ג' ימים משתקרא גזרתנו . . . ואם לא יהיה בעיר (viz. 'Akko) שום אחד מהם (viz. the Nagid and his sons) יתחייב המביא הכתבים וכו'.

The date is given there (p. 171) as ליצירה ה'מ'ו which should be המ"ז (5047 =1287 C. E.). Graetz (*l. c.*, 419) comes to the conclusion that the date was 1288 (ה'מ'ח) but we have also the Ḥerem from the Exilarch of Mosul, dated Iyyar 1599 Sel. (=1288 C. E., see Halberstam, Kobak's ישרון, VII, 75, bottom) and in view of the geography and the time it took for letters to travel in those days the above dating is to be preferred. David sent out from 'Akko letters to the Nasi of Damascus, to the Exilarch of Mosul and to the Gaon of Bagdād to help him to stop Solomon Petit's agitation. The earliest reply could of course come from Damascus (viz. Tammuz 1287). From the more distant Mosul, the reply was dated 10 months later (Iyyar 1288) and from the still further Bagdād in Tishri 1600 Sel. (=September, 1288, ibid., pp. 76ff.). The dates of Hillel of Verona are too vague to be used for the exact fixing of the events of which he was badly informed (as shown further on).

[17] *Jeschurun*, *l. c.*: נוסח הכתב ששלח . . . ר' שמואל הכהן ראש הישיבה . . . שלחו לחכמי עכו ולרבנו דוד בן הרב ר' אברהם נע̇.

are allusions therein to his enemies who are now silenced in fear by his assuming again his office.[17a]

David's correspondence with the authorities of Spain (e. g. with Solomon ibn Adret in connection with the above crisis in his career) and with the leaders of the Orient, chiefly in connection with the affair of Solomon Petit, has so far not been discovered. His relations with the pro-Maimunian group in Italy is illustrated by the interesting Genizah letter to him from a certain Isaac Beṣalel b. Ḥayyim (published by Harkavy, *Hakkedem*, III, 111–14). The writer visited Egypt and came into contact with the Nagid whom he held in high respect. When already back to Italy (viz. Rome) the agitation of Solomon Petit became acute and the pro-Maimunists bestirred themselves to obtain from the Pope in Rome an approval of Maimonides' writings. Two rich and learned Jews, Isaiah and Meir, achieved this purpose after an outlay of nearly 100 gold pieces. The Pope had a proclamation read in the synagogue of Rome declaring that he had studied Maimonides' Moreh and had found his arguments conclusive against the theory of the eternity of Matter. Thereby, the proclamation continues, Maimonides has strengthened the basis of all monotheistic religions and, although he denied Christianity because of his being a Jew, his general theological views were useful for strengthening the faith. The Pope threatened any critic of Maimonides with a fine of 100 silver pieces.[18] The two Jews, who were instrumental in this

[17a] Davidson, גנזי שעכטער, III, 288–89, where the poem is wrongly ascribed to our David's grandson (see my remarks in *Journal of Semitic Languages*, July 1930, p. 281). Cp. especially lines 28–34.

[18] Lines 17ff.: אודיע לאדוני הרשום בכ[תב אמת] ע[ל ה]צר הצורר (evidently Solomon Petit) וגואליו ורעיו ומיודעיו חשבו מזמה בל יוכלו. והמה כרעו ונ[פלו]. ואנחנו קמנו ונתעודד. ויה[י בח]דש תמוז בחמשה לחדש. העיר י״י את [רוח ההגמון] הגדול אבי כל ההגמונים. ויעבר קול בבית הכנסת תקום נצח וגם ד[בר] כתב לאמר כה אמר ההגמון הגדול. השררה והעוז הכח והגבורה נתנו לי מאלהי השמים . . . ורוב ספרי חכמות עיינתי בהם . . . ויעירני שכלי להתעסק בספרי הרב [רבי]נו משה זצ״ל וללמוד בספר מורה נבוכים . . . ואין קצה לתכונתו. ואין תכלית לתבונתו . . . על כן ראוי לכל משכיל דורש את אלהים יתבונן תמיד בספר המורה. כי הוא יסוד התורה. וסוד המורא. לפי שהורס בניני מאמיני הקדמות בראיות גמורות. ובונה מגדלי מאמצי החידוש בפנים אחרות. ואע״פ שיש בדבריו [רמזים ה]מורים על הכחשת אמונתנו (viz. Chrisian-ity) אין לחוש על זה בכל מאדי. כי הגיד להם אשר הוא יהודי. עתה שמעו עמים כולם. מטעם הפפיור וההגמונים לאמר. כי כל איש [אשר ימ]רה את פי ולא ישמע אל דברי לכל אשר אצונו

matter, were able to obtain from the Pope an earlier decree of the Church against Maimonides' Moreh so that there would be no official record of an inimical nature.[19] Harkavy, by erroneously placing the writer in France, has failed to realize the full significance of the importance of our letter which throws new light on the machinations of Solomon Petit. Not satisfied with getting letters from French and German Rabbis in approval of his stand, he went to Rome to obtain the aid of the Church whose decree would of course hold sway in 'Akko under the control of the Crusaders! There was evidently an edict of the Papacy against Maimonides' writings as a result of their having been assigned to the flames in Montpellier about 1233 in the time of Solomon b. Abraham. This is evidently meant by the phrase ההסכמה הקדמונה הידועה. Aware of this Solomon Petit hoped to obtain in Rome from the Papacy letters of approval for his cause which letters would be presented to the Christian authorities in 'Akko. But his scheme was frustrated by the leaders of the Roman community who found in the Pope an admirer of Maimonides' views. The Moreh he no doubt read in the old Latin translation of the

יפרע מאה זקוקים כסף לחצר ההגמון. כי כל איש אשר ידבר תועה על ספר מורה נבוכים. או ימנע ה[לו]מד בו והמלמדו בין בסתר בין בגלוי. ענש יענש בקנס הנזכר.

I have given here the text as printed by Harkavy. While in Leningrad I had occasion to consult this MS. (Antonin No. 711) and for הרשום בכותב הרשום בכ[תב אמת] ע[ל ה]צר הצורר there appeared to me that we should read כי ש[ל]מה הצורר and hence there would be in the letter another explicit mention of Solomon Petit as in l. 27! There is no doubt that the Pope (known as "Bishop" (הגמון) of Rome) is meant here and not a cardinal as Harkavy thinks as an alternative (p. 114). Hence the Pope of Avignon cannot be meant, as Harkavy states, because the Papacy of Avignon only began in 1305 when David was no longer alive. Harkavy was mislead to identify the writer's country as northern France or Provence but his residence was clearly in Rome. The Pope in question is probably Nicholas IV (1288–92).

[19] Lines 26ff.: ויער יי' את רוח הרב רבי' ישעיה י"ל (= יחיה לעד). וילך אל חצר ההגמון ויקח את ספר הגלוי חתום בטבעת ההגמון הנכונה. בעדות נאמנה. ועל ידו ה[חזיק] [והרב] ר' מאיר החכם. ויקח ההסכמה הקדמונה הידועה. מאת ההגמון בצינעה. והנה [עצורה ב]אהלו. לדעה מה יעשה לו. וכשמע שלמה וסיעתו את כל הדברים האלה ויצא לבם ויחרדו [איש] אל א[חיו]. וילכו אל ההגמון לקחת כתביהם מאת ההגמון ולא שמע אליהם. ויתמרמר בחמתו עליהם. ולא מצאו כל אנשי חיל ידיהם .... ותהי מת[כנ]ת ההוצאה על ידי השרים האדירים החכמים. כב' מר' ור' ישעיה החכם וה[משכיל] וכב' מר' ור' [מאיר] החכם י"ל קרוב למאה זהובים על כל הת[שורות].

13th century.[20] Not only was any disparagement of Maimonides' Moreh within the Roman Jewry forbidden but the old hostile decree (evidently deposited in the Papal archives) was secretly handed over to the leader of the pro-Maimonists, Isaiah, who was to decide what should be its fate. It was undoubtedly consigned to the flames.

From the above letter we see how badly informed Hillel of Verona was in his isolation in Forli as he himself admitted. When writing to his friend the physician, Isaac b. Mordecai (Maestro Gajo, the Pope's court physician), he did not know at all of Solomon's stay in Rome and of his endeavors there.[21] He only expressed the fear that "perhaps his falsehoods and vanities spread also there" and that he found there some followers. Likewise did Hillel not know of the whereabouts of the Nagid David to whom he sent letters addressed to Cairo. But his correspondent in Rome knew quite well of David's stay in 'Akko and enlightened Hillel on the matter.[22] The above epistle was no doubt also dispatched to David while in 'Akko. There is an allusion there to his enemies and the wish is expressed that he be restored to his office of Nagid.[23] The action of the leaders of the

[20] See Steinschneider, *Heb. Übers*, §250 (pp. 432–4) and *Arab. Lit.*, p. 207.

[21] חמדה גנוזה, ed. Edelmann, 18b; טעם זקנים, ed. Ashkenazi, 70b: ואח"כ אודיעך כי הנני גר בעיר פורלא (פורלין .r. Forli). וביקר בל ילין. ובשבתי פה אינני יודע מן הענינים המתחדשים בעולם היהודים אלא במקרה בסור הנה לעתים רחוקות קצת אנשים שיאמרו לי כך וכך נתחדש בעולם היהודים ובמקום פלוני. וזה עתה ימים רבים ששמעתי שבא בפררא (Ferrara) אחד מאשכנז שמו שלמה פטיט (שליט in טעם זקנים) ועבר על (=אל) עכו ואז לא נודעו לי מהלכיו ועקבותיו. אך עתה מקרוב נודע כי עיקר עקבותיו והליכותיו היו להלחם בה' ובמשה עבדו . . . ובשומעי ספקתי כף על כף על שלא ידעתי זה מידי עוברו באלה הגלילות שאילו ידעתי הייתי פונה מכל עסקי ורץ אחריו עד אנקונה (Ancona wherefrom Solomon embarked for 'Akko) וכו'.

Hillel continues: ולכן מפחדתי פן נתפשטו הבליו ושקריו גם שם ב ק ה ל ר ו מ י ושמא נטתה שום כת סכלות אחריו אמרתי אל לבי להזהירך ולהשכילך וכו'.

[22] Cp. Hillel's second letter to Isaac (חמדה גנוזה, 21a, bottom): אבל אמרתי לריק יגעתי כי כתבתי אגרות גדולות לקהל אלכסנדריאה שישלחום אל הר' דוד אל אלקיירא שהיא העיר אשר דר בה ומסרתים ביד סוחר א' מגינואה (Genoa) אוהבי שמצאתי בעיר בולונייא (Bologna) שהוא מעותד לעבור באלכסנדריאה והלך לו אל יינאה עם האגרות. ובשובו אל פורליץ (פורלין .r) הגיע אגרתך אלי אשר בה הודעתני שהר' דוד בא על (=אל) עכו. ואולי עדיין תגיע אגרתי לידו בשום זמן ויברכוני (ויברכני .r).

[23] Line 40: [ירים יד]ך על [אויביך]. והיה שדי בצר[יך]. יחזיק ב[יד] ימינך. ו ה ש י ב ך ע ל כ נ ך. Greetings are sent to the Nagid's 2 sons (שני הכרובים), Abraham (l.35) and Solomon (of this name only letter ל visible, thus [ש]ל[מה], l.37; Harkavy

Roman community on behalf of Maimonides' Moreh naturally evoked sentiments of gratitude on behalf of the Nagid David who no doubt commended them in his letters. Thus there grew up a mutual esteem and hence when David died at a full old age in Elul 1300 his death was mourned in Rome, and on behalf of the community a letter of condolence was sent to his son and successor Abraham.[24]

The last years of David's life, since his return from 'Akko in 1289 till 1300, were years of intermittent intolerance against Jews and Christians on the part of the Egyptian Sultans, especially with regard to the employment of non-Muslims in government offices (see vol. II of our *Texts and Studies*). But how far, if at all, this affected his own office of Nagid and of court physician (if he was such) is not known. As stated above, his son Abraham was active Nagid already in 1292, assisting his father who was of advanced age. He succeeded his father in Elul 1300. A Ketubah of Tishri 13, 1301, issued under his authority, is given farther on (No. I, p. 429). In Nisan 1301 there took place a very serious attack on Jews and Christians in Egypt on the part of the fanatical Muslims (see the full account in vol. II). The leaders of the Jews had to undertake to keep all the restrictive vows enumerated in the so-called 'covenant of 'Omar'. In this connection there is mentioned the Raīs (al-Yahūd i. e. the Nagid Abraham) and the Dayyān (al-Yahūd).[25] The effects of this serious outbreak were finally removed in Elul 1310 when the closed synagogues were reopened. The common sufferings of Rabbanites and Ḳaraites alike seem to have brought the two sections together with the result that numerous Ḳaraites went over to Rabbinism realizing that in the troublesome times strength lay in unity. Estori Parḥi briefly records this event to

has wrongly the name דניאל). The third person greeted was Samuel, evidently a member of the family. About a Samuel the son of Solomon, cp. infra, p. 441.

[24] See the passage published by Goldberg from MS. Paris (מעשה נסים, XII): וכששמעו קהל הקדוש שבעיר רומי רבתי פטירת זה הנגיד רבינו דוד הנזכר זצ"ל שלחו זה הכתב לבניו הנגיד רבינו אברהם והחכם החסיד העניו רבינו שלמה וכו'.

[25] See Quatremère, *Histoire des Sultans Mamlouks*, II, pt. 2, p. 178. About the Dayyān al-Yahūd, the judge of the Nagid's supreme court, see Mann, I, 266–7, *Hebrew Union College Annual*, III, 292–3.

have taken place at the end of the calendrical cycle 267 (= 5072 or 5073 A. M. = 1312 or 1313 C. E.)[26]. Abraham Nagid is stated to have been instrumental in this matter. He must have thus been an active communal leader but of his further achievements since then till his demise we have no information.[27] Joseph ibn Kaspi came into contact with this Nagid and his family while visiting Egypt. He was impressed by the piety of the Maimunian descendants but was disappointed with their indifference towards philosophy and the sciences.[28]

[26] כפתור ופרח, ed. Luncz, p. 70: והצדוקים (viz. Ḳaraites) אינם היום בזמנינו מוסיפים גריעות אלא שרבים מהם מתיהדים תמיד וכמעשה שאירע סוף מחזור רס"ז מקהל גדול מהם שהתיהדו ביום אחד במצרים על יד הנגיד רבינו אברהם נר"ו.

Cp. also David b. Zimra (Responsa I, No. 73, end, and II, No. 796, towards end): וכן היה מעשה בסוף מחזור רס"ז שחזרו קהל גדול מהקראיין לדת האמת במצרים ע"י הנגיד רבינו אברהם החסיד ז"ל וקרוב הוא שהיה בנו של הר"מ במז"ל. ועוד היום משפחות ההם ידועות במצרים מהם כהנים וישראלים מיוחסים ולא היה אדם פוצה פה עליהם אלא אדרבא נתחתנו בהם גדולי קהלות מצרים הרבנים. המעשה הזה (viz. of their acceptance of Rabbinism) העיד עליו בעל ספר כפתור ופרח. Radbaz's remark that this Nagid was Maimonides' son is of course incorrect. In reality he was Abraham Maimuni's great-grandson (cp. also Jaffe's note in Hebrew Graetz, V, 405).

[27] The date of his death, as given by Sambari (Neub. I, 135), is hopelessly corrupt: ונפטר בשנת אלף ותקקט לשטרות היא שנת ה' וס' ליצירה, the first date being equal to 1298 C. E. (!) and the second to 1300 C. E. But we have seen before that he was very active in 1312–13 C. E. See further Brann, *M.G.W.J.*, XLIV, 20, and the suggestion of Elbogen (ibid., p. 139–40) to read the Sel. year as תקקל"ז and A. M. as ה' פ"ו so that Abraham died in 1326 C. E.

[28] See his last will to his son Solomon (published by Ashkenazi in טעם זקנים under the heading of ספר המוסר, pp. 49bff.): זה לי עשרים שנה גליתי למקום תורה לפי הנשמע שכנתי באחרית ים ירדתי מצרים בית מדרשו של הרב הגדול החכם השלום (r. השלם) המורה ומצאתי שם זרעו זרע קדש דור רביעי ובניהם חמשי (r. חמישי) כלם צדיקים אבל בחכמות לא היו מתעסקים וגם בכל המזרח לא היו שם חכמים וקראתי על עצמי הוי היורדים מצרים לעזרה (Is. 31.1) ואשב אל ארצי בבושת פנים וכל זמן עמידתי בהליכה וחזרה היו חמשה חדשים. In his קבוצת כסף (printed in Benjacob's קבוצת כסף, II, p. 11) Joseph Kaspi explicitly mentions that he came into contact while in Egypt with the Nagid Abraham. ויבקש יוסף ללכת מעבר לים כי יש שבר במצרים לראש משביר זרע קדש החכם המורה נ"ע. ויוסף הורד מצרימה עד בואו האהלה בית אלים (=אלהים) כבוד הנגיד ר' אברהם דור רביעי אל הראש נגיד החכמים (הרמב"ם). In the number of generations enumerated Maimonides' own is included, hence Abraham b. David b. Abraham Maimuni is regarded as belonging to the 4th generation. The above ethical will was written in Valencia in Elul 1332, C. E., and Joseph refers therein to his wanderings in search of knowledge that began 20 years before (1312). The trip to Egypt took place some years after the latter date.

Abraham's successor was his son Joshu'a who died in 1355 at the age of 45 years.[29] How far the intolerant attacks by the Muslim mobs on Christian and Jewish government officials[30] affected the Nagid and his family is again obscure. We are altogether uninformed about his activities except that he was regarded as a Talmudic authority, legal questions reaching him from Yemen.[31]

The last Nagid of Maimonides' family was David b. Joshu'a. For some unknown reasons we find him living for several years in Damascus and in Aleppo (about 1375–86).[32] But he seems to have continued as Nagid of Egypt. The document given as No. II (infra, p. 431ff.) was issued in Cairo under his authority. Unfortunately the date is illegible, but the addendum, wherein the same persons are mentioned, is dated in January 1409 C. E., and hence the document proper probably belongs to a time shortly before. If this be correct, then this Nagid was still alive at the beginning of the 15th century. The document in question, signed by the leaders of the congregation, confirms the sale of communal property to the physician David b. Jacob (also a prominent doctor). The community was burdened by a heavy government impost and had to borrow money to pay this tribute (Dhimma). Now there belonged to the הקדש (viz. the communal Waḳf) three pieces of real estate, known as those of a certain Elijah (evidently the donor), from which hardly any income was derived. These properties were sold to the physician David for 7000 Dirhems and applied to the payment of the tribute. Instead of the disposed properties a ruin near the Synagogue was bought and evidently equipped for communal purposes, probably to shelter the Jewish poor and the vagrants. The document describes in detail the limits of the sold properties.

Whether David Nagid ever returned to Cairo after his prolonged stay in Syria we are entirely in the dark. With him the Nagidate, vested in the Maimunian family for about two centuries, closes. The subsequent Negidim are no longer descendants of Maimonides. The reasons for this change are entirely

[29] Brann, *l. c.*, 22. [30] See vol. II of our *Texts and Studies*.
[31] Cp. Steinschneider, *M.G.W.J.*, XLV, 134–5.
[32] See Steinschneider, *M.G.W.J.*, XLV, 135–6 and Mann, II, 330–31.

obscure. Altogether we lose trace of this family. There is only one item, given by Carmoly (*Isr. Annalen*, I, 55) from a MS. of Maimonides' tract קדוש השם in his possession,[33] to the effect that our David died in Damascus and that two sons of David b. 'Obadyah b. Abraham b. Moses b. Solomon b. David b. Abraham Maimuni were taken away in 1740 Sel. (1429 C. E.) as captives.[34]

The list of the Negidim from David till the extinction of the Nagidate after the Turkish conquest of Egypt in 1517 is incomplete. In 1422 there functioned a Nagid Simon.[35] Whether he succeeded David directly or there was another holder of the office between them is unknown.[36] The next Negidim we hear of are Joseph b. Khalifa in 1465 and his son Solomon in 1481 (see Mann, *Hebrew Union College Annual*, III, 304–05). Again we are uninformed whether Joseph succeeded Simon directly or one or more persons occupied the office between them. More is known of Solomon's successors, Natan Hakkohen Shulal and his nephew Isaac Shulal.[37] The conquest of the country by the

[33] Unfortunately Carmoly did not give the passage in the original.

[34] Cp. also Steinschneider, *l. c.*, 130, who is sceptical about Carmoly's information. The latter refers to Moses Rieti (מקדש מעט, ed. Goldenthal, fol. 101) who also records the capture of these 2 members of the Maimunian family. Carmoly may have erred in the date of Rieti but in essence the reference is correct (in spite of Steinschneider's captiousness).

[35] See the document from Alexandria cited in the question to Simon b. Ṣemaḥ Duran (תשב"ץ, III, No. 66): טופס שטר הבא מנוא אמון: סהדותא דהות באופניא (בפנינו .r) אנן סהדי דחתימות ידנא לתתא סוף שטרא דנן כן הוה בזמן אחד עשר מאייר שנת חמשת אלפים ומאה ותמנין ותרי שנין ליצירה במדינת נוא אמון דעל כיף ימא (מותבה supply רשותיה דאדוננו מאור עינינו בבת) עפעפינו . . . מנהיג קהלותינו . . . מורנו ורבנו הרב ר' שמעון הרב המובהק פטיש החזק הנגיד החסיד נגיד הנגידים . . . מרדכי הזמן צנצנת המן. הרועה הנאמן וכו'. This string of appellations was usual in the case of the Egyptian Negidim.

Evidently the same Nagid is meant in the allusion of Solomon b. Simon (b. Ṣemaḥ Duran) to a responsum by his father to the Nagid of Egypt (שו"ת הרשב"ש, No. 283): וכ"כ (=וכמו כן כתב) אדוני אבי מורינו הרב נר"ו בתשובה לנגיד שבמצרים יצ"ו.

[36] The phraseology of the letter to a certain leader 'Amram concerning the Lost Ten Tribes, written about 1419 (see Kaufmann, *JQR*, IV, 506–08), is too vague to ascribe it to an Egyptian Nagid by this name as Kaufmann does (p. 505).

[37] See the data collected by Berliner, *Magazin*, XVII, 53ff. Cp. also E. Rivlin, הנגיד רבי (יהו)נתן שולאל בירושלם (Reprint from the weekly התור, Jerusalem, 1927) and Rosanes, דברי ימי ישראל בתוגרמה, I (2nd ed., 1930), 193–96.

Turks introduced a new political situation which resulted in the abolition of the Nagidate, an office that lasted since the beginning of the Fāṭimid rule (969 C. E.) for more than five and one-half centuries. This phase of the history of the Nagidate cannot, however, be further discussed in the present connection.

I.

[MS. Mosseri V 8, paper.]

(Recto)

בתלאתא בשבא דהוא תלאת עשר לירח תשרי דשנת אלפא ושית מאה ותלאת עשר שנין לשטרות[1] למנינא דרגילנא לממני ביה הכא בפסטאט מצרים דעל נהר נילוס מותבה רשותיה דאדונינו נגידינו. הודנו והדרינו. וצניף תפארתינו. ועטרת ראשינו. ומנהיג דורינו. מרנו ורבנו. אברהם דגל הרבנים נזר החכמים. מרדכי הזמן[2]. הרועה הנאמן. ר[אש] הישיבה שלתורה. ירום הודו למע[לה]. ויגדל כבודו סלה. איך הוא מרינו ורבינו יפתח[3] החתן התלמיד נזר החתנים בר̇ כ ב ו[4] כבוד ג ל ו[4] גדולת קדושת מרינו ורבינו אברהם

[1] Tishri 1301 C. E.

[2] 'The Mordecai of the (present) period', a usual title for the Nagid and for other eminent leaders (cp. Mann, II, Hebrew Index and Glossary, s. v.).

[3] The name Yiftaḥ occurs also elsewhere (cp. Mann, II, 320).

[4] Overlined, to be deleted.

(verso)

נֿעֿ אמר לה לסת אלכל[5] בת כבוד גדולת
קדושת מרינו ורבינו[6] נֿעֿ בתולתא
פוגרת[7] הואי לי לאינתי כדת משה
וישראל ואנא איפלח ואוקר ואסובר
יתיכי כהילכת גברין יהודאין דפל[חין]
וזינין ומיקרין את נשיהון בק[ושטא]
ושמעתיה כלתא דא והות ליה לאינתו
וצבי חתנ[א] דנן ויהב לה דיליה עשרה
זוזי מוקדם ואוסיף לה על עקר
כתבתאה[7]* דא עשרין זוזי מואחרי[8]
ודן נדוניא דהעלת כלתא דא מבית
אבהתה מנין[9] תשעה וחמשים
זוזי שויאן כל דינאר שלש עשר
ושליש והאוי כלל כתובתא דא
מוהרי ונדוניא ותכשיטין ומתנה
ותוספת תשעה ושמונים וקיבל
עלוהי חתנא דנן וח[סי]נת צובתא[10]
דא עלוהי ועל ירתוהי בתרוהי

[5] Sitt al-Kul, 'the mistress of all', a usual name for ladies (cp. Steinschneider, *JQR*, XI, 330–31, No. 492).

[6] The name of the bride's father is missing and also the names of the witnesses. Hence our fragment is only a draft of a Ketubah.

[7] =בוגרת, Palestinian way of interchanging ב' and פ'. Cp., e.g., in Yer. הבקר for הפקר, and see also above, p. 360, note 3.

*[7] Read כתובתה.

[8] Read מאוחרי. About the terms מוקדם and מאוחר used in Ḳaraite Ketubot see vol. II of our *Texts and Studies*. About the custom of paying part of the betrothal money in cash and of contracting the remainder (the תוספת) as a debt of the husband to his wife, cp. L. M. Epstein, *The Jewish Marriage Contract*, 1927, 84ff.

[9] The value of the 'things' which the bride brought from her parents' home was 59 Zuz (=Dirhem) calculated at 13⅓ Dirhems for a Dinār.

[10] Evidently the same as צְבָת, bundle, viz. the combined amount.

(right hand margin)

על כל שפר ארגי[11] נכסין קנין ממון דאית ליה ע[ל][12]

תחות כל שמיא בביתא ובבר[א] בין ממחירין[13]

(top of recto)

ובין ממטלטלי ואפיל[14] מגלימא דעל

כתפיה דלא כאסמכאתא ודלא כטופסי

דשטרי אלא כחומרי כל שטרי

מוחזאקי וכתקותא[15] דרבנן

(right hand margin of recto)

וקנינא מן חתנא דנן על

מא דכתיב ומפרש לעילא במנא דכשר

למקנא ביה שר[יר]

ובר[ור ו]קיים.

II.

[From photographs in the possession of Mr. Mosseri in wrapper marked 825.]

One photograph in Arabic script, evidently the verso of the Arabic document beginning on the other photograph; this verso has also the following document in Hebrew script the date of which on top is illegible. It was issued at Cairo near Fusṭāṭ

[11] The best, the choicest of (cp. Jastrow, s. v., and also Assaf, ספר השטרות לרה"ג, 15, note 4).

[12] The 'ע is doubtful and this word does not fit in here in the sentence. Perhaps the 2 letters are only the first ones of the following line.

[13] We should expect here the word מקרקעאי as in the other Ketubot. Read perhaps here ממחידין (from אחז=אחד), viz. real estate that 'can be seized'. Hence the term corresponds to קרקעאי. Cp. also the phrase אחיד used in some Ketubot (thus in the Ketubah from Mastaura in Byzantium, dated 1022 C. E., published by Mann, II, 94, ll. 7–8: ויהיבנא לך מוהר בתולייכי אחיד וקיים עליי מן נכסיי; and so also in the Ketubah from Barḳah in North Africa, dated 990, published by Assaf, *l. c.*, p. 54, l. 6).

[14] Read ואפילו.

[15] Read וכתקנתא.

in accordance with the usual legal formula under the authority of the Nagid David.

9 . . . . אדוננו מאור עינינו דוד הנגיד הגאון המעוז המגדול הרב המובהק הפטיש החזק דגל הרבנים

וראש לכל החכמים נגיד הנגידים. וגדול ליהודים. מרדכי הזמן. צנצנת המן[16]. גביר [עם לא]

אלמן. עוז המשרה. מקל התפארה. ראש ישיבתה שלתורה הטהורה וכו׳

13 . . . . . פיקול מן וצׄע כׄטה אכׄיראׄ אן למה חצל לאל

צבור מגׄרם כתׄיר פלם יגׄדו מן אין יופי פוקפו אלגׄמאעהׄ בׄרׄ יהׄי[17] אלואצׄעין כׄטוטהם ואגׄתהדו

15 ואקתרצׄו עלי דׄמתהם וכאן פי אלקדש תׄלתׄ מלך מערוף במלך הדרת רׄ אליה זׄלׄ ולם יחצל

מנה קטׄ ראיע פאבאעוה לאלחכים אלשׄ[18] דוד סׄטׄ בר כׄ מׄוׄ[19] יעקב הרופא הנכבד השר המכובד עטרת השרים ותפארת הרופאים זׄלׄ בסבע אלאף דרהם וקבצׄו מנה אלתׄמן ווזנוה

פי אלמגׄרם אלדׄי חצל עלי אלצבור מן גׄהת אלגׄואלי[20] ומן גׄהת תבטיל אלסבת[21] תׄם בעד דׄלך וגׄדו

כׄראבהׄ פי צׄהר בית הכנסת פאשתרוהא עוׄץ ען תׄלתׄ אלמלך אלמדׄכור אלדׄי אבאעוה

וצאר הדׄא אלתׄלתׄ אלמלך אלמדׄכור לר׳ דוד אלמדׄכור פי מלכה ותצרפה אדׄא באעוה לה ביע

20 בתאת זבינין שרירין וחליטין מתהום ארעא ועד רום רקיעא ותצרף פיה תצרף אלמלאך פי

[16] About this title cp. Mann, I, 256, note 1.

[17] =ברוכים יהיו.

[18] =אלשיׄך.

[19] =כבוד מרנא ורבנא.

[20] Plural of גׄאליהׄ, tribute paid by non-Muslims.

[21] This event involving the desecration of the Sabbath is obscure as we have no other corresponding source to yield more information.

אמלאכהם ודו̇ אלחקוק פי חקוקהם אד̇ צאר לה בחכם אלביע אלשרעי אלד̇י לא שרט יעלה

ולא עאיק יבטלה וחדוד הד̇א אלמלך אלמד̇כור אלחד̇ אלאוול הו אלקבלי ינתהי אלי טריק אלמסלוך מנה

אלי אלחמ̇אם ואלסויקה̈ אלד̇י הנאך ודרב קצ̇יב ואלחד אלת̇אני והו אלבחרי ינתהי אלי דאר תערף

בבורתתהא ברושאן וערפת באבן עראקי ואלחד אלת̇לאת̇ והו אלשרקי ינתהי אלי אלדרב אלד̇י הי פיה

ופיה ישרע ת̇לת̇ אבואב מן אבואבהא וטלע רושנהא אלנקי ואלרקצייאת וענד אלג̇דאר אלד̇י חדי

הד̇ה אלחד̇ ג̇מלת רושאן ואכ̇שאב אלציבאת אלד̇י הנאך ואלחד אלראבע והו אלגרבי ינתהי א[לי]

אלזקאק אלמערוף באבן גאדי ופי הד̇ה אלחד̇ ישרע אלבאב אלראבע אלמערוף בבאב אלסר̇ ותו̇צל

מנה אלי אלסטח עלי אלדאר אלמד̇כורה̈ יחד̇ ד̇לך כלה וחקוקה במא יערף בהא סר̇ והכל אמת וקיים

יצחק הכהן בר אברהם הכהן ז̇ל̇ אברהם בר פרחיה נ̇ע̇ ישועה בר שלמה הכהן נ̇ע̇ עבדיה הכהן בר יעקב הכהן ס̇ט̇

יצחק הלוי בר יוסף הלוי נ̇ע̇ שמואל בר סעדיה הכהן נ̇ע̇ עובדיה בר אברהם ז̇ל̇

[Margin; some illegible scribble towards right-hand corner.]

למא כאן בתאריך̇ כ̇אמס עשר מן חדש שבט שנת אלפא ושבע מאה ועשרין שנין לשטרות למניינא

דרגילנא לממני ביה הכא בעיר אלקאהרה̈ הסמוכה לפסטאט דעל נהר נילוס מותבה חט̇רת זקני

היושר אלי בית אלחכים אלש̇ דויד והם אלחכים ר̇ צדקה הכהן בר אברהם הכהן ז̇ל̇ אלחכים ר̇ משה הכהן בר ירושלים הכ[הן]

רׄ עובדיה בר אברהם זׄלׄ עובדיה בר יעקב הכהן סׄטׄ אברהם
בר פרחיה נׄעׄ ישועה בר שלמה הכהן נׄעׄ

אנהם קבלו ותשלמו מן אל[חכים] אלשׄ דוד תׄלאתׄהׄ גוו רמאמין
פטה ותׄלתׄ סתור חריר רהן ענדו עלי ת[ומא]ם

. . . יצחק הלוי בר יו[סף הלו]י נׄעׄ אלעזר בר דוד נבׄתׄויׄאׄ

8.

JOSEPH B. TANḤUM YERUSHALMI

The existence of this learned son of the eminent exegete and philologist, Tanḥum b. Joseph Yerushalmi, became first known by the short publication of Brody (קבץ על יד, 1893, section מטמוני מסתרים, pp. 7 and 17–19). The part of his Diwān (Brit. Mus., Or. 2588), which Brody examined, is now described in detail by Margoliouth (*Cat. of the Hebrew and Samar. MSS. in the British Museum*, III, 253–55). Brody obtained only meagre information from Harkavy of the existence of another MS. of Joseph's work in St. Petersburg (*l. c.*, p. 7, note 3). In reality there exist there 3 MSS. of various parts of Joseph's Diwān as the following extracts reveal.

There is now no doubt that he was the son of Tanḥum Yerushalmi,[1] whose death, as we learn now, occurred in Cairo on Wednesday, 21. Tammuz 5051 A. M. (= June 20, 1291 C. E.). Joseph began to compose an elegy on his distinguished father when the news reached Cairo of the conquest of ʻAkko, the last stronghold of the Crusaders in Palestine, by the Muhammedans and the ensuing slaughter of the Jewish community with its numerous scholars. This sad news induced Joseph to include in this elegy also a lament on the fallen scholars.[2] For his father's

[1] The doubt of Steinschneider (*M.G.W.J.*, XLV (1901), p. 131) is no longer repeated in *Arab. Liter.*, 234, 236–7.

[2] The Conquest of ʻAkko by al-Ashrāf Ḥalīl, the Sultan of Egypt, took place on the 18th of May 1291 (about the date, concerning which there is some variance in the sources, see Weil, *Geschichte des Abbasidenchalifats in Egypten*, I, 180, note 1). It took thus more than a month till the news of the slaughter of the Jews perpetrated there by the wild Muslim soldiery reached Cairo.

The date, given by Abraham Zacuto (ס' יוחסין, ed. Filipowski, 88b) in the name of the eye-witness Isaac of ʻAkko, the well-known Ḳabbalist, is corrupt. בחדש אדר כתב ר' יצחק דמן עכו כי עכו נחרבה בשנת חמשים לפרט ושנהרגו חסידי ישראל שם בד' מיתות ב"ד ובשנת ס"ה (1304–5) היה זה ר' יצחק דמן עכו בנבארה באיטאליה וניצל מעכו ובשנת ס"ה עצמה בא לטוליטולה.

In reality we ought to read בחדש סיון... בשנת חמשים ואחת לפרט. That the text

tombstone he composed one expressive strophe: "Hidden in this grave lies he who gathered (in himself) all praise, the leader of the age, Tanḥum the son of the eminent Joseph." His mother died on the 26th of Ab of the same year and thus he was bereaved of both parents within a little over a month. Joseph was then a man of 29 years. Already at the age of 15 (in 1277) he gave evidence of his ability as a poet by composing a work ערוגות הבשמים after the manner of Moses ibn Ezra's Tarshish.

Of his occupation we have no information but it may be surmised that he was supported by the Nagid David and his family with whom he was intimately befriended and whose praises he sang on numerous occasions. He was in fact a sort of a house poet of the Nagid's household. Also on other Egyptian dignitaries he bestowed a share of his muse. As one of the last manifestations of the poetic tradition, which the Orient shared in common with Muhammedan Spain, Joseph's Diwān deserves to be published in full in addition to the fact that it throws some light on several personalities in the second half of the 13th century. He was born in 1262 but the date of his demise is so far unknown. Besides his Diwān Harkavy (חדשים גם ישנים X, p. 7) cites a fragment of a MS. in Leningrad containing a portion of a work on philosophy and ethics whose author he identifies with our Joseph.

Extracts from the Diwān of Joseph b. Tanḥum Yeruhsalmi

1. Joseph's Diwān consisted of seven sections as we learn from MS. Firkowicz, 2. Hebrew Collection, No. 100[1]. The third section was in the form of Maḳamas like those of Ḥarizi's Taḥkemoni.[1] The fourth one contained poems of eulogy and congratulations to contemporaries of the poet with whom he ex-

is corrupt is also evident from the geographical impossibility of Navarre in Italy! Cp. also Graetz (*Geschichte*, VII, 4th ed., 433, note 1) who corrects the year but not the month. His other emendation בנבארה בקאטלניא (note 2) does not seem likely as Navarre was a separate province and not in Catalonia. However see Neubauer, *JQR*, IV, 367, bottom, where for באיטליאה the correct MS. reading is given באישטלייא, viz. Estella in Navarre!

[1] Cp. MS. British Museum, Or. 2588 (*Catalogue Margoliouth*, III, 253–4).

changed letters and poetical compositions.[2] The fifth section dealt with love and wine songs evidently in the form of strophes ending with homonyms having different meanings (like Moses ibn 'Ezra's *Tarshish*).[3] In the sixth we have elegies and dirges while the seventh section was of a miscellaneous character.

The contents of the first two sections are not known. A separate part of the Diwān was evidently the author's ספר ערוגות הבשמים in imitation of Moses ibn 'Ezra's Tarshish (or ענק). This was written in 1277 C. E. when Joseph was 15 years old, hence his year of birth can now be fixed as 1262 C. E. Like its prototype this youthful work was divided into ten portions.

We give here some extracts from the portions of the Diwān as preserved in MSS. in Leningrad with comparison of the British Museum MS. Our purpose was merely to extract a number of historical data without editing any part of the Diwān which should be made accessible in full.

2. MS. Firkowicz, 2. Hebrew Collection, No. 100[I], is very damaged and defective and the loose leaves have to be rearranged to ascertain the extent of the portions preserved. One part of the MS. is in the form of Maḳamas like those of Ḥarizi and evidently belongs to the third section of the Diwān (cp. Cat. Margoliouth, III, 253–4). The narrator styles himself אחיטוב בן חכמוני.

The sixth section is headed באב אלסאדם פי אלמראתׄי ואלמחזונאת and contains in all nine compositions. The first elegy has the heading: מן דׄלך קולה ירתׄי ר׳ יצחק נׄעׄ בר כב״ק מׄו׳[4] דויד הנגיד שׄצׄ׳[5]. The Nagid is David b. Abraham Maimuni. He had four sons and one of them, Isaac, died in his lifetime on which occasion Joseph b. Tanḥum composed the above elegy.

The sixth elegy of this section has the important heading establishing the date and the place of the demise of Tanḥum Jerushalmi.

ותופי ואלדה זצ״ל במצר יום אלדׄ אלכׄאׄ מן תמוז שנת הׄנׄאׄ
ליצירה פקאל ירתׄיה וכאן קד דׄלך באיאם קלילהׄ וצל כׄבר

[2] Ibid., 254, col. 2, top: מקארצׄהׄ אהל אלעצר מן מדח ותהניהׄ וגיר דׄלך.

[3] Ibid., p. 255, col. 1: אלבאב אלכׄאמס. פי אלגזל. ואלנסיב. ואלכׄמריאת.

Cp. the beginning of this section cited there: יקר תבל כדך וכוסך. בין ההדסים שים חלקך וכוסך (the first meaning cup and the second lot).

[4] =כבוד קדושת מרנא ורבנא. [5] =שמרו צור.

קתל גׄמאעה̈ אלחכמים אלמקימין בעכא מע גׄמלה̈ אהלהא ענד
פתוח אלישמעאלים להא פערץׄ איצׄא בנדבהם זׄל גׄמיע פקאל.

The next item has the heading:

וכתב לינקש עלי קבר אלמדׄכור זצ"ל
נגנז בקבר זה איש כל שבח אוסף
ראש הזמן תנחום בן הגביר יוסף[6].

No. 8 is for both his parents his mother having died on Ab 26th, a little over a month after his father.

תׄם תופת ואלדתה נעׄ בעד ופאת אלואלד זצ"ל
כמדה̈ שהר ודׄלך פי כׄו אב פקאל ירתׄיהמא
‿ — — — | ‿ — — — — | ‿ — — — ||

לפירודך אבי חכמה ותורה   לעד נפשי ביין יגון שכורה
ואיך אשקוט ומעי יהמיון   ואיך אבליג ובצלעי מרורה וכו'

The 7th section of the Diwān (אלבאב אלסאבע) has 26 items and there follows the copyist's remark: נשלם זה הדיואן והעתקתיו מכתיבת יד המחבר. Then we have the author's ספר ערוגות הבשמים about which anon (§ 5). Among the leaves of this MS. there are also to be found letters from Joseph to the Nagid David. At the end of one such letter there is the remark:

וכתב בעדה אביאתא אולהא
שמעה דברים מדבש ערבו
ותכתב פי אלבאב אלראבע
וממא כאתבה בעץׄ אכׄואנה מע
קציד אולה היחיה איש
יכתב איצׄא פי אלבאב אלראבע.

Joseph added to one of his letters to the Nagid some verses beginning with שמעה וכו' which are not given here but are included in section 4 of the Diwān. Likewise one of Joseph's friends

[6] The metre of this strophe, to be engraven on the tombstone of his father, is || — — — ‿ — — | — — — ‿ — —.

incorporated in one of his letters a Kaṣīda beginning with היחיה איש. This composition too is placed in that section in accordance with its contents (see above, note 2).

3. MS. No. 102[2] also contains a part of this fourth section of Joseph's Diwān. It is a quire of five leaves of which fol. 1, recto, has the heading בשם אל עולם אלבאב אלראבע (verso is blank and there is a lacuna between fols. 1 and 2). Fol. 2, recto and verso, forms part of a letter to a certain Joseph (evidently הגביר יוסף in § 4) and then we have the heading: וכתב אלי אלנגיד ר̇ דויד (שׂצ̇ ענד סמאעה באתנ̇אהה אלי מצר בעד גיבתה ענהא פי עכה מדה̈ סני[ן].[7] This letter is the 10th item in order in this section. However in MS. Brit. Mus. Or. 2588 it seems that this letter, in rhymed prose intermingled with verse, formed a part of the 3rd section of the Diwān (cp. Cat. Margoliouth, III, p. 254, col. 1). The epistle was published by Brody, קבץ על יד, 1899, p. 17–19 (cp. also Mann, *Jews in Egypt*, II, 329).

4. MS. No. 85[26] (20 leaves) again contains a part of the fourth section of Joseph's Diwān. It is fuller than the copy in the British Museum, the latter having 49 poems whereas the former 58. Margoliouth in his Catalogue (III, 254–5) has not given all the headings nor has he indicated their respective Nos. in the manuscript.[8]

We give here a number of headings from MS. Firkowicz No. 85[26]. Where fol. 1, recto, begins we have the 7th poem of the section in honor of הגביר יוסף with part of the heading preserved אלי מצר בעד ספרה ענהא = No. 7 MS. Brit. Mus., fol. 11[a] (see ibid.,

[7] Cp. also the heading of the poem of section 4 (listed by Marg., *Cat.*, III, 255, col. 1, top): וכתב אלי אלנגיד ר' דויד ש"צ ענד עודתה הו וולדה ר' אברהם ס"ט אלי מצר בעד גיבתה ענהא סנין עדה̈.

David stayed away in 'Akko for several years together with his son Abraham (see note 17) who later succeeded him as Nagid.

[8] No. 2 of this section (fol. 8b) has the heading וקאל איצ̇א מאדחא. The person eulogised is a certain David (perhaps the Nagid): הוא הגביר דוד בחיר האל נדיב כל הנדיבים ראש בני יופי.

No. 3 (fol. 9a): וכתב אלי אלנגיד ר' דוד פי ערס ולדה, on the occasion of the marriage of his son (Abraham), as indicated in l. 13 of the poem: שם הגביר מה טוב ומה נעים הכי אותו על שם אב המון קראו. The other sons of David, Solomon and Isaac, are also mentioned.

No. 5 (fol. 9b): וקאל איצ̇א ימדח בעץ̇ אלרוסא.

p. 254, col. 2) with the heading: וכתב איצא לבעץ̇ אלרוסא וקד עאד אלי מצר בעד ספרה ענהא (viz. on the occasion when this leader returned to Cairo after he (the poet) had left the city). The section contains a number of Piyyuṭim for the various occasions of the year.

כט̇. ולה איצ̇א לפורים מע תעריץ̇ במדת קארי אלמגלה[9].
(acrostic: יוסף)

ל̇. ולה איצ̇א לראש חודש ניסן.

לב̇. ולה איצ̇א לחג השבועות עלי קריב מן טריק שיר השירים[10].

לג̇. ולה איצ̇א עלי הד̇ה אלטריק ערוץ̇ הראיתם ברק מן אקואל ר̇ יהודה הלוי נע̇[11].

לד̇. ולה סליחה לימי התשובה נסג̇הא עלי מנואל ברכי אצולה אלתי לר̇ יהודה הלוי[12].

לו̇. ולה איצ̇א סליחה עלי לחן יעירוני רעיוני אלתי לר̇ יהודה הלוי נע̇[13].

לז̇. וממא אלפה איצ̇א לשביעי שלפסח וקד אעיד אלנגיד ר̇ דוד אלי ריאסתה במצר פערץ̇ פי אכ̇רה בד̇לך[14].

לח̇. ולה סליחה לחן ישן אל תרדם אלתי ליהודה הלוי[15].

[9] A poem for Purim combining the praise of a certain reader of the Megillah.

[10] For Shebu'ot in a form near that of Canticles. It is rather strange that he chose that form for Pentecost when Ruth and not Canticles is recited in the synagogue.

[11] Another poem in the form and the metre ('arūṣ) of Judah Hallevi's poem הראיתם ברק (in honor of Joseph ibn Ṣaddiḳ, cp. Davidson, אוצר השירה והפיוט, II, 161, No. 1031).

[12] A Seliḥah for the ten penitential days composed after the manner of Judah Hallevi's well-known ברכי אצולה for Minḥah of Yom Kippur (for the sources cp. Davidson, *l. c.*, II, 79, No. 1746).

[13] Another Seliḥah after the tune of Judah Hallevi's יעירוני רעיוני (cp. ibid., 403, No. 3155).

[14] This was originally composed for the 7th day of Passover and when the Nagid David returned to his office (after he had come back from 'Akko) the author dealt with this matter at the end of the poem.

[15] A Seliḥah after the tune of Judah Hallevi's ישן אל תרדם (also a Seliḥah, cp. ibid., 449, No. 4132).

(There is a lacuna in the MS. and next item is No. 51.)

נ̇א̇. ת̇ם וצל אלמד̇כור[16] ש̇צ̇ אלי מצר בעד ד̇לך פקאל פי תהניתה

(The person eulogized is called Solomon, the father of three sons of whom the eldest was Samuel.[16a] This Solomon is the son of the Nagid David as the next item, No. 52, shows.)

נ̇ב̇. וקאל מהניא בערס ר̇ אברהם אכ̇יה ש̇צ̇ וכאן ד̇לך פי ג̇מעה̈
חג הסוכות בעד מג̇יה מן עכא צחבה̈ ואלדה ש̇צ̇ ואתפק
מע ד̇לך ערס צדוק ביר̇ שמואל הדיין נ̇ע̇ אלמערוף̇ באבן
אלאמשאטי פקאל פי ד̇לך[17].

(This is equal to No. 44 in MS. Brit. Mus. (fol. 26b). Abraham, the brother of Solomon mentioned in No. 51, is the son of the Nagid David as is evident from the line in the poem:

(וזרחו בו שני אורים גדולים . . . נגיד הדור ועל צדו חמודו).

נ̇ג̇. ונ̇ט̇ם איצ̇א פי תהניתה נ̇ע̇ מושח[18]. כוכב דרך מצוען
כוכבי מרום החריד וכו'

[16] The preceding poem (No. 50) must have also been composed for this person, viz. Solomon b. David Nagid.

[16a] This Samuel, the grandson of the Nagid David, is probably the person whom Estori Parḥi met in Cairo (כפתור ופרח, ed. Luncz, p. 64): ושמעתי במצרים מפי ה"ר שמואל ז"ל אחד מבני בני של הר"ם במז"ל שכשהר"ם ז"ל היה חותם שמו באגרת שלוחה היה מסיים הכותב העובר בכל יום שלשה לאוין פלוני (viz. משה בן מימון) אמרתי לו דרך חצי נחמה שמא הר"ב ז"ל היה מוכרח לעמוד שם שהיה רופא למלך מצרים. There is no need thus to change this name into Solomon as Carmoly and Steinschneider suggest (cp. *M.G.W.J.*, XLV, 134). Cp. also above, p. 424, note 23.

[17] This poem of congratulation on the occasion of the wedding of Abraham b. David Nagid was composed in the intermediate days (חול המועד) of Tabernacles when there was an assembly of the congregation. This was after he had arrived in the company of his father the Nagid from ʻAkko. At the same time there took place the wedding of Ṣadoḳ b. Samuel the Dayyān, known as ibn al-Amshāṭi (the combmaker), and Joseph introduced this event also in the same poem. In the composition there are mentioned 3 sons of Samuel the Dayyān, Elʻazar, Ṣadoḳ (the bridegroom) and a third one anonymously.

[18] And he (the poet) composed (literally: trimmed verses) again in his (Abraham's) honor a poem called Muwashshaḥ (double-rhymed). When the Diwān was copied Abraham was no longer alive, hence the remark נ̇ע̇ (=נוחו עדן).

(Therein the Nagid David and his son Abraham are mentioned.)

נד. ת̇ם אעיד אלנגיד אלמד̇כור אלי מנצב ריאסתה פנט̇ם גירה
פי ד̇לך אביאתא צ̇מן בעצ̇הא ען אלמשנה מעני קולהם
ז"ל אמרה נשביתי וטהורה אני נאמנת. פלמא סמע הו ד̇לך
קאל פי הד̇א אלמעני[19].

(This is equal to No. 47 in MS. Brit. Mus., fol. 27b).

נה. וערץ̇ לה מרץ̇ פכאן אלנגיד אלמד̇כור ואולאדה יש צור[20]
יעודוה פי מרצ̇ה פלמא אפאק כתב אליהם הד̇ה אלאביאת[21]

(= No. 48, ibid., fol. 28a).

נו. וקאל איצ̇א מהניא בערס ולד ר̇ חננאל בן אלחסיד שצ̇[22]

נז. ופי אלמעני איצ̇א ללמד̇כור מושח[23].

נח. וכתב לר' חננאל [אלמ]ד̇כור איצ̇א סט̇[24].

This is the last poem of this section.

5. The special part of the Diwān called ספר ערוגות הבשמים (contained in MS. Firkowicz No. 100[I] and also in No. 291[I]) has the following heading.

רדו[25] לערוגות בם מתי שכל   מעצבונם ימצאו תנחום
וכל מעין חכמה נטען . . .   יוסף הירושלמי בנו תנחום

[19] When the above-mentioned Nagid (either David or his son Abraham) resumed his official rank our poet composed verses inserting some which dealt with the passage in Mishnah Ket. 2.5. When the Nagid heard of this, he said concerning this item.

[20] = ישמרם צורם.

[21] When our poet was sick the Nagid and his sons visited him and after he had recovered he sent them the following stanzas.

[22] This composition was for the occasion of the wedding of a child of R. Ḥananel b. X. the Ḥasid, perhaps identical with Abraham החסיד b. Hillel cited frequently by Abraham Maimuni (cp. Mann, *Jews in Egypt*, II, 327 note 1).

[23] Another poem on the same occasion in the form of a Muwashshaḥ.

[24] = סופו טוב. This poem was sent to the same Ḥananel.

[25] The metre seems to be | | — — — — | — — — — while the Shevas are ignored.

The author outlines the contents of the work:

ואחלקה זה הספר כחלוק הענק[26] לעשר ערוגות . . . וקראתים ערוגות הבשמים

הראשונה

בזכרון מחמדי השר[27] ומעלליו. ומקצת מהלליו.

והשנית

במסבות ובזמנים. ומחמדי שרים ונוגנים.

והשלישית

בענין הגולות והגנים הנאים. וזמיר העוף בעפאים.

והרביעית

בשירי העגבים. ומחלת האהבים.

והחמישית

[בקור]ות ימי הזקנה אשר יבואו פתע. ובינם ובין המות כפֶשַׂע.

והשישית

בבגד רעי וחברתם הרשע[28]. ההפוכה כמו רגע.

והשביעית

בזכרון הגדיבים. ואורך ליל הידידים הפרודים[29].

והשמינית

במאיסת תבל ויראת האל וזכרון המות. והנסיעה אל ארץ צלמות.

והתשיעית

בשמחת האדם בחלקו. ובטחונו בנותן לחם חקו. והתכבדו לשאול מיגוניו ספקו.

והעשירית

בשבח השיר אשר פניו כל משכיל יחלה. והחכמה אשר בכתם אופיר לא תסלה.

[26] Viz. by Moses ibn Ezra (cp. ed. David Günzburg, 1886).

[27] The patron to whom the composition was dedicated.

[28] For the more correct order רֵעַי הרשע וחברתם in order to have some sort of a rhyme ending in 'ע.

[29] Here too the rhyme consists only of the final Mem.

At the end of the work we have the following three stanzas in the form of a colophon. Homonyms are used in each stanza.

|| — — | — ⏑ — — — | — ⏑ — — —

מגדי עצי דעת ברו אנשי   בין מנאום יוסף בנו תנחום
עד תפקחו עין כל חסרי לב   בהם ולנתיב האמת תנחום
שלמו[30] נגידי שיר להורם[31]   שמש זבול תתמה ותֵשע[32]
בשנת הלֿז[33] השלים מלאכתם   עלם שנותיו שש ותשע
ספר בספיר לא יסולה קח   מיד כבד לשון צעיר שנים
ורדֵה דבש מצוף ערוגות שיר   מספר חרוזיהם כשושנים[34]

נשלם ספר ערוגות הבשמים ברוך י״י

Then there follows an Arabic glossary of the homonyms used in this work.

MS. Harkavy, L, No. 47 (6 leaves), contains also the end of this Arabic glossary. On fol. 3, verso, bottom there is the copyist's remark: נשלם ערוגות הבשמים וכתבתיהו מכתיבת יד המחבר (cp. above, § 2). Then we have the beginning of a new poetical work:

והדֿה מקאמאת אלבעץֿ אלמחדתֿין[35] אסמה אבי איוב בן סהל נֿע

(fol. 4, recto)

נאם אשר בן יהודה. ויהי היום יושב בשער בקרב חביריו. וכל איש מהם משיח בדבריו. ומגיד משפטי נעוריו. וכו׳.

This Maḳama has been printed by Schorr (החלוץ, III, 154–58). Schorr identified it with the composition mentioned by Ḥarizi in his 3rd Maḳama (תחכמוני, ed. Lagarde, p. 23, ll. 47–48): וקרובו (של ר׳ יוסף בן סהל) ר׳ שלמה בן ציקבאל. גם הוא למד מלאכת השיר וקבל. והוא עשה המחברת החמודה. אשר תחלתה „נאם אשר בן יהודה״. How-

[30] The metre of lines 3–4 is — — — — | — — — — (the Shevas are ignored) while lines 5–6 have the same metre as lines 1–2.

[31] לְהוֹרָם.

[32] For שעה, to gaze.

[33] To be vocalized as הַלָּז. The numerical value is 5037 A. M. = 1277 C. E.

[34] Evidently as the numerical value of שושנים, 706.

[35] One of the narrators, story-tellers.

ever Brody (*Z.f.H.B.*, IV, 58–60) has come to the conclusion that the Maḳama, edited by Schorr, was of a later date than that of Ḥarizi. This seems now to be confirmed by the copyist's remark that the author was Solomon (Abū Ayyūb being the usual Arabic kunya for this Biblical name) b. Sahl and not Solomon b. ציקבאל as Ḥarizi calls him. The name ציקבאל in the Taḥkemoni is well established by reason of the rhyme (וקבל) and cannot be regarded as a corruption of סהל, although Solomon b. ציקבאל was a relative of Joseph b. Sahl. We have thus to assume that two poets composed Maḳamas each beginning with נאם אשר בן יהודה.

9.
MISCELLANEOUS FRAGMENTS CONCERNING EGYPTIAN PERSONALITIES

In this section there are assembled a number of data from Genizah fragments relating to several people in Egypt in order to supplement our knowledge of Jewish life in the country of the Nile during the Fāṭimid period and beyond.

1. Abraham b. Sabbatai and his Son Sabbatai b. Abraham.

As Ḥaber of the Egyptian community of Minyat Zifta Abraham b. Sabbatai figures in the important letter to the Nagid Moses b. Meborakh (Mann, I, 212 ff., II, 257–9). He seems to have been a Palestinian. We find him in Tyre in 1091. As the Palestinian academy was then established in this city, it may be assumed that he studied there and that he graduated from it with the title Ḥaber authorising him to be the spiritual leader (Ḥaber) of a community. MS. Firkowicz, 2. Hebrew-Arabic Collection, No. 2889, contains 11 leaves of a dictionary (אגרון) probably being that of David b. Abraham Alfāsi (letters 'יוד–ט)[1]. This MS. was copied by our Abraham for his own use as the colophon at the end shows: אני אברהם ברבי שבתי תנצבה כתבתי זה האגרון לעצמי ב צ ו ר מדינתא המקום בה ישימהו עלי סימן טוב סימן ברכה וחיסנא ויקירא ורחמי מן שמיא ויתן וימלא שאלותי ברצון. ונשלם האות העשירי שהוא אות י' בשנת דתתנ"א לבירייתיה דעלמא בירח אדר ראשון בכז יום בו. הרחמן ישמור צאתי ובואי ויצילני מבני אדם הרעים ומאורב בדרך וכן יהי רצון.

It seems that when writing this colophon[2] Abraham already contemplated leaving Tyre for Egypt in order to find scope

[1] About David and his Agron see especially Pinsker, לקוטי קדמוניות, 117–167, and cp. Steinschneider, *Arab. Lit.*, p. 86.

[2] A year before, he compiled for himself Aggadot from 'Erubin rendering them from Aramaic into Hebrew. See the fragment published by Ginzberg (גנזי שעכטער, II, 375–78) with the following colophon at the end (already

there for his learning. Ultimately he landed as Dayyān of Minyat Zifta where he seems to have resided to the end of his life.

Abraham's son, Sabbatai, is the signatory of a document drawn up at Minyat Zifta in Ab 1465 Sel. (= 1154 C. E.) when Abraham was no longer alive.[3] Sabbatai evidently expected to succeed his father but it is doubtful whether he was successful. A letter of his to the important Kātib, Judah Hakkohen b. El'azar, reveals his troubles when another person, Abū'l Bahā, a native of Damascus, but living in Cairo, competed forthe job at Minyat Zifta.[4] Judah Hakkohen is styled השר האדיר בישראל

given by Mann, *l. c.*, II, 259, note 7): נשלם זה הדיפתר לאברהם ברבי שבתי תנצבה בשנת דתתנ (1089–90) הקבה יזכהו ללמוד וללמד ולשמור ולעשות ויזכה לשמוח בשמחת ביאת הגואל ויתן חלקו עם מצוקי ארץ וינהילהו שני עולמות כדכת כי בי ירבו ימיך ויוסיפו לך שנות חיים (Prov. 9.11).

Ginzberg has rightly pointed out that the rendering of the Talmudic Aramaic into Hebrew in our fragment is similar to the method employed in the Hebrew version of ה' פסוקות edited by Schlossberg (ס' הלכות פסוקות או הלכות ראו, Paris 1886). This version is now recognized to be a Palestinian product (see Poznański, *RÉJ*, LXIII, 235, note 2, and J. N. Epstein, *Jb. d. jüd.-liter. Ges.*, XII, 99–100). Abraham b. Sabbatai, as a Palestinian by birth and training, thus followed the same method. It seems that in the Gaonic period there was in Palestine the tendency to make the Talmud more intelligible by rendering it into Hebrew which was well known and cultivated, whereas Aramaic went into discard. On the other hand, in Babylon, till as late as the time of Hai Gaon, Aramaic was still the spoken language in the smaller places (cp. the responsum published by Harkavy, חדשים גם ישנים, II, No. 10 = הקדם, II, p. 82: כי כיון שבבל מאז מקום לשון ארמי ולשון כשדי ועד אן (= ועדיין) בכל העיירות בלשון ארמי וכשדי מספרין הכל בין ישראל ובין הגוים). The Hebrew-Aramaic lingo of the Babylonian Talmud was regarded by the Babylonian Geonim as the language of the scholars (cp. Mann, *JQR*, *N. S.*, XI, 463, where Sherira's responsum is cited: ולפום דשאלתון מן קדמנא בלשון ארמית כמנהאנא דרבנן). This difference of attitude towards Aramaic, interesting as it is, cannot be traced further here in this connection. Cp. also infra, p. 554, note 1.

[3] Bodl. 2874.22: שבתי בירבי אברהם החבר הדיין תנצבה.

[4] The letter has been published by Gottheil-Worrell, *Fragments from the Cairo Genizah in the Freer Collection*, 1927, pp. 12–17. There are numerous misreadings in the printed text as a comparison with the facsimile attached reveals, and altogether the editors failed to understand the drift of the letter and to identify correctly the persons referred to therein. Thus Judah Hakkohen is made Dayyān of Bilbais (p. 13 top) whereas he was in reality an important figure in Cairo by reason of his position as a high government official.

and his elder son El'azar held the title of Sa'ad al-Mulk, 'the happiness of the Kingdom'.[5] He was a high government secretary (סופר המלכות, cp. עטרת הסופרים in our letter, l. 5) and naturally was a resident of Cairo, the seat of the government. Sabbatai b. Abraham mentions in his letter that he had already decided[6] to visit his influential patron when some Jewish people from Bilbais[7] who arrived at Minyat Zifta told him of what was

Herewith follow a number of textual corrections. L. 5 for נפוצות r. נפשות; l. 6 for אלהים r. אלהינו; l. 11 אן should be deleted as it was corrected on the top as אנה, the other sentence on top should read וקאלו קט ען עז אלדין ולם יפהם (the reading is doubtful) עבדה[א]; l. 14 for אלנור r. אלנזר (and so in ll. 15 and 21); l. 15, for מעלם r. אלעלם (as in l. 18) and for צוֹ r. צוֹ (=ישמרם צורם); l. 16, for אלהיא r. אלהינו; l. 17, for אלקיים r. לקיים and for ימצא r. ומצא; l. 20, for ונדכל r. וידכֿל and for עאדנן r. עארץ֗; l. 22, for עולם r. עולה and for ואלדי r. ולדי; l. 23, for אבו אלמגרבי יתם r. אבו אלמגֿד באתם; l. 26, for ואלי דל יעקוב חאלה r. ואל ידל ועקב שלום; the 2 marginal lines ought to come somewhere between lines 13–16, and in l. 1, for אליהודי r. אילהוד and in l. 2, for לעלם r. אלעלם; verso, l. 1, for וקל r. וקאל; l. 3, for תוצית ענה r. תואפית עני; l. 4 in קאלה בג there is really the word ק אלחבג though what ק is (or בן) is not clear; for ועף בשלום r. ועקב שלום.

[5] See Mann, II, 338, where after עטרת ראשי the word אלעזר has fallen out due to printer's error (thus עטרת ראשי אלעזר המכונה אלשיך֗ סעד אלמלך וכו').

[6] Line 9: ולמא כאן פי הדֿה אלגֿמעה עוֹלת עלי אלדכֿול אלי סאמיהא. The II of עול + עלי means 'to determine upon' (but cp. the translation of the editors: "I was boorishly denied entrance"!).

[7] About the community of Bilbais, cp. Mann, II, General Index, s. v. In this connection it should be pointed out how Worrell-Gottheil misread l. 4 on p. 18: תקדם כתאבי אליך מע אלבלביסי, 'my letter was forwarded to you with a man from Bilbais'. The word אלבלביסי becomes according to them אלכלבים, the dogs, supposed to be a derogatory name in the meaning of rascals! And a reviewer (A. Marmorstein, *RÉJ*, LXXXV, 101) promptly identified 'the dogs' with the Gentiles proceeding to give examples of such mutual compliments exchanged between Jews and Gentiles. All this learning (alas useless) about a misread word! Then the editors have discovered in the same document (p. 22, l. 8) a superstitious remedy for curing a drying up of the body or boils by using the Song of Songs (see p. 19 and Introduction, XVI and XXVIII)! In reality a certain Abū'l Ḥayy requests that a medical prescription should be obtained for him from the Nagid, whose official title was שַׂר הַשָּׂרִים (cp. Mann, I, 254) and who so often was a physician! The editors further made of the writer of this particular letter and of his brother, the recipient of the same, readers of the Law (קארי אלה) whereas the true reading is בן אבו אלחיי, thus Ibrahim b. Abū'l Ḥayy and his brother Abū 'Imrān Musa ibn al-Ḥayy. The latter actually appears on p. 155! In this manner the whole edition is teeming with curious readings and impossible renderings (e.g. the mysterious

going on in Cairo with regard to the appointment (of Dayyān) for the congregation of Minyat Zifta. These people from Bilbais evidently recently visited Cairo and now came to Minyat Zifta for some purpose, probably of a business character. A certain Abū'l Bahā of Damascus, living in Cairo, went to a certain Ṣalāḥ ad-Dīn (evidently an influential leader of the Cairo community) and obtained from him a promise that he would give him the appointment at Minyat Zifta. The informants also mentioned that Abū'l Bahā was trying for the appointment at Maḥalla. On top of line 11 there is a remark that the informants hardly spoke about 'Izz ad-Daula (evidently also a dignitary of influence in Cairo to settle the appointments in the provincial places).

Now this turn of affairs greatly upset our Sabbatai b. Abraham's position. He wanted to go to Cairo to complain, but the Jews of Minyat Zifta advised him first to write to his friends in Cairo about the matter, viz. to the Shaikh al-Thiḳa (i. e. Misha'el b. Isaiah)[8] and to Yehoseph al-נזר (=נזר השרים) b. Natan al-נזר (b. Samuel).[9] Of course the recipient of the present letter, Judah Hakkohen b. El'azar, is to help him and a certain al-Sa'īd Muwaffaḳ is to be taken into confidence in order to enable Sabbatai to obtain the office due to him (probably as successor of his father) instead of his rival Abū'l Bahā. The upshot of the whole matter is unknown. The letter reveals conditions in Egypt where appointments for the local communities were made by the Nagid and his Bet-Din Haggadol. The time of our letter probably falls in the period of anarchy in the centralized com-

gentleman Genesis-Exodus, Introduction, p. XVI, and p. 132, l. 37, of course disappears if we read פרשת אלא (r. אלה) שמות יום אלכ̇מיס, viz. that the letter was written on Thursday of the week of Sidra אלה שמות, Exodus 1–6.1)!

[8] See Mann, II, 319, note 9. Mishael's father, Isaiah, was an important figure in Fusṭāṭ, the author of a philosophical work on the soul and a brother-in-law of the influential Joshu'a b. Dosa. Mishael himself, known as אלשיך̇ אלת̇קה̈, was the father-in-law of Moses Maimonides and one of his sons, 'Uzziel Abū'l Ma'āli, married the sister of Maimonides (see ibid., note 13, and p. 328, note 1). Hence he belonged to the aristocracy of Fusṭāṭ Jewry.

[9] Cp. Mann, I, 227, note 1. His father Natan b. Samuel, called אלנזר=נזר החברים, was the secretary of the Nagid Samuel b. Ḥananyah. Both were greatly eulogized by Judah Hallevi (ibid., p. 225, note 1). Cp. also above, p. 259.

munal regime after the death of the Nagid Samuel b. Ḥananyah (1159) when there was a usurper Zuṭṭa who was greatly hated and with whom later on Maimonides came into conflict (see above, p. 416). Several persons named by their honorific titles, like Ṣalaḥ ad-Dīn and ʿIzz ad-Daula, cannot as yet be identified but others are known from other documents as pointed out above.

2. A Letter from a Widower.

The epistle, given under No. I (the beginning of which is missing and there is a lacuna at the bottom of recto), is from a widower who tarried already two years in a certain Egyptian locality in order to collect a debt. He left behind a mother and a daughter who were anxiously awaiting his return. The writer seems to have been a man of some learning, being able to make a living from teaching. While at the place of his enforced stay he became befriended with the local Dayyān who on his advancement to a similar position in the larger community of Alexandria urged this stranger to accompany him thither. This Ḥaber promised that he would procure for him a position as teacher of most of the young Jewish boys in Alexandria. There was even a talk of this widower marrying the niece of this Ḥaber (see ll. 20ff. and l. 8). He however refused to accept the invitation because he had to take care of a house which evidently belonged to his family. Now there is a new Dayyān in this locality, Nissim by name, who is also on good terms with the writer and whose present letter he is taking along with him, evidently to Fusṭāṭ where he is to stay a week, to hand over to the person addressed. This Nissim is constantly reproaching him for not remarrying which would involve his not returning to his mother and daughter.

Owing to the defective state of our letter neither the name of the writer nor that of the recipient can be established. The latter had two boys, Naṣr and Saʿīd. His wife expecting another child and also his daughter-in-law are mentioned. Writer and recipient were related. The date of the epistle cannot be ascertained but the appearance of the handwriting is one of the 12th century.

3. An Appeal from a Person about to Settle in Palestine.

David b. Benjamin (in the letter given under II) is about to leave for the Holy Land and appeals to a certain Pinḥas Hakkohen to hurry up and let him have the remainder of the amount that was collected (or should be collected) for his maintenance. Also a smaller amount was to be procured for David's son. A similar appeal David sent to the Dayyān Ḥananel. The latter is perhaps the recipient of the letter from Mishael b. 'Uzziel.[10]

4. An appeal from Prison.

In the letter, given under III, another David appeals to a prominent leader (evidently of the Fusṭāṭ-Cairo community), Abraham, to bring about his release from prison. David admits that he is not treated harshly by the jailers but complains that his freedom of movement is restricted and that his diet is meager. It is unknown for what cause this Jew, familiar with Bible and Rabbinics, was put in prison. I am also unable to identify this leader Abraham to whom David appealed in his distress. By the appearance of the MS. and the nature of the style, the epistle certainly dates not later than the 13th century and more likely the 12th.

5. A document from a North-African Community.

The extract from the document, dated Sivān 1138 C. E. (given under No. IV), is inserted here to preserve the memory of a community hitherto unknown. The document found its way ultimately to Fusṭāṭ where it was deposited subsequently in the Genizah. Evidently some of the persons involved therein resided in this city. In מינזאר, situated at the coast (of North-Africa), the communal leaders (זקנים) would attend to law-suits

[10] Published by Horovitz, *Z.f.H.B.*, IV, 155–58, cp. Pozn., ibid., p. 186. Cp. also Bodl. 2878.106 where there is mentioned מֹו (=מרנא ורבנא) חננאל הדַיָן המופלא.

between Jew and Jew.[11] Sa'adyah b. Meborakh, known as al-Jazāiri (viz. originating from Algiers but probably residing in מינואר), summoned Ḥayyim b. Reuben before the elders and produced a power of attorney from Berakhah[12] b. Joseph, known as al-Surti (viz. originating from Surt between Barḳah and Tripolis, but evidently residing in Fusṭāṭ), who had a claim against Ḥayyim demanding the return of 40 quarters (probably of Dinārs) which constituted the dowry of Berakhah's daughter. Either this lady, who evidently was the wife of Ḥayyim, became divorced or died without children and according to the Palestinian custom of the Ketubah half of the deceased's dowry had to be returned to her father's family.[13] Hence the present claim against Ḥayyim. The power of attorney, probably executed in Fusṭāṭ, was duly examined by the elders in מינואר to ascertain its validity. The litigant Ḥayyim denied the sum of the dowry to have been 40 quarters alleging that it amounted only to 10 quarters. The document, embodying the result of the lawsuit, was evidently forwarded by Sa'adyah b. Meborakh, who held the power of attorney, to Berakhah b. Joseph in Fusṭāṭ.

6. Memorial Lists.

Many such lists have been preserved among the Genizah fragments and a goodly number of them has already been published.[14] They give us the genealogies of many personalities in Egypt and thus are aids for placing persons, and through them corresponding events, in the proper chronological sequence. The five lists given under No. V give additional information of this sort. Of these No. 3 is not a memorial list but rather an enumeration of living persons, probably for taxation purposes similar to

[11] About similar cases mentioned in the Gaonic responsa, see Mann, *JQR*, *N. S.*, X, 340.

[12] The name ברכה was used both for males and females (cp. Mann, II, 172: ברכה ביר' רוח, and Bodl. 2805.4: Berakhah the daughter of Shemaryah).

[13] About this custom cp. Mann, II, 259, note 7, and 381.

[14] Greenstone, *JQR*, *N. S.*, I, 43–59; Gaster, *Kaufmann Gedenkbuch* 241–42; Poznański, *RÉJ*, LI, 52 ff., LXVI, 60ff; Mann, II, 50ff., 58f., 62ff., 100f., 210ff., 270f., 281ff., 313ff., 318ff., 357ff.

other such items that are found in the Genizah.[15] No. 4 contains the genealogy of the family of the famous Egyptian Nagid, Samuel b. Ḥananyah, which has been discussed by me before (II, 281ff.). The present list adds a few more details with regard to the medical profession practiced by several members of this family the outstanding one of whom was the Nagid Samuel as court physician of the Fāṭimid Caliph al-Ḥāfiẓ (see Mann, I, 228–29). Further details as to the persons mentioned are to be found in the footnotes to the texts.

7. A Compact of Perpetual Friendship.

The document given under No. VI, dated January 2, 1564 C. E., is an interesting compact of friendship between El'azar Maimon and Yom Ṭob ibn Sīd. They contract to be intimate towards each other as if they were the sons of the same parents, to help each other in time of joy and of sorrow, to make available to each other books acquired or copied and to pray together in the synagogue of the saintly Rabbi Samuel ibn Sīd. Any misunderstanding between them must be removed within 24 hours so that their mutual friendship be not impaired. The pact of friendship is to last through their lives and is extended to their future generations. The compact was agreed upon under the sanctity of an oath and by hand-shake. Five outstanding Rabbinic authorities of that age are to be notified of this compact so that their consent would have to be obtained before the compact could be invalidated, viz. Joseph Caro of Safed, the author of the Shulḥan 'Arukh, Moses de Trani (known as מבי"ט) and Israel de Curiel (both of Safed), Meir of Padua and Isaac ibn Sīd. The synagogue of Samuel ibn Sīd, referred to in our document, was in Cairo and hence the two friends lived there. Indeed Yom Tob ibn Sīd is mentioned among the Cairene Rabbis.

Such compacts, though we possess none in writing, were usual also in earlier times. Of Yeḥiel, the father of R. Asher (famous as the Rosh), it is reported that he concluded a covenant with his friend Solomon Hakkohen to share in all their doings including

[15] Cp. Mann, II, 246–7, and Gottheil-Worrell, *l. c.*, 66–70.

their pious acts. When Yeḥiel died his friend reminded him before he was lowered to his grave of their covenant to make sure of their common share in Paradise.[16] True friendship, it may be argued, needs no restraining bond of compact or covenant. But realizing human weakness, pious Jews would make sure of the constancy of their attachment by a religious sanctification in the form of such a compact as given here, a treaty of friendship not for material gain but for study, devotional prayer and deeds of loving kindness.

8. Miscellanea.

Under this heading we present a number of stray data culled from MSS. concerning Jewish life in Egypt (and also in Palestine), chiefly during the Fāṭimid period. They are trifles that do not lend themselves to separate treatment but may be of use in a larger connection when more material is available.

a) The two communities of Fusṭāṭ, the Babylonian and the Palestinian, are well-known. MS. Antonin, No. 793, contains two vellum leaves of a Pentateuch with the following colophon: מה שהקדישה ריסה בת יוסף בן נטירא על שמה ושם בעלה ללוש בר אברהם הרופא ירחמהו אל לכנסת הבבליים בפסטאט מצרים ארור גונבו ומוכרו וכו׳. The name ללוש is very rare. The leaders of the two congregations would meet occasionally when common action was needed. A very damaged fragment, MS. Adler (top and bottom, missing, handwriting probably of the 11th century) records such common action against a person who would denounce fellow Jews to the governor of the city. This person seems to have been a communal officer, a sort of Ḥazzān and scribe who drew up legal documents such as Ketubot and bills of divorce. The two communities by combined action decided to deprive that notorious person of any

[16] Cp. the ethical will of Judah b. Asher b. Yeḥiel (ed. Schechter, בית תלמוד, IV, 374): זקני הר׳ יחיאל נולד בשנת תתק״ע (1209–10 C. E.) וכשהיה כבן י״ג שנה היה לו חבר נאמן הר׳ שלמה הכהן ז״ל וכרתו ברית יחד שכל אחד יהיה לו חלק בכל מעשה חבירו הן במצות הן בעניינים אחרים ועמדו בברית כל ימיהם וכו׳.

The whole story is also repeated from Judah's will by Abraham b. Solomon of Torrutiel in his השלמת ס׳ הקבלה (ed. Neub., *Med. Jew. Chron.*, I, 104, and ed. Harkavy, חדשים גם ישנים, II, No. 2, pp. 9–10).

office in order to stop his nefarious activities.[17] However owing to the deficient state of the fragment it is not sure whether it refers to conditions in Fusṭāṭ and not to Alexandria where there also existed such two congregations (see Mann, I, 88, 89, note 1). The scourge of delation, so frequent in Mediaeval Jewish history, did not thus spare Egyptian Jewry.

b) Ṣadoḳ Hallevi b. Levi is known as a member of the Palestinian academy in the first half of the 11th century. He advanced in the course of time to the dignity of Ab of the school (Mann II, 182–4). MS. Antonin, No. 521, is a vellum leaf containing the commencement of 1 Chronicles with vocalization and Massorah. The text is written in three columns to the page. This leaf evidently formed the beginning of a codex of the Hagiographa as the colophon, written by our Ṣadoḳ, shows. The commencement of the Hagiographa with Chronicles was the Palestinian custom whereas in Babylon either this book or the Scroll of Esther was placed at the end of the third section of the Bible.[18]

The colophon reads: (1) זה הכתובים קנהו מר (2) יוסף בר דניאל מסגלת ממונו (3) ללימוד שני בניו מנצור (4) ועלי האחים הנאחים (5) בתורה האלהים יזכם (6) להגות בתורה ובמשנה (7) ויזכה את יוסף אביהם (8) לשמוח בשמחת תורתם. (9) ובשישת חתונתם. ולראות (10) בניהם ובני בניהם הוגים (11) בתורה לקיים עליהם (12) מקרא שכתוב[19] לא ימוש (13) ספר התורה הזה מפיך (14) והגית בו יומם ולילה (15) אמן סלה (16) צדוק הלוי ברבי לוי נב"ג[20] קטון תלמידי הצבי (17).[21] Whether Ṣadoḳ was himself the scribe of this code, or the owner of it, or was merely requested to write the colophon by the purchaser Joseph b. Daniel, who bought the volume for study by his boys Manṣūr and 'Alī, cannot be ascertained.

[17] The fragment reads: (1) . . . הקשה אשר יעשה והמזו[ן] (2) המצומצם אשר הוא ילשין בו אל שליט המדינה [ל]התרויח ממנו ויפסידו כל הון שיהא (3) לו וממון שירויח כל ימי ריחוקו מביתו עד אשר יהיה כלי ריק (4) חסר מכל וכל נקי יפילהו ביד השליט לסטרהו ולהענישהו ובזה (5) החודש הלשין על אנשים רבים וענשום [ז]הובים הרבה וכאשר (6) ראינו אילה הדברים נתועדנו אנחנו שתי הכניס[יות] וע[ש]ינו (7) כאגודה אחת והטלנו השלום בינותינו . . . שט . . . (8) עאני והעדנו על עצמנו האלהי[ם] . . . [שלא] (9) יהיה לזה האיש בתוכנו שום [רשות] . . . (10) כתובה אפילו בחזנות אפילו ב . . . (11) מינים שישתתפו בהן הקהל[ות] . . . (12) ואם . . . . עם מו . . נו

[18] Cp. Mann, *RÉJ*, LXXII, 163–4.

[19] Joshua 1.8. [20] = נשמתו בגן (עדן).

[21] = (Palestine) ישיבת ארץ הצבי.

Later on (in the beginning of the 12th century), this volume was acquired by Solomon Hakkohen Gaon b. Elijah, head of the school in Ḥadrak near Damascus (see Mann I ,196; II, 233–35). This we learn from a note on the righthand side of the above colophon. (1) זה המצחף כתובים (2) אנתקל במקנת כסף אלי (3) שלמה הכהן גאון בן גאון[22] (4) נין שלמה גאון נכד אהרן (5) קדוש יי' זצ̇ל̇ עלי יד יהודה (6) הלוי בן משולם בן יוסף נ̇ע̇ (7) נודע בן אלמגאזלי[23].

Hence our codex was in the interval acquired by Judah Hallevi b. Meshullam and subsequently bought by the Gaon Solomon Hakkohen.

c) As regards the members of the above priestly family of Palestinian Geonim (discussed by Mann, II, 62ff.) we find the sons of Joseph Hakkohen Ab, the brother of Elijah Gaon, established in Fusṭāṭ in the second half of the 11th century as members of the Bet-Din. Thus Solomon Hakkohen b. Joseph אב בית דין שלכל ישראל is a signatory of several documents (Mann I, 187, note 2, 208; II, 231). Another son was Merayot who is the signatory of a document found in T.-S. 12.624 (only the end is preserved, the date and place are missing), no doubt drawn up at Fusṭāṭ.[24]

Another member of this family was Judah Hakkohen Rosh Hasseder, a title given to him by the Bagdād Exilarch Hezekiah (cp. Mann, II, 101, note 2, 107, note 10, and especially 346 where his genealogy has been established). He was the author of a commentary on Sepher Yeṣīrah,[25] of responsa and other writings. A portion of the first mentioned work is found in MS. Firkowicz, 2. Hebrew-Arabic Collection, No. 385, consisting of 13 damaged leaves. The colophon at the end reads: כמל ספר יצירה ליהודה הכהן הח̇ והנ̇ בן כב̇ גד̇ מ̇ור̇ יוסף הכהן נין יהוסף הכ[והן] אב בית דין כהן צדק נין הגאונים נ[ע] כתב אהרן הלוי בר̇ יעקב המלמד ש̇צ̇ (viz. the copyist was Aaron Hallevi b. Jacob). In this commentary he cites the Shaikh Abū ʻOthmān with great respect wishing he had met him

[22] Viz. Elijah Gaon, the father of Ebyatar Hakkohen and Solomon.

[23] The maker of spindles?

[24] The signatures are on one line: מריות הכהן בירבי יוסף אב הישיבה זצ"ל. יפתח בניאמין בר אברהם נ̇ע̇. יכין בר מנחם נ̇ע̇ א[ברהם] . . . and on another line בר . . . .

[25] ר' יהודה הכהן בר' יוסף נין יהוסף הכ' (=הכהן) פי שרח ספר יצירה לאברהם אבינו נ̇ע̇ (see Mann, II, 101, note 2).

as the result would have been of mutual intellectual benefit.[26] One may venture to assume that he refers to a work on Sepher Yeṣīrah by Abū ʻOthmān Sahl b. Bishr, one of the most famous astrologers of the Middle Ages (first half of 9th century, see Steinschneider, *Arab. Liter.*, 23ff.), although we have no other reference to such a work by him. The name ʻOthmān is hardly ever found among the Jews and the only author known by the name Abū ʻOthmān is our Sahl b. Bishr.[27] Finally it should be added that MS. Mosseri, L 153, has a fragment of a letter addressed to יהודה הכהן הרב וראש הסדר ברבי יוסף החסיד ז"ל לברכה and also L 260 the address of which reads: חצרה מולאי אלשיך אלאגל אבי זכרי כגק מרור יהודה הכהן החכם והנבון בן כגק מרור יוסף הכהן הזקן הנכבד סט נין יהוסף הכהן בית דין כהנן צדקן.

d) The cosmopolitan character of the Fusṭāṭ community has been pointed out by me (vol. I, 206). Also Persian Jews were represented there as is evident from the Persian MSS. found in the Genizah. A document of 1021, C. E., drawn up in Hormshir (in the province of Khuzistān) has been found in the Genizah showing that some of the persons concerned must have settled in the old Muhammedan capital of Egypt.[28] A colophon (MS. Mosseri, C. 9, paper, Persian in Hebrew script) tells us of Nissi b. Samuel of Sirjān,[29] the older capital of the province of Kirmān, and of his son ʻAlī. It reads: (1) לעלי בן ניסי סימן טוב (2) עליך (3) כתיב ידניאל[30] (4) ברכה וטובה וישועה ואורה ושמחה (5) לניסי בן שמואל מארץ כרמאן ממדינת (6) סירגאן יחייה ויזכה וירבה לעדי עד. The first owner was Nissi b. Samuel and later on his son ʻAlī b. Nissi had

[26] Fol. 6b: וקד שרחנא דלך פי אול אלכתאב ארגע אליה פתראה פהדא קול צאחב ספר יצירה צא וחשוב שאין הפה יכול לדבר ואין האוזן יכולה לשמוע (cp. Yeṣīrah c. 4, end) ולקד תלף (=תאלף) אלשיך אבו עתמאן רחמה אללה פי הדא אלכתאב פיא לית לקינאה פלא בד ממא כאן נסתפיד מנה ויסתפיד מנא ואן כאנת אנסאמנא לם תלתקי פלא בד לנפוסנא אן תלתקי ואללה אעלם.

[27] Indeed Steinschneider (*JQR*, XI, 585, bottom) suggests that Sahl may have had a son who embraced Islam and hence he was called Abū ʻOthmān. However this is doubtful and certainly from the respectful way Judah Hakkohen speaks of Abū ʻOthmān it is clear that he had no inkling of any apostacy in the family.

[28] Bodl. 2875.24, published by D. S. Margoliouth, *JQR*, XI, 671–75.

[29] About this city see Le Strange, *Lands of the Eastern Caliphate*, 300ff.

[30] Is this a corruption of כתב יד דניאל?

this work. The latter or one of his heirs probably emigrated to Fusṭāṭ and thus the volume found a resting place in the local Genizah.

e) The struggle between Christendom and Islām for the possession of the Holy Land during the Crusades was keenly watched by the Jews as a highly interested third party. It led to several Messianic movements which have been discussed by me elsewhere.[31] The emergence of Saladin as the champion of Islām also gave occasion to some Jews to hope and dream for Israel's future. A Genizah fragment in T.-S. Box J. 2 tells of a Piyyuṭ which a certain teacher Mauhub composed in a dream concerning the defeat of Edom (Christendom) at the hands of the Egyptian Muhammedans, with the resulting redemption of Israel. The year given is 1185 C. E. Well, this dream was not too long in advance of the time, for in 1187 Saladin succeeded in destroying the Latin kingdom of Jerusalem as a result of the famous battle at Ḥiṭṭīn or Ḥaṭṭīn near Tiberias. The fragment reads: הדה אלשגעה[32] אלדי ראהא מוהוב אלמעלם[33] ווא . . . יעלמה לה פי אלחלם: שנת רצון אָתַת להגאל חנם[34] מאדום: בהנקם במו ענמים[35] נקמה מאדום: גם זו השנה היא ת ש ע מ א ו ת א ר ב ע י ם ו ח מ ש ה[36] ובסופה יהיו שופכים דם אדום: דגול יתן נקמתו באדום: ויגונן עם נמלטים מפרא[37] ואדום. The composing of verses in a dream is testified by other people. Thus Samuel ibn Nagdela dreamt in verse of the downfall of his political enemy Ibn 'Abbās.[38] Moses ibn Ezra treats of this theme in his Kitāb al-muḥāḍara wal-mudhākara.[39]

f) The moot question of the number and the identifications of the gates of Jerusalem at various periods cannot be discussed

[31] Cp. Mann, התקופה, XXIII, 243–261, XXIV, 335–358. Cp. further *RÉJ*, LXXXVIII, p. 250 ff.

[32] This word gives no meaning here (שגע means to be brave, courageous). We expect a word for strophes, verses (אלאשעאר). For אלדי r. אלתי.

[33] This reading is not certain.

[34] Cp. Is. 52.3.

[35] Egyptians (cp. Gen. 10.13), here the army of Saladin, the Sultan of Egypt, is meant.

[36] (4)945 A. M. = 1185 C. E.

[37] The Muhammedans supposedly descended from Ishmael (cp. Gen. 16.12).

[38] Samuel's Diwān (ed. Harkavy, זכרון לראשונים, I), p. 77.

[39] See translation Halper, שירת ישראל, pp. 101ff.

here. About the data of the Muhammedan geographers see Le Strange, *Palestine under the Moslems*, 212–17. Attention is only drawn here to a Genizah fragment in T.-S. Box K. 27 (2 paper leaves) containing prayers to be recited at the gates of al-Ḳuds (Jerusalem). Fol. 1, recto, top, has the heading צלואת אלאבואב פי אלקדס and goes on to enumerate these gates as follows: (1) באב אלכֹהֻן אבואב אלכמסה̈ (2) אבואב אלסתה̈ אבואב אלרחמה̈ (3) באב חנה באב יצחק (4) באב אלקנה באב אליהודה (5) באב דויד באב שלמה באב עשרין פדאלך (6). In reality less than 20 gates are enumerated unless we count in the following manner, 1) the Priestly Gate, 2) the 5 gates, 3) the 6 gates, 4) the gates of Mercy (viz. 2), making together 14 which with the following 6 gates enumerated separately round up the figure 20. What the 5, and respectively 6, gates were is not indicated. The Priestly Gate (שער הכהן) is already mentioned by the Palestinian Gaon, Aaron b. Meir (920) and also in a letter to Ephraim b. Shemaryah (first half of 11th century).[40] This gate is usually identified with the Gate of Mercy but in our list they are mentioned separately.

I.

[MS. Amram at Dropsie College, cp. Halper, *Descriptive Catalogue of Genizah Fragments in Philadelphia*, No. 386, pp. 194–195.]

(Recto)

אל נא אחי תרעו ואל נא תשליכו אותי אחרי גיווכם כי פן יהיה עליכם

חטא כי אתם יודעים כי יחיד ועני אני הנה בארץ גלותי לא קרוב ולא ריע

[40] Cp. Bornstein in Sokolow's ס' היובל, 63: ותפלותינו עליכם תדירה ועל זקני יקר שלכם בהר הזיתים מול היכל יי'י . . . ועל שער הכהן, ועל שערי מקדש יי'י.

Mann II, 179, l. 11: [כת] הרבנים אשר בשער הכהן שוכנים. It seems that the residential quarter of the Rabbanites in Jerusalem was then adjoining this gate whereas the Ḳaraites lived in 'the quarter of the Orientals' identified with the Biblical צלע האלף (Josh. 18.28) in which quarter there was shown the tomb of Zekharyah b. Yehoyada' killed by order of King Joash (see 2 Chron. 24.20–22). See the data discussed by Mann, I, 274–5, and cp. above, p. 317, note 20.

ואני יחידי biניהם כערער בערבה חס ושלום שלא אהיה כמותו[1]
בעזרת אלהינו
ואתם יודעים שאין בדעתי לעמוד הנה ואיני מעכב הנה כי אם
בעבור זה החוב
המבורך[2] שיש לי בידכם וזה רבינו נסים הדיין שבא הנה הוא
מוכיח אותי
בכל יום בדברי תוכחות ואומר לי אדם כמוך יעמוד בלא אשה
ואיך תסבול זה
העון ותשאנו ואין לי פה להשיבו אם אומר לו יש בדעתי לחזור
אומר בנפשו
זה מתלוצץ נגדי כבר עמד שתי שנים הנה ורצה לישא אשה בת
אחותו של החבר שהוא סיפר
לי ששמע קודם שבא הנה אום אוומר לו אין בדעתי לישא כל
שכן שאהיה בעיניו
כאַיִן ולא הוא לבדו אומר כך אלא כל השוכנים הנה אומרים
כמוהו ואני מפחד שמא
מרוב בושת פנים שיש לי מאילו האומרים אלי אילו הדברים אשא
אשה בעל
כורחי ואם כן הוא אנה אוליך עון אמי ובתי שהן מצפות אותי
ועיניהם לאם
הדרך ואוזניהן פתוחות שמא ישמעו ממי מגיד על ביאתי וחזירתי
אליה[3]
אליהן ואם תשמעו שנשאתי אשה הלא תקרענה בגדיהן ועיניהן
הלא תרד
דמעה ואנה אוליך העון ואם הוא כן יהיה זה מתחת ידיכם גם
אתם תשאו עון על זה הדבר

[1] Viz. like the tamarisk in the steppe (Jer. 17.6).
[2] Euphemism for 'cursed'.
[3] Beginning of next word.

ואתם ידועים ביראת אלהים ולא נאה לכם שתאחרוני כמו שעשיתם בזה ה'[3]
הפעם שכתבתם לשלמה דינר ועשרה כספים והוא יבקש שנים עשר כספים
וה[ש]לכתוני לאחור הלא כזה ראוי לכם לעשות וכל מי ששמע אמר זה פליאה
איך עשו הם דבר זאת. וגם אני נתעכבתי הנה בעבור ששמתוני שוער
הבית כי בעת שהלך החבר לאסכנדריא אמר לי פעם ופעמים הלא אמרת
לי שתלך עימי אם רצה המקום שאהיה דיין אסכנדריא[4] ועכשיו למה תתעצ'[3]
תתעצל מלבא ונשבע לי אם תבוא עימי אעשה לך פסיקא ראוייה
ותשמח בה מאד ואשימך מלמד לרוב הנערים שבאסכנדריא כמ[ו כן]
[יבו]או לך הנאות רבות ממני שלא תדע עתה אחת מהן ואמרתי לו
אדוני גם אני יודיע כן ואני יודע כי יכול תוכל וגם אני הייתי מתאווה על זאת
אכן איך אניח הבית שהניחו ברצותי לשכור ולהשכיר וזה שהוא
שכן בה היום שמא יצא למחר ואם תעמוד ולא ישכון שם אדם שמא
ירדו בה מאת השליט כמנהג המקום[5] ונמצא אפסיד להם אני
[א]ת ממונם והם בוטחים עלי כבן על האב ולא נאה לי לעשות [כזה] ושתק ונענע לי ראש

[4] Viz. if this Ḥaber will become Dayyān at Alexandria the writer of the letter will accompany him there. Halper, *l. c.*, p. 195, has misunderstood this passage as if the writer were to become Dayyān there.

[5] Empty houses were evidently confiscated by the authorities being regarded as ownerless property.

ואני הינחתי כל זאת בעבורכם כי אתם יודעים אהבת
החבר שהייתה עימי עצומה מאוד וכל מה שהיה נודר ואומר[6]

. . . .

(verso)

אלי בשמחה כי גם בנו הקטון לפני ובטובותיך[7] אל תאחרם מלשגרם אלי והזהיר האומן
שלא יעשה אותם מלוחין בעבור שלא יפסדו במהרה וכבר כתבת לי פעם ופעמים שדיברת
עם האומן ועשאם שחורים. ואחרי כל זאת אתם יודעים שליבי ואהבתי עליכם ואני שואל
טדירי[8] בשלומכם לכל יוצא ובא ושמעתי כי הגבירה קרובתי מעוברת וכלתך הגבירה וש
ושמחתי עליהן והקבה יקיים בהן קרא שכתוב בטרם תבא חבל לה והמליטה זכר[9] ונשמח
שמחה שלימה והודיעיני חודש הלידה כי שמא אוכל ללכת אליכם ואשמח עמכם כי לא
זכיתי לשמחת חופתך וליבי היה דואג וצעור עליה כי לא הודעתני בזמן הראוי ולא ראיתי כתבך
בזמן הצריך ותן שלומותי לגבירה קרובתי עד ימלא שחוק פיה ולגבירה כלתך הנעימה ההדורה
ולשני צנתרות הזהב[10] ר׳ נצר ור׳ סעיד תלמידי אשר ליבי עליהם בוער כאש יוקדת על תוקף
אהבתם ועל פרידתי מהם הקבה יזכיני לראות פ[ניכ]ם ופניהם בשמחה ובטוב לבב ושלח לי כת

[6] The letter is evidently torn off at the bottom and there is a lacuna between recto and verso.

[7] Read ובטובתך.

[8] Read תדיר.

[9] Is. 66.7.

[10] The sons of the recipient of the letter.

כתבך על יד זה רבינו ניסים[11] שאני משגר לך על ידו שהוא יחזור הנה ולא יעמוד שם כי אם שבוע
אחת בלבד ואראה כתב שלומכם כגוזר האל ותן שלומותי לר׳ פינחס ולכל ביתו אף על פי
כן שעשה נגדי שלא כהוגן על עסק הסודר שאינו משלחו לי ושלומכם ושלום כל אשר לכם יגדל
כחרדל. לעד ולא ידל. ואויבך יהא מדולדל. ומחיים נבדל.

II.

[MS. Mosseri, L 291, paper.]

(Recto)

מה אומר לאהובי הכהן הצדיק הטהור
ר׳ פנחס הנה שלחתי לך היום שטר
פיוסים וחנונים בעבור הבורא אשנר
ירא וחרד מדברו שלא תעכבני יותר
כי אנחנו על דרך ארץ ישר׳ ואין לי
שום עכבה כי אם מותר הפסיקא
שעל יד כבודך ומעתה אין להתייאש
אלא היום תתקבץ ולמחר אלך
לשם לכבודכם וכה שלחתי לכבוד
אדוני הרב הדיין ר׳ חננאל ובעבור
הבורא אל נא תאחרוני אפילו
שעה אחת חוץ מזה היום כי
אנחנו על דרכנו וכזה תדבר לגבאי
פסיקת[12] קטנה של בני היום ולא יהיה
עכוב למחר כשאלך לשם ותדע כי
שכרך הרבה מאד בזה ולבא ועין

[11] Evidently Nissim the Dayyān mentioned in l. 5.

[12] Read פסיקה or פסיקא as in l. 6.

תפלתי על כבודך בכל עת והמֹ[13] יציל
אתכם מכל צרה ומכל חמס ויתן לך
שכר פסיעותיך בעוֹ הזֹ ובעֹ[14] הבא ויזכה
אותך לבנים זכרים עוסקים בתורה
כחשק אהובך וחושקך המתפלל בעד
כבודך דוד ברֹ בנימן תֹנֹצֹבֹהֹ

Address (verso)

לכבוד הכהן החסיד רֹ פנחס.

(There is scribbling of a Piyyuṭ across the remainder of verso.)

III.

[MS. Mosseri, L 178, small parchment leaf; verso blank.]

(Recto)

למרבה המשרה. ומקל תפארה. צר תעודה חתום תורה[15]. עזרא
ביהודים האמללים מרנו ורבנו אברהם השר. המזג ממך לא
יחסר[16].
ותיכון שררותך כמי השילוח קופת הרוכלים עליך השלכתי
יהבי
ועל השם להוציא ממסגר אסיך מבית כלא אשר אני בה וזה
לי יתרון הלום מישיבת בית האסורים לבד תפילתי תמיד אל
חיקי
ואין יד הגוים תקיפה עלי אך אני לשמירה. כבחצר המטרה.
בלחם

[13] =והמקום, God.

[14] =בעולם הזה ובעולם. About the reward for every step done for a meritorious purpose, cp. Gen. R. c. 39,12: וליתן לו (לאברהם) שכר על כל פסיעה ופסיעה, and Ḳohel. R. c. 7, 9: והחי יתן אל לבו זה חי העולמים שהוא משלם שכר לבר נש על כל פסיעה ופסיעה בגמילות חסדים.

[15] Cp. Is. 8.16.

[16] Cp. Cant. 7.3, here probably in the later meaning of (good) temperament, health.

צר ומים לחץ[17] ורבנו אברהם. מאריה דאברהם[18]. יתן בלבך לעשות יותר

על מה שאתה עושה עם הטובות יומם ולילה לקיים עשה דכבוד

תורה[19]. ואדוני הנה חכם אתה מדניאל כל סתום לא עממוך[20] עינך

[ראתה] ולא זר קורותי ותלאותי והשם יערה עליך רוח ממרום

[להצילני להוציאני מהר מזה ואלהך די את פלח ליה

בתדירא הוא ישובינך[21]. עני ונכה רוח דוד.

IV.

[T.-S. Box K. 27, vellum.]

(Recto)

נחנן אלשהוד אלמסמון אספל הד̇א אלכתאב חצ̇ר אלינא ר̇ סעדיה בן מבורך נ̇ר̇ יערף

ג̇זאירי[22] ובידה וכאלה̈ מן קבל ברכה בר̇ יוסף יערף בן אלסרתי[23] תתצ̇מן טלב ר̇ חיים ביר̇

ראובן נ̇ע̇ בארבעין רבאעי[24] ען נקד[25] אבנתה סיידה̈ פטלבה אלוכיל בחצ̇רה̈ אלזקנים בעד

אתבאת̇ אלוכאלה̈ פאנכר ר̇ חיים אלמד̇כור וצול ג̇מלה̈ ד̇אלך אליה וקאל אנמא וצל אליי מן

ד̇אלך עשרה רבאעייא וכו'

[17] Cp. Jer. 37.21 and Is. 30.20.

[18] Viz. God, a well-known Talmudic expression.

[19] Cp. Ketubot 106a, top.

[20] Cp. Ezek. 28.3.

[21] Cp. Dan. 6.17.

[22] Evidently from Algiers (al-Jazāir).

[23] al-Surti, viz. from Surt (Syrt) on the North-African coast between Barḳah and Tripolis.

[24] Probably quarters of a Dinār.

[25] Dowry.

At the end there are given the date and the locality followed by the signatories:

וכאן ד̇אלך יום אל
אחד לעשרה איאם מצ̇ת מן שהר סיון שנת תתצ"ח לעולם במדינת
מיגזאר[26] אלראתבה̈ עלי אלבחר שריר ובריר וקיים.

. . . . [בן] שמואל הסופר זלה̇ה̇
משה בן יעבץ נ̇ע̇

(At the bottom there follows scribble. Verso contains a formula of a testatum by a Bet-Din in different handwriting.)

V.

Memorial Lists for the Departed.

1.

[MS. Mosseri, L 296, a paper leaf; verso contains Arabic script.]

(Recto)

כבוד ג̇ק̇[27]
מרינו ורבינו זכי הדין המופלא בית דין הגון ז"ל[28]
וחמודו כ̇ג̇ק̇ מרינו ורבינו שמואל הדין וכ"ל[29]
וחמוד[ו] כ̇ג̇ק̇ מרינו ורבנו אלעזר הדין וכ"ל[29]
ועוד זיכרן ט̇ לנ' נפ' לז' המ'[30] המיוחסות עד כג"ק

[26] This place, evidently situated on the North-African coast, I cannot identify.

[27] =גדולת קדושה.

[28] The Dayyān Zakkai is probably the one mentioned in a letter (Bodl. 2876.28), dated Marḥeshvān 1462 Sel. (=1150 C. E.). See also note 69.

[29] Read ז'ל.

[30] =טב לניחות נפשתא לזכר המשפחות.

מור' שלמה הזקן הנ'[31] ז"ל וחמוד זכר זכר צדיק לב'[32]
וחמודו זכר צדיק לברכה ז' כג"ק מור' עמרם
הזקן החסיד בעודו ז"ל וח̇ מור' נדיב[33] והשושן[34]

2.

[T.-S. Loan 136, a paper strip; verso blank.]

בש רח̇[35]
שלמה ראס אלמת̇יבה̇
ומצליח ראס אלמת̇יבה̇[36]
ועוד
יעקב הרב הגדול
ורבנו נסים הרב הגדול ראש
הסדר[37]
וג̇די לאבי[38]
נתן החבר המעֻלה בסנהדרים
גדלה
וחמודו שלמה המלמד
החכם והנבון
וג̇די לאמי[39]
משה החסיד
וג̇ד אלמיתה̇[40]
אהרן הכהן
וחמודו
עלי הכהן

[31] =הנכבד.

[32] From וחמוד the end of the line should be deleted as it is more correctly repeated on next line.

[33] For the proper name Nadīb cp. Mann II, 320: Nadīb b. Yiftaḥ, and Bodl. 2875.32. See further Gaster, *Kaufmann Gedenkbuch*, p. 242, No. XVII.

[34] The remainder of the memorial list is missing. 'The flower' was evidently a young boy who died prematurely.

[35] בשם רחמנא.

[36] The Geonim Solomon Hakkohen b. Elijah, head of the school in Ḥadrak near Damascus (1116 C. E.), and his son Maṣliaḥ, head of the school in Fusṭāṭ (1127–38 C. E.).

[37] Jacob b. Nissim of Ḳairwān and his son Nissim.

[38] The writer of this list indicates that his paternal grandfather was Natan the Ḥaber (probably of the Palestinian school) and that Natan's son was Solomon.

[39] The writer's maternal grandfather was Moses 'the pious one.'

[40] The grandfather of the departed lady, for whom this memorial list was compiled (her name was probably mentioned in the missing part of the paper strip), was Aaron Hakkohen whose son was 'Alī Hakkohen.

3.

[MS. Mosseri, L 218, verso, contains the following names. Recto forms part of a letter.]

אבו אלפרג̇ ישועה בר יוסף. אבו אלחסן בן עאדי. עלי בן שמריה.
בני חפאט̇[41] הכהנים שמריה וצדקה. בני צדוק אלסגלת[42] יהודה
ומנחם. כ̇לף אלוכיל[43] אלע[ז]ר בני אלנאמן. בני אלווזאן[44].
אלחבר בן אלסלמי[45]
וולד[ה]. אבו אלפצ̇ל בן אלחניך[46]. יפת בר טוביה. שלמה בן ארח
בן אצה. מבשר וששון בני אלצכאל[47] . . . . . אבן עמני בן
שלמה. פכ̇גק ישועה

4.

[Hebrew Union College Genizah Collection, No. 3, paper, torn.]

(Recto)

דוכ̇ טב̇ וני̇ נפ̇ לז̇ המש̇ המיוח̇ משפ̇ השרי̇
החכ̇ הנג̇[48] אשו[ר] נהגו שררה בע̇ יי׳ צב̇[49] עד
כב̇ גד̇ קד̇ הנ̇ד̇ י̇זק צפ̇ תפ̇[50] מו̇ר̇ שמריה הששי
בחבורת הצדק ז̇צ̇ל̇ ושלשת חמודיו בראשם הש̇ האד̇[51]
כ̇גק̇ מו̇ר̇ צדקה השר האד̇ ביש̇ החכ̇ והנב̇[52] ז̇ל̇
ואחיו כ̇גק̇ מו̇ר̇ סעדאל הש̇ הא̇ ביש̇ הח̇ וה[נב̇]

[41] About the name Ḥuffāẓ (חֻפָּאט̇) cp. Steinschneider, *JQR*, X, 540, top.

[42] Holding the honorific title of סגולת הישיבה (cp. Mann, I, 278).

[43] The agent. Probably for אלעזר r. ואלעזר, viz. Khalāf the agent and El'azar, the sons of a person holding the honorific title of נאמן (either נאמן בית דין or נאמן הישיבה, see Mann, II, Hebrew Glossary, s. v.).

[44] The name is also listed by Steinschneider, *l. c.*, 525, No. 164b.

[45] The Ḥaber ibn al-Salimi and his son. סלמי is also spelt סלימי (Steinschneider, *l. c.*, XI, 322, No. 470b).

[46] Probably = חניך הישיבה, the disciple of the school.

[47] The meaning of this word is not clear to me.

[48] = דוכרן טב וניחות נפשתא לזכר המשפחות המיוחסות משפחות השרים החכמים הנגידים.

[49] = בעם יי׳ צבאות.

[50] = הדרת יקרת צפירת תפארת.

[51] = השר האדיר.

[52] = האדיר בישראל החכם והנבון.

הרׄ[53] זׄלׄ ואחיו כׄגׄקׄ מרׄורׄ חנניה השר האדׄ ביׄשׄ
החסיד בעודו זׄלׄ ושני חמודיו השׄ האׄ וההׄחׄ[54]
והחסידים בראשם כׄגׄקׄ מרׄורׄ אברהם
השר האׄ ביׄשׄ החׄ והנׄ הרׄ[53] החסיד בעודו
ואחיו זׄצׄלׄ זׄחׄלׄ כׄעׄלׄ זׄ נׄגׄ לׄזׄ[54a] כׄגׄקׄ יׄקׄ צׄפׄ
תׄפׄ מרׄורׄ אדׄ נׄגׄ הודׄ והדׄ וצׄנׄ תׄפׄ ועׄטׄ
ראשׄ[55] שמואל הנגיד הגדׄ[56] נגיד עם יי׳ צבאׄ
שר השׄר ונגיד הנגידים מרדכי הזמ[ן]
ימין המלוכה עזר הנשיאות [ה]עושה
כמה חסדים וכמה טובות עם הענ[יים וע]ם
בני תורה זׄלׄ ושני חמודיו בראׄ[57] כבוד גדׄ
קדׄ מרׄ ורׄ יחיה השר האׄ ביׄשׄ החׄ והנׄ
הרופא החסיד בעׄוׄ[58] הנפטר בקצרות שנים
זׄלׄ ואחיו כׄ גדׄ קׄ מׄ ורבנא שָׂרֵינוּ נכבדי[נו] השׄוׄ[59]

(margin)

חנניה השר האדיר ביׄשׄ החכם והנׄבׄ הרוׄ[60] העושה כמה חסדים וכמה טובות
עם הענׄיׄ[61] ועם בני תורׄ וחמודו כׄ גדׄ קׄ מרׄ ורׄ שמואל השר הנכבד היקר החׄ
והנׄ הרׄ[53] נֶכֶד הנגידים גביר החסידים רוח יְיָ׳ תניחנו וכלל וגומׄ

(verso)

עׄתׄרׄהׄ אלרשיד שמואל[62]
עֲלִי וחמודו צמח וחמודו יפת

[53] = הרופא.   [54] = השרים האדירים והחכמים.

[54a] For כׄעׄלׄ r. זׄעׄלׄ and for לׄזׄ r. לׄבׄ and the whole sentence in full reads: זכר צדיק לברכה זכר חסיד לברכה זכר עניו לברכה זכר נגיד לברכה.

[55] = הודנו והדרנו וצניף תפארתנו ועטרת ראשנו.

[56] = הגדול.   [57] = בראשם.   [58] = בעודו.

[59] Read מרׄורׄ.   [60] Read הרׄוׄ = הרופא.   [61] = העניים.

[62] The family of Samuel al-Rashīd (the director), perhaps the person mentioned in the letter from Yeḥiel b. Elyaḳim (Mann, II, 302, l. 27).

עתֿרה בן עמאר עמרם וחמודו
ברכות וארבעת חמודיו בראשם
ישועה וחמודו אלעזר[63] ואחיו עמרם ואחיו עֵלִי ו[חמודו]
ברכות ואחיו שמואל[64] נתנאל[64]* וכלל [המשתתפים][65]
באבלו
וכבוד כֿגֿק מרוֹר שמואל וחמוד[יו]
וכבוד גֿק מרוֹר יהושע וכבוד גֿק מרֿ ורבֿ
חנניה השר הנכבד היקר הרופא ויזכור אלהינו[ו]
בזכרון טוב מלפניו כבוד גֿק יצֿתֿ
אדוננו נגידנו הודנו והדרנו וצניף תפארתנו
ועטרת ראשנו אברהם[66] הרב המובהק הפטיש החזק
דגל הרבנים יחיד הדור ופלאו. ממזרח שמש
עד מבואו. יחיה לו חמודיו.

5.

[Hebrew Union College Genizah Collection, No. 4, paper, faint.]

(Recto)

[ד]כרן ט[ו]ב ו[ניחו]ת נפשתא לכלל מיתנו ומיתיכו[ן]
[החכמים והשרים וה]חורים ר׳ י[67] תניחם לזכר המשפֿ המיוחֿ
[מ]שפחת הלויים ה[נא]מֿ עד כֿגֿק מרנא ורבנא יצחק
[ה]שר הנכבד החֿ והנֿ . . . . . ו כֿגֿק מרנא ורבנא
סעדיה וכלל חמודיו ברֿא הדֿ יקֿ [צפֿ] תפֿ מרנא ורבנא

[63] El'azar was the son of Yeshu'ah.

[64] 'Eli's two sons were Berakhot and Samuel.

*[64] The four sons of Berakhot are Yeshu'ah, 'Amram, 'Eli and Netanel. Before Netanel insert [ואחיו].

[65] On both sides of נתנאל there has been added in different handwriting the line ברכות... המשתתפים and the remainder of the list is continued in this handwriting. If Berakhot and his brother Samuel were the present mourners then for באבלו we should read באבלם. The word באבלו is also repeated on the margin of l. 31.

[66] Viz. the Nagid Abraham Maimuni.

[67] = רוח יי.

שמואל הזקן המשׄ המופׄ החׄ[68] המע[ולה] בית דין הגון נזר המשכילים זׄלׄ וחמודו . . . . [זכׄ צ]דיק לברכה [זכׄ עניו לברכה] זכׄ חסיד לברכ[ה] . . . . המשכיל המופלא החכם המעולה בית דין נזר המשכילים זכרו לברכה ועוד דכרן טב וניחות נפשתא לזכר המׄ המיוחׄ משפחת הזקנים הדיינים מרינו ורבינו זכאי הדיין המופלא החכם המעולה זׄלׄ[69] וחמודו כׄגׄקׄ מרנא ורבנא יתר הלוי[70] הנפׄ בשם טוב ובמעשים טובׄ ל[בית] עולמו רׄ יָיָ׳ תניחנו וחמודו כׄגׄקׄ מרנא ורבנא עלי השר הנכבד היקר החכם והנבון הסופר המהיר הנפטר בשם טוב ו[במעש]ים[71] טובים לבית עולמו וכלל מיתי משפחת המיוחס[ים] רוח יָיָ׳ תניחם ועוד דכרן טב לזכר המשפחות המיוחסות משפחת הזקינים החבירים הכהנים ראשי כניסיות מרינו ורבינו יחזקאל ושני [חמודיו] בראשם אלעזר הכהן [ואחיו] עלי הכהן

(verso)

. . . .

וחמודו כׄגׄקׄ מרׄ ורבׄ נתנ[אל] . . . . . הרופא ה הנפטר בשם טוב וחמודו כׄגׄקׄ מרׄ [ורבנא] עלי השר הנכבד החׄ והנׄ הרופא הנפטר בשם טוב ומעשים טוׄ[72] לבית עׄ[73] וחמודו כׄגׄקׄ מרׄ ורבׄ אברהם התלמיד הרופא הנחטף בקצׄ[74] שנים

[68] =המשכיל המופלא החכם. Samuel b. Sa'adyah Hallevi was Dayyān in Fusṭāṭ in the second half of the 12th century (see Mann, I, 195, note 2; II, 232, 314 and 317).

[69] This Zakkai Dayyān is perhaps the same dealt with above (note 28).

[70] Probably the elder mentioned in the letter of Tobias Hakkohen b. 'Alī (Mann, II, 368).

[71] =ובמעשים.

[72] =טובים.

[73] =עולמו.

[74] =בקצרות.

רוח יְיָ' תניחם   ועוד דכֹ טֹ לז המֹ המיוחסות
משפֹ הלויים כֹגֹק מֹ ורֹ אלעזר הנכֹ הנפטר
בשם טוב ובמֹ טובים לבית עולמו ושני חמודיו
חלפון ואחיו כֹגֹק מֹ רֹ עלה וחמודו שלמה
הנחטף בקֹ שנים ועוד דכרן טב לזכר המשפֹ [המיוחֹ]
משפחף הלויים עלי כגֹ קדֹ מרֹ ורבנא שלמה
וארבעת חמודיו בראשם שמואל הלוי חמדת הלויים
הנפֹ[75] ושני חמודיו הנפטרים בקצרות שנים רוח יי'
תניחם ואחיו כֹגֹק מרֹ ורבֹ אלעזר הלוי הנחטף בקצֹ שנים
ואחיו משה. ואחיו יעקב הנפֹ בשם טוב ומֹ טובים
לבית עולמו שהיום שלום[76] חדש לפטירתו רֹ יֹ תניחנו
ילווה עליו שלום ועל משֹ[77] יהי שלום והחֹ[78] והשלום
[ו]כלל הניחומֹ[79] יחולו על ראש כלל אביליו ועגומיו
[בראש שני] בניו שלמה הבחור האבל ואחיו אלעזר הבחור
האב[ל וכל] המתאבלים על אביהם כולם ינחמם מאבל[ם]
יסיר יגונם יעדי דאבונם ידבר על לבם ....

....

VI.

[MS. Firkowicz, 2. Hebrew Collection, No. 236[5], contains 10 leaves of various notes on Biblical and Rabbinic matters. On fol. 2, verso, there is to be found the following document.]

בע"ה[79a]

מודים אנו החתומים מטה לקשור קשר חזק ואמיץ של אהבה
ואחוה ושלֹ[80] בינינו כאלו היינו אחים מאב ואם

[75] =הנפטר.
[76] Better נשלם or שלם.
[77] =משכבו.
[78] =והחיים.
[79] =הניחומים.
[79a] =בעזרת השם.
[80] =ושלוה.

לכל ענין שנצטרכו[81] סיוע זה לזה בענין השאלת ספר זה לזה הן ממה שיש לו הן ממה שיקנה כל ימי חייו או יעתיק לא יוכל להסתיר מחברו כל זמן שישאל ממנו עד כ׳ ימים אם ללמוד בו אם להעתיק גם בענין התפלה ביחד בבית הכנסת של הרב הגדול הקדוש כמהר״ר שמואל בן סיד תנצב״ה[82] כל ימי היותנו חיים על האדמה גם בענין גמילות חסדים לגמול כל אחד לחבירו כמה שיוכל לכבדוולל . . . תו הן בענין שמחתו הן ח״ו בענינים אחרים. באופן שלא יהיה כי אם של ואהבה ואחוה אחים אמתיים כאלו היינו גופ׳[83] א׳ כאלו היינו אחים מאב ומאם מהריון ומלידה כל ימי חיינו קבלנו וקיימנו עלינו ועל זרעינו וזרע זרעינו זה הקשר החזק האמיץ הנז׳[84] לעיל בלב שלם בנפש חפצה בישוב דעתנו בלתי שום טענת אונס וכיוצא בו ומעכשיו אנו החתומים מטה מבטלים כל טענה שתוכל בשום אופן בעולם לא מינה ולא מקצתה לבטל ח״ו[85] זה הקשר החזק שעשינו בכל התנאים הנז׳ לעיל. כל טענה דאיכא למטען בבי דינא או טענת אונס וכיוצא בה או טענת מודעא עד כל הדורות כולם בטלים מעכשיו כחרס הנשבר ולפסל כל מיני עדות שימצא[86] בין בכתב בין על פה לבטל שטר זה של הקשר שעשינו כנז׳[87] לעיל דלא כאסמכתא ודלא כטופסי שטרי אלא שטר מוחזק ומושרר[88] כתיקון חז״ל

[81] Better שנצטרך.

[82] The synagogue of the Sevillians in Cairo was called by his name. Cp. about this scholar and Ḳabbalist, a refugee to Egypt after the Spanish expulsion, Sambari's Chronicle (in Neub., *Med. Jew. Chron.*, I, pp. 145, 159, and 161–62).

[83] =גופא.

[84] =הנזכר.

[85] =חס וחלילה.

[86] Better שימצאו, if referring to מיני or שתמצא, if to עדות.

[87] =כנזכר.

[88] From שריר.

בכל חיזוקי שרירין וקיימים שיש בעולם וגם קבלנו על עצמנו שאם ח"ו יגרום העון שיכעוס שום א' ממנו עם[89]

חברו שלא לעמד כ"ד שעות עד שיתפייסו ויעשו של' ואהבה יותר חזק ותקיף מהראשונה[90] וכל הנז' לעיל

קיימנו וקבלנו עלינו ועל זרעינו בכח שבועה חמורה בהזכרת הש' ית'[91] ובתקיעת כף על דעת רבים ועל דעת

הרבנים כמהר' יוסף קארו וכמהר' משה טראנה וכמהר' ישראל די קוריאל[92] וכמהר' מאיר די פאדווא[93] וכהר' יצחק ן' סיד[94] וכל [א']

לדעת חבירו לקיים כל הנז' לעיל בלב שלם מדעתנו ומרצונינו וזה היה ביום ראשון שבעה עשר יום לחדש טבת שנת

השכ"ד ליצירה[95] והכל שריר וקיים אני הצעיר אלעזר מימון[96] זעירא דמן חברייא יום טוב ן' סיד ס"ט[97].

[89] Better על.

[90] The genders are mixed up.

[91] =השם יתברך.

[92] Joseph Caro, Moses b. Joseph di Trani and Israel de Curiel were Rabbis in Safed. Israel is mentioned by Sambari, *l. c.*, 151, bottom, with משה די קוריאל next to him.

[93] The famous Rabbi of Padua, Italy, Meir b. Isaac Katzenellenbogen, died in 1565 (see about him Ghirondi, כרם חמד, III, 91–94).

[94] Isaac b. Sīd is unknown to me but he seems to have been the father of Yom Ṭob b. Sīd (see note 97). This Isaac was perhaps the son of Samuel ibn Sīd (note 82) because a Cairene MS., containing דרושים למהר"ש בן סיד (*JQR*, XVII, 643, No. 50), has the genealogy either of the author or of the owner Samuel ibn Sīd b. Mordecai b. Isaac b. החכם השלם הדיין המקובל האלהי שמואל (called החכם השלם הדיין) ן' סיד. Hence Mordecai was a brother of our Yom Ṭob ibn Sīd.

[95] =Jan. 2, 1564 C. E.

[96] El'azar Maimūn is unknown to me.

[97] =סופו טוב. Yom Ṭob b. Isaac ibn Sīd in common with other Rabbis of Cairo confirmed the ban issued against David who intrigued against Don Joseph, Duke of Naxos (cp. Responsa of Elijah b. Ḥayyim (מהראנ"ח), No. 55, printed in מים עמוקים, Berlin, 1778, fol. 56c: חתימות רבני מצרים, and about the affair see Graetz, *Geschichte*, IX, 4th ed., 364–66).

SECTION V

DOCUMENTS CONCERNING THE JEWS IN MOSUL AND ḲURDISTĀN

DOCUMENTS CONCERNING THE JEWS IN MOSUL AND ḲURDISTĀN

OUR knowledge of Jewish life in these districts is indeed very scanty although the Jewish settlements there date from very early times. Niniveh, the capital of Assyria, was situated on the eastern side of the Tigris opposite the present day Mosul and many were the exiles from the Northern Kingdom and from Judea that were settled in the province of Ashshūr (cp. Is. 11.11, 27.13). But about their vicissitudes we are entirely uninformed. Also in Talmudic times the Jewry of this locality hardly figures in our literary records. The community of Mosul becomes prominent in the Muhammedan period. In pre-Islamic times the place was known as Ḥesna 'Ebrāyā,[1] a name that was retained by the Jews even as late as the 13th century.[2] The Arabs in conquering the place in 640 C. E. found there a preponderant Jewish settlement. As the Mauṣil of the Arabs the city became a flourishing commercial junction between West and East and must have attracted many Jewish residents. The Jews identified the town with the Biblical city of Ashshūr by which name it is frequently mentioned in our medieval sources.

In Mosul there evidently lived Ḥefeṣ b. Yaṣliaḥ, the author of an extensive Sepher Hammiṣvot in Arabic.[3] He held the title

[1] See the data collected by Obermeyer, *Die Landschaft Babylonien*, 1929, pp. 135–139, which are deficient in many points as the following remarks testify.

The name Ḥesna 'Ebrāyā, the Hebrew castle, is mentioned in Syriac writings (ibid., p. 136, note 3).

[2] Thus the heading of the circular letter of 1288 by the Exilarch David of Mosul against Solomon Petit, who attacked Maimonides' philosophical writings, reads according to MS. Parma 3175, fol. 11, verso (cp. Mann, *Livre d'hommage . . . Poznański*, Hebrew part, p. 27, top): נוסח ההסכמה הבאה מאת אדוננו . . . דוד הנשיא הגדול ראש כל גליות ד ב ח ס נ א ע ב ר א ה מדינתא דאתור דעל דגלת נהרא מותבה ובית דינו וכו'.

[3] See Halper, *A Volume of the Book of Precepts by Ḥefeṣ b. Yaṣliaḥ*, 1915. In a Genizah letter his work is cited as כתב המצות למרב חפץ אלוף בן יצליח ה א ש ו ר י

of Resh Kallah, evidently bestowed upon him by one of the Babylonian academies, or rather by the Pumbedita-Bagdād academy. He probably was Dayyān of the Mosul community which seems to have stood under the jurisdiction of the above school. The Gaon Aaron (Khalāf) b. Sarjādo, the opponent of Sa'adyah in his conflict with David b. Zakkai, appointed as local Dayyān a certain Ephraim b. Saṭya.[4] This Ephraim too is cited as Resh Kallah.[5] Likewise the Gaon Ṣemaḥ Ṣedek of the Sura-Bagdād school in his letter to Elḥanan b. Shemaryah refers to his disciple Sahl Alluf, the son of the Alluf of Mosul (viz. the

(ibid., p. 12). The title Alluf is of course = ראש כלה and thus he is indeed styled in the headings of parts 4 and 5 of his work (ibid., pp. 144 and 194): ראס אלכל חפץ בן יצליח. All that can be ascertained about his time is that he lived after Sa'adyah and before the end of the so-called Gaonic period (cp. Poznański's review of Halper's work in המזרחי, No. 5, pp. 7–8).

[4] This Ephraim was a supporter of Sa'adyah during his conflict with David b. Zakkai. Evidently he then lived in Bagdād. But later on Aaron b. Sarjādo, when Gaon of the academy of Pumbedita-Bagdād (943–60), appointed him as Dayyān of Mosul. Cp. the Ḳaraite account of the Sa'adyah—David b. Zakkai conflict (printed by Harkavy, *Studien u. Mitteilungen*, V, p. 227, ll. 8ff.): ת֗ם ד֗כר אלקום אלדין תעצבו מעה פקאל ויתחברו אליו זקן פסילות (יומי בה אלי עמרון בן זלאלה) ופני עכבר (יומי בה אלי אפרים בן שטיא אלד֗י קד נצבה כ֗לף בן סרג֗אדו ד י א ן א ל מ ו צ ל). This Ḳaraite author quoted here from a Hebrew tract of Aaron b. Sarjādo against Sa'adyah and explained the allusions therein such as are indicated here in brackets. In that tract Ephraim was designated as פני עכבר. But later on, after Sa'adyah's death, the enmity disappeared and Aaron as Gaon advanced Ephraim.

[5] MS. Firkowicz, 2. Hebrew-Arabic Collection, No. 1679, contains 76 leaves of a portion of a כתאב אלמנאט֗ר. The heading reads: בסייעתא דשמיא. כתאב אלשיך֗ אבי אלכ֗יר טאבא בן צלחון אלמוצלי אלצואף (wool-dealer). The introduction begins: אתחיל בעזרת הבורא. כי הוא המבין והמורה. הד֗א שרח כתאב פיה מעאני פואסיק מתפרדה֗ פי אג֗זא אלמקרא בחג֗ה֗ אלעקל . . . תכריג֗ אלשיך֗ אלפאצ֗ל אלכ֗יר אבי אלכ֗יר טאבא בן צלחון אלצואף ת֗נצ֗בה֗ רסמה לנפסה ברסם אלתד֗כאר . . . לקבה כ ת א ב א ל מ נ א ט֗ ר ללמטאלעה מנה אלי עלום שת֗י ג֗לילה֗ שריפה֗ מכ֗תלפה֗ אלאנואע עני בהא . . . At the end we have the colophon: וכאן עמלה ואלפראג֗ מנה למולפה ב א ל מ ו צ ל פי ד֗ו אלקעדה֗ מן סנה֗ תל֗[ת֗] מאיה֗ את֗ני וסבעין. Dhul-Ḳa'da of 372 H. corresponds to April 17–May 17, 983 C. E. At beginning of ch. 3 he also quotes the year 368 H.

The author mentions that he consulted on certain points the Dayyān and Resh Kallah Ephraim (וסאלת אפרים אלדין רצ֗י אללה ענה, וסאלת אפרים ראס אלכל). There is no doubt that Ephraim is identical with the above Ephraim b. Saṭya who became the local Dayyān between 943–960. In spring 983, when Abū'l Khair wrote his work, Ephraim was no longer alive.

local Dayyān) who acted as the representative (פקיד) of the school (above, p. 146). Thus it appears that the spiritual leader of the Mosul community in the 10th century, appointed by the Gaon and school of Pumbedita-Bagdād,[5a] went about with the honorary degree of Alluf by reason of the financial support which the Mosul Jewry would lend to the upkeep of the academy. Whether Ephraim preceded Ḥefeṣ b. Yaṣliaḥ or vice-versa is not clear, though the former alternative seems more likely. In the time of Ephraim we have in Mosul a local author, Abū'l-Khair Ṭaba b. Ṣalḥon, who composed comments on scattered verses of the Bible in a rationalistic manner (note 5).

Of prominent visitors in Mosul, mention should be made of Sa'adyah during his trip from Palestine to Bagdād in about 920–21 C. E.[6] Also Elḥanan b. Shemaryah stayed there for some time.[7]

In the 11th century Mosul became the seat of an Exilarchate which existed till the end of the 13th century and perhaps beyond.[8] Benjamin of Tudela found there a community of about 7000 people, a figure which corresponds nearly to that of Petaḥyah of Ratisbon.[9] Ḥarizi had no high opinion of the intellectual standard of the Mosul community.[10]

5a However it may be that formerly Mosul was under the jurisdiction of the Sura school but, after the closing of the school subsequent to Sa'adyah's death in 942, the community came under the jurisdiction of the Pumbedita school and hence Aaron b. Sarjādo appointed Ephraim as the local Dayyān. With the reopening of the Sura academy under Ṣemaḥ Ṣedeḳ the former allegiance was reestablished and hence this Gaon refers to the Mosul Alluf as his representative.

6 That Sa'adyah passed Mosul on his way to Bagdād may be taken for granted. However the fragment in *Saadyana* (ed. Schechter, pp. 133–135), describing the itinerary of a young man of some 20 odd years from Bagdād to Aleppo via Arbela, Mosul and Nisibin, can hardly be attributed to Sa'adyah (cp. the discussion of Malter, *Saadia Gaon*, 59–62, 422, and my remarks against it in *RÉJ*, LXXIII, 106–7).

7 See above, p. 146.

8 See my remarks in *Livre d'hommage . . . Poznański*, Hebrew part, 23–24, 26–27.

9 *Sibbub*, ed. Grünhut, p. 5: ובנינוה החדשה יש קהל גדול כששת אלפים ויותר.

10 Taḥkemoni, Maḳama 46 (ed. Lagarde, 176): בבואי אליה. ראיתי קהליה. כל איש מהם בחיק הסכלות נרדם. והנה אין שם איש וקול אדם. כי אם הסוס אסור. והחמור אסור. והיה ליהודים כמו בור. ונפל שמה שור. או חמור. וביום גלו מירושלים עדת הצור. גלו החסידים לדמשק ולמצרים . . . ובאו האובדים בארץ אשור.

Cp. also Maḳama 50 (p. 201, bottom) and 24 (p. 108ff.).

The above stray data about the Jewry of Mosul are insufficient indeed for a clear picture of Jewish life and activities in this part of the near Orient. Still less information we possess about the Jews in mountainous Ḳurdistān. As a lonely instance there stands out the affair of David Alroy in 'Imādiya and his extensive Messianic movement during the 2nd Crusade in 1146–47 C. E.[11] The Messianic excitement effected the Jews not only in Ḳurdistān proper but also higher up north in Adharbayjān which whole district is designated in the Megillah of 'Obadyah the Proselyte as "the land of Khazaria" (ארץ כוריא).[12] Indeed it seems that the local Jews were carried away by the Messianic excitement that prevailed in 1096 at the commencement of the 1st Crusade.[13] Since the affair of David Alroy the history of Ḳurdistān Jewry is entirely shrouded in obscurity till modern times when occasional travellers visited this district.[14]

In view of the paucity of the material hitherto available the documents given here will be the more welcome as affording us interesting glimpses of the intellectual and social conditions prevailing among the Jewries of Mosul and Ḳurdistān. The documents extend from the 16th century and onwards. They form a collection of letters recently acquired by the Hebrew Union College Library. Herewith follows a detailed description of the contents of these epistles which are edited here with the necessary explanatory notes.

In the 16th century we have in Mosul a prominent scholar Jacob b. Judah Mizraḥi. He seems to have originated from Babylon (probably Bagdād) as the designation Mizraḥi indicates. For a time he lived in 'Imādiya as the local Rabbi and trained several disciples who in turn became the spiritual leaders

[11] See Mann, *Hatteḳufah*, XXIV, 341–49 for the latest discussion of this episode. Cp. also *RÉJ*, LXXXVII, p. 257ff..

[12] Cp. ibid.. p. 347, note 2.

[13] See ibid., XXIII, 255, note 5.

[14] Cp. Benjamin II, *Acht Jahre in Asien u. Afrika*, 3rd ed. 1860, pp. 66–82, 88–100. See also the account of the missionary Henry A. Stern, *Dawnings of Light in the East*, 1854, 215ff.

Cp. also *J. E.* s. v. Ḳurdistān, Turkey.

About Mosul see M. Sidi in Elmaleh's מזרח ומערב, I, 247ff.

of various communities in Ḳurdistān. For some reason or other Jacob moved to Mosul where he maintained a sort of a Yeshibah. In his educational work he was aided by his learned wife, the daughter of a scholar Samuel famous in Mosul and Ḳurdistān. She would teach the students while her husband was occupied with his own study, and after his death endeavored to maintain the school till her young son, Samuel, would grow up. This Yeshibah was greatly dependent on outside help and numerous appeals for support were sent out by Jacob and later on by his wife. The appeals however seem to have met with meager success.

The first 5 items of our documents deal with this topic. No. I is by Jacob from Mosul to the community of Nirwa (see note 1 to the text). The learned persons in Nirwa were David and Joseph, both former disciples of Jacob (cp. lines 10, 32–3, and 84). They are commended for their exertion in establishing a house of study in Nirwa so that the local young Jews grow not up in ignorance of Judaism. Yet Jacob complains about their neglect in not sending the community's yearly donation for the upkeep of his own school in Mosul. Since he had left 'Imādiya not one instalment reached him from Nirwa. Owing to the dangers of the road the donations sent the year before have not arrived. Jacob describes his deplorable conditions in Mosul. The representatives, sent out for collecting the monies for the school, would embezzle them and hence the larger communities like Aleppo, Bagdād, Diyār Bakr and Marāgha (see note 28 to the text) refrained from contributing further to the support of the Yeshibah. The whole letter testifies to Jacob's familiarity with Bible and Talmud and to his zeal for the study of Judaism. He urges his correspondents to send their sons to him for intensive study.

No. II, defective at the beginning, also emanates from our Jacob, although his signature is missing, since the handwriting, style and subject matter are the same as of No. I. The epistle was sent to 'Imādiya which had an upper and a lower community, viz. the former being situated higher up in the mountains (cp. notes 53, 110 and 158 to the texts). The lower community probably was formerly under the spiritual leadership of our

Jacob. Hence many local residents, headed by Salman, are mentioned in the letter. Several of them were Jacob's former disciples including Salman who figures first. After a long introduction, characteristic for its content and quotations, we have a fervid appeal for support. The writer is aware of the poverty of the 'Imādiya community (l. 108) and yet he impresses upon his correspondents their sacred duty of maintaining their former Rabbi and thus share with him the reward of the future world. After a delay of 2 years the 'Imādiya Jews promised at the season of Tabernacles to send their donation. The winter has passed and nothing was done. Jacob urges that the money be at least sent for Passover. Several other Ḳurdistān communities are enumerated, evidently being of smaller size than that of 'Imādiya. The quotas of these localities would be sent to 'Imādiya whence the combined sum would be forwarded to Mosul. Jacob would also send his appeals destined for these communities to 'Imādiya to be transmitted to their respective destinations.

Jacob further takes to task the 'Imādiya community for having asked a certain בן כאזו from שרנש to stay in their midst for the purpose of study. This person evidently was the most promising student in the school of שרנש and with his departure it would cease to function after the great labor Jacob had in establishing it. It may also be that this person's father was the main support of this school. The writer gives notice of his determination to fight this action and warns against anybody in 'Imādiya giving instruction to this young man.

Jacob's appeals to the communities of 'Imādiya and other places met with no success, as we learn from No. III, being an epistle by him to Abraham of Sandūr, evidently the local Rabbi. The latter apparently forwarded a donation on behalf of his community and in the accompanying letter advised Jacob to appeal again to 'Imādiya and שרנש or שראנש. Jacob in his reply mentions that nearly 14 years have already passed since any sum of money reached him from these places. He is very bitter in his denunciation especially of the scholars of 'Imādiya for their attitude towards him and even accuses them of suppressing his letters. Also other communities of Ḳurdistān ignored his appeals (l. 26 ff.).

Our Jacob's dates of birth, activities and death are not stated but they are to be placed in the 15th and 16th centuries by inference from No. V to be discussed forthwith. But first No. IV is to be considered which contains an appeal to 'Imādiya (l. 130) by the learned widow of our scholar. The lady endeavored valiantly to preserve the school of her late husband. The appeal, if it be her own composition, does credit to her knowledge of Hebrew and Rabbinic literature. Many troubles beset her after her husband's death. There was a debt due to Christians for a hundred Piastres (גרוש). The creditors obtained possession of her house and sold all her garments and those of her daughters. Hence the touching appeal to come to their aid. The widow describes her activities as teaching Judaism, instructing and preaching how to keep the laws of ritual ablution, Sabbath, Niddah, prayer and the like. She has no grown-up son (see note 132 to the text) to travel about in order to collect the donations, nor is she able to employ a representative. She goes on to state that her occupation was always to study and teach. Her father, the scholar Samuel Hallevi, had trained her so and when he gave her in marriage to our Jacob, he adjured him not to exact any housework from her. This promise Jacob carried out conscientiously. While our Jacob was busy with his own research and had no time to instruct his disciples, his wife would act as his substitute.

This long fervid appeal to the community of 'Imādiya again seemingly met with scanty response. This is evident from No. V written by Samuel b. Jacob Mizraḥi, clearly the son of the scholar and the lady dealt with so far. The letter no doubt dates several years after that of his mother (No. IV) wherein he was referred to as a minor. In the interval of time he advanced to manhood and must have helped his mother in teaching and writing appeals. In the present letter, sent to the two congregations of 'Imādiya, he refers to their neglect of the family of the late Rabbi (ll. 18–9, viz. his father) and in addition he has the grievance that his father's books, that remained in 'Imādiya several years since Jacob moved to Mosul, were now being stolen one by one. The stay in Mosul of the Dayyān, Mattityah b. Benjamin Zeeb Ashkenazi, afforded Samuel the opportunity of impressing the people of ʿImādiya by obtaining from this Mattityah a long postscript to his letter. The latter speaks of Samuel already as a scholar (l. 34) and refers to his learned mother (ll. 35–6). He strongly supports the request of Samuel that the communal leaders in ʿImādiya should endeavor by means of the Ḥerem to obtain possession of the books of the late R. Jacob and restore them to their rightful owner, his heir Samuel. Mattityah's style is stilted consisting of a string of Biblical phrases. It offers a characteristic contrast to the more natural and idiomatic phraseology of Jacob and of his learned wife. We notice at once the difference in handling the Hebrew language between an Oriental Jew and a European one in those days.

The presence of Mattityah b. Benjamin Zeeb in Mosul enables us to establish approximately the time of Jacob and of his family, viz. the end of the 15th and the beginning of the 16th centuries. Benjamin Zeeb Ashkenazi, a member of the prominent family of Treves, is known as the learned Rabbi of Arta (Greece) and as the author of the volume of responsa known as Benjamin Zeeb.[15] The volume was completed in MS. in Arta in 1534 (הרצ"ד A. M.) when his son Mattityah composed poems for the occasion.[16] The author had travelled to Venice to arrange for the publication of the volume and during his stay there the news reached him of the death of his son Mattityah "in a strange land."[17] Hence we can

[15] About the genealogy of Benjamin Zeeb Ashkenazi cp. N. Brüll, *Jahrbücher f. jüd. Gesch. u. Literatur*, I, 88–90.

The title page of the volume of his responsa reads: זה הספר נקרא שמו בישראל בנימין זאב חברו האלוף המר העלוב מהר"ר בנימין בכה"ר מתתיה ז"ל ונדפס פה ונזיאה רבתי בבית השר דניאל בומבירגי מאנוירשה. והיתה התחלתו יום ה' י"א תשרי שנת רצ"ט (1538) לפ"ק עם רב העיון. The printing was completed in 1. Adar רצ"ט (1539).

[16] Fol. 573a: אחר השלמת הספר עשה שירים הנבון הר"ר מתתיה נר"ו בן הגאון המחבר וישא משלו ויאמר וכו'. The acrostic is: מתתיה בן הרב רבי בנימין בן רבי מתתיה זלה"ה. The author refers to his son Mattityah on fol. 14a: רמזתי שלשה שמות אלה אני המר והעלוב בנימן בן הה"ר מתתיה ז"ל בן הה"ר יוחנן ז"ל ושם בני הה"ר מתתיה ז"ל בזכותם אקיים מקרא שכתוב לא ימושו מפיך ומפי זרעך וכו'.

[17] אחר כל זאת בא אלי בונזיא שמועה רעה ואקונן ואומר באבל ובענין רעה. בהעדר ממני הר"ר מתתיה ז"ל בני באה (r. באו) אלי עלבון וכאב לכן אקונן ואספיד על פרידת בני לזאת אקרא עלוב בנימין זאב.

In the eulogy he writes about his son (fol. 577b): בני ואור עיני הר"ר מתתיה ממני נעדר. באמת היה כולו הוד והדר. משכיל ונבון היה וחכם ... המלאך המקריב יקריב נשמתו ... יהיה לבניו ולנו למליץ ... יזכה לקבל פני השכינה המר העלוב אביו הכותב בנימן

infer that shortly after 1534 Mattityah set out from Arta for the Orient for reasons unknown. He reached Mosul and after a stay there for a certain period he departed this life some time before the completion of the printing of his father's responsa in Venice in Adar 1539.[18]

The other documents given here are of diverse contents and times. No. VI is a letter from Judah b. Simon of 'Imādiya to Yaḥya of Mosul. These persons were close friends and Judah's daughter was about to marry Yaḥya's son (recto, l. 13 ff.). A brother of Yaḥya, Manoaḥ, was living in 'Imādiya. The letter is eloquent testimony to the prevalence of augury among the Ḳurdish Jews in those days. Judah informs his correspondent of his having cast a lot as to who will become 'king' (l. 9), probably the tribal chief in the district of 'Imādiya. Ḳurdistān till the 17th century was bristling with castles, held by hereditary tribal chiefs. The Turks in conquering the province in 1514 divided the territory into Sanjaks or districts and installed the local chiefs as governors.[19] Such a governor is probably meant here by the designation of 'king.' Judah's lot fell on a certain Aḥmad Beg but since the day was cloudy he was not yet sure of the correctness of the lot. The same lot indicated that Aḥmad Beg's Wazīr was in danger of life but again the cloudiness made the result arrived at doubtful. Evidently by such auguries some Jews ingratiated themselves with the superstitious chieftains and their officials.

Judah however is certain that his augury about the date of the wedding of Yaḥya's son (evidently with Judah's daughter) was well established. This date can only be on the 14th, 15th and 16th of the month, whose identity is not indicated. Then comes an item concerning a certain Menaḥem about to visit Mosul (l. 15 ff.). He was afraid of Yaḥya's revenge because he was reputed of having been involved in a denunciation of Manoaḥ,

בכה"ר מתתיה. בעיפה ואופל ועייף וציה. על מיתת בני בארץ נכריה. ולא ראה לפניו לא אב ולא בן להספידו בארץ נכריה. שעסקו בהספדו ובקבורתו חסדו ואמתו יצו עליהם רב העליליה וכו'.

We know now that this strange land was Mosul. Mattityah left behind sons.

[18] See note 15.

[19] See *Encyclopedia Britannica*, 11th edition, s. v. Ḳurdistān.

Yaḥya's brother, which cost the latter 30 Piastres. Menaḥem denied the charge before Judah and Manoaḥ and hence both pleaded for him before Yaḥya. However, a certain David b. Naḥmū had obtained a document from 'the king' (l. 27), evidently the local governor, and was about to go to Mosul. On him Yaḥya can have his full revenge. This Yaḥya must have been quite an influential man in Mosul. He carried on an extensive trade with 'Imādiya in gall-nuts, skins, and other merchandise.

No. VII is sent to the Ḥakham of 'Imādiya, Simon Samuel Dugah (דוגה). Other persons, scholars and laymen, are mentioned by the writer who was evidently a native of 'Imādiya but now lived in some other locality. His name is not known because the document breaks off at the end. The writer informs his correspondents of his impending visit to 'Imādiya. Indeed the journey is difficult for him and he has no desire to see the place again because he has no longer any relatives there. But he is terrified by recurrent dreams in which his late sister takes him to task for not visiting their native city. Here again we have an item of superstition that held so much sway over the local Jews.

The Ḥakham Simon Dugah is the writer of No. VIII to a certain Joseph who is about to come to 'Imādiya to qualify himself as a Shoḥeṭ. Simon expresses his desire to teach Joseph all the relevant laws. No. IX is a letter addressed to the leaders of the Ḳurdistān communities headed by our Simon as Dayyān of 'Imādiya, the leading congregation. The writer was probably the Dayyān of Nirwa. An ugly case happened in this city when a scoundrel by the name of Ḥanukkah kidnapped a girl of 8, the daughter of the bearer of this letter, Nehemiah b. Simon, in order to marry her against her will and that of her parents. The kidnapper took her away to some fastness in the neighborhood of 'Imādiya, and her father could not free her for fear of the gentiles who evidently aided Ḥanukkah. The Nirwa Dayyān requests the 'Imādiya Jews to help in rescuing the girl. He also asks that all learned persons in the district be informed not to perform any marriage ceremony of this minor without her father's consent.

No. X is a circular appeal on behalf of a learned Jew of 'Imādiya, Ḥiyya b. Kaleb, who has fallen on evil times. Formerly his home was known for hospitality and as a meeting place of scholars. Now several members of his family have died off, many debts with interest were due to non-Jews and his houses were foreclosed to secure payment. Ḥiyya was now reduced to seek help from generous coreligionists.

No. XI is dated in the spring of 1768 C. E. at 'Imādīya. The letter is evidently sent to the Rabbi of Mosul concerning the affair of the late Isaac b. סאוו, a merchant of the former city. He once visited Mosul for business purposes when a local Jew, Moses b. Khalifa, obtained from him 1000 Christian Piastres (קרוש רומי) for a partnership in a certain transaction. The yield was to be divided into two halves. On a later occasion, when Isaac again visited Mosul, Moses denied that the partnership had yielded any profit, whereupon Isaac recouped himself by force for 300 Piastres of the sum invested by him. There remained still 700 Piastres in the possession of Moses and since several years neither the principal nor any profit on it has been paid by the debtor. The creditor is already dead and his minor orphans have all these years been deprived of what belongs to them by right. The person written to is requested to intervene on their behalf to 'our lord the king' (ll. 12 ff.), evidently the governor of Mosul.

On verso in different handwriting there is an item concerning Mordecai Sidon b. Eliezer, a representative from Safed to Persia to collect money for the poor (the so-called חלוקה). His brother Moses has also gone on a similar mission on 2 occasions. Mordecai was despoiled on the way by brigands and has arrived in abject poverty, evidently at 'Imādiya. He is now on his way home and a few lines on his behalf were written to Mosul apparently to help him along on his journey.

The small epistle (No. XII) is from 'Imādiya to Jonah of Mosul. Its contents deal with business transactions. Likewise No. XIII addressed to several people in an unknown locality is about merchandise consisting of gall-balls.

No. XIV is by the Dayyān of 'Imādiya, Simon b. Benjamin Hallevi, to the community of גלא. Several of its scholars and leaders are greeted. The community needed a Shoḥeṭ. Simon writes that he sent such a one in Moses b. Yedidyah who had no diploma yet because he still needed more practice. But he is allowed to slaughter temporarily under supervision of two local scholars, 'Ashael and Pinḥas. The same Dayyān of 'Imādiya issued a full diploma for a Shoḥeṭ, Maṣliaḥ b. Moses, in December 1764 C. E. (No. XV). Prior to Simon's advancement as Dayyān of the leading Ḳurdish community of 'Imādiya he evidently occupied a similar position in Sandūr as the address of a letter to him from Bagdād (No. XVI) seems to indicate.

No. XVII is from Sandūr to Jacob Benjamin of Jerusalem. The writer, whose name I could not decipher, replies to an epistle of the Jerusalem scholar and points out the difficulty of transmission of letters from Palestine to Ḳurdistān. Letters go as far as Aleppo and no further. Jacob sent a messenger to Sandūr apparently to give a Geṭ to his wife. The writer is awaiting the return from Aleppo to Sandūr of Jacob's father and son-in-law when the matter will be attended to. He disapproves of Jacob's action and remarks that he ought to have sent for his wife to come to Jerusalem. But as the decision has already been made, nothing more is to be added. The writer asks his Jerusalem correspondent to send several works for which he is willing to pay their full price. The letter dates from the spring 1702 C. E.

The next item (No. XVIII) also refers to the community of Sandūr concerning the case of betrothal of a girl by her father. Since she was no longer a minor, the question arose whether her father's betrothal without her consent was valid. A certain Abraham (evidently a Ḥakham) annulled the betrothal. But the writer, who investigated the matter on the spot, came to the conclusion that since the daughter had not protested forthwith on hearing of the betrothal, it could not subsequently be made invalid even though she now denounced it at the instigation of her own father who entered upon the betrothal agreement. The document is probably of the 18th century. There is quoted Moses Rivkes' באר הגולה to the Shulḥan 'Arukh, the editio princeps of which appeared in Amsterdam in 1661 and since then was published numerous times.

No. XIX also deals with a matrimonial affair in Sakho which reflects on the primitive conditions prevailing there. A father after marrying off his daughter needed a female person for housework. He therefore conceived the idea of obtaining a wife for his minor son. The daughter-in-law would attend to the housework till her husband would grow up. She was evidently older than he, and on realizing the situation after the wedding fled from her new home. Now her husband died of course childless, and there remained a brother of six years to whom the unfortunate woman is tied by the law of the levirate marriage. The woman has no home since her flight and there is the danger that in her plight she will become an apostate to Judaism. The writer, evidently a Ḥakham, is reporting the case to a Rabbi (perhaps in 'Imādiya). More details were contained in a previous epistle. Evidently an attempt was made to declare the first wedding as invalid owing to the minority of the dead person so that the girl be not obliged to wait for the Ḥaliṣah of his brother for another 7 years till he would become of full age.

No. XX is a letter by a certain Abraham b. Menaḥem from עקר (see note 348) to Joseph b. Menaḥem of שיך כא. Several persons in the latter place are greeted. The epistle is teeming with incorrect spellings and bad Hebrew showing that the writer was not familiar with the language. He evidently has moved recently with his family to עקר.[20] He is pleased with the change and is willing to bring over his mother-in-law in time before the New Year.

[20] A MS. at the Hebrew Union College Library (MS. Frenkel No. 249) contains the section on שחיטה וטרפה of Maimonides' Yad (ס' קדושה, הלכות שחיטה) with an Arabic translation, each Halakah is given first in the Hebrew original followed by its rendering into Arabic. (About Arabic translations of parts of the Yad, cp. Bodl. Nos. 614–16). This MS. has the following colophon dated 1484 C. E.: כמלת סיר אלדבאחה בעון אללה פי תאני שהר מרחשון סנה אתשצו לשטרות עלי יד אלעבד אלפקיר שעדיה אבן גמליאל מן גמאעה אלעקר ועבב [וכתבו] ל[נפסה]. (The abbreviation ועבב is not clear to me). This MS. was subsequently bought from the copyist Sa'adyah b. Gamliel of עקר by Benjamin b. Khalāf Hakkohen as an additional colophon shows: ה[ד]א מא אשתרי בנימן בן כלף אלכהן מן סעדיה בן גמליאל אלעקרי במבלג אשרפי דהב תכון מבארכה עליה.

Then in other script: . . . . [ועל] הקונה ועל הקורא . . . . [נ]צח סלה ועד

There follows a third colophon surrounded by a drawing with pictures of camels: על שם התלמיד הנעונים. וי[ו]לד שעשועים. וישמרהו (היינו השם) מכל פגעים רעים. הלו הו (הלא הוא .r) רחמים בן יעקוב יצ"ו הקורה (הקורא .r) בו ישמח. וגונבו שמו ימח. בזכות אברהם בן תרח האתן (האיתן .r) נצח סנה (סלה .r).

The next item (No. XXI) reveals the troubles of a certain Mordecai, apparently sent by a Ḥakham of a larger community to act as his representative in the role of religious supervisor at a settlement in Ḳurdistān. There were in the latter place a number of students of this Ḥakham who had authorization to act as Shoḥeṭim. The newcomer had instructions not to allow these people to slaughter animals except in groups of two persons at a time according to the law when there is a doubt about the expertness of a Shoḥeṭ. A certain Moses took this amiss when he was asked to bring along with him his colleague Judah. Moses' father, Abraham, slandered Mordecai to the Ḥakham whose subsequent letter of verification of Mordecai's instructions was hidden. The writer lost his temper and it came to a brawl. He pitifully asks his correspondent to help him leave this place where he was shamefully maltreated.

Finally in No. XXII we have a letter of appeal from Aleppo[21] on behalf of a Ḥakham by the name of Benjamin Mizraḥi, the bearer of the epistle. His eyesight has failed him and his wife died leaving behind 3 sons of whom the youngest is an infant at the breast. The child was given to a non-Jewish nurse for the fee of 2 Piastres per month and there is the danger that, if the stipulated sum be not paid regularly, the nurse would bring about the apostacy of the infant. Benjamin was travelling from place to place to find healing and monetary help. In Aleppo he obtained the present letter of introduction.

These texts give us glimpses of the internal life of several communities in Ḳurdistān, a district of mountain fastnesses difficult to approach. Some contact with outside Jewry was main-

[21] In connection with this well-known community attention is drawn to a liturgical MS. at the Hebrew Union College Library (MS. Frenkel No. A 30) containing the rite of this locality (מנהג ארם צובה) which bears marks of the influence of the old Palestinian order of service of the synagogue. Thus the 12th benediction of the 'Amidah has a reference to the Christians (ולנצרים) as is the case with the Genizah fragments of the Palestinian liturgy (cp. Mann, *H. U. C. Annual*, II, 295ff.). This MS. has the following colophon dating 1410 C. E.: וכאן אלפראג̇ מנה אכ̇ר נהר אלכ̇מיס ה̇ פי שהר שבט שנת א̇ת̇שׁכ̇א לשׁ (=לשטרות) במידנת (במדינת .r) צובה דעל נהר קוקיון מותבה. והד̇א מא עלקה העבד הרש (supply המחכה) לישע דר בשמי עליה אברהם בר שלמה בר אברהם נ̇ע.

tained via Mosul.[22] In spite of the unfavorable cultural and economic conditions of the environment there was still a residue of knowledge of Judaism among the Ḥakhamim and the teachers who endeavored to raise disciples and preserve Judaism for the future generations. The success of their efforts is to be found in the preservation of this Jewry to the present day.

I.

[Two paper leaves.]

(Fol. 1, recto)

לקק נירוא יצ̇[ו][1]
שלומך כשושנה יפרח. ואורך תמיד יוזרח
יוזרח[2]. וסרח העודף לאחריך תסרח[3].
החסיד הענו ידיד ה̇ ישכון לבטח צדיק
צדקות אהב. בסופה את והב[4]. כמ̇[5] דוד יצו
ויהי דוד בכל דרכיו משכיל וה̇ עמו ועוז
גאותו שחקים ברום. כי ירום חסידות
יעשה קציר כמו נטע ותארכנה פארותיו
וסרעפיו בין העבותים[6] מילדותו ינחנה[7].

[22] Another community of the district of upper Mesopotamia (Jazīrah) is mentioned in a leaf among our collection of letters. It contains the end of a legal document dated Ṭebet (5)362 A. M. (=1601 C. E.) פה כרכוך. Karkūk was near Daḳūḳā (cp. Le Strange, *Lands of the Eastern Caliphate*, 92, note 1, and Map II facing p. 25).

[1] ישמרה צורה וגואלה. Nirwa, "a fortress in the district of Zawwazān belonging to the ruler of Mosul" (Yaḳūt, s. v.).

[2] Repeated in MS.

[3] Cp. Ex. 26.12, but here in the meaning of material plenty, abundance.

[4] Cp. Deut. 33.12, Ps. 11.7, Num. 21.14 (the order of the words is changed for the sake of the rhyme); about the verse in Num. cp. the well-known Aggadah in Ḳidd. 30b, top.

[5] =כבוד מרנא.

[6] Cp. Job 14.9, Ezek. 31.5.

[7] Referring to his piety (חסידות).

או כי שצמחו[8] הלבנים בלחייו נתקדש בקדושה עליונה. גם על תלמידי מ̇ יוסף יצ̇ו כבר ידעתי על צדיקותכם ונדיבותכם עליתם על כל ביראת ה̇ ובענוה והיה אמונה אזור חלציכם וצדק אזור מתניכם[9] והצלחתם בהצלחה ששמתם המדרש[10] וזאת הפגימה היתה בקהלתכם ומלאתם אותה וגדרתם הפרצה ואת הנטישות הרפות התזתם[11] הסירותם חרפה מעליכם ושמחתי. ג״כ[12] את אלקי השמחתם ללמוד בנעם שלא יצאו בורים ערירים מן התורה עתה הרימותם דגליכם והצלתם עצמכם מיד ה̇ כי היה עליכם קצף גדול וידעתם כל קהל שאין בה ת̇ת̇[13] מחריבין אותה א̇ד̇[14] מחרימין אותה[15] ותזהרו במדרש שלא תתבטל שישמע קול תינוקות מביניכם וג̇כ̇ בניכם לא יצאו בורים ויקללו אתכם ותנצלו מקללתם ונאמר[16] ארור אשר לא יקים ד̇ת̇ הזאת והוא בכלל ארור. אמנם לענין נדבתי זה כמה שכחתם אותי ולא באתני נדבתכם מימיכם אכלנו מכחכם ולא נסוגותם אחור ולא מעדו קרסוליכם מפרנסתינו ואל תאמרו נתרחק ממנו ונשכחנו ע̇ז̇כ̇[17]

[8] =כשצמחו, i.e., when he became gray.

[9] Cp. Is. 11.5. [10] Established a school. [11] Cp. Is. 18.5.

[12] =גם כן. [13] =תלמוד תורה. [14] =איכא דאמרי.

[15] Cp. Sabbath 119b, bottom, and דקדוקי סופרים, a.l.

[16] Deut. 27.26 and cp. Soṭah 37a bottom: ארור בכלל וארור בפרט.

[17] =על זה כתוב. The verse is incorrectly quoted (cp. Deut. 6.12; 8.11). The Rabbinic inference את לרבות הרב is in connection with another verse (Deut. 6.13). Cp. Pes. 22b: עד שבא ר״ע ודרש את ה׳ אלהיך לרבות תלמידי חכמים

לא תשכח את ה֟ אלקיך לרבות הרב
שאסור לשכחו ותדעו מיום שיצאתי משם[18]
לא בא לידי פרוטה מנדבתכם אשתקד
שלחתם לא הגיעה לידי אם בשנים
אחרות ובשנים קדמוניות לא ראיתי ולא
שמעתי א֟כ֟[19] מה תועלת לי ולכם תשלחו
לא אתם תזכו ג֟כ֟ אני לא אהנה מכם
ואז֟ל֟[20] אין הצדקה נגמרת אלא לפי חסד

(verso)

ש֟[21] זרעו לכם לצדקה וקצרו לפי חסד ופרש֟י֟[22]
ז֟ל אין מעשה הצדקה נגמר אלא להגיעה
ליד המקבל הזורע ספק אוכל ספק אינו
אוכל אבל הקוצר ודאי אוכל וכן תרצו
תרבה[23] זכותכם תגיעוני הנאתכם ותשלחו
נדבתכם בכתב ליד איש נאמן ותכתבוה
ותמסרוה ליד איש נאמן תשביעוהו שיגיע
לידי ואין לי שליח נאמן לשלוח לקהלות
ואשלח כתבים לא יגיעני דבר וזהו זכותכם
אע״פ שאני רחוק מכם שתעשו נדבתי
אע״פ שלא תראוני וזו המצוה לשמה שאין
בה פסול ופגימה ומצוה פגומה שיעשה
האדם מבושה או מיראה או לכבוד
האדם וזו אינה מצוה ועזא[24] התנא וכל

[18] viz. from ʻImādiya.

[19] =אם כן.

[20] =ואמרו (חכמינו) זכרם לברכה, Sukkah 49b.

[21] =שנאמר, Hos. 10.12.

[22] =ופרש רש״י. Cp. Rashi's comment: הנתינה היא הצדקה והטורח הוא החסד כגון מוליכה לביתו וכו׳.

[23] Read שתרבה.

[24] Read ועז״א = ועל זה אמר (התנא), cp. Abot 2.12.

מעשיך יהיו לש"ש[25] וכתב בעל ס' חובת הלבבות[26] גדול עונש העובד אדם מעובד הצלמים כי עובד הצלמים עובד דבר שאינו מכעיס ועובד האדם עובד דבר המכעיס ועוד וזה מוזהר עליו וזה אינו מוזהר וכתב לשם טעמים רבים יעויין שם. סוף דבר זהו זכותכם ומעלתכם שתעשו מצוה שלא מחנופת האדם בזה יקובל[27] נדבתכם אך באופן שתגיעני. ועניני ידוע ונגלה לכל יושב בזו המדינה מדוחק ומצער בעניות ובצמצום יין ושכר לא יבוא לפי ערום וחסר כל אשלח שליח גונב הכל ממני לפיכך נמנעים הקהלות מלהשגיח עלי ואם לא היה מפחד זה לא הייתי צריך לכם כלל היו שולחים לי נדבות מקהלות גדולות מצובה ומבבל ומדיאר בכר וממראגא[28] לא היו מונעין ממני הכל אוהבים דברי לא יסובו אחור ממני ולא ימנעו ממני ואז"ל[29] [יר]מ[י]ה התפלל על אנשי ענתות שלא יזמין להם חכמים צדיקים לעשות עמהם שלא יקבלו שכר עליהם ש'[30] ויהיו מוכשלים לפניך בכל עת בעת אפך עשה בהם ופי' רש"י[30a] אע"פ שבאים לעשות צדקה הכשילם בבני אדם שאינם מהוגנים שלא

[25] =לשם שמים. [26] See שער יחוד המעשה, ch. 4. [27] Read תקובל.

[28] Aleppo, Bagdād, Diyār Bakr and Marāghah (about the last two towns see Le Strange, *Lands of the Eastern Caliphate*, 86ff., 108, and 164).

[29] B. Batra 9b, bottom. [30] =שנאמר, Jer. 18.23.

[30a] The passage is not in our text of Rashi.

(fol. 2, recto)

שלא יקבלו עליהם שכר. הואיל שאתם צדיקים טוב שיאכלו צדיקים מלחמכם מכחכם אם כל העולם ישכחוני אתם אין ראוי לכם לשכחני אע"פ שאני רחוק אהיה זכור בפיכם ואוכל מפרי ידיכם ואברך אתכם הואיל שאתם תלמידי ועוד יש לכם קורבה עמנו כמו ששמענו מקדמונים ומֹ דוד יודע בקרבה[31] ונאמר מבשרך לא תתעלם[32] והגבוהה[33] העולה באחרונה אתם צדיקים וממון צדיקים לצדיק ואמר החכם[34] פעולת צדיק לחיים ותבואת רשע לחטאת ר"ל[35] פעולת הצדיק לאנשי חיים דהיינו צדיקים ולא לרשעים שהצדיקים נקראים חיים שֹ[36] ובניהו בן איש חי שאפילו במותו נקרא חי רב פעלים מקבצאל שריבה פעולים לתורה[37] ותבואת רשע לחטאת לאנשי חטאת דהיינו רשעים שנקראים מתים שֹ[38] והמתים אינם יודעים מאומה מכירין רבונם ומורדים בו וכמֹשו"ל[39] בשר טלה לבטן אדם ובשר חמור לבטן כלב טהור לטהורים[40] טמא לבטן טמאים וכן ממון

[31] Read בקורבה, viz. David, to whom the letter was addressed, knows of this relationship.

[32] Is. 58.7.

[33] To be understood as the highest reason for my support, adduced here as the last instance, is that you are righteous people.

[34] Prov. 10.16. [35] =רצונו לומר. [36] 2 Sam. 23.20.

[37] Cp. Ber. 18a, bottom, b, top.

[38] Kohel. 9.5 and cp. Ber. 18b.

[39] Read וכמו שאמרו (החכמים) זכרם לברכה=וכמשז"ל.

[40] Read לבטן טהורים.

צדיקים לחכמים הצדיקים וממון הרשעים לרשעים ר"ל ממון הצדיק הולך לג̇ אנשים ס̇י א̇צ̇י̇ אלקים צדיקים ישראל וממון רשעים למ̇גר למלכים לגוים ולרשעים. ותדרשו בקהל לענין נדבתי ולמעני יקום מ̇ דוד בקהל וידרוש על נדבתי ותעשוה כסף וצרור כסף תשלחוהו לידי וכמה שלחתי[41] אם יש לכם בן יודע תשלחוהו אצלי ואלמד אותו שאיני רוצה שתפחת התורה מזרעכם ומביתכם לא יכרת מעונה[42] ויהיה לכם ער בחכמים ועונה בתלמידים[43] בלתי שיבוא אצלי לא יושלם בתורה הלמוד[44] אחרים בטעות ולמוד זקנים אמתי ואני תמיד איחל והוספתי על כל תהלותיכם ושמכם בפי. במו פי אתחנן[45] לצור שיעמיד מכם חכמים ושלמים וכן רבים בתורה והיו אד[46] אך למאור להעלות נר תמיד[47] כנפש המעתיר יעקב בכה"ר יאודה ס̇ט̇[48]

(verso is blank).

II.

[Two paper leaves, damaged.]

(Fol. 1, recto)

. . . . ים במתי. ולהעניק השפעות לעדתי. נועה [ונדה] לא מריתי. מלהתפלל ואחור לא נסוגותי].

[41] Read שלחתם. [42] Cp. Zeph. 3.7. [43] Cp. Mal. 2.12.

[44] Read למוד.

[45] Cp. Job 19.16. [46] To be deleted. [47] Cp. Exod. 27.20.

[48] The last two words are doubtful as only the tops of the letters have been preserved. ס̇ט̇ = סופו טוב.

מלישא כפי לתלמידי יונקי משדי תו[רתי].
משתעשעים על ברכי חכמתי. שואבי [מי]
תבונות מבאר השכלתי. לוקטים משדה
מדעי. עתה אקום על ברכי ואשתחוה
לאלקי השמים המאציל מאור אצילו[49] חנו
לחכמים המתדפקים על תורתו ומעטה
האור לנשמות היראים מושכים מאצילו
המתאצל מאור הצח והמצוחצח ומתחל[ק]
לכמה חלקים הבלתי מתחלקים מסוד
ע"ב גשרים[50] ברוחניות ובפנימיות החסדים
הנאחדים בחמשים אפיקים בגאות התבו[נה][51]
אריקם אציקם אאביקם אבהיקם אזיקם[52]
עליכם ק"ק תחתון[53]. היושבים בטדי[54] ואיתון.
בראשם השרים הגבירים תלמידי שלמן יצ"ו
והשר הנכבד יקיר ליקירים נחום יצ"ו ולשלמ[ן]
ומֿ עבדולא יצֿו ולהזקן עבדיה יצֿו ולידיד
נפשי אברהם הלוי ולחמודי ברימו יצֿו ולגא[ן]
ויבארי יצֿו ונחום אבארי יצֿו ולמנדו יצֿו ולעלוון יצֿו ולעבדלו
י[צֿו]
ולהחסיד מוסא בן רומי יצֿו ולתלמידי מוסא

[49] אציל is taken here as אצילות, emanation.

[50] The 72 'bridges' are not clear to me but they are evidently connected with the mystical שם ע"ב.

[51] The reference here is to "the 50 gates of understanding" (נ' שערי בינה, Ned. 38a).

[52] Paiṭanic phrases (אאביקם from אבק, viz. as plentiful as dust; אבהיקם from בהק, to shine; אזיקם evidently formed from זיק, a spark).

[53] 'Imādiya was divided into two parts, the upper one high in the mountains and the lower one (cp. infra, notes 110, 158). That the letter was sent to 'Imādiya is evident from l. 134.

[54] Evidently in the meaning of strength synonymous to איתון. Cp. also Ben-Jehuda, *Thesaurus*, IV, *s. v.* טֶדי, note 2.

ומרדר יצׄו ומשה יצׄו ועלון ולרחמים יצׄו ולמקדסי נחום יצ[ו]
ולאבכו יצׄו ולאחז[55] יצׄו ולבבכונא רהוכי יצׄו ולב[נו]
ולמשה בן מׄ נסים יצׄו ולכהן כׄוגו יצׄו וליסב[56]
ולאחיו יצחק בני נאנדו יצׄו ולברימו בן ברמא
ולחנן יצׄו ולשלמה זנמי יצׄו ול[57]
ולשאר הנשארים שנשמטו מפי עטי. ב[הם]
לא ממעטי. גם הם בתוך שטי. מה אמרי[ץ]
במלין ידעתם מה עמדי וגורלכם עמי
בעדן אלקים בתוך מדרשי והיכלי תתענג[ו]
על רב טוב הצפון ליריאיו כי הׄ דבר טו[ב]
לחסידיו וממלא אוצרותיהם מכל טוב
גם חלק לנערים ההולכים עמו הם יקחו
חלקם[57a] חלק כחלק יאכלו לבד ממכריו [על]
האבות מלשון אבי יבחן איוב[58] כפי חפ[צם]
והצביון המגיע אל המוכר והקונה אל המו[כר]

(verso)

. . . . .אל האורים
. . . . . בתשבץ שם יתנו צדקות הׄ צדקות
[פרז]ונו בישראל פיזר נתן לאביונים יאכל
[מ]שולחן המלכים הנקובים מאן מלכי רבנן
[ו]שם יחלק מנות אשפר ואשישה הבו
דלא לוסיף עלה ואז יקבלו פרס מבית
המלך לפי מתנתו מה דיהיב יהבין ליה

[55] The name Aḥaz is rather strange being after a Biblical king of ill repute. Read perhaps ולאחיו.

[56] Probably = Yūsuf.

[57] The first 2 letters of the next word.

[57a] Cp. Gen. 14.24, but here the allusion is to the young men who walk in God's way.

[58] Cp. Deut. 18.8. In a peculiar manner he connects the word אבות with Job 34.36 in the meaning of desire.

ושם חלקתכם ספונה אתי תאכלו
בראש הקרואים[59] ומאמר חז״ל[60] דור ודורשיו
דור וחכמיו דור ומנהיגיו כשם שבעה״ז
האדם מאכיל קרוביו ורעיו ואוהביו כן
המדה לעה״ב דמדה טובה מרובה ועוד
עשיריה בה מילתא אלבישייהו יקירא
וכן אמרו חכמי החקירה קק[61] מהשמש שהוא
בגלגל רביעי שהוא מחלק האור לז ככבי
לכת וכל הככבים ממנו מאירים ועז״כ[62] ואוהביו
כצאת השמש בגבורתו ק״ו[63] לצדיק שהוא
מאיר לדובקיו ולעוזריו ולאנשי חברתו
אם הרחוק הנזור יתעלם ממנו האור
כמרחק הירח מנכחיות השמש יתכהה
קדרות וז״ש[64] אך קרוב ליריאיו ישעו לשכון
כבוד בארצנו ר״ל כבוד של יריאים
ישכון בארצינו וכן אז״ל[65] פני משה כפני
חמה ופני יהושע כפני לבנה וכן אז״ל[66]
גֹעַ מדורות מדורות הוא כל צדיק
יש לו מדור עם תלמידיו ואנשי דורו. ועתה
[ב]אתי לגלות לכם זה הסוד על עה״ב מימי
[ל]א גליתי לשום אדם ואדם בזה הדור

[59] The drift of these lines, consisting of Biblical and Talmudic phrases, is that his correspondents by supporting the writer and his school will have a share with him in the future world.

[60] Cp. Sanh. 38b.

[61] Crossed out with correction ק״י on top which reading is not certain.

[62] Judges 5.31.

[63] =קל וחומר.

[64] =וזה שכתוב, Ps. 85.10.

[65] B. Batra 75a, bottom.

[66] See Sabb. 152a, bottom, B. M. 83b. Cp. also the Midrashic versions of the dimensions of Paradise (אוצר מדרשים, I, 83ff., 255–6).

[ל]א השיגו אלא א׳[67] מני אלף שרידים אשר [ה׳] קורא דעו שעה״ב שאז״ל[68] עין לא ראתה [א]לקים זולתך אינה תחת כיפה ר״ל תחת [שק]ערירות הז׳ גלגלים אלא היא חוץ מכיפה [של] השמים ומשטחם כולם כזרת של הב״ה ית׳[69] שנאמ׳ שמים בזרת תכן[70] ושעור עה״ב שהיא תחת הכסא הכבוד סביב [ב]אויר הכיפה בעודפיות הכסא והוא שיעור ל״ו פרסאות שנ׳[71] שרפים עומדים

(fol. 2, recto)

ממעל לו ר״ל עומדים במרחק ממנו שיעור ל״ו פרסאות וכל פרסה ח׳ מלין וכל מיל אלף אלפים אמה צא וחשוב אבד חשבון[72] והכיפה כולה חצי אמה אכ״ אל יתמהו המתמיהין היכן ידורו כל צבאות המלאכים וכל המון הנשמות הצדיקים והרשעים מיום שנברא העולם ועד המלך המשיח היכן ילכו היכן ידורו ואז״ל[73] עתיד להנחיל לכל צדיק וצדיק יש עולמות וכתב הרמב״ם ז״ל[74] ש״י פעמים כנגד טוב של עה״ז והיא העולם הבא אין לה שיעור ומדה וקצבה לבד האל היושב בה ואמר[75] אלף אלפין ישמשוני רבוא רבוון מן קדמוהי

[67] =אחד.   [68] Cp. Is. 64.3 and Ber. 34b.

[69] =הקדוש ברוך הוא יתברך.

[70] Is. 40.12.   [71] Is. 6.2.

[72] A pun on Num. 21.30, here in the meaning that the calculation of the size of this עולם הבא is impossible.

[73] ʿUkṣin, end.

[74] In his Mishnah commentary, a. l.

[75] Dan. 7.10.

יקומון אז״ל לנהר דינור אבל לגדודין אין מספר[76] וגליתי לכם זה הסוד מאהבתי עמכם עוד שתדעו שכרכם הצפון לכם ולא יקשו עליכם מאמרי חז״ל ועוד תהיה דעתכם שלמה לעה״ב לפי שהאדם משיג לעה״ב כפי דעתו משל להד׳ לא[77] שלא ראה קושטדינא וספרו לו כך וכך שעריה וכך מבואותיה וכך מגדליהם במקום פלוני ארמון המלך ובמקום פלוני מעין ובמקום פלוני השוק כשילך לשם אע״פ שלא ראה אותה מימיו הולך על דרך שספרו לו ולא יטעה אבל מי שלא ראה ג״כ לא ישמע לא מבוא שער המדינה בלי שיראוהו לא ילך ולא יוכל ליכנס בה[78a] ולפיכך יש כמה צדיקים לא ילכו אצל המלך בלי שליח ומורה הדרך ויש כמה צדיקים שהולכים דרך נכוחה שידעו ושמעו הדרך של עה״ב ולא יטעו וז״ש[79] הא דעיילי בבר הא דעיילי בלא בר ר״ל בלא רשות זוטרי נינהו[80] כר׳ חייא ובניו שעולה גוהרקא שלו בלא שליח עמו כדאיתא

באמונת חכמים[78]

[76] Cp. Ḥag. 13b, bottom. [77] =למה הדבר דומה לאחד.

[78] It is not clear where in the text this marginal note fits in. To assume that there is here an indication that our parable is found in a work אמונת חכמים, is rather difficult because the only 2 works known by this name, one by Abi‘ad Sar Shalom Basila (editio princeps, Mantua, 1730) and the other by Abraham Ḥayyim Viterbo (edited in Ashkenazi's טעם זקנים, 19ff.), are much later in date than our epistle (see above, p. 484). Moreover I could not find this משל in these works.

[78a] This passage is corrupt. Read perhaps: ולא יטעה מבוא שער המדינה בלי שיראוהו אבל מי שלא ראה וג״כ לא שמע לא ילך ולא יוכל ליכנס בה.

[79] =וזה שאמרו, Sukkah 45b, Sanh. 97b.

[80] זוטרי נינהו refers to those who enter only after permission (דעיילי בבר) whereas R. Ḥiyya and his sons are those who enter without permission.

בבתרא[81]. כבר יצאתי מכונה[82] אבוא לענייני ומה יענה יעקב[83] עוד ידעתי דלותכם אמנם יש לנו חלק עמכם כשם שאתם יש לכם חלק עמי בעהֹבֹ בשכר הרוחני והאמתי כך אני יש לי חלק בידכם ובכחכם לפרנסני

(verso)

ומעתה אל תתעצלו בנדבה שלי ותשלחוה לי לפסח ואתם שלחתם לי בחג[84] נעשה לך נדבה עבר החורף היכן הבטחתכם ותאחרו נדבתי של שתי שנים ואחֹכֹ תאמרו עכשו שלחנוה לא תאמרו של אשתקד ודאשתקד היתה אלא תחשבוה לשנה הבאה ועוד לא היתה שלכם של נירוא וביתנורי[85] היתה לקחתם אותה נתתם אותה לרמֹ יצוֹ ושלחתם תמורתה ולא ידעתי כונת מֹ שלמן יצוֹ. נא שלח למזורן[86] לנדבתי צדקו דברי מֹ[87] ספתו שאמר עתה תראה אנו היינו לוקחים לך נדבה וכופין אותם וכמה שנים קֹקֹ שוכו[88] לא ראיתם מהם פרוטה ולא קהל ברוריים[89] והנה שלחתי

[81] Read במציעא, viz. B. M. 85b.

[82] מְכֻוָּנָה, i.e. from the purpose of my letter.

[83] Viz. the author of our letter.

[84] Tabernacles.

[85] About Nirwa see above, note 1. Bēt-Nuri is probably identical with Bait-al-Nār which Yaḳūt states was a large village belonging to the district of Irbil from which it was distant 80 miles. Benjamin II (*Acht Jahre in Asien u. Afrika*, 3rd ed., 68) calls the place Tanura.

[86] Spelt in l. 130 מזוראן which I cannot identify.

[87] =מר.

[88] Probably identical with Sakho (cp. Benjamin II, *l. c.*, 63ff.: Sachu).

[89] I cannot identify this locality.

אליך כתבים תשלחם לכל קהל וקהל
לנירוא ולביתנורי ותקחו נדבתי ותשלחו
לי ואתם מתעצלים בענייני ושלמן הי'[89a]
צדיק אבל עצל ורפה הוא ותשלח
כתבי למזוראן ולענין קׄ שרנש[90] ידעתם
שקצו אצבעותי מכתבים[91] עד שהושבתי
ביניהם המדרש ובניתי היסוד למה
תהרסו יסודותי ובנייני ששלחתם להביא
בן כאזו יצֹו אליכם לא די לכם בני עמדיא
גם תהרסו יסוד שבניתי אם בן כאזו יצא
ממדרש תבטל המדרש והשבעתי אתכם
אם תעשו זה תהרסו המדרש על המלמד[92]
תדעו אלחום עמכם לא אקבל מכם זה
הדבר אל תפרצו סייגי אל תעברו על גזרתי
אל איקל בעיניכם אם אחרים יפרצו בי
אתם בני אל תקילוני ועוד החכם באחור
ישבחנה[93] ודי באזהרה מועט אעֹפֹ שישלחנו
אביו ישוב אחור וכל שילמדנו אות יהיה
לאות. ויתכסה בלאות[94]. ויובא בלילאות[95].
לא ירום לבי לומר עליכם דבר תנואות. כמֹשֹ
הרמבֹן על הראבֹעֹ זהב יוצק גרונו[96]. אם לא

[89a] השם ישמרהו=.

[90] Likewise unknown to me; קׄ=קהל. In letter III, 1.10, the spelling is שראנש.

[91] A peculiar expression, "my fingers abhor letters", viz. are tired of the many epistles written to this community.

[92] On account of the loss of an important student called בן כאזו.

[93] Cp. Prov. 29.11 in connection with the beginning of the verse: כל רוחו יוציא כסיל.

[94] Rags.

[95] In bonds (for לילאות read לולאות).

[96] The famous remark of Naḥmanides in his Pentateuch commentary on several occasions when disagreeing with Ibn Ezra.

למעני למענו. שלא יפול בניינו. כל זה היין תשתו קשה היה בעיניכם לזוכרני בקנקן א֗ עם יוסב[97] גאן ומוקא שבאו בידים ריקניות. חוץ מאברהם אדם אחר לא יזכרני למי אשא עיני זולתכם כל שיארך הזמן הפרידה[98] אשכח מלבכם עבדיה יצ֗ו וברימו[99] וזולתו לא יזכרוני במעט ממון כל התלמידים ראיתי מהם כבוד חוץ ממוקא בן עבדיה אחור הנ[ו]לך כנגד [פניו] . . . .

(right hand margin)

. . . עשו ממני שאני זקנתי לא נשאר בי כח ובנותי הקטנות למען ה׳ אם תהיה פחד תצילוני מן הצרה ואל תעלימו עינכם ממני ושלום.

III.

[One paper leaf, torn and very faded. Verso contains scribble besides the address.]

Address (verso)

ב֗ה֗[100]

אל מול פני המנורה
הטהורה המאירה
לארץ ולדרים כה״ר אברהם נר״ו
ופגי״ן דרגמ֗ה֗ לזר[101].
מאשור לסנדור
יע֗א֗[102].

[97] Probably = Yūsuf (cp. above, note 56).

[98] Read זמן הפרידה.

[99] Mentioned in lines 19 and 20.

[100] = ברוך השם.

[101] ופני״ן = ופורץ גדר ישכנו נחש (Koh. 10.8). Here נחש is taken as the abbreviation of נדוי חרם שמתא; דרגמ״ה = דרבנו גרשום מאור הגולה, viz. the well-known Ḥerem of R. Gershom against the opening and reading of other people's correspondence.

[102] From Mosul to Sandūr (about the latter place cp. Benjamin II, *l. c.*, p. 68); יע״א = ינן עליהן אלהים.

(Recto)

גברא רבא איקלע לנהר דעֲהֹ[103] תושע לו ימינו כמו אל . . . . .
ימים . . . ל
על התורה ועל העבודה להכינה ול . . . . . אליהו[103]* הרב[103]*
כתובה יכולת תע . . .
והארש[104] תענה. מתחת זרועות עולם ישאו יחד קולם יברכו שם
כבודו ברכות
שמים מעל תבאתה לראש המשביר כ"ר אחי אשר כנפשי החכם
השלם כה"ר אברהם נרו. מגן אברהם יהי בעזרו. ועליו יציץ נזרו.
אכי"ר[105].
אחרי עתרת החיים והשלום בעדו ובעד כל אשר לו מסביב מענין
מכתב אצבעותיך המסולאים כפז האירו אל עבר פני ששלחת ביד
שי'[106] יעקוב ברוך אתה לה' שהשגחת ממעון קדשך לאחיך בן
בריתך
וכמה שאמר כ"ת[107] שאכתוב שטרות[108] לעמדיא עשיתי כאשר
אמרת
וגם כתבתי שטר לשראנש[109] ויגיעו לידך עם שי'[109a] יעקוב הלוי.
הנה השלכתי יהבי על ה' ועל כ"ת שתשתדל בכל עוז ותעזרני
בכחך
כי זה קרוב לי"ד שנים שלא שלחו לי שום דבר וכל הקהילות
ברוכים יהיו

[103] Pun on Nehardea in Babylon.

*[103] The reading is doubtful.

[104] Pun on ארץ (cp. Hos. 2.24). אר'ש is evidently an abbreviation of ארשת שפתינו.

[105] =אמן כן יהי רצון.

[106] =שיך.

[107] =כבוד תורתו.

[108] In the meaning of letters asking for support. About the expression שטר for letter, cp. also Mr. David Sassoon, הצופה לחכמת ישראל, IX, 209.

[109] Cp. above, note 90.

[109a] =שיך.

השגיחו עלינו ואלו הג̇ קהילות[110] פנו אלי עורף ולא פנים ואיני צועק וקובל רק על הת"ח שביניהם שהם הרחיקוני מגבולי וקפחו פרנסתי חוטאים ומחטיאים לא די שהם ממאנים להשגיח עלי רק לכל מקום שיראו אגרותי מעלימים אותם ואני עושה עצמי כמחריש[111] כי כן קבלתי מרבותי[112] כל מי שיש לו דין צעקת לגימה על חבירו ושותק שוכן עדי עד עושה לו דין וכמה פעמים השי'[113] גילה חרפתם והיה לאל ידם[114] לקעקע ביצתם עכ"ז עשיתי לפנים משורת הדין והארכתי אפי ויצא מפי שלא אשאל מהם עוד וע"ע[115] ממקום אחר ישלח שלומיו וסוף סוף שהם יכי[נרו] שבלי ספק רוח הקדושים אשר בארץ אינה נוחה מהם וכמה פעמי' היתה יד ה̇ בם ל[רעה] ולא השגיחו ואמרו דרך מקרה הוא אכן כיום שראיתי אחי אוהב חסד כדרך אבינו הראשון[116] כשמו כן הוא שלח שאכתוב להם לא מנעתי והכל כדי שידע אחי כמה עיניהם רעה בשל אחרים ומבטח אני באלקי אבי ואדוני שכל מי שיקפח פרנסתי

[110] Evidently the 2 congregations of ʻImādiya (upper and lower) and the one of שראנש.

[111] Reading uncertain.

[112] See Giṭṭin 7a.

[113] =השם יתברך.

[114] Read ידי.

[115] =ועד עולם. But reading is uncertain. The context would require some such words as והש"י.

[116] The Patriarch Abraham whose namesake was the recipient of the letter.

ומחיתי יקפח בניו ויראו עיניו פידו גם מענין ביתנורי[117] לא שלחו לי
שום דבר ואשתקד דאשתקד כתבתי ושלחתי להם ולגלא[118] ולניריא[119] ולכאכא[120]
ונפלו ביד מקפחנ[י] דרכים וקפחום ויישהום אצלם בבית נכותם ועוד
כתבים כאלו של זו השנה כתבתי להם אבל בזה הפעם איני חושדם
שקפחום לפי שלא נודע לי האמת אבל לא שמעתי מהם עד היום

(Continued on right hand margin; the writing is very faded and hardly any connected sentence can be deciphered.)

IV.

[Two paper leaves the second of which is cut off in the middle.]

(Fol. 1, recto)

פשוט ומרובע[121]

שמעו החכמים מלי ונמנים[122] יאזינו אלי
צירי מחלתי אשמיע אולי ישוב כחי חילי
על תורה אזעק אנאקה כי נעדרה מכל גבולי
נתכסה ניצוץ מאיר תוך ענן מעון מקהלי
אפסו מושכי עיון אישי חכמה מעמקי מושכלי
נסגרו שערי הבינה לא נודעו ארחי ושבילי

[117] See above, note 85.

[118] This locality is unknown to me. It is also mentioned in text No. XIV.

[119] The reading is uncertain and can be ניהיא, but if ניריא be correct, then read נירוא, Nirwa (see note 1).

[120] Unknown to me.

[121] The metre is || — — — — | — — — — while all moving Shevas are ignored; Ḥaṭafs are even sometimes regarded as syllables. Hence the indication פשוט (viz. without יתד) and מרבע (viz. that each foot has 4 syllables).

[122] Read ונבונים

הדור אפל אין מוכיח   אבכה לזמני גם חדלי[122]*
אני עמדתי במצב צרות   הקיפוני את ידי רגלי
תכנתי עמודי ארץ   אז אציב דינים בפלילי
גם סגרתי הנפרצות   מדרש ותפלה בגלילי
הטרידו שכלי במבוכת   הרבות עונש שלי [ע]ולי
הציגוני ריק הפשיטו   את שמלת אדר ומעילי
קראתי חנוני רעי   כי צר[123] אללי אללי לי
ולמי מקדושים אפנה   לנדיבים רופאי מחלי
אתם חסידים חמלו נא אל   תורת אלי צורי פועלי
לא אל הודי או תועלתי   היא בכייתי או תוללי[124]
גם לא אל צורך ביתי או   אל מלבושי ומאכלי
אך אל קיום המדרשות   שלא יפיץ מני חילי
חיילים אגביר אל תורה   על זאת מתני מלאו חלחלי[124]*
אקים סוכה הנופלת   אסירה את כל מבדילי
על זאת יחרד כל איש משכיל   גם נבון יחרד למלולי
אם עשיר אם עני ישלח   צרי אל לבי ולכסלי
אפס עוזר סומך אין   גם אח קרוב מגואלי
אך לנדיבי ישראל אל   הרי עזרתם אשא קולי[125]
הרבה מוטים אל ההרג   הצלתם התירו שלשלי
שלא תכבה גחלת ה׳   הר ניצוץ דולק בזך שיכלי
ולהרים קרן מדבר שמם   וחייתה נפשי בגללי
אל דמעתי אל תחשו   ישישו נא כל חלילי
אעשה חיל ארבה כי   באתי בכתב משאלי

*[122] For חלדי to suit the rhyme.

[123] Insert here לי to complete the metre.

[124] תולל (from ילל), lament. Cp. also Ps. 137.3.

*[124] For חלחלה to suit the rhyme (cp. Is. 21.3).

[125] Here there is one superfluous syllable unless we assume that עזרתם was vocalised עֶזְרָתָם with the moving Sheva having been ignored and likewise in l. 25 שַׁלְשְׁלַי.

וזכותכם נאדרת עד רום שחק אל ראש מגדלי
שמכם יוחק במרום שחק קרן הודכם לגדולי
אם יפוצו תלמידי אל תבל מה הם יומי לילי
לכן שמעו החסידים אנשי צדק האזינו אלי

אשא עיני אל ההרים. הרי ישראל הנדיבים והשרים. אפתחה לפניהם
עניני וכל הדברים. אולי יכמרו רחמיהם. וינחמוני בדבריהם.

(verso)

ויחזקוני בפיוסיהם. ויעזרוני בתנחומיהם. ויאמרו לי בפיהם
ובמכתביהם. חזקי והתאמצי ולבך מדאגות עולם אל ימס. הן אל
כביר לא ימאס. וישיש ויתעלס. כי עזרך אלקיך כי כבר רצה את
מעשיך. וידינו עמך בכל לעזריך. עד יצא לאור צדקיך. וכלפיד
יבער ישעיך. כי לאקים[126] פעוליך והדרך.[126*] אתם בחכמתכם ובתורתכם
ואני בהוננו נעזריך. והיה הטוב ההוא אשר יטיב ה׳ והטבנו לך כי
תיטיבו עמנו בתורתכם ולעה״ב בעדן אלקים נשב בצל אביך ובעליך
זלהה בחופת החכמים. אצל הצדיקים והתמימים. כי זה הוא מובחן
ומנוסה. לא יפלא ולא יכוסה. המחזיק ביד חכמים בזה יחלוק
עמהם בחלקם ובגורלם אם נכבד אם נבזה חלק כחלק יאכלו.
הלומד עם המחזיק יחדו יגילו. [וכ]ן ראיתי בספר מספרים[127] ברבינו
יחיאל אביו של הראש ז׳ל שעש[ה] תנאי וברית עם א׳ מעשירים שהיה

[126] =לאלהים.

*[126] Read והדריך. For the phrase, cp. Ps. 90.16.

[127] This story is related by Judah b. Asher in his Ethical Will (ed. Schechter, בית תלמוד, IV, 374). Cp. also above, p. 453 f..

משרתו ומאכילו שיהיה עמו לעֹ[הֹ] וישב במדרשו וכשנפטר רֹ
יחיאל זֹלֹ
בא העשיר ועמד עליו ושאלו אם ע[ו]מד על תנאו ונאמנותו אם
לא והעידו
כמה חכמים ותלמידים אשר על[י]ו עומדים שהרים ראשו ושחק
ונענע
בראשו לומר שעומד על תנאו ודבריו ולא ישוב מאומרו ומעתה
עליכם קֹקֹ יהי שלוה בחיליכם. ושלו[ו]ם בארמנותיכם. והיה
ה׳ בכסליכם. וכסף תועפות לכם. ופה אשמיעכם עוד לענין צרתי
ותפיסתי
שתפסוני והממוני אלו רומיים[128] רשע[י]ם כשנפטר הרב זֹלֹ[129]
שלחו מאצל
קאצֹי רֹלֹ שופט ותפסו הבית ולקחו המפתח אלו הכופרים ומכרו
בי כל
בגדי ובגדי בנותי יצֹוֹ אפילו ספרים שהיו לפני ונפלו עלי בחוב
מאה קרוש[130]
ואין לי מנוסה ופליטה לשום מקום אלא רחמי שמים ורחמיכם
שתרחמוני
בעבור קבר אבא זֹלֹ והרב זֹלֹ שלא תתבטל תורתם ושמם מאילו
קהלות
שאני נשארתי מלמדת תורה ומוכחת ודורשת לטבילה ולשבת
ולנדה
ולתפלה וכיוצא ואני בזו הצרה שנפלו עלי כמה חובות ברבית
סֹךֹ[131]
הנזכר ואלו מאה קרושים במ... אותם אין לי דבר למכור ולא בן

[128] Christians.
[129] Her husband.
[130] =גרוש, plural of גרש, غرش, piastre.
[131] The abbreviation marks should be deleted.

גדול[132] או שליח שיחזור לנו לקהל[ות] ג"כ אין דרכה של אשה
לחזור לקהלות
שׁ[133] כל כבודה בת מלך פנימה משבצות זהב לבושה ואני מיומי
מפתח ביתי
לחוץ לא יצאתי בת מלך ישראל הייתי מאן מלכי רבנן בין ברכי
חכמים גדלתי מעונגת לאבי זל הייתי שום מעשה ומלאכה לא
למדני
חוץ ממלאכת שמים לקיים משנא[134] והגית בו יומם ולילה בעונות
הרבים . . . .
לא היו לו בנים כא בנות וג"כ השביע את בן זוגי זל לבלתי עשות בי
מלאכה וכן עשה כאשר ציוהו [ו]מתחלה הרב זל טרוד היה בעיונו
ולא . . . .
היה לו פנאי ללמד התלמידים כי אני הייתי מלמדת אותם במקומו
עוזרת
הייתי כנגדו עתה בעונות הרבים הלך הוא למנוחות. ועזב אותי
והילדים

(fol. 2, recto)

לאנחות. ואין לנו לא חונן ומחנן ולא . . . .
ועוד קק אשור[135] יעא הרבה טובה עשו . . . .
ממני שמעי בתוך מדרשי ועברו לפ . . . .
למלכות יב קרוש מצד ענישה ואחר . . . .
בעליך זל במדרש כבתחלה כל מה . . . .
יגדל בנך בעזרת האל וישועתו השי יי . . . .
ובזכותכם תגין עליו ולא ינחלו אחרים . . . .
החובות הקהלות שהם סביבי היו משגי[חים] . . . .
חירום ותגרות בין מלכים ואין להם פנא[י] . . . .

[132] A young son is referred to in l. 76.

[133] =שנאמר, Ps. 45.14.

[134] =מה שנאמר, Josh. 1.8.

[135] Mosul.

תלוי בכם אתם הצדיקים ואין לי אלא . . . .
ת֗ח השקדנים כמ֗ש[136] בן זומא ברוך שבר[א כל אלו לשמשני] . . . .
כל האדם לא נברא אלא בשביל הצד[יקים ש֗[137] כי לה֗ מצקי ארץ אלו צדיקים]
וישת עליהם תבל אלו עשירים ה . . . . [מצקי ארץ]
ר֗ל צדיקים שהם חוזק העולם וישת על[יהם תבל . . . . [תשעה]
נכנסו לג֗ע בחייהם[138] חנוך בן ירד בנימן ן֗ יעקב] . . . .
אליעזר עבד אברהם כלאב בן דוד ע[בד מלך הכושי ויעבץ] . . .
ותראו שזכו אלו הצדיקים לג֗ע בחיי[הם] . . . .
חנוך בן ירד לפי שהיה משרת לפני . . . .
בנימן ן֗ יעקב שהיה ליעקב אביו יותר . . . .
יוסף שיוסף היה משרת לאביו הרבה . . . .
ליעקב אבינו אליעזר שהיה משרת לא[ברהם אבינו ועשה ליצחק אבינו נחת]
רוח שהביא אשה לו כלאב שהציל אב[יו בהלכה ממפיבושת[139] עבד מלך הכושי שהעלה]
לירמיה מבור הטיט[140] יעבץ ג֗כ שמש [לפני ר׳ יהודה הנשיא אביו מזה]
למדנו שבזכות הצדיקים ובשמוש ה[חכמים] . . . .
כמו שראית באלה הט֗ צדיקים שמנו ח֗[ז֗ל] . . . .
לצדיקים ואז֗ל המתעצל בצורך ת֗[ח] . . . .
בצרתו להצילן בין בגופו בין . . . . [וזה]
{ שז֗ל[141] כל המתעצל בהספד של ת֗ח ראוי [לקוברו בחייו וכן מצינו ביהושע] . . .

[136] =כמו שאמר, Ber. 58a, top. [137] 1 Sam. 2.8.

[138] See Derekh Ereṣ Zuṭṭa, c. 1, end (ed. Tawrogi, pp. 8–9). None of the texts cited there have Benjamin and Kilab, but cp. B. Batra 17a where among the four, who died by reason of the original sin (בעטיו של נחש), Benjamin and Kilab are enumerated.

[139] Cp. Ber. 4a. [140] Cp. Jer. 38.7ff., 39.15–18.

[141] =שאמרו זכרם לברכה, Sabbath 105b, bottom.

שלא הספידוהו כהלכה וגעש עליהם הנ[הר ש[142] מצפון להר געש מלמד]

שגעש עליהם להרגם וכן מצינו בנ[יוסף שכל ישראל היו עסוקים בבזה של מצרים]

ומרעֹהֹ נטפל בארונו של יוסף[143] ואנ[זל[144] מפני מה כתיב בני חת י' פעמים מפני]

שבררו עסקו של אא[145] בקנין המערה העלנ[ה את שם בני חת י' פעמים כנגד י' הדברות]

וכן הֹ פעמים כתיב ולבני ברזלי הגלעד[י] . . . .

ופירות ומאכל כשברח מפני אבשלום בנ[נו][146] . . . .

הצדיק ויפדינו משבי ומשלל ומתפיסנ[ה] . . . .

שהיה בנו של רֹ ישמעאל[147] שבוי בידהש . . . .

ואפדה לבן הצדיק מיד הגוים עד שנה . . . .

(verso)

. . . . .טו]רחות טרח שנצטרך לנס לקרוע גנאי נהיה

. . . . להצלת תֹחֹ וילדיהם ואלמנותיהם שחיי

. . . . יחס ואזֹלֹ להנאת הדור יכול צדיק בצרה

. . . . להאכילו ולטרוח שאם לא יהי נצרך

. . . . . נ[שֹ ישב עולם לפ]ני אלקים חסד ואמת מן ינצרוהו[148] רֹלֹ

. . . . שירות אֹכֹ חסד ואמת מי ינצרם וישמרם[149]

142 =שנאמר, Josh. 24.30.

143 Cp. Mekhilta to פ' בשלח, and Mekh. de R. Simon b. Yoḥai, ed. Hoffmann, p. 39, top.

144 The passage cited here till l. 104 is taken from Genesis R., c. 58, end, though it is here rephrased.

145 =אברהם אבינו.

146 Cp. 2 Sam. 17.27–29.

147 The source of this story I could not locate. For another story of a son and a daughter of R. Ishmael, who were taken captive, cp. Giṭṭin 58a.

148 Ps. 61.8.

149 Evidently reference is made here to the homily of Rabba b. Mari in 'Erubin 86a, top, cp. also Exod. R. c. 31, 5, end.

. . . . י יעשו חסד וצדקה אם החרש תחרישי
[בעת הזאת רוח והצלה יעמוד ליהודי]ם את ובית אביך תאבדו[150]
רׄלׄ אמ׳ מרדכי
[לאסתר] . . . . . הש״י שזכית למלאכה אינה לתועלת אדרבה
. . . . זו לעת כזאת ולזו הצרה ראה השיׄתׄ
. . . . רוח והצלה יעמוד ליהודים מצד אחר
. . . . העולם שנתעצלת בהצלת ישראל הרי
. . . . תׄחׄ ויתומים ואלמנות שהם בצרה מה
. . . . בלתו ואמרינן במׄ[151] ברכות אמׄ רב חנינא
[משמיה דרב כל שאפשר לו לבקש ר]חמים על חבירו ואינו מבקש
נקרא
[חוטא שׄ[152] גם אנכי חלילה לי מחטא ל]הׄ להתפלל בעדכם אמׄ
רבא אם תׄחׄ הוא
[צריך שיחלה עצמו עליו מׄטׄ אילימא] משום דכתי׳ אין חולה מכם
עלי ואין גולה
[את אזני דלמא מלך שאני אלא מהכא] ואני בחלותם לבושי שק
רׄלׄ[153] אמר כל שאפשר
. . . . ק ולא יעשה לו הצלה ומנוחה נקרא חוטא
. . . . על הצדיקים ובזה הלשון אומרת קלני
[מראשי קלני מזרועי[153a] שהמקום בׄהׄ מצ]טער על מיתת הצדיקים
ועל צערם ולצרתם
. . . . [ע]ונש קשה יותר מהם ומעתה אליכם אישים
. . . . [קׄקׄ עמדי]א יעׄאׄ ועמהם תשכון הנדיבות
. . . . [ח]נינה לעמילי התורה ולהוגיה בראשם
. . . . על הנעלה כבוד מׄ זכריה יצׄוׄ ועל האהוב

[150] Esther 4.14.
[151] =במסכת, Ber. 12b. Cp. ד״ס, a. l.
[152] 1 Sam. 12.23.
[153] This statement of Resh Laḳish is not in our text of Berakot.
[153a] Cp. Sanh. 6.5.

. . . . [יצ]ו ועל כוגא הרון יצ֗ו ועל כוגא דניאל יצ֗ו
. . . . ם והשרים וכל קק מקטנים ועד גדולים
. . . . והתפלות והתהלות והן ליהוי ידיע לכם
. . . . [א]שר הרדיפוני מנוחה מפטירת מארי
[הרב ז"ל] . . . . וש ונודע זה בישראל ואני רכה ומעוננת
. . . . [אנ]י בעול היתומים אוי לי מהם אוי לי מבעלי
. . . . אתם קהלות הרמות תרימו יד הרמה
. . . . רק תקבלו פני כתבי כאלו פני הולכים
. . . . [הה]רי עליכם להתיר כבלי לכן אחלה פני החכמים
. . . . ומכתי אלא על תח שיחממו ראשם בחמימי
. . . . . . [עיני] בנאמני ארץ לשבת עמדי[154] והיו באוכלי שולחני
. . . . כרצון המעתרת בקול תחנה אל הרנה אשר
. . . . מהר שמואל הלוי זלהה[155] ועבדכם נושק ידיכם[156]
. . . . [שמואל בן מהר] יעקב זלהה

V.

(Address, fol. 1, recto)

ב"ה
ליד עמי ועדתי קק
עמדיא יע"א וגזרתי
מפי קדישי מעלה
ופגין דרגמה[157] על
מי שמעלימו מן הקק
כא[158] יקראוהו בתוך
קק עליונה ואחכ

[154] Cp. Ps. 101.6.

[155] This is probably the name of the lady's father (see l. 65ff.).

[156] This is probably her young son (see note 132). His name was Samuel, after his grandfather, as the next letter (No. V) shows.

[157] See above, note 101.

[158] =כי אם. Here both the upper and lower communities are referred to (cp. above, notes 53 and 110).

לתחתונה וכל הקורא
אותו יחיד יהיה בגזי'[159]
נח"ש אלא ברבים בתוך
הקק. מאשור יעֹאֹ.

(Fol. 1, verso, blank; fol. 2, recto)

וגזרתי מפי קדישי עליונים ושרפי מעלה
על מי שלא יקרא כתבי על ראש קק עליונה
ותחתונה והמעלימו יעלם ויהיה בנח"ש אכי"ר[160]
שלמא וחינא וחסדא מן קדם מארי עלמא אתם עמי ועדתי קק קורדישתאן ובפרט עיר ואם בישראל קק עמדיא
עליונה ותחתונה ובראשם החכמים השלימים שרים ונכבדים זקינים טפסרים שוטרים ממונים העוסקים
עם הצבור לשש"[161] יהיה להם חמלה וחנינה מלפני שוכן מעונה אכי"ר
מדוע יצאתי ואין איש קראתי ואין עונה ושלחתי לכם כמה כתבים ולא חשבתם אותם לכלום ומיום שנפטר הרב
לא זכרתם את גוזליו ולא ריחמתם עליהם וכל הקהלות זכרו אותנו ואתם לא כן עמדי ולא די שלא
זכרתם אותי ולא השיבותם את תשובת כתבי ועשיתם בי אלו המעשים והוספתם להכעיס אותי וגזלתם
אותי וחמסתם ששביתם הספרים שלי כשבויות חרב וכל אֹ מכם לקח נייר אחד מהם ועל מלבושי
השלכתם גורל ועתה די לכם באלו הדברים שקרבה שנת ישע והגאולה מיהרה[161]* ועתה די לכם באלו
הדברים ורחמו כדי שירחם[162] עליכם ועתה ראו ושמעו התוכחות של האלקי המסובל הדיין מורנא ורבנא

[159] =בגזירת; נח"ש =נדוי חרם שמתא. [160] =אמן כן יהי רצון. [161] =לשם שמים.

*[161] Perhaps the reference here is to the Messianic expectation in connection with the activities of David Reubeni and Solomon Molkho

[162] Viz. God, cp. Sabbath 151b, bottom.

עטרת ראשינו החכם השלם כמוהר"ר מתתיה יצו̇ האשכנזי אשר זרח אורו עלינו אור השכינה אשר בא

להוכיח אתכם על מעשיכם. הרחוקים שלא ראיתים ולא ראוני כשרואים אותי מרחמים עלי ואתם בחשבון

עמי ועדתי ולא ריחמתם עלי ולחכמייא ברמזא אני עבד ת̇ח̇ הצעיר שמואל בכה̇ר̇

יעקב מזרחי

ועתה תקבצו הספרי' ותניחום אצלכם בפקדון

עד שאשלח אחריהם ואביאם לאצלי וזה הסדכם ועתה

תשיבו תשובה ברה ונכונה כחפצי.

וכשכתבתי הכתב בצער

הייתי בכאב הראש.

עמודי עולם אנשי קודש כולם יראי חטא אנשי אמת שונאי בצע הה̇[163] ק̇ק̇ קורדישתאן ובראשם זר זר שם

החכמים השלימים והגבירים הנכבדים וכל ישרי לב עדה הקדושה דק̇ק̇ עמדיא יצו̇ כל א̇ וא̇ כפי מעלתו

ומדרגתו רוחניות וגשמיות ושלום וישע רב.

אד̇ש̇[164] וטובתכם כל הימים הנה יצאתי בשברון מתנים ובמרירות לב על הקרות[165] והשתנות הזמן של

האי צורבא דרבנן היקר ומאד נעלה מזה בן מזה כה̇ר̇ שמואל הנ̇ז̇[166] שצועק ככרוכי'[167] ושיאו עולה

שמים ובוקע כמה רקיעים על אשר זה כמה שנים שעזבתם אותו ואת אמו אשת חבר

הדומה לחבר שלא זכרתם אותם אפי'[168] בשוה פרוטה כשאר בני ישראל רחמנים בני רחמנים אשר

[163] =הלא הם. [164] =אחרי דרישת שלומכם.

[165] Read הקורות or perhaps the writer formed a noun הַקְּרוֹת, happening.

[166] =הנזכר.

[167] =ככרוכיא. [168] =אפילו.

מרחמים עליהם בכל שעה והם כחותם על לבם ולא כחותם על זרועם שפעמים נראה ופעמי׳

אינה[169] והלואי שהעליתם אותם כחותם על זרועכם ולא זו אף זו שמענו אשר פגעו איזה

אנשים וקמו בתחבולות רעים לעקור שורש האילן וענף בלי שריד ולהופכו על פניו לפשוט יד

בגזל ובחמס בספרי הקודש של הרב אביו ז״ל וכוונתם עולה לשלי שלי ושלך שלי[170] אשר על זה ארץ

רעשה ומוסדי הרים ירגזו דא לדא נקשן גם נטפו דם ואש ותמרות עשן השמש בצאתו חשך

אורו וככבים אספו נגהם מלאכי שלום מר יבכיון אבל יהמיון גם בני איש יחרדו וכצפור יחד

אבות ובנים נאקת חלל נואקים מראש הרים יצווחו ואצל כל פינה פעם בחוץ פעם ברחובות

יתנו קולם מפרץ הרים ומשבר סלעים קול מכאובות לקול המולה גדולה מילולן של מרגלים

הציתו אש מקודם ועתה תמיד המדורה ע׳ מעשיהם המקולקלים הנה נשמע וכל עוברי דרך

והולכי אורח עוף השמים ובעל כנפים מעידים הדברים אשר על זה ידוו כל הדיוים[171] וכף

על ירך יכו וכל בית ישראל יבכו כי הוסג אחור משפט ואמת השלח אמת ארצה ועליה שקר

הונחה. עשתה פרי גם הצליחה. והנה באתי בשורתיים אלו לעושה הטוב ולהחזיקה[172] באמת

ובצדקה אשר להם זרוע עם גבורה לעלות בפרצות ולגדור גדר במשמרת מצוה ותורה

[169] Supply נראה. Cp. Ta'anit 4a, bottom, and Cant. R. c. 8,5.
[170] Cp. Abot 5.10.
[171] Read הדווים, those who grieve.
[172] For לעושה r. לעושי, and for ולהחזיקה r. ולמחזיקים.

(verso)

לשובב נתיבות וסוכה נופלת להקים אשר מגערתם ינוסון משנאי ה̇ מתעבי משפט
מדיחי הנשי'[173] שתרפאו פצעי חנם ותראו מדנים דמעת העשוקים ותשיבו נפשות
האביונים הנאנקים ותעשו כרוז בבתי כנסיות בגזרת נח̇ש חווי'[174] דרבנן
שתכף ומיד יחזרו הגניבה או הגזילה לבעליו ומשם ואילך כל יד המרבה
לבדוק יקצץ[175] והנגע בהם ע̇מ̇[176] להתלבש בטלית שאינו שלו או ליקחם ולעשם[177] עטרה
לעצמו ינשכנו מלך בני עמון[178] ועליכם ק̇ק̇ חכמים וגבירים פרנסי הקהל מוטל
הדבר למען כבוד רבכם שתדריכו בני עמכם להרים צור מכשול ואבן נגף
לסקל ברצועה ומקל ובזכות זה אל חי ישים בקרבכם אהבה ואחו'[179] ושלום
וריעות ויסיר מכם האבן הנגף הנגוף אותנו כעתירת הצעיר מתתיהו
באא̇[180] הגאון בנימין זאב אשכנזי[181]

[173] =הנשיה.

[174] =חיויא, "the serpent of the Rabbis", viz. the Ḥerem with allusion to נח'ש (=נדוי חרם שמתא).

[175] Cp. Niddah 2.1, of course here in a different meaning.

[176] =על מנת.

[177] Better לקחתם ולעשותם.

[178] Evidently a pun on עמנו, our people (cp. l. 56 בני עמכם). Perhaps the secular authorities are meant here.

[179] =ואחוה.

[180] =בן אדוני אבי.

[181] There is some calligraphic embellishment under this signature which I could not decipher.

VI.

[Paper leaf. See Facsimile XXIII, A and B, infra, pp. 723–24.]

Address (verso)

יגיע לייד[181a] אחירם ואחיפנ[182] הגדול
ה"ה הגביר המרומם כה"ר שי'[183]
[י]חיא יצ"ו מעמדיא
יע"א
לא[שור] יע"א ולזר
נחש[184] ועורב[185]

(Recto)

שלום רב. וישע יקרב. יחול ויאתה לראש אהובי וחביבי הה
הגביר המרומם ביתו בית ועד לחכמים מוקיר ודחיל
רבנן כה"ר שי' יחייא יצו ה אתו הברכה חיים עד העולם כיר[186]
ועל ראש כלל אנשי ביתו ברוך בכלל וברוך בפרט[187] כיר
ואחדש"ו[188] שיסגא לעד ידיע להוי למר שכתבך הגיעני
כפול[189] וראיתי כל הכתוב בו לחיים ממצב שלומכם
כי טוב ושמחתי כעל כל הון כן[190] מלא וידיע להוי לאחירם
שהשלכתי גורל ונפל הגורל על אחמד בג[191] שיהיה
מלך אבל יום מעונן היה ואם יעזור השם אשלח לך
כתב אחר מכל הענינים ויודע לך שפקיד שלו דהיינו
משנה שלו צריך לשמור נפשו כי כך יצא בגורל אבל

181a Read ליד or אלי יד.

182 =ואחי פנים, a peculiar combination evidently on the model of נשוא פנים.

183 =שיך.

184 =נדוי חרם שמתא.

185 Pun on the Hebrew words 'serpent and raven' taken here as abbreviations; ועורב=ועונשו רב (see previous note).

186 =כן יהי רצון.

187 See Soṭah 37a, bottom.

188 =ואחרי דרישת שלומו וטובתו.

189 Folded, viz. unopened.

190 =כף נחת, cp. Kohel. 4.6.

191 Aḥmad Beg.

עדיין איני מאמין מפני שיום מעונן היה כשהשלכתי הגורל. ומענין נישואי בנך היוֹ[192] אם נעשה אותם לא נעשה אותם כי אם ביוֹד או בטוֹ או ביוֹ לחודש כי זה הענין מכבר ראיתי וחפשתי עליו והוא נכון. ועוד יודע לאחי כי מ׳ מנחם רוצה לבוא לאשור ומתירא מפניך בא ונשתטח לפני רגלי מנוח ולפני בבית הכנסת שנכתוב לך כתב שלא תדבר עליו רעה הנה אחלינו[193] ירובו למען הֹ ולמען כבוד אחיך מנוח ולמעני שלא תדבר עמו כי די לו צרתו ולא הייתי כותב ליו[194] שום דבר אבל מנוח הפציר בי[195]

ועוד הוא לא היה בתוך הנועדים לענין שלושים יוזלג[196]

(continued across right hand side)

שלקחו מן מנוח. וחייך הטובים כי חייך קודמין לחיי אם היה מֹ מנחם בתוך הענין

שלקחו מן מנוח שלשים קרוש אני הייתי כותב לך כתב [ש]תעשה בו משפטי

נקמות ומנוח גֹכֹ היה כותב לך הכתב כי אחי יודע אינני מסתיר ממנו שום דבר

חזרתי על המקרא[197] למען הקב״ה ותורתו ולמעננו אני ומנוח שלא תדבר עליו שום

רעה. ומענין דוד ןֹ[198] נחמו לקח לו כתב מאת המלך ויבוא לאשור על זה הרשות

נתונה בידך ותנקום נקמתך ממנו ובכן אין להאריך כי אם בשלומך שיסגא לעד וש״ש[199]

192 =השם יחיהו וישמרהו.

193 From אַחֲלַי (2 Kings 5.3, Ps. 119.5).

194 Read לו.

195 The rest of the line is crossed out and is undecipherable.

196 Evidently a Ḳurdish name for קרוש (l. 24) =גרוש.

197 Evidently for the purpose of casting a lot.

198 =בן.

199 =ושלום שלום.

ממני הצעיר יאודה ויוספ׳[201] ושמואל מנשקים ידיך והחברים
בכהר׳ שמעון סט׳[200]
שואלים בשלומך וכתב אחר אשלח לך מכל הענינים וסוד
השם ליראיו
ומהרסי[202] שבתי פורס סוכת שלום עליך ויודע לך שהיה רוצה
לשלוח לך כשיעור
כ׳ קנטאר עפצים ויותר אבל אשתו כנפשי[203] חייה למור ולבניו
שבקה ומפני זה
לא שלח ועכ׳פ׳[204] נשלח לו כ׳ מנים אסטים פרנגי עם אדר הראשון
ובעה׳[205] אחר
השבת ישלח לך עפצים וש״ש[199] ועוד יא אחי לענין כתב ששלח לך
טבו ן׳ אסווד לענין
שנשלח לו עורות עכ׳פ׳ נעשה לו רצונו.

VII.

[Paper leaf; verso contains a text in Persian.]

(Recto)

מאן דעסיק באוריתא תדירא. עימיה שריא נהורא.
מי לא יירא לגשת בארשת[206] שפתיו ולדבר דבורא.
חד בדרא. ארי שבחבורה. אספקלריא המאירה. הה׳
הח׳ הש׳[207] הדיין המצויין מורי ורבי ועטרת ראשי
כמוהרר׳[208] חכם רבי שמעון שמואל דוגה יצו׳ נרו

[200] =סופו טוב.

[201] =יוסף or Yūsuf. Joseph and Samuel are probably the sons of the writer.

[202] This is probably some name unknown to me. The reading can also be ומורסי and perhaps it is an abbreviation for ומרנא ורבנא סיניור. Cp. next note.

[203] Evidently the name of Sabbatai's wife who died: חַיָּיה למור (= למרנא ורבנא) וכו׳.

[204] =ועל כל פנים. [205] =ובעזרת השם.

[206] This line and a half is also repeated on the top.

[207] =החכם השלם.

[208] =כבוד מורנו הרב ר׳.

יאיר כזיהרא דשמשא כיר״א[209] ועוד אטה כנרה[210] שלום מאת שוכן מרום ע״כ[211] הטוה השני כבוד חכם יהודא יצ״ו וע״כ הטור השלישי. אודם תרשישי. כה״ח[212] מנחם יצ״ו וע״כ בנן של קדושים כה״ח שמואל יצ״ו וע״כ אחי ואור עיני מ״ו מצליח יצ״ו וע״כ שיך יוסף אברם יצ״ו וע״כ מנוח נחום ובנו דויד יצ״ו וע״כ יונה יצ״ו וע״כ אבו[213] אליה יצ״ו וע״כ יצחק כירו ובנו משה יצ״ו וע״כ נתן קינו ובניו יצ״ו וע״כ בראהים[214] ובנו שלמה יצ״ו וכל מי ששואל בשלומינו יהיה באלף נחלי שלום ואחד״שו שיסגיה[215] לעד יוודע להוי למעכ״ת[216] מעיניין[217] הצעיר הייתי רוצה לבוא עם ר׳ נחום אליה לא נסתייעא מלתא ואם יעזור השם בעזרתו יתברך שבוע[213] אחר שבוע אחד עולה לעמדיא והשם יודע עלייתי לעמדיא הרבה כבד עלי אבל מה אעשה שהבהילוני החלומות וכל יום[218] שרו[י] בתענית מפני אחותי שעושה עמי קטטה בחלום ואם לא כן לא הייתי דע[219] עמדייא אלף שנים וכי מה עסק יש לי בעמדיא ומה נשאר בית או כלים או אבי ואמי מצפים לי ועינם על הדרך אימתי יראו אותי אין לי אלא השם יתברך שמו ויתעלה ואין לי זולתו כי

(Here the MS. breaks off.)

209 =כן יהי רצון אמן.

210 Read כנהר.

211 =על כבוד. For הטוה read הטור.

212 =כבוד חכם.

213 This word is doubtful.

214 =אברהים.

215 Read שיסגא.

216 =למעלת כבוד תורתכם.

217 =מענין, about the affair of the insignificant one (viz. myself).

218 Supply אני.

219 Read יודע.

VIII.

[Narrow strip of paper; verso blank.]

(Recto)

שלום רב. וישע יקרב. על כבוד
אהובי יוסף יצ"ו
ועל כלל אנשי ביתו שלום
רב כי"ר[220]
ואחדשו שיסגא לעד להוי
ידיע לך הנה בא גוי
אחד ואמר לי משמך יוסף
רוצה לבא לכאן ללמוד תורה
ודיני הלכות שחיטה ואני
גֹכֹ כתבתי שתי שורות אלו
לכבודך ואני רוצה שתבוא
לכאן ללמוד תורה ודיני הלכות שחיטה
והלכות טרפיות ובלבד שתהא
ירא שמים ואוהב תורה ומצותיה
ואני גֹכֹ איני מקצר עמך
ואלמד אותך תורה וכל מה
שתרצה אעשה עמך טובה
בעז"ה בלמוד התורה כה דברי נאֹהֹ ודשׁוֹ[221]
הצעיר שמעון
דוגה יצֹוֹ

[220] =כן יהי רצון.

[221] =נאם החותם ודורש שלומו וטובתו.

IX.

[Paper leaf; verso blank.]

(Recto)

ב"ה

כגון דא מצוה רבא לאודועי לחכמי ומנהיגי הקהלות הקדושות כורדיסאתן יע"א ועילא מינהון ידין[222]

ה"ה החכם השלם הדיין המצויין כה"ר שמעון דוגא יצ"ו יהי שלום בחילו נסו[223]

על דברת מוביל כתבא דנא ושמו נחמיה ן שמעון ממתא נירווא שיש לו בת קטנה כבת

שמנה שנים ואיש אחד שמו חנוכה רע מעללים נתן עיניו בה וחטף אותה והוליך אותה

לכורך[224]. ואין יד אביה משגת להשיבה אליו מאימת הגוים אילי הארץ אליכם אישים אקרא שתודיעו

למעלמין[225] אשר סביבותיכם שלא יקדשו אותה ולא יכתבו לה כתובה ואם קידשו אותה בלא רצון

אביה שאינה מקודשת וכל מי שידו משגת להציל עשוק מיד עושקו השג ישיג והצל יציל

להשיבה אל אביה יבורך מפי עליון ושכמה[226] ועליו תבוא ברכת טוב הלא כה דברי נאה[227] כנהר שלום

הצעיר משה בן[228] . . . .

סט

[222] =ידיד נפשי.

[223] =נצח סלה ועד.

[224] This locality is unknown to me. Perhaps read לבורג, Arabic for castle, tower.

[225] Plural of Mu'allim, teacher, scholar.

[226] =ושכרו כפול מן השמים.

[227] =נאם הנוטה.

[228] The signature is given with calligraphic embellishments which I could not decipher entirely. A photograph, somewhat enlarged, is adjoined here. See Facsimile XXIV, infra, p. 725.

X.

[Stout brownish paper, torn off at bottom; verso blank.]

(Recto)

בה̇

ראשי עם בני ישראל הפחות והסגנים זקני עם ועם שלומי אמוני
ישראל. אראלים ותרשישים כולם תחכמונים
ורבי פעלים פינות צבאות קדושים קהל ועדה מישראל. שיאי
המטות הם העומדים על הפקודים המתנדבים
בעם הקהלות הקדושות די בכל אתר ואתר אשר דבר המלך
מלכו של עולם מגיע לפני יקר תפארת גדולת
מעלתם הה̇ הגבירים הרמים פרנסים גזברים ממונים וכל
העוסקים עם הצבור לשם שמים ועטרותיהם
בראשיהם המה המאורות הגדולים החכמים השלימים הדיינים
המצויינים ואחריהם כל ישרי לב כי כל
העדה כולם קדושים ובתוכם ה̇ אתה ה̇ תשמרם וכבוד והדר
תעטרם עטרת ישועה ורחמים גם בניהם
עדי עד יחיו דגן ויפרחו כגפן פוריה כי"ר.
אחר עלות קול רינה ותפילה לפני שוכן מעונה ידינו לעושיהן
יעשו תפילה ובקשה לפני שוכן שמים שיזכו להדין
תלתא דמ̇נינו רבנן בדיבורייהו רב חי̇יא ורב הונ̇א ורב בנ̇ייא[229]
גם עושר גם כבוד עד זקנה ושיבה אלדים[229a] אל
תעזבם אכי̇ר.
אות̇ותינו אלה מעידין ומגידין בעד מוביל כתבא דנא הה̇ החכם
השלם כה̇ר חייא בכ̇ר כלב נ̇ע̇ והוא מתושבי
ק̇ק̇ עמדיא יע̇א̇ אשר מקדמת דנא ביתו היה פתוח לרוחה והיה
בית ועד לחכמים ופיתו היתה מצויה לעוברים

[229] A pun on the names of the three Rabbis Ḥiyya, Huna and Benayah, viz. long life (חַיָּא), much wealth (הוּנָא) and many children (בְּנָיָא).

[229a] =אלהים, cp. Ps. 71.18.

ושבים ועתה בעוה̇[230] נהפך עליו הזמן ופגעה בו מדה̇[231] ומתו אחיו
ואביו וכמה נפשות מביתו ונפלו עליו חובות
הרבה בנשך ותרבית וכשל כח הסבל ובתים שלו ג̇כ̇ לקחו אותם
הגוים ונשאר בעירום ובחוסר כל והוא
מטופל בילדים ואין לאל ידו נודדים ללחם ואיה על כן פשט לו
הרגל לדפוק על בתי נדיבים עם אלד̇י̇
אברהם רחמנים בני רחמנים והדבר אין אתו[232] ומסוה הבושה על
פניו וליתיה בשאלה עתה באנו באו̇תו̇ת שתים
להיות לו לפה ולמליץ שאל כל מקום אשר תדרוך כף רגלו
יפרישו לו מממוכם[233] מנה הראויה
להתכבד כל איש אשר ידבנו לבו יביאה את תרומת ה̇ ימלא את
ידו מלא חופניה טיבותא העשיר לו̇ ירבה[234]
והדל לא ימעיט וסמך שתי ידיו עליו במדה גדושה לא נצרכה
אלא להעדפה להחזיק את ידו לתומכו
ולסעדו וליתן לו אכסניא נאה ולהדריכו עם אנשים נאמנים והאי
גברא קים לן בגופה דגבר צניע ומעלי ובעל
תורה הוא ולאו כל שעתא ושעתא מתרחיש לכו כי האי גברא
זכו בו סכו בו[235] ולא כתנו[236] להזהיר אלא להזכיר
ובשכר זאת אל ש̇די.[*236] יריק לכם ברכה עד בלי די. ויאמר
לצרותינו ולצרותיכם די. וישלח ברכה במעןשה ידיכם]

. . . .

[230] =בעונותינו הרבים.

[231] =מדת הדין.

[232] Cp. Jer. 5.13, but here in the meaning of lack of speech owing to shame.

[233] Read מממונכם.

[234] Pun on Exod. 30.15.

[235] Cp. Lev. R. c. 34,7: א'ר זעירא אפי' שיחתן של בני א"י תורה היא. הא כיצד? אדם אומר לחבירו זכי בי . . . ר' חגי אמר סכי בי אסתכל בי סכי בי מא הוינא ואסתכל בי מה אנא.

[236] Read כתבנו.

[*236] Probably = שאמר (לעולמו) די in accordance with the well-known Agadic interpretation of the Divine name שדי (see, e. g., Gen. R. c. 46,2).

XI.

[One paper leaf.]

(Recto)

[ב]ראשית הטור[237] הגשה לתפילה באנו להודיע מענין גביר אחד שהיה בכאן והיה שמו יצחק בכר סאוו ופעם אחד הלך לאשור לסחורה ופגע בו משה ן כליפא אותו שהוא לשם[238] ולקח ממנו אלף קרוש רומי למחצית הפירות בעידות שי'[239] יוסף יונה ושי' חיים ממי[*239] וכל הקק של אשור יודעים בגופא דעובדא

ולקח הממון והלך לו פעם אחרת פגעו זה בזה ג"כ באשור ואמר לו על ענין מחצית הפירות ואמר שלא יש כלום ולקח ממנו בחזקה שלש מאות ק[240] ושבע מאות נשארו עליו ומאותו היום ועד עכשיו לא שלח עוד פק[241] לא קרן ולא פירות ויצחק הנז'[242] נפטר אלו שלשה ארבעה שנים והניח יתומים קטנים ומשה הנז'

אכל המעות אלו כמה שנים על היתומים ואין מנחם ואין מרחם[*242] וידענו שאדונינו המלך חפץ חסד הוא ומרבה להטיב לכן[243] בשורותיים אלו להפיל תחינה לפני אדונינו המלך שישאל ויחקור וידרוש על זה הענין ויציל עשוק מיד עושקו וכתר[244] עשינו אותו פקיד על זה הדבר שישתדל על זה הענין ויקח ממון של יתומים ממנו וימסור אותו ביד זה המוביל חכם יאודה ולכתר תחשב לצדקה ושכומה[245] שגם בני שלשים

237 This word is doubtful.
238 Viz. who resides in אשור, Mosul.
239 =שיך.
*239 Evidently a cognomen of Ḥayyim.
240 =קרוש.
241 =פרוטה קטנה. 242 =הנזכר.
*242 Supply עליהם.
243 Supply באנו. 244 =וכבוד תורתו.
245 =ושכרו כפל וכפלים מן השמים.

יולדו על ברכיו בנים מורי הוראות בישראל ואת מלכים לכסא חיים עד העולם כי״ר כד״[246] עמוסי התלאות דמצלין לחיי מלכא ובנוהי החותמים פה עמדיא יעׂא בסדר ונשא אהרן את משפט בני ישראל וכו׳[247] שנת התקכ״ח[248] ליצירה ושלם על כל זרע ישראל.

Address (verso)

גלילות אצבעותיו הקדש כמה הביאו ספריו וחפיצים עלו וכמה חנן אותם מידו הרחבה והמלאה בשכר מצוה ואת ברכת הדיוט קל[ה] שגם בני שלשים יולדו על ברכיו בנים מורי הוראות בישראל ואת מלכים לכסא ויאריך על ממשלתו הוא ובניו בקרב ישראל.

(Different handwriting.)

בהיות איך עבר עלינו והאיר אל עבר פנינו הח׳ השלם כמוהר״ר מרדכי סידון בן לאותו צדיק וחסיד החכם השלם והכולל כמהר״ר אליעזר זלהה״ אחיו של הח׳ הש׳ והכו׳[249] כמהר״ר משה סי׳[250] שבא שני פעמים בשליחת עיר צפת תו׳[251] וגם זה הח׳ הנז׳ בא בשליחות ערי פרס ויצאו שוללים לדרכו ושללו אותו ולא הניחו לו לא כסף ולא שוה כסף וה . . . . השטרות שהיו בידו ובא למחנינו ק״[252] והיה
ועשינו עמו טובה
רוצה לחזור ואנחנו לא הנחנו שאמרנו

[246] =כה דברי.
[247] Exod. 28.30, hence the letter was written in the week of Sidra תצוה.
[248] 1768 C. E.
[249] =החכם השלם והכולל.
[250] Evidently =סידון.
[251] =תבנה ותכונן.
[252] =קדוש, cp. Deut. 23.15.

לו איך תחזור לבית בידים ריקניות וחלה
פנינו לכתוב שורותיים אלו יען שמסוה
הבושה על פניו ופה אין לו לדבר כי
כבד פה וכבד לשון הוא ומסוה . . . .

(Across the righthand margin there is the remainder of a legal document disqualifying any protest against a Geṭ. The witnesses are Moses b. Isaac and Jesse b. Elijah.)

XII.

[Piece of paper.]

Address (verso)

יגיע ליד השם הטוב
יונה מעמדיא לאשור
ולזר נ֗חש ופגיין[253] . . .

(Recto)

שלומות רבות מפי אכי[254] חזקו בן
אבטליון על כבוד השם הטוב יונה
יא יונה
ועל כבוד ג֗מעא[255] ואחרי השלום יגיעו
לך חמשה עשר צאלי[256] טובים עם גרדו[257]
ותמכור אותם בכל מה שתדע ויגיעו
לך שלושים וחמשה סקי[258] של ג֗כמי
עם אבדל רחמן[259] עם ארבעה קד֗י
וַבַסְכָא פֵיגָ֗אִ֗י אחת ואותם דמי אלו
החפצים ותמכור אותם ותתן אותם

[253] See above, note 101.
[254] Read perhaps אבי, Abū.
[255] Arabic, congregation.
[256] The meaning of this word is not clear to me (cp. also l. 11).
[257] Evidently the name of a Ḳurd.
[258] Sacks of a certain merchandise.
[259] Corrupt for עבד אלרחמן, 'Abdul-Raḥman.

בָגְלָדֵי כַף[260] ואם לא יהיו גלדי ותתן
אותם בָתוּרָא אחת צָאלַי קוֹרמֶס
ולא תשכח בשביל בסכא פיגיי
ואין להאריך כי אם בשלומיכם
הנעים . . .[261]

XIII.

[Narrow strip of paper; verso blank.]

(Recto)

שלום רב. וישע יקרב. מפנ̇ין
אלעזר וחיו[262] על ראש הה̇
כ̇שי̇[263] ח̇ בנימין יצ̇ו ועל
ראש שי̇[264] עלוון יצ̇ו ועל
ראש שי̇ו̇[265] וישלח לו רפואה
שלימה רחמני יצ̇ו ועל כל
אנשי ביתם יצ̇ו א̇כי̇ר̇
ואחד̇שו̇ יא אחי יודע לכם
עפצים הגיעו יט̇ כונכריי
ונתתי להם ד̇ ק̇[265a] ובבלי
שכירות ויוודע לכם לא היו
שוים ששה ק̇ ה̇[266] יודע אבל
קבלנו אותו בששה ק̇
ושכירות עליכם ויגיע לכם
דמי רביע נייר ורביע
צוקר ואין להאריך ושש̇[267]

[260] Leather gloves.

[261] Here are 2 letters, the same as in the address, l. 3, after ופניין, which I could not decipher.

[262] Read perhaps יחיה. [263] Perhaps = כבוד שיך חכם. [264] Perhaps = שיך.

[265] Perhaps = שם (השם) יחיהו וישמרהו and hence above ש״י is also = שם (השם) יחיהו.

[265a] = ד׳ קרוש. [266] = השם, God. [267] = ושלום שלום.

XIV.

[Paper leaf.]

(Recto)

טוביינא דחכימו. מרגניתא דלית לה טימו. ונהורא שרי עימו. מר ניהו
רבא דעמו. מדברנא דאומתו. ומשתמען ליה כל בני מאתו
וסיעתו. עביד גבורן עם בעלי תריסין ונצח להון ברוח גבורתו. דין
הוא הׄהׄ הׄהׄ[268] הרׄ חׄ[269] פינחס היו והרׄ חׄ עשאל היו והׄהׄ הרׄ ידידייא
היו והׄהׄ הרׄ חׄ אחווא היו והׄהׄ חׄ אהרן היו והׄהׄ יאושע[270] היו
והׄהׄ סימן טוב היו והׄהׄ יחזקאל ומיכאל היו והׄהׄ אליי[271] היו והׄהׄ
זכרייא היו והׄהׄ שלמה היו והׄהׄ יעקב היו ועׄכׄ כׄמׄ קׄקׄ[272]
גׄלא[273] כׄיבׄנׄש כׄיׄרׄא
ואחדשׄו וכׄו[274] ידוע למעלת כת״ר[275] ששלחתי את הׄהׄ ה״ר משה
בכה״ר ידידייא למח״ק[276] והרשיתי אותו שתאכלו משיחיטתו[277]
משחיטה ובדיקת הריאה ושבעים טריפיות והגם שלא כתבתי
לו סמיכה עדיין עד שיחזור פעם אחרת אצלי ואחזק אותו

[268] To be deleted as repetition.

[269] =חכם.

[270] =יהושע.

[271] =אליה.

[272] =ועל כל כבוד מעלת קהל קודש.

[273] This locality is also mentioned above, No. III, l. 27. The next abbreviation is not clear to me; perhaps כיבנ״ש = כן יבנה במהרה נוה שלום, viz. Jerusalem; כיר״א = כן יהי רצון אמן.

[274] =ואחרי דרישת שלומכם וטובתכם וכוליה.

[275] =כבוד תורתכם.

[276] =למחניכם קדוש (cp. above, note 252).

[277] Read משחיטתו.

בטוב יע"ה[278] ועכשיו אם תצטרכו לשחוט תשחטו בו ותאכלו
משחיטתו

וג"כ תבדקו סכין שלו אתה ה֗ עשאל והר֗ ה֗ פינחס הי"ו
ותבדקו אחריו ותנסו אותו ואין מזהירין אלא לנזהר ובכן
יוסף ה֗ עליכם ככם אלף פעמים ואתם שלום וביתכם שלום כה
דברי עבדא דרבנן
הצעיר שמעון
בכ"ה ח֗[279] בנימן
תמ"ך[280] יצ֗ו

(Verso contains an account.)

XV.

[Paper leaf; verso blank.]

(Recto)

בהיות אמת וצדק איך בא לפני כה֗ר מצליח בכה֗ר משה נ֗ע
למ[דינתנו]

וקרא ושנה ושמש ת֗ח ולמדתיו ג֗כ שחיטה ובדיקה ועתה הוא בקי
ב[שחיזת]

הסכין ובדיקתה ומרגיש בהרגשה דקה מן הדקה וחלי ומרגיש
אבשר[א]

ואטופרא ואתלת רוחתא[281] ובקי בשבעים טריפיות שמנו רבותינו
זכרונם לב[רכה]

ויודע הלכות שחיטה וגם הוא בקי באימון ידים שוחט ואינו מתעלף
על כן

כראותי כך מעתה ומעכשיו שמתי אני החתום למטה את ידי עליו
לסומכו

[278] =יגן עליו השם.   [279] =בן כבוד הרב חכם.

[280] =תהי מנוחתו כבוד.

[281] See Ḥullin 17b.

ולתומכו לחזקו ולאמצו ונתתי לו רשות לשחוט ולבדוק בינו לבין עצמו בין

בהמה בין חיה ובין עוף ומותר לאכול משחיטתו לאכול ולהאכיל ומכאן והלאה

אנש לא ימחא בידיה מן דנא ולעלם ולראיית אמת וצדק ולהיות בידו מכתב

לחזקיהו[282] כתבתי וחתמתי שמי פה העירה עמדיא יעא בס[283] ובשנת וטבח טבח

והכן כי אתי יאכלו וכו לפק[284] והיה זה שלם כה נאם הצעיר שמעון בר בנימן

זלה"ה בית

הלוי[284a]

(In different script.)

הצעיר יעקב

בכהר' עבדיה

תנצב"ה

XVI.

[Two paper leaves, much torn. Scribble on all sides. Of letter on fol. 1, verso, only left side edge remains; address on fol. 2, verso.]

[י]עלה [אל מו]ל פני המנורה [הטהורה].

שרגא דנהורא. מרנא ורבנא [כהר' חכם]

[282] Pun on Is. 38.9. Vocalise here of course לְחַזְקִיָהוּ.

[283] =בסדר, viz. in the week of Sidra מקץ, the verse cited here being Gen. 43.16.

[284] =לפרט קטן. The numerical value of the large letters is 525, i.e. 5525 A. M. Since the Sidra מקץ usually falls in December, the corresponding Christian year is 1764.

[284a] A somewhat enlarged photograph of his signature is adjoined here. See Facsimile XXV, infra, p. 726.

שמעון לבית הלוי נרו מגן אב[רהם]
יהיה בעזרו. ושחרו כרועה עדרו.
אכי"ר
מבגדאד לסנדור
יעׄאׄ יעׄאׄ
ולזר נחׄש ופגׄין
דרגמׄאׄ[285]
והלבׄיא חׄמׄה קרׄובׄץׄ[286]

XVII.

[2 paper leaves.]

(Fol. 1, recto)

בׄהׄ

יקר רוח איש תבונה. חידׄודׄה קודם לליבונה[287]. ליבון אשפׄיר[288]
ספיר גזרתו ומעונתו בצׄיון ההלכה[289]
הנסוכה ערוכה בכל הוא ידיד נפש הנעלה לתהלה כה"ר חכם
יעקב נר"ו ואתו עמו סיעת
מרחמוהי בכלל החיים והשלום מעתה ועד עולם אמן.
מאשר יקרת בעיני נכבדת ואני אהבתיך לכן יגל לבי באותיותיך
מעשה אצבעותיך ודבר
שפתיך כי נעים מי השלׄוׄח ההולכים לאט[290] והנה עתך עׄט
דודים[291] אמנם היתה שמחה מצד

[285] Read דרגמ"ה. See above, note 101.

[286] =והמגיעו לידו ברוך יהיה אמן. חמ"ה. קול רנה וישועה באהלי צדיקים. The abbreviation חמ"ה is not clear to me.

[287] Cp. Ḥullin 8a, here in the meaning that the correspondent's intellect (תבונה) is sharp.

[288] Cp. Sanh. 106a.

[289] Pun on Ps. 76.3, here in the meaning that the correspondent is at home in Halakhic scholarship. Cp. Ber. 8a: שערים המצויינים בהלכה.

[290] Pun on Is. 8.6, here in the meaning of sending (שִׁלּוּחַ).

[291] Pun on Ez. 16.8 where עת.

ודאגה מצד לשמע אזן מלין תבחן[292] לאמר שעזבנוך ושכחנוך ולא בא זכרונך לפנינו לידע
מה אתנו יודע עד[293] מה דרך גבר בעלמא אם לשלום ואם למלחמה. והלא אם היתה מגעת
תשורת שורת מנחת מרחשׂת שפתים[294] וניב צׄרי הנוטף מעצי הכתׄב[295] אל מול פניך היית טוען
משא על כתפך[296] וחוזר מימים קדמונים אכן מה אעשה שהכתבים ממשמשים ובאים
עד צובא יע״א ומשם נבלעים במקומם וא״כ איך ולמה תהיה קובל שלא הגיעוך כתבים
מידינו כי זו היא הדרך וזו הנתיבה אשר ראו עיניך במקום שאין השיירות מצויות מפה לפה
ולעת הזאת אודיעך קשט אמרי נועם איך השליח של הי״ב[297] הגיע אלינו ערב פסח אמנם לפי
שעדיין מר אביך נר״ו וחתנך הנה הנם עדיין בצובא יע״א לכן לא[298] יגיע לפרק התׄקבל[299] עד
שיבואו לשלום ועתה אחרי שהשחת ובלעת את נחלתך[300] מה ארבה עוד לדבר שמן הראוי
היה לך לשלוח ולהוליכה ומ״מ[301] כיון שכבר נחתם ונגמר נביאהו לפרק הנז׳[302] ואם תשאל
עלינו של[303] כלנו במצב הבריאות והשלימות יושבים בשובה ונחת כן נשמע ונתבשר

[292] Cp. Job 12.11.

[293] These four words should evidently be deleted and the sentence should read לידע מה דרך גבר בעלמא (pun on Prov. 30.19).

[294] Pun on Lev. 2.7. Cp. further Yer. Ber. II, 4b, bottom: שפתותיו רוחשות.

[295] Pun on עצי הקטף, resin trees.

[296] Read כתפי.

[297] This abbreviation is not clear to me. Perhaps = החכם יגדל בתורה.

[298] Viz. this messenger?

[299] Pun on ch. 9 (המקבל) of B. Meṣi'a.

[300] Referring to his wife.

[301] = ומכל מקום.

[302] = הנזכר.

[303] = שלום.

משלומך כי טוב הוא ועכ"פ תשתדל בכל עז לשלוח לי ספר לוחות הברית[304] וספר מגני

ארץ[305] וס' שפתי חכמים[306] ובהגיעם לידי בין עם המוביל בין עם אחר בע"ה[307] אשלח דמיהם לידך

וגם לרבות לחם משנה[308] ושירי כנסת הגדולה[309] וספרי הרב אשכנזי זלהה[310] כל מה שתמצא

על הכל תשתדל בכל מאמצי כחך לשלחם לידי ודמיהם בע"ה יהיה מוכן ומזומן ואין לי

פנאי להאריך כא[311] בשלומך שיגדל כנפשך הרמה וכנפש דורש שלום ואמת פה סנדור

יע"א י"ג לחדש ד' לסדר ושלח את הצפר החיה[312] שנת התס"ב[313] ליצירה

הצעיר[314]

(More cursive writing.)

ומצדי תפרוש כנהר שלום על ידיד נפש החכם השלם כמה"ר

בנימן כהן נר"ו נא אל ישכח אהבת קדומים ואלף שלומים

מאת אחיו הקטן משה.

[304] Probably the well-known work שני לוחות הברית by R. Isaiah Horowitz

[305] Viz. Shulḥan ‘Arukh Oraḥ Ḥayyim with the 2 well-known commentaries Magen Abraham by Abraham of Kalish and Magen David by David Hallevi (author of Ṭure Zahab).

[306] On Rashi to the Pentateuch by Sabbatai Bass of Prague.

[307] =בעזרת השם.

[308] On Maimonides' Mishneh Torah by Abraham de Boton.

[309] By Ḥayyim Benveniste.

[310] viz. the works of Isaac Lurya (האר"י).

[311] =כי אם.

[312] Lev. 14.7, viz. Sidra מצורע.

[313] =1702 C. E.

[314] The signature with calligraphic embellishments I could not decipher. Herewith is adjoined a somewhat enlarged photograph of it. See Facsimile XXVI, infra, p. 727.

(Fol. 1, verso, and fol. 2, recto, are blank. Address on fol. 2, verso.)

נ[ל]עה"ק[315] ירושלם תובב"א[316]
ליד ידיד נפש החכם ונבון כה"ר
יעקב בנימן נר"ו והלביא[317]
והזר הקרב חש"ן ילבש[318]

XVIII.

[Paper leaf.]

(Recto)

שלום על כל הקהל מגדולם ועד קטנם כי"ר[319]

יודע לך מ' אברהם שבא זה היאודנ[י]ם̇[320] אצלי ואמר לי שזה האשה אשר אירסתי לי

אמר מ̇ אברהם אינה מקודשת ותלך ותנשא לכל אשר תרצה ואני אמרתי יישר כוחו

שהוא סומך על חכמתו הגדולה ולא ישאל מגדול ממנו וכמדומה שאין כמוהו מורה

שילך ויתן רשות לאשת איש שתנשא לאחר וירבה ממזרים בישראל וכן לא יעשה בישראל

ועתה אכתוב לך מה שראו עיני כשדנתי זה הדין בעיר סנדור יעא̇ כשבאתי לסנדור

בא מרדכי אבי הבת ושאל לי על עסקי קידושי בתו ואמר מה שאמר אמרתי

315 =לעיר הקודש.

316 =תבנה ותכונן במהרה בימינו אמן.

317 =והמגיעו לידו ברוך יהיה אמן.

318 Pun on the חשן worn by Aaron. Here=חרם שמתא נדוי for anyone who would read this letter.

319 =כן יהי רצון.

320 Dot on ם indicates that the letter should be deleted.

לו אם כדבריך הבת אינה מקודשת ויהי ממחורת[321] קרא לי הגוי שחני[*321] שלכם ואמר

לי תבוא ותדין לנו זה הדין נראה זה הבת מקודשת היא אם לאו והלכתי לבית

. . . .

יעקב ן̇ חוה[**321] נע̇ ונאספו כל אנשי סנדור וגם חר̇[322] יאודה נע̇ בא עמהם ושאלתי את

אנשי סנדור כיצד היית[323] המעשה אמרו אנשי סנדור אנחנו נדע זה מרדכי נתן בתו

לבן דוד ודוד ג̇כ̇ נתן את בתו לבן מרדכי והלך זה מרדכי הנז̇ עם אנשיו לסוכי[324]

לקדש את בתו לבן דויד ודויד ג̇כ̇ יקדש את בתו לבן מרדכי ואמרתי לאנשי סנדור

הידעתם אם בת מרדכי רוצה היית בזה הקידושין אם לאו אמרו אנשי סנדור לא שמענו שמיחתה

ואמרה איני רוצה אמרתי לאנשי סנדור כשהלך זה מרדכי לקדש את בתו לבן

לבן[325] דויד שום אדם הרגיש בזה הקידושין אמרו כל אנשי סנדור כולנו ידענו כשהלך

זה מרדכי לקדש את בתו לבן דויד ועוד אמרתי להם כשהלך זה מרדכי לקדש את

בתו לבן דויד בת מרדכי הנז̇ בעיר היית אמרו אנשי סנדור הן בעיר היית הבת

אמרתי להם שום אדם לא שמע כשהלך זה מרדכי לקדש את בתו הבת אמרה

[321] Read ממחרת.

*[321] Probably = Shiḥna in Arabic, prefect of police.

**[321] Can also be read אוה.

[322] = חכם ר'. When this statement was written he was no longer alive.

[323] = היתה, but more correct היה.

[324] Probably = סוכו, Sakho (see above, note 88).

[325] Repeated in MS.

[איני רוצה אם] לאו אמרו אנשי סנדור לא שמענו שהבת אמרה איני רוצה ועוד

[אמרתי להם] ....

....

(verso)

ברתיה[326] של[יח] מילתא

והיכא דקדיש ראובן בתו בוגרת ולא שויתיה וי]דיע דאבוה קידשה ושמעון שגר סבלונות לברתיה

אעָג[327] דלית ליה לאבוה רשותא לקדושא אי קבלינהו לסבלונות איכא למיחש דילמא מצטבא

להנהו קידושין וצריכא גט מספיקא ואעָג דלענין ברא לא חיישונן לקידושי אבוהי כההוא

דהוי שתי חמרא תותי ציפי דבבל שמא נתרצה לא אמרינן[328] הא איכא למימר איתתא בכל דהוא

ניחא לה ואפי׳ לא שדר לה סבלונות צריכא גט מספיקא והכי שדר גאון עכ׳ל והביאו הטור

אהָ[329] סי ל״ו וכתבה הבי׳[330] בשולחנו הקצר בשם יש מי שאומר בסי׳ הנז סעי׳ יא עָש[331] נראה

אם האב קידש אשה לבנו ולא ידע הבן אינה מקודשת אבל אם האב קידש את בתו הבוגרת

שלא מידיעתה הבת היא מקודשת מספק מפני שהאשה ניחא לה בכל דהוא וכתב

באר הגולה בסי׳ להָ בסק[332] ג וז׳ל אבל האשה ניחא לה בכל דהוא כדאמר ריש לקיש[333] טב למיתב טן דו

[326] The Hebrew בתו is corrected on top by the Aramaic ברתיה.

[327] =אף על גב.

[328] Cp. Ḳidd. 45a, bottom, 45b, top.

[329] =אבן העזר.

[330] =הבית יוסף.

[331] =עיין שם.

[332] =בסעיף קטן.

[333] Ḳidd. 7a and frequently.

עֹכֹ[334] [ו]אצל הבן כתב אֹהֹ סי׳ להֹ סעיף הֹ וז״ל יש מי שאומר שאם האב הרצה הדברים

לפני הבן שהוא רוצה לקדש לו ושתק [ה]בן והלך האב וקידשה לו הרי זו מקודשת

דמחמת כיסופא דאב שתק ועשאו שליח לקדש לו עֹכֹ עֹשֹ אבל אם האב הרצה הדברים

לפני בתו הבוגרת ושתקה ולא מיחתה והלך וקידשה ודאי מקודשת היא קידושין גמורין

וכן הוא הנדון דידן שזה מרדכי אבי הבת שלושה ימים קודם הקידושין היה נושא ונותן בקידושי[ן]

בתו ובתו היית רואה שאביה רוצה לקדש אותה ולא מיחתה והלך אביה לעיר

אחרת לקדש אותה ולא מיחתה ודאי רוצה היית בקידושי

אביה לא כל שכן שהלכו העדים ואמרו לה שאביה הלך לקדש ולא מיחתה אעֹפֹ

שהלכו העדים זה שלא בפני זה ועוד שלחו לה סבלונות ועשו להם משתה כנהוג

ועוד עשו לה שמחה וריקודין וזמר ולא מיחתה לפחות עד אחר ששה חודשים

אמרו[335] איני רוצה בו ועוד היא לא אמרה איני רוצה בו אלא אביה הטעה אותה

ואמר לה תאמרי איני רוצה [בו] כך ספרו אנשי סנדור וכתב הבאר היטב בסי׳ לו

סעי׳ ד׳ וז״ל דחיישינן שמא נתרצה לקידושי אביה אעֹגֹ דשמא נתרצה הבן

[לא אמרינן ממֹ איהי ניחא בכל דהו] ....

334 =עד כאן.

335 Read אמרה.

XIX.

[2 leaves of paper; fols. 1, recto, and fol. 2, verso, are blank except for scribble; fol. 2 is cut off in the middle.]

(Fol. 1, verso)

[336]כי יח̇ מדו[337]

בהיות כי אחרו גלילות יק̇[338] ולא שלח לי כתר̇[339] תשובה הנה אמרתי אפשר כתבים ששלחתי לכתר̇ לא הגיעו לידו ומפני זה לא שלח לי כתר̇ תשובה ומפני זה הוצרכתי לשלוח לכתר̇ שתי שורות אלו לכתר̇ להודיע לו גופא דעובדא הה̇[340] בקיצור מענין המעשה שעשיתי בשוכו̇ הנה כשהלכתי לשוכו̇ קבצתי כל יחידי קק̇ שוכו במעמד אנשי העיר ואבי הבן עמהם אמרתי לאבי הבן ספר נא לי כיצד היו נשואי בנך הקטן אמר לי במעמד אנשי העיר היה לי בת גדולה ו[341] והשיאתי[342] אותה והיה לי בן קטן אמרתי אתן בתי לאיש ואביא אשה לבני חליפי בתי לעבודת הבית עד שיגדל בני ותהי לו לאשה אמרתי בנך ידע בכל אלה שתביא אשה לבנך או הוא אמר לך שתביא לו אשה ובנך היה יודע בט[י]ב אשה מה היא ענה אבי הבן ואמר לי בני לא היה יודע בטיב אשה ולא אמרתי לו שאביא לך אשה ולא היה יודע אשה מה היא אלא אני אמרתי ללבי אביא אשה לבני חליפי בתי לעבודת הבית עד שיגדל ותהי̇ לו לאשה וכל אנשי העיר שהיו במעמד ההוא אמרו

[336] Before this word there is some calligraphic embellishment which I could not decipher.

[337] This abbreviation is not clear to me.

[338] =יקרתו.

[339] =כבוד תורתו.

[340] =היכי הוא.

[341] To be deleted.

[342] Read והשאתי.

כך היה המעשה לא אמר לבנו שאביא לך אשה ולא היה יודע בנו אשה מה היא אלא הוא בעצמו נמלך והביא אשה לעבודת הבית חליפי בתו אמרתי לו בן כמה שנים היה בנך כשהביאתה אשה לבנך אמר איני יודע קם אחד[343] היה לו כמו יד׳ שנה הן חסר הן יתר ואדם[344] גכ׳ אמר היה כמו בן יד׳ שנה אמרתי לאבי הזה כשהשיאתה[345] אשה לבנך הביא שש[346] או לאו כל העם שהיו שם אמרו לא הביא שש כשהשיא אשה לבנו אמרתי להם אפשר אחכ׳ הביא שש אמרו אין אנחנו יודעים קם אדם אחד ואמר כשברחה אשתו מאצלו ואמרה איני רוצה בו שאינו כשאר בני אדם בדקתי אותו בבית הערוה בפני בני אדם ולא ראיתי בו שום שערות שהיה כילד קטן בלא שערות וכל זה היה בפסח כשברחה אשתו ובדק אותו . . . . [ולא היו לו]

(fol. 2, recto)

לא שערות ולא גומות בבית הערוה ובדו[ק] . . . [עד] כאן סוף השאלה ובכתב ששלחתי לכת״ר קוד[ם] . . . . מזה כל גופא דעובדא וכאן קיצרתי . . . . והבן חלש[347] ונפלה לפני יבם קטן בן ו׳ [שנים] . . . . אין לה מנוח לכף רגלה ואין שום אדם . . . . בסכנה גדולה עד שרוצה להמיר דתה . . . . בכתב שקודם זה בארוכה.

(On fol. 1, recto, there is on the left side edge the indication: אני הצעיר שמעון, perhaps by the author of this epistle.)

343 Supply ואמר.

344 Supply אחר.

345 Read כשהשאת.

346 =שתי שערות.

347 =חיים לרבנן שבק.

XX.

[Paper leaf; scribble on verso.]

Address (verso)

יגיע ליד יוסף ן̇ מנחם מן עקר[348] אלי שיך̇ כ̇א[349]
יע̇א̇[350] ק̇רו̇ב̇ץ̇[351] יע̇א̇

(Recto)

אברך [את] ה̇ [אשר] יעצני ובדרך אמת הנחני כי מיום עומדי על דעתי חמודי החבל[352] הלא תכלה הזמן והיריעה ותקצר אשר עשה אתי חמודתו [ול]אשר תחזינה מישרים עטרת החיים והשלום

שלמא רבא לגברא רבא וחביבה וחיבה יתירא ורוב שלום לקראת ומ̇ע̇[353] ה̇ה̇ כבוד ח̇ר̇ שמואל הי̇ו̇ ועל הטור השיני ח̇ יוסף הי̇ו̇ ועל ה̇ח̇ צורבא מרבנן בנימן וע̇[354] ה̇ה̇ א̇ח̇[355] עזיז רחמים הי̇ו̇ וע̇ הה̇ אחי הגדול יוסף ואנשי ביתו הי̇ו̇ וע̇ מ̇ע̇ זלפה הי̇ו̇ וע̇ ה̇ה̇ בזבו אחי ונחום ומרדכי בן לאנו הי̇ו̇ וע̇ כל ק̇ק̇ שיך̇ כ̇א אתה השם תשמרם כי̇ר̇א̇ השם ייטיב לכים.

ואחדשו[356] וכו׳ יא קהל קדוש ידוע[357] לכם ענין ביאתנו ליעקר[358] לשלום הגיענו בשמחה ובששון ובלב חפיצה לו[359] יש לנו

[348] There are several places by this name. Our place is probably the one lying between Taḳrīt and Mosul forming a station for the caravans (see Yaḳūt, s. v.).

[349] This place is unknown to me.

[350] This refers to עקר.

[351] See above, note 286.

[352] The letter is very carelessly written. The writer meant to say that were he to describe God's kindness to him, time would pass and paper would be short for this purpose. For ותקצר read תקצר.

[353] Read מ̇ע̇ = מעלת; ה̇ה̇ = הרב החכם; ח̇ר̇ = חכם ר̇.

[354] = ועל.

[355] Probably read אל, viz. אלעזיז.

[356] = ואחרי דרישת שלומכם וטובתכם.

[357] Read יודע.

[358] = לעקר.

[359] Read לא.

שום צער לו[359] משום אכילה ולו[360] משום שתיה ולו[360] משום
מלבוש ותומרא[361] לחומותי[362] אים היא רוצה תבא אצלי
אשלח אחריה ה̇ ימים קודם ר̇ה̇ ויצחק ומנחם
ינשק ידכים ואני אברך אתכים בשם ה̇ ושים שלום
ורח̇ני ומכ̇מורי[363] הרביה הצעיר אברהם
שואלים בשלומכים כולכים בן מנחם יצ̇ו ס̇ט̇

XXI.

[Narrow strip of paper.]

(Recto)

[ב]ן יוחי לשוק שתשאלו לאותו
[הר]שע אדוני להיכן הוא או תראוהו
בשוק או א׳ מקרוביו שיבואו
אחרי ויביאו פרדה כי הרבה
צער הגיע עלי השם יודע מיום
שבאתי מאצלך לא דברתי עם
התלמידים גדולים
מטוב ועד רע אבל חכם אמר
אל ישחטו בעצמם יום ח̇
א א[364] אמרתי לאותו
טפש משה שיחזור מ̇ יהודה
עמך וא̇ח̇ך̇[365] תשחוט הלך אביו
ושקר אצל חכם ואמר מ׳
מרדכי[365a] נתקנא בבני ואינו

[360] Read ולא. [361] Read ותאמרו.

[362] Read לחמותי.

[363] Evidently names of persons, perhaps the writer's wife and daughter just as Isaac and Menaḥem are probably his sons.

[364] Smudges after each letter, probably to be deleted.

[365] =ואחרי כן.

[365a] Evidently the name of the writer of our epistle.

מניח שישחוט וכתב חכם
כתב ושלח אצלי וראו כי
שקר דברו והחביאו מכתב
ולא הראוהו לשום אדם
ואחר שלושה ימים שמעתי
אמרו חכם כועס עליך
וכיון שמעתי כעסתי אני
ואמרתי טפשים תביאו כתב
של חכם הראוהו אל תחביאו
אותו וכין שאמרתי כך קם זה
הרשע אברהם[365b] להכות אותי
[אם לא] היו אוחזין אותו ולא נשא׳[366]
שום קללה שלא קללני באבי
[וב]אמי

(verso)

וג"כ ותעשה[367] חסד ותתן
קרוש א׳ לחכם דמי אגרה[368]
במהרה ואל תעכב ולאלו
הדברים תעשה משא עליך
כי הרבה הכוני וקללוני כי
אין לי פנים לדור בין ב׳
אנשים והם אינם מניחים
לשכוב בהמה מכאן
וכמדומי[369] אני אני[370] שהם

[365b] Probably the father of Moses (l. 11) who wanted to act as Shoḥeṭ by himself.

[366] =נשארה.

[367] Read תעשה.

[368] =אגרת.

[369] Read וכמדומה.

[370] Repeated in MS., to be deleted.

משתדלים להפסיד ממוני
פעם אחרת הלואי לא
ירדתי משם והכל סבה
מן חכם שאחז אותם
התלמידים ואם הייתי
יודע לא הייתי יורד משם
ובלבול מעשים ממנו הוא

XXII.

[Paper leaf, faded and torn; verso contains scribble.]

(Recto)

בֿהֿ

השרידים אשר הֿ קורא אחינו בית ישראל אחי ומרחמי די בכל אתר ואתר מוי[371] וכי את[ום אנשי]

חסד רודפי צדק אשרי נוצרי י״י. המה הגבירים הרמים גוברין גוברי י״י. ועטרותיהם ברא[שם]

הרבנים המובהקים אילין נטורי י״י. הכל בכלל יזהירו כזוהר הרקיע דנפיש זהורי י״י.

אכי״ר

בראש כל אמרי י״י. מבאין[372] שלמים וכן רבים נחל נהרי י״י. גם ברכות יתברכון משופרי י״י.

הדא אמרה דברי אלה יעידון יגידון על האיש מוביל כתבא דנא איש מסכן

חכם כהֿרֿ בניימין מזרחי יצֿוֿ ההוא אמר מפיו ומכתב כן נמצא כתוב שהיה

[371] These 2 letters should be deleted.

[372] Read מובאין, a combined pun on Beṣah 2.4 and Nah. 1.12, here in the meaning of greetings of peace.

בביתו שקט ושאנן כתמר טב דיתיב על דורדיא[373] עוסק בתורה תורה שיש עמה [דרך ארץ]

ובע"ה[374] התהפך עליו בלהות הזמן ונשתנה לגריעותא שנחלה בחולי הענים וכמעט [שעיניו]

כהות ב"מ[375] ואין יכול לצאת ולבא הא במילי דעלמא הא במילי דשמייא זאת ועוד זאת

שלא שקעה שמשה של צרה וצרה זורחת שמתה אשתו והניחה אחריה שלשה בנים

והקטן צריך להניק והשכיר לו מניקת גוייה מדי חדש בחדשו שני גרושוש ובודאי יפול חֿו

שאם לא יפרע לה שכרה תמיר דתו בֿמ[375] וזה לו ימים רבים גולה ומטולטל ממקום למקום

וכל אשר קבץ על יד הוציא אותו בשן בהמות[376] ובמיני תרופות ולא הועיל בהם וכ[שהגיע]

פה אצֿו[377] יעֿא ולרש אין כל ואנן בדידן חזינן להאי גברא שייף עייל שייף נפיק[378] לא [ימוש]

מתוך האהל דאסבורי ליה מסבר וחזותו מוכיח עליו שיראת הֿ בלבבו ומ. . . . .

פניו איש תם וישר וירא אלהים לכן המצוה הזאת אליכם שבכל מקום אשר תדרך כף רגלו

הצג על הארץ יענק יעניקוהו מגרני צדקתם במזון וצידה ובאכסניא נאה ובמנה

הראויה לפי חומר הנושא העשיר לוֹ ירבה והדל לא ימעיט[379] ובפרט אם [יזדמן לו]

[373] Like good wine resting on its lees. Cp. Meg. 12b.

[374] =ובעונותינו הרבים.

[375] =בר מינן.

[376] viz. for travelling on animals.

[377] =ארם צובה, Aleppo.

[378] Cp. Sanh. 88b.

[379] Cp. above, note 234.

רופא אומן יודע לרפאת את עיניו יעמדו לימינו ויחזקו אותו ברצי
כ[סף אולי ימצא]

תרופה וכגון דא מצוה רבה ועצומה אין קץ למתן שכרה ובשכר
זה תאכלו מטוב

האדמה כרבות הטובה דשנים ורעננים כנפשכם הרמה והפתוחה . .
ה̇ וכנפש נאה דשו̇ החו̇[380] פה צובה יע̇א̇ בסדר ובשנת לכל נדבותם
א̇ש̇ר̇ יקרי[נבו][381]

. . . .

הדיין זלהה̇[382]

(Postscript in different hand.)

ולזה אוותה נפשו לעלות אל ערי קדשנו ואל מקום משכן בית
אלהינו ולהתאבק בעפר ציון אולי יחנון ה̇ וישוב[

מחרון אפו ומחשבה טובה מצרפה למעשה וכאשר ראה אדוניו
מחשבתו וכוונתו קם עליו זה הגוי עז [פנים]

רשע ובליעל ושלל וביזה כל אשר נשאר לו מיתר הפליטה דהיינו
חפציו וכלי תשמישו וספריו שהיה לו . . . [עם]

כל זה לא ביטל מחשבתו וכוונתו הטובה

. . . . . בס̇ ובש̇[383] ויאמר חזק ו̇אמץ

(Verso contains scribble.)

[380] נאם הכותב דורש שלומכם וטובתכם החותם=

[381] Lev. 22.18, hence the Sidra was אמור. The numerical value of א̇ש̇ר̇ is (5)501 A. M. = 1741 C. E.

[382] The signature above this line I could not decipher owing to calligraphic embellishments. A somewhat enlarged photograph is adjoined here. See Facsimile XXVII, infra, p. 728.

[383] = בסדר ובשנת. The verse is Deut. 31.23, hence in Sidra וילך. The year cannot be ascertained owing to the lacuna.

[illegible Hebrew text]

25 . . . .

[illegible Hebrew text]

(Postscript in different hand.)

[illegible Hebrew text]

30 [illegible Hebrew text]

(Verso contains scribble.)

[illegible] = [illegible Hebrew]

[illegible] Lev. 22.18, hence the Sidra was אמור. The numerical value of [illegible] is (5)501 A. M. = 1741 C. E.

[illegible] The signature above this line I could not decipher owing to calligraphic embellishments. A somewhat enlarged photograph is adjoined here. See Facsimile XXVII, infra, p. 728.

[illegible] = [illegible Hebrew]. The verse is Deut. 31.23, hence in Sidra וילך. The year cannot be ascertained owing to the lacuna.

SECTION VI

FRAGMENTS OF LEGALISTIC WRITINGS OF THE GAONIC PERIOD

FRAGMENTS OF LEGALISTIC WRITINGS OF THE GAONIC PERIOD

In this section a number of fragments are edited which add to our knowledge of the literary activities in the field of Halakah and interpretation of the Talmud. One item originally intended for this section, has since found its place elsewhere. The 'Sepher Ha-Ma'asim of the Palestinian Jews', an important compilation of law and ritual as prevalent in Palestine in the Byzantine period, throws some light on the legal practices after the conclusion of the Palestinian Talmud and probably after that of the Babylonian Talmud. A portion of it has been edited by me (תרביץ, I, No. 3, 1ff.) in supplementation of the other fragments edited by Lewin and Epstein (ibid., No. I, 79ff., and No. II, 33 ff.). Another item containing portions of Hai Gaon's valuable commentary on Berakhot was originally intended for another occasion and the introductory remarks were given in Hebrew. Owing to the indefinite delay of this publication the paper is inserted here as item 4 of this section.

The fragments given below comprise 1) Formulae of Proclamations of the Bet-Din, evidently of the early Gaonic period, 2) a characteristic responsum by Naḥshon, Gaon of Sura, to Ḳairwān, 3) a portion of Sherira Gaon's commentary to Baba Batra, 4) portions of Hai's commentary to Berakhot, and 5) a list of questions sent to a Gaon. The last two items (6 and 7) belong to authorities who had intimate connections with Hai Gaon, viz. a portion of R. Nissim's Mafteaḥ in Arabic to Nedarim and Gittin and a section of Samuel ibn Nagdela's Halakhic work הלכתא גבראתא which has hitherto only been known from quotations.

1.

FORMULAE OF PROCLAMATIONS FROM A BABYLONIAN BET-DIN

The adjoining fragment contains six formulae, of which the first and the last ones are defective. They are a welcome addition to those published by Aptowitzer (*JQR*, *N. S.*, IV, 23–51, cp. also the fragment edited by Mann, ibid., XI, 460–61). They afford us a glimpse of the procedure of the Bet-Din in supervising individual and communal affairs. Their style is pure Aramaic which presupposes that it was the common language of the people for whom these proclamations were intended. Such was the case in Babylon during almost the entire Gaonic period. Only towards its end did Arabic become the everyday language of the people, especially in the larger cities like Bagdād, Baṣrah and others.[1] Such proclamations were no doubt made public at the synagogue during the Sabbath morning service when the attendance was numerous.

The purpose of No. I is not evident owing to its defective condition, except that the people are urged not to neglect the meritorious deed asked of them. The following items deal with cases of lost property, libel, slander of a fellow-Jew before non-Jewish authorities, recommending a respectable person, formerly in comfortable but now in straitened circumstances, to the sympathy of coreligionists and finally condemning the action of

[1] Cp. the interesting responsum of Hai Gaon (published by Harkavy, *Hakkedem*, II, 82): כי כיון שבבל מאז מקום לשון ארמי ולשון כשדי ועד אן (=ועדיין) בכל העיירות (viz. in the small cities and villages) בלשון ארמי וכשדי מספרין הכל בין ישראל ובין הגוים אף במדינות שחידשום ישמעאלים רוב השמות ארמי מרוכך הוא. Hai states further in another responsum that Aramaic proverbs, mentioned in the Babylonian Talmud, were popular in his own time (see Gaonic Responsa, ed. Hark., No. 33: אילו משלים הן שמצויין בפי הכל בבבל). On the other hand we find legal questions from Baṣrah to Hai in Arabic (*Geon.*, II, 71, cp. ed. Hark., No. 422, end).

In Palestine the tendency was to render even the Aramaic of the Babylonian Talmud into Hebrew (see above, p. 446, note 2).

א ל ס ד ר פחכם ראס אלגאלות וראס אלסדר באן ליס עלי אבן אלפראת אן יעטי אלאדראהם ויג̇ב לה אן יאכ̇ד̇ במא ג̇רם עלי כ̇לאץ אלמאל: וחכם דיאן אלבאב אן יג̇ב עלי אבן נוח אן יעטי אבן פראת*[1] דנאניר אבריזיה̈ ויג̇ב עלי אבן נוח פראת**[1] אן יתחסב לה במא יכון . . . (last line) . . . פאמא י ו ס ף ר א ס א ל מ ת̇ י ב ה̈ פאנה קאל אן] (fol. 5a) לם יכן לה אן ירד אלאדראהם . . . (he goes on to quote the Gaon's whole legal argument; l. 3 from bottom) ואמא ע מ ר ם ד י א ן א ל ב א ב פאנה[קאל אן אבן נוח לם יאמר אברהם . . . (continues on fol. 5b the [whole legal argument of 'Amram Ab-Bet-Din).

All this is quoted to prove the difference of opinion among the Rabbinic authorities (פהאד̇ה קיאסתהם ואסתנבאטהם ועליהם יבנון אמורהם פי אחכאמהם). He goes on to remark (l. 3 from bottom): ווג̇דו בעץ̇ ר ו ו ס א ל מ ת̇ א י ב א ל מ ת ק ד מ י ן קד חכם פיהא בחכם מא ואן לם יתעלק בדליל עמלו עלי ד̇לך אלחכם וג̇עלה אצלא יעמלון עליה כמא תעלק ע מ ר ם בקול ר' נחמן לתקוני שויתך ולא (fol. 6a) לעויתי (Ḳidd. 42b, top).

Which R. Joseph Gaon is meant here is difficult to say. Should we say that Joseph b. Saṭya, the nominee of David b. Zakkai during his conflict with Sa'adyah, is referred to here? Then the Exilarch would be our David. The Ab-Bet-Din 'Amram may be of the Sura school or the Exilarch's Dayyān al-Bāb. It is interesting to note that also the Rosh Hasseder of the school was asked to give his opinion. Indeed we find a Rosh Hasseder sending responsa to Ḳairwān (*Geonica*, II, 59: למרב חזקיה בן שמואל ראש סדר נכד פלטוי ראש הישיבה מנחה שלוחה למרב בהלול בן מרב יוסף זצ"ל). Ginzberg's assumption (p. 54) that he did not live in Babylon and his further argument (*Geon.*, I, 7, note 1) that only the Gaon of the school was entitled to send responsa now hardly need refutation. Above (pp. 116 and 152 f.) we have had Asaf Rosh Hasseder playing a prominent role under Hai and Joseph under Israel b. Samuel b. Ḥofni.

The chief point of interest in our polemical tract is in the section adjoined here containing a characteristic responsum by Naḥshon Gaon to Ḳairwān. The Ḳaraite author gives this responsum in the original accompanied by an Arabic translation for the benefit of his fellow-sectaries unfamiliar with the Talmudic

*[1] These four words are between the lines, evidently meant as a correction.

**[1] This word is between the lines as a correction, viz. Ibn Furāt instead of Ibn Nūḥ.

style of a mixture of Aramaic and Hebrew employed by the Geonim. The case concerned the estate of a married woman (נכסי מלוג) whose husband is entitled to its usufruct and also to inherit this estate in case she died before him. The resolution at the meetings of Usha, after the cessation of the Hadrianic persecutions, was that if the wife sold such property in her lifetime, her husband could after her demise reclaim the property from the purchasers (Ket. 50a: אמר ר' יוסי בר חנינא באושא התקינו האשה שמכרה בנכסי מלוג בחיי בעלה ומתה הבעל מוציא מיד הלקוחות). However the Talmudic report left it obscure whether the buyers had to be compensated for the amount of their purchase money or whether they forfeited it because of the invalidity of the sale from its very beginning. This point formed the subject of discussion of several Geonim of both academies.[2] Three Sura Geonim in succession, Naṭronai, 'Amram and Naḥshon, were for the latter alternative whereas another Sura Gaon, Hilai, as well as the Pumbedita Gaon Mattityah and the chief Judge Ṣemaḥ b. Solomon held that the purchasers should be compensated. This problem also formed the subject of discussion by the later Geonim like Samuel b. Ḥofni and Hai and also by Meshullam b. Ḳalonymos of Lucca in Italy.[3]

[2] Louis M. Epstein, *The Jewish Marriage Contract*, 1927, p. 110 ff., entirely failed to take into consideration the views of the Geonim on the subject.

[3] See 'Iṭṭur, ed. Lemberg, I, 45d: איתשיל ממר רב עמרם הבעל מוציא מיד הלקוחות בדמים אי לא, ואמר בלא דמים. וכן אמר (better: אמרו) רב נחשון ורב נטרונאי. ומר רב מתיבתה (צ"ל: מתתיה) ומר רב הילאי אמר (better: אמרו) בדמים כדרבא דאמר הכיר בה שאינה שלו ולקחה מעות יש לו שבח אין לו (ב"מ ט"ו, ע"ב). וכן אמר רב צמח בר שלמה בר דיינא דבבא חוזר וגובה הדמים מבעלה של אשה בשעה שמוציאין מידו וכו' (delete בר).

Cp. the corresponding statement in Gaonic Responsa, ed. Harkavy, No. 544, where in line 5 the missing name should be Hilai (וכן אמר רב [הילאי] גאון בדמים כהכיר בה שאינה שלו). Harkavy, pp. 387–8, erroneously suggests to fill in the lacuna with Samuel b. Ḥofni.

As to the title of Ṣemaḥ b. Solomon there is much confusion in the sources. Whereas he is known as the דיינא דבבא of the Exilarch Ḥisdai b. Naṭronai (cp. Dukes, *Ben Chananja*, IV, 141–2, Harkavy, *l. c.*, p. 389) and is styled as such in the above passage in 'Iṭṭur, he is called Gaon in the corresponding passage in ed. Harkavy (וכן אמר רב צמח גאון ביר' שלמה דיאנא) and likewise in No. 266 (probably by Hai, cp. 'Iṭṭur, I, 45d, bottom, where for ור"ח read ור"ה): אשר ראיתם דברי מר רב מתתיה ורב צמח הגאונים. Cp. also the passage in ס' המתיבות (edited by Assaf, תה"ג מתוך ה.גניזה', 227, lines 42–3): הכי אמר מרב צמח גא' בר שלמה דינא דבבא,

In our responsum by Naḥshon the Gaon expresses his indignation with his Ḳairwān questioners for sending the same question both to the Sura and the Pumbedita academies. Such a procedure would only lead to quarrels because if different decisions would be given by the two academies, as in our case, the dissatisfied litigants would cling to the opinion of the Gaon that was in their favor. Naḥshon reminds the Ḳairwān scholars

making his father Solomon to have been the דיינא דבבא, and see further Epstein, *Haggoren*, III, 79, and Büchler, *RÉJ*, L, 175–6.

But such a Gaon Ṣemaḥ b. Solomon is never mentioned for example by Sherira in his 'Letter'. In our responsum by Naḥshon Ṣemaḥ is mentioned before Mattityah but neither is indicated by the title Gaon; however in the corresponding responsum in שערי צדק, fol. 69a, No. 71 (cp. infra, note 4 to our text) Ṣemaḥ is again styled Gaon (שדר רב צמח גאון). But if R. Naḥshon referred to a Ṣemaḥ Gaon, he could have only had in mind his contemporary Ṣemaḥ b. Palṭoi, who became Gaon of Pumbedita in 872, two years before him, and not Ṣemaḥ b. Solomon.

It must be assumed that the title Gaon has erroneously crept in in connection with Ṣemaḥ b. Solomon owing to his namesakes, the Geonim Ṣemaḥ b. Ḥayyim of Sura and Ṣemaḥ b. Palṭoi of Pumbedita. On the other hand 'Amram refers in several of his responsa to a Ṣemaḥ Ab-Bet-Din (cp. the headings of the responsa in ed. Lyck, No. 56, *Geonica*, II, 326, Seder R. 'Amram, beginning, and Mann, *JQR*, *N. S.*, XI, 446, note 9). Of course it is possible that there were at the same time a Ṣemaḥ b. Solomon דיינא דבבא of the Exilarch and a Ṣemaḥ Ab-Bet-Din (=דיינא דבבא) of the Sura School. But it is more likely that, owing to the strong influence of the Exilarchate on the Sura school and owing to the prestige of Ṣemaḥ b. Solomon, there was such an arrangement that the chief judge of the Exilarch's court was also the chief judge of the court of the Sura school, or that 'Amram had to mention Ṣemaḥ in the responsa issued by his school. Who knows whether, during his conflict with Naṭronai as rival Gaon (see Sherira's Letter, ed. Lewin, p. 115), 'Amram was not aided by Ṣemaḥ b. Solomon with the consent of the Exilarch and hence such an agreement was reached upon? Or we may argue the opposite way that Naṭronai had the Exilarch's support whereas 'Amram was joined by Ṣemaḥ b. Solomon, the latter relinquishing his office of chief judge of the Exilarch's court and becoming instead Ab-Bet-Din of 'Amram's rival school. Be this as it may, there is reason to identify Ṣemaḥ b. Solomon with Ṣemaḥ Ab mentioned by 'Amram (against Ginzberg's objections, *Geon.*, II, 303, note 2). At any rate Ginzberg's solution that the latter is identical with Ṣemaḥ b. Ḥayyim, the later Sura Gaon, is certainly unlikely because if he was already Ab under 'Amram, he would have naturally succeeded him as Gaon and not have first made way for his half-brother Naḥshon. It is more natural to explain the situation in the Sura school that Ṣemaḥ b. Solomon, the Ab, died before 'Amram whereupon Naḥshon

that their predecessors, like Natan b. Ḥananyah and others, never adopted such a procedure and warns them that if such a case would recur, they would receive an answer from neither school. The responsum reveals the fact that there was no interchange of opinions between the schools and that the contents of responsa sent out from Sura were unknown to Pumbedita and vice versa. We also learn that the distance between the two places was about 28 parasangs.[4] The Ḳaraite author deserves our thanks for having preserved this responsum that furnishes interesting information concerning the mutual relations of the schools and their connections with the Ḳairwān community and finally affords us a glimpse into the personality of the Gaon R. Naḥshon.

(דף ו׳, ע״א, שורה ט׳)

ולקד צג מן דאלך נחשון ראס אלמתיבה צגיגא עטימא וכאן מן
צאלחי אלדיאנין וממן לא יסתחל אן יתזיד ענד מא סאלוה מן אלקירואן
ען נכסי מלוג וקאלו לה אנא קד כנא סאלנא לצמח ראס אלמתיבה ומתתיה
ראס אלמתיבה ען רגל באעת אמראתה עקאר ורתתה בלא אמר זוגהא
ומאתת וגאא אלזוג יטאלב באלעקאר ויקול הו לי [וקאלו לה]
אן יסתרגע אלעקאר [ויררד] מא אכדת אמראתה ללמשתרי וסאלנא

advanced to the office of Ab and succeeded ʻAmram as Gaon. Under Naḥshon his half-brother Ṣemaḥ b. Ḥayyim served as Ab and in his turn succeeded Naḥshon as Gaon.

Hilai Gaon mentioned above was probably Hilai b. Naṭronai who succeeded Hai b. Naḥshon. Had one of the earlier Sura Geonim, Hilai b. Mari or Hilai b. Ḥananyah, given an opinion on this subject, his view would have probably been mentioned in our responsum of Naḥshon.

About the views of Samuel b. Ḥofni and Hai, cp. שערי צדק, 79b, No. 9, and 82a-b, No. 20, and for that of Meshullam b. Kalonymos, see Ginzberg, גנזי שעכטער, II, 219.

[4] Cp. also Obermeyer, *Die Landschaft Babylonien*, 250, and Assaf, קרית ספר, VII, 62.

למר̇ ר̇ עמרם פקאל לה אן יסתרג̇ע אלעקאר ולא ירו[ד] אלת̇מן וענדנא דיאנין קד חכמו באן ליס לה אן יסתרד אלעקאר חתי יכ̇ד̇ מא אכ̇ד̇תה אמראתה פערפנא אנת מא ענדך פי ד̇לך פכתב להם מא אנא ד̇אכרה וששאלתם אתתא דזבנית נכסי מלוג בחיי בעלה ופרישתון שדר מר̇ צמח בדמים ושדר̇ מר̇ מתתיהו[1] בלא דמים ואית גבן רבנן דאמרין בדמים ומתרצין כי אמור רבנן[2] אהו[3] דאפסיד נפשיה דלא איבעי ליה למזבן מן אנתתא דיתבי תחות גברא ולאו לגמרי (ע"ב) אפסיד נפשיה אילא ל[ענין שיהא] מקחו מקח טעות ולעולם בדמים: אנן השתא כמאן נעביו[ד כ]מר̇ עמרם דאמר בלא דמים או דלמ̇[3a] כמר̇ צמח וכמר̇ [מתתיה דאמרי] בדמים[4]. הכין חזינא דלא לנ[יכת]ב לכון בהדא שאילתא [שום מידע]ם ואנתון גופיכון שלא כדין ולא כשורה קא [עבדיתון דעברתון על] בלא[5] דרבנן דא[מרי[6] נשאל]

1 צריך להוסיף: „בדמים ושדר מר̇ עמרם" (וכן ברור מתרגום הערבי למעלה, שורה 11 ושורה 15, וגם מע"ב, שורה 2—3).

2 עיין בבבא בתרא, קל"ט, ע"ב.

3 צ"ל: „איהו". 3a=דלמא.

4 שאלה זו נזכרת בתה"ג שערי צדק (דף ס"ט, ע"א, סי' ע"א) באופן מקוצר: „הא דאמור רבנן נכסי מלוג בחיי בעלה ומתה הבעל מוציא מיד הלקוחות שדר רב צמח גאון בדמים ושדר רב מתתיה בדמים ואשכחן בשאלתות רב עמרם גאון בלא דמים ואית גבן דאמרי בדמים אנן השתא כמאי (צ"ל: כמאן) נעביד". כל התשובה המענינת של רב נחשון גאון שלפנינו חסרה שם ונמצאה רק ההכרעה שלו: „מסתברא בדמים" (וצ"ל: „בלא דמים"). ועיין ר"י מיללער, מפתח לתה"ג, צד 44, הערה ט"ו לסי' רס"ו, אבל השערתו לאחד תשובת רה"ג (תה"ג, הוצ' הרכבי, סי' רס"ו) עם זו שלפנינו אי־נכונה עתה אחרי שידענו שהיא לר' נחשון.

5 צ"ל „מלא".

6 ע"ז ז', ע"א.

לחכם ואסר [לא ישאל לחכם ויתיר נשאל לחכם וטימא לא] ישאל
לחכם ויטהר [ואי האכי למן נגנ]ה למר עמרם או למר צמח
ולמֹ מתתיה האיי [עובדא בישת]א הוא דקא עבדתון שלימו להי[7]
שאלאתכון דבעיתון למשאל הדא שאילתא מן ארבעה גאונים
ועוד קא בעיתון למשרא[8] מחלוקת ביני ישראל דלא סלקא מן אתריכון
לעולם: אנחנא כחד מנהון כתבינא לכון כד מאטיא שאילתא[9]
תמן תיבע[10] אומֹ כגאון פלוני דמקבילנא. ותיבע אומֹ כאידך גאון
מאי[11] [מקבילנא והויא] מינה לא[12] סָלִיק דינא לעולם מי מכריע ואו אית
רבנן גביכו[ון] אומרין בדמים ומתרצין הכין הני מתיבתא
למא לכון לפסקון שאילאתא רבנן דתמן. ודקא כתביתון
שאילאתא לקדמנא ולמתיבתא דפום ואיכא בין דילנא לדילהון
קרוב לכהֹ פרסי לא ידענא מאי כתבין ולא אינן[13] ידעין מאי
כתיבננא סוף סוף סברא דליבא הוא אית מדי[14] דאנחנא חזיננא
חד אנפא ואינון חאזין חד אנפא לא האוי חלול השם תמן דאמריתון
קא פלגין על הדאדי רֹ נתן בר רֹ חנניה[15] ניחא נפשו בעדן ורבנן קדימי
דילכון דהות כונתן לשמים לא עבדו מעולם הכין דכי הידנא[16] לז

7 הלשון מגומגם פה כפי הנראה ע"י טעותו של המעתיק הקראי.
8 צ"ל: לְמַשְׁרֵי (בנין אפעל).
9 היינו תשובתנו על השאלה.
10 צ"ל: „תובע" אומר . . . „ותובע" אומר.
11 צ"ל: „קא".
12 צ"ל: „דלא".
13 בכ"י „אינ̊ין" וישנו תקון על הגליון „אנין".
14 צ"ל: „מידי".
15 אודות הרב הזה בקירואן, שהיה בקשר מכתבים עם רב נטרונאי גאון סורא ועם גאוני בבל אחרים, עיין פוזנאנסקי, אנשי קירואן, סי' כ"ג ול"ט, והשוה למעלה, צד 64, הערה 4.
16 =האידנא.

(דף ז', ע"א)

שני דהות כתבין שאילתא או כ[להון] לקדמננא או כלהון לפום או מקצת
לקדמנא ומקצת לפום אבל [למכתיב חדא] נוסחא בשאילה מן תרתין
מתיבתא לא עבדו הכין לע[ו]לם ולא מיכשר מ[ן] שמיא למעבד כמעשה
ב[ת]למאי המלך[17]: השתא נמי אי [לאו רבנא ש]למה בר רבנא יצחק
ו[רבנא] משה הכהן בן רבנא אהרן[18] דמבעו מינ[נ]א דאמרו דחדא
זימנא בלחו[ד] הוא דהויא] . . . . הכין לא הוה
כתבינא יתהון[19] [והשתא נמי] קא מתרינא בכ[ו]ן דאי[ן] שאילתון חד נוסחא
מן קדמנא ומן פום לא מיכתיב לכון שם[20] מד[ו]עם ב[ע]למא לא מן פום
ולא מן קדמנא[21]: שהמלך ברחמיו יזכיכם ללמוד וללמד ולשמור
ולעשות ולהבין בתלמוד ולדין דין אמת לאמתו: ותפסיר דׄאלך
הו אנה קאל קד ראינא אן לא נגׄיבכם ען האדׄה אלמסלהׄ בשַׁיְא אצלא
לאנכם מא עמלתם באלחק ואלאסתקאמהׄ וכׄאלפתם אלרבנין פי קולהם

17 עיין מגלה ט', ע"א: „מעשה בתלמי המלך שכינס ע"ב זקנים והכניסן בע"ב בתים ולא גילה להם על מה כינסן ונכנס אצל כל אחד ואמר להם כתבו לי תורת משה רבכם וכו'". מסגנון הספור כנראה הוציא רב נחשון כעין בקורת על מעשה תלמאי שעשה שלא כהוגן לשאול אותו הדבר לחכמים שונים. אז אירע נס ש„נתן הקב"ה בלב כל אחד ואחד עצה והסכימו כולן לדעת אחת", אבל לאו בכל יומא מתרחיש ניסא ולא יכשר לעשות דבר כזה.

18 אי אפשר להחליט אם שני החכמים האלה, ר' שלמה בר ר' יצחק ור' משה הכהן בר ר' אהרן, גרו בקירואן וכתבו לרב נחשון בבקשה להשיב על השאלה או שהיו מחכמי ישיבת סורא והשפיעו על הגאון למחול לחכמי קירואן מפני שעשו ככה רק פעם אחת בלבד.

19 צ"ל „יתכון".

20 צ"ל: „שום".

21 עקר התשובה חסר פה וכבר ראינו למעלה (הערה 4) שרב נחשון פסק שלא בדמים. מן „שהמלך ברחמיו" הוא הסגנון הרגיל בסוף תשובות הגאונים.

אד̇א סאל אלאנסאן לחָכָם ען שְׁיִא וחט̇רה עליה לא יסאל חכם אאכ̇ר

ויביחה ד̇אלך ואן הו סאלה ען שְׁיִא פנג̇סה לא יסאל אאכ̇ר ויטהרה פאד̇

הכד̇א פנחנן למן נְגָהִל למר̇ עמרם או למר̇ צמח ומר̇ מתתיה

האד̇א ד̇נב עט̇ים קד פעלתמוה פי מסלתכם ען שאילה לארבעה

רווס מת̇איב וקד אכ̇ד̇תם איקאע[22] אלאנקסאם פי ישראל ומא לא יזול

אלי אלאבד ונחן פאן כתבנא אליכם פי האד̇א שיאא פאנמא הו מת̇ל

ואחד ממן כתב אליכם ואד̇א מצ̇י אגוא̇[23] אליכם פאלמטאלב יקול לא

אעמל אלא בקול הד̇ה אלגהה̈ ואלמטאלב יקול לא אעמל אלא בקול

האד̇א אלגהה̈ ועלי האד̇א לא יכ̇רג̇ אלחכם אלי אלאבד ואד̇א כאן

(ע"ב)

ענדכם ראבנין קד קאלו אן [להדא אלרג̇ל יס]תרג̇ע אלעקאר באלת̇מן אלד̇י

אכ̇ד̇תה אמראתה למא לכם . . . . מת̇איב יקטעון שאילתכם.

ומכאתבתכם לנא ול[למת̇יבה̈ פום ובי]ננא ובינהם מסירה̈ ח̇ וכ̇ פרסכא

והם לא יערפון מא [נג̇יב לכם ולא נח]ן נערף מא יג̇יבוכם לאנה . .

אלקלב פנחנן נט̇[ר] . . . . . דון מן וג̇ה . . . .

ענד ורו . . . . כאן פי מא תקדם

ענד מא כאן ר̇ נ[תן נ̇נ̇[24] ו]רבאנין אלקדמא קבלכם וכאנו יקצדון במא

22 צ"ל: „אוקאע". 23 =אגואב.
24 =נוחו נפש או צריך להשלים „נ"ע"=נוחו עדן.

יסאלון ענה מא . . . לה מא עמלו מתֹל מא עמלתם קט ואערף
מנד

לוֹ[25] סנה אנהם כאנו יכתבון שאילאת אמא גֹמיעהא אלינא או
גֹמיעהא

[10] אלי מתֹיבהֹ פום או בעצֹהא אלינא ובעצֹהא אלי מתֹיבהֹ פום
פֹאמא נסכהֹ

ואחדהֹ אלי אלמתֹיבתין פֹאנהם מא עמלו הכדֹא קט ולא יחל מן
אלסמאא

אן יעמל כמא עמל תלמאי המלך ולולא שלמה ומשה אנהם טלבו
אן יכתב אליכם האדה אלרקעהֹ לם נכאתבכם ואלאן פהודֹא
נתרי[26]

בכם פֹאן אנתם סאלתם ען מסאלהֹ ואחדהֹ ללמתֹבתין לם נגֹיבכם
לא

[15] נחן ולא מתֹיבהֹ פום ֹאצל. פֹמא דֹכרנאה מן קול מר נחשון מן
אדֹל דליל

עלי בטלאן קול מן זעם אן גֹמיע מא יחכמון בה אלרבאנין פהו
מנזל

מן אלסמא אדֹ קד פצח באנהם מסתדלין ואנה סיברא דֹליבא הוא
ואן אלרבא[27] נהו אן יסתפתי רגֹל לעאלמין לקול נשאל לחכם
ואסר

לא ישאל לחכם ויתיר נשאל לחכם וטמא לא ישאל לחכם ויטהר:

[20] ואדֹ אלאמר הכדֹא פקד צֹח אן חאל אלרבאנין
ואלקראיין ואלעאניהֹ חאל

ואחדה ואן אלגֹמאעהֹ פי וקתנא האדֹא פי אכתֹר אלאמור אכלֹו
(דף ח', ע"א)

מראתבהם מן טריק אלאסתדלאל לא מן [וטריק] אלנקל.

25 בתשובה (למעלה, דף ו', ע"ב, שורה 21) המספר הוא ל"ז.
26 מלה זו לקוחה מן ארמית „אתרי".
27 =אלרבאנין.

3.

A PORTION OF SHERIRA GAON'S COMMENTARY TO BABA BATRA

The commentary of Sherira Gaon to Baba Batra, viz. to the first 3 chapters, was hitherto only known from citations in other sources. These citations have been collected by J. N. Epstein (*REJ*, LXIV, 210–14). Only quite recently have the Genizah fragments yielded portions of the actual commentary. Assaf (תה"ג מתוך ה„גניזה", 1928, pp. 195–207) has edited a section covering the comments on B. B., fols. 22–27, from a MS. Firkowicz in Leningrad. It very likely emanates from the Fusṭāṭ Genizah as Firkowicz must have obtained from this source many fragments (cp. Steinschneider, *Arab. Liter. d. Juden*, XXVII).

The fragment edited here from a Genizah MS., originally in the possession of Dr. L. Blau of Budapest and now belonging to the Library of the Hebrew Union College in Cincinnati, covers the comments on B. B., fols. 14–17. There is little doubt that the Leningrad MS. constitutes the continuation of our fragment.

Besides its intrinsic value as emanating from Sherira and as offering textual variants of the Talmudic text, the commentary contains also valuable allusions to other Geonim and members of the schools (see, e.g., note 5 to the text). Let us hope that more portions of the commentary will come to light with the progress of making the Genizah fragments accessible to the student.

[מכ"י הגניזה במוסד Hebrew Union College, שני דפים קרועים של נייר].

(דף א', ע"א)

עורות איקרו קנלף] . . . . הכין אהדריה רב גידל[1]
ששה שכיון שנעב הוא] הוי הקיפו כארכו. ובקלף

1 צ"ל: בגויל. ב"ב, י"ד, ע"א, למעלה. בנוסח הדפוס: שאלו את רבי, אבל נוסחת רש"ג כנראה היתה: שאלו את רב. אמנם בהלכות ס"ת שפרסם אדלר (גנזי מצרים, צד 14, 16, 20) הנוסחא היא ג"כ „רבי".

איני [יודע] דכיון] דקליש לא ידעינן כמה אתי הקיפו כיון דבעינן למהוה הקיפו כארכו לא ידעינן כמה [נ]שוייה לארכו ואנחנא לא חזי לנא מעולם ספר תורה דקלף ולאו מצוה מן המובחר למעבדיה ורקי[1a] שהוא חיפא הכשירו מר רב משה נא׳[2] גאון מחסייה ולא הודו לו חכמי דורו כמות מה[3] רב יוסף גאון בר מר רב רבי בן דודנו[4] נוחם עדן אף חכמי ישיבתו כמו מר רב נחשון גאון ז״ל ואף אשר אחריהם.[5]

ארבעה מיתו בעיטו שלנחש[6] שלא היה להם חט[א ולא] מתו אלא בההיא גזרה דנחשא . . . . . ני ומפרשא בכמה בהמה[7] ושמעינן [מינה] דיש מיתה בלא חטא ופירוש עיטו

(דף א׳, ע״ב)

מלשון עט שיכתבו [על אדם] בעט מיתה מגזירת נחש[8]. פרק בֿ לא [יחפור].

[1a] „רק״ בערבית, קלף דק.

[2] צ״ל: נ״ע=נוחו עדן. [3] צ״ל: מר.

[4] עיין אגרת רש״ג (הוצ׳ לוין, נוסח צרפתי צד 112): ואחתיה על מרב יוסף בר מרב רבי . . . ובן דודנו הוה בר בריה דמרב אבה גאון זקנינו.

[5] פסקא זו נזכרת ג״כ בשם רש״ג באשכול, הלכות ס״ת (ח״ב, צד 37). הנוסחא שם משובשת מאד ויש לתקנה ע״פ פרוש רש״ג שלפנינו.

רש״ג מזכיר פה את רב נחשון, גאון סורא, ובכן כל הפלפול של ר״ל גינצברג (גנזי שעכטער, ח״ב, צד 530) נופל מאליו. רואים אנו אפוא שחכמי ישיבת סורא בזמנו של רב נחשון ואחרי כן אסרו ג״כ ספר תורה שנעשה מחיפא (רק בערבית). השוה ג״כ פרוש רב מתתיה גאון ב„גנזי מצרים״, צד 14.

[6] ב״ב, י״ז, ע״א, סוף פ״א.

[7] שבת נ״ה, ע״ב, למעלה.

[8] פירוש זה מזכיר בשם רש״ג ר׳ יהודה אבן גֿנאח (ספר השרשים, הוצ׳ באכער, צד 364, ערך „עט״): ופרש בו רבינו שרירא ז״ל בקלמוסו שנכתב בו המות על בני אדם (השוה ג״כ אפשטין בהריוי הצרפתית, כרך ס״ד, צד 212).

עיין ג״כ בערוך ערך „עט״: ד׳ מתו בעוטיו של נחש פי׳ קולמסו שנכתב בו המות כמו עט סופר; פירוש אחר בעצתו. הפירוש הראשון בלתי ספק לקוח מפירושו של רש״ג, ובודאי באמצעותו של פי׳ ר״ח לב״ב (וכבר העיר אסף, תה״ג מתוך ה„גניזה״, צד 196, שר״ח השתמש בפירוש רש״ג). אמנם בפי׳ ר״ח לשבת אין שום פירוש למאמר זה.

פ׳ תח בבור וסיים ב[כות]ל[9]. כיון ששנה בראשה לא יחפור אדם בור סמוך לבורו [של] חבירו היה ראוי לסיים אלא אם כן הר[חיק] מבורו ומדוע שנה מכותלו אמ̇ אביי ואיתימא רב יהודה שכך תירוץ המשנה אלא אם כן הרחיק מכותל בורו שלחבירו שנמצא מרחיק בור מבור ששה טפח̇[10] שלשה לכותל זו ושלשה לכותל זה ולמדנו ממנו בעסק מקח וממכר שכותל [אח]ד שלשה טפח̇ ובהיות שתי שדות סמוכות זו לזו אחת לראובן ואחת לשמעון ומצר מפסיק ביניהן ואין ביניהן כותל ובקש ראובן לחפור בור בתוך שלו בצד המצר מבלי להו[רחיק] ממנו שלשה טפח̇ נאמרו בה שני לשונות מ. . . . . אם[*10] יחפור בצד המצר אם יבקש שכנו לח[פור] . . .

(דף ב׳, ע״א)

והכין איצטריכינין לעיוני בה דקא מהדרינן לאותוביה לאביי ו . . . ה פשיטא הילכתא כרבא הא סוגיין בעלמא [כ]ואתיה ומאי אית לן לאותובי׳ לאביי ר׳ יהודה או̇מ סלע הבא בידים ופריק אביי מאי דפרישניה ולא שמעינן משם גאון דילן נ̇ע̇ כמאן עבדינן. ואית מן רבנן[11] דסלקא אדעתיהון דהילכתא כאביי. מיגו דאיתקשו ליה ופריק ואיתקשו לרבא ובטילו פירוקיה אלא מיהו הא כבר פרישנן דאף על גב דדחיאתיה בטילן לא הויא תיובתיה והכי סבירא לן דכיון דלא

9 ב״ב י״ז, ע״ב, למעלה.

10 =טפחים.

*10 קריאת מלה זו היא בספק.

11 היינו רבנן של ישיבת פומבדיתא. בעטור (דפוס לבוב, ח״א, נ״ג, ע״ב) הנוסחא משובשת ויש לתקנה ע״פ הכ״י שלפנינו.

. . . ה ולא על אביי תיובתא עבדינן כרבא ולא
שבקינן ליה לחפור בצד המצר חדא דאמ̇רינן[12]
דאהדרינן לכללא[13] דהילכתא כרבא ועוד טובא
. . . . טעמיה דקא מרעי ליה לארעא.
. . . . [מ]שום דדלמא מצטריך אחרינא למיחפר
. . . . . . א דמנעינן ליה דאילו בההיא ליכא

(דף ב׳, ע״ב)

גירא ולא אפילו גראמא דשכיח והילכ̇[14] כר̇ יוסי דאמ̇[15] זה חופר בתוך שלו [וזה נ]וטע בתוך שלו אלא משום גיריה דשכיח בההוא עידאנא מן ארפיתא דארעא ובהא מילתא לר̇ יוסי וכל שכן לרבנן הזק גדול וגירא היא והכין סלקא.

ובריכת הכובסין[15a] נקראת בלשון ישמעאלי תגאר אלקצארין[16] תנן ועושין נברכת במועד ואמרינן[17] מאי נברכת אמ̇ רב זה הבקיע וזה[18] תניא הנברכת זה[19] בקיע אמ̇ אביי ואי תימא רב כהנא גיהאה ובר גיהאה והן הן המחמצן והמְנַדְנַן[20] המחמצן גיהאה מרחיקו ג̇ טפח̇ ששורין בו [את] הבגדים והמחמצין[21] אותן והמנדון דהא בר גיהאה מרחיקו ד̇ אמות שבו מכבסין ומנפצין את הבגדים ואזלו ניצוצות על הכותל דמיא

12 הנקודות מורות שצריך למחוק מלה זו.
13 היינו הכלל שאביי ורבא הלכה כרבא חוץ מיע״ל קג״ם (עיין ב״מ, כ״ב, ע״ב, וש״נ).
14 =והילכתא.
15 =דאמר, שם, י״ח, ע״ב.
15a שם י״ט, ע״א, למעלה. נוסחת הדפוס: נברכת הכובסין.
16 تغار القصارين, The boiler of the laundrymen.
17 מועד קטן, ח׳, ע״ב, והנוסחא שם: אמר רב יהודה זו בקיע.
18 צ״ל: והא.
19 צ״ל: והבקיע.
20 בב״ב הנוסחא: הנדיין, ועיין בערוך, ערך „בקע״.
21 צ״ל: ומחמצין.

ונאדו על אשיאתו וכיון שנותזין ני[צו]צות דמיא] על הכותל צריך להרחיק ד׳ אמות . . . .

[ההמשך של פירושנו מב״ב, כ״ב ב׳ והלאה, בכ״י אחר נתפרסם ע״י מר ש. אסף, תשובות הגאונים מתוך ה„גניזה״, צד 196—207].

4.

קטעים חדשים מפירושו של רב האיי גאון למסכת ברכות.

הפירוש החשוב הזה של הגאון הגדול הזה הולך ונתפרסם לפנינו יותר ויותר לרגלי חקירת כ"י ה„גניזה" המפוזרים ההולכת ומתקדמת. לפני שמונה שנים פרסמתי ב„הצופה לחכמת ישראל" (שנה ו', 1922, צד 187—204) שני קטעים גדולים שמצאתי בקבוצת הגניזה הגדולה אשר בקמברידזי[1]. באותו הזמן פרסם הד"ר לוין ב„גנזי קדם" שלו (ח"א, צד 11—14, 19—25, 49—64) ג' קטעים אחרים מהפירוש הזה (ואחד מהם היה מקביל בקצתו למה שנדפס על ידי), וחזר להוציא לאור קטעים חדשים ב„גנזי קדם", ח"ב (צד 21—26). כל הקטעים האלה נקבצו עתה ב„אוצר הגאונים" שלו (כרך א': מסכת ברכות, תרפ"ח).

אמנם כדאי היה לקבוע שם (בחלק הפירושים) מקום מיוחד לפירושו של רה"ג ולא לפזר אותו בין שאר הפירושים הנובעים מגאונים אחרים. לכל הפחות כדאי היה לבחור בסדר זה בנוגע לקטעים שנמצאו בגניזה מפני שהם נותנים לנו הסגנון כמו שיצא מידי הגאון בעצמו. הצִיטָטִים הרבים מפירוש הגאון שמביא, למשל, הרשב"א בפירושו לברכות, וכמו"כ המחברים האחרים, לקוים מצד זה שנותנים לנו ברובם רק תוכן דברי רה"ג או „תורף פירוש הגאון" (כמו שזהיר הרשב"א לפעמים להזכיר בפירוש) ולא הדברים כלשונם וסגנונם. מפני כמה טעמים מדעיים (למשל מצד האורטוגרפיה, נוסחאות התלמוד וכו') חביבים עלינו עתה

1 וחבל שכמה טעיות הדפוס עלו במאמרי זה מפני שלא נשלחו לי גליוני־ההגהה, וגם התקונים ששלחתי אח"כ למערכת „הצופה" לא נדפסו מפני איזו סבה אי־ידועה לי.

דברי הגאונים דוקא בשלמותם ובאופן כתיבתם בלי הקצור והקטוע שנהגו בהם המחברים המאוחרים להם.

זה מקרוב הוציא לאור הרב ש. אסף קטע חדש מכ"י הרכבי בלֶנינגרַד („תשובות הגאונים מתוך הגניזה", תרפ"ט, צד 207—210, והשוה להלן צד 12). בקיץ של שנת 1928 מצאתי ג' קטעים חדשים בקמברידז וגם בקבוצת הגניזה אשר תחת רשותו של מר יעקב מוֹסֶרִי בקהיר, מצרים, אשר אני מציע בזה לפני הקוראים. כל הקטעים האלה, שנובעים מכ"י שונים ומקבילים במקצת זה לזה, מראים שפירושו של רה"ג היה מפורסם במצרים בימי הבינים ושרבים השתמשו בו, ומפני זה הרבו הסופרים להעתיק אותו בכמה אכסמפלרים. גם במרכזים היהודים אשר לאורך חוף אפריקא הצפונית ובספרד השתמשו הלמדנים בו, והיה ידוע ג"כ לר' נתן בעל „הערוך" ברומי. רק לצרפת ולגרמניה כנראה לא חדרה ההשתמשות בפירושו של הגאון, ומפעלו הכביר של רש"י בפרשנות התלמוד גרם ג"כ שהפירוש שלפנינו נאבד ברוב הימים.

לע"ע יש לנו הקטעים האלה מהגניזה:

1) לברכות, דף ב', ע"א („אוצר הגאונים", ח' הפירושים, צד 2; סגנון הקטע מורה שהוא חלק מן הפירוש, אע"פ שהמו"ל מסופק בדבר).

2) לדף ה', ע"ב (שם, צד 7—8, כמו שהעיר המו"ל בצדק).

3) לדף י"ד, ע"ב—ט"ז, ע"ב (שם, צד 15—22).

4) לדף כ"ד, ע"ב (שם, צד 31).

5) לדף כ"ו, ע"ב (שם, צד 33—34).

6) לדף ל', ע"א—ל"ב, ע"א (שם, צד 41—47).

7) לדף ל"ד, ע"א—ל"ה, ע"א (שם, צד 48—49).

8) לדף מ"ו, ע"א (קטע א', להלן, צד 583—587).

9) לדף נ"ו, ע"ב—ס"ג, ע"א, למטה (קטע ב' וג' להלן בצרוף עם מה שנדפס מקודם, השוה ביחוד להלן, צד 590).

ויש להוסיף לזה כל התשובות של רש"ג ורה"ג לברכות שנכתבו קודם חבור הפירוש שבודאי נספחו לתוכו כמו שנראה להלן.

והנה אודות אופן חבור הפירוש ישנן שלש שאלות שדורשות פתרון: 1) מתי נכתב, אם בעת היות רב האיי כבר גאון ישיבת פומבדיתא—בגדאד או מקודם בעת שהיה עוד אב"ד משנת 885 לספה"נ ועד 1004 כשנתמנה לגאון שנתים לפני פטירת אביו רש"ג בשנת 1006[2]. 2) אם התשובות של רה"ג לכמה פסקאות בברכות שמקבילות לפירושו, כפי שנמצא לפנינו, נכתבו מקודם ונספחו לתוך הפירוש או שאחרי חבור הפירוש שאב הגאון ממנו כדי להשיב על השאלות אודות פסקאות ידועות במסכתא זו. 3) מדוע הפירוש אינו משתרע בשלמות על כל המסכתא; כמה פעמים ישנו הפסק גדול בין סוגיא לסוגיא המבוארות בפירוש, וישנה ג"כ אריכות בפירוש איזה פסקאות ולאידך גיסא קצור גמור בפירוש ענינים אחרים.

פתרון שאלה ב' כנראה יתן לנו האפשרות לתרץ לכל הפחות שאלה ג' גם כן. ישנה קבוצה שלמה של תשובות לקירואן בשנת אלף ש"ג (לשטרות=992 לספה"נ), שיצאה מתחת ידי רש"ג ושבודאי השתתף בכתיבתה רב האיי בנו בתור אב"ד („תשובות הגאונים", הוצ' הרכבי, סי' שע"ב—תי"ח), אשר ממנה מצאו מקום בפירוש שלפנינו סי' שצ"ד, שצ"ז, ת"א ות"ח (עין להלן, הערות 17, 115, 128, 138). רק סי' ת"ז חסר בפירושנו, אבל בעצם הדבר המלה מפורשת שם באותו מובן כמו בתשובה זו (עין להלן, הערה 113). ובלתי ספק הוא ששאר התשובות מקבוצה זו אודות ענינים במסכת ברכות נלקחו לתוך חלקי הפירוש החסרים עוד, והיינו סי' שע"ט, שצ"א—שצ"ג, שצ"ה—שצ"ו, שצ"ח—ת', ת"ב—ת"ו, ת"ט—תי"ד. מפני שקבוצה זו יצאה מתחת ידי רש"ג מובן מאליו שרב האיי שאב ממנה בעת חבור הפירוש ולא להיפך שרש"ג השתמש בפירוש

2 אודות קביעת התאריך של פטירת רש"ג בתשרי אשי"ח לשטרות (=1006 לספה"נ) עיין למעלה, צד 109.

בנו כדי להשיב על השאלות שבאו מקירואן בשנת 992 לספה"נ. כמו"כ אודות ענין רב ספרא (ברכות דף ס"ב, ע"ב, למעלה) ישנה תשובה מרש"ג ובנו רב האיי אב"ד שתמציתה נלקחה אח"כ לתוך הפירוש שלפנינו (עין להלן, הערה 127). גם יש לקבל כודאי שהתשובה המענינת בנוגע לזועות (ברכות נ"ט, ע"א) מצאה מקום אח"כ בשלמותה בפירוש (השוה „אוצר הגאונים", ח' התשובות, צד 130—132, וח' הפירושים, צד 91—94).

לאידך גיסא ישנן תשובות מרה"ג שלא מצאו מקום בפירושו, למשל בנוגע לד' אמות של תפלה (שם, ח' התשובות צד 74, והשוה ח' הפירושים, צד 44), ובנוגע לרב ששת ורב חסדא (שם, ח' התשובות, צד 72, והשוה ח' הפירושים צד 41). אבל עובדא זו יש לפרש בנקל, והיינו שהתשובות האלה נכתבו אחרי גמר הפירוש, ובאמת רה"ג רומז לפירושו זה באיזו מתשובותיו (שם, ח' התשובות, צד 50, וצד 141).

ובכלל נראים הדברים שבאיזה זמן הגיע רב האיי לידי הרעיון, ואולי ע"י דרישת אחד השואלים, לקבץ את כל התשובות של אביו ושלו (ובכמה מהן השתתפו האב והבן ביחד) אודות פסקאות בברכות ולעשות מהן פירוש מיוחד למסכתא זו. אפשר להכיר מכמה מבטאים שנמצאו בפירושנו שבתחלה הדברים היו מכונים לשואלים שהתקשו בפירוש פסקא זו או אחרת. למשל בקטע שפרסמתי ב„הצופה לחכמת ישראל" (=שם, ח' הפירושים, צד 41): ומאי איכא בין הבינונו לתפלה קצרה פ ש י ט א (היינו שאיננו זקוק לפירוש), או (שם, צד 43): וכל ההלכות שנאמרו אחר כך נכוחות ואין בהן קושיא לפרשהו; וכמו"כ (שם, צד 45, למעלה): כל אילו ההלכות נכוחות ונבונות אין בדבריהם צורך לפירוש, ושאר דראשי יש בהן נכוחים ויש בהן הגדות רחוקות... ואית בהו מילי שאנו מזכירין ברמז ואמרום גאונים[3]

3 מזה שמזכיר פה „גאונים שלפנינו" אין להוציא אפוא המסקנא שרה"ג כתב את הדברים האלה בעת היותו כבר גאון מפני שאין אנו יודעים מתי נכתבה התשובה שנספחה כאן לתוך

שלפנינו... הכין פרישו רבנן אילין ואף את (היינו אתה השואל) פריש כל שכיוצא בהם כסדר הזה וכדרך הזאת; וכמו"כ (שם, צד 49, למעלה): כל ההלכות הללו.. דלית בהי ספיקא ולא צריכין פירושי. סגנון כזה של משיב לשואל יש לנו בקטע ג' (להלן, צד 594): ודילמא אית אנפא אחרינא דמן שמיא ידעין ליה ואנן לא ידעינן ליה... ואף כבד אין אנו יודעין בו דרך הכעס. גם סגנון הפירוש של פסקא בנוגע ל„זועות" הוא כזה של משיב לשואל, וכבר העירונו למעלה שהתשובה אודות הענין הזה קדמה לחבור הפירוש. (השוה עוד להלן, הערה 112[a], בנוגע לסגנון שלקוח מדברי השואל).

עובדא זו שרב האיי קבץ תשובותיו של אביו ושלו לברכות ועשה מהן פירוש מבארת ג"כ יחוס הפירוש הזה לרש"ג (עין מה שהעיר הפרופ' י. נ. אפשטין ב„הצופה לחכמת ישראל", שנה ז', צד 96), וכמו"כ נתיחס לו פירוש רה"ג לשבת וגם פירושו לחגיגה[4]. אמנם נכנסו כמה מתשובות רש"ג לתוך הפירושים האלה, ולוּ נמצאת הקדמת הפירוש לברכות, למשל, יש לשער שרב האיי בודאי הזכיר שם את שמו של אביו הגדול שבפרי תורתו השתמש כל כך ושהשתתף עמו שנים רבות כל כך.

ובזה אנו באים לפתרון השאלה השלישית שהזכרנו למעלה (צד 575). מפני שהפירוש הוא בעקרו קבוץ של התשובות לפסקאות בברכות נשתלשל הדבר שישנם הפסקים בין סוגיא לסוגיא, וישנה אריכות במקום אחד וקצור גמור במקום שני. נבדיק נא את החלק המשתרע מדף נ"ו, ע"ב, ועד ס"ג, ע"א, שנמצא עתה בידינו בשלמות (קטע ב' וג' להלן בצרוף עם מה שנדפס מקודם). הגאון מבאר את המאמר „הרואה גמל בחלום" (ברכות נ"ו, ע"ב, למטה) ופוסח אח"כ לדף נ"ז, ע"ב, למעלה, אודות „ג' חכמים וג'

הפירוש, ואולי נכתבה ע"י רש"ג ביחד עם בנו האב"ד, ובכן רש"ג בתור גאון רומז לגאונים שלפניו.

4 קטעים מהגניזה מפירוש רה"ג לשבת נתפרסמו ע"י לוין, גנזי קדם, ח"א, צד 9–10, וח"ב, צד 44–45.

תלמידים" שמבאר בקצור גמור ש„דוגמה קתני". הוא מבאר ביותר אריכות המאמר „ששה דברים מרפאין את החולה" והפירוש לקוח מתשובת רש"ג כמו שהזכרנו למעלה (צד 2). אח"כ ישנו הפסק גדול עד דף נ"ח, ע"ב, בנוגע ל„זיקין" מפני שכן אירע שלא היו תשובות מאביו וממנו עד אותו המקום. אחרי שהשלים לדון בפירושו על עניני זיקין, זועות ורעמים (דף נ"ח, ע"ב, למטה, ונ"ט, ע"א, למעלה) הוא דן בקיצור גמור על הבריתא בדף נ"ט, ע"ב, למעלה, ופונה להאריך מאוד בפסקא „על הגשמים" (דף נ"ט, ע"ב, וס', ע"א). כל החלק הארוך הזה לקוח בלי ספק מתשובה להשיב קושיות איזה שואל. אח"כ ישנו עוד הפעם הפסק גדול ואין שום פירוש עד דף ס"א, ע"א, פסקא „ויבן ד' אלהים את הצלע". כמו"כ ישנו הפסק בפירוש לדף ס"א, ע"ב, וישנה אריכות לפסקא בעמוד זה למטה אודות „לא יקל אדם וכו'"; וכן בדף ס"ב, ע"א, ישנו הפסק עד שבא הגאון לפרש דברי בן עזאי (דף ס"ב, ע"א, למטה, וע"ב, למעלה) ופה מופיעה עוד הפעם האריכות. וכן באחרונה אחרי ענין דרב ספרא ישנו הפסק עד דף ס"ג, ע"א, פסקא „חותמי ברכות שבמקדש", שמבוארת באריכות.

נתוח החלק הזה של הפירוש, שנמצא עתה בידינו בשלמות, מראה בעליל את אופן חבורו, היינו קבוץ של תשובות שונות שנכתבו בזמנים שונים ולשואלים שונים, ועי"ז נשתלשל הדבר בהכרח שהפירוש לא היה חבור שלם ושטתי ולא נתכון להשתרע על כל המסכתא בהדרגה ממאמר למאמר ומסוגיא לסוגיא, אלא שהסדר היה יותר בתכונה מקרית כפי התשובות שהיו בנמצא על פסקאות שונות בסירוגין ממקום למקום. וכמו כן אירע שאחרי חבור הפירוש, הגאון נשאל להשיב תשובות חדשות על מקומות שנתקשו בהם השואלים שלא נתפרשו בפירוש שלפנינו (כמו שהזכרנו למעלה, צד 576).

אופן החבור כזה יש לשער ג"כ בנוגע לפירושים לשאר המסכתות המיוחסים לרה"ג או לרש"ג.

קשה להחליט מתי התחיל רב האיי בשטה זו לקבץ התשובות השונות של אביו ושלו כדי לחברן לפירושים מיוחדים לאיזו מסכתות. אולי ע"י דרישת איזה שואלים, למשל בין חכמי קירואן, נתנה הדחיפה הזאת כמו שאירע בכמה מחבורי הגאונים. הבה נקוה שע"י התגלות קטעים חדשים תפתר השאלה הזאת בברור.

יש עתה להעיר בקצור על איזה פרטים שאפשר להוציא מתוכן ג' הקטעים שלפנינו. בנוגע לאגדות אנו מוצאים אותה רוח הבקרת שאפשר להכיר משאר דבריו ודברי אביו רש"ג. ישנה ההשתדלות להדגיש שבעלי האגדות לא חשבו כלל שהמקראות, שמביאים בתור סיוע לדבריהם, רמזו לדעותיהם אלא שהשתמשו בהם רק ל„זכרון דברים בעלמא" (להלן, צד 588). כמו"כ רב האיי מביט על כמה אגדות שרק „מילי נינהו ולא מדקדק בהו" (להלן, צד 593 f.)[5]. מדברי הפירוש נשקף ג"כ הרציונליסמוס הממוצע, למשל, בנוגע לרפואות שזוכרים בעלי התלמוד שאין לקבלן כמוסכמות בזמן הזה, ובכן „אין לסמוך עכשיו על אותן רפואות" (להלן, צד 588 f.). פסקא זו נובעת מתשובות רש"ג ומתאימה לדבריו בתשובה מענינת אחרת אודות הרפואות שבגטין (דף ס"ח, ע"ב–ע', ע"ב) שפרסם לוין ב„תחכמוני" (ח"א, בֶּרן 1910, צד 41): ודשאלתון למכתב לכון הנהי אסותא דמי שאחזו קורדיאקוס מן רב ושמואל עד פסקא דמתני' היאך קרייתו. תשובה. צריכין אנן למימר לכון דרבנן לאו אסותא אינון ומילין בעלמא דחזונין בזמניהן וכחד חד קצירא אמרונין ולא דברי מצוה אינון הילכך לא תסמכון על אילין אסותא וליכא דעביד מנהון מידעם אלא בתר דמבדיק וידע בודאי מחמת רופאים בקיאים דההיא מלתא לא מעיקא לה וליכא דליתי נפשיה לידי סכנה. והכין אגמרו יתנא ואמרו לנא אבות וסבי דילנא (היינו: מישיבת פומבדיתא) דלא

[5] עין מה שכתבתי על ענין זה ב„הצופה לחכמת ישראל", ש"ו, צד 188.

למעבד מן אילין אסותא אלא מאי דאיתיה כגון קיבלא דקים ליה לההוא דעביד ליה דלית ביה עקתא.

לאידך גיסא רב האיי מאמין שבעלי התלמוד ידעו איזה לחשים („קיבלי") „ברזי דשמיעין מן מלאכים ומפמליא שלמעלה" (להלן, צד 600) ושלרוחות יש יצר ופה ומנהגים שונים (צד 601). אף שרב האיי התנגד לכמה דברי גוזמא של בעלי המסתורין, כידוע מתשובתו החשובה שנתפרסמה ב„טעם זקנים" לר"א אשכנזי (צד 54 והלאה), עכ"ז לא דחה את תורת המסתורין בשתי ידים והאמין, למשל, בפעולת הקמיעות אלא שמשתדל לצמצם את כח השפעתם, כנראה מדבריו (שם, צד 56): אבל קמיען מומחין לרפואות ולחכמה ולשמירה ולדברים אחרים יש, ורובן תלוין בכותב ויתמחי (צ"ל: ואתמחי) גברא שפיר שכיח ואתמחי קמיעה. הוא האמין ג"כ בדעות אודות מעשה מרכבה ובכתבים של „יורדי מרכבה", כגון היכלות רבתי וכו', שנובעים מן התנאים (שם, וביחוד בתשובתו ב„תשובות הגאונים", דפוס ליק, סי' צ"ט), ובפרט האמין בכוחו הגדול של שם המפורש. כל זה מתאים לשטת הרציונליסמוס הממוצע שאחזו בה רב האיי ואביו רש"ג בהתנגדות להרציונליסמוס הקיצוני שחדר ג"כ לתוך החוג של חכמי הישיבות ושהשפיע, למשל, גם על רב שמואל בן חפני (השוה דברי רה"ג נגדו, שם, סי' צ"ט, צד 32, למטה)[6].

מענין ביחוד הוא הפירוש לברכות ס"ג, ע"א, אודות חתימת הברכות שבמקדש ואודות שאילת שלום בשם. רב האיי מבאר שחתימת הברכה במקדש לפני התקנה היתה: „ברוך אתה יי' עד העולם שאותך ביראה נעבוד". ברכה זו היא רק לדוגמא כי באופן כזה היתה חתימת שאר הברכות כנראה מתענית ט"ז, ע"ב, (אלא ששם נזכרה כבר החתימה במקדש אחרי התקנה, היינו „מן העולם ועד העולם"). מפירושנו יש לראות שנוסחת רב האיי

6 במקום אחר נדון בשלמות על הענין החשוב הזה של הרציונליסמוס והראקציה נגדו משך תקופת הגאונים ושלאחריה.

היתה „עד העולם" כפי נוסחת המשנה שלפנינו בבבלי, ולא „מן העולם" כפי נוסחת המשנה שבירושלמי וכפי נוסחאות כמה כ"י בבבלי (עין „דקדוקי סופרים"). רב האיי אינו מבאר את הטעם של תקנה זו מפני שכבר נמצא במשנה, אף שהיה מענין לדעת את מחשבתו של הגאון כנגד איזה מן המינים מכונת תקנה זו. לאידך גיסא טעמה של תקנת שאילת שלום בשם לא נמצא במשנה ולא בתלמוד, והגאון מבאר באופן מענין מאוד שהתקנה היתה מכונת נגד הנוצרים שהיו רגילים לשאול בשלום בעלי דתם בצורה כזו: „בריך מר לאבא וברא ורוחא קדישא, ואצריכו רבנן למימר „יברכך ד'" למיהוה שם שמים תדיר ביניהון" (היינו בין היהודים, ובפרט בין עם הארץ שביניהם). מזה יש ללמוד שבנוסחת המשנה שלפני רב האיי נכתב „משקלקלו המינין" (ולא „הצדוקים", וכן הוא באמת ברוב כ"י), כי אין לחשוב שרב האיי יִחֵס לצדוקים את האמונה בדוֹגמָה הנוצרית הזאת.

ובאמת אחדים מן המלומדים המודרנים השתדלו לבאר תקנת שאילת שלום בשם באופן כזה שמכונת נגד הנוצרים (עין מאמרו של אברהם הלוי, בית תלמוד, שנה שנייה, צד 62—63, ור"א שווארץ בפירושו „הגיון אריה" לתוספתא ברכות, צד 58—59), וקובעים את תאריך התקנה בזמנה של מרידת בר כוכבא. אבל הפירוש הזה דחוק מאוד כי התקנה הראשונה בנוגע לחתימת הברכות היא בודאי נגד הצדוקים (וכן היא דעת רוב החוקרים נגד דעתו של גיגר שהיא נגד כת הדוסתאים של השומרונים, השוה „קבוצת מאמרים" לר"א גיגר, הוצ' פוזננסקי, צד 123, הערה 3, וצד 403, וגם הר"א שווארץ בעצמו מבאר את התקנה הזאת ככה ב„הגיון אריה", צד 57, הערה קפ"ט). שנוי זה בחתימת הברכה להדגיש עקר האמונה בעוה"ב נגד הצדוקים אירע בסוף זמן בית שני כאשר העיר בצדק הר"א ביכלר (בספרו Priester u. Cultus, צד 176). באותו הזמן נתקנה ג"כ תקנת שאילת שלום בשם כמו שנראה מסגנון המשנה: „משקלקלו הצדוקים (או: המינים) התקינו . .

והתקינו", וגם רה"ג מיחס התקנה השניה לקלקול המינים. אמנם „קלקול הצדוקים" שאמרו „אין עולם אלא אחד" אין לו שייכות לקלקולם שהיה סבת התקנה השניה נגדם. והנה לעהמאן (בהריוי הצרפתית, כרך ל"א, צד 31 והלאה) השתדל באריכות לבאר את טעם התקנה ולא עמד על תכלית הענין. לאידך גיסא בֵּנֶט (בספר Ursprung d. Ṣadoḳäer u. Boëthosäer ,1882, צד 48 והלאה) השתדל בצדק למצוא קשר בין תקנה זו ודעות הצדוקים בנוגע להשגחת הבורא, אלא שבמשך דבריו נסתבך הקשר הזה באופן כזה שאי אפשר להוציא השקפה ברורה ממנו, ובאחרונה מסים (צד 61) שהצדוקים השתמשו בשאילת שלום במבטא „יברכוך טובים" ועי"ז השתדלו מתנגדיהם, הפרושים, להנהיג מחדש המבטא הישן „יברכך ד'". אודות מסקנא זו יש לאמר, כפי הפתגם הידוע, „עקר חסר מן הספר". הענין הוא יותר פשוט. כפי שמודיענו יוסף הכהן (קדמוניות י"ג, ה', סי' ט', והשוה מלחמות, ב' ח', סי' י"ד) כחשו הצדוקים בגזרה הקדומה ואחזו ברעיון שהאדם בעצמו הוא סבת אשרו ואסונו, נגד דעת הפרושים שהאמינו שהכל צפוי מאת השם אף שאינם שוללים לגמרי את הבחירה מצד האדם לעשות את הטוב ואת הרע (מתאים למאמרו הידוע של ר"ע ש„הכל צפוי והרשות נתונה"). דברי יוסף הכהן, שהתקשו בהם חוקרים שונים (עין למשל שירר בספרו הידוע, ח"ב, הוצ' ד', צד 460 והלאה), יש להבין (כמו שהעיר בצדק פרופ' קלוזנר, היסטוריה ישראלית, ח"ב, תרפ"ד, צד 111) שהצדוקים כפרו ב„השגחה פרטית", היינו שהשם אינו מתערב בעניני האדם הפרטי להשפיע עליהם לטובה או לרעה, אלא שהשגחתו היא רק באופן כללי על העולם ועל האומות השונות בתור קבוצים חברתיים. קלוזנר לא מצא סמוכים לדעה זו של הצדוקים בתלמוד ובמדרש (כאשר העיר בפרוש). אבל בתקנה זו שלפנינו נמצאו הסמוכים מפני שהיא מכונת כנראה נגד דעה זו. לפי דעת הצדוקים היה כעין חלול השם להזכיר שמו של הבורא

בקשר עם צרכי האדם הפרטיים ולברך איש את חברו שיצליח השם את דרכו או שישפיע עליו לטובה, כי הלא השם אינו מתערב כלל בענינים הקטנטנים של האדם הפרטי. כמחאה נגד דעה זו של „קטני אמונה" וכדי להדגיש הרעיון של השגחה פרטית התקינו החכמים הפרושים לשאול תמיד בשלום חברו בשם.

והנה ישנם חוקרים (כגיגר, והר"א שווארץ ב„הגיון אריה", וגם בעל המאמר ב„בית תלמוד" שנזכר למעלה) שמבארים „בשם" במובן „שם המפורש". אבל בכלל קשה להעלות על הדעת שהותרה ההשתמשות בשם המפורש אף בשאילת שלום גרידא. גם רב האיי מבאר רק שהתקינו „למימר יברכך ד'". ובאמת לפי הטעם שהזכרנו למעלה להדגיש רעיון „השגחה פרטית" נגד הצדוקים, עקר התקנה היה הזכרת השם שיכולה להיות בכל כנוי שהיו רגילים בו באותם הימים ולא דוקא בשם המפורש.

I.

קטע א' לברכות מ"ו, ע"א.

[סימן הכ"י T.-S. 10 F 4[4], דף אחד של נייר].

(עמוד א')

זימון לא יצאו איצטריכו לאודועאנן עד היכא מחייבין למיהוא דחבירין[1]

עם הדאדי בברכה ונפקין ידי חובת זימון ומיכן[2] ואילך או ניחא להון לאיפרודי

מן הדדי וסדרי כל חד וחד מינהון ברכה דיליה שפיר דאמ[י] והאוי דנפקו להו

ידי זימון וידי ברכה ואיצטריכנן למימר רב נחמן אמ̇ עד נברך דאיכא דאיתרמו

1 צ"ל „חבירין".

2 =ומכאן.

שלשה שאכלו כאחד וגמרו סעודותיהו כיון דאתחיל גדול שבהן ואמֹ נברך
אם עמד אחד משלשה והלך ונשתייר המברך והשני עמו גומר את ברכתו
ועונה השני אחריו אמן ואין לחוש לאותו שעמד שאעֹפֹ שהלך אחד משלשה
ועמד והלך לו אין פוגם את הברכה אלא כיון שהיה בשעה שהתחיל המברך
בברכה ואמר נברך ועמד לאחר מיכן אין בכך כלום ולא נפגמה הברכה
והכין סבאריה דרב נחמן דאמֹ עד נברך דצריך שיהוא שלשה לברכת הזימן
אבל מן נברך ואילך אם עמד אחד מהן אין בכך כלום ורב ששת אמֹ עד
הזן דסבירא ליה דצריכין שיהו שלשה שנזדמנו לברכת הזימון עד שיאמר
המברך הזן את הכל שאם עמד אחד מהן קודם הזן נפגמה הברכה אבל
אם עמד אחר הזן לא נפגמה הברכה והכין טעמיה דרב ששת וקא האוו
בה רבנן וקא אמרי לימֹ טעמיהו דרב נחמן ורב ששת בברכת הזימון בפלוגתא
דהני תנאיי דקא מיפלגין דתנו[3] חדא שנים ושלשה מברכין ברכת הזימון
ותניא אידך שלשה וארבעה ואידי ואידי בגברי קא אמרין ולאו בברכות[4]

[3] צ״ל „דתניא״.

[4] נוסחא זו מביא ג״כ הרשב״א בחדושיו: „והכי גרסינן בספרים ישנים ובספרי הגאונים ז״ל נימא כתנאי דתני חדא ב׳ ג׳ מברכין ברכת הזימון ותניא אידך ג׳ וד׳״. ותמוה הדבר שהרשב״א מוסיף: „ופירשה רב האיי גאון ז״ל שהם ברכות וכו׳״, ופה אנו מוצאים שהגאון

ואמרינן סברוה בין הני תנאיי ובין רב נחמן ורב ששת דברכת הטוב

והמטיב לאו דאוריתא משום דלא קא מצרכין לה למלתא למיהוי תלתה

גברי עד דחתים הטוב והמטיב ואמרינן מאי לאו בהא [קא] מיפלגי דמאן

דאמ׳ שנים ושלשה קא סבר עד הזן להוו בתלתה גוברי ד[עד הזן] הוא מצות

[זימון] ומיכאן ואילך אם עמד אחד ונותרו שנים גומרין א[ת] הברכה והינו שני[ם]

[ושלשה ו]מאן דאמ׳ שלשה וארבעה קא סבר עד נברך ברכת זי[מון דאם]

[בברכת הזי]מון היו ד׳ אנשים מזומנין לברכה כיון שעמד אחד מ[הן] לאחר

[שאמר נ]ברך ונותר המברך ושנים עמו שהן כולם שלשה גומרין את]

[הברכה ואין ב]כך כלום ומדחינן ואמרינן לא לאו בכי הדין סברא דתהיי[5]

אומר בפירוש: „ואידי ואידי בגברי קא אמרין ולאו בברכות" וכמו"כ בעמוד ב׳ שו׳ 15–16: „הולכך בגברי קא אמרינן ... ולא בברכות". אמנם גם מדברי הרי"ף נראה שהקדמונים (וכנראה גם רה"ג בכלל) חשבו שהמספרים ב׳ וג׳ וד׳ רומזים לברכות מפני שכותב: „הא שמעתא שקלו וטרו בה קמאי ז"ל (היינו הגאונים ובכללם רה"ג) ולא סלקא להו כל עיקר משום דסבירא להו דהא דתניא שנים ושלשה ברכות אינון וקשיא להו היכי תני להו בלשון זכר ולא אשכחו בה פירוקא". אבל מדברי ר׳ יונה אבן גנאח (הרקמה, צד 207) נראה שגם בין הגאונים היתה פלוגתא בנוגע למובן בריתא זאת ושלא כולם הבינוה שרומזת לברכות כמו שיש להוציא מסגנונו של הרי"ף, ואלה הם דבריו: „וכבר רבתה המחלוקת בין הגאונים בפירוש הבריתא מהם מי שברח משומם (היינו המספרים) ברכות בעבור ההא ומהם מי ששמם ברכות ואמר שאינו יודע עלת ההא". לפני הרשב"א היה כנראה פירושו של רה"ג בשלמותו והוא מזכיר אותו הרבה פעמים, וכדי להסיר הקושי אפשר לשער שרה"ג אחרי שמציע בפרוש הסוגיא כפי שנמצא בקטע שלפננו דחה אח"כ בחלק שחסר פה את הפרוש הזה והציע פרוש חדש באופן שהבריתא רומזת ל„ברכות", ומסקנא זו של הגאון מזכיר הרשב"א בחדושיו.

5 הכ"י מטושטש פה ובודאי צ"ל „דתנאיי".

נמיפלגי רב נחמן ו]רב ששת מיהא תרויהו סבירא להו כי הני תנאיי

(עמוד ב')

וכל חד וחד מתריץ ליה לטעמיהו דהני תנאיי בסבארא דנפשיה ולא מפיק

נפשיה מסבארא דחד מינהון דקא אמרינן רב נחמן מתריץ לטעמיה ורב

ששת מתריץ לטעמיה רב נחמן מתריץ לטעמיה דכולי עלמא הני תנאיי סבירא

ל ה ו[6] עד נברך סבירא להון ומאן דאמ׳ ארבעה[7] שפיר דכיון דהאוו ארבעה אף[6]

על פי שעמד אחד מהן לאחר נברך ונשתיירו שלשה משום דקא סבר הטוב

והמטיב דאוריתא ובענין תלתה דמשתיירו לאו משום ברכת הזימון אלא

משום הטוב והמטיב ומאן דאמ׳[8] שלשה אעפ׳ שעמד אחד ונשתיירו שניים

לאו משום דסבירא ליה דהטוב והמטיב לאו דאוריתא ולא קא מצריך לה

שלשה אלא הכא בברכת פועלים עסיקנן דפועלין לא קא מחייבין לה בהטוב

והמטיב דאמ׳ מר הפועלים כולל בונה ירושלם בברכת הארץ וחו[ותם בברכת]

הארץ[9] ורב ששת נמי מתריץ לטעמיה דכולי עלמא הני תנאיי עד הזן סבירא

להון ומאן דאמ׳ שלשה שפיר שכיון שהיה בשעת הזימון שלשה וישבו שלשתן

[6] הקוים למעלה מורים שיש למחוק שתי המלים האלה.

[7] היינו שלשה וארבעה.

[8] היינו שנים ושלשה.

[9] עיין הנוסחאות בדקדוקי סופרים.

עד הזן אם עמד אחד מהן לאחר הזן ונשתיירו שלשה[10] שפיר דאמי ומאן דאמֹ

ארבעה שפיר קא סבר הטוב והמטיב דאוריתא שכיון שהן ארבעה אם

עמד אחד מהן ונותרו שלשה עד הטוב והמטיב גומרין את הברכה הולכך

בגברי קא אמרינן שנים ושלשה שלשה וארבעה ולא בברכות וכן רב נחמן

ורב ששת פלוגתיהן בגברי ניהו דרב נחמן סבירא ליה הכין דצריכ[ין]

למהוה שלשה עד נברך ואפילו נמי האוו ארבעה וחמשה ובאעו למיפק

ידי זימון [קא] מחייבין לברוכי כולם כאחד עד נברך ומיכן ואילך אם רצה

לעמ[וד ולילך] ולברך כל אחד ואחד לעצמו או שנתייר מהן מנ[י] שנש[תייר]

[ואפי]ל[ו] אח[ד] המברך גומר את הברכה והנותר עונה אחריו אמן. . .

. . . בו[10*] פסיר[10*] וכולם יצאו ידי זימון וידי ברכה ורב ששת סביר[א דציריכין]

להו [למיהוי] שלשה עד הזן את הכל ולענין מחלוקת רב נחמן ורב ש[שת רב]

ששת אמֹ עד הזן משום דעד הזן דמינכרא מילתא דזימנ[ו]ן [ואם נשתיירו]

עד הזן מיכן ואילך עד עמד אחד מהן גומר המברך [ואין בכך כלום]

(פה סוף העמוד וחסר ההמשך).

10 צ״ל „שנים״.

10* הכ״י מטושטש פה.

II.

קטע ב׳ לברכות נ״ו ע״ב—נ״ח ע״ב ונ״ט ע״ב—ס״א ע״א.

[סימן הכ״י T.-S.10 F 4[3], שני דפים של נייר וחסרים ביניהם כמה דפים].

(דף, א׳, ע״א)

לאיו למיגמר מן הדין קרא הרואה גמל בחלומו[11] מאי האוי אלה[12] לזכרון דברים בעלמא כגון שיצא מן המיתה כמה שנצלו בנ[י] יעקב ממצרים והכין כדא[מ]רון רנ[ב]נן מאי קראה פירושה סימנ[א] דמילתא לאידכוריה כגון רב יוסף תחתון מתקנן[13] ששמין זכר לדבר ויוסף הורד מצרימה יוסף הורד יוסף תחתון וכגון מ[צו]ה להתפלל עם דמדומי חמה וקראה ייראוך עם שמש[14] וכגון ההוא דחלק[15] אין בן דויד בא עד שתהפך מלכות כולה למינות וקראה כלו הפך לבן טהור הוא. שלשה חכמים ושלשה תלמידים[16] דוגמה קתני. ששה[17] דברים מרפאין את החולה לא כעינין רפואות שהיו הראשונים עושין רפואות שלעכשיו ויש כמה דברים שהיו[18] הראשונים עושין רפואות שלעכשיו ויש כמה דברים שהיו הראשונים יודעין שיש במאכל זה שאין יודעין אותו עכשיו ואין לתמוך[19] עכשיו על

11 ברכות נ״ו ע״ב, למטה.

12 =אלא.

13 ב״מ קי״ז ע״א. נוסחתנו היא: „רבי אלעי משום רבי חייא בר יוסי אמר התחתון מתקן״ אבל עיין בד״ס הנוסחא „רב חייא בר יוסף״ וגירסת רה״ג כנראה היתה „רב יוסף״.

14 ברכות ט׳ ע״ב.

15 סנהדרין צ״ז, ע״א, למטה.

16 ברכות נ״ז ע״ב.

17 כל הפיסקא הזאת עד ע״ב, שו׳ 12, נמצאת ג״כ בתשובות הגאונים, הוצ׳ הרכבי, סי׳ שצ״ד, (השוה „אוצר הגאונים״, הוצ׳ לוין, ח״א, ח׳ התשובות, צד 103—104).

18 מן „שהיו״ עד „דברים״ בשורה הבאה כנראה מיותר הוא ונכפל בטעות ע״י המעתיק, ובאמת לא נמצא בתשובת הגאון.

19 צ״ל „לסמוך״.

אותן רפואות לפי שאין אנו יודעין היאך רפואה בהן ועוד אין לך דבר מיוחד שהוא מרפא לכל חלי אלא כל אחד יש בו רפואה לדבר אחד וזה שהוצרכו[20] להזכיר ששה דברים אילו לומר כי יש בהן מזון ואף יש בהן רפואה. כרוב בלשון ישמעאל כרנב[21] יש בו הועיל מן השכרות וגם משלשל הוא ומימיו מתירין את הבטן[22] ויש בהן מי רוק ומועילין

(עמוד ב׳)

לפתח סיבור[23] שבכבד ומועילין בכבד הטחול. מי סיסין יבשה מפרשין אותו מיא דקובלי והן עשבים שנקראין בלשון ערבית באבונג[24] שורין אותו במים ורוחצין במימיהן ושותין נמי מהן והן סגלגלין ודומין לסיסין מפרש במי שאחזו קורדיקוס[25] למישרא סיסין יבשתא במיא למיסר סיסין רטיבתא במיא קיבה לא הקיבה[26] שבבהמה קטנה והיא הנקראת אנ[פ]חה[27] שמעמידין בה את הגבינה יש בה כמה מיני הועיל להברות ולהעלות בשר. ר״ת אמרו חתיכה קטנה יתירה שוֹמ[28] שנמצאת על ליבן שלכבשים קטנים שיונקים[29] חלב ונקרא

20 היינו בעלי התלמוד, ונוסחא זו „שהוצרכו" יותר טובה מהנוסחא בתשובת הגאון „שהוצרכנו".

21 וכן תקן בצדק הרכבי את הנוסחא בתשובת הגאון.

22 חסר פה המשפט בנוגע לתרדין כמו בתשובת הגאון: „תרדין בלשון ישמעאלי סלק אף הן מימיהן מתירין את הבטן ויש בהן מירוק וכו׳ ". הרכבי הדפיס „מירוק" במלה אחת אבל לא בארה. לפי הכ״י פה צ״ל „מי רוק", היינו כעין ציר דומה לרוק של הפה.

23 כך הוא בכ״י אלא שאין לו מובן, וכנראה יותר נכון לקרוא „סיכור" (היינו סתימה שבכבד) כמו בתשובת הגאון. גם תחת „בכבד הטחול" יותר נכון „בכאב הטחול" כמו שם.

24 כבר העיר הרכבי, בסמכו על לאוו, שהעשב שנקרא בארמית „קובלי" (מוטטערקרויט) נקרא בערבית באבונג.

25 גטין ס״ט ע״ב.

26 חסר פה וצ״ל כמו בתשובת הגאון: „לא הקיבה שבבהמה גדולה היא אלא שבבהמה קטנה וכו׳ ".

27 בערבית.

28 כנראה שוֹמ=שומן, אבל מלה זו חסרה בתשובת הגאון ואולי צ״ל פה „שנמ", היינו תחלת המלה הראשונה בשורה הבאה כרגיל בכ״י.

29 כאן מתחיל כ״י אוכספורד שפרסם לוין ב„גנזי קדם" ח״א (השוה „אוצר הגאונים" שלו, ח׳ הפירושים, צד 90).

אללבלאב ונקראת אלחלוה ויש בה כמה מיני הועיל. יותרת הכבד כמשמעה מרפאין בה את בעלי שבדדין[30] שבעין שנקראו בלשון ישמעאל אלעשא ואלשבכרה. ודתנן על הזיקין ואיתמר עלה מאי זיקין אמ׳ שמואל כוכבא דשא׳ דשאביט פירוש זיקיו אש שמתקדחת למעלה ונראה לה אור כענין שנ׳ קודחי אש מאזרי זיקות ובזיקות בערתם[31] והעמודין שלאש הללו שנראין למעלה ברום העולם הן הזיקין שאנו חייבין לברך עליהן ברוך שכוחו מלא עולם ומאז בני אדם קורין להם כוכבא דשאביט ואומרין עד כוכבא דצארי שאביט מלשון שבט שעומד כשבט וכעמוד ומכן[32]

נפה סוף דף א׳ של קטע ב׳ שלפנינו וחסרים בינו ובין דף ב׳ כמה דפים שאפשר עתה להשלימם ע״י קטעים אחרים שנדפסו על ידי וע״י לוין וגינצבורג ועתה גם ע״י אסף. כשנצרף כל הקטעים יש לנו עתה חלק הגון מפירושו של רה״ג לסוף המסכתא מדף נ״ו ע״ב עד ס״ג ע״א, למטה, החל מהקטע שלפנינו, דף א׳ ע״א, ועד סוף קטע ג׳ שיבא להלן. ההמשך של הדף שלפנינו בנוגע ל„זיקין״ נמצא בכ״י קמברידז, שפרסמתי ב„הצופה״, ובכ״י אוכספורד שפרסם לוין ב„גנזי קדם״ (השוה עתה „אוצר הגאונים״, הוצ׳ לוין, כרך א׳, חלק הפירושים, צד 91 והלאה). כמו שהעיר לוין בצדק, סופו של כ״י קמברידז ב„הצופה״, שקרוע ומטושטש מאוד, אפשר להשלים ע״י הקטע שפרסם גינצברג ב„גיאוניקא״, ח״ב, צד 275—276.

והנה עתה פרסם הר״ש אסף („תשובות הגאונים מתוך הגניזה״, תרפ״ט, צד 208 והלאה) קטע חדש מכ״י הרכבי שמשלים באמת

30 צ״ל „שברירין״ כמו בתשובת הגאון.

31 כאן מתחיל כ״י קמברידז שפרסמתי ב„הצופה לחכמת ישראל״, שנה ו׳, צד 199 והלאה.

32 =ומכאן, אבל בכ״י אוכספורד יותר נכון „ומק׳ כת׳ ״ (=ומקרא כתוב).

את הקטע שב„גיאניקא", אף שהמו"ל לא עמד על זה כי החליף את סדר העמודים ומה שנדפס שם כדף א', ע"ב, צריך להיות ע"א ולהפך מה ששם ע"א צ"ל ע"ב. הקטע שב„גיאוניקא" (אוצר הגאונים, צד 96 למטה) חותם במלים „שקנה פעם אחת אין" (צ"ל ואין), ובאותן המלים דוקא מתחיל הקטע מכ"י הרכבי, דף א' ע"ב (שצ"ל באמת ע"א). דף זה מכ"י הרכבי, משורה 15 („כיון שקנה") עד סופו, מקביל לדף ב' של הקטע שלפנינו שיבא להלן (עד ע"א, שו' 17: „סבירא להו")].

(דף ב', ע"א, לברכות נ"ט ע"ב, למטה, וס' ע"א, למעלה).

[כיון ש]קנה אחרים חדשים מברך והדין [פי]רושה הכין [סאליק כדאמרינן] דאסיקנן אדעתא דבתחלת קנינו[ו עסיקנן וקאמ̇ רבנן] ד[א]ף על גב דליכא הכין בגמרא כיון ד[לא סליק גירסא דרבנן איל]א הכין שמעינן דהכין היא מילתא דלא לאט̇ [לאטעויי גירסא] דרבנן ואפילו[33] הכין מנא לן דכיון דפליגי ביש [לו מכלל דס]בירא להו קנה וחזר וקנה אין צריך לברך ועוד רב[נן דגארסי] מיכלל דתרויהו סבירא להו קנה וחזר וקנה דברי [ה]כל צריך לא יאכיל לשוויה לקושיא לר' יוחנן דהא ר̇ יוחנן הכי קאמ̇ וליכא עליה קושיא ומכל מקום הילכתא כר̇ יוחנן אפילו בלישנא בתרא אבל פירושא דשמעתא או נאקטת דוקה מינה מחלפת ליה לקושיא לרב הונא ולא צריכת לאפוקי לא מתניתין ולא בריתא מן פשאטיה ולא לאסופי מידעם ואו משוית ליה לקושיא לר̇ יוחנן כי דקא מיגריס צריכת לאסוקי על דעתך מאי דלא מפרש דבתחלת קנין עסיקינן ודר̇ יוחנן קא מפריק[34] בדין הוא דאפילו קנין שנין[35]

[33] כאן מתחיל עמוד ב' האמתי בקטע הרכבי (תשובות הגאונים, הוצ' אסף, צד 209): „[ואפילו] הכין וכו'", ויש לתקן שם שורות 5–10 ע"פ הנוסחא השלמה פה בשורות 8–12.

[34] בכ"י הרכבי „מפריך" בטעות.

[35] צ"ל „שני".

הכין הלכתיה ודאמרין דל[ישנא][36] בתרא מיכלל דתרויהו סבירא להו[37] קנה ויש לו דברי הכל אין צריך לברך לא ברוך[38] מנא להון האי כללא ועוד דגאריס דברי הכל הכי לא מצי . . . בלישנא בתרא לאסוקי בפירוקא להודיעך כוחו דר׳ יהודה דאפילו קנה ויש לו נמי צריך לברך והכין הוא דהאי דגרסי׳

(עמוד ב׳)

דגרסינן מיכלל דתרויהו סבירא להו ק[נה ו]ח[זר וקנה צר]יך [לברך] . . . דודאי ודגרסינן אין צריך לברך מן . . . . . . לאסוקי קושיא לר׳ יוחנן ולא קא [ס]לקא ומאן[39] דגרי[ס] . . . פירושא צריך לאתותובי ולעיוני טובא. [ויבן יי׳ אלה] את הצלע. רב ושמואל[40] חד אמ׳ פרצוף וחד אמ׳ זנב מא[י] פירושה מאן דאמ׳ פרצוף הכי קאמ׳ שני פרצ[ופות ברא] הקב״ה לאדם יש לו פנים מלפניו ויש לו פנים מ[אחוריו] וכשלקח הקב״ה אותו נשאר פרצוף אחד ומפרש אחור וקדם צרתני שנברא מעיקרא שני פרצופות אחור וקדם וכת׳ וייצר בתרין יוד ומפרש עוד האי דכת׳ מעיקרה זכר ונקבה בראם שברא גוף אחד שיש בו שני פרצופות ומפרש ויסגר בשר תחתנה שכשנטל פרצוף אחד סגר בשר מאחור. ומאן דאמ׳ זנב הכי קאמ׳ זנב ברא הקב״ה לאדם מתחלה והוא שנטלו ובנה ממנו את חוה והיינו דכתיב ויבן וזה מוציא מקראותיו שלז[ה] למדרשות אחרים וזה מוציא מקראותיו שלזה ל[מדרש]ות אחרים כי דמפרש

36 צ״ל „בלישנא״.

37 כאן מפסיק כ״י הרכבי.

38 צ״ל „ברור״.

39 כאן מתחיל כ״י מוצרי בקהיר, מצרים (עין למטה אצל קטע ג׳), ושם בשורה הראשונה המטושטשת אפשר לקרוא: „[ו]מאן דגר[יס] על ... ן פירושא צריך לא[תותובי] (2) ולעיונ[י ביה] טובא״.

40 ברכות ס״א, ע״א.

בגמרא. והא דאמ̇[41] יצר הרע דומה לזבוב ו[יו]שב על מפתחי לב שמואל אמ̇ דומה לחטה שנ̇ לפתח חטאת רובץ האי לפתח חטאת רובץ דשמואל סימן הוא לחטה וטעמיהו שנהו]א דבר קטן כזבוב או כחטה

III.

קטע ג׳ לברכות דף ס״א ע״א—ס״ג ע״א, למטה.

[כ״י מוצרי בקהיר, מצרים, סימן C 9, ח׳ דפים של נייר מטושטשים וקרועים. דף א׳, ע״א, מקביל לקטע שלמעלה מן ע״ב, שו׳ 3 („ומאן דגריס״) עד שו׳ 19 („חטאת רובץ״) ומפני זה לא נדפס פה כדי שלא להכפיל הדברים].

(דף א׳, ע״ב)

ה[אי] לפתח חטאת רובץ דשמואל [סימן] הוא לחטה וטעמיהו שהוא דבר קטן דומה [לזבוב א]ו כחטה[42] . . . ו דבר גדול ובזמן שאדם דוחה . . . ה וכדאמרינן[43] [יצר הרע בתחלה דומה לחוט] שלבוביה והוא כחבלי השוא לבסוף [כע]בות העגלה וזה [ש]הסמיכוהו ללב אף על פי שהמחשבה מן הכבד מפני שהמחשבה . . . ן בלב הוא והכתוב הסמיכו ללב דכת̇[44] כי יצ̇ר ל̇ב האדם ר̇ע̇ וכל יצר מחשבות לב[45] ומפרש̇[46] בכל לבבך בשני יצריך. והא דתאנו רבנן הלב מבין כליות יועצ̇ו[47] הני כולהי מילי

41 בכ״י מוצרי: „דאמ ראבא״=ר̇ אבא=רב כמו שהוא בנוסחה שלנו, ועיין ג״כ בר״ס, הערה ס׳.

42 ב׳ השורות האלה מקבילות לסופו של כ״י קמברידז.

43 סוכה נ״ב ע״א, סנהדרין צ״ט, ע״ב.

44 בראשית ח׳, כ״א; ו׳ ה׳.

45 צ״ל „לבו״.

46 ברכות נ״ד, ע״א.

47 =יועצות.

נינהו ולא מדקדק ביה מיהו כליות יועצות קרא קאמ׳[48] אף לילות יסרוני כליותי ודילמא אית אנפא אחרינא דמן שמיא ידעין ליה ואנן לא ידעינן ליה וקרא אחרינא נמי שיש מחשבה בכליות אני יי׳ חוקר לב ובוחן כליות[49] וקרא אחרינא בוחן כליות ולב[50] ואף כבד אין אנו יודעין בו דרך הכעס אילא שאומרין כשרותיח דם לב ובו הכעס אף הכבד מרגשת ויוקפת[51] והדם שבה רותח ומוסיף לדם שבלב והכעס. לי.[10*] ידי[10*] ורגלין[52] בני אדם ל[ומר א]דם קפדן כבדאני וכשמעמידו[53] על [דעו]תיו אומרין קדקאנ[י] . . . [מ]רה

(דף ב׳, ע״א)

והמרה ה . . . ה מזקקת את הדם ומושכת ממנו דם המרה הירוק[54] אלעמה[55] והי בודאי מנחת את הכבד כי כל זמן שהמרה היר[וקה] משרבת בדם קרוב להרתי[ח] ולעורר כעס ובזמן שמזוקק מן המרה קשה לכעוס.

ותנן[56] לא יקל אדם את ראש[57] כנגד שער המזרח אמ׳ רב יהודה לא אסרו אלא מן [הצופ]ים ולפנים וברואה איתמר נמי אמ׳ ר׳ אבא בריה דר׳ חייא[58] אמ׳ ר׳ יוחנן לא אסרו אלא מן הצופים ולפנים וברואה ובמקום שאין שם גדר

48 תהלים ט״ז, ז׳. 49 ירמיה, י״ז, י׳.

50 ירמיה, י״א, כ׳.

51 אולי צ״ל „ויוקדת״. 52 =ורגילין.

53 יותר טוב „וכשעומד״.

54 צ״ל „הירוקה״.

55 מובן המלה הערבית הזאת איידוע לי.

56 פה מתחיל כ״י הרכבי, דף ב׳, ע״א (שפרסם אסף ב„תשובות הגאונים״, צד 209) ושם תחת „והתנן״ צ״ל „ודתנן״. השוה ג״כ רשימת התשובות בכ״י דרופסי (אוצר הגאונים, ח״א, נספחים, צד 83).

57 =ראשו. בנוגע לשנויי נוסחאות בפסקא זו עיין ד״ס.

58 בכ״י הרכבי „חייא בר אבא״ ועיין ד״ס.

ובזמן שהשכינה שורה ואית רבנן דגרסי לה תניא נמי הכי לא אסרו אלא מן הצופים ולפנים וברו[59] וכול והכין פירושה קלות ראש מילתא ידעתא היא דתנן[60] שחוק וקלות ראש מרגילין לחודיה[61] וכנגדה אין עומדין להתפלל אלא מתוך כובד ראש[62] וצופים זה שאמר כן[63] מקום שהיה על שערי ירושלם ושמה[64] היה בו מקום לצופים ובני ארץ ישר׳ קורין לו הצופית[65] ועליו שנינו במשנתינו[66] וכן מי שיצא מירושלם ו[ראה] שיש בידו בשר

(דף ב׳, ע״ב)

הקדש אם עיבר הצופים וכול ו[ב]רואה שאמרו מקום המקדש נראה משם דתנן[67] קדשי קדשים נאכלים לפנים מן הקלעים קדשים קלים ומעשר שני בכל הרואה כי בית המקדש גבוה הרבה היה ונראה מרחוק ולענין רואה אמרינן[68] אמ׳ ר׳ אלעזר אמ׳ ר׳ הושעיא דאמ׳ קרא פן תעלה עולותיך בכל מקום אשר תראה. במקום שאתה רואה אי אתה מעלה אבל אתה אוכל במקום שאתה רואה ואמרינן נמי רבי אבהו אמ׳ קרא בן פורת יוסף בן פורת עלי עין שלא ראתה[69]

59 =וברואה. 60 אבות ג׳, י״ג.

61 צ״ל „לערוה״.

62 ברכות ל׳, ע״ב. 63 =כאן.

64 =ושמא.

65 לפי דברי יוסף הכהן (קדמונית, ספר י״א, פ״ח, סי׳ ה׳) ההר הזה נקרא „צָפִין (Σαφίν) לפי כ״י היותר טובים), היינו בארמית מקביל לשם העברי „צופים״ וביונית „סקופוס״ (השוה שִׁיךְר, ח״א, צד 604, הערה י״ד). פה הגאון נותן לנו שם חדש שכפי הנראה השתמשו בו בני ארץ ישראל בזמנו.

66 פסחים ג׳, ח׳. 67 זבחים י״ד, ו׳.

68 זבחים קי״ח, ע״א וע״ב.

69 לפנינו בזבחים „רצתה״.

ליהנות ממה שאינה שלה תוכה ותאכל כל קדשים במלוא עיניה ותניא הרואה שאמרו רואה כולו ולא שיהא דבר מפסיק בינו לבינה[70] אמׄ ליה רׄ שמעון בן אליקים לרׄ אלעזר[71] אסברה לי אמׄ ליה כגון בי כנישתא דמעון אמׄ רב פפא רואה שאמרו אפילו מקצתו בעי רב פפא עומד ורואה יושב ואינו רואה מאי בעי רׄ ירמיה על גב הנחל רואה מאי תיקו וכאן קאמר רבנן לא יקל אדם

(דף ג׳, ע״א)

את ראשו [בז]מן שהוא רואה את השער המזרחי ללישנא דרב יהודה אמׄ רב וללישנא דרבי יוחנן במקום שהוא יכול לראות משם את השער ה[מז]רחי ובזמן שאין שם גדר ובזמן שהשכינה שורה.

ובתרה תנו רבנן הנפנה בכל מקום[72] לא יפנה מזרח ומערב אלא צפון ודרום רׄ יוסי אוׄ לא אמׄ אמרו אלא ברואה רׄ בנימין אוׄ בזמן שהשכינה שורה אסורה[72a] אין השכינה שורה מותר וחכׄ אומרין בכל מקום חכׄ היינו תנא קמא איכא ביניהו צדדין. וכן פירושה הנפנה לא ישב להפנות לא כשפניו נגד מערב ולא כשאחוריו כנגד מערב אלא פניו כלפי דרום או כלפי צפון רׄ יוסי סבר הני מילי ברואה אבל כשמרוחק ישב אפילו כלפי מזרח ומערב. ורׄ בנימין סבר הני מילי בזמן שהשכינה שורה בלחוד וחכׄ דאומרים בכל מקום אסור להפנות בשרם כלפי

70 צ״ל „לבינו״. 71 כאן סוף כ״י הרכבי.

72 לפנינו „ביהודה״ אבל עיין בד״ס גם בנוגע לשאר השנויים בנוסחאות.

72a הנקודה על הה״א מורה שצ״ל „אסור״.

מזרח או כלפי מערב מקשונן היינו תנא קמא דקאמ̇ הנפנה בכל מקום ומפרקינן איכא ביניהו צדדין ומפרשי רבנן[73] דתנא

(דף ג', ע"ב)

קמא קא שארי בכל מקום להפנות צפון ודרום דאיכא צדדין וחכ̇ לא קא שארו להפנות בכל מקום צפון ודרום אלא קאסרי' מזרח ומערב ולא פרישו בהדי מימרא צפון ודרום והכין סבירא להון דמזרח ומערב לעולם אסור בכל מקום אבל צפון ודרום במקום שארץ ישראל מכוונות כנגד צפון ודרום בודאי אף אינון אסורין לא ישב כלפי[74] צדדין לא מזרח ומערב מכונים ולא צפון ודרום מכונים אלא מצדיד פנים לצד שהוא בינתים מקום שאינו לא כנגד מזרח ומערב ולא כנגד בית המקדש כי מזרח ומערב מקומות ידועין הן שהחמה זורחת משם ושוקעת שם מראש תקופת תמוז ועד ראש תקופת טבת וצפון ודרום מקומות קצרין הן ומה שבין[75] צפון ודרום ועד קצה המזרח והמערב הוא הצדדים וההוא דתניא[76] מקום שהחמה יוצא[77] ביום ארוך ושוקעת ביום ארוך זה הוא פני צפון חמה יוצא[77] ביום קצר ושוקעת ביום קצר זה הוא פני דרום בתקופת ניסן ובתקופת תשרי

73 היינו חכמי הישיבות בבבל.

74 כאן מתחיל כ"י אדלר שפרסם לוין ב„גנזי קדם", ח"ב (=„אוצר הגאונים", ח' הפירושים, צד 97–99).

75 אצל לוין בטעות „ומחשבין".

76 עירובין נ"ו, ע"א (ולוין, שם, אינו מציין את המקור ושם גם בטעות „מקום מקום" וגם „זורחת").

77 צ"ל „יוצאה".

(דף ד', ע"א)

חמה יוצא[77] [ב]חצי מזרח ושוקעת בחצי מערב ליתה דאמ̇ רב משרשיה ליתנהו להני כלאלי דתניא לעולם לא יצאה חמה מקרן מזרחית דרומית ושקעה בקרן מזרחית[78] ומעולם לא יצאה מקרן מזרחית צפונית ושקעה בקרן מערבית דרומית[79] וודאי בניסן ותשרי חמה בחצי מזרח ובחצי מערב מניסן[80] ועד תקופת תמוז ומתשרי ועד תקופת טבת כל אלה מזרח ומערב המה ואסור להפנות כנגדן בכל מקום והוא מילתא דקאמ̇ תנא קמה[81] לא יפנה אדם מזרח ומערב וקאמרי חכמים הכין אבל תנא קמה דקאמ̇[82] אלא צפון ודרום אמ̇ לך בכל מקום שרי להפנות בכל צד אף עלפי שהוא מכון כנגד בית המקדש ומשם[83] כנגדו ומתפללין וחכמ̇ דקאמרי לא יפנה מזרח ומערב ולא קאמרי אלא[84] צפון ודרום סבירא להון כי הרוח שמתפללין כנגדה מאותו מקום לא יפנה אדם לא מאחוריו ולא מלפניו. ובתרה[85] תניא אידך ביהודה לא יפנה מזרח ומערב אלא צפון ודרום[86] נמי אסור

78 צ"ל „מערבית דרומית" כמו בכ"י אדלר.

79 כמו"כ בכ"י אדלר אבל לפנינו בעירובין „מערבית צפונית".

80 צ"ל „ומניסן" כמו בכ"י אדלר.

81 =קמא.

82 חסר בכ"י אדלר.

83 בכ"י אדלר בטעות „ומשום".

84 בכ"י אדלר בטעות „לא".

85 היינו אחרי הבריתא הקודמת.

86 צריך להוסיף פה ע"פ כ"י אדלר: „ובגליל אפילו צפון ודרום" נמי אסור (והשוה למטה, ע"ב, שורה 6–7).

(דף ד', ע"ב)

ר' יוסי או' לא אסרו אלא ברואה [ו]ר' יהודה או' בזמן שבית המק' קיים אסור אין בית המק' [קיי]ם מותר ור' עקיבה או' בכל מקום היינו תנא קמא איכא ביניהו חוצה לארץ. וזו ברורה היא תנא קמא על ארץ ישר' בלחוד קאמ' דהכי קאמ' יהודה וגליל והאי דקאמ' בגליל אפילו צפון ודרום דילמא צפוני ודרומי[87] דגליל כנגד ירושלם קאיי והולכך לא יפנה שם אלא לצדדין מקומות שבין מזרח ומערב לצפון ודרום מידפרישנא[88] לעילא ור' יוסי סבר אל[89] אסירא האי מילתא אבל[90] ברואה ור' יהודה סבר אפילו ברואה[91] לא איסיר אלא שבית המק' קיים ור' עקיבה סבר אפילו בחוצה לארץ לא יפנה מזרח ומערב ומשמעתה דרבה גמרינן דהלכה כר' עקיבה ואפילו בזמן הזה שאין בית המק' קיים דהוה זקיפן ליה הנך לבני מזרח ומערב דהוה מיפני עילויהו לצפון ודרום כשבנויות ככירים [בנוי]ה לקדירה אחת משוכה כלפי מזרח ואחת משוכה כלפי מערב שיושב עליהן רגלו אחת עליו כלפי מערב או ממזרח[92] ורגלו אחת כנגדה נמצא

(דף ה', ע"א)

ידיו כלפי מזרח ומערב ופניו ואחוריו כלפי צפון ודרום ומבבל ירושלם כלפי מערב היא וכי אזל אביי אפכינהי איקפד רבה ואמ'

87 צ"ל „צפונו ודרומו" כמו בכ"י אדלר.
88 בכ"י אדלר „כדפרישנא".
89 צ"ל „לא".
90 צ"ל „אלא".
91 בכ"י אדלר בטעות „בחוצה".
92 צ"ל „מזרח".

מאן קא מצער לי אנא כר̇ עקיבה סבירא לי דאמ̇ בכל מקום נמי אסור ולענין צפון ודרום וצדדין דפליגי תנא קמא דמאמא[93] וחכ̇ לא פסקא הלכה ומי שדרכה[94] להחמיר על עצמו אין נפנה בכל מקום כנגד בית[95] התפלה.

יוצאין חוץ לפתח בית הבד[96] משום טהרה היקלו בצניעות והא דקאמ̇ בן עזאי משמש ושב[97] ואל תשב ותמשמש שכל היושב וממשמש אפילו הוא כאן ועושין לא[98] כשפים באספמ[יא] מועלין[99] פירושה בזמן שאדם מבקש לישב במקום לעשות צרכיו ממשמש תחלו[100] באותו מקום אם יש בו צרור או נמי טנופת יסירנה ואחר כך ישב ואל ישב במקום ואחר כך ימשמש תחתיו וגמירי דהא מילתא מהניא בכשפים ואו אתיב[101] והדר ממשמש מאי תקנתיה נימא הכי לא לי לא לי או נמי חוס חוס ואל תחתים והני קיבלי דאמרי להו רבנן בשמעתא

(דף ה', ע"ב)

דמעלי נקוטי וגמורי דמעלי למימר הכי ברזי דשמיען מן מלאכים ומפמליא שלמעלה כי כמו שיש רוחות שהלכן[102] הוה מועיל בהם[103] ומוסר אותן לטובה ולרעה ומהני בהו לפי יצירתם

93 בכ"י אדלר „דסתמא".
94 צ"ל „שדרכו" ובכ"י אדלר „שרוצה".
95 בכ"י אדלר בטעות „פני".
96 ברכות ס"ב, ע"א.
97 בצוי „מַשְׁמֵשׁ ושֵׁב" ובכ"י אדלר בטעות „ממשמש ויושב".
98 צ"ל „לו".
99 =מועילין.
100 צ"ל „תחלה".
101 צ"ל „יתיב" כמו בכ"י אדלר.
102 בכ"י אדלר „שבלשון" ויותר טוב היה „שהלשון".
103 כאן סוף כ"י אדלר.

כי דמהני מיני זמר בבן אדם שהוא שומיע קול פעמים מתחנן ופעמים שהוא שוחק שהוא בוכה ופעמים שמוציא חרוץ[104] ושמחה ופעמים שמוציא עצבות ועצלות ופעמים ששותק ודומם ופעמים שמתנדנד ומרקד ואף עלפי שאין דבר נוגני[105] בגופו אלא קולות בעולם הוא שומע בחיבורין אף לבריות הללו יצרים ושכיסות[106] ופיפיות ומנהגות שהדברים הללו מועילין בהן ואף עלפי שאין נודע בפרט על אי זה אופן מפני שבריים[106a] סתורה ממנו ומפני שמועה אתו רבנן בהני קיבלי ודאמ׳ על כל מושב שב חוץ מן הקורה והשכיבה על הקרקע בזמן[107] שם מחצלת ולא מצע יחוצץ יש בה דבר רע ולא[108] פורש לנו מה הוא מי לאו[109] קאמרי משום זוי[110] שתי ביצים ושני קישואים ושני איגוזים ודבר אחר הלכה למשה מסיני

(דף ו', ע"א)

ונזרו רבנן לכולהו זוי[110] משום ההוא דבר אחר להודיעך דהני מילי אית בהיי[111] מפי נביאים

104 צ"ל „חדוה". 105 צ"ל „נונע".

106 מובן המלה הזאת איידוע לי, אמנם אפשר לקרוא „שביסות" (השוה ישעיה, ג', י"ח), אבל גם לזה אין מובן פה.

106a =שבריאתם. 107 צריך להוסיף „שאין".

108 מן „ולא" עד „הלכה למשה מסיני" (דף ו', ע"א, שו' 3) נמצא ג"כ בערוך ע' שב בשם „הגאון" (היינו רה"ג), אבל פה הנוסחא ביותר שלמות.

109 בערוך „מאי לאו דקאמרי", ולפי הערת אפשטיין (ב„אוצר הגאונים", ח"א, ח' הפירושים, צד 99, הערה ג') צריך לקרוא כמו בדפוס פיזרו וכו': „מי"=מיהו, ובכן: מיהו לאו דקאמרי וכו'. אמנם גם זה אינו מקיל המובן פה לפי ההמשך, כי איזו שיכות יש לענין שלפנינו עם המאמר בפסחים אודות „זוגות"? ויותר נכון לקרוא כמו פה „מי לא (או: לאו) קאמרי", היינו הכי לא אמרו רבנן בנוגע ל„זוגות" שישנה קבלה עתיקה? וכמו כן פה כל הדברים האלה הם מיוסדים על איזו שמועה אלא שאין אנו יודעים הטעם.

110 צ"ל „זוגי" והכונה למאמר בפסחים ק"י, ע"ב.

111 צ"ל „בהו".

ואית בה[111] הלכה למשה מסיני. ודאמ̇ שמואל שינה בעבור[112] השחר כצטמא לפרזלא דבר זה יש ללמדו[112a] ופירוש צטמא בלשון ישמע̇[113] אלפולאד וממה[114] ששנת שחרים נעימה מאד כלולה עם דברים שמוציאין את האדם מן העולם וודאי דרך ארץ שלא ללמד אדם את עצמו כך אבל בעמוד השחר מותר. מילי[115] דמזבין בר קפרא בדינרי שהיה ממשל משלים ללמוד[116] מוסר ודרך ארץ ודרכי ניהוג העולם ונוטל שכר על זאת אדכפנת אכול עודך רעב רעב[117] אכול כשם שהרעב אם אוכל בשעה שהוא רעב או אחרי כן כמעט הרי הוא אוכל בתאוה ונהנה במאכלו ואם מעכב[118] המרה הירוקה גוברת עליו וכוחו כחש וכשבא לאכול אין יכול לאכול [הר]בה כך בעסקי העולם הזה והעולם הבא כענין שכת̇[119] כל אשר תמצא ידך לעשות בכחך עשה. ופתרונו בזמן שכוחך עליך וכדתניא[119*] ר' שמעון בן אלעזר או̇ עשה עד

112 צ"ל „בעמוד".

112a כנראה „דבר זה יש ללמדו" לקוח מן השאלה של השואל שהתקשה במובן מאמר זה דשמואל. הגאון השיב על שאלה זו, ותשובתו זאת נספחה אח"כ לתוך הפירוש (עין למעלה, צד 575 והלאה).

113 =ישמעאל; ובערבית „פולאד" הוא ברזל נקי או ברזל עשות, והמלה הזאת נלקחה מפרסית. בתשובות הגאונים, הוצ' הרכבי, סי' ת"ז, נמצא פרוש יותר שלם למלה זאת אבל מובן „שאבורקאן" בפרסית היא ברזל עשות כמו פולאד̇.

114 מפה ועד „מותר" (שו' 9) נמצא ג"כ בערוך ע' אסטמה בשם רה"ג (עין „אוצר הגאונים", שם).

115 מן פה ועד „כי כן טוב לך" (דף ז', ע"א, שו' 3–4) נמצא ג"כ בתשובות הגאונים, הוצ' הרכבי, ס' שצ"ז (=„אוצר הגאונים", הוצ' לוין, ח"א, ח' התשובות צד 139).

116 צ"ל „ללמד".

117 נכפל בכ"י בטעות.

118 יש להוסיף פה „הרבה" כמו בהוצ' הרכבי.

119 קהלת ט', י'.

119* שבת קנ"א, ע"ב.

(דף ו׳, ע״ב)

שאתה מוצא ומצוי לך ועודן בידך ואם תניח צרכי היום וחובותיו למחר דיו ליום השני לעמוד בצרכיו וחובותיו ואיך יעמד בשלא תמולן[120] כש[ום ש]הרעב ברעב[121] ודוחה אכילתו לרעב[121] שני אין יכול לאכול אפילו אכילה שלעת אחד וכל שכן לכמה עתים כך פתרון אדכפנת אכול ואדצחית שתה דברי חכמים יפים במשל שמצוי תמיד וידוע לכל ופירוש אדרתחה קידרך שפוך גם כענין הזה בזמן שבידך עושר שאתה יכול לפזר ממנו ולעשות חסדים שנמצא מה שבידך כמים רותחים בקדירה ונשפכים לחוץ כי הקדירה לא מכילם לפיכך מה שנטל מן הקדירה באותה שעה הרי הוא נשמר ויכולין בעליו לעשות בו [כל] חפציו[122] ולהאכיל ממנו עניים אם נוטלין ממנו ומחסרין[123] את הקדירה בדע[ת ואם] מעלימין עין הרי הוא נשפך ארצה כי אין הקדירה מכילה אותו ואבד מבעליו וכך משל שלממון. קרנא ברומי קריא היה

(דף ז׳, ע״א)

מפרש כי רגילין ברומי להכריז בקול קרנא משרוקיתא ולומר כך בן מוכר תאנים מכור תאנים דאבוך[124] ואל תשנה מאומנותו כי כן טוב

120 מלה אחת „בשלאתמולן" ונפסקה לשתים בטעות.

121 צ"ל „בערב" וכן „לערב".

122 צ"ל „חפצם".

123 צ"ל „מחסרין".

124 צ"ל „כאבוך" כמו בהוצ' הרכבי.

לך[125] ודרב ספרא הכין גרסין לה רבנן רב ספרא הוה [יתיב] בבית הכסא אתא ר׳ אבא נהר אמ׳ ליה ניעול מר אמ׳ ליה אכתי לא עיילת לשעיר גמרת לך מילי דשפיר[126] מי לא תנן מצאו נעול בידוע ששם אדם מצאו פתוח בידוע שאין שם: ורב ספרא סבר דר׳ אבא מסוכן הוא כדתניא רבן שמעון בן [גמ]ליאל או׳ עמוד החוזר מביא את אדם [לידי] הדרוקין סילון החוזר מביא את אדם [לידי] ירקון וברורה היא[127] ודרוקין[128] בלשון ישמע׳ [אלאסתקא][129] ושלשה מינין של אבר[130] קוראים [אותן הרופאים עכשו אלטב]לי ואללחמי ואלזקי והא [דתנן[131] חותמי ברכ]ות שבמקדש היו[132] עד העולם [והאי ברכ]ה הכי הויא ברוך אתה יי׳ עד העולם שאותך ביראה נעבד ותקינו הכי בר׳ אתה יי׳ מן העולם ועד העולם והא מילתא

(דף ז׳, ע״ב)

קבלה היא ומפי שמועה אמרוה וראיה מן קומו וברכו אסמכתא בעלמא והא קא [דמ]דכרי רבנן מאי דהוה רגילי מעיקרא

125 כאן סוף התשובה, הוצ׳ הרכבי. 126 צ״ל „דשעיר״.

127 אודות ענין רב ספרא עין התשובה ב„גיאוניקא״, ח״ב, צד 4, שו׳ 5 והלאה, והתשובה שם אינה בשלמות כי ישנו הפסק בין דף א׳ ודף ב׳ של הכ״י. תשובה זו וגם זו שלפניה בנוגע ל„אסימון״ נזכרות בין התשובות ששלחו רב שרירא ובנו רב האיי, בעת היותו עוד אב״ד, לרב משולם בן רב קלונימוס מלוקא (שם צד 57, סי׳ ג׳: ודמפרשי רבנן אסימון מעות הניתנין, וסי׳ ד׳: ודאמרינן לענין בית הכסא).

128 מפה ועד „אלזקי״ (שו׳ 15) נמצא בתשובות הגאונים, הוצ׳ הרכבי, סי׳ ת״א, ועל פיה השלמתי מה שחסר פה בכ״י.

129 בערבית חולי המים (וואססערזוכט), הערת הרכבי.

130 בהוצ׳ הרכבי „שלו״ תחת „של אבר״.

131 ברכות ס״ג, ע״א. השוה ג״כ רשימת התשובות בכ״י דרופסי (אוצר הגאונים, ח״א, נספחים, צד 83).

132 צריך להוסיף „אומרים״.

ותקנתא וקרא כי תקנתא הוא להודיעך דאסמכתא היא ולענין א[מן אמן במ]קדש לא קאמ׳ שאין אומרין אמן כל עיקר אילא [לא] כסדר הוה דילנא אבל אומרין [אמ]ן והללויי עם אמן נותנין תהלה בפר[ט] על כל ברכה וברכה ולאיו קבע דילהון בתר כל ברכה למימר בר׳ שם כבוד מלכותו לעולם ועד ומאן דאמ׳ אמן ברוך שם כבוד מלכותו או נמי ברוך י״י לעולם אמן ואמן שפיר ד[מי]

ולענין אל תבוז כי זקנה אמך הכינן פירושה] דלפום מ[אי] דקאמ׳ ראבא האי [קרא מרישיה] לסופיה מ[דריש מסופיה לרישיה מדריש וזה] תורף שלה משקלק[לו המינים התקי]נו שיהא אדם שואל את שלום חבירו בשם וטעמא דמילתא כיון ד[משום] קלקולא דמילתא חזו רבנן דצריך עלמא למיהוה שם שמים

(דף ח׳, ע״א)

תדיר בני[133] בני אדם דהוה אמרין בשאילת שלום בריך מר לאבא ובברא ורוחא דקודשא ואצריכו רבנן למימר יברכך י״י למיהו[וה שם] [שמים תדיר] ביניהון והא תקנתא דהות בהנך יומי כיון . . . . . מצינו אבותינו ששאלו שלום בשם שנ׳ והנה בעׄז באׄ ככתׄ[134] ויאמׄר אל ה וג׳ . . . . . [מצ]אנו בשעת צורך יש לנו לתקין כזאת ואו[135] י״י עמך [ג]בור החיל מאי ואומר הכי קאמר׳ רב[נן][136] . . . . . תקנו תקנה זו אם תאמר שבועז

133 צ״ל „בין׳. 134 צ״ל וכתׄ=וכתיב; רות ב׳, ד׳.
135 =ואומר; שופטים ו׳, י״ב.
136 היינו חכמי הישיבות.

שוטה הנ[יה] כששאל שלום בשם ואין מעשיו
[מוכיחין תא] שמע שהמלאך אומר
[לגדעון יי׳ עמך] גבור החיל ואומר אל ת[בוז]
[כי זקנה אמך ואומר] עת לעשות ליי׳ הפרו
[תורתך] . . . . אף הכי קאמרי
. . . . הוא
. . . . [ה]סמיכו על ידו . . . . . .
. . . . . [בני] אדם שואלין [בשלום חב]ירו
בשם . . . . . . [ש]מע לאביך זה ילדך[137] משמיא
קא מפקדי [לך לשמוע ל]דברי חכמ׳ ולא תבוז לדורות
דב . . . . תימא דאיכא שינוי מנהג

(דף ח׳, ע״ב)

דהא כת׳ עת לעשות לי״י וג׳ מדא . . . .
לי״י עשינו דבר זה משום . . . .
להפר תורתו ויהיו עם הארץ . . . .
גידוף המינים בעבודה זרה ואין [שם שמים]
תדור בפיהם . . . .
הפרנו מנהג הראשונים בשאי[לת שלום]
מפני שהוא עת לעשות ליי׳ ו . . . .
ומעשה בעז ומלאך ראיה. . . . .
אפילו היה בה הפרת תורה. . . . .
שלא תופר התורה ואם אית מאן [דיימר מאי]
שנא הא תקנתא מכולה דתק[נו] . . . .
[דאצ]טריכו בה לכולי האי. . . . .
. . . בין ללמוד את לשונ[ם] . . . .
. . . . . ה גם הוצרכו . . . .
. . . .
. . . .

137 משלי כ״ג, כ״ב.

מן התקנות. פירוש מ[חטא דתלמיותא][138] . . .
איחוי הנקרא כן בלשון יש[מעאל אלר]פו
ומעשה דר׳ אבהו מש[תע׳] . . . . דאמ׳ להו
חנניה בן אחי ר׳ יהושע [בן חנניה] . . . .
(פה סוף העמוד וחסר ההמשך).

138 הפירוש הזה של מחטא דתלמיותא (ברכות ס״ג ע״א) נמצא בתשובות הגאונים, הוצ׳ הרכבי, סי׳ ת״ח, ועל פיה השלמתי מה שחסר פה.

5.

A LIST OF QUESTIONS SENT TO A GAON

Several lists of Gaonic responsa have been published by various authors (Wertheimer, קהלת שלמה, 69–73; Ginzberg, *Geonica*, II, 56–71, גנזי שעכטער, II, 416–31; Marmorstein, תשובות הגאונים, 39–52; Lewin, גנזי קדם I, 7–8, II, 43–44, אוצר הגאונים, I, נספחים, 83). They are all of value as giving indications of many responsa that have been lost. So far no list has been published of questions sent to a Gaon in their full form because in the other lists the questions are only indicated briefly at the beginning of each responsum (cp. especially קהלת שלמה, 69–70). The subjoined fragment will therefore be of some interest as giving us such a list of questions. I have been unable to find any responsum in answer to any of these questions and therefore their place of provenance and the name of the Gaon, to whom they were addressed, is impossible to ascertain.

In my opinion the list of questions on difficulties in the Pentateuch (published by Ginzberg, גנזי שעכטער, I, 230–34) also represents a questionnaire sent to a Gaon. Ginzberg's remarks that the author lived before Ḥiwi al-Balkhi as well as his opinion on the character of the poems on the Bible difficulties (published by Schechter, *JQR*, XIII, 345 ff.) are unacceptable (see Mann, *Journal of Semitic Languages and Literatures*, July 1930, p. 268–69, and especially vol. II of our *Texts and Studies*).

רשימה של שאלות לגאונים.

[סימן הכ"י T.-S. 8 G 7^{10}, ב' דפים של נייר, כתב מרובע].

(דף א', ע"א)

I אלא הנ[א]נו ארבסר דמתקרי ראשון. אימא
מאורתא מכי עייל ארבסר. ביום כת̇. בימּמא.
אימא מצפרא. אך חלק הכתוב. דהוה ליה

מתחילת שבע. ועבדו רבנן הרחקה דליבער מתחילת
שש דלא לינגע באיסורא דאורייתא. וכולי[1].
כאי זה צד הוא האי אך דחלק הכת

II והא דתניא[2] האומר סלע זו לצדקה בשביל שיחיו
בניי[3] ובשביל שאזכה בה לעולם הבא[4] הרי זה צדיק
גמור. מפני מה הוא צדיק גמור. בשביל
סלע צדקה. קשיא.

III והאי דגמרינן[5] ארבעה מתו בעטיו של נחש.
ואלו הן בנימן בן יעקב ועמרם אבי משה וישי אבי
דוד. וכלאב בן דוד. וכולהו גמרא לבד מישי אבי
דוד דמפריש ביה קרא. [ד]כ׳ ואת עמשא שם אבשלו[ם]
תחת יואב על הצבא. ועמשא בן איש ושמו יתרא
הישמעאלי[6] אשר בא אל אביגיל בת נחש אחות צרוי[ה]
אם יואב. וכי בת נחש היא. והלא בת ישי היא
אלא בת מי שמת בעטיו של נחש. מאי עט[יו]

IV שלנחש[7]. והאי דגמרינן[8]

(ע״ב)

ב
לעניין[9] רוב וקרוב הלך אחר הרוב. א׳ אביי. אף
אנן נמן תניינא. דם הנמצא בפרוסדור ספיקו
טמא שחזקתו מן המקור. ואפעל גב דאיכא עלייה

1 =וכוליה. פסחים ה׳, ע״א למעלה. נוסחת הדפוס משונה לגמרי מזו שלפנינו.

2 פסחים, ח׳, ע״א, למטה וע״ב למעלה, ר״ה ד׳, ע״א, בבא בתרא, י׳, ע״ב.

3 בנוסחת הדפוס בלשון יחיד אבל לפי הנראה גם לרש״י היתה נוסחא בל״ר (עיין ד״ה „הרי זה צדיק גמור" בסוף).

4 בנוסחת הדפוס „או שאהיה בן העוה״ב", אבל בפיר״ח „ובשביל שאזכה לעוה״ב" (וכן בכ״י מינכן, עיין בד״ס).

5 ב״ב, י״ז, ע״א, שבת נ״ה, ע״ב.

6 בנוסחת הדפוס „הישראלי" כפי הפסוק בשמואל ב׳, י״ז, כ״ה, אבל בד״ה א, ב׳, י״ז, אבי עמשא נקרא „יתר הישמעאלי".

7 עיין למעלה (צד 20) בפירושו של רש״ג לב״ב.

8 ב״ב, כ״ד, ע״א, ואודות שנויי הנוסחאות עיין בד״ס.

9 אות ב׳ למעלה מורה שצ״ל „בעניין".

דמיקרבא. א' ליה רבא רוב ומצוי קא אמרת. רוב ומצוי ליכא למאן דאמ'. תני ר' חייה דם הנמצא בפרוסדור חייבין עליו על ביאת מקדש ושורפין עליו את התרומה. א' רבא. שמ' מי[10] מדר' חייה תלת'[11] שמ' מ' רוב וקרוב הלך אחר הרוב. ושמ' מי רובה דאורייתא. ושמ' מי איתה לר' זירא. דאמ' אפעל גב שדלתות מדינה נעולות. דהא אשה כדלתות מדינה נעולות דמייא. ואפילו הכי אזלינן] בתר רובה.

דבר זה צריך עיון:

V והאי דלעינין[12] רוניא זבן ארעא אמיצרא דרבינא. סבר רבינא לסלוקיה משום דינא דבר מיצרא. א' ליה רב ספרא בריה דרב ייבא לרבינא אמרי אינשי ארבעי[13] לצלא וארבע לצללא.

מאי האי דאמ'[14] ליה ושתק.

VI [ו]האי דכ'[15]. עללת נפקת בכד. תעדה כתר חברתה [מינ]ה. או יבעון נשריא לקיניהון. זמנין

(דף ב', ע"א)

א' להו. יבעון נשרייא לקיניהון. וזמנין א' להו תעדה כתר חברתה מינה ותהא עללת בכד כאילפא.

VII דאזלת בלב ים. והאי דר' יוסי בר אבין דהוה אמר עבדו לי שור משפט בטור מסכין.

VIII והאי דתנן[16] הביאו לו מליח בתחילה ופת עימו מברך על המליח ופוטר את הפת שהפת

10 =שמע מינה. 11 =תלתא.

12 ב"ב, ה', ע"א.

13 צ"ל ארבע. 14 =דאמר.

15 =דכתיב, ערובין נ"ג, ע"ב, ועיין בד"ס בנוגע לשנויי הנוסחאות.

16 ברכות, מ"ד, ע"א, והשוה התשובה על ענין זה ב„אוצר הגאונים" לברכות (הוצ' לוין, חלק התשובות, צד 98).

טפלה לו זה הכלל כל שהוא עיקר ועימו טפילה
מברך על העיקר ופוטר את הטפילה.

כאי זה צד המליח עיקר והפת טפל
וכבר גמרינן[17] פת פוטרת כל מיני מאכל יין פוטר
כל מיני משקה. וכי האי גוונא קשיא.

IX וטוט אסר טוט שרי דגמרינן[18]
לעניין שמתא מאי הוא:

X והאי דגמרינן[19]. כך היה מנהגו
שלר׳ יהודה ביר׳ אילעאי בערב שבת מביאין לו
עריבה מליאה חמין ורוחץ בה פניו ידיו ורגליו
ומתעטף בסדין המצוייץ ודומה למלאך ייי׳ צב[א]
והיו תלמידיו מחבין ממנו כנפי כסותו אׄ להן
בניי לא כך שניתי לכם סדין בציצית בית [שמאי]
(ע״ב)
פוטרין ובית הלל מחייבין. והלכה כבית הלל. וכול.

כנפי כסותו גמרינן ליה או כנפי כסותן.
ובין כך ובין כך מפני מה היו מחבין אותן.

XI והא דתנייא[20]. ושכב איש אותה שכבת זרע.
אׄ רׄ מאׄ[21]. אותה ולא את אחותה. אותה ולא את
הערווה. וכן בדין. ומה אם כשבא איסור הקל
על איסור הקלה אסר את אוסריו כשבא איסור
חמור על איסור חמורה אינו דין שיהא אוסר
את אוסריו תלׄ לו[22]. אותה. אותה ולא את
אחותה אותה ולא את הערווה:

17 ברכות, מ״א, ע״ב.
18 מו״ק, ט״ז, ע״א.
19 שבת, כ״ה, ע״ב, ועיין בד״ס אודות שנויי הנוסחאות.
20 ספרי נשא, סי׳ ז׳.
21 =אמר רבי מאיר.
22 =תלמוד לומר, במדבר ה׳, ט״ו.

מאי איסור קל וקלה. וחמור וחמורה ומאי אסר את אוסריו. ודין הוא שיהא אוסר את אוסריו.

XII ומה היה עניין מחלוקת קרח[22a] עם רבינו משה מה עיקר העסק הקשר הגדול ההוא.

XIII ולמה קצף משה רבינו על שעיר החטאת[23]. ומה תשובה השיב לו אהרן שלא היה יודע משה רבינו ושתק ושמע וייטב בעיניו.

XIV ותוב אשכחנן בגמרא בדוכתיה[24].

22a במדבר ט'ז.

23 ויקרא י', ט'ז–כ'.

24 כנראה הכונה פה לשקלא וטריא של התלמוד על ענין זה זבחים, ק'א, ע'א.

6.

A PORTION OF THE MAFTEAḤ TO NEDARIM AND GIṬṬIN BY NISSIM B. JACOB OF ḲAIRWĀN

R. Nissim's 'Key to the Locks of the Talmud' was written originally in Arabic[1] and extended over the whole of Talmud Babli. Whereas the Hebrew translation of the work on Berakhot, Sabbath and 'Erubin has been known since 1847 through the edition of Goldenthal,[2] portions of the original in Arabic, as preserved in Genizah fragments, have only recently been made accessible. A British Museum fragment of 2 leaves has been edited by Marmorstein (גנזי קדם, I, 81–82) and 2 more leaves from the Adler Collection were added by Ginzberg (גנזי שעכטער, II, 339–343). In T.-S. Collection I have found 4 more leaves which upon examination turned out to be of the same MS. as the other 4 leaves, viz. the Adler fragment formed the outer leaves of the T.-S. leaves which in turn were the outer leaves of the British Museum fragment. All the 8 leaves are given here together as they form a unit extending from Nedarim 28a—to Giṭṭin 2b. Marmorstein edited his text in his usual faulty fashion as the comparison with the version here on the basis of a photostat will reveal.

[1] כתאב מפתאח מגאלק אלתלמוד, thus R. Nissim cites the work himself in the Arabic original of his Sepher Ma'asiyot (see Harkavy, חדשים גם ישנים, No. 8 (in *Steinschneider Festschrift*), p. 21, bottom). Cp. further Poznański, אנשי קירואן, p. 37, and Ginzberg, *Geonica*, II, 273, where there is cited from a T.-S. fragment the passage: פירש אותם רבינו נסים זצ"ל בחבורו שקראו מפתאח ומגאלק אלתלמוד[ו] המחובר בלשון ישמעאלי.

[2] ספר המפתח של מנעולי התלמוד, Wien 1847.

The Hebrew passage on Sanhedrin 16a–b (published by Lévi, *RÉJ*, XLIV, 294–97, and re-edited by Lewin, גנזי קדם, I, 17–18) is not from our work as it was not his custom to give long explanations in the Mafteaḥ but rather to indicate the sources for Talmudic passages as they occur elsewhere in both Talmudim. Indeed this is stated to be taken from a separate commentary of his on the first 2 chapters of Sanhedrin (מן פירוש אלפרקין אלאולין מן סנהדרין). For another such commentary on the 1st Mishnah of R. H. in Arabic, see the passage cited by Mann, *JQR, N. S.*, XI, 453.

In addition Ginzberg has published a section on Ketubot (ibid., 333–39); see also the passage on Sabbath (p. 287–8). In *Catalogue Adler*, p. 19 (Commentaries), there are also listed portions on Ḥagigah and Mo'ed Ḳaṭon. In our text R. Nissim refers to his remarks on Yebamot, Ketubot, and Nazir.[3] The value of R. Nissim's work lies chiefly in the textual variants it offers to many passages all over both Talmudim.

[3] After the completion of this volume new extracts from R. Nissim's Mafteaḥ have been edited by J. N. Epstein, תרביץ, II, 1 ff.

[MS. Adler 5079, גנזי שעכטער, II, 339–41.]

(דף א', ע"א)

שבלב אינם דברים[1] [אצל דלך פי שבועות בפרק שלישי[2] אמר שמואל גמר בלבו צריך שיוציא בשפתיו] שנ' לבטא בשפתים כוול[3]. וקאלו פי] קידושין פרק האיש מקדש פי אלמשנה[4] ובכולם] אף על פי שאמרה בלבי היה [להתקדש כול וכן היא] שה[טע]תו. וקאל[5] פי אלתלמוד ההוא גברא דזבנינהו לנכסיה אדעתא למיסק ל[ארץ ישראל] בעידנא דזבין לא אמ' לסוף לא סליק [אמר רבא] האי דברים שבלב ודברים שבלב אינן [דברים] כול: הניחא[6] למאן דאמ' אינה חוזרת [אבל] למאן דאמ' חוזרת מאי איכא למימר: אצל דלך פי קידושין בפרק האומר לחבירו[7]:

1 נדרים כ"ח, ע"א. כל הציונים למקומות בתלמוד בדף א', ע"א וע"ב, נמצאים בההערות של גינצברג.

2 כך יש להשלים החסר ולא כמו שמשלים גינצברג (שם, צד 339, הערה לשורה 2). המאמר הוא בשבועות כ"ו, ע"ב.

3 גינצברג מנסח „מו' ", אבל אין ספק שצ"ל „כול"=כוליה וגם יש להשלים החסר כמו למעלה.

4 קדושין מ"ט, ע"ב. גינצברג לא השלים החסר „ובכולם".

5 צ"ל: וקאלו. 6 נדרים כ"ט, ע"ב.

7 קידושין נ"ח, ע"ב, ונ"ט, ע"א.

האומר לאשה התקדשי לי לאחר שלשים יום ובא אחר וקידשה בתוך שלשים יום מקודשת לשני לא בא אחר וקידשה בתוך שלשים יום מהו: רב ושמואל דאמרי תרויהו מקודשת ואף על פי שנתאכלו מעות כול׳. לא בא אחר וקידשה וחזרה בה מהו ר׳ יוחנן אמ׳ חוזרת ריש לקיש אמ׳ אינה חוזרת כול:

(דף א׳, ע״ב)

[סליק פרקא דאר]בעה נדרים:

[פרק רבי]עי: אין בין מודר הנאה

[דקא מהני ליה פרו]טה[8] דרב יוסף פי בבא קמא [בפרק הכונס פי] אלתלמוד[9] קאלו איתמר שומר [אבדה ר]בה אמ׳ כשומר חנם דאמי ורב יוסף [אמ׳ כש]ומר שכר דאמי רבה אמ׳ כשומר [חנם דא]מי מאי הנאה קא מאטי ליה רב יוסף [אמ׳] כשומר שכר דאמי בההיא הנאה דלא [בעיי] למיתב ריפתא לעני הוי עליה שומר שכר:

מאי שנא מדרש דלא[10] דכת׳ ואותי צוה יי׳ בעת ההיא וגו׳ פי מסכת בכורות בפרק עד כמה ישראל חייבין שנינו[11] הנוטל שכרו לדון דיניו בטלין. וקאלו פי אלתלמוד מנא הני מילי אמ׳ רב יהודה אמ׳ רב אמ׳ קרא ראה למדת׳ אתכם וגו׳ מה אני בחנם אף אתם בחנם

תניא נמי הכי כאשר צוני יי׳ אלהי׳ מה אני בחנם אף אתם בחנם: ומנין שאם לא מצא בחנם ילמד בשכר תל׳ לומ׳ אמת קנה ומנין שלא יאמר כשם שלמדתי בשכר

8 נדרים ל״ג, ע״ב.
9 ב״ק נ״ו, ע״ב.
10 נדרים ל״ז, ע״א.
11 בכורות כ״ט, ע״א.

[סימן הכ"י T.-S. 10 F 4[5], ד' דפים של נייר].

(דף ב', ע"א)

אך[12] אלמדה בשכר תל לומׄ אנ[מ]ות קנה ואל תמכור: גבור[13] דכתׄ ויפרוש את האהל על המשכן ואמׄ מר משה רבינו פרשו דכתׄ עשר אמות אורך הקרש: אצל דׄלך פי מסכת בכורות בפרק מומים אילו[14] אמׄ רב משה רבנו עשר אמות היה גובה קומתו[15] שנׄ ויפרוש את האהל על המשכן וכתׄ עשר אמות אורך הקרש ופרשו אמׄ ליה [רב[16] שימי בר חייא לרב אכׄ ע[ו]שיתן בעל מום [למשה רבינו דתנן גופו] גדול מאבריו או קטן מאבריו אמׄ ליה שימי באמה של קודש קא אמינא[17]. במערבא[18] אמרי כוס שלבית המרחץ. שרחו פי מסכת שבת[19] בפרק רׄ אליעזר אומׄ תולין את המשמרת: תנו רבנן עושין יינמילין בשבת ואין עושין אלנתית ואילו הן יינמילין ואלו הן אלנתית יינמילין יין דבש ופלפלין. אלנתית יין ישן ומים צלולים ואפרסמון: למאי עבדין ליה כי נפקי ואתו מבי מסותא שתוׄ למיקר. אמׄ רב יוסף יומא חד עיילי לבתר מר עוקבא לבי בני כי נפק ואתאי אשקיאן חד כסא וחַשִׁי בנפשאי מביניתא דראשי ועד טופרא דכרעי. ופי תלמוד ארץ ישראל יסמונה

12 צ"ל „כך". בנוסחת הדפוס „למדתיה . . . אלמדנה".

13 נדרים ל"ח, ע"א.

14 עקר דבר זה במסכת בכורות (מ"ד, ע"א).

15 „גובה קומתו" חסר בנוסחת הדפוס.

16 מן „רב שימי" ועד „אמׄ ליה" נמצא על הגליון בצד ימין של הכ"י.

17 נוסחא זו יותר טובה מנוסחת הדפוס: „באמה של קדש קאמר" (עיין ג"כ בשטה מקובצת).

18 נדרים ל"ח, ע"ב למטה.

19 פרשו במסכת שבת (ק"מ, ע"א). אודות שנויי הנוסחאות עיין ג"כ בד"ס.

(דף ב׳, ע״ב)

קונדיטון כמא קאלו פי פרק שמונה שרצים[20] חד בר נש שאל לר׳ שמעון בר כרסנה מהו למישתי קונדיטון בשבתא אמ׳ ליה אם להתענג מותר ואם לרפואה אסור. ופי נדרים קאלו[21] הנודר מן היין מותר בקונדיטון. אלא אמ׳[22] הינו טע׳ דר׳ יוסי גזירה משום מתנת בית חורון

אצל ד׳לך פי פרק השותפין אלד׳י בין ידינא[23] מעשה בבית חורון באחד שהיה נודר אביו הנאה ממנו. כול׳. סליק פרקא אין בין מודר הנאה:

פרק חמישי השותפין.

אמ׳ רב אשי[24] ומאן לימא לון דסודרא אי תפיס ליה לא מיתפיס. פי בבא מציעא בפרק שנים אוחזין בטלית תג׳ד[25] אמ׳ רב אשי[26] השתא דאמרת זה נוטל עד מקום שידו מגעת וזה נוטל עד מקום שידו מגעת כמאן דפסיקא דמיא. האי סודרא כיון דתפיס שלש על שלש כמאן דפסיק דאמי וקאני ולא בענן[26a] עד דמשיך ליה כוליה: סליק פרקא השותפין:

(דף ג׳, ע״א)

פרק ששי: הנודר מן המבושל:

הד׳א אלד׳י פי אלמשנה[27] הנודר מן החלב מותר בקום

20 ובתלמוד ארץ ישראל קוראים כוס כזה קונדיטון כמו שאמרו בפרק שמונה שרצים (ירושלמי שבת, פי״ד, ה״ג, דף י״ד, ע״ג).

21 ובנדרים (בירושלמי, פ״ו הי״ג בסוף, דף מ׳, ע״א למטה) אמרו.

22 צריך להוסיף „רבא", נדרים מ״ג, ע״ב.

23 מקור דבר זה בפרק השותפין אשר לפנינו (היינו הפרק הבא), נדרים מ״ח, ע״א.

24 שם, מ״ח, ע״ב.

25 בבבא מציעא בפרק שנים אוחזין בטלית (ז׳, ע״א) תמצא „אמר רב אשי" וכו׳.

26 וכן בכ״י מינכן (עיין בד״ס). מן „השתא" ועד „דמיא" לא נמצא בנוסחת הדפוס וגם לא בכ״י שמביא בעל ד״ס.

26a צ״ל „בעינן", ועיין בד״ס.

27 זה אשר במשנה (נדרים נ״א, ע״ב למטה).

פי תלמוד ארץ ישראל קאלו[28]. מהו בקום חלבה מקטרה. מה טעׄ דרׄ יוסה שם אביו קרוי עליו. וקולהם איצׄא[29] מן העדשים אסור בחשישים[30]. שרחוה פי תלמוד ארץ ישראל[30a]. וקאלו רׄ יסא אזל לגבי חסא דאישתמוע[31] ואפיק קומוי טלפחין מקליין וטחנין ומגבלין בדבש ומטגנין: אמׄ ליה אילין אינון אשישישין[32] שאמׄ חכמׄ. מן שית מילי איעתר רׄ עקיבא[33]. הדה אלסתה קד שרחו מנהא ההנא תׄלתׄה[34] בר כלבא שבוע. ואיילא דספינתא וגווזא. ואמא קצׄה אשתו שלרופוס וקטיעא בר שלום ומטרוניתא לם תשרח ההנא. פאמא[35] קצׄה קטיעא בר שלום פהי משרוחׄה פי מסכת עבודה זרה פי אלפרק אלאול. ההוא קיסר דהוה סאני להו ליהודאי אמׄ להן לחשיבי דמלכותא מי שעלה לו נומה[36] ברגלו יקטענה ויחיה או יניחנה ויצטער אמרו לו יקטענה ויחיה. אמׄ ליה קטיעא

28 בתלמוד א״י אמרו (פ״ו, ה״ח בראשיתה, דף ל״ט, ע״ד).

29 ומאמרם ג״כ (במשנה, נ״ג, ע״ב).

30 צ״ל „באשישים״.

30a בארו אותו בתלמוד א״י (פ״ו, הט״ז, דף מ׳, ע״א למטה) ואמרו.

31 בנוסחת הדפוס „רבי יוסי״ אבל פה „חסא״ (בלי שם התואר רבי: השם „חסא״ נזכר ג״כ ביבמות, קכ״א, ע״ב למטה). האיש הזה היה גר ב„אישתמוע״. המקום הזה היה בנחלת יהודה והיה עיר הלוים (עיין בד״ה א׳, ו׳, מ״ב; ביהושע ט״ו, נ׳, העיר נקראת אשתמה). המקום הזה הוא אלסַמוּע לדרום חברון (עיין הורוביץ, ארץ ישראל ושכנותיה, כרך א׳, צד 99, ד״ה אשתמה או אשתמע). והנה למדנו מנוסחא זו שלפנינו שהיה ישוב יהודי באשתמוע בזמנו של ר׳ יסא.

32 צ״ל אשישין.

33 נדרים נ׳, ע״א.

34 בנוגע לששת הדברים האלה הנה בארו שלשה מהם פה: בר כלבא שבוע ואיילא דספינתא וגווזא, אבל הספור של אשתו שלרופוס וקטיעא בר שלום ומטרוניתא אינו מבואר פה.

35 והנה ספור של קטיעא בר שלום מפורש בע״ז, פרק א׳ (י׳, ע״ב).

36 ולא „נימא״ כבנוסחת הדפוס, עיין ג״כ ערוך ערך נם ד׳. אודות שאר שנויי הנוסחאות עיין בד״ס.

(דף ג׳, ע״ב)

בר שלום חדא דלא מצית להו לכולהו דכת׳ כי כארבע רוחות השמים וג׳ מאי קאמ׳ או לימא דבדרתינכו בארבע רוחי עלמא האי בארבע רוחות מיבעי ליה אלא כשם שאי איפשר לעולם בלא רוחות כך אי אפשר לעולם בלא ישראל. ועוד קרו לך מלכותא קטיעא אמ׳ ליה שפיר קא אמרת מיהו כל דזכי למלכא שרו ליה לקמוניא חלילא כד נקטין ליה ואזלין אמרה ליה מטרוניתא וָיי לה לאילפא דאזלא בלא מכס שקל סכינא וקטעה לערלתיה. ואיכא דאמרין נפל על ראשה דערלתיה וקטעה בשיניה אמ׳ יהבית מכסי חלפית ועברית כי קא שדו ליה אמ׳ כל נכסאי לר׳ עקיבה וחביריו יצא ר׳ עקיבא ודרש והיתה לאהרן ולבניו מחצה לאהרן ומחצה לבניו: ובעד ד׳לך[37] פי אכ׳ר הד׳א אלפרק. קאלו מעשה בר׳ עקיבא שראה אשת טורנוס רופוס הרשע רק שחק ובכה רק שהיא מטפה סרוחה. שחק דעתידא דמגיירא ונסיב לה

סליק פרקא הנודר מן המבושל:

[MS. Brit. Mus., Or. 5558 H, fols. 51–52, גנזי קדם, I, 81–2.]

(דף ד׳, ע״א)

פרק שביעי: הנודר מן הירק:

אסור בפול מצרי לח[38]. פי תלמ[וד] ארץ ישראל

37 ואח״כ בסוף הפרק הזה אמרו (ע״ז, כ׳, ע״א למטה).

38 במשנה, נ״ד, ע״א.

במסכת כלאים ובמסכת שבת[39] קאלו דין הן פול מצרי כד ה"[40] הוא רטוב אינון צוחין ליה לובי כד הוא נגיב אינון צוחין ליה פול מצרי.

הנודר מן התבואה אינו אסור אלא מחמש[ת] המינין[41]. יעני[42] חטין ושעורין וכוסמין ושיבולת שועל ושיפון: ופי[43] מסכת פסחים בפרק כל שעה. שרחו כוסמין מין חטין. שיבולת שועל ושיפון מין שעורין. כוסמין גולבא. שיפון דשרא שבולת שועל שובלי[44] תעלא: תניא[45] הנודר מן הדגן אסור בפול מצרי יבש ומותר בלח ומותר באורז בחלקה בטרגס וטיסני. פי[46] מסכת משקין בפרק מי שהפך את זיתיו: שרחה[47] אמֹ אביי חלקה חדא לתרתי טרגס חדא לתלת טיסני חדא לארבעי. כי אתא רב דימי אמֹ כונאתא. וא. דס . . קול רב דימי וצח תפֿסיר אביי[48]. הנודר[49] מן הבית אין אסור אלא מן האגף ולפנים. פי[50] מסכת פסחים בפרק

(דף ד', ע"ב)

כיצד צולין שאנו[51] מן האגף ולפנים: כלפנים מן האגף ולחוץ כלחוץ. שני[52] אוכל שני טועם מותר

39 בתלמוד א"י במסכת כלאים (פ"ח, ה"ד, דף ל"א, ע"ג) ובמסכת שבת (פ"ה, ה"א, דף ז', ע"ב) אמרו.

40 צריך למחוק אות זו.

41 במשנה, נ"ה, ע"א.

42 היינו.

43 ובמסכת פסחים (ל"ה, ע"א) בארו.

44 ולא „שבילי" כמו שלפנינו, ועיין בד"ס.

45 נדרים נ"ה, ע"ב למעלה.

46 במו"ק (י"ג, ע"ב) בארו.

47 צ"ל „שרחו".

48 ודחו (כנראה כן מובן המלה הערבית שהיא מטושטשת בכ"י) מאמר רב דימי ופרוש אביי הוא הנכון (היינו שהגמרא מסיימת ב„קשיא" על פרוש רב דימי).

49 במשנה נ"ו, ע"ב.

50 במסכת פסחים (פ"ה, ע"ב).

51 היינו במשנה שם.

52 =„שאני" (פעמים), במשנה נ"ז, ע"א.

בחילופיהן ובגידוליהן בדבר שזרעו כלה. אבל בדבר שאין זרעו כלה גידולי גידוליו אסורין:

ואי זה[53] הוא דבר שאין זרעו כלה כגון הלוף והשום והבצלים. דתניא[54] ר שמעון אומ כל דבר שיש לו מתירין כול אצל הדה אלבריתא פי[55] תוספת תרומות בפרק הלוקט דלעת:

סליק פרקא הנודר מן הירק:

פרק שמיני קונם יין:

אמ רבא[56] שרי ליה לצורבא מרבנן למימר לא יהיבנא אכרגא דכת מנדה בלו והלך וג׳ ואמ רב יהודה כול[57] תגד פי בבא בתרא[58] בפרק השותפין רב נחמן בר רב חסדא רמא אכרגא ארבנן. אמ ליה רב נחמן בר רב יצחק עבר מר אדאוריתא ואדנביי ואדכתיבי אדאוריתא דכת׳ אף חובב עמים וג אמ משה לפני הקבה רבונו שלעולם בשעה שאתה מחבב עמים כל קדושיו יהיו בידיך וג׳ דנביי

(דף ה׳, ע״א)

דכת גם כי יתנו בגויים עתה אקבצם וג׳

ואמ עולא פסוק זה בלשון ארמי נאמר אם כולם יתנו בגויים עתה אקבצם ואם לאו ויחלו מעט ממשא מלך שרים[59]. דכתיב מנדה בלו והלך לא שליט למרמא עליהון. ואמ רב יהודה

53 המעתיק השמיט פה כנראה שורה שלמה: „אצל דלך פי מסכת תרומות בפרק תשיעי״ (תרומות ט׳, ו׳).

54 נדרים, נ״ז, ע״ב, ונ״ח, ע״א.

55 עקרה של בריתא זו בתוספתא תרומות (ה׳, ט״ו).

56 נדרים ס״ב, ע״ב.

57 =כוליה.

58 תמצא בב״ב (ח׳, ע״א למעלה).

59 וכן היא הנוסחא בכ״י מינכן (עיין בד״ס).

מנדה זו מנת המלך. בלו זה כסף גולגלתא והלך זה ארנונא: סליק פרקא קונם [יין]:

פרק תשיעי ר׳ אליעזר אומ׳ פותחין:

שמעת מינה[60] מטלטלי משתעבדי לכתובה. קדי[61] דכרנא דלך פי כתובות. שמעת מינה[62] אין מסדרין בבעל חוב. פי׳[63] בבא מציעא בפרק המקבל. קאלו איבעיא להו מהו שיסדרו בבעל חוב[64] גמר מיכה מערכין או לא. תא שמע דשלח ראבין באיגרתיה דבר זה שאלתי לכל רבותי ולא אמרו לי דבר ברם כך היתה השאלה האומר הרי עלי מנה לבדק הבית נגנבו או שאבדו[65] מהו שמסדרין ר׳ יעקב משמיה דבר פדא ור׳ ירמיה

(דף ה׳, ע״ב)

משמא דאילפא אמרו קל וחומר ומה בעל חוב שמחזירין אין מסדירין הקדש שאין מחזירין אינו דין שאין מסדירין: ור׳ יוחנן אמ׳ נדר בערכין כתיב כול וקאלו[66] אשכחיה רבה בר אבוה לאליהו דהוה קאיי בבית הקברות של גויים אמ׳ ליה מהו שמסדירין בבעל חוב אמ׳ ליה גמר מיכה מערכים. אמ׳ רבא[67] ר׳ שמעון היא דאמ׳ עד שיאמר שבועה

60 נדרים ס״ה, ע״ב, למטה. לפנינו הנוסחא: „מטלטלי מי מישתעבדי לכתובה״ אבל נוסחת רש״י היתה כמו למעלה.

61 הנה זכרנו ענין זה בכתובות (היינו במפתח למסכתא זו, לדף פ״א, ע״ב, למטה).

62 שם בנדרים.

63 בב״מ (קי״ד, ע״א למעלה) אמרו.

64 צריך להוסיף „מי״ גמר.

65 מן „נגנבו״ חסר בנוסחת הדפוס, וישנם גם שאר שנויים בנוסחאות.

66 ואמרו (בב״מ שם, למטה).

67 נדרים ס״ו, ע״א.

לכל אחד ואחד. אצל קול[68] ר̇ שמעון פי משנת שבועות בפרק שבועת הפקדון: היו חמשה תובעין אותו ואומרין לו תן לנו פקדון שיש לנו בידך שבועה שאין לכם בידי אינו חייב אלא אחת שבועה שאין לך בידי לא לך ולא לך ולא[69] חייב על כל אחת ואחת ר̇ אליעזר אומ̇ עד שיאמר שבועה באחרונה ר̇ שמע̇ אומ̇ עד שיאמר שבועה לכל אחד ואחד:

סליק פרקא ר̇ אליעזר אומ̇ פותחין לאדם:

פר[ק] עשירי נערה המאורסה:

הינו דר̇ זורא[70] דאמ̇ כל הראוי לַבְּלָה: אצל

[T.-S. 10 F 4[5].]

(דף ו׳, ע״א)

אצלי[71] קול ר̇ זורא פי מסכת מנחות בסוף מסכתא: וקד ד̇כרנא ד̇לך פי מא תקדם. ור̇ אליעזר[72] סבר לה כבית שמאי פי משנת[73] יבמות בפרק ארבעה אחין. שלשה אחין שנים מהן נשואין שתי אחיות ואחד מופנה ומת אחד מבעלי אחיות ועשה בה מופנה מאמר ואחר כך מת אחיו השני בית שמאי אומרין אשתו עמו והלזו תצא משום אחות אשה. וכד̇לך איצ̇א[74] קול

68 עקר מאמר ר׳ שמעון במשנה שבועות (ה׳, ג׳).

69 צריך למחוק „ולא״ או להוסיף „ולא לך״.

70 נדרים ע״ג, ע״א.

71 נכפל בכ״י. המובן הוא: עקר מאמר ר׳ זירא במנחות (ק״ג, ע״ב למטה). והנה זכרנו את זה למעלה (היינו במפתח ליבמות ק״ד, ע״ב).

72 נדרים ע״ד, ע״א.

73 במשנה יבמות (ג׳, ה׳).

74 וכן נ״כ מאמר ר׳ אליעזר שאמר (שם בנדרים) . . . שם בפרק ארבעה אחים (יבמות כ״ט, ע״א) עקר דבריו.

ר׳ אליעזר אלדׄי קאל מאמר לבית שמאי אינו קונה אלא לדחות בצדה לבד הנאך פי ארבעה ארבעה אחים אצל קולה. לבית שמאי[75] דאמרי אין שאלה בהקדש. קד שרחנא[76] אצל דׄלך פי נזירות נסתגי[77] ען אעאתדה: סליק פרקא

נערה המאורסה: פרק אחד עשר:

ואילו נדרים:

אלמא[78] טובת הנאה אינה ממון: אעלם[79] אן אלתרומה ואלמעשר אלדׄי אוגׄב אללה עלי ישראל אכׄראגׄהם ואטאעהם ללכהן וללוי קד גׄעל אללה תעׄ[80] לאצחאבהם פיהם חטׄ אן יעטיהם למן יכׄתארוה מן אלכהנים ואללוים. ואצל דׄלך[81]

(דף ו׳, ע״ב)

פי אלמנצוץ כמא גׄא פי סיפרי ואיש את קדשיו לו יהיו. מגיד שטובת קדשים לבעליהן: ופי תוספת פאה[82] בפרק נטל מקצת פיאה שנינו ארבע מתנות בכרם הפרט והשכחה והפאה[83] כולן אין בהן טובת הנאה לבעלים: אפילו עני שבישראל מוציא את שלו מידו ושאר מתנות כהונה ולוייה כגון הזרוע

75 נדרים ע״ח, ע״א.

76 מפני שכבר בארנו עקר ענין זה במסכת נזיר (היינו במפתח למסכתא זו, דף ט׳, ע״א) אין אנו חפצים להכפילו הנה.

77 צ״ל נסתגני (מן غني).

78 נדרים פ״ד, ע״ב.

79 דע שהתרומה והמעשר, אשר השם הטיל כחובה על ישראל להוציאם ולתתם לכהן וללוי, נתן השם יתברך זכות לבעליהם שיתנום למי שיבחרו מן הכהנים והלוים.

80 =תעאלי.

81 ועקר דבר זה מן הקבלה כמו שנאמר בספרי (נשא, פי׳ ו׳, הוצ׳ הורוביץ, צד 10).

82 ובתוספתא פאה (ב׳, י״ג).

83 צריך להוסיף „והעוללת". השוה שינויי הנוסחאות בין הפיסקא שלפנינו ובין הוצ׳ צוקרמנדל, צד 20, ועיין ג״כ חולין קל״א, ע״א.

והקיבה יש בהן טובת הנאה לבעלין ונותנין לכל כהן שירצה כול ותגׄדהאׄ[84] מדוונהׄ פי מסכת שחיטת חולין בפרק הזרוע והלחיים והקבה. והנאךביינו אלאדלהׄ עלי גׄמיעהא.

אמׄ רבא[85] רׄ שמעון היא דאמׄ עד שיאמר שבועה לכל אחד ואחד. קד[86] דׄכרנא פי הדׄה אלמסכת בפרק רׄ אליעזר אצל קול רבי שמעון. כמאן אזלא[87] הא שמעתיה דרב כרׄ מאיר דאמׄ יד אשה כיד בעלה:

פי[88] תלמוד ארץ ישראל קאלו עלי הדׄה

(דף ז׳, ע״א)

הדׄה[89] אלמשנה ולא ליך אמׄ ר׳ זעורה[90] מא[ן ולא] ליך רׄ מאיר דרׄ מאיר ע[נב]ד יד העבד כיד רבו מפני שאמׄ ולא ליך הא אם לא אמׄ ולא ליך זכת האשה זכה בעלה. פדל[91] עלי אן הדׄה אלמשנה לר׳ מאיר והו ידׄהב אן יד ה[אש]ה כיד בעלה. ולדׄלך תרצוה בהדׄא אלתירוץ. וקאלו תני לא ליך. וקול[92] רׄ מאיר יד עבד כיד רבו פי משנת קידושין בפרק האשה נקנית. עבד כנעני נקנה בכסף ובשטר ובחזקה וקונה את עצמו בכסף על ידי אחרים בשטר על ידי עצמו

84 ותמצא אותה (היינו תוספתא זו) מפורשת במסכת חולין (קל״א, ע״א) ושם בארו הענין בשביל כל המקומות (אשר בהם נזכר ענין זה של טובת הנאה).

85 נדרים פ״ז, ע״ב.

86 כבר הזכרנו מקור מאמר ר׳ שמעון במסכתא זו בפרק ט׳ (עיין למעלה הערה 68).

87 נדרים פ״ח, ע״ב, למעלה.

88 בירושלמי (פי״א, ה״ח, דף מ״ב, ע״ד) אמרו על משנה זו.

89 נכפלה בכ״י.

90 בנוסחת הדפוס חסר שם האמורא.

91 ורמז שמשנה זו כר׳ מאיר ודעתו היא שיד האשה כיד בעל, ולכן תרצוה באותו תירוץ ואמרו.

92 ומאמר ר׳ מאיר במשנה קדושין (א׳, ב׳).

דברי ר׳ מאיר: וקאלו פי אלתלמוד[93] נימא בהא קא מפלגי דר׳ מאיר סבר אין קנין לעבד בלא רבו ואין קנין לאשה בלא בעלה כול. תשע[94] נערות נדריהן קיימין. קאלו[95] פי תלמוד ארץ ישראל. אמ׳ ר׳ יוחנן שתים הן ולמה תנינן תשע בשביל לחדד את התלמידים וכו׳ יהוד[נ]ה שלש. השמים[96] ביני לבינך. שרחו[97] פי תלמוד ארץ ישראל כמא דשמיא רחיקין[98] כן תהא ההיא אתתא רחיקה מן ההוא גברא. ושרחו[99]

(דף ז׳, ע״ב)

איצא יעשו דרך בקשה. אמ׳ ר׳ הונא יעשו סעודה והן מתרגלין לבא דרך סעודה: סליק פרקא

ואילו נדרים: וסליקא מסכתא:

מסכתא דגטים: פרק ראשון:

המביא גט:

אי נמי[100] איתיה חד ממדינה למדינה בארץ ישראל. אצל[101] דלך פי אלמשנה. בפירקין המביא גט בארץ ישראל אינו צריך שיאמר בפניי נכתב ובפניי נחתם. עד אחד[102] נאמן באיסורין תג׳ד[103] פי אול פרק האשה רבה. אלא עד אחד דמהימן סברא היא. מידי דהוה אחתיכה.

93 ואמרו בגמרא (שם, דף כ״ג, ע״ב).
94 נדרים פ״ט, ע״א (במשנה).
95 אמרו בירושלמי (פי״א, הי״א, דף מ״ב, ע״ד).
96 נדרים צ׳, ע״ב (במשנה).
97 בארו בירושלמי (שם, הי״ג).
98 צריך להוסיף „מן ארעא".
99 ובארו נ״כ (שם).
100 גטין ב׳, ע״ב ובנוסחת הדפוס ליתא „איתייה חד" (תחת „איתייה" צ״ל „אייתיה").
101 מקור זה במשנה בפרק שלנו (א׳, ג׳).
102 שם בנטין.
103 תמצא בתחלת פרק האשה רבה (יבמות פ״ח, ע״א למעלה).

ספק שלחלב ספק שלשומן ואתא עד אחד ואמׄ בארי לי דשומן הוא דמהימן. ואפילו[104] לרׄ מאיר דחייש למיעוט. קד[105] דׄכרנא אצל קול ר' מאיר פי מא קד תקדם. ותגׄדה[106] פי יבמות בפרק האשה שהלך בעלה וצרתה. דתניא קטן וקטנה לא חולצין ולא מייבמין דברי רׄ מאיר אמרו לרׄ מאיר יפה אמרת שאין חולצין איש כתוב בפרשה ומקשינן אשה לאיש. ואלא מה טעם אין מיבמין אמׄ להן קטן שמא ימצא סרים

[MS. Adler 5079, גנזי שעכטער, II, 341–43.]

(דף ח', ע"א)

וקטנה שמא תימצא [אילונית ונמצא פוגעים] בערוה פמן [דׄלך אלאדלהׄ דחייש רׄ מאיר][107] למיעוט. אלדי[108] . . . . . [ורבנן סברי זיל בתר][109] רוב קטנים ורוב קטניוׄם לאו סריסי נינהו זיל] בתר רוב קטנות ורו[ב] קטנות לאו א[ילונית נינהו] דאזלי רבנן בתר רוב[א] ולא חיישי למי[עוטא אצל][110] הדׄא אלקול מדׄכור פי עידהׄ מואצׄע מן [אלתלמוד:] ואין דבר בערוה פחות משנים[111] פי [אלמשנה] סוטה דׄכרו דׄלך בפרק מי שקינא לה ו[קאלו[112] ומה]

104 שם בגטין.

105 כבר הזכרנו עקר מאמר ר' מאיר למעלה (היינו במפתח ליבמות).

106 ותמצא אותו ביבמות (קי"ט, ע"א).

107 כך צריך להשלים החסר וגינצברג לא העיר על זה. והמובן: ומן מאמר זה הראיה שר' מאיר חייש למיעוט.

108 כנראה איזה ט"ס. 109 כך צריך להשלים.

110 כך צריך להשלים, היינו שמקור מאמר זה (לא חיישינן למיעוטא) נזכר במספר מקומות בתלמוד (ותחת עידהׄ צ"ל עדׄהׄ).

111 שם בגטין. שאר הציונים על המקומות בתלמוד נמצאים בהערות גינצברג.

112 כך צריך להשלים ולא „ואמרו" כהשלמת גינצברג מפני שרבנו נסים משתמש במלה ערבית ולא עברית.

עדות הראשונה ש[אי]ן אוסרתה איסור עולם [כול][113] אינו דין שתתקיים בנ[ע]ד אחד תל׳ לומ׳ כי מצ׳א בה ערוׄת דבר ולהלן [ה]וא אומ׳ על פי שני [עדים] או על פי שלשה עדים יקום דבר מה דבר ה[אמור] להלן על פי שנים אף ד[בר] האמור כאן על פי שנים וקד ד׳כרו הד׳ה אלמו[צ׳ע]ה׳ פי אלפרק אלאול מן סוטה ותג׳ד איצ׳א פי אכ׳ר מסכת גטין מת׳ל ד׳לך. הכא אשה מהיימנא. אצל ד׳לך פי אלמשנה ב[פרק] שני אף הנשים שאין נאמנות לומר מתו בעליהן נאמנות להביא [את גי]טה חמותה ובת חמותה וצרתה ויבמתה ובת בעלה. וכד׳לך איצ׳א קולהם

(דף ח׳, ע״ב)

[הכא בעל דבר מהימן][114] אצלה פי הד׳ה אלמשנה [האשה עצמה מביאה את ג]טה ובלבד שצריכה [לומר בפני נכתב ובפני]נחתם: ואין העדים [חותמין על] הגט [אלא מפני] תיקון העולם אצל [ד׳לך] [פי אל]משנה[115] בפרק השולח גט לאשתו. העדים חותמין על הגט מפני תיקון העולם [וקאלו] פי אלתלמוד מפני תיקון העולם [דאורית]א היא וכתׄוב בסׄפר וחתׄום והעׄ׳ עדים: אמר רבה לא צריכא לר׳ לעזר דאמ׳ עידי מסירה כרתי ת[קינ]ו רבנן עידי חתימה [דז]מנין דמיתי סהד[י א]ו נמי זמנין דאזלי [למד]ינת הים. רב יו[ס]ף אמ׳ אפילו תימא ר׳ מאיר דאמ׳ עידי [חתי]מה כרתי התקינו שיהו העדים מפר[שין] שמותיהן בגטין מפני

113 כך צריך להשלים כמו הרבה פעמים למעלה ולא כהשלמת גינצברג.
114 גינצברג לא השלים החסר.
115 כך צריך להשלים מפני שווי אורך השורות ולא כהשלמת גינצברג.

תיקון העולם. כי [דתני]א בראשונה אני עד[116] ואם מת עד אם היה כתב ידו יוצא ממקום אחר כשר ואם לאו [פסו]ל התקינו שיהו כותבין שמותן מפ[ני] תיקון העולם אמ׳ רבן שמעון בן [גמלי]אל תקנה גדולה

116 היינו שלא פרש שמו. כנראה צריך להוסיף ,היה כותב׳ אני עד.

7.

A PORTION OF THE WORK הלכתא גבראתא BY SAMUEL IBN NAGDELA OF GRANADA

The occasion for this work has been described by Samuel himself in a poem recently published by Mr. David Sassoon of London, who is now editing the complete Diwān of the Nagid (ספר מֹעט דֹבשׁ, Oxford 1928, pp. 18–21). In 1056 C. E. the army of Granada, which Samuel accompanied to battle, was defeated through the treachery of the people of Malaga and as a result Samuel was captured by the enemy and was in great danger of life. After his rescue he vowed to compose a Halakhic work called הלכאתא גבראתא (cp. Ber. 31a, bottom).[1] In this poem he alludes to the Ḳaraites (who also spread to Spain) and their perversion of the laws of Judaism. Samuel declares that the purpose of his Rabbinic studies was to refute them and explain what the

[1] Cp. heading of poem (p. 18): ויצא דבר המלכות לצאת המחנות עלי גולה המקום באייר שנת תתי"ו ונצל המקום בבגד אנשי מאלקה למחנותינו על הר פומיש יום ה' אחרון לאייר ונאבדו במלחמה אנשי החיל ונלכד בה אבי י"א (= ירחמהו אלהים) אחר כן הצילו השם בנסים ונפלאות אשר לא נשמעו כמוהם ונדר בעת ההיא לחבר הלכאתא גבראתא ואמר בזכרון חברו אותם ובספור המלחמה ההיא והצלתו ממנה.

This heading is by his son Joseph, who collected his father's poems, and is evidently a translation from the Arabic. However the date Iyyar, (4)816 A. M. is to be doubted as his death occurred in the same year at an advanced age (cp. also above, p. 204). Perhaps for תתי"ו we should read תת"ט, 1049 C. E.

See further ll. 66–69 of the poem:

נתתני בידם ותהי לי — למגדל עוז ולמצדות בצורות
ותפשו בי בידים ואולם — אני על במתי עבים יקרות
והאיצו להרגני בחיצים — כמו זיקות ובחניתות כקורות
וחשבו כי בידם להרג בם — והנה מאחוריהם קשורות.

L. 80ff.:

ביום שמו בבור מות וחרוץ — וכליון לבבי במגורות
ביום דלקו שאול ובנות עלוקה — לחייתי כמו נשים מאירות
ויום צרחי במר מגיא הרוגה — עניתני בחיים מסערות.

true laws were.[2] This aim he certainly could not achieve by his הלכתא גבראתא as far as its contents hitherto known indicate, because these topics were hardly the subject of discussion between Rabbanites and Ḳaraites. But perhaps the work contained other matters of more controversial character.[3]

Samuel goes on to state in this poem that he bases his work on the Talmud supplemented by the Gaonic opinions, especially by those of Hai Gaon.[4] Yet with all his reverence for the Geonim, and for Hai in particular, he dares criticise their views although he is aware that he will be reproached for his critical attitude.[5] Thus this work was intended to collect the views of the Geonim, especially of Hai, on selected topics of the Talmud[6] and to examine them critically, a feature that is evident from the text given here.

Sassoon (pp. 3 and 6–7) lists the authorities quoting the Nagid's work, but the original has hitherto been unknown. Here again the Genizah is partly supplying this addendum. The text presented here consists of 4 leaves unfortunately very damaged. The language is partly in Talmudic style and partly in Arabic.

[2] L. 35ff.:

ולכן חזקו מינים זרוע   ודלה דת וקלו החמורות
והרחיבו והפטירו שפתם   ושלחו יד מתי ידות קצרות
והשחירו צדקות הלבנות   והלבינו רשעות השחורות
ולכן הנני חוקר בדת אל   כפי יכלי ושכלי עוד הקירות
ומזכיר התעיות להניאם   וכותב להקימם ההדורות
וחוקק אשר אין בו חלוקה   בלשון צח ובדרכים נברות.

[3] The passage cited in ס' העתים, p. 267, with the allusion to the Ḳaraites in Spain, probably emanates from the הלכתא גבראתא because it begins with הכי אמר שמואל הלוי just as in our text his comments to one section begin with קאל שמואל הלוי (fol. 1, verso, l. 1). Sassoon (p. 3) also rightly surmised so.

[4] L. 42ff.:

והתלמוד אני שם על דברי   מקום מולד וארץ המכורות
ואסמוך באשר אתוה ואכתוב   עלי אמרות גאונים הבחורות
ורב האיי גדול כלם אשו לי   פליאות להתפאר צפירות
ומבורו אני שואב ופתו   אני אוכל ולא אמצא מרורות.

[5] L. 51ff.:

ולא אהדר פני רם כי פני כל   אשר חנף לאל רם לא הדורות
ואדע כי גבוהה עוד ועתק   תדבר בי עדת דעות חסרות
וינדילו ויניעו בראשם   מתי חמד ומלוחם נעורות
ויאמרו מי ידבר כי שגגה   בפי גאון ודברי איש שררות.

[6] Cp. second poem (p. 21, l. 1):

בספר תחזה דברי קדומים   ואחרונים ולא תטרח לחפש.

It is difficult to ascertain from this fragment what plan Samuel adopted in composing the work because there is no order in the selection of the topics discussed, one passage dealing with a Halakhah in Ketubot, and the next one with one in Sukkah while a third section takes up the discussion of a passage in Yebamot. Of course a definite opinion on the character and value of the work must be held in abeyance till more of it will be made accessible as the result of new finds. In its complete form the work would be valuable not only on account of its illustrious author but still more because it incorporated many responsa by Hai and other citations from Gaonic writings.

It should finally be remarked that the work was evidently begun before 1056 because he cites R. Hai as still living (fol. 1, verso, l. 2), hence this part must have been written before 1038. However in another section (fol. 4, verso, ll. 11–12) Hai is quoted as already departed. It must therefore be assumed that Samuel busied himself with the study of Hai's responsa and other Gaonic writings for several years, as far as his busy life left him leisure, and only in 1056 he decided to collect his annotations to the opinions of the Geonim including Hai in the form of a work which he called הלכתא גבראתא.

[סימן הכ"י T.-S. Loan 173, ד' דפים של קלף קרועים ומטושטשים מאד].

(דף א', ע"א)

ועומד לטביחה[1] ואמ̇ לך רבה הא נמי מוקימנא לה בשור לחרישה ועומד
לחר[נישה] כד אוקמתה לדשמואל הדר אותבוי אי הכי אדתאני סופא
לקח זה בשלו וזה בשלו ונתערבו זה נוטל לפי מעותיו וזה נוטל לפי
מעותיו אי הויא קמייתא באנפא דקא אמרת בלחוד אדמפליג הכי
הוה מפליג בדידה ותאני במ̇ דב̇ אמ̇[2] בשור לחרישה ועומד לחרישה

1 כתובות, צ"ג, ע"א, וע"ב. 2 —במה דברים אמורים.

ומדפסקה להדיא שמעינן דבין בהא אנפא ובין בהא אנפא השכר לאמ׳[3]

ופריק רבה דחסורי מחסרא והכי דקא תאני לקח זה בשלו וזה בשלו

ונתערבו הוא הדין למאי דאמ׳[4] דאו כד ח[ש]יבו למיעבד עבדו שותפותן

קיימת והשכר לאמצע ואו לא יכלו למיעבד מ[א] דחשיבו ואשתתפו

אדעתיה אילא איצטריכו למילתא אחרניתא כבר איס[תל]ק[א] לה שותפותם

דחשיבו והוה ליה זה לקח בשלו [וזה לקח בשלו וסליקא לה הא שמע]תא

והילכתא כרבה ודקא מותבינן [תנן וכן שלשה שהטילו לכיס פחתו]

או הותירו כך הן חולקין איכא דק[א משוו לה קושיא לרבה דקא]

אמרינן היכא דהטילו לכיס זה מנא[5] וזה [מאתים ולקחו שור לחרישה]

ובתר הכין אימליכו עליה לטביחה הוה [ליה כל]קח [זה בשלו וזה בשלו]

ונתערבו ואקשו להא מתניתין דהטילו לכיס [תנן ולא קא מפלינ]

בה ותנן כך הן חולקין דאלמא כל אחד [לפי] מעותיו [כהיו שם שלש]

מאות ואנחנא חזינא דהאי [קושיא על עיקר דשמואל היא דקאמ׳]

השכר לאמצע וקא מקשו [ליה הא מתניתין דאלמא השכר לכל]

אחד [לפי מעותיו ופריק שמואל שאם הותירו דזבנו בזוזא וזבינו]

בזוז[א ודנקא השכר לאמצע והכא במאי עסקינן כגון דזבנו]

3 =לאמצע.

4 =דאמרי.

5 =מנה.

[באסתירי רצינאתא דאינון עתיקתא כי ההיא דמפרשינן התם]
[מאי הלמו אמׄ רב נחמן רצינאתא וזבינו כזוזי חדתי דטפי עדיפי ופחתו]

(ע"ב)

איפכא[6] . . . . . קאלי[7] שמואל הלוי. כד מעיננן בפירושיה דנהוריה
דעלמא ריבוננא מר רב האיי יתקיים לעלמין דפריש [להה]יא
שמעתא אמרינן בה אמׄ שמואל שנים שהטילו לכיס זה מנא וזה
מאתים מיתחזי לן בה פירכא דבאעי צילותא וברישא אמרינן
דאשכחנא בנוסחא דפירושא דפריש ורב המנונא אמׄ אפילו לקחו
שור לחרישה ועומד לטביחה אם מצאו ריוח זה נוטל מן הריוח לפי
מעותיו וזה נוטל מן הריוח לפי מעותיו[8] וממילה מיסתבר דהא
טעות סופר היא והכי אשכחן בנוסחין דילנא ורב המנונא אמׄ אפילו
שור לחרישה ועו[מד] לטביחה השכר לאמצע וכד בדקניה בספר

[6] כל הפרוש הזה בשם רה"ג נמצא בתור תשובה בתה"ג, הוצ' הרכבי, סי' פ"א (צד 50), אלא ששם קצר המעתיק התחלת הפרוש. ע"פ תשובה זו השלמתי את החסר בכ"י שלפנינו (ועיין הערות הרכבי).
תשובה זו היא האחרונה בקובץ של ס"ז תשובות שנשלחו לרב יוסף בן רב עמרם, ראש בי"ד של קהלת סגלמאסה (במורוקו). עיין הכתובת בצד 32 לפני סי' ס"ח (ושם תחת „ורבנו דתלמידי" צ"ל „ורבנן ותלמידי"). כבר העיר הרכבי (צד 353, לסי' ע"ג) שתשובה זו (ובכן כל הקובץ של הט"ז תשובות) היא בודאי או לרש"ג או לרה"ג, ועתה מכ"י שלפנינו נתברר שיש ליחסן לרה"ג.

[7] בעברית: אמר.

[8] ונוסחא זו באמת בתשובת רה"ג שהזכרנו למעלה (הערה 6).

השותפ[ות דמר רב שמואל גאון נוחו] עד[9] אשכחן
נמי כד אשכחן בנוסחין . . . .
[דילנא] . . . . מדכתיב בפירושא דרבנא האיי
. . . . [אמ׳ שמואל שנים שהטילו] לכיס זה מנא וזה מאתים השכר
[לאמצע] . . . . פסיק ולא קא משני בין שור לחרישה
[ועומד לחרישה ובין שור לחרישה] ועומד לטביחה וכיון דתיובתא
[דרבה הילכתא כרב המנונא[10] דמ]תניתין מסייעא ליה לרב
המנונא ועוד מתחזי . . .
[כנוסחין דילנא מדק]אמ׳ ורב המנונא אמ׳ אפילו שור לחרישה
ועומד . . . .
[לטביחה השכר לאמצע] מאי אפילו [והא] רבא בשור לחרישה
ועומד לטביחה
. . . . חשיבו למיעבד עבדי
. . . . יכולין למיעבד מאי דחשיבו
. . . .
. . . .
. . . .

(דף ב׳, ע״א)

ו. . . . .
דלא . . . .
משכחת . . . .
לה מי מיש . . . .

9 =עדן. ספר השותפות לר׳ שמואל בן חפני, גאון סורא, נזכר בספר העיטור (הוצ׳ לבוב, ח״א, ט״ו, ע״א למעלה) לנדון שלפנינו: ורבינו שמואל בן חפני כתבא (צ״ל: כתב) בספר השותפות אע״פ שלא נתערב ממון השותפות זה עם זה נכנס לכלל השיתוף והריוח לאמצע, והרב אלפס חלק עליו בתשובה ואמר דדוקא שהטילו שניהם לכיס אחד ונתערב הממון הא נאו (צ״ל: לאו) הכי לא וכו׳. השוה ג״כ למטה, צד 670.

10 וכן היא דעתם של ר״ח ור״י אלפאסי (עיין ברא״ש לכתובות פ״י, סי׳ י׳ בסוף: ורבינו חננאל ורב אלפס ז״ל פסקו כרב המנונא. ועיין ברי״ף: הלכה כשמואל ואליבא דרב המנונא) והרמב״ם. ועתה נודע שגם ר׳ שמואל הנגיד בין הפוסקים האלה נגד דעתו של רה״ג שההלכה כרבה.

קושיא זו היינו . . . .

ואפיק לנא בין [אליבא . . . .

לרבה ובין אליבא דקא משוי לה . . . .

דמשוי לה קושיא לרבה דקאמ׳ . . . .

ולקחו שור לחרישה ואימליכו [עליה לטביחה זה נוטל לפי מעותיו וזה נוטל]

לפי מעותיו ואי סל[11] דע . . . ה . . . .

והא מתניתין אדעתיהו כל אח[ד] . . . .

ואי אמרת משום דלא אפליג ב . . . .

דקשיא לרבה לחודיה והא כי הי . . . .

קשיא ליה לרב המנונא דקאמ׳ ל[עולם השכר לאמצע] . . . .

וכי תימא רב המנונא בתרי באבי כל אח[ד] נוטל מן הריוח לפי מעותיו]

סבירא ליה וההיא דלעיל לאו טעות סופר היא אי [הכי] . . . . . .

מאן מותיב לה אי רבנן אליבא דרב המנונא . . . .

הואיל ולית ליה השכר לאמצע כלל . . . .

אמאי אמרינן תי[ו]בתא דרבה] . . . .

מיבעי ליה דר[ב המנונא] . . . .

[רי]שא קשיא . . . .

[אמ]רינ[ן] . . . .

(ע"ב)

[א]מ׳ . . . .

. . . .

[ר]בנא הא יי . . . .

חולק[12] כך הן [פחתום או הותיר]ום . . . .

שלוש מאות אם . . . .

דהאי בבא . . . .

11 =סלקא.

12 =חולקין.

. . . . דהאי בבא לאו משום דכל אחת נוטלת
. . . . אחרינא אי לשמו[13] כדאית ליה
. . . . מסלקינן הנך שינויי מן היו שם
[שלש מאות] . . . . [ע]יקר [הא] טובא מרחק מאי דפיש
. . . . אמר[13*] כלל דבאבא דהיו שם שלוש
[מאות] . . . . ספרא[13*] אבל וכן שלשה שהטילו
[לכים] . . . . שינויא אלא בראיה ברורה דהאי
. . . . חושבנא אתא אלא לאוקומי עיקר
. . . . אתא והוה ליה היו שם שלש מאות טפילה
הוא עיקר ומאן דאמׄ דעיקר שלשה שהטילו
[לכים] . . . . מהדין טפילה מרחק טעמיה טובא וכלשון
. . . . [היו] שם שלש מאות תוספת על העיקר
. . . . שות ושמא יש
. . . . [ר]בנא האי . . . .
. . . . נו
. . . .
[בין דף ב', ע"ב, ודף ג', ע"א, חסרים ב' דפים או יותר].

(דף ג', ע"א)

רבא אמׄ האמ[ת] וה[ש]לום אהבו[14]. מאי פירושיה. פירושיה כופרא[15] כפניות

הנקראות בלשון [יש]מעׄ[16] אלגפרי[17] וקא . . . . כפות תמרים וליכא

אימ[18] כופרא שמא כפניות אמׄ לנו ליטול והן [כפות] תמרים אמר אביי מפני

13 =לשמואל. 13* קריאת מלה זו היא בספק.
14 סוכה ל"ב, ע"ב.
15 שם, ל"ב, ע"א (ותחת „פירושיה" צ"ל „פירוש" כמו שמורות הנקודות על שתי האותיות האחרונות).
16 =ישמעאל.
17 מלה זו מסופקת מפני קרע בכ"י. 18 =אימא.

שדרכי התורה דרכי נועם [וכל נתיבותיה שלום שאין דר]כן שלכפניות לבוא

אלא בניסן והרבה כבד שכל יחיד ויח[יד] . . . . . ן עד החג ליטול אותן.

ומכמה תעלה בידו אחת או . . . . כשיעבור עליה

הקיץ ונמצא צריך לטורח גדול ואין [זה] דרכי [נו]עם ונתיבות שלום.

הילכך לא כך אמרה תורה מפני שד[רכיה דרכי נו]עם.

והירדוף[19] בלשון

משנה הרדופני[19a] דתנן בואילו טו[רפות[20] ושאכ]לה [הר]דופני והוא עץ שֶעָליו

רחבים מֶעָלין שלהדס אלא שהוא עבות וע . . . . הוא

מכוער במראה וריחו רע ביותר והרבה . . קורין אותו אלדפלה̇[21]

וכששאלו שמא עליו אמֹ תורה עץ עבות [אמר א]ב[יי] שאין התורה

מזהרת ליטול כזה שריחו רע ומאוס הוא ביותר ובני אדם בדילין ממנו

כי אין אילו דרכי נועם ונתיבות שלום ו[התו]רה כתוב בה דרכיה דרכי נועם

וכל נתיבותיה שלום והכין נמי ביבמות ביש [מות]רות לבעל[יהן][22] דאמר ליה

רב יהודה מדיסקרתא לרבא דין[23] שאינו נוח הכין אהדר ליה רב[א] והל[א]

דרכי נוֹעםֹ תורה הואיל וכתוב בה דרכיה דרכי נועם וכל [נתיבותיה ש]לום.

19 שם, ל״ב, ע״ב.

19a בנגוד לפרוש זה, שהוא נ״כ של רש״י, עיין בתוספות, ד״ה: האמת והשלום אהבו.

20 חולין נ׳, ה׳.

21 בערבית, ובאנגלית: Oleander, rhododendron.

22 יבמות פ״ז, ע״ב.

23 היינו קל וחומר.

ביע אלארוסה לאמלאכהא אלתי ורתת . . . הא זוג̇ת . . .
ודכ̇לת אליה . . . . . אלבעל אפסאק ד̇לך אל . . . . ב ע ̇ץ
אלגאונים ד̇כר כד

(הפסק הזה נמשך מדף ג', ע"א, שורה י"ח, עד דף ד', ע"ב, שורה י"א, ומפני שהכ"י קרוע ומטושטש מאוד לא העתקתי אותו, ואני נותן רק את ההמשך מדף ד', ע"ב, שורה י"א, עד סוף העמוד, שבו נמצא פירוש מרב האיי גאון).

(דף ד', ע"ב, שורה י"א)

......................רבינו האיי
גא̇ זצ̇ל יבמות. והא דתנן[24] שנים [ש]קידשו שתי נשים ובשעת
כניסתן לחופה וכו̇ל הא דמשני רב עמרם[25] אמרי בירב בשופעת
מתוך שלש לאחר שלש לאחר שלש[26] לאיחובי אינהו ואיכא דרך לשש עשרה
ח[טאות ואו]ף על גב דליתיה [ד]רך טעמא קמא סגיא או אית טעמא אחרינא
[הכי]ן חזינא דלפום אוקמתא שנייה דאמרינן איב̇ אימ̇[27] כולה באיסור בת
[אח]ת ואליבא דר̇ שמע̇[28] לית ליה אנפא לנידה אלא כדרב חיסדא[29] דאמר
בירב לגבי שש עשרה חטאות לא משכחת לה אלא אליבא דמאן דא[מר]
ברישא מאן האי תנא דאית ליה איסור כולל ואיסור מוסיף ואיסור [בת]
[אחת] אמ̇ רב יהודה אמ̇ רב ר̇ מאיר היא דתנן יש אוכל אכילה אחת

24 יבמות ל"ג, ע"ב (במשנה).

25 שם, ל"ד, ע"א, ובנוסחת הדפוס: אמר רב עמרם אמר רב.

26 נכפל בכ"י וצריך למחוק. נוסחא זו נזכרת ג"כ ע"י ר"ת כפי ספר בשר על גבי גחלים (עיין בתוספות, ד"ה: מתוך י"ג).

27 =איבעית אימא. 28 שמעון.

29 צ"ל: כדרב עמרם, כמו למעלה (שורה 13).

ו[חייב] עליה ארבע חטאות ואשם אחד וכול שא[יס]ור חל על
איסור בחיובו[ו]

ה[וא] כולל או מוסיף וכל שכן אם שני האיסורין באין לאותו אדם
ובח[יוב]

א[חד וכבר] פירשנום ביאור נכון אל קירואן. ומאן
דאית ליה האי

SECTION VII

GENIZAH INVENTORIES OF BOOKS

BOOK-LISTS

The importance of these old book-lists, especially if emanating from the Genizah, for the history of Jewish literature has been recognized by several scholars. Frequently they contain the only records of works entirely lost to posterity or they throw new light on those previously known; in addition they illustrate the tastes and the interests of the reading public in those days and also testify to the respective popularity of certain literary productions. All the previous publications of such lists are discussed by Poznański (*Z.f.H.B.*, XII (1908), p. 111 ff.) who himself edited there a number of new fragments. Thirteen years afterwards six additional lists were made accessible by me (*RÉJ*, LXXII, 163–183) whereas Poznański contributed a rather recent list of 28 Ḳaraite works (ibid., 184–91). Quite recently Prof. Gottheil augmented the number of these literary inventories by 5 more Genizah book-lists (*Jewish Studies in memory of Israel Abrahams*, 1927, 149–69).[1] Finally there is the Fihrist of Sa'adyah's works, unfortunately incomplete, drawn up by his sons (Mann, *JQR, N. S.*, XI, 423–28; cp. Poznański's remarks, ibid., XIII, 369–96).

The new fragments of this kind given here are a welcome addition. No. I is especially instructive because the compiler, not venturing to state his own identification, has scrupulously given us the beginning of each item listed. Thereby we now obtain definite information how, e.g., Mekilta de R. Simon b. Yoḥai commenced (see note 24), and how probably also the Mekilta to Numbers (see especially note 92) and the Yelamdenu to Genesis (see note 32).

No. II is a very extensive list although still incomplete. No. III, just as the previous ones, also emanates from the Genizah. However No. IV is rather a late Ḳaraite compilation discovered

[1] The editor has misread many words and also his notes leave much to be desired.

by Firkowicz. Pinsker (ל"ק, נספחים, 191, note 2) has extracted from it some items. I have found it in Leningrad among the MSS. belonging to the late Dr. Harkavy. There is no record how this list came into his private possession.[2] Its importance is by far inferior to the lists coming from the Genizah. The item of a complete commentary on the Pentateuch by Hai Gaon (see note 340) would be of much interest and the loss of it greatly to be regretted, if all doubts about the veracity of this item, by reason of the lateness of the MS. and its having passed through the magic hands of Firkowicz, could be dissipated. However the whole list should not be regarded as a forgery because its genuineness otherwise (apart from the item listing a grammar in Arabic by Ḳimḥi, note 347) is evident. Moreover Hai's commentary may well have existed, although never heard of before, just as we learned for the first time from the genuine Genizah book-list (Mann, *RÉJ*, LXXII, 164) of Jacob b. Nissim (of Ḳairwān) having composed a commentary to the second half of Genesis and R. Ḥushiel of the same city to Exodus.[3]

[2] The other list (cited by Pinsker, *l. c.*, 192, note) I could not locate.

[3] תפֿ ויצא לרֹ יעקב ראס כלה ז"ל (viz. from Gen. 28.10–end) and כראס ואלה שמות מן פירֹ ר' חושיאל ז"ל. The last item would indicate that Ḥushiel's comments extended to other books of the Pentateuch, only that this pamphlet comprised merely the interpretation of Exodus.

I.

[T.-S. Loan 149, 6 paper leaves. Each item in the book-list is divided by a line.]

(Fol. 1, recto)

*דפתר[1] אבתדאה שאילות אנשי
קירואן ששאלו מלפני שרירא
דפתר[2] אבתדאה על שמך רחמנא אגדה
דשמואל. עת לעשות ליי' הפרו תורתך
כתאב אלאמאנאת ואלאעתקאדאת[3]
כתאב[4] אבתדאה חשוכי בגדים יריד בה

*On account of their abundance and size the notes have been placed behind the texts.

מן ומא בהם כ̇ארג̇ת מן אלנג̇אסה̇
כתאב אבתדאה השותפין שרצו לעשות
מחיצ̇[5] בחצר בונין
כתאב אבתדאה בראשית שאילתא
דחייבין בית ישראל למינח ביומא דשבתא[6]
תפסיר תהלות[7] ואבתדאה פצ̇להא במא
אודעהא מן עט̇ים חכמתה

(verso)

[כתאב אב]תדאה בשם שומע לחשים.
[נת]חיל סדר קדשים: כל הזבחים שניזבחו[8]
דפתר[9] פי ורק דמשקי מַשְׁנָה פיה מן אול
אלמשנה אלי סליק מסכתא דברכות והו
תשעה פרקא
כתאב תרג̇מתה פתרון חומש [אל]ה ה[דברים]
ושפטים שפתר דניאל בן משה זכ[רו לברכה][10]
דפתר אבתדאה ואלה שמות בני ישר[אל]
זה שאמר הכתוב בשמך אלהים וג̇ מלך בשר ודם[11]
כתאב תרג̇מתה פרוש סדר טהרות
ואבתדאה וחשוכי בגדים פירושן[12]
כתאב מכלה̇[13] ואבתדאה לפי שנאמר
בכל קודש לא תגע יכול אף במעשר

(fol. 2, recto)

תפסיר דניאל[14] בג̇לד אחמד ואבתדאה
כתאב אלממאלך ואלמלאחם יכון פי
אלף שפ̇ו סנה̇
כתאב אבתדאה לעולם יי׳ דברך נצב בש̇
תני בשם רב̇ אליעזר בעשרים וחמשה
באלול נברא העולם[15]
דפתר[16] אבתדאה ספר זרעים ברכות

תוספה [וג̇ז]ו עלי ט̇הרה תוספה
על המשנה כולו
כתאב פיה תפסיר משלי וגירה
ואבתדאה כ̇רג̇ פי אלאסת קום יתכ̇דון
אעיאדהם עלי רויא אלהלאל[17]
כתאב אבתדאה אילו דברים שבין
בית שמאי ובית הלל בסעודה[18]
כתאב אבתדאה וידבר יי׳ אל משה
במדבר סיני וג̇ מה ראה הדבר הזה
להכתב באי זה יום באי זה חדש[19]
(verso)
כתאב אבתדאה יציאות השבת
שתים שהן ארבע בפנים ושתים[20]
[ג̇ז]ו פיה ברכות תלמוד ואבתדאה
אנו תינינה משעה שהכהנים[21]
כתאב אבתדאה אגדה דאלה הדברים
אלה הדברים זה הוא שאמר הכתוב
אז ידלג כאיל פסח וג̇ מי היה זה משה[22]
כתאב אחכאם אלאמלאך [תא]ליף̇ אדנינו
שמואל הכהן[23]
כתאב אבתדאה ומשה היה רעה וג̇
וירא מלאך יי׳ אליו בלבת אש רב̇ שמעון[24]
כתאב כביר אבתדאה ערב
פסחים סמוך למנחה לא יאכל אדם[25]
כתאב אבתדאה שביעית כתוב
ששת ימים תעשה מעשיך[26]
(fol. 3, recto)
כתאב תורת כהנים ואבתדא[ה]
רב̇ ישמעאל אומר משו[ל]ש עשרה מדות[27]

כתאב אבתדאה מקאלה̈ אלפהא ראס
אלמתׄיבה̈ אהרן הכהן בן יוסף לצהרה
חין אלתמס מנה תפסיר וזאת הברכה[28]
כתאב אבתדאה ר̇ תנחום בר חנילאי
פתח ברכו יי׳ מלאכיו אמר ר׳ תנחום[29]
כתאב [א]בתדאה אלה פירושי השמועות
הקשות אשר במסכתא דברכות[30]
כתאב[31] כביר אבתדאה תפסיר אלנצף
אלאכׄיר מן אלגזו אלכׄמס מן אלתורה
עלי תופיק אללה קאל מכׄרגׄה מן אלעבראני
כתאב אבתדאה בראשית ברא אלהים
ילמדינו רבינו י״י בחכמה יסד ארץ
כשברא הקדש ב̇ה̇ את עולמו[32]

(verso)

כ[תא]ב אבתדאה חמש עשרה נשים
פוטרות צרותיהן וצרות צרותיהן[33]
כתאב אבתדאה רחמנא סייען
אמ̇ רב שמעון בן לקיש שנים עשר
מזלות ברא הק̇ב̇ בעולמו וכל מזל[34]
כתאב אבתדאה מאבוי שגבוה
מעשרים אמה ימעט רב̇ יהודה אומר[35]
כתאב אבתדאה ביצה ש[נול]דה ביום[35a]
בית שמאי אומר תאכל ובית הלל
אומ̇ לא תאכל[36]
כתאב נסך̇ אלשטרות וכבותות[37]
ואבתדאה בכך וכך בשבת בכך וכך
לחדש[38]
כתאב פרקי תשעה באב: כתב
מזמור לאסף אלהים באו גוים[39]

כתאב אבתדאה הכל חייבין בראיה
חוץ מחרש שוטה וקטן וטומטום[40]
(fol. 4, recto)
כתאב אבתדאה תאליף שמואל[41]
ואיצֿא כתאב אלעדד וכתאב אלשרוט[42]
מצחף אבתדאה בשם אל שוכן מעונה.
נתחיל בסדר החמישי תוספת המשנה[43]
כתאב אכֿר אבתדאה יציאות השבת
שתים שהן ארבע בפנים ושתים שהן
ארבע בחוץ: שאלנו בתלמוד של[44]
מצחף [א]בתדאה דיני ממונות
בשלשה ורבי אומר בחמשה ביד[45]:
כתאב אבתדאה כתאב אלביוע
תאליף מרנא שמואל הכהן ראש הישיבה[46]
כתאב אכֿר לטיף כתאב בעיף כיף
צאר מנתחלי אלבחתֿ אלי אלבהת[47]
גֿזו פיה תפסיר ויהיו חיי שרה
בגֿלד אכֿוד בחלקהֿ פצֿהֿ[48]
(verso)
גזו לטיף בגֿלד אחמד חסירות
ויתירות ו[אבת]דאה ברוך י׳׳ לעולם.
אל נצב על הסולם[49].
כתאב אחכאם אלזוגֿיהֿ
ואבתדאה תאליף מרנא שמואל
הכהן[50]
כתאב גֿאמע אלצלואת ואלתסאביח[51]
כתאב אגדת משלי: משלי שלמה
בן דויד מלך ישראל. רבֿ תנחום בֿ הנולאי[52]
כתאב אכֿר אבתדאה חמש עשרה

נשים פוטרות[53]
כתאב תרגׄמתה מסכת יומא
ומסכת עבודה זרה וגׄ אפראק
ואבתדאה אמר להן הממונה צאו וראו[54]
(fol. 5, recto)
כתאב אכׄר משנה פיה מאמתי קורין
אלי חסלת מסכת ברכות[55]
כתאב אבתדאה מגלה נקראת באחד
עשר בשנים עשר[56]
כתאב פיה נדרים גמארא ונזירות
וקידושין: ואבתדאה כל כינויי נדרים
כנדרים חרמים כחרמים[57]
כתאב סדר קדשים[58]
כתאב אלנצף אלתׄאני מן כתאב אלכשף
ממא אלפה אברהם בן מומר אלצירפי
תלמיד ראס אלמתׄיבהׄ אלפיומי[59]
גׄזו אבתדאה אלקול פי אלצלאהׄ
וגׄובהא[60]
גׄזו פיה אלפאטׄ משנה וגירהא
גׄזו אכׄר אלפאטׄ משנה וגירהא[61]
(verso)
כתאב בכׄט גליט אבתדאה תמיין[61a]
מדׄהב אלחק מן אלבאטל פי אתׄבאת
אלאעיאד[62]
כתאב אבתדאה אסתדראך אלפהן[63]
אלמוגׄוד פי כתב ראס אלמתׄיבהׄ
אלפיומי תאליף מבשר הלוי בן נסי
אלמערוף באבן עשבהׄ[64]
פרקים דרב אליעזר: ואבתדאה

רבֿ אליעזר בן הרקנוס פתח מי ימלל[65]
גֿזו כביר תפסיר אלגֿזו אלתֿאני מן
אלספר אלאול מן ספור אלתורה[66]
גֿזו כביר תפסיר ויקרא ואחרי מות
אבתדאה תפסיר אלגֿזו אלתֿאלתֿ חסב מא
קדם[67]
גֿזו כביר פיה הלכות גדולות
ואבתדאה ברוך אתה י״י אלהינו מלך
העולם אשר קדשנו במצותיו וצונו על
דברי תורה[68]
(fol. 6, recto)
גֿזו פיה אותיות רבֿ עקיבה ואבתדאה
אמר רֿ עקיבה אילו עשרים ושתים אותיות
שבהן נתנה כל התורה כולה לשבטי ישראל[69]
כתאב אלאימאן: ואבתדאה כתאב
מכֿתצר פי שרח אלגֿמל ואלאצול מן פקה[70]
תפסיר משלי לסעדיה ואבתדאה כת[אב]
טלב אלחכמה[71]
כתאב הלכות פסוקות דסדר מועד
הלכות שבת: תנו רבנן לדעת כי אני יי׳ מקֿ[72]:
גֿזו לטיף בגֿלד אסוד אבתדאה תפסיר
אלגֿזו אלתֿאני מן אלספר אלאול מן ספור אלתורה[73]
כתאב שחיטת חולין ואבתדאה וסליק
פירֿ הכל שוחטין ושחיטתן כשרה[74]
גֿזו לטיף מגֿלד בלוח ואבתדאה בשלשים
ושתים נתיבות פלאות חכמה[75]
(verso)
גֿזו כביר אבתדאה לגיעולי גויים או
דלמא כיון דאפיה ישראל שרי [76]

ג̇זו פיה תפסיר פרשת אחרי מות
ואבתדאה תפסיר אלנצף אלת̇אני מן אלג̇זו
אלת̇אלת[77]
ג̇זו הלכות שחיטה ואבתדאה
אוג̇ב מא אבתדי בה פאתחה כל מקאלון[78]
כתאב פיה מן אכ̇באר אדם ואלי אלמגר
מן כתאב גריון ואבתדאה אדם
הוליד את שת ושת הוליד את אנוש[79]
ג̇זו תפסיר ויאמר י״י אל אברם לך לך
ואבתדאה אול מא עמלת וצלת אלסבב[80]
ג̇זו לטיף[81] ואבתדאה עת לעשות לי״י הפרו
תורתך. תנ̇י בשם ר̇ נתן מסרס את המקרא
הפרו תורתך

II.

[T.-S. 10. K. 20.9, 4 paper leaves in quires of 2 leaves each, and T.-S. Loan 147 also containing 2 leaves. These 3 quires probably fitted into each other but their sequence cannot now be established. The first two quires (T.-S. 10. K. 20.9) have been published by me in *RÉJ*, LXXII (1921), 169ff., but are reproduced here again in connection with the new fragment (T.-S. Loan 147) which is a part of the same MS. The beginning and end of this very extensive inventory of books are still missing. The explanatory notes are taken over from *RÉJ* but are here modified in several instances. The 3 quires of our MS. are given here under A, B and C.]

A.

(Fol. 1, recto)

מצחף תפסיר ויצא יעקב[82] מצחף סידור[83]
מצחף תלמוד נשים ונזיקים והלכות קצובות[84]
מצחף מקרא נביאים כאמל[85] מצחף שאילתות
לר̇ אחא[86] סתה̇ דפאתר תלמוד בבא מציעה

הוריות ומגלה בכורות ערכים[87] אלבֿ[88] בבא בתרא
סנהדרין ומכות אכֿר עבודה זרה אכֿר
בבא קמא שבועות הוריות מצחף[89] כראריס
תלמוד שבת כראריס מסכת נדה
מצחף גיר מגֿלד ראש השנה וכיפורים
דפתר מסכת שבת דפתר מנחות
אכֿר יום טוב וראש השנה וסוכה ותעניות
אכֿר כֿמסהֿ כראריס נתֿר תלמוד נזיקים[90]
דיפתר[91] כראסין שקלים מצחף בלא מגֿלד
מסכת ברכות אכֿר איצֿא בגיר מגֿלד
נדרים ונזירות

(verso)

וגטים כראריס מכאלהֿ וידבר[92] כראריס
תרגום[93] כֿמסהֿ עשר רזמהֿ כראריס נפץֿ[94]
דפתר תפסיר בראשית דפתר תפסיר איוב[95]
שתהֿ[96] עשר כראס אפתתחאת עלי
אלפראריש[97] רזמהֿ כראריס רקוק וכאגר
תשובת שאילות[98] דפתר תשובות ואכראראת
תסעהֿ עשר כראס[99] דפתר כראס
אלמדכֿל תלמוד[100] כתאב אחכאם אלוכאלהֿ[101]
תפתר[102] אכֿבאר אלמהרי דפתר נקל חנין
אבן אסחק[103] דפתר תשובת שאילות[104]
כתאב אלכֿלאף בין סורא ואלאנבאר[105] כתאב
אלטֿא ואלצֿאד[106] כתאב בריתא[107] כתאב
תדביר אלרגֿל למנזלה[108] כתאב תפסיר

(fol. 2, recto)

השותפין[109] כתאב אגדה לתורה[110]
דפתר תלמוד עבודה זרה[111] ארבעה
אפראק תלמוד מן שבת כראסהֿ דינים[112]

רזמה̈ כראריס מכאתבאת[113] דפתר ארבעה אפראק מן יבמות[114] כראריס מכאתבאת דפתר שימות[115] גזו מן תפסיר קוהלת[116] דפתר תפסיר אלכב̇[117] תפתר רסאלה̈ אלכנדי[118] כראסה̈ מאסרה̈ אלתרגום[119] דפתר עיבור[120] דפתר הלכות גדולות[121] דפתר עזא עלי אלף בֵית[122] כראסה̈ לקוטים מן תלמוד[123] דפתר תפסיר מגלה ואמרו דפתר תפסיר מגלה אשרי דפתר

(verso)

תפסיר מגלה תפלה[124] דפתר מסכת פסחים[125] דפתר שופטים ושוטרים לאבן סרג̇דו[126] דפתר כתאב אלאזהאר[127] תפתר תפסיר ויקח קרח וזאת וראשי המטות[128] כתאב מג̇רד ותשובות ללסג̇למאסיין[129] דפתר זאד אלמסאפר[130] דפתר אלשהאדאת [ל]שמואל[131] דפתר מאסרה̈ אכלה ואכלה[132] דפתר אלסבעין לפצ̇ה̈ לראש אלמת̇יבה̈[133] דפתר סדר עולם ותפאסיר[134] דפתר עירובים תלמוד[135] דפתר נסכ̇ה̈ אלמלכים[136] תפתר תפסיר אלתורה שרח[137] דפתר אלנצף אלאול מן תרי עשר[138] תפסיר[139]

B.

(Fol. 1, recto)

תפסיר דניאל[140] תפסיר מגלה כאייל[141] דפתר אלכ̇[142] אלכתאב דפתר מסאיל בן עטא וכתב לשמואל בן חפני[143]

דפתר שרוט אלאויה[144] דפתר כ̇מסה̈
אפראק מן יבמות דפתר סבעה̈
אפראק איצ̀א תפסיר יבמות[145] דפתר
זאד אלמסאפר אלג̇זו אלאול[146] דפתר
פיה ארבעה̈ כתב אלשהאדאת ואלות̇איק
ואלודאיע[147] דפתר תפסיר אלנצף̇ אלב̇ מן
תרי עשרה[148] דפתר תפסיר שיר השירים[149]
דפתר קדמוניות[150] דפתר ישעיה תפסיריה[151]
כראסה̈ רסאלה̈ לעילי החבר[152] כתאב
[אלא]סכנדר[153]

(verso)

כתאב מסאראת[154] כתאב תפסיר אלה המשפטים[155]
כראס אלפאט̇[156] כראס מכאתבה̈ אלמת̇איב[157] כתאב
אפתתחאת[158] כראס עיבור[159] כראריס שטאראת[160]
כראס אלפאט̇ זרעים[161] דפתרין רסאלאת[162]
כראס משמרות[163] דפתר כתב[164] אלאמאנאת
כנאש ללנביאים ואלכתובים[165] דפתר כתאב
אלטלאק לשמואל[166] דפתר תפסיר סתה̈
אפראק מן עירובים[167] דפתר אלפאט̇
אלנביאים[168] דפתר מגלה תענית[169] דפתר
תפסיר[170] דפתר אלפאט̇ הלכות
גדולות[171] דפתר כתאב אלעדר ואלחדוד
ואלשראיע[173] דפתר תפסיר יחזקאל[174]
דפתר שרח אלתורה[175] דפתר תפסיר אחרי מות
וקדושים[176] תפתר תשובות להיי מנסוכ̇ה̈
אלי נסים[177]

(fol. 2, recto)

דפתר כתאב אלביוע ואלאשריה̈[178] דפתר
תפסיר אלה נוח[179] דפתר ארבעה̈

אפראק מן מסכת שבת[180] כתאב אלשבועות[181] כתאב אלשופעה להייא[182] ושאילות ללחנן[183] כראס תפסיר משלי כראס פרק מן ספרים כראס מגלה דפתר שטרות[184] כראס מסכת יום טוב דפתר האזינו[185] דפתר הלכת[186] שחיטה דפתר[187] טריפות דפתר עבודה זרה דפתר תשובות[188] רזמה̈ כרארים ז̇ כרארים אלרד עלי אלקראיין[189] כרארים אלפאט̇ טהרות כרארים שימות[190] כרארים משלי קראן אלפאט̇[191] כרארים שימות יד̇ כראס ואיצ̇א כרארים שימות[192] ח̇ כרארים אלפאט̇ אלמשנה כראס אלפאט̇ זרעים

(verso)

ואלפאט̇ שבת[193] כראס מגלה תלמוד כרארים מדרשות[194] דרג̇ עיבור ג̇זו פסחים ויום טוב כרארים מן עיבור[195] כראס פיה נסך̇ אלשרע[196] כרארים מן גטים ונזיקים[197] דפתר תשובות לעמרם בן ששנה[198] דפתר מסאיל רזמה̈ כרארים[199] דפתר תשובות אבן שאפול[200] דפתר מדרש[201] כראס ג̇ואב מסאיל ראס אלמת̇יבה̈ אבן מאיר[202] דפתר רד עלי אלמתחאמל[203] דפתר כתאב מג̇אורת לר̇ שמואל[204] דפתר כתאב אלשרוט ואלקניין ואלכ̇לוב[205] דפתר תפסיר ויהי בשלח[206] ג̇זו פיה מן אלעיבור[207] דפתר אגדה אלה שמות[208]

C.

(Fol. 1, recto)

[דפֿ][209] שיר השירים וקהלת ואחשורוש מקֿ[210]
דפֿ כתאב מסאיל נסי בן חסן אלבצרי[211]
דפֿ תפסיר תרי עשרה במעאני[212] דפֿ מסכת
כתובות[213] דפֿ פיה תֿלתֿהֿ כתב אלמנטק[214]
דפֿ נואדר מן אלתלמוד[215] דפֿ מסא[יל] לסעדיה[216]
דפתר כתאב אלכֿלק[217] דפתר דקדוק אלמקרא[218]
דפֿ אגדה רות[219] דפֿ אלאסתחקאקאת
וטומאה וטהרה[220] דפֿ תפסיר שלח לך[221]
דפֿ מאסרהֿ תרגום אלתורה[222] דפֿ כתאב
אלאספאת[223] דפֿ מדרש לרֿ תנחומה[224]
דפֿ תפסיר ויקרא במעאני[225] דפֿ תפסיר
מגלתין מן תהלות[226] דפֿ חזאנהֿ וגיר דֿלך[227]
דפֿ תפסיר שיר השירים[228] דפֿ אלגזו אלבֿ
מן כתאב אלרהק[229] דפֿ אלנצף אלאכֿיר מן
תפסיר לשלמה[230]

(verso)

דפֿ תפסיר מסכת ברכות דפתר [מסאיל]
לשרירה[231] דפתר כתב אלאימאן ואלש[רוט]
ואלקניין[232] דפֿ תפסיר ואלה שמות אלי ויהי בשלח[233]
דפֿ אותיות לרֿ עקיבה[234] דפֿ אלשהאדאת
ואלותֿאיק[235] דפֿ תחציל אלשראיע לסעדיה[336]
דפֿ תפסיר שיר השירים[237] דפֿ תשובות[238]
דפֿ צדר אלתהלות ותפסיר מזאמיר[239]
דפֿ אגדה קוהלת[240] דפֿ תפסיר ואלה
שמות וארא וכי אני הרבֿ[241] דפֿ ו מקאלאת
מן אללגהֿ[242] דפתר כתאב אלהדאיהֿ[243] דפֿ
מכֿתצר לאבן שעדאן פי אלנחו[244] דפֿ תפסיר

איכה[245] כתאב אלאסכאלת[246] כתאב תפסיר וירא בלק ופינחס[247] כתאב אלהבהׄ ואלאמלאך[248] כתאב תפסיר נשוא[249] כתאב קנסר וסדר עולם[250]

(fol. 2, recto)

כתאב אלסאלף אלחאתמיי[251] דפתר סידור עמרם בן ששנה[252] דפתר תפסיר תהלות[253] שרח דפתר צנעהׄ אלטיב[254] דפתר תפסיר ויקרא[255] דפתר כׄלף בן נפתלי[256] דפתר טבי ללראזי למן . . . ה . . . ה טביב[257] דפתר תפסיר אשה כי תזריע[258] דפתר שאילות[259] דפתר כתאב אלשופעהׄ לר׳ שמואל[260] דפתר אגדה לה דפתר אפסאקאת[261] דפתר אלה שמות ללפיומי[262] דפתר תפסיר עזרה[263] דפתר בבא בתרא[264] דפתר [תפסיר] בראשית וויצא[265] דפתר כתאב[266] . . . . . . דפתר כתאב אלתמייז[267] ודׄלך . . . . . דפתר תפסיר אלצלאהׄ לראס אלמתׄיבהׄ[268] ועדד אלחרף אלקרא[269]

(verso)

תפסיר רות[270] דפׄ כתאב פי אלסראגׄ וכתאב אלאימאן להייא[271] דפׄ תפסיר שיר השירים[272] דפׄ תפסיר ויקרא וצו ויהי ביום השמיני[273] דפׄ אפסאקאת אלשאמיין[274] דפׄ אלחמש מקרא[275] דפׄ תהילות מקרא[276] דפׄ כתאב אחרף אללין ודׄואת אלמתׄלין ופיה שרוט אלנקט[277] דפׄ פיה תשובות[278] דפׄ מעשה מרכבה[279] דפׄ פיה תחיית המתים ומילה[280] דפׄ ספר הגלוי[281] דפׄ תפסיר עשרים וארבע מתנות כהונה[282] דפׄ

כתאב אלאלחאן ואלמבאדי[283] דפ̇ כתאב
אלחרף אלהנדי ושמם אלמעאלי[284] דפ̇ תפסיר
[ויד]בר[285] דפ̇ תפסיר תהלות[286] דפתר איוב
ומשלי מקרא[287] דפ̇ אכ̇באר בני אלעבאס
ואלבראמכה̈[288] דפ̇ תפסיר בראשית[289] דפ̇
תפסיר כי תצא והאזינו וזאת הברכ[ה][290]

III.

[Mosseri Collection, Li, marked I, paper.]

(Recto)

שר[ח אל]תורה ירמיה ותרי עשר יהושע
ושפטי̇ ובעץ̇ שמואל אלג̇מיע קרא[291]
פיר̇ בעץ̇ אלפרק אלאול מן שבת לרבנו
שמואל גאון[292] יר̇ ה̇[293] בבא בתרא ופירשהא
לר̇ שלמה[294] אלערוך מנה אלי אלבאב אלנון[295]
אלמחזור בכ̇ט בן אלשראר[296] כנאש בן סראפיון
פי אלטב רק[297]
ג̇זו ואלה שמות וויקרא

בכ̇ט אלשיך̇ אבולעז[298]	מג̇לד פי אללגה̈ ט
	מקאלאת לרב̇ סעדיה[299]
תפס̇ אחרי וקדשים	
לרב̇ סעדיה במעא̇[300]	פצול בקראט[301a] תנפיר
מקאלאת לקסטא	גאלינוס[302] פי̇ ראש השנה[303]
בן לוקא פי אלטב[301]	קואנין[304] סדור רב̇ סעדיה[305]
	אלג̇מע פי כראסין רק
אגרון נסכ̇תין	
לבן אלרביע אחדהמא[306]	כת̇ אחכאם אלקרצ̇ה̈[308]
תפסיר אלה מסעי[307]	תד̇כרה̈ אלכחאלין לחנין
	כ̇ט עבראני[309]

תֿדֿכרהֿ אלכחאלין

כֿטי לעיס[310]   בעץֿ היל ראו[312]

כתׄ פי צֿרב אלהנדי   כתׄ טומאה וטהרה[313]

כֿט ערבי[311] . . . . .

כתׄ תמייז[314]   מגֿמוע פיה אבות

אלמדֿהב . . . כֿט עֿ[315]   ותפסיר האזינו לבן אלעאקולי[316]

(verso)

כתׄ ואלה שמות כתׄ ואלה המשפטים

כתׄ ויקרא[317] אלעבור לבן עלון זׄ כראריס[318]

[Another fragment, marked II.]

(Column 1)

ספר דינין מכֿתצר

גֿז[319]

כראריס פיהם סליחות[320]

מגֿמע סליחות ותפלות

גֿז[321]

מגלת סתרים וגירהא[322]

גֿז

(Column 2)

אלעיבור לרֿ האיי[323]

גֿז

שרח אחרי מות במעני[324]

גֿז

מסכת [מ]גלה ויום טוב[325]

גֿז

כתאב אלאמאנאת ואל[326]

גֿז

IV.

[MS. Harkavy, K, No. 5; 6 leaves. Extracts from this MS. are cited in Pinsker, לקוטי קדמוניות, נספחים, 191, note 2.]

(Fol. 1, recto)[327]

שרח	משלי לסעדיה גאון נע[328]
חומש	תורה משרח ערבי לסעדיה גאון מגלד[329]
מגלדין	שרח ישעיה עה ליפת נע תמאם[330]
שרח	אלעתידות פי תלאת מגלדאת[331]
שרח	ירמיהו עה תמאם פי מגלד ואחד[332]
שרח	שיר השירים מגלד גדיד תמאם[333]
גזוין	מגלדאת מן שרח שמואל הנ עה אלאול אולה מן חזק ונתחזקה ואכרה ותעצר המגפה מעל ישראל. ואלתאני אולה ויאמר יהונתן אל דוד. ואכרה ויעש דוד כאשר[334]
שרח	קהלת אכר[335]
שרח	נצף מלכים אלא מגלד לר יפת נע[336]
שרח	דניאל עה מגלד ואחד ופי אכרה רסאלה מליחה לשמואל הרופא נע[337]
שרח	יחזקאל הנ עה פי מגלד ואחד[338]

(verso)

שרח	תרי עשר נביאים עה פי מגלדין תמאם[339]
שרח	משלי פי מגלדין לנא וואחד למוסי[339a]
פירוש	עלי אלתורה לר האיי מגלד תמאם[340]
פירוש	עלי אלתורה מגלד פיה ספרין בראשית ושמות לר בחיי זל[341]
פירוש	משלי ותהלים מגלד לדוד קמחי זל[342]
שרח	אלמגלה אלאולה מן אלמזאמיר לר יפת נע מגלדה[343]

(Fols. 2, recto and verso, and 3, recto, are blank; fol. 3, verso)

אלאצואלאת ואלדקדוקים[344]

ספר מאיר נתיב לשון קדש[345]

ספר אגרון ערבי אצול אלמקרא[346]

ספר דקדוק ערבי לקמחי נ̇ע̇[347]

ספר אכ̇ר איצ̇א דקדוק ערבי[348]

ספר דקדוק לשון קדש[349]

ספר יסמא ד̇רד̇ק̇י פי אצול אלכלאם[350]

ספר שרשים ללקמחי לשון קדש[351]

ספר אהל מועד יסמא ישתמל
עלי מנאאבהאת אלכלאם[332]

מג̇לד תרג̇מה̈ אלפאט̇ באלערבי נביאים
ראשונים ואחרונים ואלכתובים ג̇מיע[353]

(Fol. 4, recto, is blank; fol. 4, verso)

ביאן ספרי מצות[354]

מג̇לד פיה ארבע מקאלאת ליפת בן צעיר נב̇ע̇[355]
אדרת אליהו לשון קדש ללאסטנבוליין[356]

ספר ללאסטנבוליין לאהרן בכ"ר אליהו ז"ל
העתקת התורה וחלוקת
הקראים והרבנים יסמי עץ חיים[357]

ספר דינים אסמה שער יהודה[358]

כתאב ליהודה האבל לשון קדש פי
ת̇לאת̇ מג̇לדאת בתמאמה̈[359]

ספר לאליהו הדיין ויתבעה כתאב
ללמלמד פאצ̇ל ופי אכ̇רה שרח
האזינו אלג̇מיע פי מג̇לד ואחד[360]

(fol. 5, recto)

ספרי מצות ת̇לאת̇ה̈ מג̇לדאת מתמ̈מאת
למר̇י ורב̇י שמואל הרופא
המערבי ת̇נצ̇ב̇ה̇[361]

מג̇לד פיה ה̇ מקאלאת לר̇ יפת בן צעיר
נב̇ע̇ כ̇ט אלפקיר צאר גמלה̈
מא ענדנא מנה ט̇ מקאלאת[362]

(The rest of fol. 5, recto and verso, is blank; fol. 6, recto)

אלתפלות ואלמקדמאת[363]

סדור אול פי ימי החול. ליל ונהאר.
ושבת. וחדש. תמאם

סדור ת̇אני אולה מן אלפסח חג השבועות
וארבעין איכה. אכ̇רה לשבת נחמו.

סדור ת̇אלת̇ מן אול יו̇[363a] כפור ליום תרועה[364]

סדור אולה מן חג הסוכות. ושמיני עצרת.
ושמחת תורה וצלואת אלצומות. ופורים.
והנא. ועזא. וג̇מיע מא יחתאג̇ אלאמר[365]

סדור אולה מן חג השבועות ואכ̇רה יום תרועה[366]

תפלת יום הכפורים ורקהא קטע כאמל

תפלת ליל הכפורים מג̇לדה̈[367]

תפלת יום הכפורים ורקהא קטע כאמל
בקר. וצהרים. ורחמים. אואיל
אלכלאם מג̇זוף באחמר[368]

(verso)

תפלת יום הכפורים בקר קטע אלרבע[369]

איצ̇א ואחדה̈ אכ̇רה מת̇להא קאידה̈ צהרים[370]

מקדמאת עלי אלפרשיות מתממאת
אלאולאניאת ואלת̇אניאת[371]

(The rest is blank.)

NOTES ON THE BOOKS LISTED.

[1] A volume bearing the heading: Questions of the people of Ḳairwān sent to Sherira Gaon. Evidently the volume contained the Gaon's responsa to the queries (for such responsa cp., e.g., Gaonic Responsa, ed. Harkavy, pp. 97, 107, 188).

[2] A volume beginning with על שמך רחמנא, one of the usual introductory phrases of a scribe commencing his copy, together with the indication that the volume contains the Midrash to Samuel which opens with a comment on Ps. 119.126 (cp. ed. Buber, Introduction, p. 7, for the various designations of this Midrash). Another copy is also mentioned at the end of our fragment.

[3] Sa'adyah's well-known work on Jewish religious philosophy, the Hebrew equivalent being ס' האמונות והדעות.

[4] A work beginning with חשוכי בגדים (Kelim 1.2) and continuing with some explanation of it which is not clear from the few words cited. The same work seems to recur in the book-lists published by Gottheil (*Jewish Studies in Memory of Israel Abrahams*, 1927, p. 150, l.3, and p. 154, l. 8). Cp. also infra, note 12.

[5] =מחיצה. The work began with Baba Batra 1. 1. Whether it contained the Mishnah or the Gemara or a commentary to B. B. (e.g. Sherira Gaon's, above, p. 568 ff.) is not stated.

[6] Sheeltot of R. Aḥai of Shabḥa.

[7] A commentary on Psalms. From the commencement cited here it seems that the volume was defective at the beginning.

[8] Mishnah of Seder Ḳodashim beginning with Zeb. 1.1.

[9] A volume in Damascene paper containing the whole Mishnah of Berakot.

[10] The commentary on Deuteronomy by Daniel al-Ḳūmisi. Cp. my remarks on this item in *JQR, N. S.*, XII, 436. Marmorstein (הצופה לחכמת ישראל, XIV (1930), 27) has appropriated my remarks as his own.

[11] Tanḥuma to Exodus (cp. ed. Buber).

[12] The Gaonic commentary on Mishnah Seder Ṭaharot. Our copy did not contain the introduction (cp. ed. J. N. Epstein, p. 8).

[13] A Mekilta to Numbers beginning with a comment on Lev. 12.4 (=Sifre Zuṭṭa, ed. Horovitz, *Siphre d'be Rab*, p. 227). Cp. infra, note 92.

[14] A commentary on Daniel in a fine binding, the heading of the work being "the book of the kingdoms and the wars that will be in the year 1386" (Sel.=1074–5 C. E.). We have here evidently a commentary that interpreted Daniel to foretell events leading up to the Messianic age to be ushered in in 1074–5. I surmise that it was written in Palestine and was inspired by the fights between the Fāṭimids and the Seljūḳs who conquered Jerusalem in 1071 C. E. How easy it was to interpret the classical ch. 11, in which there is depicted the struggle between "the king of the South" with "the king of the

North," to refer to the conflict for the possession of the Holy Land between the Fāṭimid Caliph of Egypt ("the South") and the Seljūḳ Turks who came from the North! The Messianic expectations of those days, which our commentary seems to reflect, had evidently repercussions in the Diaspora. The Messianic movement in France centering in Lyon (about which Maimonides reports, see my remarks in *Hattekūfah*, XXIV, pp. 356–8, and cp. above, p. 32) should now be connected with this struggle between the Fāṭimids and the Seljūḳs.

[15] Cp. Pesiḳta d. R. Kahana, No. 23 (ed. Buber, 149b), and Lev. Rabba, c. 29, which quote this Baraita in the name of R. Eli'ezer (b. Hyrkanos) headed by Ps. 119.89. Cp. also A. Epstein, מקדמוניות היהודים, p. 22. Whether our work contained this early Baraita dealing evidently with the rules of calendation, which the authors of the Pesiḳta, Lev. R. and also Pirḳe de R. Eli'ezer utilised, is difficult to ascertain.

[16] A volume beginning with Tosefta Berakot and a pamphlet on the back of which there was stated that it contained the complete Tosefta.

[17] A book containing a commentary on Proverbs and other matter. It began with the statement that people arose in אלאסח (this word is not clear to me) adopting their festivals according to lunar observation. Evidently this is directed against the Ḳaraites. The book seems to have been defective at the beginning as a commentary on Prov. was hardly likely to begin abruptly with such a statement.

[18] A work beginning with Mishnah Berakot 8.1. Whether it contained ch. 8 of Babli or some other code dealing with this topic is not stated.

[19] A work beginning with comments on Num. 1.1 evidently in the nature of a Midrash. Neither Rabba nor Tanḥuma to Num. begin in this manner, though as to the substance cp. Rabba, § 1, end, and Tanḥuma (ed. Buber), § 1, end. See also Tobias b. Eli'ezer's לקח טוב to Numbers, beginning: ומה ראה הדיבור לומר באיזה זמן באיזה מקום בכמה בחדש באיזה חדש באיזה שנה טוביהו ברבי אליעזר זצ"ל אמר באיזה זמן וכו'. Probably this work is identical with the Mekilta to Numbers (see infra, note 92).

[20] A book beginning with Sabbath 1.1; whether Mishnah, Gemara or a code on the laws of Sabbath is not stated.

[21] A pamphlet containing Talmud Yer. to Berakot.

[22] A book called "Aggadah (=Midrash) of Deuteronomy." Neither Rabba nor Tanḥuma have the beginning as given here.

[23] The work on the laws of possessions by Samuel b. Ḥofni. It is also cited in the Fihrist of the Gaon's works (*JQR*, XIV, 311, line 3 from bottom) where for כתאב אלמלאך evidently read כתאב [אחכאם] אלאמלאך. Cp. also the book-list (*JQR*, XIII, 54, l. 43) where it is cited as כת' אלאמלאך. See also infra, note 248.

[24] This work is no doubt the Mekilta of R. Simon b. Yoḥai which began with Ex. 3.2 (the verse about the burning bush) and hence this Mekilta is cited as מכילתא דסניא. Our item fully corroborates the correct interpretation of מכילתא דסניא as given by Chajes (*Rivista Israelitica*, VI (1909), 198, note 3). Cp. also מכילתא דרשב"י, ed. Hoffmann, p. 1. See further below, note 92.

[25] A large book beginning with Pes. 10.1.

[26] A book containing Yer. to Shebi'it.

[27] Siphra to Leviticus beginning with R. Ishmael's 13 hermeneutic rules.

[28] A book bearing the heading: "a tract which the Gaon Aaron Hakkohen b. Joseph (i.e. Khalāf ibn Sarjādo) composed for his son-in-law when he requested of him a commentary on Deut. 33–34." About Aaron's commentary to the second half of Deut., which appeared in the form of pamphlets for the Sidrot of the week, cp. my remarks in *JQR, N. S.*, XI, 426, note 10; Poznański, ibid., XIII, 377–8.

[29] A volume commencing with the opening Aggadah of Levit. R., evidently comprising the whole of this Midrash.

[30] This book containing explanations of the difficult passages in Berakot is unknown to me.

[31] A large volume having the heading "Commentary (Tafsīr) of the second half of the fifth part (Deuteronomy) of the Torah" (about the division of the books of the Pentateuch into halves, see my remarks in *Journal of Jewish Lore and Philosophy*, I, 348, note 6, and *JQR, N. S.*, XI, 436–7). There is also given the first line of the work which shows that it was an Arabic translation of a Hebrew commentary. But Tafsīr can also denote a translation and hence only the Biblical text was rendered into Arabic.

[32] Yelamdenu to Genesis which began with Prov. 3.19. Evidently the beginning of Tanḥuma: זה שאמר הכתוב ה׳ בחכמה יסד ארץ וכשברא הקב״ה את עולמו נתיעץ בתורה וכו׳ emanates from our Yelamdenu; the passage in Tanḥuma, ed. Buber, § 15, in comment on this verse is not to Gen. 1.1 but to 2.4. The question beginning with ילמדנו evidently was: כשברא הקב״ה את עולמו במה נתיעץ? נתיעץ בתורה וכו׳.

[33] A volume beginning with Yeb. 1.1; whether Mishnah, Talmud or commentary to this tractate is not stated.

[34] A volume beginning with רחמנא סייען, one of the usual introductory phrases of the scribes, and the commencement of a treatise on the signs of the Zodiac. Cp.ברייתא דמזלות (in Wertheimer's אוצר מדרשים כתבי״ד, I, 1).

[35] A volume beginning with 'Erubin 1.1.

[35a] Supply טוב.

[36] Likewise one beginning with Beṣah 1.1.

[37] Read וכתובות.

[38] A volume containing copies of legal documents.

[39] A book called "Chapters of the 9th of Ab," evidently a sort of a Midrash for this day; it began with a homily on Ps. 79.1. Perhaps it contained the section of Seder Eliyahu Rabba (ed. Friedmann, p. 147ff.) beginning with this verse.

[40] A volume beginning with Ḥag. 1.1.

[41] A volume headed as "the work of Samuel" (i. e. Samuel b. Ḥofni). The nature of it is not stated.

[42] Another volume contained this Gaon's Kitāb al-'Idad and Kitāb al-Shurūṭ. The full title of the latter work is given in the book-list (*JQR*,

XIV, 311, l. 2) as כ' אחכאם אלשרוט, viz. on the laws of contracts. Probably the first book's full title was also כ' אחכאם אלעדד but its nature is not clear. In Muhammedan law 'iddah is the legal period of retirement assigned to a widow or divorced woman before she may marry again. See infra, note 173. (The כתאב אלעדד is also mentioned in the list edited by Gottheil, *l. c.*, 151, top).

[43] A volume containing the Tosefta to Ḳodashim.

[44] Another volume containing comments on Sabbath.

[45] Read כדי. The volume began with Tos. Sanh. 1.1.

[46] A volume containing Samuel b. Ḥofni's work on the laws of sale (see Poznański, *Zur jüd.–arab. Litteratur*, p. 57).

[47] Another nice volume; the meaning of the sentence from בעיף onwards is not clear to me (for בעיף read perhaps כשף).

[48] A pamphlet containing a commentary on Gen. 23–25.18 in a binding fastened by a silver buckle.

[49] A nice pamphlet, beautifully bound, containing Midrash Ḥaserot viserot (cp. ed. Marmorstein, 1917).

[50] Samuel b. Ḥofni's work on the laws of marriage (cp. *JQR*, XVI, 411).

[51] A volume containing a collection of prayers and praisegivings (Hebrew תפלות ותשבחות), evidently by Sa'adyah (cp. Malter, *l. c.*, 330). Also MS. Mosseri, P. 745, contains a fragment beginning with: כתאב גֹאמע אלצלואת ואלתסאביח ממא ענא בתרתיבה רבנו סעדיה גאון רוח י'י תניחנו. The work is evidently his Siddur.

[52] Midrash Proverbs. For הנולאי read חנילאי.

[53] Another volume beginning with Yeb. 1.1.

[54] A volume containing Yoma, 'Abodah Zarah and 3 chapters of a tractate omitted by the copyist by oversight. The volume was incomplete as it began with Yoma 3.1.

[55] Another volume containing the complete Mishnah of Berakot.

[56] A volume beginning with Meg. 1.1.

[57] A volume containing Babli of Ned., Nazir and Ḳiddushin.

[58] A volume containing Mishnah to Ḳodashim.

[59] A volume containing the second half of Kitāb al-Kashf (inspection, discovery) composed by Abraham b. Mumar, the money-changer; our Abraham was a disciple of Sa'adyah Gaon. The nature of the work is unknown (cp. Poznański, *Schechter's Saadyana*, p. 20; in *Saadyana* אלנצף is wrongly printed as אלוצף).

[60] A pamphlet containing a treatise on prayer and its duties. Such works were written by Sa'adyah (cp. Malter, *l. c.*, 330) and by Israel Hakkohen b. Samuel b. Ḥofni (Mann *JQR*, *N. S.*, XI, 415–16).

[61] Two pamphlets containing a glossary of Mishnah and of other writings.

[61a] Read תמייז.

[62] A volume in coarse handwriting containing a treatise differentiating between the true opinion and the false one concerning the fixing of the festivals. It evidently dealt with the problem of the Jewish calendar; whether from a Ḳaraite or anti-Ḳaraite point of view is impossible to ascertain.

[63] Read אלסהו.

[64] A volume containing the rectification of the errors found in the writings of Sa'adyah Gaon composed by Mebasser Hallevi b. Nissi known as ibn עשבה. Parts of this work of criticism on Sa'adyah have been published by Harkavy from a MS. in Leningrad (2. Firkowicz Collection, Hebrew-Arabic, No. 326). Cp. Pozn., ibid., p. 20.

[65] Pirḳe de R. Eli'ezer beginning with c. 3. As is well-known the first 2 chapters are a later addition incorporating the account of R. Eli'ezer's early career as a student as found in Abot de R. Nathan, c. 6 (2nd version, c. 13, ed. Schechter, p. 30).

[66] A large volume containing a commentary on the second half of Genesis (i. e. from ויצא to ויחי). Cp. also note 73.

[67] Another large volume containing a commentary on both halves of Leviticus commencing with ויקרא and אחרי מות respectively. There is given the first line of the commentary; it is evidently by Sa'adyah because the commentary on the second half of Lev. also commences with חסב מא וכו' (*JQR, N. S.*, VI, 372). Cp. also note 77.

[68] A large volume containing Halakot Gedolot beginning with a benediction for the study of the Torah (cp. ed. Hildesheimer, p. 8).

[69] A volume containing Otiyot de R. 'Aḳiba (cp. version 2 in ed. Wertheimer, מדרש אותיות דרבי עקיבא השלם, p. 59).

[70] Hai Gaon's work on oaths (cp. Steinschneider, *l. c.*, p. 99, and Poznański *l. c.*, p. 52).

The full title is given here as כתאב מכתצר פי שרח אלגמל ואלאצול מן פקה וגוב ואלאימאן. In *JQR*, XVI, 412, top, the title is quoted as כ' אלגמל ואלאצול פי אלפקה עלי אלאימאן. T.-S. Loan 157 contains a portion of the work on the colophon of which the title is given as כתאב מכתצר פי פקה וגוב אלאימאן תצניף אדונינו האיי ראש הישיבה שלגולה בן שרירא ראש הישיבה שלגולה. The owner was Netanel b. Yefet (לנתנאל בר יפת נע׳). It was subsequently acquired by another person whose name is crossed out (אנתקל בחכם . . .). On the top of the colophon there is listed another owner of whose names only the words אלעזר הכהן are still legible.

An anonymous Hebrew translation of this work (Bodl. 813.2 and not 313 as given by Steinschneider, *l. c.*) renders this title as ס' מחובר בקוצר מן הדינין בביאור כללים ועיקרים בחלקי חיוב השבועה.

[71] Sa'adyah's commentary on Proverbs (cp. Derenbourg, *Oeuvres Complètes de R. Saadia*, VI, p. 1).

[72] Thus begins this section in הלכות גדולות (ed. Hildesheimer, p. 78). Here the work is called ה' פסוקות meaning evidently R. Yehudai's work on the basis of which Simon Ḳayyara later on issued a larger work under the title of ה' גדולות. The fact that the Mo'ed section of ה' פסוקות began as in ה' גדולות tends to show that the two works also corresponded to each other by beginning with הלכות ברכות (cp. Poznański, *RÉJ*, LXIII, 235–6); Epstein's remarks, *Jb. jüd.-liter. Ges.*, XII, 100, need therefore correction.

[73] A nice volume in black binding containing a commentary on the second half of Genesis. Cp. also note 66.

74 A commentary on Ḥullin; the copy was defective as it commenced with the indication that the comments on ch. I of the tractate were completed.

75 A nice volume bound in boards containing Sepher Yeṣīrah.

76 A large volume evidently defective at the beginning which starts in the middle of a sentence pertaining to an item of ה' עבודה זרה.

77 A volume containing a commentary on Lev. 16 ff., evidently extending to the end of the book and thus comprising its whole second half. Perhaps it was by Sa'adyah (cp. *JQR*, *N. S.*, VI, 372). See also note 67.

78 A volume containing the laws of Sheḥiṭah in Arabic.

79 A volume containing the well-known Yosippon.

80 An Arabic commentary on Gen. 12.1.

81 A nice volume containing Midrash Samuel (see note 2).

82 A volume containing a commentary of Gen. 28.10, probably extending to the end of the book and thus comprising the second half of Genesis.

83 A volume containing a Siddur.

84 A volume containing the Talmud to Nashim and Neziḳin and also the work הלכות קצובות attributed to Yehudai Gaon (cp. תורתן של ראשונים, ed. Horowitz, I, p. 14, and *M. G. W. J.*, LXIX, p. 32; see also Epstein, *Haggoren*, III, 68–69, whose remarks need now modification especially about הלכות קצובות דבני מערבא).

85 A complete volume containing the text of the Prophets.

86 The Sheeltot of R. Aḥa of Shabḥa.

87 Six volumes containing 5 tractates of Talmud, evidently Baba Meṣia was in two parts owing to its size.

88 Probably read אכר as in l. 6, viz. another volume contained B. B., Sanh. and Makkot, which must have rendered it very bulky; two others contained 'A. Z. and B. Ḳ., Sheb. and Horayot respectively.

89 A volume in pamphlets consisted of Sabbath, other pamphlets comprised Niddah and likewise there were volumes of other Talmudical tractates (ll. 10–11).

90 Another volume in 5 loose parts comprised the Talmud to Seder Neziḳin.

91 =דפתר, this volume in 2 pamphlets contained Sheḳalim, another one, unbound, Berak. and a third, likewise unbound, Ned., Nazir and Giṭṭin.

92 Such a Mekilta is also mentioned in another book-list (*JQR*, XIII, p. 53, No. 16): מכלתא דוידבר. Now by it our Sifre could be meant which begins with Num. 5.1 (וידבר ה'). However it is usually called ספרי דבי רב (cp. Hoffmann, *Einleitung*, 51–2). On the other hand וידבר, without any further indication, refers to the whole book of Numbers by reason of its beginning with וידבר (1.1). Hence the Mekilta of the school of R. Ishmael is meant here which extended over Exodus, Leviticus, Numbers and Deuteronomy as Maimonides reported (Introduction to Yad: ורבי ישמעאל פירש מאלה שמות עד סוף התורה והוא הנקרא מכילתא).

Now above (p. 646, ll. 41–43, cp. note 19) we have had an item of a work beginning with: וידבר יי' אל משה במדבר סיני וג' מה ראה הדבר הזה להכתב באי זה יום באי זה חדש, hence commencing the comments with Num. 1.1. There is thus reason to believe that this is the commencement of our very Mekilta to Numbers and hence the indication מכאלה֞ וידבר or מכלתא דוידבר fits in exactly. Our Siphre to Numbers, although having the essential character of a Tannaitic Midrash of R. Ishmael's school (as demonstrated by Hoffmann, *l. c.*, 52 ff., cp. also ed. Horovitz, VIff.), contains also matter from other sources (cp. especially Horovitz, p. XI) and no longer preserves R. Ishmael's Mekilta to Numbers in its purity. Anyhow the beginning of this Mekilta from Num. 1.1 to 5.1, being merely Aggadic in nature, has been entirely omitted. Perhaps this omission was caused by analogy to Sifre Zuṭṭa, known as וישלחו זוטא and ספרי של פנים אחרים (in reality belonging to R. ʻAḳiba's school, although erroneously quoted by Maimonides as מכילתא דר' ישמעאל, as shown by Hoffmann, *l. c.*, 59 ff., Horovitz, *l. c.*, XVff.), which actually commenced only with the Halakic portion to Num. 5.1 as evident from the item (above, p. 645, ll. 25–26): כתאב מכלה֞ ואבתדאה לפי שנאמר בכל קודש לא תגע יכול אף במעשר (cp. ed. Horovitz, p. 227).

Who knows whether the Mekilta to Exodus did not actually begin with Exod. 1.1 (as the words of Maimonides ור' ישמעאל פירש מאלה שמות would seem to indicate) and only later on the purely Aggadic part till 12.1 was left out? Mekilta of R. Simon b. Yoḥai also began with the Aggadic section from Exod. 3.1 (see above, note 24). The subject cannot be further discussed here except that reference should be made to the remarks of Dr. J. Z. Lauterbach (*JQR*, *N. S.*, XI, 169 ff., *H. U. C. Annual*, I, 432 ff.) who so positively denies the above theories which, however, are now strengthened by the items in our book-lists.

93 Pamphlets containing Targum; there is no indication as to which part of the Bible.

94 Fifteen bundles of discarded pamphlets (this seems to be the meaning here of נפץ֞).

95 A volume containing a commentary on Genesis and another one on Job.

96 =סתה֞.

97 Sixteen pamphlets comprising Aggadic homilies (פתיחתות=אפתתחאת) on the Sidrot of the week (פרשיות=פראריש); cp. *RÉJ*, XL, 55, note 2. See also infra, note 158.

98 A bundle of pamphlets in vellum and paper (for וכאנר read וכאגד, كاغد in Persian meaning paper) containing (Gaonic) responsa.

99 A volume in 19 pamphlets containing Gaonic responsa and proclamations (for ואכראראת probably read ואכראזאת=הכרזות, viz. הכרזות בית דין). Cp. the book-list in *RÉJ*, XXXIX, 200, nos. 16, 48 and 49. Bacher (ibid., 208 and XL, 55, note 2) explains אכראזאת to mean sermons, but the above explanation as denoting proclamations of the Bet-Din is more likely. Specimens of such proclamations are found in the fragment printed above, p. 555 ff.

100 A volume in pamphlet form containing an introduction to the Talmud. Saʻadyah wrote such an introduction (cp. Malter, *Saadia Gaon*, 341–2), but here evidently the similar work by Samuel b. Ḥofni is meant because the next item also contains a work of his (see note 101). About Samuel's Introduction to the Talmud, cp. Harkavy, זכרון הגאון רשב"ח, pp. 4–5, whose arguments that this Gaon was the first one to compose such a work are now untenable.

T.-S. Loan 108 contains a considerable part of this work which comprised 145 chapters. This copy was made in Jerusalem in מרחשון ד̇ת̇ש̇צ̇ו (=fall of 1035 C. E., yet the ו is doubtful), and hence not long after the Gaon's death in 1013.

After the Introduction there follows in this MS. another of Samuel's works with the heading: כתאב אלשרכה̈ ואלמצ̇ארבה̈ תאליף רבינו שמואל הכהן ראס אלמת̇יבה̈ נ̇ע̇. This work on partnership and limited partnership (commandite) is quoted by 'Iṭṭur (ed. Lemberg, I, 15a, top): ורבינו שמואל בן חפני כתבא (r. כתבו) בספר השותפות וכו'. See further above, p. 635, and cp. also Harkavy, *l. c.*, note 96. From the above Arabic title it is evident that the ס' השותפות cannot be identified with his כתאב אלקסמה̈, as Poznański (*Zur jüd.-arab. Litteratur*, p. 58) would like to do.

[101] The same volume contained also Samuel's work on the laws of agency or power of attorney (also mentioned in the Fihrist of his works, *JQR*, XIV, 311).

[102] =דפתר, a volume containing the history of the Mahdi (for אלמהרי read אלמהדי), probably of 'Ubaid Allah the Mahdi, the founder of the Fāṭimid Caliphate in North-Africa. In l. 168–9 we have an item listing the history of the 'Abbāsids and the Barmakids. We thus see an interest in Jewish circles in the history of their Arab rulers.

[103] A volume containing a translation into Arabic of a work by Ḥunain b. Isḥāḳ (cp. Steinschneider, *Hebr. Übersetzungen*, s. v.).

[104] A volume of (Gaonic) responsa.

[105] A book on the differences (חלופים) between Sura and Pumbedita (= al-Anbār, see *JQR*, XVII, 756, note 3). Probably the work dealt with the Massoretic differences between סוראי and נהרדעאי (the latter being attached to the Pumbedita school, cp. Mann, *JQR, N. S.*, VIII, 352–3). There were also differences in law and custom between these two schools (cp. the enumeration in Assaf, חלופי מנהגים והוראות בין ישיבות סורא ופומבדיתא, reprint from התור, 1912), but of a special work listing these differences (similar to the חלוף מנהגים בין בני בבל לבני א"י) we have no knowledge.

[106] A grammatical work on the letters Ẓā and Ḍād, evidently emanating from the massoretic school of Tiberias. In the commentary to Sepher Yeṣīrah (attributed to Jacob b. Nissim of Ḳairwān but probably by his townsman Dunāsh b. Tamim, cp. above, p. 74, note 25) we read according to MS. Parma 3018, fol. 89, recto, col. 1: ויש אצל הערביים הברות שאינם נמצאות אצל העבריים, והם הצדי מן קצ̇יב והטא מן עט̇ים. פי' קצ̇יב שבט או שרביט ונכתב בצדי ונקודה מלמעלה והיא הברה בפני עצמה וגם היא דומה להברת דלת ברפי. ופי' עט̇ים עצום ונכתב בטית ונקודה מלמעלה והיא הברה בפני עצמה וגם היא דומה להברת דלת ברפי . . . והיה רבנא יצחק בן רבנא שלמה ז"ל אומר כי יש בלשון העבריים אצל (viz. the famous court physician Isaak Israeli) הטבריים הטא והצדי והיה קורא ויטע אהלי אפט̇נו (Dan. 11.45) והיה מיסד הט̇א בלשונו והיא בכתב דלת. והיה קורא ויצ̇רכו את לשונם (Jer. 9.2) והיה מייסד הצ̇אד בלשונו והיא בכתב דלת. וכל זה למה מפני שהיה בקי בקריאת בני טבריה. Cp. also Dukes, קונטרס המסרת, p. 73. The other version given there (p. 9) is corrupt and still more the one printed by Grossberg (ספר יצירה, London, 1902, p. 22). From our

item we learn of a separate treatise on the peculiar Tiberian way of pronunciation of the דלת sometimes as Ẓa and sometimes as Ḍād. From the above remarks of Dunāsh b. Tamim we learn that the pronunciation of both Ẓa and Ḍād was similar to the pronunciation of Hebrew דלת when Raphe. Hence Kahle's remark (*Massoreten des Westens*, I, 50) is to be rectified. Cp. further Segal, יסודי הפוניטיקה העברית, Jerusalem 1928, p. 35, note.

[107] A book containing the Baraita, i. e. the Tosefta.

[108] A work entitled "A man's management of his house", evidently being an Arabic translation of a part of Aristotle's Ethics. Aristotle's theory of government (הנהגה=תדביר) was divided into 3 parts, 1) self-government (הנהגת האדם את עצמו), viz. ethics, 2) management of the home (הנהגת הבית) and 3) government of country (הנהגת המדינה) i.e. politics, cp. Steinschneider, *l. c.*, p. 209.

[109] A book containing a translation into Arabic of ch. 1 of Baba Batra.

[110] A Midrash to the Pentateuch.

[111] A volume containing 'A. Z. and evidently also 4 chapters of Sabbath (cp. also note 180).

[112] A pamphlet containing laws (דינים) of unknown nature.

[113] A bundle of pamphlets containing letters, perhaps Gaonic.

[114] A volume containing 4 chapters of Yebamot. See note 145.

[115] Pamphlets of correspondence, perhaps Gaonic.

[115a] A volume containing "names", either Divine names (and hence of a mystical nature) or the names of members of the community (of Fusṭāṭ) listing their contributions to charity or their payments of the government tax, the Kharāj. For such lists, cp. Mann, *Jews in Egypt*, II, 246–47, and Gottheil-Worrell, *Fragments from the Cairo Genizah in the Freer Collection*, 1927, 66 ff. Cp. also above, p. 452 f.

[116] A part of an Arabic translation of Ḳohelet. Three such Tafsīrs by Isaac ibn Gayyat, by Judah ibn Bala'am and by an anonymous author are itemised in a book-list (*RÉJ*, LXXII, 166).

[117] If the reading is correct, then 'אלכביר=אלכ, viz. a volume containing a large Tafsīr but with no indication as to its nature. Perhaps read 'אלרבות=אלר, hence an Arabic translation of Midrash Rabba, but we should have expected a more explicit indication. Cp. also note 142.

[118] A volume containing a tract by the famous Arab philosopher Ya'ḳūb b. Isḥāḳ al-Kindi (1st half of 9th century, cp. Steinschneider, *l. c.*, §351, p. 562 ff.).

[119] A pamphlet containing the Massorah to Targum (Onkelos). Cp. Berliner, *Die Massorah zum Targum Onkelos*, 1877. Cp. infra, note 222.

[120] A volume containing either a calendar or a treatise on calendation. In the book-list (*RÉJ*, XXXIX, p. 200, no. 20) we have the item: וג'זו פיה אלעיבור which Bacher identifies with Sa'adyah's treatise on the calendar. But here the definite article is missing. See also infra, note 159.

[121] A volume of Halakot Gedolot. An Arabic glossary of this work is listed infra, ll. 77–78.

[122] A volume containing poems of condolence arranged after the Alphabet

[123] A pamphlet of extracts from the (Babylonian) Talmud.

[124] Three volumes containing Arabic translations of 3 out of the 5 divisions of Psalms, viz. 1) beginning with Ps. 107.1 (for ואמרו read יאמרו, Ps. 107.2, this being here the indication since 107.1 הודו occurs also elsewhere in Psalms), 2) beginning with 1.1 and 3) with 90.1. In ll. 55–56 another part is listed תפסיר מגלה כאייל, viz. 42.2 (since למנצח (42.1) would be an indistinct indication owing to its frequency in the book). Cp. also infra, note 226.

The designation of the divisions of the Psalms as מגלה is familiar from the Talmudic literature where the expression מגלה for a portion of a Biblical book occurs frequently (cp. Blau, *Studien zum althebr. Buchwesen*, p. 66 ff.). See further infra, note 343, where the first division of Psalms is listed as מגלה.

[125] A copy of Pesaḥim.

[126] The commentary of Aaron (Khalāf) ibn Sarjādo, Gaon of Pumbedita-Bagdād, to the second half of Deut., beginning with 16.18. Cp. Mann, *JQR*, *N. S.*, XI, 426, note 10, where it is shown that this Gaon's commentary was split up into pamphlets for the Sidrot. Cp. also above, note 28.

[127] Sa'adyah's Kitāb al-Azhār (book of splendor), cp. Poznański, *JQR*, *N. S.*, XII, 379 ff.

[128] An Arabic translation of Numbers 16.1–22.1, 30.2–32.42.

[129] An unbound book (for מגרד cp. Bacher, *RÉJ*, XXXIX, 201), but no indication of its contents is given, and also Gaonic responsa to correspondents in Sajalmāsa (Morocco, cp. about this community Mann, *JQR*, *N. S.*, VII, 485).

[130] A volume containing the *Viaticum* by Jezzar (cp. Steinschneider, *l. c.*, p. 703 ff.). See also infra, lines 60–61.

[131] Samuel b. Ḥofni's work on the law of evidence (cp. also the Fihrist n *JQR*, XIV, 311).

[132] A volume containing the Massoretic work Okhlah veokhlah (ed. Frensdorff, Hannover 1864).

[133] Sa'adyah's explanation of the 70 Biblical hapaxlegomena (cp. Malter, *l. c.*, 307–08); לפטה=לפצה.

[134] Seder 'Olam with Arabic translations (or with translation and commentary).

[135] A copy of Babli 'Erubin.

[136] A copy of Kings.

[137] Here it is expressly mentioned that the Tafsīr to the Pentateuch was a commentary (שרח). See also l. 80 for another copy.

[138] A volume containing the 1st half of Minor Prophets. The second half is listed in ll. 63–64.

[139] The nature of this Tafsīr was indicated on the next leaf which is missing as there is a lacuna between A and B.

[140] An Arabic translation of Daniel.

[141] See note 124.

[142] The reading is uncertain. If אלכביר=אלכֿ, then there would be missing the indication of the character of this work. Perhaps אלכאמל=אלכֿ, but the

construction ought to be דפתר אלכתאב אלכאמל, viz. a volume containing the whole Bible. Cp. also note 117.

[143] Questions which ibn 'Aṭa, viz. Ibrahīm b. 'Aṭa, Nagid of Ḳairwān, sent to Samuel b. Ḥofni. About this Nagid cp. Mann, *JQR*, *N. S.*, XI, 429 ff.

[144] A volume of the laws of אויה, evidently a grammatical work dealing with the rules of the letters אהוי.

[145] Two volumes containing 5 and 7 chapters of Yebamot respectively. Above, ll. 32–3, another volume of 4 chapters was listed, hence the 3 volumes comprised the complete text of this tractate consisting, as it does, of 16 chapters.

[146] The first part of Jezzar's *Viaticum* (cp. above, note 130).

[147] A volume containing three (for ארבעה evidently read תֿלאתֿה) works on the laws of 1) evidence, 2) contracts and 3) pledges, evidently by Sa'adyah (see Malter, *l. c.*, pp. 345–6). In the Fihrist of Sa'adyah's works (*JQR*, *N. S.*, XI, 425, ll. 21–22) thus read: וכתאב אלשהאדאת וכתב (r. וכתאב) אלודאיע וכתאב אלוותאיק (but see Poznański, ibid., XII, 392).

[148] See note 138.

[149] A translation of Canticles.

[150] A copy of the first books of the Prophets (Joshua-Kings) called here קדמוניות, but usually styled נביאים ראשונים.

[151] A copy of Isaiah with its 2 Tafsīrs (viz. translation and commentary), probably Sa'adyah's.

[152] A pamphlet containing a tract by 'Alī the Ḥaber.

[153] The story of Alexander the Great (cp. Steinschneider, *l. c.*, §540).

[154] A work on Massorah.

[155] An Arabic translation of the second half of Exodus beginning with 21.1.

[156] A pamphlet of words, viz. a vocabulary, with no indication of its nature.

[157] A pamphlet of correspondence from the (Babylonian) academies (מתיבתות =אלמתֿאיב).

[158] A pamphlet of Aggadic homilies (פתיחתות) to the Sidrot of the week (see note 97).

[159] A pamphlet containing a calendar (cp. note 120).

[160] Pamphlets containing legal documents (שטרות).

[161] A pamphlet containing an Arabic glossary to Mishnah Seder Zera'im.

[162] Two volumes containing tracts without indication of their authorship.

[163] A pamphlet of משמרות, evidently liturgical pieces to be recited in the morning in memory of the organization of משמרות ומעמדות at the Temple (cp *Seder R. 'Amram*, I, 16a–17b, on the מעמדות). However perhaps the famous Piyyuṭ of Ḳalīr on the 24 divisions of the Priesthood is meant here (cp. Klein, *Die Barajta der 24 Priesterabteilungen*, 97 ff.).

[164] Read כתאב, viz. Sa'adyah's famous religious philosophical work known in Hebrew as Emunot Ve-De'ot.

165 A compendium to the Prophets and Hagiographa. For the term כנאש to indicate pandects, cp. Steinschneider, *H. Ü.*, p. 729, bottom, and note 500b. Cp. also infra, note 297.

166 Samuel b. Ḥofni's work on the laws of divorce (cp. also Harkavy, *l. c.*, note 92).

167 An Arabic translation of six chapters of 'Erubin.

168 An Arabic vocabulary to the Prophets.

169 A copy of Megillat Ta'anit.

170 Here is a blank in the MS., the copyist evidently omitting to indicate the nature of this Tafsīr.

171 A vocabulary to Halakot Gedolot.

173 These works seem to emanate from Samuel b. Ḥofni. A כתאב אלעדד was mentioned above (note 42), hence here too we should read אלעדד for אלעדד. However no suitable meaning could be found for the work. Perhaps read here and there אלעדר, غدر meaning menstruation), hence on the laws of נדה. However the next item אלחדוד, the limits, is unknown to me. Its juxtaposition rather suggests the reading ואלעדד in the meaning of numbers, hence a work on the numbers, the limits and the laws (of Rabbinic legislation?). Or should we say that the work dealt with the שיעורין of the Talmudic laws? A כתאב אלשראיע by Samuel b. Ḥofni is known. Poznański's view (*Zur jüd.-arab. Litteratur*, p. 55 ff.) that the numerous legal works of this Gaon are only subtitles of his comprehensive work on Rabbinic legalism going by the mame of כתאב אלשראיע, is now refuted by the description of this very work on the basis of Genizah fragments given by Harkavy in *Haḳḳedem*, III, 107 ff. Cp. also Israelsohn, ibid., German part, p. 40.

174 A Tafsīr on Ezekiel.

175 An Arabic translation of the Pentateuch.

176 A Tafsīr on Leviticus, chs. 16–20.

177 A volume of Responsa by Hai Gaon copied (or composed) for Nissim b. Jacob of Ḳairwān. About Hai's relations with R. Nissim see above, p. 137.

178 A volume containing a work of the laws of buying and selling, evidently Hai Gaon's treatise of which we possess a Hebrew translation (מקח וממכר) by Issac b. Reuben of Barcelona (cp. Steinschneider, *Arab. Liter. d. Juden*, p. 99, no. 1). Fragments of the Arabic original are found in the T.-S. Collection (see *JQR*, XVI, 411, bottom). Also Samuel b. Ḥofni wrote a כתאב אלביוע (see Poznański, *Zur jüd.-arab. Litter.*, 57, no. 11). Cp. also above, note 46.

179 A Tafsīr on Gen. 6.9–11.32.

180 A volume containing 4 chapters of Tractate Sabbath (see also above, ll. 30–31).

181 Evidently Hai Gaon's work on oaths known also as כתאב אלאימאן (see above, note 70).

182 Hai's work on the laws of adjacent fields and real estate (מצרנות, cp. also Steinschneider, *l. c.*, p. 100, no. 3). A כתאב אלשופעה by Samuel b. Ḥofni is also listed in the Fihrist (*JQR*, XIV, 311). Cp. infra, note 260.

[183] This volume also contained Hai's responsa to Elḥanan (b. Shemaryah of Fusṭāṭ). The copyist mistook the אל in אלחנן for the Arabic definite article and hence we have ללחנן.

[184] One pamphlet contained a Tafsīr to Proverbs, a second a chapter from Mass. Sopherim, a third a scroll (perhaps the book of Esther), whereas a volume consisted of legal documents.

[185] A pamphlet containing tractate Beṣah and a volume Sidra Haazinu (Deut. 32.1–52).

[186] =הלכות.

[187] Supply הלכות. Two volumes containing the laws of Sheḥiṭah and Ṭerefot respectively. Such works were written by various authorities. Thus Sa'adyah Gaon (cp. Malter, *l. c.*, 347). To the fragments listed there should be added MS. Mosseri, Ch. No. 1 (2 leaves, of which fol. 1, recto, is blank). Fol. 1, verso, has the heading: בשֿמ רחֿמ נתחיל [הילכות] שחיטה לרבינו סעדיה גאון ז"ל. נסכֿהֿ כתאב אלפה ראס אלמתיבתא אלפיומי ז לבר֗ [מ]כֿתצר פי אלטריפות . . . Also MS. British Museum (Or. 5565, D., fol. 23, verso) has the heading: בשֿמ רחֿמ תצניף הילכות שחֿי (=שחיטה) תצניף סידנא ראס אלמתֿיבהֿ אלפיומי פי תצפיהֿ אללחם (cp. Bodl. 2854 A. 7).

Further Hai Gaon seems to have composed a treatise on the laws of Sheḥiṭah, for in the Booklist (*JQR*, XIII, 54, No. 47) probably read היל' שחיטה ללהאיי for היל' שמיטה ללהאיי.

About a similar work by Joseph b. Hezekiah the Exilarch, cp. Mann, *Jews in Egypt*, II, 145, note 7.

[188] A copy of 'A. Z. and a volume of (Gaonic) responsa.

[189] A bundle of pamphlets 7 of which contained a polemical work against the Ḳaraites. While Sa'adyah wrote several such Kitābs (viz. against 'Anan, Ibn Saḳawaihi etc., cp. Malter, *l. c.*, 380 ff., 398 ff.) there is no work of his mentioned bearing the general title of "the book of refutation of the Ḳaraites," unless we identify it with his Kitāb al-Tamyīz or we assume that his various polemical works against individual Ḳaraites were combined under one comprehensive title. We have probably to identify this work with another author, perhaps with Samuel b. Ḥofni.

[190] Pamphlets containing a vocabulary of Mishnah Seder Ṭaharot; others containing 'Names' (see above, note 115).

[191] Read ואלפאטֿ, viz. pamphlets containing Proverbs, text (Ḳurān!) and Arabic glossary. For the designation of the Bible text as Ḳurān, cp. Bodl. 2862.27c where Sa'adyah's work on the hapaxlegomena is given as שרח אלסבעין לפטֿהֿ מן מפרדאת אלקראן.

[192] 14 pamphlets of 'Names' and again other pamphlets of the same contents.

[193] 8 pamphlets of an Arabic glossary to the Mishnah, another pamphlet of the same contents for Seder Zera'im and a third for Sabbath.

[194] A copy of tractate Megillah and pamphlets containing Midrashim.

[195] A quire containing a calendar; a fragment of tractates Pes. and Beṣah; other pamphlets of calendars.

[196] A pamphlet containing Samuel b. Ḥofni's polemical work on the problem of the abolition of the Law. The full title of the work was: כתאב נסך אלשרע ואצול אלדין ופרועה (cp. Harkavy, *l. c.*, p. 6). Hence one part was polemical against those who argued that Judaism was superseded by Christianity or Islām and another dealt with the roots and branches of the (Jewish) religion.

[197] Pamphlets of Giṭṭin and Neziḳin (probably the Mishnah text).

[198] A volume of responsa by R. 'Amram, Gaon of Sura.

[199] A volume of questions (to the Geonim) in a bundle of pamphlets.

[200] A volume of responsa by (or to) Ibn שאפול; the last 3 letters are doubtful and the word can also be read שאתוק. This person is unknown to me.

[201] A volume containing a Midrash.

[202] A pamphlet containing responsa by the Palestinian Gaon (Aaron) b. Meir, famous for his calendar controversy with Sa'adyah; גואב מסאיל=תשובת שאילות (cp. l. 25).

[203] A volume containing Sa'adyah's 'refutation of the overbearing' (opponent). Cp. Malter, *l. c.*, 266–7, 384.

[204] Samuel b. Ḥofni's work on the laws of neighbors (שכנים). It is also cited as כ' אחכאם אלמגאוראת and כ' אלמגאורה̈ (see Poznański, *l. c.*, 57, no. 3).

[205] A volume containing a threefold work on the laws of 1) contracts (תנאים=שרוט), 2) acquisition (קנין) and 3) wounds (דיני קנסות), no doubt by Samuel b. Ḥofni since the first 2 items are listed in his Fihrist (*JQR*, XIV, 311) as כתאב אחכאם אלשרוט and כתאב אחכאם אלקנין. About the first work see also above, note 42. It is also cited by Hai Gaon in a responsum as ספר התנאים (שערי צדק, fol. 88a, No. 21; cp. also Harkavy, *l. c.*, notes 23 and 95). See further infra, notes 232 and 248.

[206] A volume containing a Tafsīr to Exodus 13.17–17.16.

[207] A fragment containing a treatise on the calendar, perhaps of Sa'adyah's כתאב אלעבור, also called אקאמאת אלעיבור in the Fihrist of Sa'adyah's writings (*JQR*, *N. S.*, XI, 425, l. 24; see Poznański, ibid., XIII, 395, no. 3).

[208] A volume containing a Midrash on Exodus.

[209] =דפתר.

[210] =מקרא, thus this volume contained the text of Cant., Kohelet and Esther.

[211] A work containing the questions of Nissi b. Ḥasan al-Baṣri, unknown to me. Should we say that he is identical with Nissi b. Nūḥ the Ḳaraite author, and that Ḥasan is the Arabic Kunya of Nūḥ?

[212] A Tafsīr of Minor Prophets with commentary.

[213] A copy of tractate Ketubot.

[214] A volume containing 3 books on logic.

[215] A volume containing curiosities (curious stories) or witticisms (viz. popular proverbs) from the Talmud.

[216] Responsa by Sa'adyah Gaon, but perhaps here the work is meant as listed in the Fihrist of his writings (*JQR*, *N. S.*, XI, 425, l. 16): מסאיל מן תרי עשר ומן אלתוריה (cp. Pozn., ibid., XIII, 382 and 379).

[217] Such a work is cited in *JQR*, XVI, 412, bottom, as existing in the T.-S. Collection.

[218] A grammar of Biblical Hebrew.

[219] A Midrash to Ruth.

[220] A volume containing a work on merits (זכיות) and also on the laws of purity and impurity. The latter is quoted among Sa'adyah's works (cp. Malter, *l. c.*, 348) but the former is unknown to me.

[221] A Tafsīr to Numbers 13–15.

[222] A Massorah to Targum Onkelos (cp. note 119).

[223] The פ is doubtful. Probably read אלאסכאה, viz. 'the book that silences' (an opponent). Such a polemical work is cited among Sa'adyah's works (cp. Malter, *l. c.*, 402, no. 16).

[224] A copy of Midrash Tanḥuma.

[225] A Tafsīr to Levit. with a commentary.

[226] A Tafsīr of 2 sections of Psalms (cp. above, note 124).

[227] A volume of Piyyūṭim (thus Yannai's compositions are called חזאנה ינאי) and other matter.

[228] A Tafsīr of Canticles.

[229] The second part of 'the work of malice', evidently of a polemical nature. Unknown from elsewhere.

[230] The second half of a Tafsīr by Solomon (Rashi?).

[231] A Tafsīr to Berakot and Responsa by Sherira Gaon.

[232] Samuel b. Ḥofni's works on the laws of oaths, contracts and acquisition (see above, note 205). His Kitāb al-Īmān is listed in the Fihrist (*JQR.*, XIV, 311). See also note 248.

[233] A Tafsīr on 1st half of Exodus (1–17).

[234] The work Otiyot attributed to R. 'Aḳiba (see above, note 69).

[235] Sa'adyah's work on the laws of evidence and contracts (cp. Malter, *l. c.*, 345, no. 3). See also above, note 147.

[236] The full title of this work by Sa'adyah is כתאב תחציל אלשראיע אלסמעיה, the book of the summary of the traditional laws. About the various views concerning the identity of the work see Malter, *l. c.*, 400–401. Cp. also Pozn., *JQR, N. S.*, XIII, 393, 395.

[237] A Tafsīr to Canticles.

[238] A volume of (Gaonic) Responsa.

[239] A volume containing the beginning of Psalms (evidently an introduction to this Biblical book) and a Tafsīr to Ps. 120–150 called here מזאמיר (=זמירות) because these Psalms were read at the morning service as פסוקי דזמרא. About these Psalms as part of the Palestinian morning ritual cp. Mann, *H. U. C. Annual*, II, 293, top.

But perhaps by מזאמיר all the Psalms are meant and hence Sa'adyah's commentary is listed which had an extensive introduction as stated in the Fihrist (*JQR, N. S.*, XI, 425, ll. 17–8): ומן אלכתובים תלים ולה צדר מפרש כביר. Cp. also Pozn., ibid., XIII, 383.

[240] A Midrash to Ḳohelet.

241 =הרביתי=Sidra בא, hence a Tafsīr to Ex. 1–13.16.

242 A volume containing six treatises on (Hebrew) philology.

243 Baḥya's Kitāb al-Hidāya ilā Farāiḍ al-Ḳulūb (famous by the Hebrew translation חובות הלבבות).

244 A volume containing a digest of Ibn Sha'adan's work on syntax. The author is unknown to me.

245 A Tafsīr to Lamentations.

246 The nature of this work is unknown to me. Read perhaps אלאסכאת (see above, note 223).

247 A Tafsīr to Num. 22.2–30.1.

248 Samuel b. Ḥofni's work on the laws of gifts (מתנה) and of possessions (probably the latter is identical with his כ' אחכאם אלקנין). About the former cp. Pozn., *Zur jüd.-arab. Litter.*, 56; and about the latter above, notes 23, 205, 232.

249 A Tafsīr on Num. 4.21–7.89.

250 A volume containing the Kitāb קנסר (lots=ס' גורלות, cp. vol. II of our *Texts and Studies*) and Seder 'Olam.

251 The 'book of the decisive braggart,' evidently a polemical work. Author and the person alluded to are unknown to me.

252 Siddur R. 'Amram Gaon.

253 A commentary on Psalms.

254 A volume on "the work (employment) of the physician" or it may mean "the preparation of perfume." Unknown to me.

255 A Tafsīr on Leviticus.

256 A volume containing the Massoretic differences (חלופים) between Ben-Naphtali and Ben Asher.

257 One of al-Rāzi's treatises on medicine (see Steinsch., *H. Ü.*, 722 ff.). Perhaps the work is identical with his defence of the respected doctor against the quack (ibid., p. 732, no. 10).

258 A Tafsīr to Lev. 12–13.

259 A volume of questions to (and responsa from) the Geonim.

260 Samuel b. Ḥofni's work on the laws of adjacent fields and real estate (מצרנות). See above, note 182, and Harkavy, זכרון רשב"ח, p. 5 and note 80. It consisted of 20 chapters. The MS. containing the 3 works of Samuel on the laws of 1) maturity of minors (כתאב אלבלוג ואלאדראך), 2) Ṣiṣit (כתאב אחכאם שרע אלציצית) and 3) adjacent property (כתאב אלשפעה), described by Harkavy (*l. c.*, notes 76, 77 and 80), is now MS. Firkowicz, 2. Hebrew-Arabic Collection, No. 1467 (vellum). The colophons read as follows:

(fol. 1, recto; verso is blank)

קנה זה (r. זו) הנוסחה כבוד גד' מר' ורב'
עובדיה החכם והנבון הרופא הנכבד
ביר' שלמה המבין מלך ברחמיו
יזכהו ללמוד (בו הוא ו)בניו ובני
בניו וכן יהי רצון

(fol. 2, recto; verso is blank)

כתאב אלבלוג ואלאדראך
וכתאב אחכאם שרע
אלציצית
וכתאב אלשפעה
אלעזר הלוי ביר׳ יוסף ביר׳
אברהם ביר׳ מבורך החבר
המעולה בסנהדרין גדולה זכרם
לחיי עד אמן נצח סלה בשנת את״ל
לשטרות
עובדיה ביר׳ שלמה ס״ט מה שקנה שמואל הלוי
בר׳ סעדיה
דוד ביר׳ אלעזר ס״ט ביר׳ אלעזר רי״ת
קדש עלי ועל זרעי אחרי ואחריהם
על כנסת בני מקרא אני שמואל בן מר׳
ור׳ שלמה בן מר׳ור׳ שמואל בן מר׳ור׳ משה
כאזרוני ס״ט ארור מוכרו וקונהו [וממשכנו]
וגונבו וברוך הקורא בו ומחזירו למקומו אנ״ס (= אמן נצח סלה).

This codex thus had several owners. Written by El'azar Hallevi b. Joseph b. Abraham b. Meborakh the Ḥaber in 1118–19 C. E., it was bought by the physician 'Obadyah b. Solomon and later on by Samuel Hallevi b. Sa'adyah, then by David b. El'azar b. El'azar and finally by a Ḳaraite Samuel b. Solomon b. Samuel b. Solomon כאזרוני. Samuel donated it to the Ḳaraite community in Fusṭāṭ. About the Ḳaraite family of כאזרוני see vol. II of *Texts and Studies*.

Samuel b. Sa'adyah Hallevi is known as the buyer of other MSS. (cp. *Saadyana*, p. 116; Bodl. 2862.28). He lived in the second half of the 12th century (cp. Bodl. *Catalogue* II, Index, s. v.).

The heading of the first work (fol. 3, recto) reads: כתאב אלבלוג ואלאדראך לר׳ שמואל הכהן גאון בן אב בן גאון י״י. On fol. 45, recto, bottom, there ends the second work כתאב אחכאם שרע אלציצית. A colophon at the bottom is cut off, but on fol. 45, verso, we read the following badly written colophon: הד׳א אלמצחף אכ׳ד׳תו מן אלקודש והוא הקדש מן בנהת (Hark. reads כנסת) דאר שמחה תב׳ ות׳ (= תבנה ותכונן) ארדת אני אקרא פיה מצות ציצית והו תאליף חכמי הרבנים. ארור מוכרו וגונבו וברוך הקורא בו ומחזירו למקומו אנ״ס.

The heading of the third work (fol. 46, recto) reads: כתאב אלשפעה תאליף שמואל גאון בן גאון אלחופני בן אב גאון (which is a corruption of שמואל גאון בן חופני אב בן גאון).

Portions of the work on Ṣiṣit have been published by Israelsohn (*Haḳḳedem*, III, Germ. part, 40–43) and by Herzog (*JQR*, *N.S.*, V, 17 ff.).

[261] A volume containing a Midrash to which there belonged another one containing Pesiḳtot (פסיִקְתָא=אפסאקאת), evidently Pesiḳta de R. Kahana because Pesiḳta Rabbati is mentioned infra, l. 159.

[262] Sa'adyah's commentary on Exodus.

[263] A Tafsīr on Ezra.

[264] A copy of tractate B. Batra.

[265] A Tafsīr on both halves of Genesis.

[266] The nature of this Kitāb is impossible to ascertain owing to the lacuna.

[267] Sa'adyah's Kitāb al-Tamyīz against the Ḳaraites (see Malter, *l. c.*, 380 ff.).

[268] Sa'adyah's commentary on the liturgy forming a part of his Siddur (see *l. c.*, 329 ff.).

[269] The same volume also contained a treatise on the number of the letters of the Bible (viz. on the Alphabet). Evidently the same item as given in *Saadyana*, p. 52, containing the beginning of his Piyyūṭ on the Alphabet with the heading: אעדאד אחרף אלמקרא תצניף רבנו סעדיה גאון מחסיה. Cp. Malter, *l. c.*, 339 ff.

[270] A Tafsīr on Ruth.

[271] A volume containing a work on the question of the Sabbath light (נר שבת) and Hai's work on laws of oaths (שבועות). The former was probably by Sa'adyah against the Ḳaraite prohibition of lights on Sabbath eve (listed in the Fihrist, *JQR*, *N. S.*, XI, 425, l. 23, as כתאב גׄמע אלחגׄה ללסורגׄ; also called מקאלה̈ פי סראגׄ אלסבת, cp. p. 428, and Pozn., ibid., XIII, 394–5). About Hai's work see above, note 70.

[272] A Tafsīr on Canticles.

[273] A Tafsīr on Lev. 1–11.

[274] "The Pesiḳta of the Palestinians," probably Pesiḳta Rabbati is referred to here which was redacted by a follower of the Abele Zion in Jerusalem in the 9th century (cp. Mann, *Jews in Egypt*, I, 47–8).

[275] A copy of the Pentateuch.

[276] A copy of Psalms.

[277] Ḥayyūj's works on 1) weak verbs, 2) the double lettered ones (כפולים) and 3) on the laws of punctuation. The last is also known as כתאב אלנקט or ספר הנקוד (cp. Poznański, *JQR*, *N. S.*, XVI, 258 and 260).

[278] A volume of Gaonic responsa.

[279] A volume containing the mystical work called מעשה מרכבה (quoted by Rashi to Ḥag. 13a, see Abraham Wilna, רב פעלים, p. 84), evidently forming a part of the so-called Hekhalot literature.

[280] A volume containing matters on the resurrection and on circumcision, a curious combination of subjects. Perhaps it dealt among others with the point concerning boys, who died before the performance of the Abrahamic rite whether they would share in the resurrection. R. Naḥshon, Gaon of Sura, reports of the custom to circumcise such a child at the grave and to give it a name for the purpose of resurrection (cp. Caro, בית יוסף, to Ṭūr Yoreh De'ah, § 263, end). Perhaps in our treatise the theological aspect of this point was dealt with.

[281] Sa'adyah's Sepher Haggalui.

[282] Sa'adyah's treatise on the laws concerning the 24 kinds of perquisites of the priesthood (also cited in *Saadyana*, p. 53, bottom; cp. Malter, *l. c.*, 348, No. 9).

[283] A work on the value of words (or on intonation) and manifestations (evidently on rhetoric).

284 A work on Indian plant and fine scents (medical).

285 A Tafsīr on Numbers.

286 A Tafsīr on Psalms.

287 A copy of Job and Proverbs.

288 The history of the 'Abbāsids and Barmakids. See above, note 102.

289 A Tafsīr of Genesis.

290 A Tafsīr on Deut. 21.10–25.19; 32–34.

291 A commentary on Pent., Jer., the Minor Prophets, Joshua and Judges, and part of the text of Samuel.

292 A commentary (פירוש=פי׳) on some of the first chapters of Sabbath by Samuel b. Ḥofni. In a letter (above, p. 159) this Gaon refers to his commentaries on Tractates of Mishnah and Talmud.

293 =ירחמהו ה׳.

294 A copy of B. Batra with Rashi.

295 Natan's 'Arukh till letter נון.

296 A Maḥzor in the handwriting of Ibn אלשראר.

297 The Pandects of Ibn Serapion on medicine; cp. Steinschneider, *H. Ü.*, § 474 (see p. 737, note 539). The copy was of vellum (רק).

298 A part of Exodus and Numbers in the handwriting of Abū'l 'Izz.

299 A bound volume dealing with Hebrew philology containing 9 treatises by Sa'adyah Gaon. This work is unknown to me.

300 Sa'adyah's commentary on Lev. 16–20; במעא֗=במעאני.

301 Treatises on medicine by Ḳosta b. Luḳa, a Christian philosopher, mathematician and physician of Baalbek (9th century); see Steinsch., *l. c.*, §§ 157, 342.

301a The Aphorisms of Hippocrates translated into Arabic by Ḥunain b. Isḥāḳ under the title כתאב אלפצול (see Steinschneider, *H. Ü.*, p. 658).

302 A work by Galen called תנפיר, evidently in Arabic translation, but the work is unknown to me. About Galen in Hebrew literature see Steinschneider, *l. c.*, p. 650 ff.

303 A commentary on R. Hashana.

304 The canons, evidently of Avicenna, on medicine. There is the large canon consisting of 5 books (see Steinschneider, *H. Ü.*, p. 678 ff.) and there is a small canon (אלקאנון אלצגיר, ibid., p. 695).

305 Sa'adyah's Siddur, complete in 2 vellum pamphlets.

306 Sa'adyah's Agron in 2 copies one of which belonged to a certain Ibn al-Rabi'a.

307 A Tafsīr to Num. 33–36.

308 A work (כתאב=כת֗) on the laws of loans (הלואה or perhaps רבית), probably by Samuel b. Ḥofni.

309 A list of the kinds of koḥl (antimony, stibium) by Ḥunain b. Isḥāḳ in Hebrew letters.

310 Another such list "(in) my handwriting" (viz. in that of the compiler of this book-list). The author was a certain 'Īsa.

311 A work in Arabic letters on Indian (=decimal) multiplication.

312 Some of the Hilkhot ראו (see ed. Schlossberg, ה' פסוקות או ה' ראו, 1886).

313 Probably Sa'adyah's work on the laws of purity and impurity (see Malter, *l. c.*, 348).

314 Sa'adyah's polemical work against Ḳaraism known as al-Tamyīz (see above, note 267).

315 A certain work in Hebrew or Arabic handwriting (עברי= עבראני or ערבי).

316 A collection in which were to be found Pirḳe Abot and a Tafsīr on Deut. 32 by Ibn al-'Ākūli. An Ibn al-'Ākūli is mentioned as a writer against the theory of eternity of matter (see Munk, *Le Guide des Égares*, I, 462).

317 Copies of Exodus (both halves) and of Leviticus.

318 Seven pamphlets containing a work on calendation by ibn 'Alvān. Read perhaps עלאן for עלון, thus the author was Joshu'a b. 'Alān, a Rabbanite authority on the calendar, cited by the Ḳaraite Ben Mashiaḥ (see Harkavy, *Haggoren*, IV, 75–80).

319 =נוז. A fragment of a digest of Dinim.

320 Pamphlets containing Seliḥot.

321 A part of a collection of Seliḥot and prayers.

322 A part containing Megillat Setarim (by Nissim b. Jacob of Ḳairwān, cp. Poznański, לקוטים מן ס' מגלת סתרים, in הצופה לחכמת ישראל, vols. VI and VII) and other matter.

323 Hai's work on calendation (probably by Hai b. David, cp. Harkavy, *Haggoren*, IV, 80).

324 A commentary of Lev. 16–end, probably by Sa'adyah (see above, note 67).

325 A copy of Megillah and Beṣah.

326 Saadyah's well-known religious-philosophical work (after אל supply אעתקאדאת).

327 The beginning of this book-list is evidently missing because each section contains a heading according to its subject-matter (see ll. 24, 36, 54) and this heading is lacking here to the section of Bible commentaries. See also note 335.

328 Sa'adyah's commentary to Proverbs (cp. *Oeuvres Complètes*, ed. Derenbourg, vol. VI, 1894).

329 Sa'adyah's Arabic translation of the Pentateuch, bound (cp. *l. c.*, vol. I, 1893).

330 Two bound volumes containing Yefet b. 'Alī's commentary on Isaiah, complete.

331 A commentary on 'the future events' (viz. on Is. 40–66), in 3 bound volumes, also by Yefet b. 'Alī.

332 A commentary on Jeremiah in one bound volume, complete.

333 A commentary on Canticles, newly bound, complete.

334 2 bound parts of a commentary on Samuel, the first of which extending from 2 Sam. 10.12 (our text reads ונתחזק but in 1 Chr. 19.13 ונתחזקה) to the end and the other from 1 Sam. 20.12 to 2 Sam. 5.25 (insert כן after דוד, but cp. 1 Chr. 14.16!).

335 Another commentary on Ḳohelet (evidently one such commentary was listed before in the missing part).

336 A commentary, bound, on a half of 1 Kings by Yefet b. 'Alī.

337 One bound volume contained a commentary on Daniel (perhaps also by Yefet, cp. ed. D. S. Margoliouth, *Anecdota Oxoniensia*, Semitic Series, Vol. 1—Part III, 1889).

At the end there was a nice treatise (Risāla) by Samuel the physician, probably Samuel b. Moses al-Maghribi, the author of al-Murshid (15th century), cp. Poznański, *Ḳaraite Literary Opponents of Saadya*, 81–2. See infra, note 361.

338 A commentary in Arabic on Ezekiel in one bound volume (הנ׳=הנביא).

339 A commentary on the Minor Prophets in 2 bound volumes, complete.

339a A commentary on Proverbs in 2 bound volumes, one (insert ואחד before לנא) belonging "to us" (viz. to the compiler of the book-list) and another to a certain Mūsa.

340 A commentary on the Pentateuch by Hai Gaon, bound and complete. This work is unknown. From the designation פירוש it seems it was in Hebrew.

341 A bound volume containing Baḥya b. Asher's commentary on Genesis and Exodus (printed).

342 A bound volume containing David Ḳimḥi's commentary on Proverbs and Psalms.

343 An Arabic commentary, bound, on the first section (chs. 1–41) of Psalms by Yefet b. 'Alī. About the term מגלה see above, note 124.

344 Dictionaries and Grammars.

345 Evidently the Biblical concordance of Isaac Nathan b. Ḳalonymos, compiled in 1437–45 (cp. Bacher, *J. E.*, IV, 204).

346 A dictionary (Agron) of the roots of Biblical Hebrew in Arabic, perhaps the Agron of David b. Abraham al-Fāsi (cp. Steinschneider, *Arab. Liter. d. Juden*, § 47).

347 David Ḳimḥi's grammar (viz. the מכלול) was of course written in Hebrew and not in Arabic. As in our list a Hebrew work is indicated by לשון קדש we cannot here assume that ערבי is a mistake for עברי. Some other grammatical work in Arabic has therefore been wrongly attributed to Ḳimḥi. His dictionary is listed in l. 31. and evidently his Mikhlol is meant in l. 29.

348 Another Hebrew grammar in Arabic.

349 Probably Ḳimḥi's Mikhlol (see note 347).

350 A book called דרדקי on the roots of the (Hebrew) language. Evidently a primer for elementary school children and hence the title of the work.

351 Ḳimḥi's dictionary of Biblical Hebrew.

352 A book called אהל מועד dealing with topics (memoranda) of the Hebrew language. Probably the work by David Kohen de Lara on the Rabbinic synonyms (see Ben-Jacob, s. v.).

353 A bound volume containing an Arabic glossary of the Prophets and Hagiographa.

354 Explanation of codes.

355 A bound volume containing 4 treatises by Yefet b. Ṣa'īr (Steinschneider,

l. c., § 185), author of a ספר מצות in 10 Maḳālāt (cp. Pinsker, נספחים, ל״ק, 188). See also infra, note 362.

[356] Elijah Bashiazi's Aderet. The compiler of the list indicates that this work emanates from the Constantinople Ḳaraites.

[357] The well-known work Eṣ Ḥayyim by Elijah (II) b. Aaron (cp. ed. Delitzsch, 1841) is here given also with the title העתקת התורה וחלוקת הקראים והרבנים. The latter title is given to a work by Elijah Bashiazi.

[358] A book on legalism called שער יהודה, evidently the work by Judah b. Eliezer Poki on the laws of permitted and prohibited marriages (printed Constantinople 1581, cp. Fürst, *Bibliotheca Hebraica*, III, 108, bottom).

[359] Elijah Hadassi's Eshkol Hakkofer in 3 bound volumes, complete.

[360] One bound volume contained 1) a work by Elijah the judge followed by 2) a work of the teacher (אלמעלם) Fādhil and at the end there was 3) a commentary on Deut. 33. Cp. Poznański, *MGWJ*, LXV (1921), 133 ff.

[361] Three bound volumes, complete, containing the Murshid of Samuel al-Maghribi. Cp. note 337.

[362] A bound volume containing 5 sections of Yefet b. Ṣa'īr's Sefer Hammiṣvot which with the 4 listed above, l. 37 (see note 355), make 9 sections, all in the handwriting of the compiler of the list.

[363] Prayers and Introductions (to the Sidrot of the week).

[363a] =יום.

[364] Three volumes of Siddurim. The first one contained the prayers for the weekdays (evening and morning), Sabbath and Rosh Ḥodesh. Complete.

The second began with the liturgy for Passover, then Pentecost, the 40 איכה (evidently compositions for the 9th of Ab) whereas the end of the volume comprised items for Sabbath נחמו.

The third volume covered the ritual from the beginning of Yom Kippur to Rosh Hashanah. The order is peculiar and we would expect the reverse from Rosh Hashanah to Yom Kippur.

[365] The next Siddur covered the liturgical items for the remainder of the year, viz. for Sukkot, Shemini 'Aṣeret, Simḥat Torah, the prayers for the Fasts and for Purim. In addition there were Piyyuṭim of congratulation (for weddings and circumcisions, etc.) and consolation (for mourning) and other items. By Simḥat Torah Sabbath בראשית is meant. Cp. the מנהגים of Joseph b. Mordecai (סדור התפלות כמנהג הקראים, ed. Wilna, I, 462, No. 45): בשמחת התורה שהיא שבת התחלת התורה וכו'.

[366] A Siddur beginning with Shebu'ot and ending with Rosh Hashanah.

[367] A bound copy of the liturgy for Yom Kippur eve.

[368] A copy of the liturgy for Yom Kippur Day divided into 1) morning, 2) afternoon and 3) mercy prayers, the latter corresponding to Ne'ilah. It was in vellum, a complete fragment. Each section had the first words tinged in red.

[369] A copy of the liturgy of Yom Kippur morning, in 4 parts.

[370] Another one containing the liturgy for Yom Kippur afternoon.

[371] Complete introductions to the Sidrot, the first and second ones (evidently there were 2 such compositions to each Sidra).

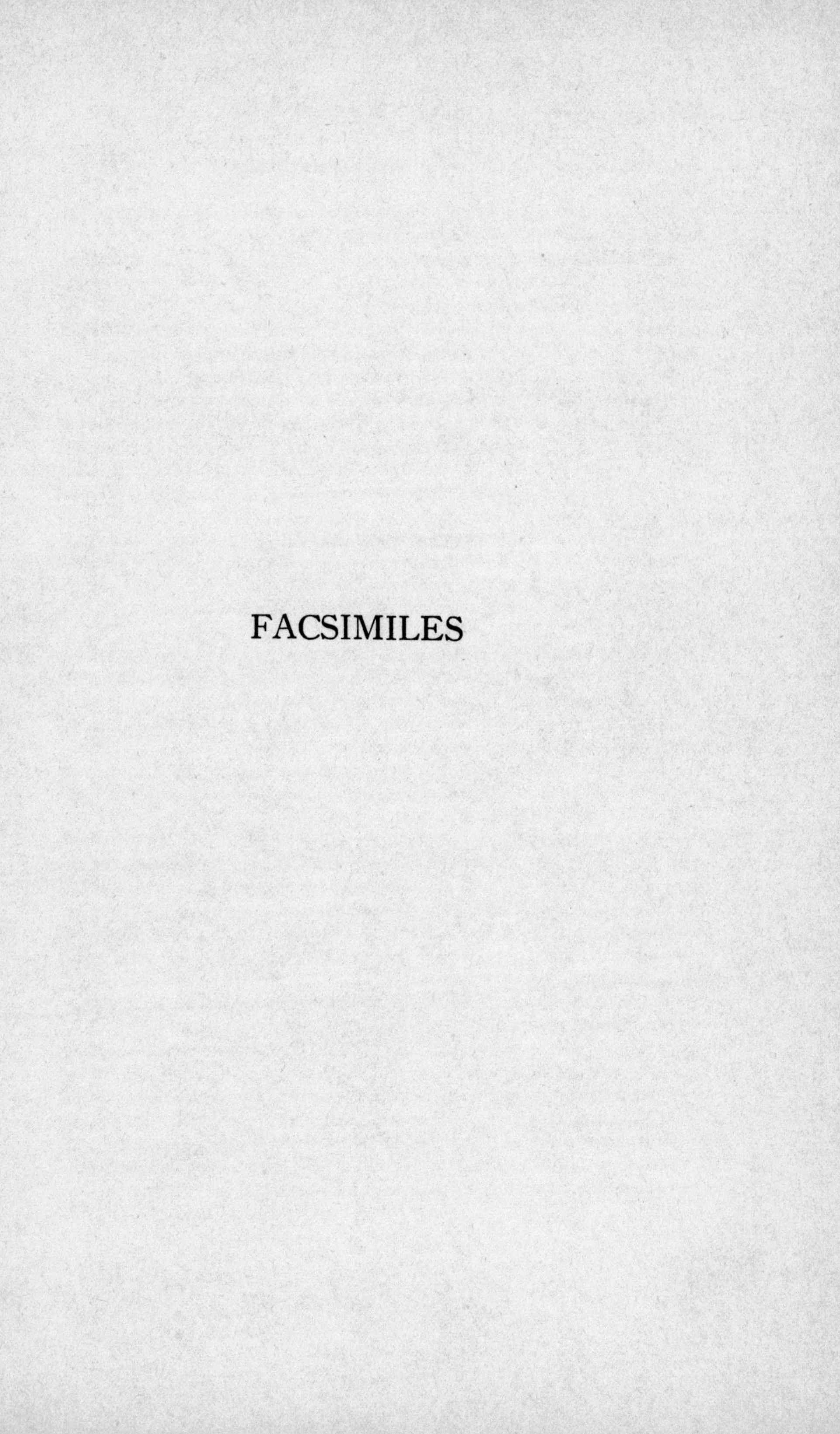

FACSIMILES

FACSIMILE I, A

(Verso) (Recto)

From a letter of Sherira Gaon and his son Hai Ab

(*see above*, *pp.* 99–100)

FACSIMILE I, B

(Verso)

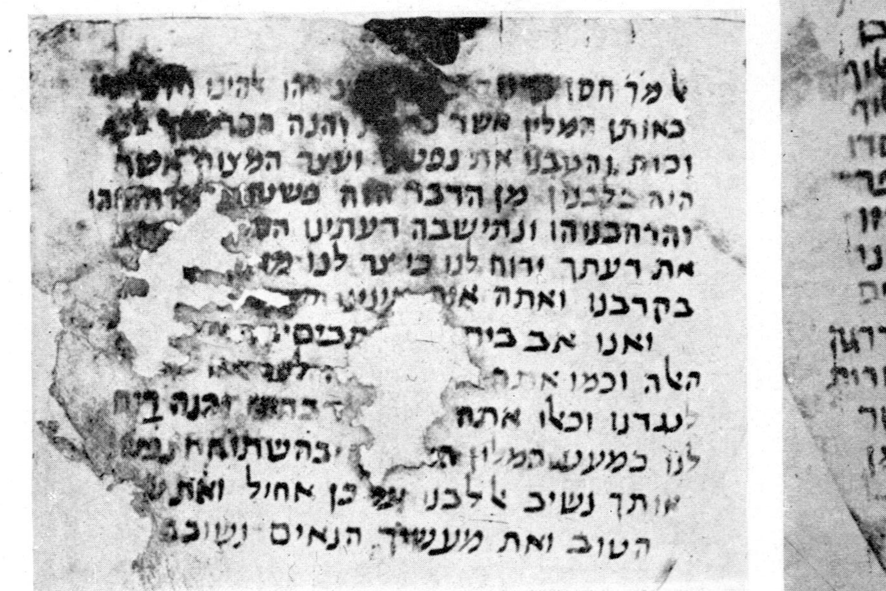

(Recto)

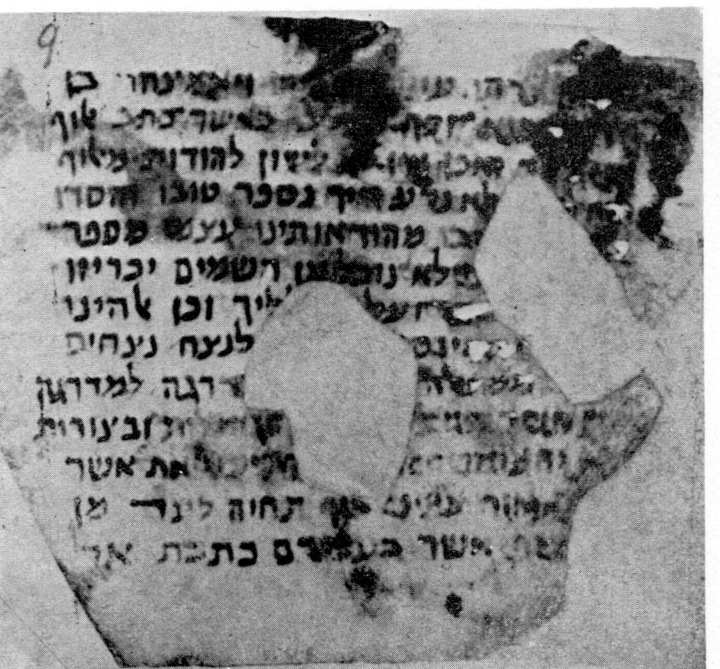

From a letter of Sherira Gaon and his son Hai Ab
(*see above, pp. 100–101*)

FACSIMILE I, C

(Verso)

(Recto)

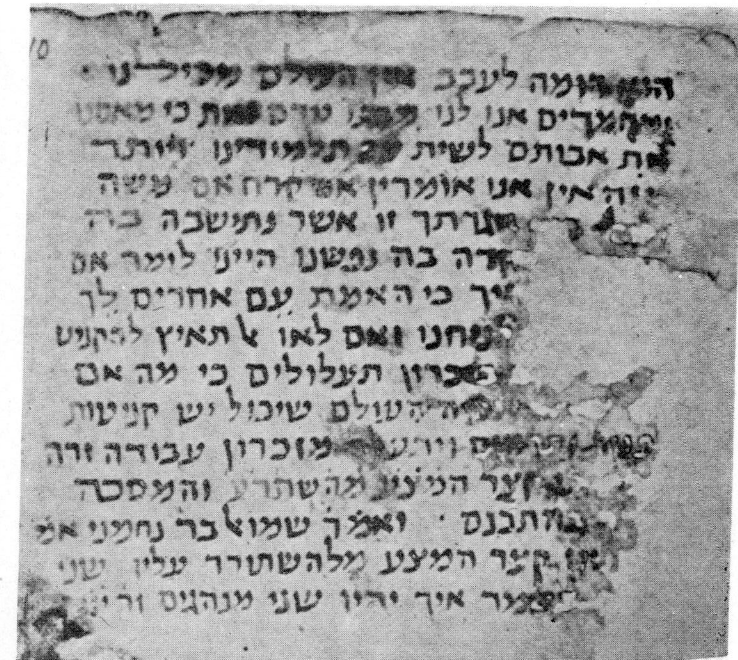

From a letter of Sherira Gaon and his son Hai Ab

(*see above*, *pp. 102–103*)

FACSIMILE I, D

(Verso) (Recto)

From a letter of Sherira Gaon and his son Hai Ab
(*see above, pp. 103–104*)

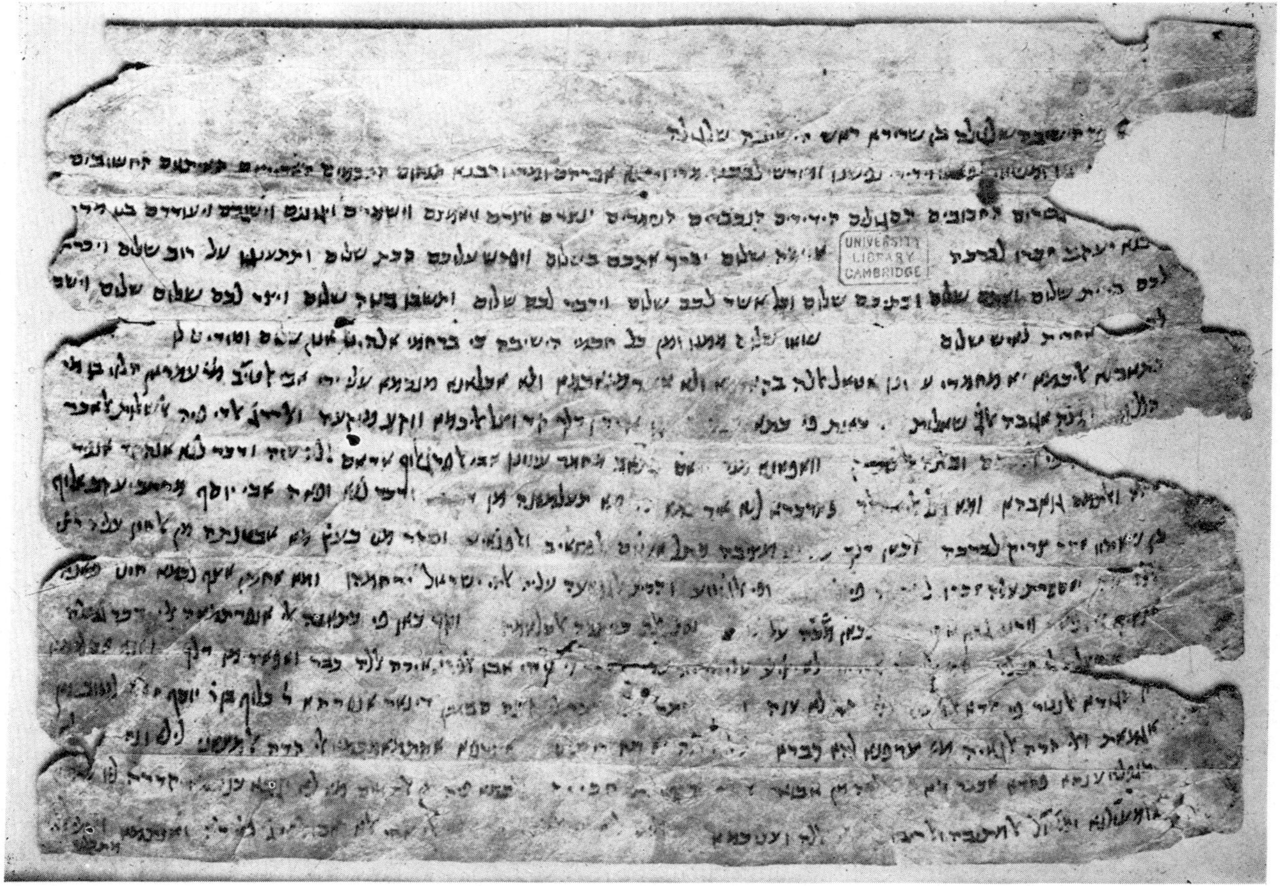

FACSIMILE II, A

(Recto)

Letter of Hai Gaon, dated Adar 19, 1007 C. E. (*see above, pp. 123–26*)

FACSIMILE II, B

(Verso)

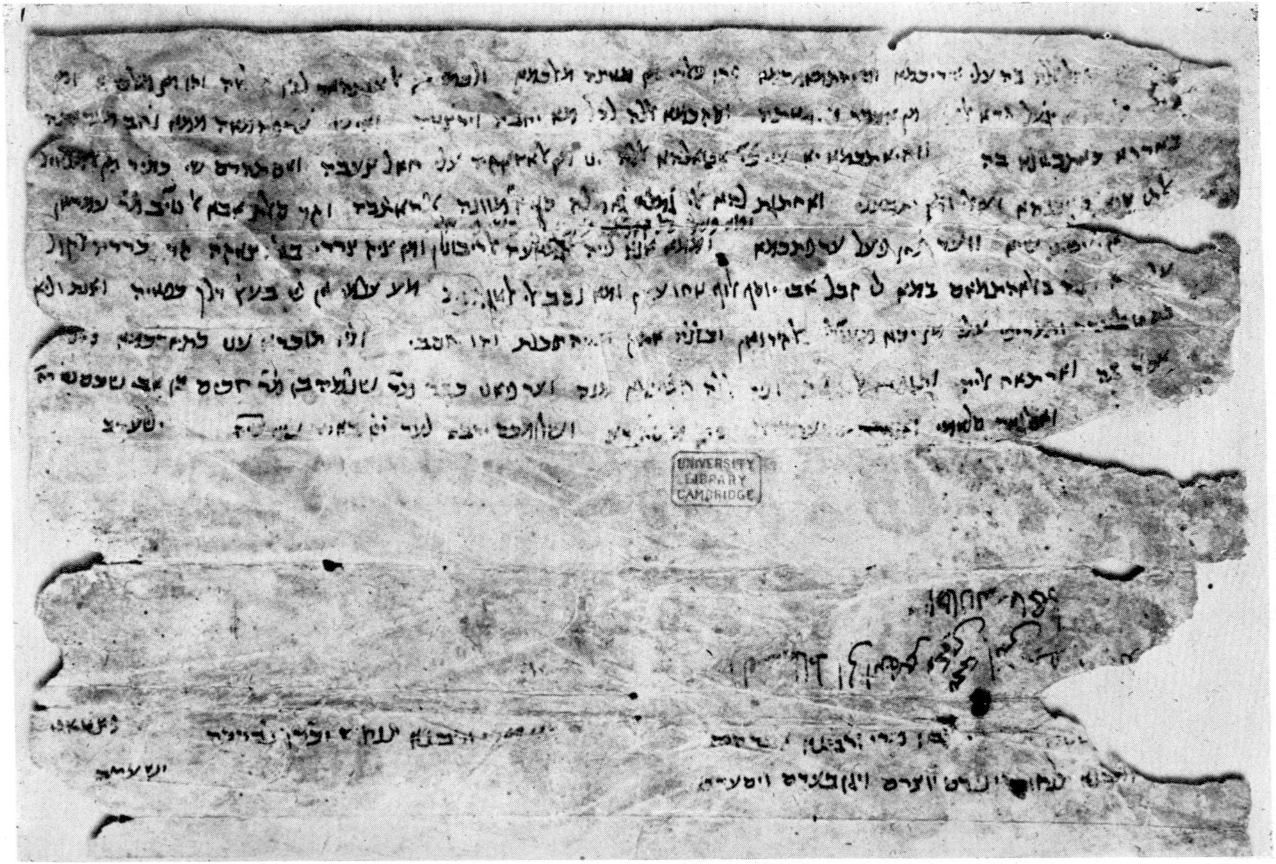

Letter of Hai Gaon, dated Adar 19, 1007 C. E. (*see above, pp. 123–26*)

(Fol. 1, recto)

FACSIMILE III, A

(Fol. 3, verso)

From a letter of Hai Gaon (*see above, pp. 126 ff.*)

FACSIMILE III, B

(Fol. 3, recto) (Fol. 1, verso)

From a letter of Hai Gaon (*see above, pp. 126 ff.*)

FACSIMILE III, C

(Fol. 2, recto) (Fol. 2, verso)

From a letter of Hai Gaon (*see above, pp. 129-32*)

FACSIMILE IV

Letter of Hai Gaon, dated Shebaṭ 19, 1018 C. E. (*see above, pp. 135–36*)

FACSIMILE V

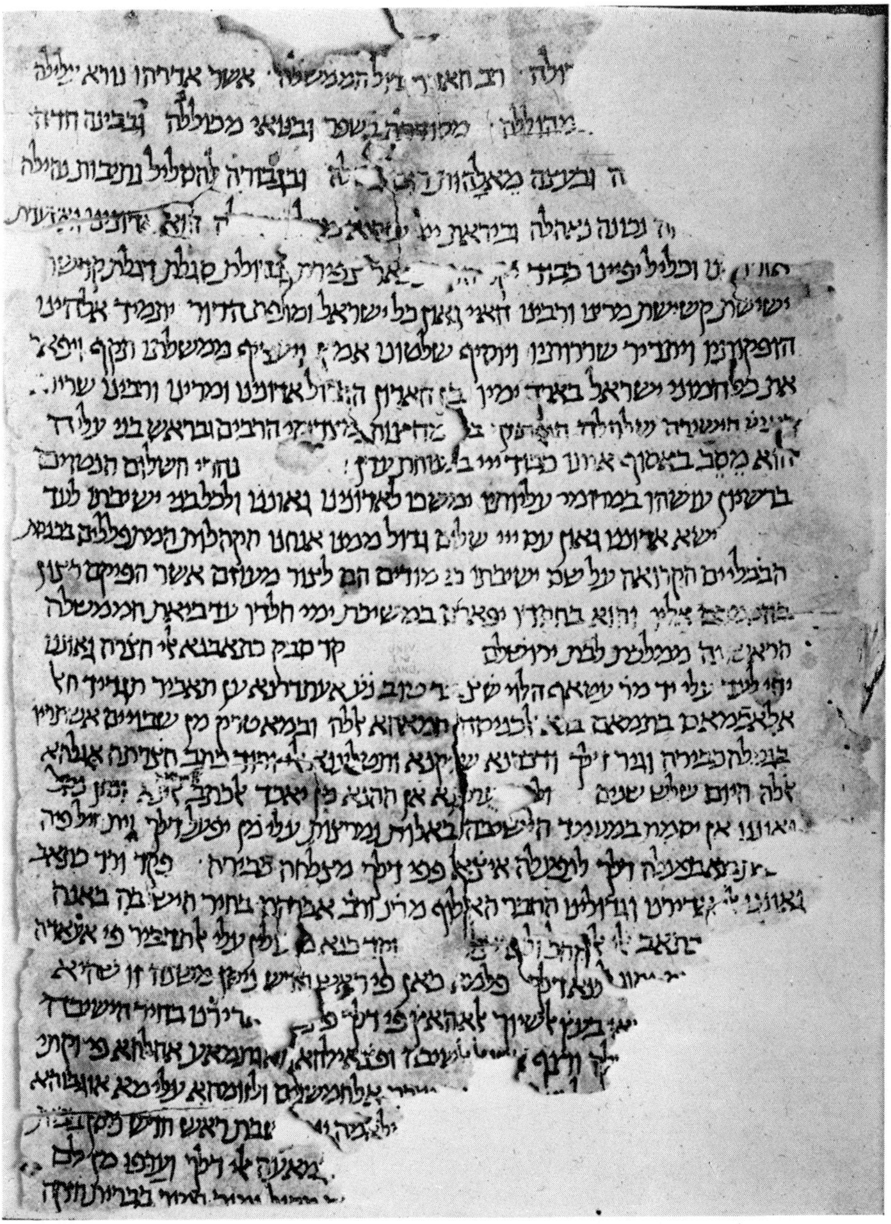

Letter from Fusṭāṭ to Hai Gaon

(*see above, pp. 138–40*)

FACSIMILE VI

(Recto)

Letter from Ḳābes to Fusṭāṭ
(*see above, pp. 140–41*)

A FACSIMILE VII, A AND B (Recto)

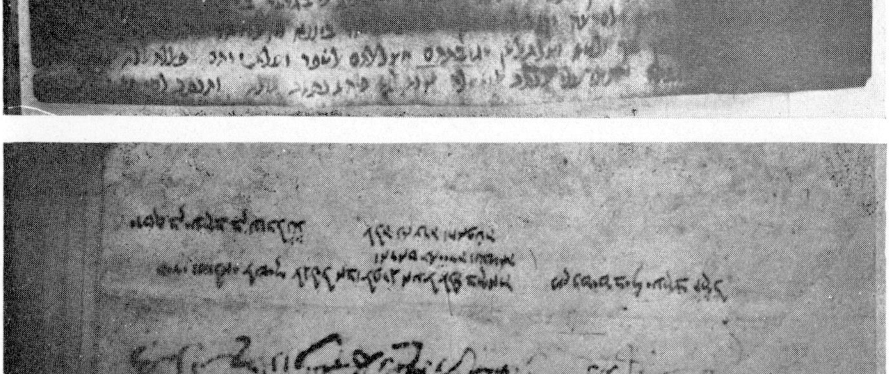

(Verso)

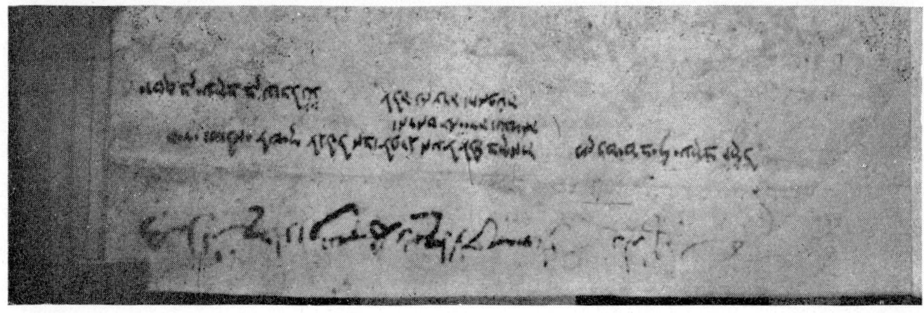

B

Letter from Nissim b. Jacob of Ḳairwān to Joseph b. Jacob of Fusṭāṭ

(*see above, pp. 142–45*)

FACSIMILE VIII

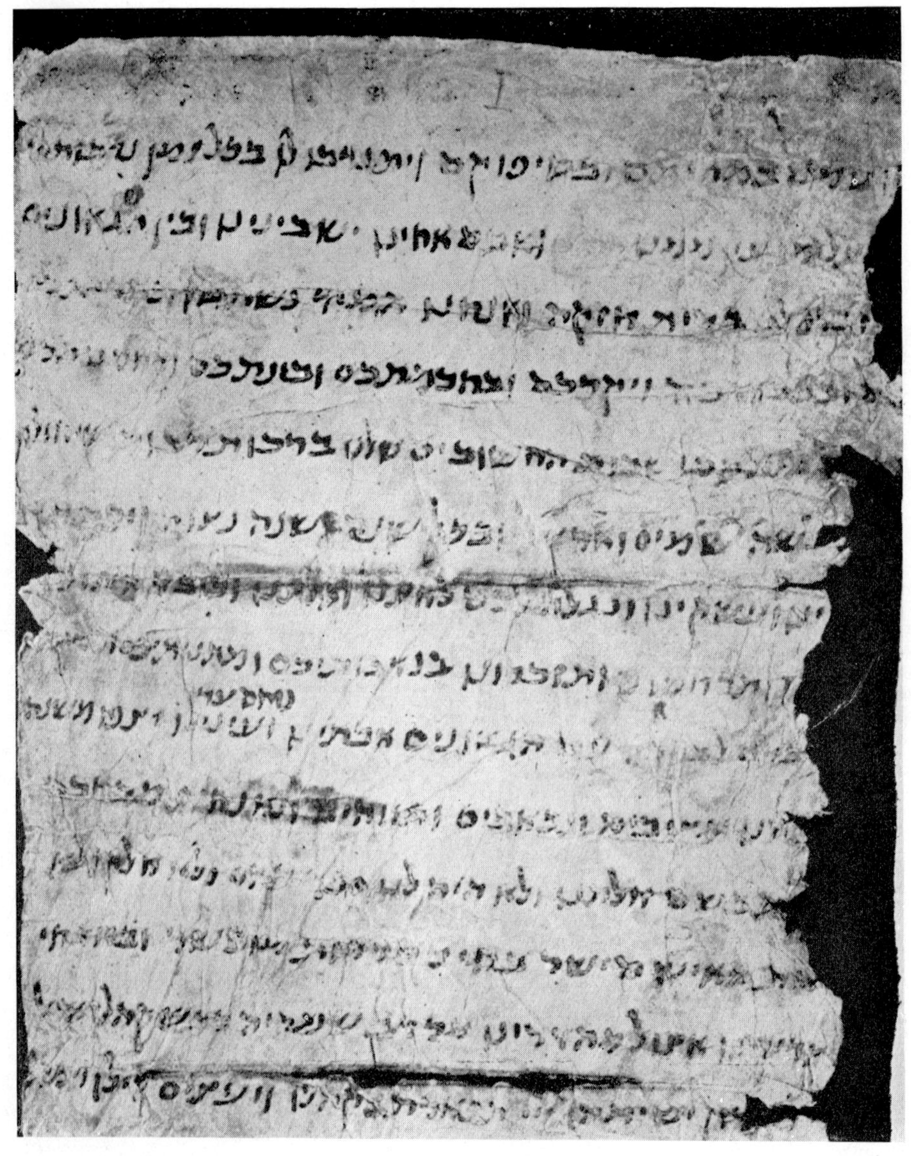

Letter of Samuel b. Ḥofni, dated Tammuz 977 C. E.
(*see above, pp. 155–56*)

FACSIMILE VIII (continuation)

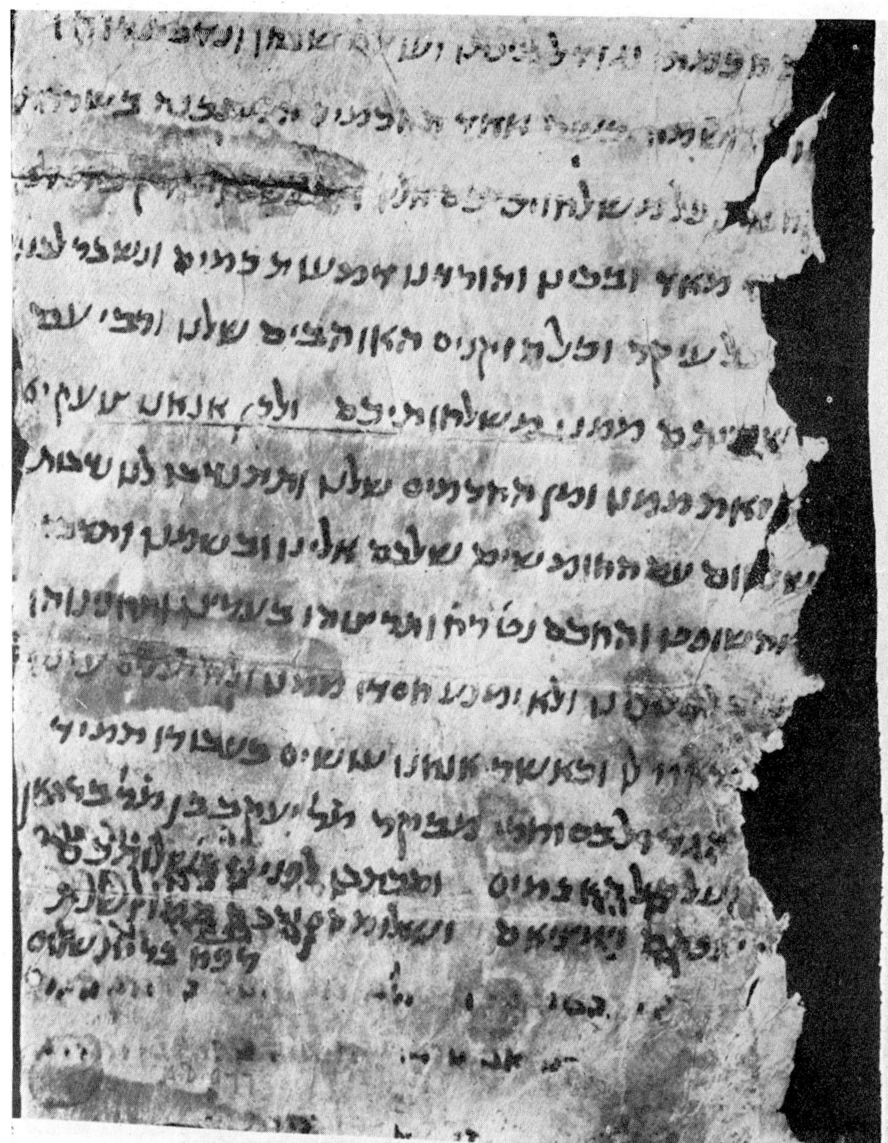

Letter of Samuel b. Ḥofni, dated Tammuz 977 C. E.
(*see above, pp. 155–56*)

FACSIMILE IX, A

(Recto)

Letter of Samuel b. Ḥofni
(*see above, pp. 160–61*)

FACSIMILE IX, B

(Verso)

Letter of Samuel b. Ḥofni
(*see above, pp. 162–63*)

FACSIMILE X

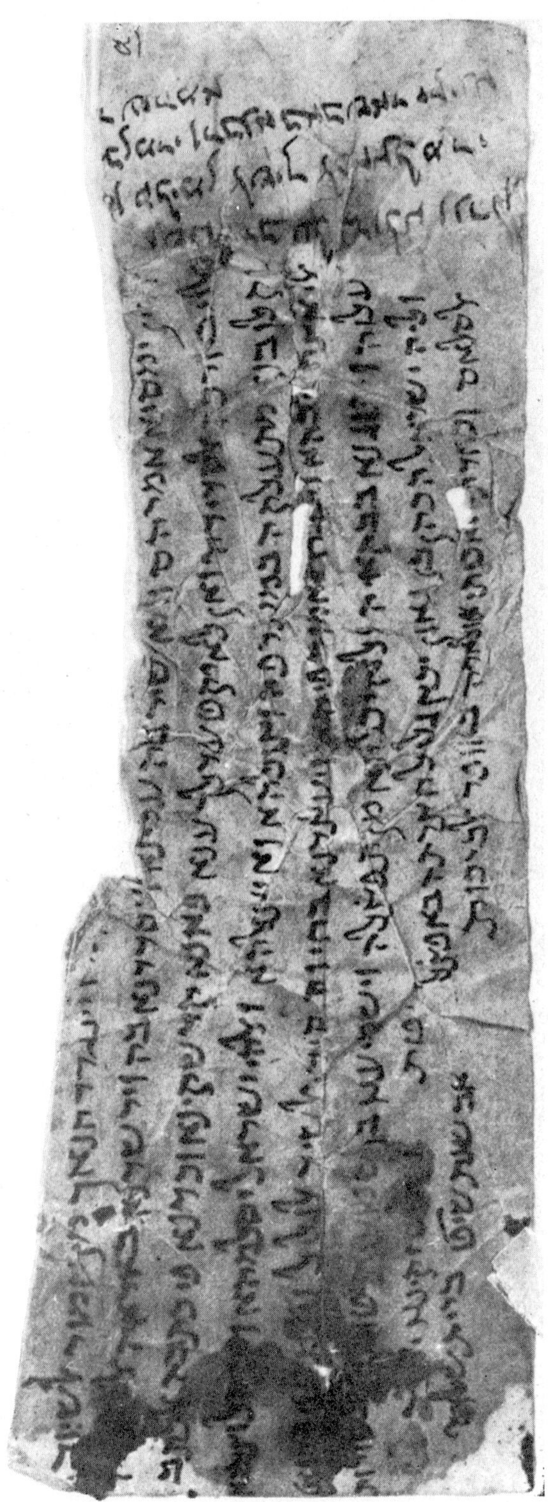

Letter of Samuel b. Ḥofni, dated Ab 1008 C. E.

(*see above, pp. 163–64*)

FACSIMILE XI

Letter of Samuel b. Ḥofni, dated Elul 1004 C. E.
(*see above, pp. 165–66*)

FACSIMILE XII

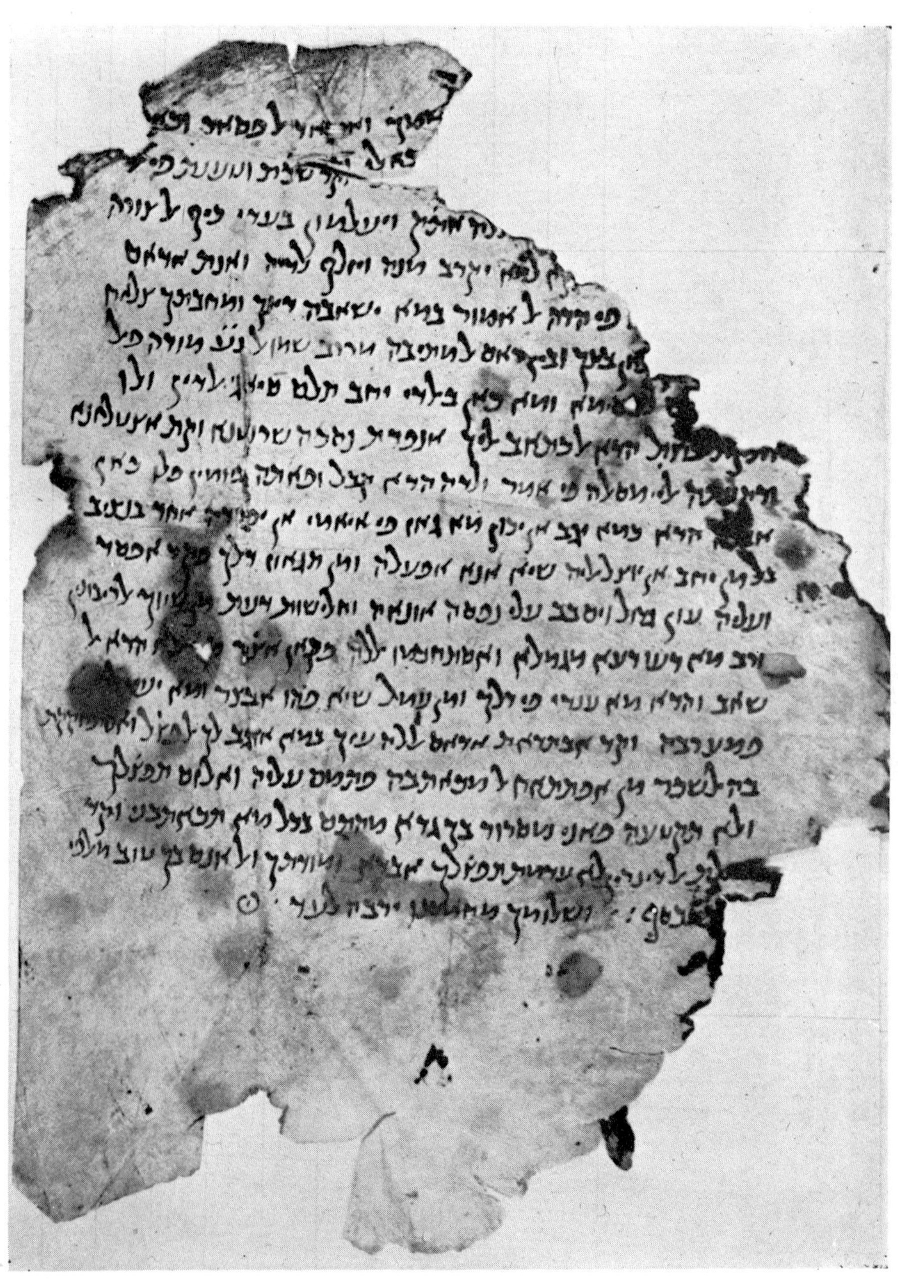

Letter of Dosa Gaon b. Sa'adyah Gaon
(*see above, pp. 166–67*)

(Fol. 1, verso) FACSIMILE XIII, A (Fol. 1, recto)

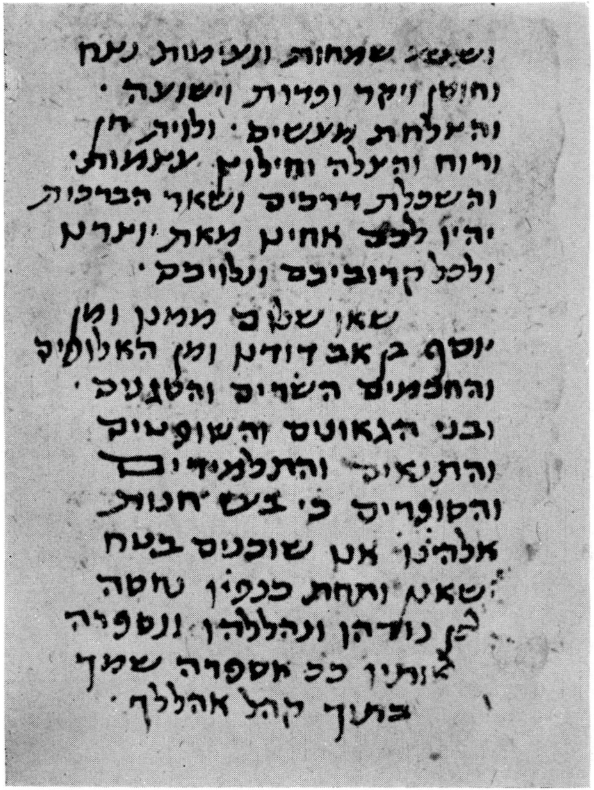

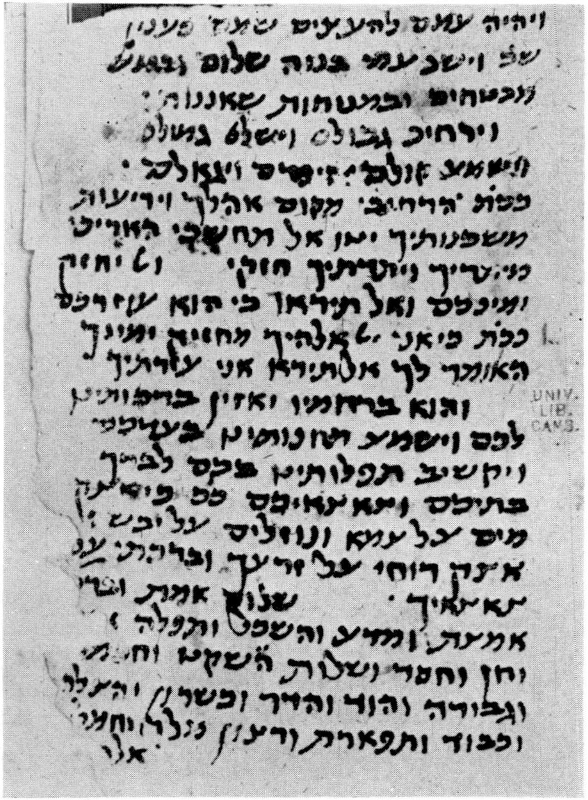

From a letter of Israel Gaon b. Samuel b. Ḥofni (*see above, pp. 167–69*)

(Fol. 2, verso) FACSIMILE XIII, B (Fol. 2, recto)

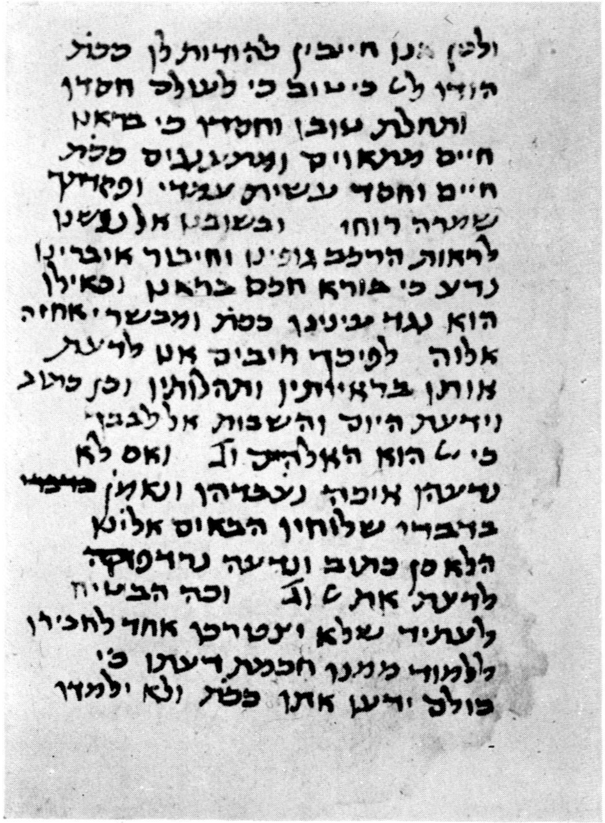
ולכן אנו חייבין להודות לו ככת'
הודו ליי כי טוב כי לעולם חסדו
ותחלת טובו וחסדיו כי בראנו
חיים מתאווים ומתענגים ככת'
חיים וחסד עשית עמדי ופקודתך
שמרה רוחי ובשובנו אל נפשנו
לראות הרכב גופינו וחיבור איברינו
נדע כי בורא חכם בראנו וכאילו
הוא נגד עינינו ככת' ומבשרי אחזה
אלוה לפיכך חייבים אנו לדעת
אותו בראיותיו ותהלותיו וכן כתוב
וידעת היום והשבות אל לבבך
כי יי הוא האלהים וג' ואם לא
ידענו איכה נעבדהו ונאמן בדברי
בדברי שלוחיו הבאים אלינו
הלא כן כתוב ונדעה נרדפה
לדעת את יי וג' וכה הבטיח
לעתיד שלא יצטרכו אחד לחבירו
ללמוד ממנו חכמת דעתו כי
כולם ידעו אותו ככת' ולא ילמדו

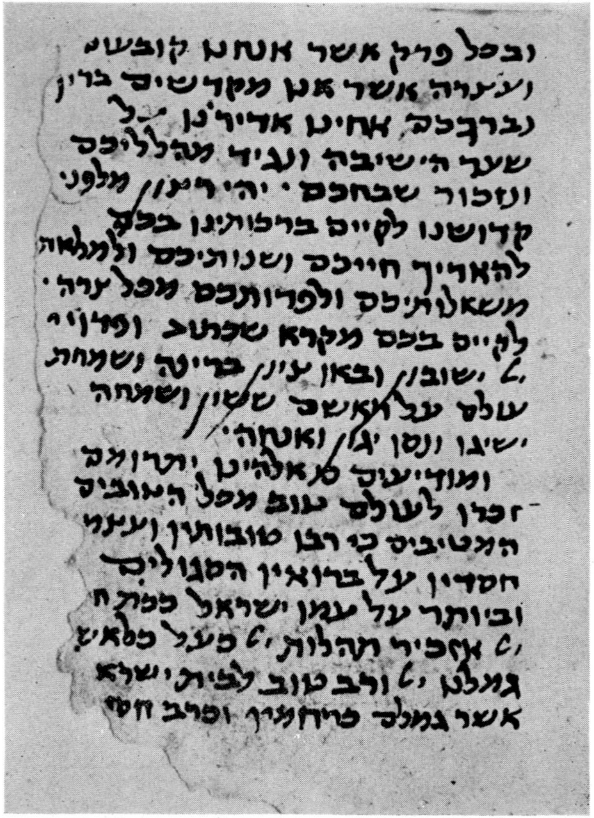
ובכל פרק אשר אתנו קובעים
ועצרה אשר אנו מקדשים ברין
נברככם אחינו אדירינו על
שערי הישיבה ועיד מהלליכם
ונזכור שבחכם · יהי רצון מלפני
קדושנו לקיים ברכותינו בכם
להאריך חייכם ושנותיכם ולמלאות
משאלותיכם ולפרותכם מכל צרה ·
לקיים בכם מקרא שכתוב ופדויי
יי ישובון ובאו ציון ברינה ושמחת
עולם על ראשם ששון ושמחה
ישיגו ונסו יגון ואנחה ·
ומודיעים לאלהינו יתרומם
זכרו לעולם טוב מכל המטיבים
המטיבים כי רבו טובותיו ועצמו
חסדיו על ברואיו הסגולים
וביותר על עמו ישראל כמ"ש
יי אזכיר תהלות יי כעל כל אשר
גמלנו יי ורב טוב לבית ישראל
אשר גמלם כרחמיו וכרב חסדיו

From a letter of Israel Gaon b. Samuel b. Ḥofni (*see above, pp. 169–70*)

FACSIMILE XIII, C

(Fol. 3, verso)

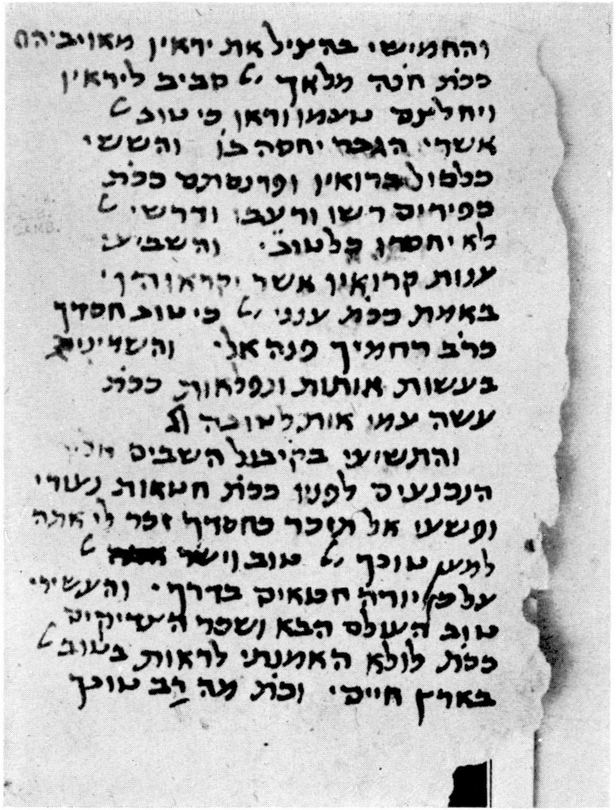

והחמישי בהציל את יראיו מאויביהם
ככת׳ חונה מלאך ה׳ סביב ליראיו
ויחלצם טעמו וראו כי טוב ה׳
אשרי הגבר יחסה בו והששי
כלכלת יראיו ופרנסתם ככת׳
כפירים רשו ורעבו ודרשי ה׳
לא יחסרו כל טוב׳ והשביעי
ענות קרואיו אשר יקראוהו
באמת ככת׳ ענני ה׳ כי טוב חסדך
כרב רחמיך פנה אלי והשמיני
בעשות אותות ונפלאות ככת׳
עשה עמי אות לטובה וגו׳
והתשיעי בקיבול השבים אליו
הנכנעים לפניו ככת׳ חטאות נעורי
ופשעי אל תזכר כחסדך זכר לי אתה
למען טובך ה׳ טוב וישר [illegible] ה׳
על כן יורה חטאים בדרך׳ והעשירי
טוב העולם הבא ושכר הצדיקים
ככת׳ לולא האמנתי לראות בטוב ה׳
בארץ חיים׳ וכת׳ מה רב טובך

(Fol. 3, recto)

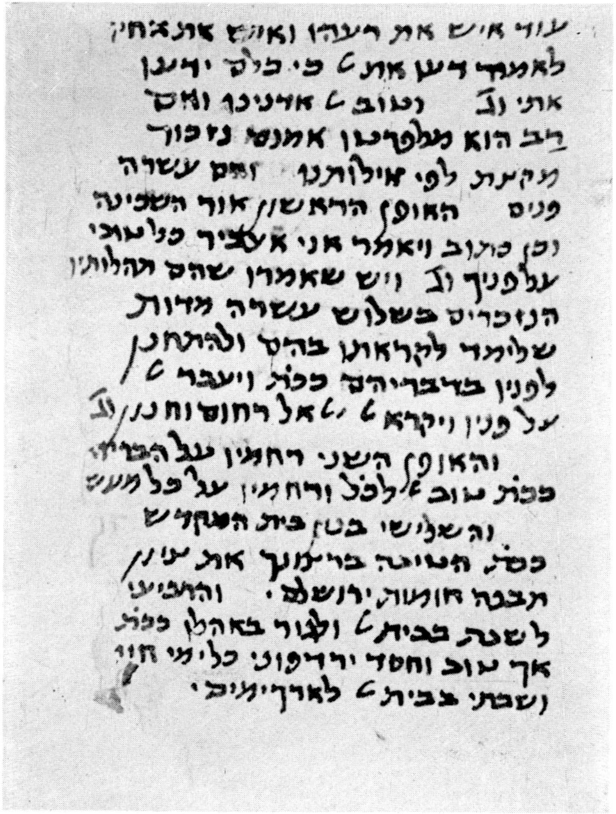

עוד איש את רעהו ואיש את אחיו
לאמר דעו את ה׳ כי כולם ידעו
אותי וגו׳ ונטוב ה׳ אדונינו ואם
רב הוא מלספרו אמנם נזכור
מקצת לפי אילותנו ושם עשרה
פנים האופן הראשון אור השכינה
וכן כתוב ויאמר אני אעביר כל טובי
על פניך וגו׳ ויש שאמרו שהם תהלותיו
הנזכרים בשלוש עשרה מדות
שלומד לקוראו בהם ולהתחנן
לפניו בדבריהם ככת׳ ויעבר ה׳
על פניו ויקרא ה׳ ה׳ אל רחום וחנון וגו׳
והאופן השני רחמיו על בריותיו
ככת׳ טוב ה׳ לכל ורחמיו על כל מעשיו
והשלישי בטוב בית המקדש
ככת׳ הטיבה ברצונך את ציון
תבנה חומות ירושלם׳ והרביעי
לשבת בבית ה׳ ולגור באהלו ככת׳
אך טוב וחסד ירדפוני כל ימי חיי
ושבתי בבית ה׳ לאורך ימים׳

From a letter of Israel Gaon b. Samuel b. Ḥofni (*see above, pp. 171–72*)

(Fol. 4, verso) FACSIMILE XIII, D (Fol. 4, recto)

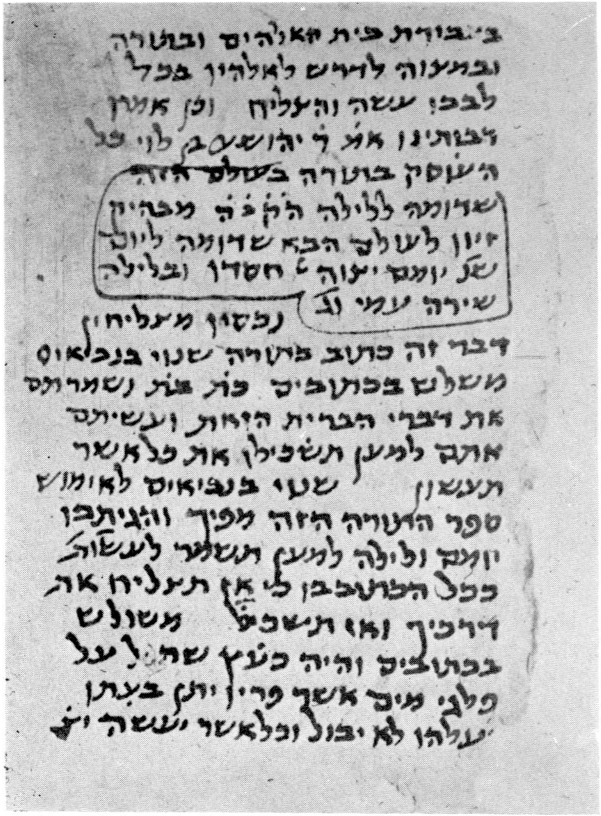

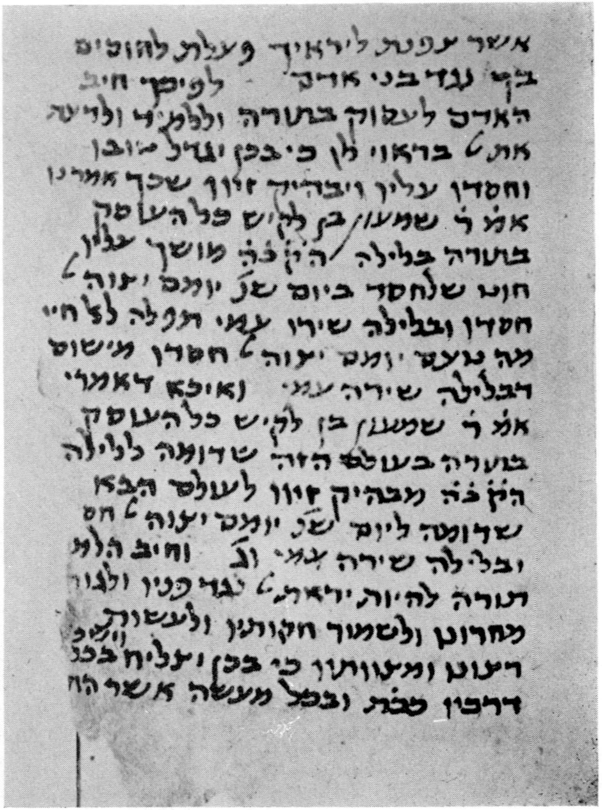

From a letter of Israel Gaon b. Samuel b. Ḥofni (*see above, pp. 172–74*)

(Fol. 5, verso) FACSIMILE XIII, E (Fol. 5, recto)

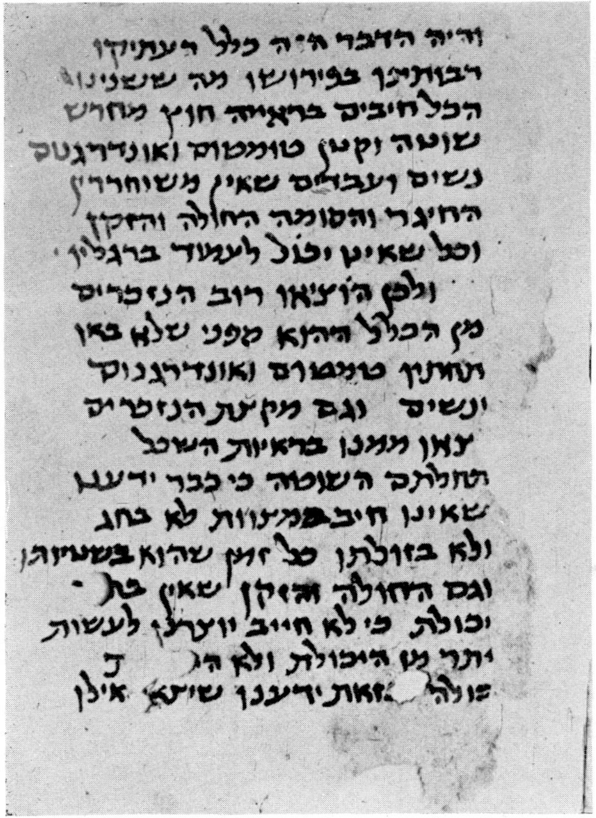

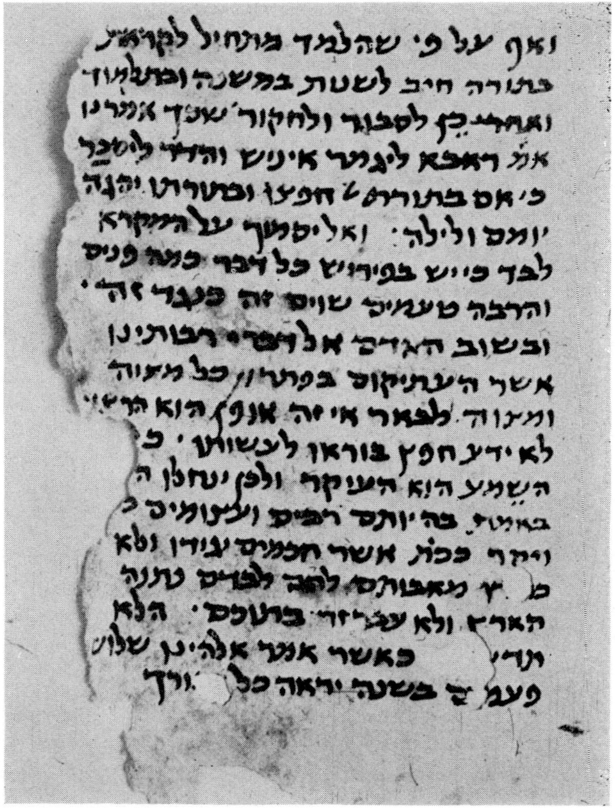

From a letter of Israel Gaon b. Samuel b. Ḥofni (*see above, pp. 174–76*)

(Fol. 6, verso) FACSIMILE XIII, F (Fol. 6, recto)

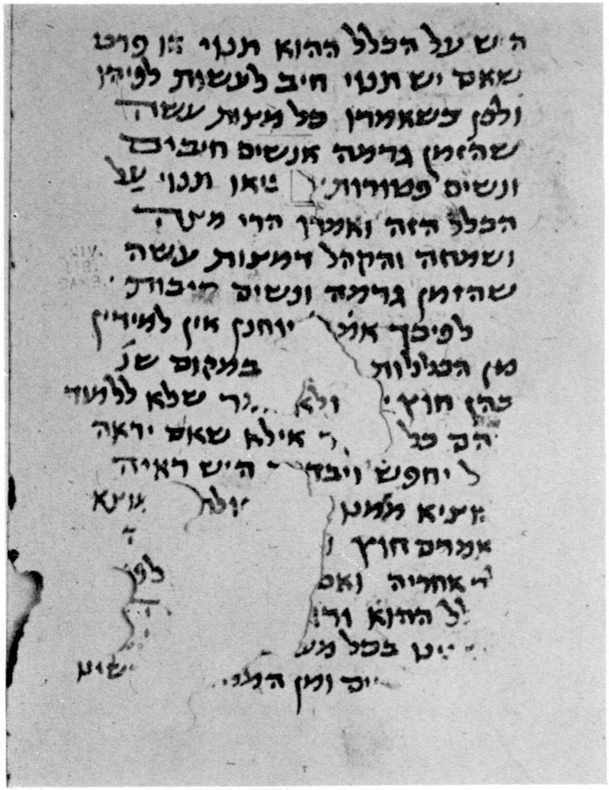

היש על הכלל ההוא תנוי הן פרט
שאם יש תנוי חיב לעשות לפיכן
ולכן כשאמרו כל מצות עשה
שהזמן גרמה אנשים חיבים
ונשים פטורות [illegible] ואן תנוי על
הכלל הזה ואמרו הרי מצה
ושמחה והקהל דמצות עשה
שהזמן גרמה ונשים חיבות
לפיכך אומ' יוחנן אין למידין
מן הכללות במקום של
[illegible]

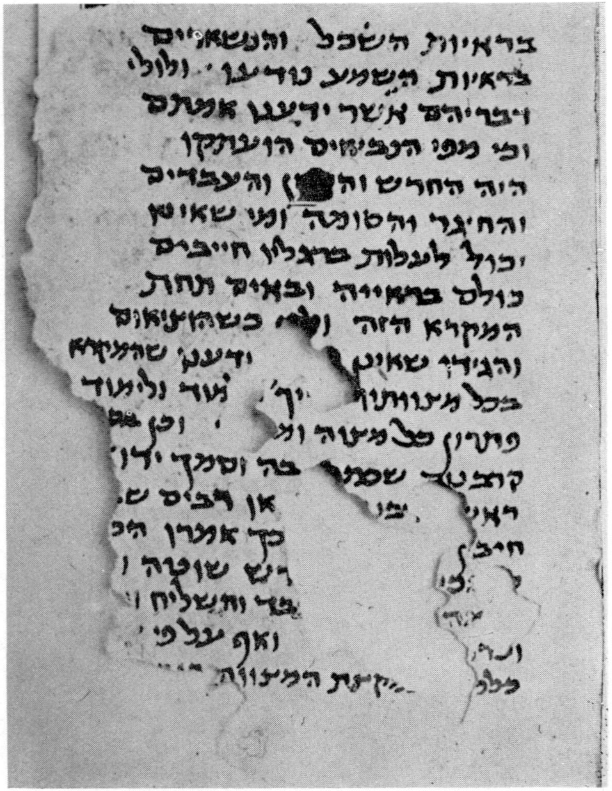

בראיות השכל והנשואים
בראיות השמע נודיעו. ולולי
דבריהם אשר ידענו אותם
ומי מפי הנביאים הועתקו
היה החרש וה[illegible] והעבדים
והחיגר והסומא ומי שאינו
יכול לעלות ברגליו חייבים
כולם בראייה ובאים תחת
המקרא הזה [illegible]
[illegible]

From a letter of Israel Gaon b. Samuel b. Ḥofni (*see above, pp. 176–77*)

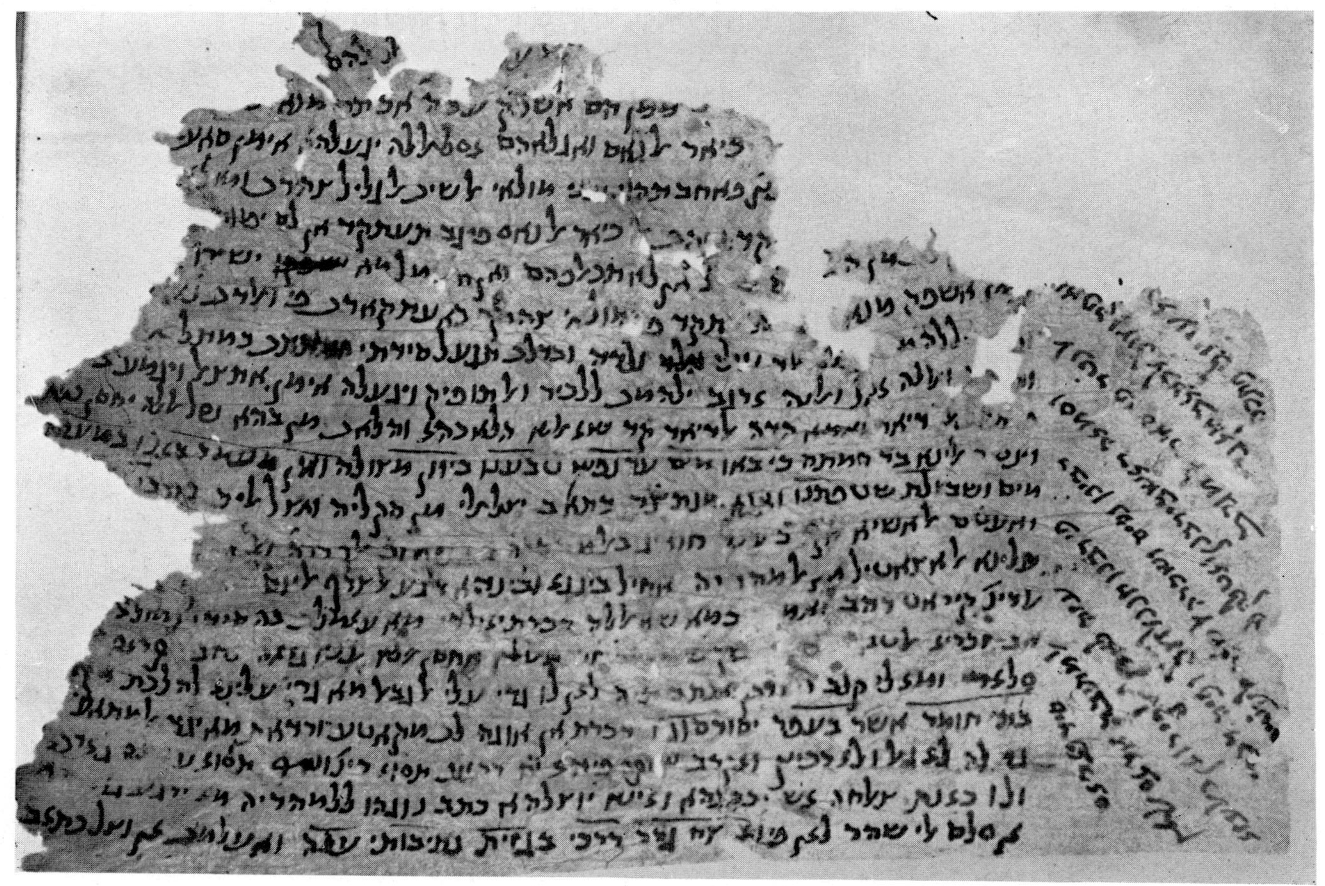

Letter from North-Africa to Fusṭāṭ (*see above, pp. 244–46*)

FACSIMILE XIV, B (Verso)

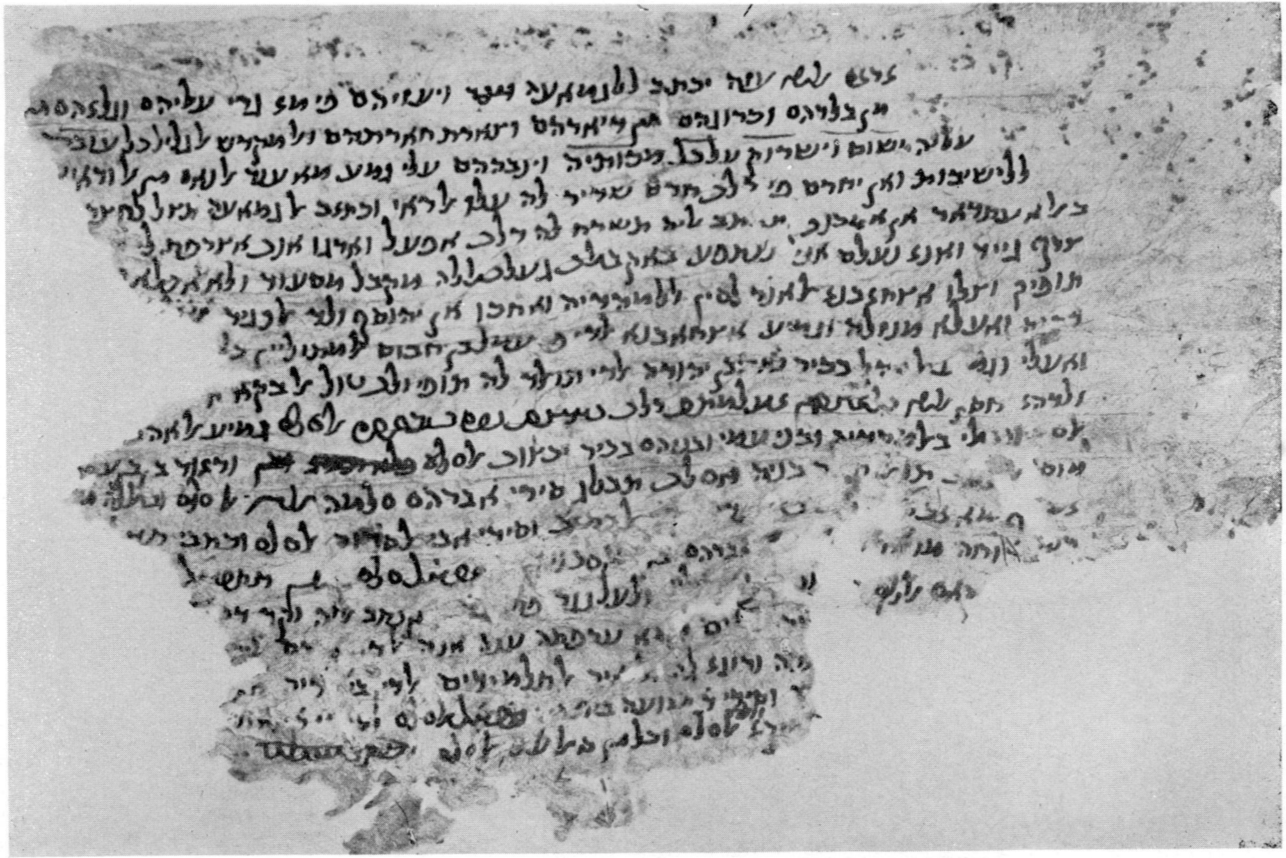

Letter from North-Africa to Fusṭāṭ (*see above*, *pp.* 246–48)

FACSIMILE XV

(Recto)

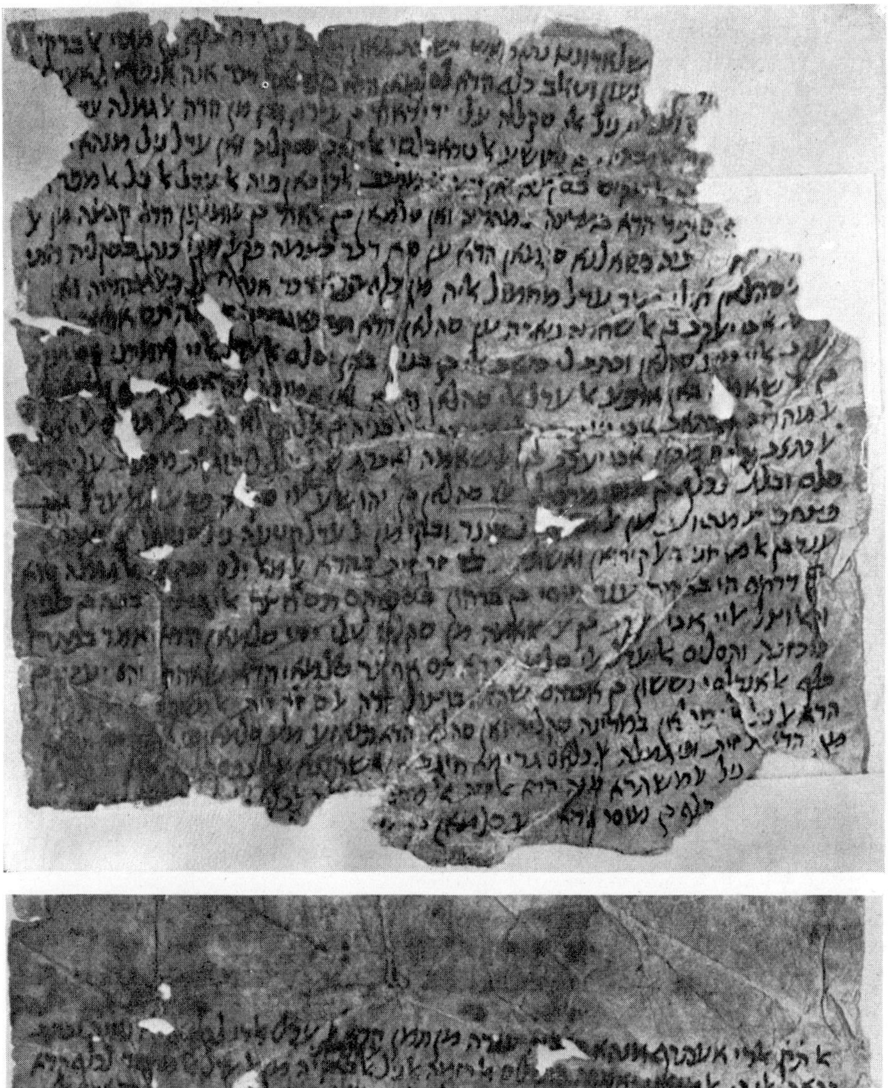

(Verso)

Legal Document, dated Adar 1040 C. E.

(*see above, pp. 343–45*)

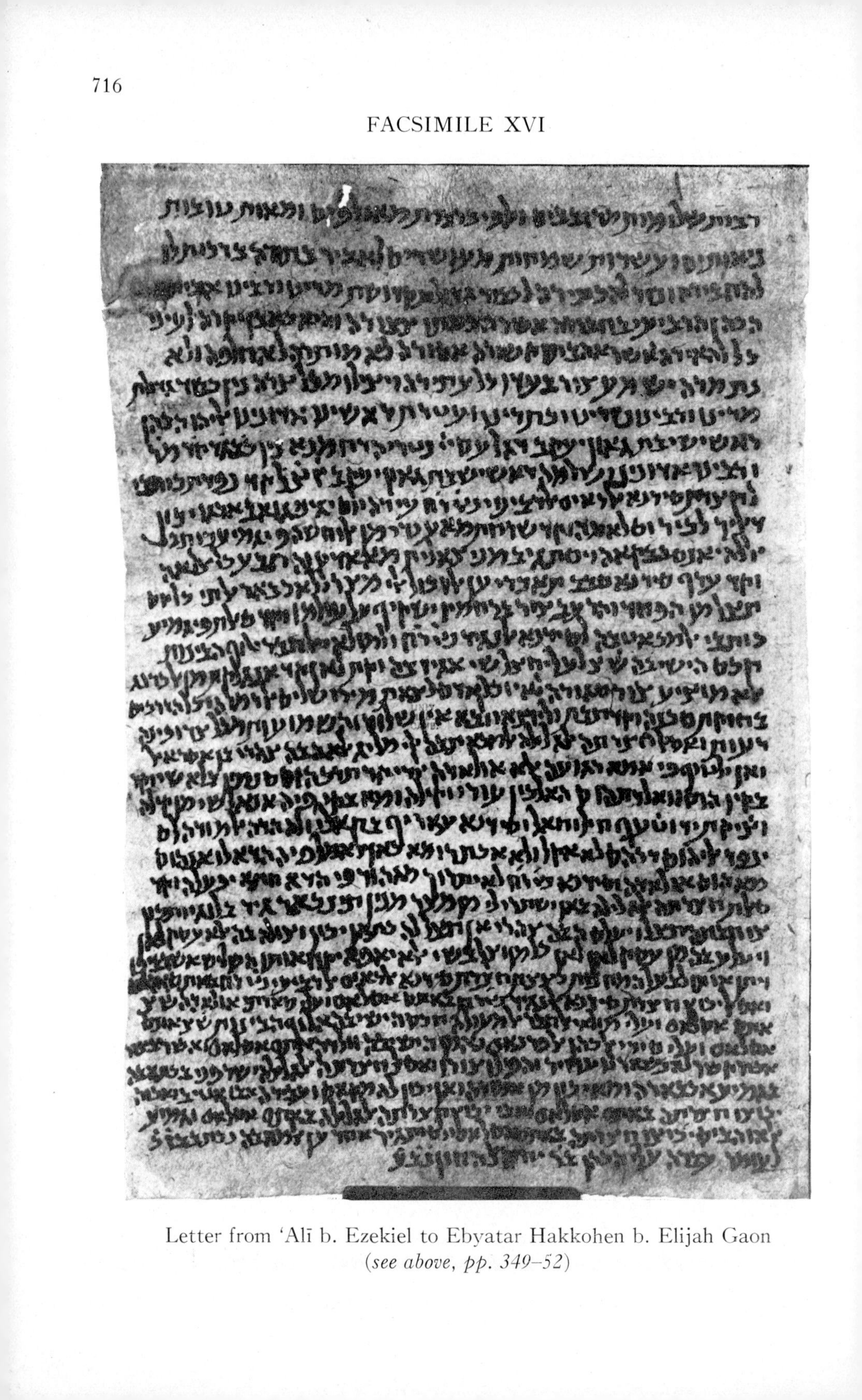

FACSIMILE XVI

Letter from ʿAlī b. Ezekiel to Ebyatar Hakkohen b. Elijah Gaon
(*see above, pp. 349–52*)

FACSIMILE XVII

Letter of Abraham Ab-Bet-Din b. Isaac Alluf (*see above, pp. 352–54*)

FACSIMILE XVIII

Legal Document, dated Sivan 12, 967 C. E.
(*see above, pp. 360–61*)

FACSIMILE XIX

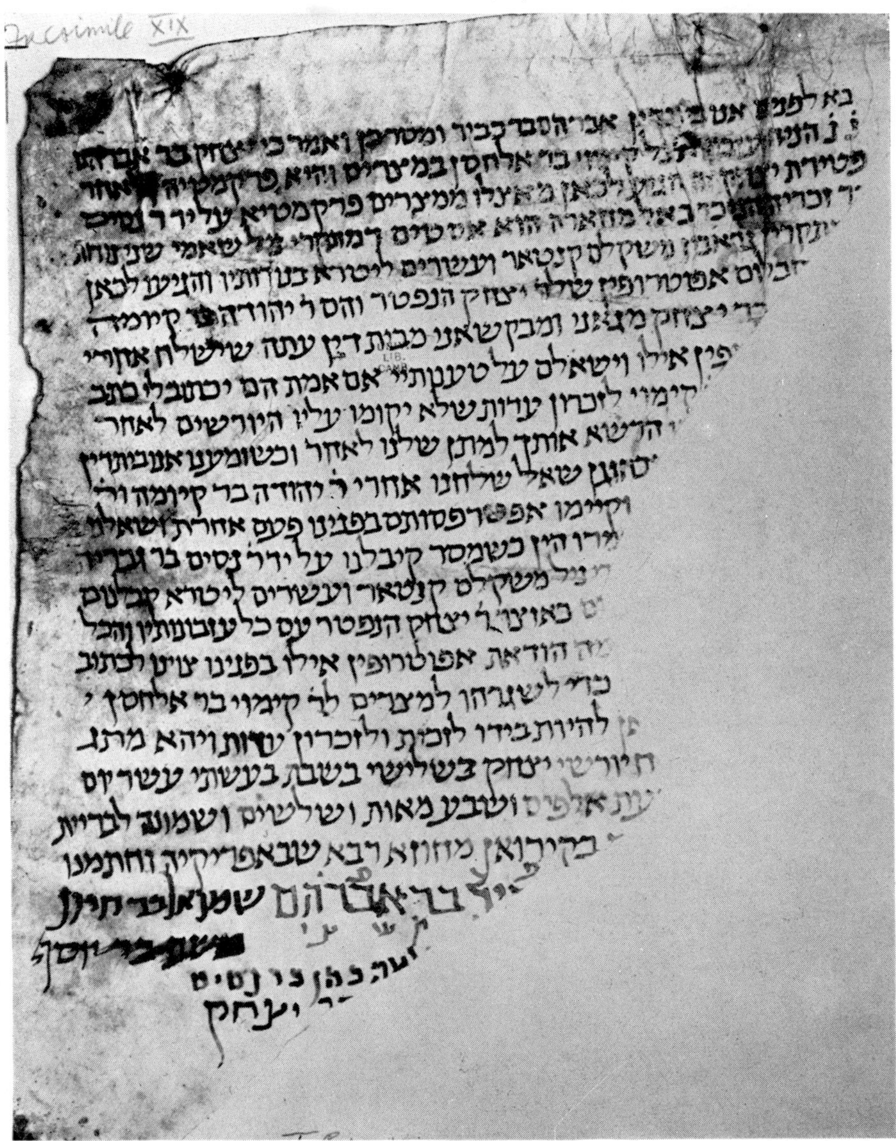

Legal Document, dated 977–78 C. E.

(*see above, pp. 361–63*)

FACSIMILE XX

Legal Document, dated Sivan 29, 982 C. E. (*see above, pp. 363–65*)

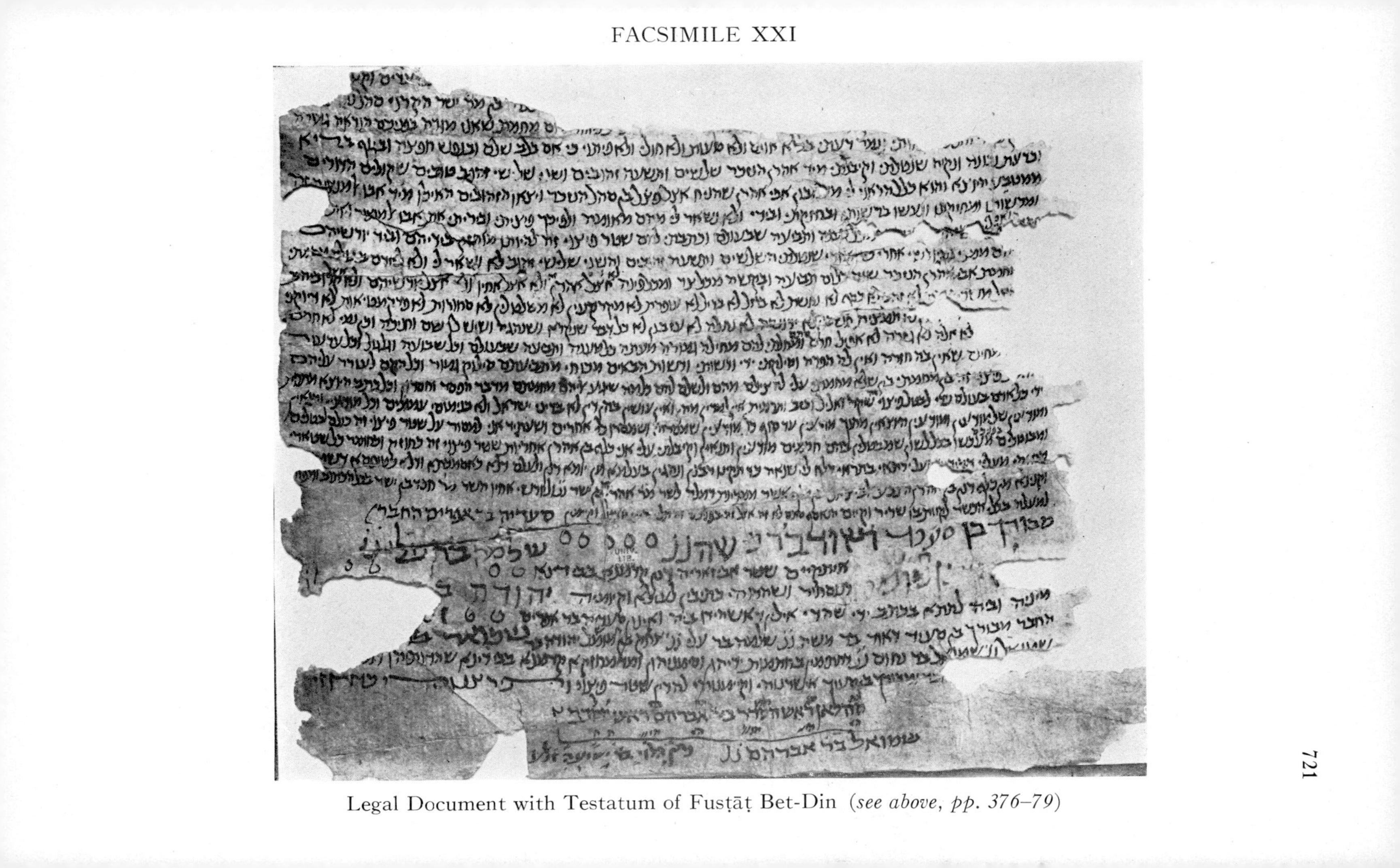

FACSIMILE XXI

Legal Document with Testatum of Fusṭāṭ Bet-Din (*see above, pp. 376–79*)

FACSIMILE XXII

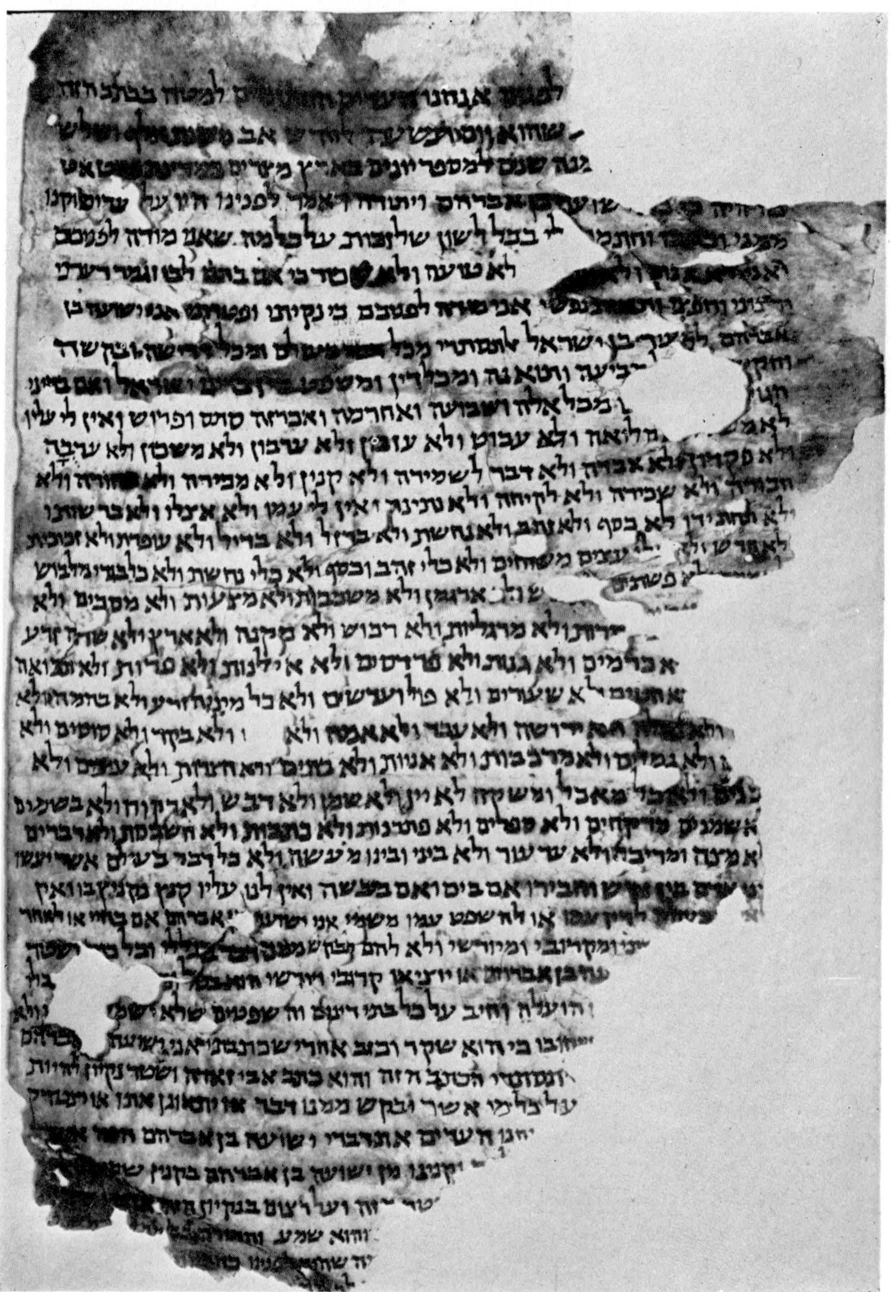

Ḳaraite Legal Document of 11th Century

(*see above, pp. 381–82*)

FACSIMILE XXIII, A (Address, verso)

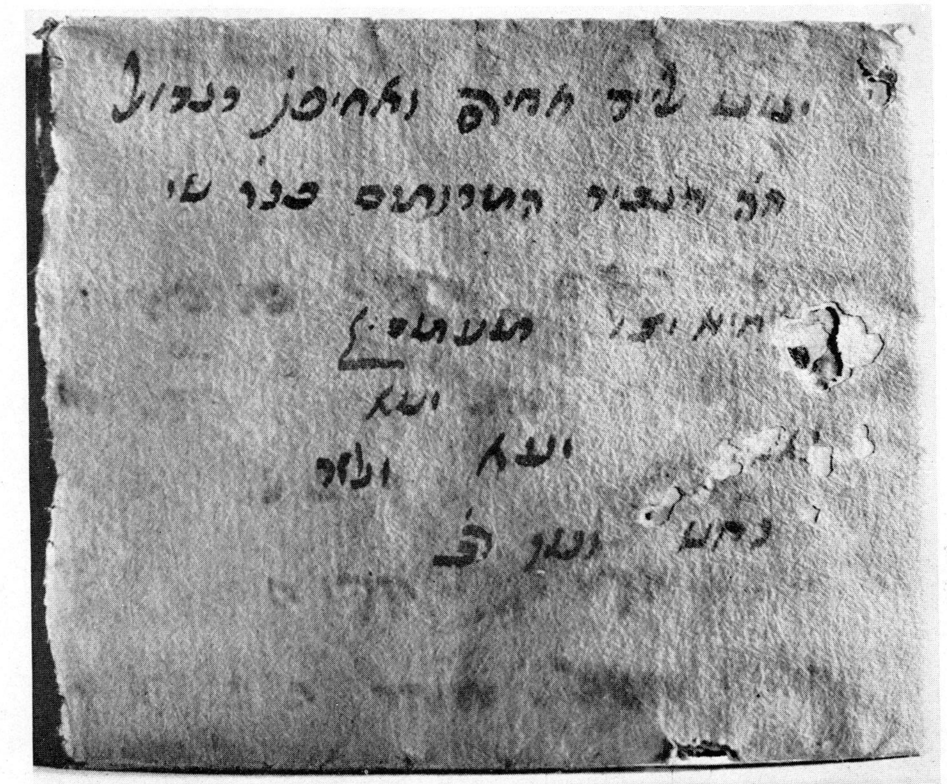

Letter from ʿImādiya in Ḳurdistān to Mosul (*see above, p. 520*)

(Recto)

FACSIMILE XXIII, B

Letter from ʿImādiya in Ḳurdistān to Mosul (*see above*, *pp.* 520–22)

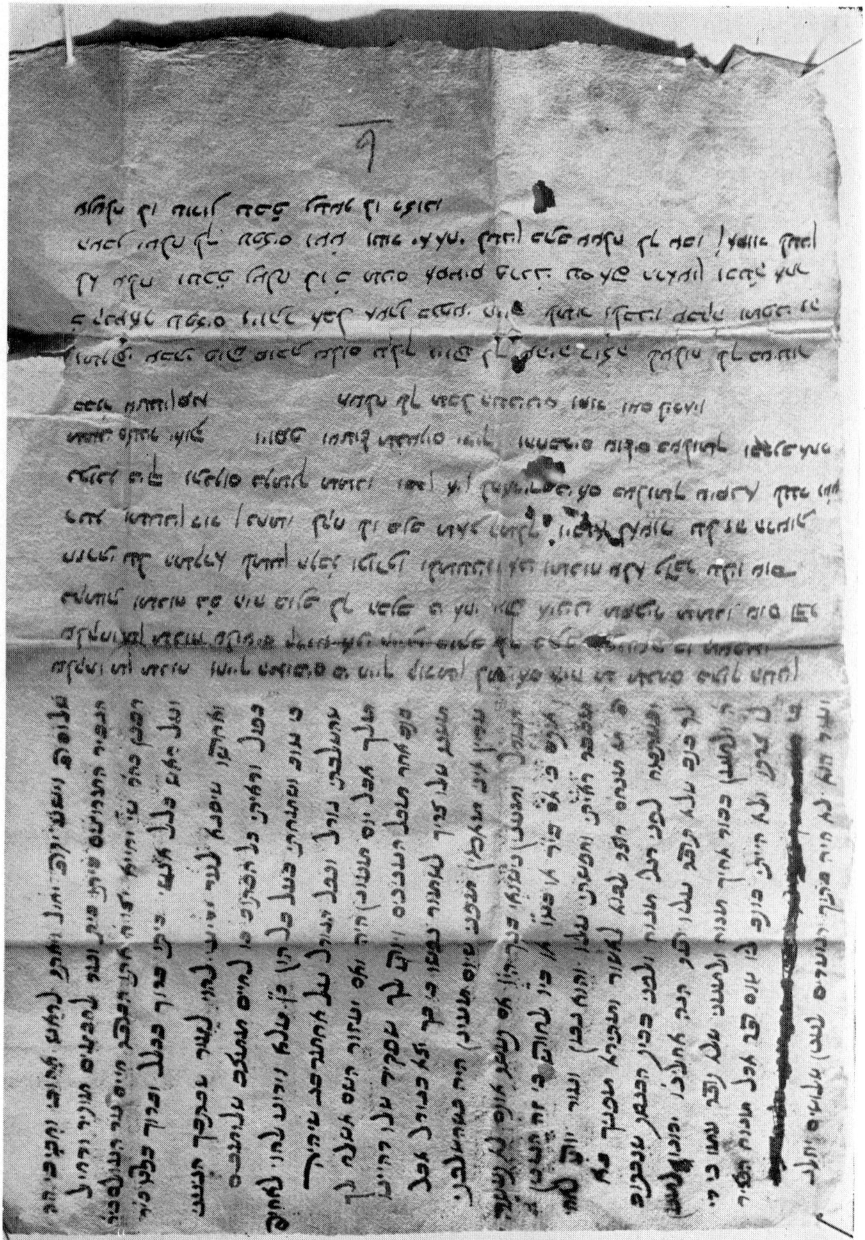

FACSIMILE XXIV

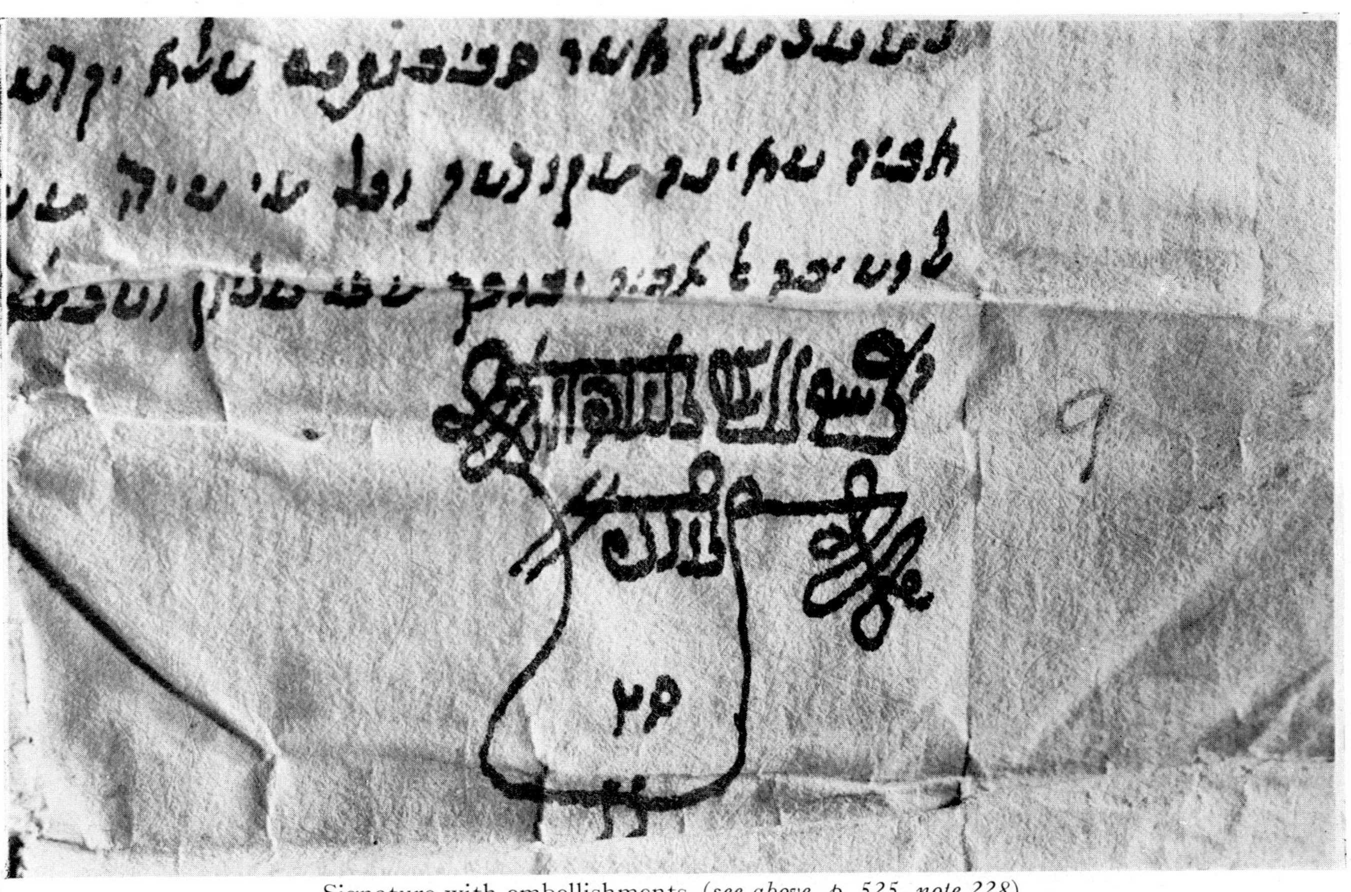

Signature with embellishments (*see above, p. 525, note 228*)

FACSIMILE XXV

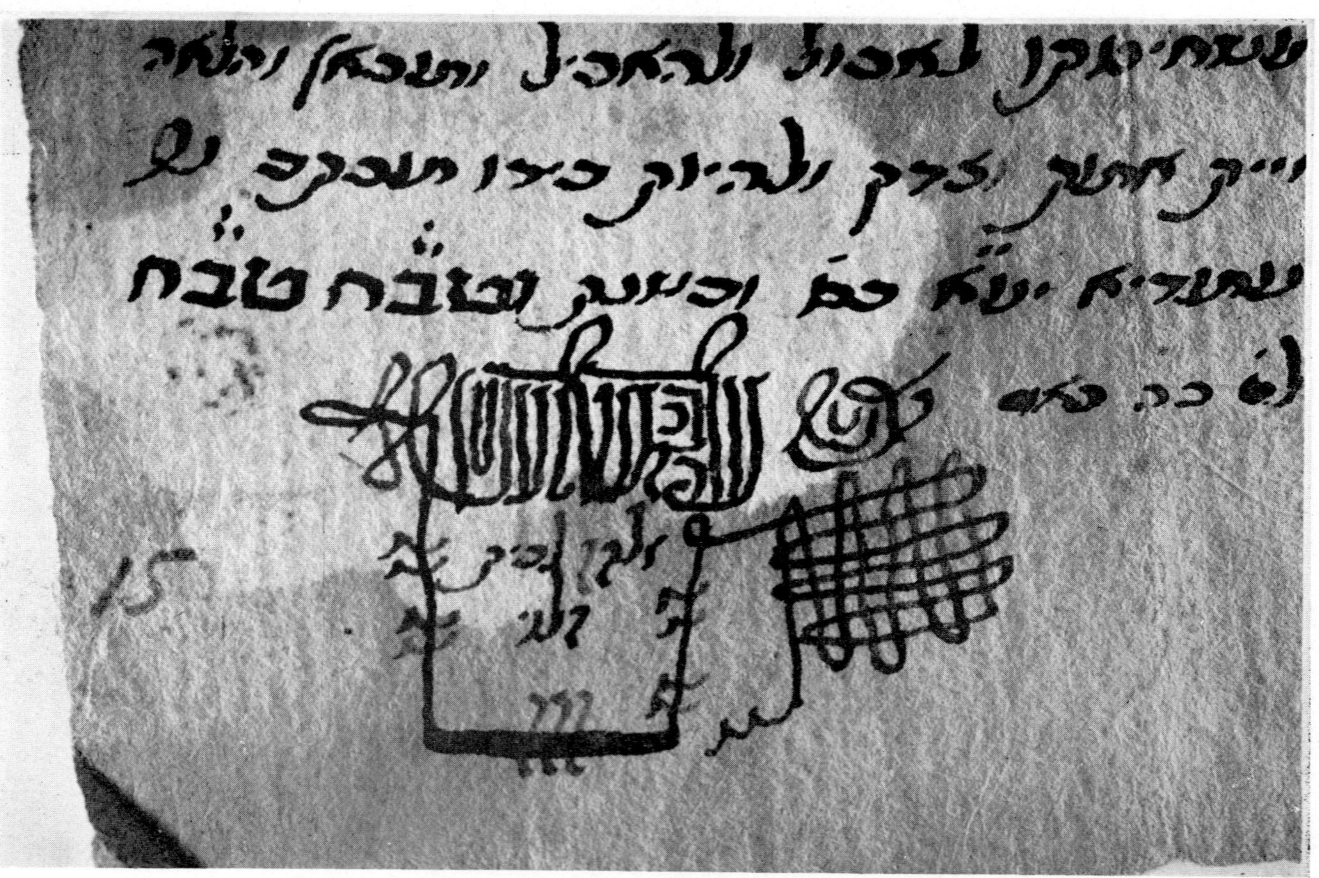

Signature with embellishments (*see above, p. 534, note 284a*)

FACSIMILE XXVI

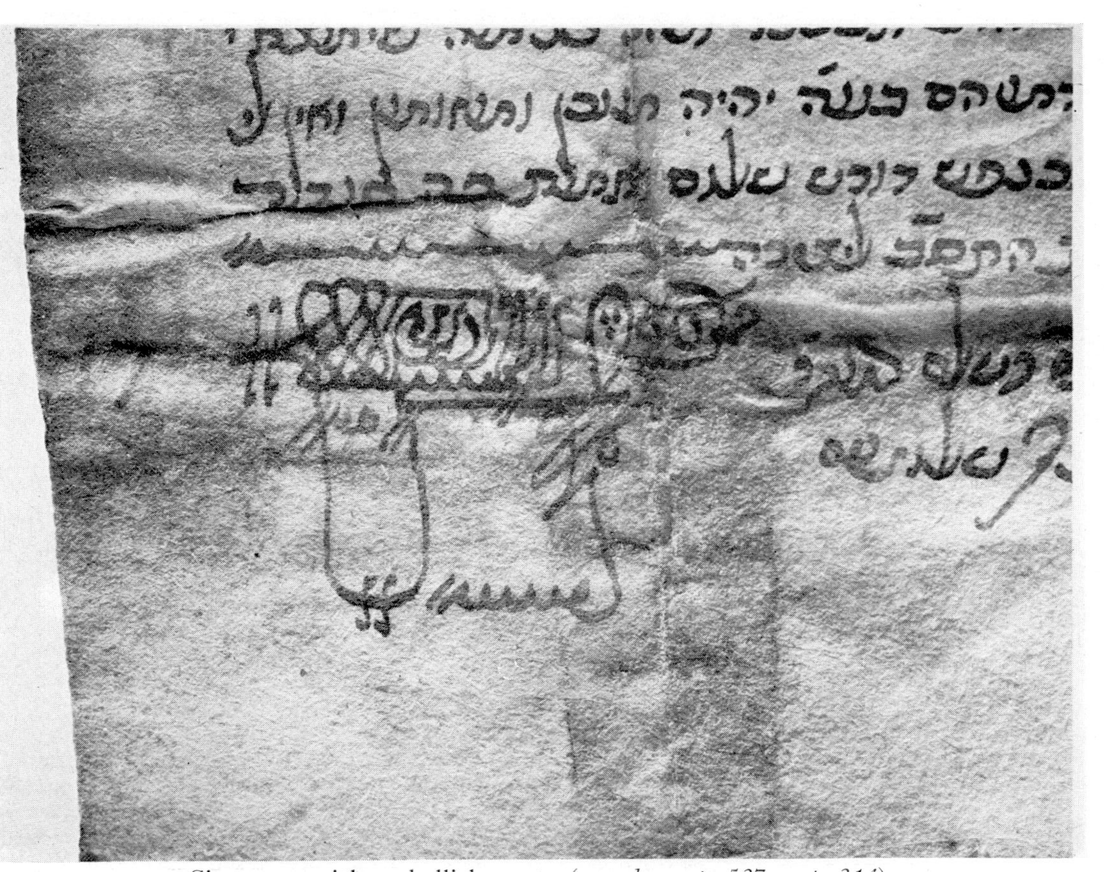

Signature with embellishments (*see above, p. 537, note 314*)

FACSIMILE XXVII

Signature with embellishments (*see above, p. 549, note 382*)